MONEY, BANKING, AND MONETARY POLICY

MONEY, BANKING, AND MONETARY POLICY

READINGS IN DOMESTIC AND INTERNATIONAL POLICY

HAROLD R. WILLIAMS
Kent State University

HENRY W. WOUDENBERG
Kent State University

HARPER & ROW, PUBLISHERS
New York, Evanston, and London

Money, Banking, and Monetary Policy:
Readings in Domestic and International Policy
Copyright © 1970 by Harper & Row, Publishers, Inc.

Library of Congress Catalog Card Number: 69-18492

CONTENTS

Preface ix

PART I. AN INTRODUCTION TO MONEY, DEBT, AND
FINANCIAL INTERMEDIARIES 1

  1. The Merits and Drawbacks of Money, Dennis H. Robertson 3
  2. Before the Introduction of Coins, Arthur R. Burns 13
  3. Debt—and the Economy, Federal Reserve Bank of Chicago 31
  4. Postwar Developments among Financial Intermediaries,
    J. A. Cacy 58

PART II. COMMERCIAL BANKING 69

  5. Recent Bank Failures—Why?, Federal Reserve Bank of
    Richmond 71
  6. Correspondent Banking, Federal Reserve Bank of Kansas City 79
  7. Is Banking Unique?, Phillip E. Coldwell 91
  8. Competition in Banking: The Issues, Federal Reserve Bank
    of Chicago 99
  9. Banking Structure and Competition, Howard D. Crosse 111
 10. What Price Liquidity?, Federal Reserve Bank of Philadelphia 120
 11. Theories of Cyclical Liquidity Management of Commercial
    Banks, G. Walter Woodworth 128
 12. The Federal-Funds Market, G. Walter Woodworth 154
 13. Impact of Credit Cards on Commercial Banks, Federal Reserve
    Bank of Boston 168

PART III. INSTRUMENTS OF MONETARY MANAGEMENT 179

 14. Why a Central Bank?, J. Keith Horsefield 181
 15. The Mysterious World of the Fed, Delbert C. Hastings
    and Ross M. Robertson 189
 16. The Instruments of Monetary Control, Warren L. Smith 200
 17. The Dealer Market for U.S. Government Securities and
    Monetary Policy, Federal Reserve Bank of Cleveland 241
 18. Some Issues in Federal Reserve Discount Policy,
    Lester V. Chandler 254
 19. Reappraisal of Federal Reserve Discount Policy,
    George W. Mitchell 267

PART IV. THE PROBLEMS AND CONTROVERSY OF MONETARY
POLICY 277*

A. Debt Management and Monetary Policy

 20. Federal Reserve-Treasury Controversies, Clay J. Anderson 280

21. The Changing Views on Debt Management, William E. Laird   293

B. Financial Intermediaries and Their Effects on Banking and Monetary Policy
22. Commercial Banks as Creators of "Money," James Tobin   308
23. Financial Intermediaries and the Saving-Investment Process, John G. Gurley and Edward S. Shaw   319
24. Can Monetary Policy Influence the Availability of Credit?, A. Dale Tussing   339

C. The Question of Rules Versus Authority in Monetary Policy
25. The Money Supply Controversy, William N. Cox, III   354
26. Rules Versus Authority in Monetary Policy, Milton Friedman   363
27. Reflections on Central Banking, Paul Samuelson   372
28. Rules Versus Authority in Monetary Policy, Henry C. Wallich   390
29. Rules Versus Authority in Monetary Policy, Richard D. Selden   402
30. Controlling Money, Allan H. Meltzer   409

PART V. MONETARY AND FISCAL STABILIZATION POLICY   427

A. Inflation and Unemployment
31. The Employment Act Objectives—After 20 years, Henry C. Wallich   430
32. A Look at Some Measures of Inflation, Sheldon W. Stahl   439
33. The Gains and Losses from Inflation, Staff Report of Joint Economic Committee   451
34. Cost and Demand Inflation: Implications for Monetary Policy, William McChesney Martin   462
35. The Relation Between Prices and Employment: Two Views, Roger W. Spencer   474

B. Monetary and Fiscal Policy: Optimum Mix and Effectiveness
36. Fiscal-Monetary Policies: What Mix?, Clay J. Anderson   488
37. Monetary Versus Fiscal Policy, Warren L. Smith   501
38. Lags in Monetary and Fiscal Policy, Mark H. Willes   525
39. Monetary and Fiscal Actions: A Test of Their Relative Importance in Economic Stabilization, Leonall C. Andersen and Jerry L. Jordan   536

PART VI. INTERNATIONAL MONETARY RELATIONS

A. Nature and Defects of the International Monetary System
40. The Foreign Exchange Market, United States Treasury Department   570
41. The International Monetary System and Adjustment of Payments Imbalances, United States Treasury Department   581
42. Guidelines for International Monetary Reform, Warren L. Smith   598

B. Reforming the International Monetary System

43. The Long-Run Evolution of Our International Monetary System, Robert Triffin 617
44. Flexible Exchange Rates, Milton Friedman 630
45. Exchange Rates: How Flexible Should They Be?, Henry C. Wallich 641
46. The New International Monetary Plan in Perspective, Thomas E. Davis 647

C. The Dollar Problem and Related Considerations

47. U.S. Balance of Payments—The Record to Date, United States Treasury Department 639
48. Balance of Payments: Statement by the President Outlining a Program of Action—January 1, 1968, President Lyndon B. Johnson 669
49. The Price of Gold Is Not the Problem, William McChesney Martin 677
50. Rapid Inflation and International Payments, Graeme S. Dorrance 687
51. Eurodollars—An Important Source of Funds for American Banks, Federal Reserve Bank of Chicago 693
52. The Appropriate Use of Monetary and Fiscal Policy for Internal and External Stability, Robert A. Mundell 706

Index 715

PREFACE

Analyzed in the context of current and significant national and international problems, the material in Money and Banking courses can be extremely interesting and rewarding. Weaving theory, policy, and current problems into a logical, cohesive unit of knowledge accomplishes two objectives. It not only results in a superior understanding of monetary theory and policy per se but also yields the student greater personal satisfaction. He now is better able to comprehend and evaluate the crucial social and economic issues of our time. Indeed, from this view there is little room for debate. Today it is difficult to find any significant public policy issue not directly related to money and banking. The problems of inflation, unemployment, economic growth, and balance of payments equilibrium are intricately interwoven with central banking and multiple money systems.

This reader brings together a relatively comprehensive collection of papers presenting current and significant issues in money, banking, and monetary policy. Although all standard areas of money and banking are covered, heavy emphasis is placed on monetary *policy*, both domestic and international. Theoretical articles per se are not included. Most money and banking texts contain an adequate treatment of the theoretical material, as well as the institutional and historical, that forms the base for courses in money and banking. Such texts do not, however, provide breadth and depth on specific aspects of the subject or the flavor and subtleties issuing from debates over controversial matters. More importantly, they fail to expose students to adequate discussion and analysis of public policy applications of the theory. Discussion and analysis must be furnished by the instructor and by supplemental readings. It is in this respect that this compilation of readings can play an important role in the student's edification.

The readings are classified into six major parts. Each has an introduction describing what it is, why it is important, and how it ties in with prior and subsequent sections. Parts IV through VI are further subdivided into two or three smaller sections. This will assist the reader in organizing, comparing, and extracting central ideas from the readings. In addition, the role of each article and its relationship to others in the class are discussed briefly. There is no attempt, however, to state the full conclusion and supporting points to each paper.

With few exceptions, articles are presented in their entirety. Where length and/or organization of an item necessitates the use of excerpts, the author's style and originality is kept. For a few selections all or some of the footnotes have been deleted, but only in cases where the notes are not essential to understanding the article. In addition, at least two articles are presented on controversial issues, one on each side of the debate. By so doing we hope to avoid giving the student a biased and perhaps minority view on crucial issues. Throughout the readings every effort is made to ensure that both generally accepted and controversial views are set in proper prespective. Certainly not all economists would have selected the same papers. This would be true even using the criteria we used (given the constraints mentioned): the level of difficulty, presentation of important views, interest and readability, and up-to-dateness of the articles. Undoubtedly, our beliefs, preferences, and biases affected the choice of articles. We did try, however, to present *present* positions, logic, and facts surrounding controversial issues as fairly as possible.

Our many thanks to the authors and publishers who so graciously permitted us to reprint their articles in part or in full. It is they who deserve credit for any merits found in this compilation of readings.

Harold R. Williams
Henry W. Woundenberg

AN
INTRODUCTION
TO MONEY,
DEBT,
AND
FINANCIAL
INTERMEDIARIES

PART I

This introductory part is specifically directed at providing a perspective on the significance of the relationships of money and debt to economic activity. The first two selections deal primarily with the roles and development of money, and the last two selections examine the relationship of money and debt to the growth and competition of the financial businesses that create debt.

As a student of money and banking, it is imperative that you thoroughly understand the underlying functions and importance of money to economic activity. This analysis is concisely presented in the first selection by Robertson on the roles of money and its relationship to economic decisions. By reading Burns' enlightening and amusing examination of early monies in the second selection, you will gain an historical perspective on the relevance of functional money in the early development of economies.

Debt, a part of which we call money, has grown very rapidly in the United States particularly in the period following World War II. The importance of this growth of debt, the changes in its composition, and its relationship to money are the general area of investigation of the last two articles in this first part. The article by the Federal Reserve Bank of Chicago traces the growth of both public and private debt, relevant changes in its composition, and its ever-increasing importance to the United States economy. As a preview to Part II and because of its importance to the subject of money and banking, the last article of this section specifically investigates the growth and competition of commercial banks and other financial institutions for the rapidly expanding credit business. The Cacy article provides a perspective on the relationships, important differences, and competition between commercial banks and nonbank financial intermediaries. It also briefly discusses the implications of this competition for monetary policy. Articles containing a more complete analysis of the relative effects of financial institutions on the effectiveness of monetary policy will be incorporated in Part IV after you more fully understand the U.S. banking system (Part II) and how it is controlled (Part III).

DENNIS H. ROBERTSON

THE MERITS AND
DRAWBACKS
OF MONEY

1

"Crabs and all sorts of things," said the Sheep: "plenty of choice, only make up your mind. Now what do you want to buy?" —Through the Looking-glass.

1. INTRODUCTORY

Money is not such a vital subject as is often supposed; nevertheless, it is an interesting and important branch of the study of economics. It is necessary for the economics student to try from the start to pierce the monetary veil in which most business transactions are shrouded, and to see what is happening in terms of real goods and services; indeed so far as possible he must try to penetrate further, and to see what is happening in terms of real sacrifices and satisfactions. But having done this he must return and examine the effects exercised upon the creation and distribution of real economic welfare by the twin facts that we do use the mechanism of money, and that we have learnt so imperfectly to control it.

And this is specially necessary at a time when the money systems of the world have ceased to work with the comparative ease and smoothness to which we had become accustomed, and are indeed for the most part thoroughly out of order. Almost everybody is directly affected by, and acutely conscious of, the violent changes which have taken place in the purchasing power of money over the things which he wishes to buy; and most people are also, though less vividly, aware of the violent changes which have taken place in the purchasing power of the money of their own country over the money of other countries. This disorganization of the world's monetary apparatus has become a breeding ground of real dangers and disharmonies, and to some extent also of illusory hopes and aspirations. It is necessary, therefore, to explore it thoroughly, if only to clear the approach to those more vital questions of the creation and apportionment of real wealth with which the later volumes of this series will be concerned. A monetary system is like some internal

Reprinted by permission of James Nisbet and Co., Ltd., and Cambridge University Press from Sir Dennis H. Robertson, "The Merits and Drawbacks of Money," *Money*, 1957, pp. 1–13.

organ; it should not be allowed to take up very much of our thoughts when it goes right, but it needs a deal of attention when it goes wrong.

2. A DEFINITION OF MONEY

It is clearly desirable to arrive at an early understanding of what we mean by money. There is no very general agreement upon this point; but as with so many other economic terms, it does not matter very much what meaning we adopt as long as we stick to it, or at any rate do not change it without being aware that we are doing so. In this [article], the term money will be used to denote anything which is widely accepted in payment for goods, or in discharge of other kinds of business obligation. If things which are intended to be money—the notes of certain Governments, for instance—cease to be widely accepted in discharge of obligations, they cease to function as money, and, from the point of view of the student at any rate, to *be* money. On the other hand, if things which have not been hitherto considered as money, such as tobacco or cattle or tins of bully-beef, become widely accepted in discharge of obligations, they become, in our present sense, money.[1]

This property of being widely acceptable generally, though not always, involves another, namely the property of being expressed in units, in terms of which it is common to reckon the value of all those goods and services which men are in the habit of exchanging with one another. This is what the textbooks on money mean to convey when they say that money is not only a "medium of exchange" but a "standard of value." But that statement as it stands does not quite fit in with the definition of money which we have chosen. It is not necessary that everything which is used as a medium of exchange should itself be also a standard of value, but only that it should be expressed in terms of something which *is* a standard of value. For instance, John Smith's checks may be widely accepted in discharge of his obligations, and are therefore rightly regarded, according to the definition which we have chosen, as money: and Bank of England five-pound notes are universally accepted in the United Kingdom in discharge of obligations, and are certainly money. But nobody reckons his income or conducts his business dealings in

---

[1] Of the beer in which in effect wages were partly paid in the Staffordshire coal-mines in the middle of the nineteenth century, a recent historian remarks: "This currency was very popular and highly liquid, but it was issued to excess and difficult to store," Fay, *Life and Labor in the Nineteenth Century*, p. 197.

terms of John Smith's checks or even of Bank of England notes: people reckon their incomes and conduct their transactions in terms of the pounds sterling of which John Smith's checks and Bank of England notes are expressed as multiples.

Money then is anything which is widely acceptable in discharge of obligations; but a thing will not as a rule be widely acceptable for this purpose unless it is expressed as a multiple of some unit which is regarded as a measure or standard of the value of things in general. This conception of a "standard of value" raises some difficulties, to which we must return later. And we must also postpone for the present a consideration of the different *kinds* of money which exist, and of the ways in which various money systems are built up out of them. Meanwhile what there is to be said applies to *all* money, defined as we have defined it.

3. THE ADVANTAGE OF MONEY TO THE CONSUMER

The next question for our consideration is "What is the point of using money?" We have become so accustomed to the use of money that it requires a little exercise of imagination to realize how much we owe to it. But over large parts of the world to-day people have been deprived of the advantages of a sound system of money, and are finding out how inconvenient and even paralyzing the consequences may be.

The first great achievement of money is that it enables man as consumer to generalize his purchasing power, and to make his claims on society in the form which suits him best. If there were no money, people would have to be paid for their services in kind; and whether they were strictly rationed, or whether they were allowed to help themselves to an unlimited extent, in either case there would be waste. For in the former case they would be encouraged to take more of certain goods and services, and forced to take less of others, than they really require, and in the latter case they would be tempted to be extravagant all round. The existence of a monetary economy helps society to discover what people want and how much they want it, and so to decide what shall be produced and in what quantities, and to make the best use of its limited productive power. And it helps each member of society to insure that the *means* of enjoyment to which he has access yield him the greatest amount of *actual* enjoyment which is within his reach—it gives him the chance of not surfeiting himself with car rides, or stinting himself unduly of the countenance of Charlie Chaplin.

How fully he avails himself of this opportunity depends on his

aptitude for judging accurately of the relative amounts of enjoyment which different ways of spending a penny or a dollar would
afford him, and on his strength of mind in acting on his judgment.
Some people exploit to the full this opportunity of "making the
most of their income"; others settle down to a comfortable habit
of customary expenditure, and regard immunity from excessive
brain-wear about the spending of money, and from the keeping of
meticulous accounts, as worth some leakage of material enjoyment.
To waste satisfaction by "going on the burst" may even be itself a
source of satisfaction. But in any case man values highly this privilege of spending his money income, that is of taking his real income, as he pleases—how highly you may see if you read the story
of the fight against the truck system of paying wages, or watch the
faces of an engaged couple as they open the parcel containing their
seventeenth writing-case.

There are indeed some services, such as the use of the roads,
which we all of us receive without making specific payment. Further,
in some callings, such as the army or domestic service, a more extensive payment in kind is generally recognized to be for the convenience of everybody concerned: and those who have given rein
to their fancy in delineating the ideal economic society of the
future have often contemplated some system of doles or rationing
for the distribution of those staple commodities of which all human
beings stand in need. But since even such an ideal society would not
be likely to be infinitely rich, the total claim which any individual
could make upon it would still have to be limited: and since individual tastes and requirements would presumably continue to
differ, people would still have to be given a certain amount of latitude and discretion with regard to the form in which they presented
part, at any rate, of their claims. In other words, money of some
kind—certificates, that is to say, of a general title to real income,
to be interpreted and particularized by the individual—would have
to persist. The need for money then seems to be fundamental, if a
given volume of productive power—a given poise of mankind in his
relations with nature—is to be made to yield the greatest harvest of
individual satisfaction which it is capable of yielding.

4. THE ADVANTAGE OF MONEY TO THE PRODUCER

The second great achievement of money is that it enables man as
producer to concentrate his attention on his own job, and so to add
more effectively to the general flow of goods and services which
constitutes the real income of society. Historically, the process of

"commutation" of payments in kind into payments in money is found to be very closely bound up with the process of "differentiation" of various crafts and occupations: and logically the intimate connection between the two is not difficult to understand. The specialization and division of labor on which our economic structure is founded would be impossible if every man had to spend a large part of his time and energies in bartering his products for the materials of his industry and the goods which he requires for his own consumption.

This is especially true of the system of large-scale "capitalistic" production which is dominant to-day. The various forms which this system takes must be discussed in more detail in a future volume: but for our present purposes it is sufficiently accurate to describe it as one under which a large number of workmen work for wages under the orders of a "capitalist," who is responsible for the disposal of their joint product, and who allocates a share of the proceeds to the individual workmen. Now it would as a rule be intolerable from a business point of view if every large "capitalist"—say an iron-master or the managing director of a railway company—had to lay in a store of all things his workmen are likely to want and to dole them out to them. In certain conditions indeed, as experience shows, a partial arrangement of this kind may be put into force, either because it is a source of illicit profit to the "capitalist" (as under the old truck system), or because it furnishes a special incentive to the workman (as in the case of the special butter wages allowed in 1919 to coal miners in Germany) or because (as in domestic service) it is manifestly to the convenience of both parties. But speaking generally it is far simpler, and is indeed the only practicable course, for the "capitalist" to pay his workmen money wages, which they accept in the confident expectation of being able to obtain with them the things which they require. The existence of money then seems to be a necessary condition for any great development of the division of labor not merely as between those who follow different crafts, but as between those who plan and initiate and control and those who do the day-work of the world. Whether this is a thing for money to be proud of is of course another matter: all that is urged here is that in so far as the capitalistic system of industry has been an indispensable instrument of material progress, money has been so too.

The third great achievement of money is closely allied to the second. It consists in this, that money immensely facilitates the making of loans and payments in advance of all kinds. Wage payments, which have been mentioned above, are in essence one form of such payment in advance. The "capitalist" will not be able to dispose finally of his product till it is in a finished state; but the work-men engaged on the preliminary stages must be enabled to live meanwhile, and money facilitates arrangements being made for this. The making of advances by one kind of businessman to another is also rendered much easier by the existence of money; so is the investment or loaning of its savings by the general public. Saving, and the lending of savings by one person to another, means in the last resort the saving and lending of real things, and it may exist without money: but so long at any rate as we rely for it upon indi-viduals, it would be very cumbrous and difficult to arrange on a large scale without the aid of money. So for this reason, too, the existence of money seems to be essential to our modern system of production, which rests so largely upon the willingness of one man to transfer command over goods to another, in the expectation of being repaid either by that other or by some third party at a future date.

5. THE DANGEROUS EASE OF BORROWING AND LENDING MONEY

But this third great achievement of a monetary economy is also one of its two great drawbacks and dangers. For it makes it so fatally easy to lend and to borrow—or to appear to lend and to borrow—things which are not really in existence at all, or even likely to come into existence. How this happens we shall see more clearly when we come to examine in detail the structure of modern monetary systems: but it may be convenient to give here one or two preliminary illustrations of what is meant. In the early days of the war the British Government wanted in effect, to borrow from private citizens various things—lumps of steel and cloth and hay and such like—for the prosecution of the war. But all it could do in fact was to borrow money, because that is the only thing which people are used to lending. And with the money so obtained it expected, with a touch-ing confidence born of long years of the smooth working of a mone-tary economy, to be able to obtain everything it wanted. But it soon found that it could not do so, and that it would have to make special and elaborate ordinances in order to obtain the things which it wanted, and even in some cases itself to undertake their production.

Our second illustration is from the ordinary conduct of industry. When there is a "boom" in the constructional trades—steel, ship-building, engineering, and the rest—"capitalists" in these trades bid for the services of workpeople by offering them plentiful money wages. As was explained above, these wages are really in the nature of an advance, backed by the estimates made by the "capitalists" of the value which society will set on the buildings and ships and so forth which are in process of production. But what the workman wants these money advances for is to obtain the necessaries and conventional comforts of his life: and under a money-system there is no guarantee that these are being turned out as fast as the money wages are being handed over. Hence we may get a state of affairs when industry is active and wages high, but the necessaries of life are scarce; and then there is outcry and unrest: which is broadly what was happening during the two years after the armistice. If every businessman had to make arrangements himself for feeding and clothing and amusing his employees before he embarked on any venture, as he might have to do if he were building a railway, say over the Andes, hundreds of miles from civilization, such maladjustments would not occur; but of course industrial progress would be very slow and difficult. As it is, the ease with which advances of every kind can be made in money oils the wheels of material progress: but the result is that people tend to confuse the pieces of money, which are mere certificates of a right to draw goods which may not even exist, with the goods themselves, and to lay up all sorts of trouble and disillusionment for themselves. Adam Smith once compared money to a road, over which all the produce of a district passes to market, but which does not itself produce a single blade of anything. Nobody would be so foolish as to expect to eat a road: yet man is always being surprised afresh by the discovery that he cannot eat money, as the Turks are said to be surprised afresh each year by the advent of winter. He is so pleased with his ingenious invention that he is always expecting too much of it.

6. THE EVIL EFFECTS OF MONETARY INSTABILITY ON THE DISTRIBUTION OF WEALTH

The second great disadvantage of money is one of which everybody to-day is acutely aware, namely that its value does not remain stable. We shall have to examine more carefully in a moment what we mean by this phrase, "the value of money": for the present we may define it provisionally as the power of money to purchase the things people want. Now all of us, from landowner to laborer, are enabled to live because other people want our services; if we take that word in an extended sense to include the use of our possessions: and if the power of other people's money to buy our services always varied in exactly the same degree as the power of our money to buy other people's services, there is no reason why these variations in the purchasing power of money should matter to any of us. But in fact that is not the way things happen. Some people sell their services on conditions which are fixed, by legal contract or by the force of custom, for a long time ahead in terms of money: other people are easily enabled or forced, as the case may be, to bring about alterations in the prices of the services they sell. The former group of people are clearly benefited by a rise and injured by a fall in the value of money: for in the former case they receive a greater and in the latter case a smaller power of command than they expected over the things which they require. The latter group of people tend to gain by a fall and to lose by a rise in the value of money: for they make use, whether for purposes of further production or for their own enjoyment, of the services of people whose money rewards are fixed, while their own money rewards are variable. Any change therefore, however, slight, in the value of money, so long as it is not perfectly forseen, leads to a certain redistribution of the real income of society between these two groups of persons.

A few years ago it was possible to lay down fairly definitely the classes of which each of these two groups was composed. Broadly speaking, the former comprised wage earners, professional people (such as Government officials and schoolmasters), and those who had made loans, whether to Governments or to industrial companies, at a fixed rate of money interest. The latter group comprised the "business classes," those, that is, who derived an income from venturing and planning and controlling the production and sale of goods: for their money expenses for the hire of labor and capital remained relatively fixed, while their money incomes fluctuated with the prices of the things they sold. This generalization is still partially true, but the situation has been greatly complicated by the increased power of certain sections of Labor and by the piecemeal interventions of the State. The violent fall in the value of money between 1914 and 1920 led to a great and often arbitrary redistribution of income not only between different social and industrial classes, but between the members of different callings in the same class. The reader, however, will probably recognize without much difficulty to which group he belongs. If he is a railway shareholder or an elementary school teacher or a certain type of skilled artisan, he will probably hold that he was "hit" by the fall in the value of money: if he is a shipowner or a railway porter he will probably admit to himself, though not to the world, that things did not work out so badly.

7. THE EVIL EFFECTS OF MONETARY INSTABILITY ON THE CREATION OF WEALTH

But this is not all. If the effects of the instability of the value of money were confined to distribution, they might not be of such fundamental importance: for though the consequent changes might not bear much relation to social justice, they would not necessarily diminish the total economic welfare of society, and might even substantially increase it. The loss of some would be the gain of others: and the others might on the whole be the more necessitous and even the more deserving. But in fact any violent or prolonged exhibition of instability in the value of money affects not only the distribution but also the creation of real wealth: for it threatens to undermine the basis of contract and business expectation on which our economic order is built up. That order is largely based on the institution of *contract*—on the fact, that is, that people enter into voluntary but binding agreements with one another to perform certain actions at a future date, for a remuneration which is fixed here and now in terms of money. And a violent or prolonged change in the value of money saps the confidence with which people make or accept undertakings of this nature. Nothing has been more significant in post-war business history than the wholesale attempts which have been made in certain industries and countries to repudiate contracts—to decline to make delivery of goods which were ordered when prices were lower, or to accept delivery of goods which were ordered when prices were higher. It is of course conceivable that contracts should be framed in terms of something other than money: it is even conceivable, or so some people assure us, that society should come to rely on some other method than free contract, such as the fiat of an industrial autocrat or the promptings of spontaneous benevolence, for getting its work done. But so long as reliance on the method of contract as we know it persists, so long are the vagaries of the value of money a potential cause of disaster.

None of us, however, can reduce the whole of his working life within the sphere of definite and formal contract; for the rest we live by calculation, expectation, faith. And these too are threatened, both by the instability of the value of money and by the attempts, necessarily impromptu and incomplete, which are made by society to minimize its evil results. For society, even when scrupulously regardful of contract, cannot always afford to be very tender towards more indefinite expectations. It was, for instance, inevitable, though not altogether fortunate, that during the war those "capitalists" in Great Britain who were concerned with the rendering of the most indisputably necessary services—the provision of coal, of railway transport, of houseroom—should be singled out for the most drastic attentions of the State and the Trade Unions. The present situation is indeed somewhat paradoxical. Just as the more obviously useful and important the industry in which a workman is employed, the more odium he incurs if he strikes to better his position, because he is "holding up society to ransom"; so the more obviously useful and important the direction in which a man has invested his savings, or exercised his brain power, or shouldered the burden of risk, the greater precautions the State will take that the instability of the value of money should operate to his hurt. *Noblesse oblige:* but it is not altogether astonishing if those thus put under obligation grow peevish and threaten to refuse to play. Thus monetary disease and improvised remedy alike strike at those roots of undefined but not unreasonable anticipation from which the tree of industry is still expected to derive so large a proportion of its sustenance.

Nor is it only changes in the power of money to purchase goods and services that play havoc with expectation and reasoned action. The ordinary citizen, unless he happens to have served in one of the Armies of Occupation, does not as a rule regard himself as directly interested in changes in the power of our money to buy the money of other countries: nevertheless, they affect him deeply, in so far as his economic welfare depends on the operations of foreign trade. For the tendency of these fluctuations in the foreign exchanges, as they are called, is to change the basis of foreign trade from a reasoned calculation of needs and resources to a chaotic speculation in foreign moneys. To some extent indeed the business world has already adapted itself to this perplexing environment. It has become more and more possible for those who only wish to deal in goods to protect themselves against the antics of the foreign exchanges by sloughing off the risks of monetary vagaries on to the specialized dealers in foreign money. But in so far as this device is still imperfectly known or used, the course of international trade is still warped. For to whom shall we export? Not to those who most require our goods, but to those who will pay us in a money which we hope to be able to sell dearly for the money of our own country. From whom shall we import? Not from those who have what we most need, but from those who will accept payment in a money which we hope to be able to buy cheaply with the money of our own country. Indeed, shall we export or import at all, seeing that the whole profits of a legitimate and beneficent interchange of goods may be wiped out by a turn of the money exchanges?

Thus money, which is a source of so many blessings to mankind becomes also, unless we can control it, a source of peril and confusion.

ARTHUR R. BURNS

BEFORE THE
INTRODUCTION
OF COINS

2

1. THE FIRST STAGES IN THE ORGANIZATION OF EXCHANGE

The idea of coining is one of the most important, if not the most important, single contribution to the heritage of economic knowledge that underlies the complex co-operation upon which modern life is based. But the idea did not flash suddenly upon the world; it came by such gradual stages that, as we retrace them, very much in the dark, we can never be sure which of them marks the beginning of the story. Coinage evolved, with almost incredible slowness, out of pre-existing conditions: we cannot, therefore, begin a discussion of money with the invention of coining: we are forced to consider the economic conditions in the earliest times of which there is record, that we may know the environment in which the new institution developed and which shaped its early career.

Economists have always suggested that money developed out of the priority in exchange obtained by some commodity in primitive times. Every book on economics introduces the reader to the subject of money by way of an account of the trials and troubles of life in a community where unorganized barter is the only method of ex-

Reprinted by permission of Routledge & Kegan Paul Ltd. from Arthur R. Burns, "Before the Introduction of Coins," *Money and Monetary Policy in Early Times*, 1927, pp. 1–28.

change. A community without a medium of exchange or a unit of value has, however, never been found, and the stage is one imagined for simplicity of exposition of the merits of money; it must not be taken seriously. The next supposed stage is where one or a small number of commodities has emerged as a general medium of exchange. The commodity, or one of the commodities so selected, would form one side of every exchange. But in very early times such commodities were often bulky and troublesome to deal with, and it is evident that time and energy would often be wasted in taking over the medium of exchange to pass it on again. Where it was impossible for the goods and services offered and wanted by one party to be fitted to those wanted and offered by the other, some such intermediate commodity might be required. But in early times it must very frequently have occurred that each party to the negotiations could offer a commodity desired by the other, and the real problem was to determine the ratio of exchange. The verb "to sell" corresponds to words in various ancient Teutonic languages meaning to give, to deliver up, to offer, to sacrifice; in its original use it carried no reference to exchange for currency or any common medium of exchange. The first stage in the organization of exchange was the development of a unit of value in terms of which barter could be arranged. The commodity upon which the unit was based was actually transferred in a relatively small number of the exchanges effected, but the preservation of the unit would require that the commodity selected should be one exchanged with some frequency. There is no reason why all the people in a community should use the same unit of value when it is not represented by a medium of exchange. Where a number of sheep are to be exchanged for corn, one man may value corn and sheep in oxen, and the other in bars of bronze, and without any risk of disagreement arising out of the use of different units of value. Specialized persons selling a single commodity would be apt to make all valuations in terms of some easily defined quantity of their produce. In fact, units of value in common use merely developed out of commodities in frequent exchange, and the appearance of a general medium of exchange in the sense of a commodity handed over in settlement of one side of most bargains is a later stage of economic evolution. Such a medium arose only when a commodity was available which was easily portable, divisible, and capable of preservation without difficulty. For this reason the metals provided the first medium of exchange. The introduction of metals may have given rise to a new unit of value, but more probably older units of value were translated into the new material. But the pursuit of this aspect of the evolution of money will take us too far forward into the subject. It is desirable first to investigate the commodities used in early times as mediums of exchange, and the basis of units of value.

References to these commodities by economists have been supported by casual quotations from classical authors, but their general description of primitive conditions of exchange has been mainly coloured by travellers' stories of the habits of primitive peoples in more recent times. Excavation has proceeded at a very rapid rate during the past half century, and the progress of archæological research makes possible some, although a very blurred, picture of conditions in early times.

If the commodities which figured largely in primitive exchange furnished the earliest units of value, these latter must have varied from place to place as the staple commodities in exchange varied. Palæolithic man lived mainly by hunting, at least in colder areas, and, so far as exchange occurred, furs and skins must have dominated commerce. In the colder climates they would be valued for clothing and would be less perishable than meat, the other important product of the chase. There is much evidence that furs and skins were so used in later historical times in the ancient world. The cavemen of this Old Stone or an early Neolithic Age have left another suggestion of a common medium of exchange. Buried with the most ancient remains of the human race which have been found in Europe are shells. They must have travelled far from their source of production and have posessed considerable value. In consequence, it is not improbable that they were very early a form of money. The use of tortoise and cowry shells as money in China is well authenticated both by mention in early books and by relics of their use which linger in the written and spoken language. The ideogram pei (shell) means wealth and riches, and appears in all the words relating to purchase, sale, prices, cheap, and dear, and the expression kuei hwo (tortoise-shell money) is still used as an elegant expression for coin. Tortoise shells of various species and sizes were used for greater values which would have required too many cowries. But this shell money did not come into use in China until 2000 to 1500 B.C. It is well known that in more recent times cowry shells have been very common instruments of barter in widely scattered parts of Asia and Africa, but it is doubtful when they came into use. It has been said that "shells or necklets of shells are found to be used everywhere in the earliest stages," but the New English Dictionary offers no encouragement to the quotation of the English phrase "to shell out" in support of the use of shell money in England at any time. For shells to be used as a medium of exchange they must have possessed value. But the demand for shells cannot have been narrowly utilitarian, for they play no direct part in the struggle of man with his environment; they must have appealed to the cave man and woman's passion for adornment. But to ask why their passion should have lighted upon and been satisfied by shells is to strain our archæological resources more than they can at present stand. Professor Elliot Smith holds that primitive people saw in the cowry shell a resemblance to "the portal by which a child enters the world." In consequence, they regarded the shell as a giver of life and used it as a fertility charm. The demand for shells consequent upon the spread of this practice resulted in a great traffic in them in prehistoric times, and they attained a position in commerce that fitted them for use as a medium of exchange and the foundation for a unit of value. Professor Seligman, on the other hand, states that primitive peoples now more often see in cowry shells a resemblance to an eye and use them to represent eyes in mummies. Because of this resemblance they are used as charms to ward off the evil eye. The reasons which moved primitive men to desire cowry shells are unknown, but it is clear that they were fairly common in exchange in early times. Nevertheless, they seem to have left no impress upon money as it subsequently evolved, for there is no trace of the influence of any shell unit of value. Possibly shells were never more than subsidiary currency.

The Neolithic period is characterized by the cultivation of the soil and the taming of animals. The substitution of settled life for hunting produced the small aggregations of people who first faced the problems of social organization. On the economic side accumulations of agricultural knowledge, the harnessing of the energy of beasts and the development of exchange are the most striking aspects of this new but primitive civilization. It is with the last that we are here concerned. The more durable agricultural products such as grain and oil are known to have been frequently exchanged, but fluctuations in the supply of such products caused by variations in the harvest must have rendered them unsuitable as the basis of a unit of value. Fishing communities have used dried fish in early historical times, and may well have done so soon after the process of preserving by drying and salting was discovered. When some men began to make weapons of superior material, for example, axes of jade instead of stone, these also may have been used as a medium of exchange. Social conditions were doubtless responsible for the use of a great variety of commodities as more or less common mediums of exchange in early as in more recent primitive communities. Some such commodities may have given birth in later times to units of value, and others have left their impress upon the face of the coins, but most of them were swept away when invention or importation presented units that fitted more easily into the needs of the time.

2. THE OX UNIT OF VALUE

One among the units of this age was the product, not of local conditions, but of features which characterized the civilization as a whole. The taming of animals, their use for food and sometimes for draught, brought them into the market, and made them the subject of frequent exchanges. The ox, in particular, provided the basis of a standard of value more widely used, particularly among the Aryan races, than any previous unit. Moreover, it persisted long after man had become acquainted with the metals, and into the periods of which records are available.

Representations of the heads of oxen on an inscribed clay tablet, from Knossos, part of a palace inventory, probably indicate the use of an ox unit in Crete in Minoan times. In the Homeric poems values are constantly expressed in oxen. The arms of Diomed are stated to have been worth nine oxen, while those of Glaucos were valued at one hundred. A woman slave skilled in industry was worth four oxen, and the three-legged pot, the first prize for wrestlers in the 23rd *Iliad*, was valued at twelve. A cargo of Lemnian wine, which reached the Greek camp before Troy, the chiefs purchased for cattle and hides. Towards the end of the 7th century, the fines fixed in the laws of Draco at Athens were stated in cattle. In the time of Æschylus (the 5th century B.C.), it was said of a man whose silence had been bought, that he "had an ox on his tongue." The Aryans of the *Rig-Veda*, who dwelt in the North-West Punjab, in about the 6th or 7th centuries B.C., also measured values in sheep and cattle. In ancient Persia payment in cows and sheep was common, and in the Zoroastrian *Zend-Avesta*, which was revised and partly re-written at the beginning of the 3rd century A.D., cattle units were still in use concurrently with metallic money. According to the *Vendidad* during the transition from one measure to the other cattle and sheep were still acceptable in all payments, but coins were also accepted at specified rates. Among the first inhabitants of Italy everything was valued and paid for in cattle and sheep, the full grown cow being the principal unit of value, in which accounts were kept both there and in Sicily. The Tarpeian Law of about 452 B.C provided, for the first time, for penalties fixed in cattle and sheep to be paid in pieces of marked copper. Some twenty years later a tax was substituted by law for the fines expressed in cattle, which probably means that the fines were expressed directly in copper. At Syracuse the cow was the rateable unit until the end of the 4th century B.C. Written record is supplemented by indirect evidence. Representations of a whole or part of an ox appear on many coins issued on both the west and east coasts of Greece, on the coast of Asia Minor, and also in Central Italy, and have been claimed as evidence that these coins superseded an ox unit; but the evidence is weak. More assistance is obtained by tracing the derivation of words relating to money and monetary transactions. It is well known that the Latin *pecunia* is derived from *pecus* (cattle), and "peculation," says Festus, "as a name for public theft, was derived from *pecus* because that was the earliest kind of fraud." The English *fee* is traced through Anglo-Saxon to the Gothic *faihu*, meaning cattle. Another Gothic word for cattle, *skatts*, comes in its Anglo-Saxon form of *skeat* to mean treasure or money. The Indian *rupee* can be traced to a Sanskrit word *rûpya*, which again is derived from a word meaning cattle. These words all became so generally related to cattle, used as a medium of exchange, that they were applied to anything else which was so used when, in its turn, the cattle medium was superseded.

The wide use of the ox unit shows that it met the needs of the age. As a means of payment, and a form in which purchasing power could be accumulated, cattle were troublesome, requiring care and some degree of skill in their preservation. For overseas trade they were particularly unsuited, but they were not so radically disqualified for use in local and continental trade. They were not quickly perishable, and their capacity for multiplication, for work, and the supply of milk, all counterbalanced the disadvantage that they were costly to maintain. Their bulk was no great disadvantage, as they provided their own transport. But, in spite of their capacity to become current in the most literal sense, they were probably much more used as a unit of value than a medium of exchange—a probability which is supported by such evidence as is available. The size of the ox unit must have limited its usefulness in either capacity. In Homeric times oxen were owned mainly by kings, nobles, and the wealthier classes, the simple man having only goats and sheep, and, as a currency, oxen were limited to the settlement of larger bargains. But in more primitive economic conditions, small transactions are much less frequent and important than in modern times, and there is little doubt that they were effected by some other form of currency. These latter forms of currency doubtless supplied small value units as well. As the basis of a standard of value, the ox was not all that could be desired. But its disadvantages are different in kind from those attaching to its use as a currency. As a value unit it would be as useful as any other in foreign trade, which was not of great importance to most early communities, and must always have been effected by barter. But it is essential in a standard that it shall possess stability, and that it shall be capable of easy and precise definition. Cattle were probably more stable in value than agricultural products and many of the other primitive standards, since the stock of cattle was greater in proportion to the annual accessions to that stock than can be said of agricultural produce. But the stock was liable to sudden reduction owing to epidemic diseases and shortage of fodder, which tended to cause temporary and local enhancement of the value of the unit. Stability of the unit of value must, however, have been of much less importance in primitive communities, where the number of bargains for future fulfilment, made in the terms of the unit, was probably very small, and their duration usually short. It is the increase in the number of such bargains, and in the length of the period between the time of agreement and the time of execution, that renders stability of the unit of value of such primary importance at the present time. Oxen are not uniform in value, and an ox unit of value must be an abstract unit. The abstract unit necessitated precise definition of both quality and quantity. If the word "ox" was applied only to the full-grown beast, a rough natural definition of quantity was obtained. The definition of quality was very much more difficult. The long and searching discussion involved in the negotiation of the sale of an ox in a modern country market shows that the fixing of the values of cattle, which appear to the untrained eye to be of similar quality, is no simple business. Oxen cannot have changed much in this respect, even in three or four thousand years, and the definition of the typical or "money-ox," which was to be the one carried in the mind when values were being quoted, presented great difficulties. Although men probably did not then attempt the exact measurement of values to which the long use of the metals has accustomed us, they did make some attempts to render their unit less vague. Generally the "standard ox" was one of a stated age. But the difficulty of making out of the ox any sharply defined standard of value must have proved insuperable, and probably accounts for the willingness of most progressive communities to turn to the metals and allow the old ox-unit to be superseded.

3. METALLIC MEDIUMS OF EXCHANGE

The next stage in the evolution of exchange technique accompanied the abandonment of stone tools in favour of bronze. The pursuit of agriculture in the Neolithic Age brought with it the problem of agricultural machinery in its most primitive form. The need for tools was doubtless an incentive in the search for a more tractable material than stone, and the metals provided that material. Gold and bronze are of great age. The latter dates at least from the 4th millennium B.C., and its discovery revolutionized economic life: the Stone Age gave place to the Age of Bronze. The metal which was so useful in providing new implements attained an important position in exchange, and was probably among the first commodities that can properly be described as mediums of exchange. Gold was the other metal to be so used; known, perhaps, even earlier than bronze, it met less urgent economic needs, but became a more universal exchange medium. Silver is rarely found native, and its isolation called for considerable metallurgical skill; in consequence, it was a much later exchange medium than gold. Still greater skill, both in smelting and working, was necessary before iron could replace bronze as a medium for tools and open the Iron Age. Methods of working iron were probably discovered in the north of Syria during the 2nd millennium B.C., and among the civilized peoples of the East the Iron Age began with the 1st millennium B.C. Gold, bronze, silver, and iron are the principal metals which were used as mediums of exchange. Other metals have been used, but not over long periods or large areas, and, as they have had no appreciable effect on the subsequent history of money, they can be ignored.

The three most ancient civilizations which have left records— Egypt, Babylon, and China—were all acquainted with bronze, and have left evidence that it was used as a currency. This evidence takes the form either of literary record or the discovery of bronze made up in forms suggestive of currency use. The Egyptians worked the rich copper mines of the peninsula of Sinai from about the beginning of the 4th millennium B.C. Supplies were also obtained from Cyprus and Syria, and the metal was fairly plentiful. Gold, though also fairly plentiful, was too valuable to furnish a convenient unit for the settlement of day-to-day transactions; silver, in very early times, was even more valuable than gold, owing to its greater scarcity, all supplies having to come from a distance. In consequence, when a medium of exchange and unit of value was formally adopted in the middle kingdom about the 12th century B.C. copper was selected. Down to the 6th century B.C. it was a common practice to cast copper in moulds made to contain a unit weight, but, as the resulting bricks of the metal were not uniform in size, they were usually weighed out. The values of goods and cattle are recorded in copper by weight, and wages were expresed in the same terms. In the records of the tomb robberies about the 13th century B.C. values are also reported in terms of copper, and this basis of reckoning continued down to the 3rd century B.C.

Copper was known to the civilizers of China in the 23rd century B.C., and they learnt the use of bronze some five hundred years later. There is more certainty that in China copper supplied an early currency. "Originally any metallic tool or implement of small size, or even a lump of metal, was used in barter. The convenience of this practice led gradually to the practice of casting sham tools or implements for the purpose of exchange only." From at least the 7th century B.C., and most probably very much earlier, small round tongue-like plates of copper, generally regarded as hoes and spades, were in common use as currency. The thinness of the later issues of spades is evidence that they were never intended for use in agriculture. Copper knives were also very commonly used as money. Their issue began in Shantung in the 7th century B.C., and they seem originally to have been graving knives, the point of which was used for writing and the blade for erasing, as they follow the legal regulations as to the length of these knives. The ring shape, which has proved so universally popular a shape for ingots of the monetary metal, is also mentioned in China in the middle of the 10th century B.C., when commutation of punishments and fines was enacted, and the penalties were expressed in terms of rings of copper weighing six ounces. These rings do not appear to have been so widely acceptable as spades and knives, and several unsuccessful attempts were made to popularize them before success was attained in 221 B.C. The *Rig-Veda* testifies to the use of copper among the peoples of North-West Punjab in the 7th century B.C. In Assyria and Babylon pieces of copper of fixed weight circulated together with the precious metals and were in very common use. That copper was held in considerable esteem appears from the prominence given to bricks, plates, and utensils of copper in the accounts of the treasure obtained by Assyrian conquerors as a result of their depredations in Syria and Asia Minor in the 12th and 9th centuries B.C.

In Crete, the half-way house between Egypt and Greece, the Bronze Age began about 2400 to 2100 B.C., and by the middle of the 2nd millennium B.C. the Mycenæan offshoot of the Cretan civilization appeared on the mainland of Greece. Between 1400 and 1200 the Minoan civilization fell, but in its Mycenæan form survived for a brief period of two or three hundred years, using bronze for currency as well as tools and weapons. In the district to the west and south of the isthmus of Corinth (Argolis) there has been found beneath the Palace of Mycenæ a copper ingot about 2½ feet long in a shape which is said to represent a hide stretched to dry (with no head or tail). This may even be as old as the 14th century B.C., and suggests a transition from the live ox unit to metals by way of a representation of the shape of the hide. Other specimens found off the coast of Eubœa suggest that the circulation of the ingots extended to Attica. A tablet found by Sir Arthur Evans at Knossos, which seems to equate ox-hide ingots of copper with talents of gold, points to their circulation in Crete. These ingots are of a shape that cannot have rendered them particularly useful; they may have been so shaped to make them convenient to lash. They were of fixed weights which formed a series of multiples, and they often bore a stamp, and it is probable that bronze in this form circulated as a currency in the Eastern Mediterranean for six or seven hundred years into the Homeric Age when copper was certainly used for many payments.

Further west bronze was used by the primitive peoples of Central and North Italy. These peoples, who were making their way to Italy at the beginning of the 2nd millennium B.C., had in circulation from at least 1000 B.C. amorphous lumps of bronze of various sizes, the value of which must have been measured by their bulk. Later it became customary to cast it in more regular form. Flat pieces, some oblong, and others square, and weighing from one ounce to twelve pounds, have been found, very frequently in votive deposits to the divinities of fountains. Bronze was probably also made up into foot lengths, divided by transverse marks into twelve inches. Still later it began to pass by weight and was made up into pieces of one pound weight. The advent of weighing made it possible to dispense with definition by measurement, and then the pieces lost their old shape. These lumps or bars, known to ancient writers as *as rude* (raw copper), were, according to Pliny, the common means of payment until the time of Servius Tullius (in the middle of the 6th century B.C.). By 451 B.C. the *as* must have been common as a means of payment, for in that year the Tarpeian Law, while continuing to express fines in terms of sheep and cattle, made provision for their payment in marked *asses*. The three Commissioners sent to Athens in 454 B.C., to study the laws there, doubtless reported that Solon had provided that the fines expressed in the laws of Draco in sheep and cattle might be paid in money, and the Tarpeian Law was copied from Athens. A year or two later, when the twelve tables of laws were drawn up, some penalties were made payable in *asses* and *sesterces* of copper, no mention of payment in cattle being made. But the cattle unit died hard, for twenty years later it was necessary to order by law (the lex Papiria) that payments in copper should replace payments in cattle. Cicero ascribed this law to the fact that "the Censors had, through the vigorous imposition of fines of cattle, converted many private herds to the public use," and in consequence "a light tax in lieu of a fine of cattle was substituted." This may, however, only mean that payment in cattle was inconvenient, owing to the difficulty of disposing profitably of the cattle: it probably marks the end of the practice of assessing fines in cattle and sheep. There is, therefore, no doubt as to the existence of a bronze medium of exchange and standard of value. In fact, the habit of expressing values in terms of copper or *aes* gave rise to the verb *æstimare* and to our words to *esteem* and to *estimate*. A medium similar to the Italian *libra*, or pound, of bronze was used in Sicily, where it was called a *litra*, and circulated in rods similar to those used in Italy. In the Caucasus and Russian Armenia, in certain parts of the Urals, and along the banks of the Volga, bronze rings were in use in prehistoric times. Specimens found there in burial grounds are regular and graduated according to the system of weights. In Scandinavia, and generally in Central European countries, bracelets of copper and bronze were in use during the Bronze Age as a standard of value. Specimens are frequently spiral in form, and the fact that they often appear to have been intentionally broken at one or both ends suggests that the settlement of small transactions was effected by breaking off pieces from the rings. Rings of this kind were also in use among the Saxons, Danes, and other North European peoples until the beginning of the Middle Ages. Bronze probably circulated in other forms too, in double axe heads in Central Europe and in celts in Gaul.

Acquaintance with gold is of such great age that we do not know where or when it was first used. It was often found native, especially in the beds of streams, and the most primitive men in gold-yielding areas must have been familiar with its appearance. The ease with which the metal was shaped must also have been discovered in a remote age. But it was not suited for the making of weapons or tools, and the only explanation of the value which it attained is that it proved attractive for personal adornment. It could be of no use as a currency or to provide a value standard until some demand for it had arisen and it had become valuable and frequently exchanged. Though a pure speculation, it is not unlikely that very early men picked small nuggets out of the streams and used them as trinkets in much the same spirit as they used shells. When they discovered that the new material was easy to work, more complicated trinkets were possible, and they may at first have made imita-

tions of the shells then fashionable. But we must be on our guard
when we regard the beautiful lustre of the precious metals as sufficient explanation for their original appeal to man, for social convention and habit make it impossible for us to look with the un-
sophisticated eyes of primitive man on the many beautiful things
produced by nature and to choose impartially. Many attempts have
been made to discover the impulses in primitive men to which gold
made its successful appeal, thus securing a place in his subsequent
economic history out of all proportion to the assistance it has given
in his struggle with Nature. He may have seen in the metal a resemblance to the sun which he had already come to see as the author
of all life; or its association with the springs of life may have been
by its association with the cowry shell; for if, as Professor Elliot
Smith suggests, the cowry shell was widely regarded as a giver of
life, peoples living at some distance from the sea must have found
difficulty in obtaining supplies of the shells. It is supposed that,
rather than pay the high prices demanded, they made gold imitations of cowry shells and, finding them to be good, they continued
to use them. Later ideas as to the source of the magical properties
of the charm became confused, and those properties were associated
with the metal and no longer with its shape. Gold was now launched
on its long career in the satisfaction of the human desire for personal adornment, and it slipped easily into the position occupied
by shells as a medium of exchange. It has often been claimed for
gold that it is the source of life and immortality and that it preserves the body. These beliefs are found particularly in Chinese
and Indian literature; Western peoples have made humbler claims.
Pliny says, "Gold boiled in honey with melanthum and applied as
a liniment to the navel acts as a gentle purgative upon the bowels.
M. Varro assures us that gold is a cure for warts."

It is, however, probable, and even to be expected that, when men
discovered gold, their first efforts would be directed to the imitation
of shapes with which they were acquainted, and, in particular,
shapes already regarded as attractive. Gold imitations of cowry
shells have, in fact, been found, and the Egyptians so far associated
gold with these shells that "the earliest hieroglyphic sign for gold
was a picture of a necklace of amulets" (of shells).

That men began to work gold solely for the purpose of imitating
cowry shells, the core of Prof. Elliot Smith's theory from the economic point of view, is entirely unproved. Some modern psychol-
ogists contend that metal coins in general, but gold in particular,
are valued because, for definite psychological reasons, they are particularly associated with our sense of possession. The popular con-

fusion between money and wealth is not, therefore, to be ascribed alone to inadequate diffusion of economic knowledge. The importance attached to the gold standard, on the other hand, is not the result of pure economic thought; it also is the product of this symbolism. The psychological factors behind the present high value of gold are somewhat different from those of primitive times. The most important modern demand arises out of its monetary use, either directly in coins or indirectly in reserves. This use is founded on the relative stability in the value of gold which results from the absence in recent years (if we many exclude years of war) of rapid variations in either the demand for or the supply of gold. The psychological reasons behind the general, but now questioned, adherence to gold as a basis for currencies are best sought in treatises on currency theory. The industrial demand for gold is based on the physical qualities of the metal, and these, in particular the fact that it does not corrode, are considerable. Probably a fall in the price of gold would reveal capacity for a very great extension of these uses, and gold would then cease to be regarded as more ornamental than useful. The individual demand for gold is now confined mainly to its use for decoration and jewellery, for the latter of which it is still in great demand—a demand doubtless based in part upon its pleasant colour and lustre. In these, however, it is by no means alone, especially among the metals, although in its freedom from tendency to tarnish it is more uncommon. But the demand probably once based on natural qualities of beauty has caused a rise in value, and gold is now by reason of its value used also as a means of ostentation, a certificate not only of wealth, but of the ability to keep possessions in a form unproductive of economic gain. This motive is indicated by the recent tendency to supersede gold by platinum in jewellery. Platinum, while being harder, is much less attractive in appearance than silver, which possesses a finer lustre, yet silver has already fallen into disuse for jewelry. Gold, if once used as a magical means of securing good luck, is now a certificate of its enjoyment.

The part played by gold has been, and continues to be, of such importance in economic life generally and in currency arrangements in particular, that is origins must be of the greatest interest. It must be confessed, however, that the theories put forward need specialist examination, and, for the economist, the primary facts are that gold was known in very early times, and, for reasons yet not explained, man chose to work gold and make ornaments. In consequence it became a commodity of value, and, in times of recorded history, we find it in use almost everywhere as a medium of exchange. But in these later ages of which there is record, silver was frequently used side by side with gold. It has already been said that silver came into use much later than gold. In common with gold it has rarely been found in directly utilitarian use in ancient times, and the main use of both has been for ornament and as an exchange medium. Less attempt has been made to account for the appeal of silver. When it was isolated, gold had long been used, and men were more sophisticated than when they first worked gold. Nevertheless, while gold is said to have made its appeal because of its resemblance to the sun, silver was thought to resemble the moon, and attempts have been made to associate the relation between the periodicity of the sun and moon with the relative values of gold and silver. How any causal connection can be established between the two relations is inconceivable.

The ancient civilizations offer plenty of evidence of the use of gold and silver in exchange. In Egypt gold was playing a part at the very dawn of history and silver came into use considerably later. Both metals were made up in unit weights, sometimes in the form of bricks, but more commonly in rings carefully graduated in weight down to the smallest units. These rings are frequently mentioned in Egyptian texts. The museum at Leyden contains a number of specimens which were found in Egypt: they are perfectly regular, made of pieces of wire bent round into circles, or into "S" form, but of six different sizes; they are of such small dimensions that they could not have been meant for use as jewellery but must have been instruments of exchange. They did not, however, bear any guarantee of weight, and it appears from temple paintings that they were verified in the balance. Some of these paintings show great sales of corn being settled by means of gold rings which are being heaped up in the scales to be weighed. These rings were probably used to settle the larger transactions, but copper remained the measure of value, and gold and silver were taken at their current value in copper. In a hieratic papyrus in the Louvre a number of receipts in *sicles* (*shekels*) of silver are mentioned "at the rate of three-quarters of an *outen* of copper to the *sicle*," the *outen* being the unit of weight for copper. The units of weight upon which the rings are made come from Asia, and it is, therefore, probable that the rings were current there as well; perhaps, as Babelon suggests, they came as tribute from Palestine or Syria. From the 12th to the 7th centuries before our era gold, silver, and copper were all circulating in this form in Egypt, but silver composed the mass of the currency and regulated prices.

The Chinese have been using gold and silver in exchange since about 2100 B.C., and as early as eleven centuries before our era gold in one inch cubes (or *kin*), weighing one pound, is mentioned as a unit, but historical references to its use are very rare. It was probably restricted to the purchase of jewels and to presents from princes and wealthy persons. Both gold and silver also circulated in rings, and attempts to popularize this form, probably introduced from Egypt, were made in 1032 B.C. Ring money is mentioned in connection with commutation of punishments in 947 B.C. Again in 523 B.C. an unsuccessful attempt was made to circulate rings, but in 221 B.C. metal in this form was definitely adopted as currency. Small bean-shaped ingots or metallic cowries, circulated 613–590 B.C. Japan presents a very striking contrast to China, for there a state of pure barter, without the use of metals in any form, is believed to have persisted until the 5th century A.D. The peoples of North-West India of Vedic times (about the 6th or 7th century B.C.) had a gold unit of their own before they knew the use of silver.

In Babylon both gold and silver were known. Gold was scarce and but rarely used in business transactions, although it appears more frequently in temple offerings. Silver provided a generally accepted unit of value at the end of the 3rd millennium B.C. The laws of Hammurabi then set down fixed wages, prices, and fines in considerable detail, and frequently in silver by weight. Both metals at first circulated in irregular ingots, but were later made up into small pieces of exact weight, and must, therefore, have been used as exchange mediums. After the sacking of Babylon by the Hittites, silver served as a unit of value, but much less frequently as a medium of exchange, bargains being settled frequently in corn, and to some extent also in slaves, animals, weapons, and garments.

The Minoan peoples must have used gold, if not silver, from the 3rd millennium B.C., for they were in close communication with Egypt. Recent discoveries reveal how close an approach was attained in Mycenæ and Cyprus, as well as Crete, to the making of coins. The precious metals circulated in lumps, and gold even in discs, the weights of which indicate that they were based upon an organized system of weights. Moreover, when the King of Knossos caused an inventory to be made of his treasure, its value in copper talents was converted into gold.

The Phœnicians, whose culture was probably an early offshoot of the Minoan, rose to power at the decline of the Cretan power in the 12th century B.C., when they were using both gold and silver. So prominent were their possessions of the precious metals that a tradition grew up among the Greeks that the Phœnician ships had anchors of gold.

Among the Jews of the early centuries, the last millennium B.C., all three metals circulated by weight. Gold and silver are mentioned very early in the Hebrew scriptures. Abraham came back from Egypt "very rich in cattle, in silver, and in gold," and Solomon accepted tribute payments in these metals; he received "vessels of silver and vessels of gold." Probably the metals were frequently in the form of rings, and sometimes bars and bricks. Gold, however, was not used so much for money as for personal ornaments and in connection with the temple. The gift made by the servant of Abraham to Rebekah of a "golden earring of half a *shekel* weight and two bracelets for her hands of ten *shekels* weight of gold" suggests that jewellery was made up of unit weights so that it could be used in lieu of money. A statement of the weight of the ornament would have been the most suitable way of conveying the value of the gifts, but it does not follow that the exact weight is given. Although gold and silver rings were a common form of early currency over a great part of the ancient world, the common medium among the Jews was silver measured by weight. When Abraham purchased from Ephron the cave of Machpelah as a burial place for Sarah, he "weighed to Ephron the silver which he had named in the audience of the sons of Heth four hundred *shekels* of silver current money with the merchant." Although "money" is referred to, since it had to be weighed out, it could not have been coined money, of which there is no mention in the Hebrew scriptures. In the law of Moses the prices of slaves and cattle, fines for offences, contributions to the temple, sacrifices of animals, are all regulated by the value of silver.

Numerous other passages in the scriptures bear evidence of the use of gold and silver by weight, although it is probable "that the balance was not called into operation for every small transaction, but that little beads or bullets of silver and of gold of fixed weight, but without any official mark, and, therefore, not coins, were often counted out by tale, larger amounts being always weighed. Such small lumps of gold and silver served the purposes of a currency." In Mycenæan Greece, and also in the dark ages succeeding the Dorian invasion of Greece from the north in about 1200 B.C., both gold and silver were in use, but conditions were very primitive and older units long survived. Later, gold came into more common use as a medium and was dealt in by weight. A special unit (the *talent*) was used for weighing it, and it was probably kept in ingots of *talent* or half-*talent* weight. Two round bullets of gold, which have been found in a late Mycenæan tomb in Cyprus, are believed to be half-*talents*. No single piece of coined money has, however, come down from these times. In Italy, in early times, although copper was the principal medium of exchange, gold and silver were in use in small ingots or bricks, and were probably used to settle larger transactions. There was a considerable supply of gold in England, probably from Ireland, in the middle of the Bronze Age (towards the end of the 2nd millennium B.C.). There is no sign of its use for currency. Thin crescent-shaped sheets are found with bronze celts; a gold plated breastplate intended for a pony indicates the possibility of the use of gold in religious ritual, and the crescents may have been associated with moon worship.

Iron seems to have been first worked in the district to the west of the Taurus Mountains: during the 2nd millennium B.C. knowledge of the process passed eastward with the Vannic peoples who lived in what is now Armenia. During the first two or three hundred years of the last millennium B.C., probably at the end of the 8th century owing to the northern campaigns of Sargon, it passed to Assyria, where iron extensively replaced bronze. To the west the Hattic peoples, who lived in Cappadocia to the north of Syria, knew of the use of iron probably from the middle of the 2nd millennium B.C., and, by the beginning of the 1st millennium B.C., the knowledge had passed southward to the Hittite Carchemish and to Palestine. The general replacement of bronze by iron did not occur in the Eastern Mediterranean until the early part of the 1st millennium B.C., when the civilizations of Egypt and Assyria were beginning to crumble and that of Crete had already fallen. By that time bronze and gold and silver were well established in their use as mediums of exchange. Although the new metal made great changes in economic life, it probably had no marked general effect upon primitive currency. Specimens of iron currency and weapons are much more rare than those of bronze, not only because it was late in coming into use, but also because it so easily oxidizes. In Greece, however, there is definite evidence of the use of iron as an exchange medium. The Dorian peoples from somewhere in the neighborhood of the wilds of Albania came down into Greece at the beginning of the 12th century B.C., leaving a trail of ruins from Corinth to Sparta. They laid waste Mycenæ, and the native peoples fled. Destructive as they were of the old civilization they brought the seeds of a new, for they possessed a knowledge of the use of iron, and, on their arrival, the Bronze Age in Greece gave way to one of iron. The weapons and implements of Homeric Greece were of iron, which was then held in high regard. It was an important article of commerce, and there is a little doubt that it provided the staple currency of the Peloponnese for two or three hundred years down to the beginning of the 7th century B.C. In about 600 B.C. the laws of Lycurgus prohibited the introduction of gold, silver, or even copper in Sparta for commercial circulation. Iron alone was allowed, and that circulated in long bars weighing about 1¾ lbs. troy. The broken remains of such bars have been found in excavations at Sparta. The Homeric poems also mention the circulation of iron bars concurrently with precious metals and cattle. Aristotle records that Pheidon dedicated specimens of iron nails or spits in the Heræum, and subsequent excavations on the site of the temple have brought to light a bundle of rounded iron bars about four feet long and pointed at one end. The reason for the dedication is in some doubt. The nails were most probably the form in which iron was used as currency, and their dedication may have been a way of preserving official standards of weight and length for the uncoined metal in circulation. More probably the nails were dedicated as specimens of obsolete currency which had been superseded by the coins which Pheidon is believed to have introduced into Peloponnesus, or perhaps still more likely as obsolete apparatus of the period before the introduction of coins which was no longer required. Such a dedication is in accordance with a prevalent custom of offering up in the temple old and obsolete implements that had ceased to please the owner. The nails, or *obols*, are worth something less than a penny of our money (in gold equivalent), and six of them made a handful, or *drachma*, which has since become an historic currency unit. Small change was probably obtained by breaking pieces off the bars, much as apparently the early farthings were intended to be obtained by breaking coins into four in England. Aristotle referred to iron *obols* in his lost constitution of the Sicyonians, and Rhodopis, the Greek courtesan of Naucratis, is reported to have dedicated a great quantity of iron spits, "such as are fit for roasting oxen," at Delphi. At the beginning of the 7th century this iron currency was probably superseded, at least in large payments, by the silver coins of Egina. . . .

FEDERAL RESERVE BANK OF CHICAGO

DEBT—AND THE ECONOMY

3

This article is concerned with an area about which nearly everyone has something to say, and usually from a fairly fixed and passionate point of view. At the same time, it is an area, unfortunately, about which economists and economic literature have provided relatively little that can be taken as authoritative and definitive. Over and above the fact that the economy needs debt to function—on this point there is virtually no disagreement—there is little in the way of benchmarks or yardsticks suggesting *how much debt* the economy *ought to have* or *can have*. Because of the lack of standards or benchmarks, there is wide disagreement as to how debt can be meaningfully measured or evaluated, for example, regarding its growth and composition. The confusion and diverse opinions that sprout whenever debt is discussed are suggested by the following quotation:

> Not long ago one of our elder statesmen made a campaign speech in which he announced with rage and shock, "the debts of the American people today are higher than ever before in our history!" It is an effective point and he delivered it well—as he should. He has been saying it for years. It is a line that suggests evil doings in high places and has the special political advantage that it is almost always true. It is virtually an economic law and its corollary is that we are almost always upset about it.
>
> A few years ago we were shocked by the rapid growth of farm debt, then we were dismayed by the expansion of business debt, then Congress got worried about housing debt, and the President became concerned about consumer debt.
>
> Meanwhile, when things became slack, we all fussed about the national debt. But why? Why do we continue to accumulate debts when they cause us so much concern?[1]

Reprinted from "Debt—and the Economy," *Economic Review* (September 1965), pp. 3–23, Federal Reserve Bank of Chicago.
[1] See Marshall A. Robinson, *Debt and the American Economy* (Washington, D. C.: The Brookings Institution, 1959), p. 1.

THE ECONOMICS OF DEBT

This section attempts, perhaps heroically, to come to grips with the question posed in the foregoing quotation. The creation of debt is part of a process by which the surplus purchasing power of savers is placed in the hands of deficit spenders. In other words, the creation of debt involves a transfer of purchasing power from those spending units—individuals, families, business concerns, government bodies, etc.—that save a part of their current incomes to those spending units desiring to make outlays in excess of their current incomes. Such transfers of purchasing power involve the incurrence of debt, that is, an obligation on the part of a borrower to make repayment at some future time. But, simultaneously, such transfers of present purchasing power also involve the creation of a financial asset held by the lender, that is, a claim to future purchasing power. Thus, the creation of debt involves the simultaneous creation of offsetting assets and liabilities.

Debt is created (and accumulated) because it is essential to the proper functioning of an economy such as that of the U.S. Economic growth, which is one important measure of economic performance, depends to a large extent on a nation's willingness to forego the immediate consumption of part of its current output in favor of acquiring the means of producing a larger output for future consumption. Stated somewhat differently, satisfactory economic growth depends on adequate levels of savings and capital formation. Another, though less measurable, index of economic performance is the extent to which scarce resources are allocated to the most productive uses. Optimum savings and investment levels and an efficient redistribution of savings, which involves shifting control over resources to those best able to determine their use, are facilitated by the process of debt creation.

Consider, for example, an economy in which a debt process does not exist; that is, consider an economy in which no spending unit is able to spend more than the sum of its current income and financial savings. Surely, some saving and, therefore, capital accumulation will take place. The levels of savings and investment, however, would almost certainly be less than optimum. Some spending units that foresee profitable investment opportunities would be restrained by a lack of purchasing power. Other units, having no such desirable opportunities, would have to choose between consuming all their current income, hoarding a portion of such income in the form of generalized purchasing power, or making less productive investments. In any event, a less than optimum share of scarce resources would be devoted to capital formation.

Suppose now that debt creation becomes possible. Spending units with profitable investment opportunities would compete with each other to acquire necessary purchasing power from saving units. The latter, as a general matter, might be inclined to transfer purchasing power to these units for any of several reasons. First, because they expect to share in the returns earned on the investment, such units stand ready to receive a larger amount of future purchasing power —an amount, perhaps, sufficient to cause individuals to forego some present consumption. Second, the opportunity cost of hoarding rises considerably as excess funds can earn an interest return. Finally, by lending to those perhaps more qualified to make investments, savers now have opportunities to earn better returns than the returns formerly earned on capital they themselves had acquired. In summary, then, the economy benefits by encouraging, through the process of debt creation, a separation between the function of saving and the function of investment.

The transfer of funds from savers to investors is facilitated by the existence of financial institutions and financial markets. The principal function of financial institutions such as commercial banks, mutual savings banks, insurance companies, and savings and loan associations, among others, is to perform as intermediaries in the transfer of purchasing power between ultimate lenders and ultimate borrowers. More specifically, the principal function of financial intermediaries is to purchase the debt instruments of ultimate borrowers and to issue their own debt instruments for the portfolios of ultimate lenders. Individual savers, therefore, have a choice of acquiring claims either on the ultimate borrower or on an intermediary institution.

As implied, the existence and development of financial intermediaries tend to raise the level of savings and investment and, at the same time, to increase the efficiency of resource allocation. Consider, in this connection, the following statement pertaining to intermediation:

> Financial intermediaries exploit economies of scale in lending and borrowing. On the lending side, the intermediary can invest and manage investments in primary securities (i.e., debt instruments issued by ultimate borrowers) at unit costs far below the experience of most individual lenders. The sheer size of its portfolio permits a significant reduction in risks through diversification. It can schedule maturities so chances of liquidity crises are minimized. . . . On the borrowing side, the intermediary with a large number of depositors can normally rely on a pre-

dictable schedule of claims for repayment and so can get along with a portfolio that is relatively illiquid. The advantages of large-scale borrowing and lending with numerous creditors (i.e., holders of claims on the intermediary) and debtors (those whose debt instruments are held by the intermediary) can be distributed to the intermediary's debtors in the form of favorable terms of lending, to its creditors in the form of interest payments and other benefits, and to its stockholders in the form of sufficient dividends to attract additional capital funds.[2]

Individual lenders and borrowers are less likely to agree easily upon terms (concerning the type of debt security, duration of loan, repayment procedure, etc.) that are suitable for both parties. This, together with the risks attached to a lack of portfolio diversification, would likely result in lower rates of saving and capital formation. Intermediation by financial institutions, however, "give(s) lenders a wide variety of financial assets particularly suited to their needs, and . . . also make(s) it less necessary for borrowers to issue these types of securities, which are ill-adapted to their own businesses."[3]

Most observers would agree, at least in principle, that debt plays a particularly important and beneficial role in our economy. In considering specific aspects of debt, however, all semblance of agreement vanishes. Thus, an active and continuous debate rages regarding such questions as how much debt the economy ought to have, and how this debt should be distributed among different sectors of the economy. Unfortunately, economists have yet to provide adequate answers to these important public policy questions.

To gain some perspective on the magnitudes and relationships associated with debt, the following pages are devoted to the "numbers" and some of their implications. Unfortunately, there are no answers provided—if there are "answers." The discussion centers on aggregate data—the broad or global statistics—as well as disaggregated data—the major sectors of the economy.

THE BIG PICTURE

As indicated in Chart 1, at the end of 1964, total debt in the economy had reached nearly $1.3 trillion, which admittedly is an astronomical figure. Total debt had thus doubled since 1953, and had increased nearly three times since the end of World War II (the average annual rate of growth during 1947–1964, inclusive, amounted

[2] See J. G. Gurley and E. S. Shaw, *Money in a Theory of Finance* (Washington, D. C.: The Brookings Institution, 1960), p. 194.
[3] *Ibid.* p. 197.

CHART 1   Debt and Economic Activity (*end of year*)

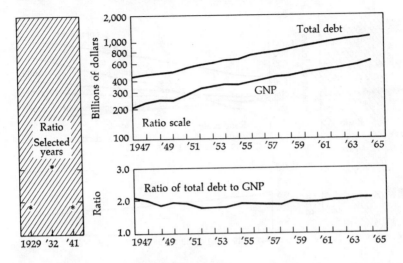

SOURCE OF DATA: U.S. Department of Commerce.

to 6.06 percent). In the way of historical comparison, total debt had amounted to $228 billion in 1941, $179 billion in 1932 (the low level during the 1930s) and $196 billion in 1929. Admittedly, magnitudes such as these—outside of sheer size—do not mean very much by themselves; they should be compared with or contrasted to other relevant magnitudes.

A comparison often made is that with the Gross National Product in order to get an impression of the magnitude of debt in terms of the total value of the nation's current output as well as the nation's ability to service debt out of current production. As Chart 1 shows, the movements of total debt and GNP, although characterized by some unevenness, have been largely parallel, especially in recent years. This is confirmed by the ratio of total debt to GNP, shown in the bottom panel of the chart. In 1964, the total debt/GNP ratio was 2.04, not much higher than during most of the postwar period and actually below 1946. (The annual growth rate of GNP, in current dollars, during 1947–1964, inclusive, was 5.92 percent.) As the ratio line indicates, the debt/GNP ratio has tended to decline, or increase less, during recession periods (1948, 1953, 1957), as debt has increased less, or has fallen more, than GNP. Again for historical interest, and as shown in the left-hand panel, the debt/GNP ratio was 1.9 in 1929, 3.1 in 1932 (when GNP had de-

CHART 2   Public and Private Debt *(end of year)*

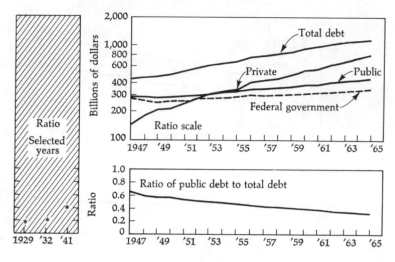

SOURCE OF DATA: U.S. Department of Commerce.

clined drastically), and 1.8 in 1941. There is implicit in these figures an important phenomenon. . . . The rapid expansion in total debt since World War II really has not represented "a breakthrough to unprecedentedly high levels relative either to GNP or to after-tax income. Rather, this expansion has represented a process of catching-up."[4] In other words, rising debt—and, as will be seen, this applies only to private debt—has been making up ground lost during the depression of the 1930s and the war years. (All of the net increase in total debt from 1930–1945 was accounted for by the Federal Government.)

PUBLIC AND PRIVATE DEBT

One way to analyze total debt is to separate public and private debt. As Chart 2 shows, private debt clearly accounts for a larger proportion of total debt; since private debt has been increasing faster than public debt, the proportion has risen in each year of the postwar period. (Since 1947, private debt has increased at an average annual rate of 9.34 percent and public debt at 2.67 percent.) At the

---

[4] See C. Canby Balderston, "Borrowing Short and Lending Long," address before the Fiftieth Annual Fall Conference of the Robert Morris Associates, Montreal, Canada, Sept. 28, 1964, p. 5 (mimeographed).

end of 1964, private debt amounted to $819 billion, or about 65 percent of total debt. Private debt more than doubled from 1955 through 1964 and increased more than four times during 1947–1964, inclusive. While private debt as a ratio of total debt was 0.65 in 1964, it had been 0.50 in 1952 and about 0.40 in 1947. In connection with this increase, the catching-up of private debt referred to earlier should be recalled. As a ratio of total debt, private debt amounted to 0.60 in 1941—which was the prewar *low*—and 0.82 in 1929. As indicated earlier, total private debt actually began to decline in 1929; there was no increase again until the very late 1930s, and private debt did not regain its 1929 level until 1947.

From Chart 2, some observations about public debt are readily apparent. First, public debt as a ratio of total debt amounted to 0.35 at the end of 1964. (See lower panel of Chart 2.) In comparison with private debt, public debt has increased moderately since World War II, becoming a much smaller proportion of total debt—and GNP. In the case of the latter, it means that public debt is presently less of a burden for the economy than earlier. Within total public debt, Federal debt has not increased anywhere as fast as that of state and local governments (during 1947–1964, inclusive, Federal debt increased at an average annual rate of 1.65 percent and that of state and local governments at 10.56 percent). This is revealed by the widening gap between Federal debt and total public debt in Chart 2. At the end of 1964, gross Federal debt amounted to $356 billion, and was 20 percent larger than in 1955 (private debt had doubled over the same period) and was about one-third higher than in 1947 (private debt had increased more than four times). State and local debt amounted to $92 billion in 1964, had more than doubled since 1955, and had increased more than five times since 1947.

PRIVATE DEBT, LIQUIDITY, AND INCOME

On the basis of the foregoing numbers, it would seem not unreasonable to suggest that if debt in the economy is a matter of concern—as to problems of servicing it, as to quality, or rates of growth—the area to be concerned with is private debt. In Chart 3, the following series are potted: (1) total private debt, (2) liquid assets held by the nonbank public—money, savings deposits and shares, and the like, and (3) private GNP.[5]

The relationship of private debt to private GNP provides an indication of the private sector's ability to service debt out of current

---

[5] Total GNP less Government purchases of goods and services.

CHART 3   Private Debt, Liquid Assets, and Income *(end of year)*

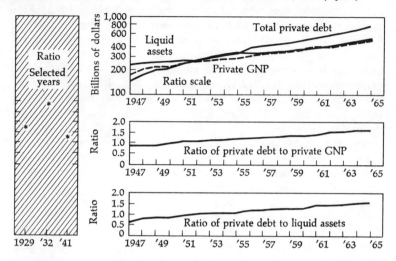

SOURCES OF DATA: U.S. Department of Commerce and Board of Governors of the Federal Reserve System.

income. Private debt in relation to liquid assets provides some indication of the private sector's ability to adjust to an unexpected adverse turn of economic events. If income is maintained at high and growing levels, the ability to handle debt out of current income is obviously enhanced; this ability is importantly backstopped by the accumulation of liquid assets, which by definition are readily convertible into cash.

If one looks at the numbers, some *casual* observations can be made. The word "casual" is emphasized because it is in this connection that existing knowledge is probably most deficient. For example, it is not known what relationship between income and debt is appropriate or desirable or sustainable, and what volume of liquid assets is sufficient. It is generally agreed among most observers that if income continues to advance strongly, the likelihood of problems emerging from debt is considerably reduced—or if there are problems, they would be concealed or deferred.

With reference to the numbers, private debt, on balance, has been obviously out-stripping both private GNP and liquid assets, a pattern that has pretty much characterized the postwar period. However, in recent years, increases in the ratio of private debt to liquidity have slackened, as indicated in Chart 3. This suggests that the private sector of the economy is nearly holding its own in building a cushion against its debt, which cannot help but be a favorable thing. On the other hand, the ratio of private debt to private GNP has continued to increase throughout the postwar period. As Chart 3 shows, that ratio has almost doubled in the postwar period, rising from 0.87 in 1947 to 1.66 in 1964. While the ratio for 1964 was virtually the same as that for 1929, it was more than one-third lower than for 1932, which was the peak year during the 1930s. The ratio declined appreciably during World War II, reflecting sharp increases in income.

If historical comparisons mean anything—and they may not— the current ratio of private debt to private GNP is relatively low. Moreover, the transformation of the economy—the built-in correction factors and the improved institutional arrangements—would suggest that the economy can handle more debt than it could earlier. At least this would appear to be the case when considering the broad aggregates. What the case is within or behind the broad statistics on private debt may or may not be another matter. The rest of this article is concerned with the major components of private debt.

HOUSEHOLD DEBT

Private debt is the sum of corporate debt and of individual and noncorporate debt. The latter, in turn, includes consumer debt and residential nonfarm mortgages—here referred to jointly as "household debt"—along with several categories that are not dealt with in this article, such as farm debt and other noncorporate business debt.

Currently, about one-half of total private debt is owed by corporations, while household debt—as defined here—represents one-third of the total (see Chart 4). Household debt, however, has grown faster than corporate debt during the postwar years, with an accompanying shift in the proportions of total private debt accounted for by the two major segments. A sevenfold rise in household debt to $264 billion during 1947–1964, inclusive, contrasted to a less than fourfold advance in corporate debt to $402 billion.

Nonfarm residential mortgages, the long-term portion of household debt, account for about seven out of every ten dollars of household indebtedness, or about the same proportion as in 1947. The growth of residential mortgage debt during the postwar period from close to $27 billion in 1947 to $187 billion in 1964 has been steady and virtually uninterrupted, reflecting a fairly steady increase in private home ownership. While residential mortgage debt has con-

CHART 4 Total Private Debt—Net *(end of year)*

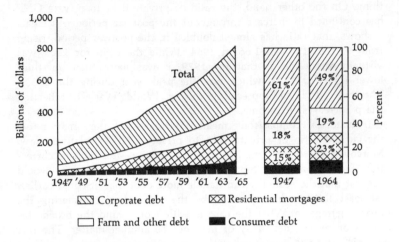

SOURCES OF DATA: U.S. Department of Commerce and Board of Governors of the Federal Reserve System.

tributed a large share of the growth of total household debt, its rise appears to have created less concern than has the expansion of consumer debt, except perhaps for the growing practice of refinancing mortgages for purposes other than the financing of home ownership. Anticipated acceleration in the rate of family formations over the next few years can be expected to speed up the growth in residential mortgage debt.

Consumer Credit

Consumer credit, which represents the short- and medium-term portion of household debt and contributes three out of every ten dollars to the total, tends to occupy a larger place in discussions on debt than might be warranted by its size, which is less than one-tenth of total private debt. Its growth from $11.6 billion to $76.8 billion during 1947–1964, inclusive, was accompanied by shifts in the relative shares of its two major components, instalment and noninstalment credit, as well as among the several types of instalment credit. (See Table I.)

From Chart 5, it is apparent that the use of instalment credit by consumers has increased during the postwar period at a much faster rate than the use of noninstalment credit (see also Table I). In part, this reflects the catching up of instalment debt for consumer

TABLE I Consumer Credit Outstanding, 1947 and 1964 (*end of year*)

	1947		1964		1964 as a multiple of 1947
	Amount (billions)	Percent of total	Amount (billions)	Percent of total	
Total	$11.6	100.0%	$76.8	100.0%	6.7
Noninstalment	4.9	42.3	17.4	22.7	3.6
Instalment	6.7	57.7	59.4	77.3	8.9
Automobile paper	1.9	16.6	24.5	31.9	12.9
Other consumer goods paper	2.2	18.5	15.3	19.9	7.0
Repair and modernization loans	0.7	6.2	3.5	4.6	5.0
Personal loans	1.9	16.4	16.1	20.9	8.5

SOURCE: Board of Governors of the Federal Reserve System.

CHART 5   Components of Consumer Credit Outstanding *(end of year)*

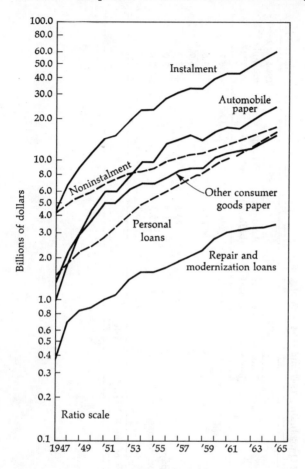

SOURCE OF DATA: Board of Governors of the Federal Reserve System.

items that had been in limited supply during the war. For example, the large rise in automobile loans—a nearly thirteenfold increase between 1947 and 1964—was partly the result of a rapid recovery in automobile loans from a very low base during the early postwar years as production began to catch up with pent-up demand for cars. But even after the readjustment, automobile credit has been a major force in the continued rise in the volume of instalment credit, sharing that role with personal loans, which have expanded even faster than automobile debt due largely to the growing variety of purposes for which personal loans have come to be used.

Instalment credit is sensitive to changes in business conditions, as the data in Chart 5 illustrate. The strength of consumer demand is closely related to the general level of economic activity; the willingness of consumers to commit a portion of expected future income for the purchase of automobiles or other high cost items, for which instalment credit is generally used, reflects consumers' confidence in current and future income levels. The slowdown or reduction in instalment credit, notably for automobile and other consumer goods, that occurs during periods of business decline—for example, 1954, 1958, 1961—can be seen in Chart 5.[6] Conversely, the increase, or acceleration, in the same series during recovery periods, as consumer confidence is restored, is also suggested in the chart. At the same time, it is significant that the volume of personal loans has continued to rise virtually uninterrupted even during periods of business recession.

The growing use of instalment credit has been facilitated by a generally favorable economic climate during much of the postwar period, particularly by rising consumer income and its discretionary portion, which has served to augment the debt-carrying capacity of consumers. An adequate supply of lendable funds, offered by a growing number of financial institutions on terms acceptable to consumers, has been an important contributing factor. Undoubtedly, also, the adoption of highly alluring methods designed to put consumers into a buying mood has helped to carry the "buy now, pay later" way of life into new territory, in some cases perhaps beyond limits of prudence.

On the other hand, the creation of additional consumer buying power by means of credit has tended to stimulate economic activity by increasing current demand for many types of consumer goods and services. It may well be questioned, for example, whether the production and sale of seven or eight million automobiles per year— including the beneficial effects reaching far beyond the automotive industry—would be feasible, or possible, without extensive use of consumer credit. Nevertheless, it is legitimate to ask whether consumer debt is growing too fast in relation to the general growth of the economy and whether corrective or preventive measures should be considered to forestall possible economic dislocations.

[6] This relationship would, of course, be more precisely demonstrated by the use of monthly data.

CHART 6   Consumer Debt Income and Liquid Assets *(end of year)*

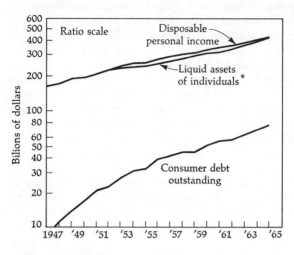

*Data not available prior to 1950.
SOURCES OF DATA: U.S. Department of Commerce; Securities and Exchange Commission; Board of Governors of the Federal Reserve System.

Too Much Consumer Debt?

Due to the lack of generally accepted standards by which current levels of consumer credit could be measured, and tagged either "safe" or "dangerous," there are no clear-cut answers to those questions. However, it is perhaps helpful to consider consumer credit along with economic variables—personal income after taxes and liquid assets—that reflect the ability of consumers to carry and/or liquidate their debts.

As Chart 6 indicates, consumer credit outstanding amounts to only a fraction of total annual disposable income. The size of that fraction, however, has grown from one-fifteenth to more than one-sixth of disposable income during the postwar period, a reminder of the rising popularity of consumer credit as a method of financing large purchases. Instalment credit, which, as previously stated, has grown faster than noninstalment credit, has accounted for the major share of the inroad of consumer credit upon disposable income. (See Table II.)

Since the terms of maturity vary for consumer credit, especially for the instalment portion, debt repayments, rather than the amount of debt outstanding, offer a better measure of the proportion of

TABLE II   Consumer Credit and Components as Percentages of Disposable Personal Income

Year	Total consumer credit[a]	Instalment credit[a]	Non-instalment credit[a]	Instalment credit repayments[b]
1947	6.8%	3.9%	2.9%	6.0%
1948	7.6	4.8	2.9	7.0
1949	9.2	6.1	3.0	8.2
1950	10.3	7.1	3.3	8.9
1951	10.0	6.7	3.3	10.1
1952	11.5	8.1	3.4	10.7
1953	12.4	9.1	3.3	11.0
1954	12.6	9.2	3.5	11.8
1955	14.2	10.5	3.6	12.3
1956	14.5	10.8	3.6	12.7
1957	14.6	11.0	3.6	12.9
1958	14.2	10.6	3.6	12.7
1959	15.3	11.6	3.6	12.6
1960	16.0	12.2	3.8	13.1
1961	15.8	11.9	3.9	13.1
1962	16.4	12.5	3.9	13.2
1963	17.4	13.4	4.0	13.7
1964	17.8	13.8	4.0	14.0

[a] Outstanding at end of period.
[b] Annual totals.
NOTE: Due to rounding, percentages for instalment and noninstalment credit do not in all cases add up to total consumer credit.
SOURCES: Board of Governors of the Federal Reserve System; U. S. Department of Commerce.

current spendable income that is required to pay for past purchases and is thus unavailable as current consumer purchasing power. As shown in Table II, the increase in repayments as a proportion of disposable income, while somewhat less than the increase in total instalment credit outstanding as related to income, has been steady. This development has been viewed with alarm by some observers at different times. No convincing reason has as yet been presented for considering the present ratio of about 14 percent—or the previous 12 percent or 13 percent—as an absolute upper limit. There is, furthermore, no assurance that the expected rise in the number of young families, who commonly rely heavily upon instalment credit, will not cause a further increase in that ratio in the years to come.

TABLE III Debts and Liquid Assets of Consumers—*Year-end Data (In Billions of Dollars)*

Year	Annual increase			Net change	
	Liquid assets	Consumer debt outstanding	Household debt outstanding*	Liquid assets against consumer debt	Liquid assets against household debt
1951	$ 6.5	$1.2	$ 7.4	$+ 5.3	$− 0.9
1952	10.6	4.8	11.3	+ 5.8	− 0.7
1953	9.0	4.0	11.2	+ 5.0	− 2.2
1954	8.6	1.1	10.2	+ 7.5	− 1.6
1955	10.7	6.4	18.3	+ 4.3	− 7.6
1956	11.2	3.6	13.9	+ 7.6	− 2.7
1957	11.7	2.3	10.4	+ 9.4	+ 1.3
1958	12.7	0.3	9.9	+12.4	+ 2.8
1959	19.4	6.4	18.9	+13.0	+ 0.5
1960	8.0	4.5	14.4	+ 3.5	− 6.4
1961	17.5	1.7	12.6	+15.8	+ 4.9
1962	28.8	5.5	17.6	+23.3	+11.2
1963	30.9	6.7	21.0	+24.2	+ 9.9
1964	33.0	6.9	22.4	+26.1	+10.6

* Includes consumer credit and nonfarm residential mortgages.
sources: U. S. Securities and Exchange Commission; U. S. Department of Commerce; Board of Governors of the Federal Reserve System.

The making of repayments causes an individual borrower to suffer an actual reduction in his personal current spending power. A proportionate restraint, however, does not necessarily apply to all spending units, taken as a whole, since not all families are using instalment credit.

In times of declining incomes, consumers can, if necessary, fall back upon their reserves to meet loan repayments. As shown in Chart 6, liquid assets held by individuals have been increasing virtually *pari passu* with income. Of special importance is the fact— shown by the data in Table III—that consumers in the aggregate have added a larger amount to their liquid assets than to their total debt in each of the 14 years since 1950 (see the "net change" column of liquid assets against consumer debt). If comparison is made between liquid assets and total household debt (mortgages plus consumer debt), the result shows that debt has outpaced liquid assets in seven of the ten years from 1951 to 1960. After 1960, however, asset accumulation accelerated to produce an excess of liquid asset growth over growth in household debt, averaging over $10 billion annually for the last three years. This development serves to demonstrate the ability of consumers—at least during a period of sustained high income—to step up accumulation of liquid reserves despite a growing level of debt and a 14 percent toll on current incomes for instalment credit repayments.

DETERIORATION OF QUALITY?

The increasing use and growing amount of household debt, in the opinion of some, tend by definition to lower its quality. Lengthening of terms of maturity, lower downpayments, and lower standards in the screening of applicants for loans are generally cited as evidence of deterioration that will lead to growth in delinquencies. The recent record on this point is not conclusive. While the foreclosure rate on nonfarm mortgages has doubled during the last ten years, delinquency rates on instalment credit held by banks have moved horizontally during that interval. The growing number of personal bankruptcies, on the other hand, suggests that—aside from cases of misfortune or fraud—some borrowers, as well as their lenders, may have failed to exercise prudence.

ARE AGGREGATES MISLEADING?

The broad aggregates—debt, income, assets—do not necessarily portray potential weaknesses in the debt structure. For example, in the absence of specific knowledge as to who owes the debt and who owns the liquid assets or earns the income, it might be erroneously assumed that the sum total of liquid assets could be made to serve as a backstop for debt repayments, when in reality those assets might be owned largely by consumers without any debt at all.

The use of instalment credit is less than universal. Furthermore, as revealed in periodic polls by the University of Michigan's Survey Research Center, the proportion of all families that do use it, and the percentages of spendable income tied up in instalment debt repayments, vary considerably among different income classes. (See upper panel of Chart 7.) About 60 percent of middle-income families reported using instalment credit in early 1964, but less than 40 percent of the families in the highest income group and only about one-fourth of the lowest income families were doing so, albeit for different reasons.

As Chart 7 further indicates, families in the lower income brackets carried the heaviest debt burdens relative to income. For example, 12 percent of all families in the lowest income class and 17 percent of all families with $3,000–$4,999 income—representing a large proportion of the debt-carrying families in those two income brackets —were committed to annual payments equal to at least 20 percent of disposable income. The higher absolute amounts of repayment, of course, were concentrated in the higher income groups, where

CHART 7 Instalment Debt *(percent distribution of family units by amount of annual payments as a percent of disposable income)*

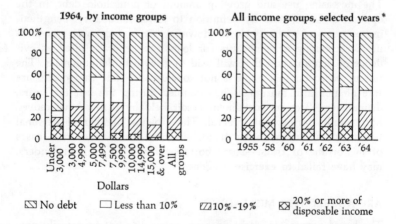

*Data prior to 1964 are based on spending units rather than family units.
SOURCE OF DATA: Survey Research Center, University of Michigan.

they represented a smaller percentage of income and, presumably a lighter burden.

The general picture of the use and distribution of instalment credit does not appear to have changed appreciably over the past ten years, if results of previous surveys are compared with the most recent one. As the data in the lower panel of Chart 7 indicate, the average percentage of all spending units reporting use of instalment credit—47 percent in 1964—has remained fairly constant while the proportion of families with a debt burden of at least 20 percent of disposable income—one family in ten in 1964—is slightly lower than in most earlier surveys.

A previous survey had also shown that three out of four families in 1963 held some liquid assets, thus reinforcing their debt-carrying ability (see Table IV). As would be expected, the proportion of families with liquid assets and the size of individual holdings per family increase with the size of spendable income. From the data in Table V, it appears that both the proportion of families with assets and, to a smaller extent, the amount of liquid reserves per family (if not necessarily the rates of reserves to incomes) have tended to grow during the postwar period, which is consistent with the rise in aggregate totals discussed previously. A direct comparison of specific amounts of liquid assets with specific instalment debt burdens carried by individual families, however, is not possible on the basis of the data. Thus, the possibility that families holding assets are the ones with little or no instalment debt and those without assets carry the heaviest debt burdens relative to income, remains strong. It is further strengthened by statistical inferences indicating that a family with low financial reserves is more likely than a more affluent family to owe instalment debt and, if so, to carry a heavier relative debt burden.

While some of the individual data may appear to be cause for concern, particularly in the event of a decline in income levels, it should be remembered that important institutional changes have occurred in the economy that affect debt-income-liquid assets relationships and the debt-carrying capacity of consumers in general. Auxiliary assets (such as pension funds, unemployment compensation, including supplemental benefits under private agreements, and health and other insurance plans) have built in some protection, albeit small, for income maintenance, and have perhaps lessened the need for the same measure of liquid assets as protection in case of retirement, loss of employment, or prolonged illness. Growth of auxiliary assets helps to release liquid reserves for other purposes, including the repayment of consumer debt when necessary.

TABLE IV Liquid Assets of Consumers, 1963, by Income Groups and by Amount of Assets
(percent distribution of spending units within income groups)

| Liquid assets | Spending units with annual income of: | | | | | All spending units |
	Under $3,000	$3,000– $4,999	$5,000– $7,499	$7,500– $9,999	$10,000 and over	
None	49%	28%	27%	7%	1%	24%
Less than $500	24	33	30	29	16	29
$500–$1,999	13	17	21	34	24	21
$2,000–$4,999	8	12	12	15	23	13
$5,000 and over	6	10	10	15	36	13

SOURCE: Survey Research Center, University of Michigan.

TABLE V Liquid Assets of Consumers in Selected Years (percent distribution of spending units by size of assets)

Liquid assets	1947–1949 average	1951–1953 average	1955–1957 average	1958–1960 average	1963
None	27%	29%	27%	25%	24%
Less than $500	27	29	29	30	29
$500–$1,999	25	22	22	22	21
$2,000–$4,999	13	11	12	12	13
$5,000 and over	8	9	10	11	13

SOURCE: Survey Research Center, University of Michigan.

CHART 8 Corporate Debt and Corporate Gross Product *(nonfinancial corporations—end of year)*

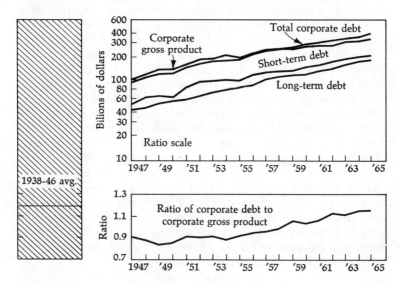

SOURCE OF DATA: U.S. Department of Commerce.

CORPORATE DEBT

Total debt of nonfinancial corporations has increased without interruption in every year in the postwar period, reaching a total of $402 billion at the end of 1964. While corporate debt has accounted for an increasing proportion of total debt, as indicated earlier, it has constituted a steadily declining share of private debt—falling from three-fifths to less than one-half of the total.

The trend of corporate debt is depicted in Chart 8, with totals for the short- and long-term components shown separately. Although the two components have represented fairly consistent shares of the total, the long-term portion has grown steadily while the short-term portion has moved upward more irregularly—a pattern largely associated with reductions in borrowing requirements during periods of business recession, for example, 1949, 1954, 1958. The recent relationship between short- and long-term corporate debt is the reverse of the pattern that prevailed in prewar years, when long-term borrowing consistently exceeded short-term debt, and reflects the changing character of corporate needs for funds.

A comparison of corporate debt with Corporate Gross Product

(a proxy for corporate income) shows that, during 1947–1957, the total of corporate product, although slowed twice by business recessions, was consistently larger than the volume of corporate debt, with the debt/corporate product ratio averaging about 0.9. Since 1957, however, corporate debt has risen considerably faster than corporate product, with the result that the ratio averaged 1.11 during 1958–1964, and reached a high of 1.16 in 1964. The 1964 figure, while a high for the postwar period, does not compare unfavorably with an average ratio of 1.20 in the 1938–1946 period.[7]

Before reviewing other corporate debt relationships, some comment should be made concerning the "catching-up process" that was mentioned earlier in connection with total private debt. As a result of a number of factors, nonfinancial corporations emerged from the war years in a hyperliquid condition, with debt levels low in relation to output, and with a need for funds to finance both the replacement of badly worn plant and equipment and the new expenditures required to gear operations to rising levels of economic activity. Increasing needs for funds, coupled with growing corporate preference for borrowed funds, have undergirded the steady rise in corporate debt since the end of the war.

SOURCES AND USES OF FUNDS

The postwar trend in corporate indebtedness is probably best explained by the changing composition of both sources and uses of corporate funds (see Chart 9). As is clearly evident, corporate demands for funds are strongly influenced by the business cycle, with demands increasing sharply during early stages of business expansion and contracting noticeably prior to and during recessions. Of importance is the steadily growing volume of funds generated internally. Since the end of the war, three-fifths of total corporate requirements have come from internal sources, that is, retained earnings and depreciation charges. In recent years, tax concessions in the form of liberalized depreciation allowances, investment tax credit, and reduction in corporate income taxes, have augmented the internal flow of funds. The rising flow of internally generated funds has been almost exactly matched by the need for funds to finance plant and equipment.

Periods of business expansion have been characterized by sharply enlarged demands for funds for inventory accumulation and for additions to financial assets—principally accounts receivable. These

[7] The earliest year for which Corporate Gross Product estimates are available is 1938.

CHART 9 Sources and Uses of Corporate Funds *(annual totals)*

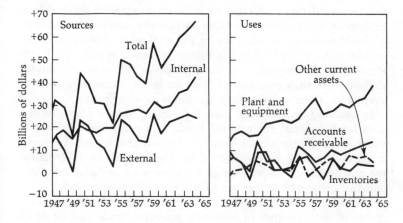

SOURCE OF DATA: U.S. Department of Commerce.

demands have usually slackened as the pace of expansion slowed, receding to low levels during recessions, as additions to inventories and financial assets are curtailed. It has been, in fact, the volatile changes in current assets (principally inventories and accounts receivable) that have accounted for most of the swings in corporate demands for funds during the postwar period. Despite this volatility, however, total demands for funds have trended upward (especially after 1954), and the demand for external financing has continued to grow. While funds from external sources supplied only two-fifths of total requirements during 1947–1964, 85 percent of external funds have represented additions to corporate debt.[8] Furthermore, 56 percent of the addition to corporate indebtedness was accounted for by short-term obligations, with the remainder of course coming from long-term sources.

The period since 1961 has been characterized by continuous business expansion—already the longest peacetime expansion on record. With a sustained rise in levels of output, corporate demands for funds have also risen continuously, reaching a record level in 1964.

[8] Since external sources of funds include the net new stock issues of investment companies (totaling about $2 billion annually in recent years), debt as a proportion of external funds of nonfinancial corporations is understated. The total for other current assets as a use of funds is correspondingly overstated, due to the inclusion of the net new investments of these companies.

The volume of internally generated funds has continued to satisfy about three-fifths of total requirements, and has almost matched the volume of funds allocated to additions to physical assets (plant, equipment, and inventories). More importantly, however, the volume of funds required for additions to financial assets has been sizable in each year, in contrast to the pattern in earlier expansions. Funds allocated to the increase in financial assets in 1961–1964 constituted slightly more than one-third of total funds used, compared with an average of about one-fourth in the entire postwar period.

In recent years, growing need for current financing has further stimulated demands for external funds, and corporations have met these requirements almost entirely through the use of borrowed monies. Additions to corporate debt during 1961–1964 accounted for nine-tenths of the volume of funds raised externally, compared with an average of 85 percent in the entire postwar period.

Marked corporate preference for debt has reflected both the availability of large amounts of internally generated funds, part of which adds to the corporate equity base, and the lower costs associated with borrowed funds, as compared with equity financing. Moreover, a higher proportion of borrowed funds usually exerts favorable leverage on a corporation's net income, especially during periods when total income is rising steadily.

Recent growth in corporate debt, therefore, has been associated in large part with the steady, although not necessarily excessive, accumulation of inventories and an unusually large buildup in financial assets. The bulk of the increase in financial assets has been centered in accounts receivable, while holdings of cash, U. S. Government securities, and other financial assets (including an undetermined amount of other types of negotiable securities) have expanded more moderately. A major part of growing working capital requirements has been satisfied by an increase in short-term borrowing—principally notes and accounts payable and bank loans—but increasing amounts of long-term borrowing have been used in recent years.

ACCOUNTS RECEIVABLE

As a result of the increasing proportion of corporate funds allocated to investment in accounts receivable in the postwar period, the volume of accounts receivable outstanding has expanded nearly five times, accounting for nearly one-half of total current assets at the end of 1964, compared with only 31 percent in 1946. This large expansion in the volume of trade credit is reflected in the current liabilities section of the corporate balance sheet in the nearly four-fold increase in notes and accounts payable. The slower rate of growth in accounts payable would seem to indicate, however, that nonfinancial corporations have been extending larger amounts of credit to their customers than they have been receiving from their suppliers. The ratio of accounts receivable to accounts payable has risen steadily (from 102 percent in 1946 to 124 percent in 1964). The sharp expansion in trade credit is a natural consequence of the increasingly competitive business climate, with the availability of larger amounts of interim financing serving as an additional incentive to corporate customers.

The sustained rise in the volume of trade credit extended has raised questions in some quarters about possible deterioration in the quality of such credit. Data collected by the Credit Research Foundation indicate that the average collection period for the accounts receivable of manufacturing corporations has lengthened considerably during the current business expansion.[9] The average number of calendar days' sales outstanding has risen steadily, from about 34 days in early 1961 to nearly 38 days in March 1965. Despite this trend toward more liberal terms, however, the percentage of manufacturers' receivables that are current, that is, within terms, was actually somewhat higher during the past year (averaging 84 percent) than in earlier years of the expansion. Looking at the repayment record in another way, the proportion of accounts receivable volume that is over 90 days past due has averaged only 2.8 percent during the past year, which is slightly below the average for the entire expansion.

These comparisons bring into sharper focus the growing role of corporations in providing current financing to their customers, indicating that more liberal credit terms are becoming standard practice and are being accepted by corporations as an added cost of doing business.

CORPORATE DEBT AND ASSET SIZE

The growth in debt of nonfinancial corporations can be broken down by asset size of borrower.[10] This is done on the premise that increased use of debt by corporations would be potentially more

[9] See *National Summary of Domestic Trade Receivables*, published quarterly by the Credit Research Foundation, Inc.

[10] Data were taken from *Statistics of Income*, Internal Revenue Service, U. S. Treasury Department. Most recent data available are for corporations with accounting periods ended July 1961–June 1962.

Percentage Distribution of Corporate Debt by Asset Size Class, 1951 and 1961

Year	Under $1 million	$1 million to $10 million	$10 million to $100 million	Over $100 million	Total
1951	17.8%	15.7%	19.1%	47.4%	100.0%
1961	20.8	14.3	14.5	50.4	100.0

dangerous if a disproportionate amount of the increase were accounted for by smaller firms, among which the likelihood of failure is considerably higher. The record of the 1951–1961 period indicates that the increase in debt of nonfinancial corporations was centered most heavily in small and large firms. While debt of all corporations increased by 146 percent during the period, small firms (under $1 million in assets) reported an increase in debt of 187 percent, and large firms (over $100 million in assets) an increase of 162 percent. Corporations in the intermediate size classes added debt at a more moderate rate. As a result of the faster rates of growth in debt of corporations at the two extremes of the size range, corporate debt in 1961 was more heavily concentrated among large and small firms than in 1951. While comparable data for recent years are not available, it is unlikely that these relationships have changed significantly.[11]

Growing corporate preference for debt as the principal source of external funds has brought pronounced changes in the relationships between corporate debt and other items in the corporate balance sheet. Chart 10 shows the postwar growth in corporate debt, compared with the increases in both total assets and net worth of nonfinancial corporations. The increase in corporate debt has outpaced gains in both assets and net worth, and, as the bottom panel indicates, debt has represented a steadily increasing proportion of both items. Although completely comparable historical data are not available, reasonably reliable estimates indicate that the ratios of debt to assets and net worth are currently at record levels, exceeding even those that prevailed in the 1929–1933 period.

[11] This assumption is supported by analysis of recent trends in the increase of debt of manufacturing corporations. Although the distribution of debt among manufacturing firms is not the same as for all nonfinancial corporations, debt increases of manufacturing companies in recent years (1961–1964) have followed the same pattern as during earlier postwar years.

CHART 10   Total Corporate Debt in Relation to Total Assets and Net Worth *(nonfinancial corporations—end of year)*

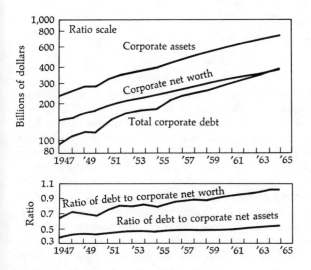

SOURCES OF DATA: U.S. Department of Commerce and U.S. Department of the Treasury.

While such comparisons serve to place the upward spiral of corporate debt in somewhat better perspective, they do not provide conclusive evidence that such debt has reached excessive or unmanageable proportions. The record of business failures during the present expansion has improved steadily, with the number of failures and the rate of failure per 10,000 concerns in 1964 at the lowest levels in five years. The sustained rise of corporate profits during the current business expansion is further evidence that corporations have encountered little difficulty in servicing a growing volume of debt. In addition, a substantial increase in the volume of internally generated funds (which reached a record annual rate of $51 billion in the first quarter of this year) is working to keep the inflow of borrowed funds from reaching unmanageable proportions. While a protracted period of business recession would probably strain the capacity of corporations to service debt, the continued exercise of public and private initiative to promote a sustainable and sufficient rate of economic growth is good insurance against such an eventuality in the corporate sector, as well as in the household sector and in the economy at large.

J. A. CACY

POSTWAR DEVELOPMENTS AMONG FINANCIAL INTERMEDIARIES

4

Most financial intermediaries have benefited from as well as contributed to the rapid growth of the U. S. economy since World War II, but the growth records of various types of intermediaries have varied substantially. The growth of financial intermediaries depends primarily on the growth of their liabilities or the claims that they issue—claims which are financial assets of the individuals, businesses, and governments that hold them. This article examines some aspects of the postwar behavior of claims against major financial intermediaries—commercial banks, mutual savings banks, and savings and loan associations. Perspective on the postwar period is provided by reference to developments over a longer time span.

The major developments discussed are the following. (1) Total claims against intermediaries (demand deposits at commercial banks, time deposits at commercial banks, time deposits at mutual savings banks, and shares at savings and loan associations) have increased very rapidly during the postwar period, and the rate of growth has accelerated during the 1960s. (2) The public has undertaken a steady rearrangement of its portfolio of total claims—shifting away from demand deposits and toward time intermediary claims. (3) The relative shift away from demand deposits has exceeded a shift toward time deposits at commercial banks so that relative holdings of claims against commercial banks have declined throughout the period. (4) There has been a relative shift away from time deposits at commercial banks and mutual savings banks and toward shares at savings and loan associations.

FRAMEWORK OF DISCUSSION

As is the case with most economic phenomena, a discussion of intermediary claims may proceed in the framework of supply and demand. One or the other may be stressed. If the supply of claims

Reprinted from J. A. Cacy, "Postwar Developments Among Financial Intermediaries," *Monthly Review* (May 1968), pp. 3–8, Federal Reserve Bank of Kansas City.

were stressed, the focus would be on the behavior of financial intermediaries as they issue claims against themselves. The discussion might begin by examining those factors which affect the willingness and ability of financial intermediaries to issue claims. If the demand for claims were stressed, reference would be made to the behavior of the public as they adjust their holdings of intermediary claims. In this case, the discussion might begin by examining those factors which determine the volume of claims which the public wishes to hold. Of course, a complete description would include both aspects and would culminate in a treatment of the interaction between demand and supply forces. Demand aspects are stressed in this article and the focus is on the behavior of the public as it alters its holdings of intermediary claims.

In connection with research into the theory of the demand for money, monetary economists have developed a framework that is useful for the analysis of the demand for all types of assets. The framework has two essential elements. The first element begins with the observation that an individual or group of economic units, at any point in time, possesses a certain stock of wealth, and this wealth is held in various forms. The sum of the amounts of wealth held in various forms cannot, of course, exceed or fall short of total wealth. The significance of this simple fact is that a change in total wealth will result in a change in the amount of wealth held in some particular form. This line of reasoning leads to the proposition that the amount held of any particular form of wealth will be related to the total volume of wealth possessed. Thus total wealth is said to serve two interrelated purposes: as a constraint on the amount held of any particular type of wealth in the sense that the sum of the parts must equal the total, and as an important determinant of the amounts held of particular forms of wealth.

The second important element of the analysis is that the individual allocates his total wealth on the basis of characteristics of the various forms which are attractive to him. Relevant characteristics of assets include liquidity, marketability, and rate of return.

In using wealth as a reference point in a discussion of claims against intermediaries, the concepts of gross and net wealth may be distinguished. Gross wealth refers to total assets, while net wealth refers to total assets minus total liabilities. In the formulation of the theory of asset holdings, net wealth is the relevant concept. However, gross wealth concepts may usefully be employed under certain circumstances. In this article, wealth held in the form of financial assets is used as a point of reference. Also, in discussing various types of claims, reference is made to total intermediary claims. Both total financial assets and total intermediary claims are gross wealth concepts. Gross concepts, such as the volume of financial assets, may be employed by supposing that the public makes two decisions, which may be treated as independent of each other for purposes of discussion. First, there is the decision concerning the volume of total financial assets to be held. This decision may be thought of as being influenced by the magnitude of the public's net wealth. The second decision concerns the composition of the total financial asset portfolio, or, in the context of this article, the decision concerning the proportion of gross financial wealth which is to be held in the form of claims against intermediaries.

GROWTH OF TOTAL CLAIMS

The public has increased its portfolio of intermediary claims quite rapidly since the end of World War II. (In this article, the public includes households, nonfinancial businesses, financial businesses

TABLE 1 Financial Intermediary Claims Held by the Public

	Level (billions of dollars)	Rate of change (percent)	Intermediary claims as a percent of financial assets
1900	8.0		14.2
1912	17.7	6.9	15.4
1922	38.7	8.1	14.8
1929	55.0	5.2	11.8
1933	41.0	7.1	12.3
1939	58.1	6.0	16.0
1945	124.2	13.5	18.0
1946*	137.9	(†)	25.1
1950	158.0	3.5	22.4
1955	211.4	6.0	19.7
1960	272.9	5.2	18.9
1967	483.9	8.5	20.2†

* Data for 1946 through 1967 not strictly comparable with earlier data.
† This is the ratio for 1966.
sources: Raymond Goldsmith, *Financial Intermediaries in the American Economy Since 1900, National Bureau of Economic Research, New York*, (Princeton, N.J.: Princeton University Press, 1958), and Board of Governors of the Federal Reserve System.

other than those intermediaries whose claims are being discussed, and state and local governments.) From 1946 to 1967, these assets increased from $137.9 billion to $483.9 billion. As shown by Table 1, the rate of growth has accelerated in the 1960s. It may be noted from the table that there have been several periods in which the public has increased its holdings of intermediary claims at a more rapid rate than during the 1946–60 period, but the growth rate of the 1960s is unprecedented, except for the World War II years.

Intermediary claims have increased less rapidly than total financial assets held by the public; that is, the ratio of intermediary claims to total financial assets has declined since the end of World War II (this is not true for the 1960s, however).[1] At the end of the war, the public's portfolio of financial assets was apparently "overloaded" with intermediary claims. Table 1 shows that the percentage of financial assets held in the form of these claims increased considerably during the 1939–45 period. Judging from available data, the volume of intermediary claims held by the public, relative to

TABLE 2   Intermediary Claims as a Percent of Financial Assets

	Excluding life insurance and pension fund reserves		Including life insurance and pension fund reserves	
	1946	1966	1946	1966
Households	27.7%	25.9%	42.8%	45.0%
Nonfinancial businesses	31.2	16.3	31.2	16.3
Finance	4.1	2.2	8.7	3.9
State and local	29.5	24.8	29.5	24.8
Total	25.1	20.2	38.8	36.2

NOTE: Available data for sectors provides totals for currency plus demand deposits, but does not provide a further breakdown. In arriving at series on intermediary claims by sectors, it was assumed that the ratio of currency to demand deposits is the same for each sector and is equal to the currency-demand deposits ratio for the public as a whole.
SOURCE: Board of Governors of the Federal Reserve System.

[1] Financial assets include, besides intermediary claims, currency, life insurance and pension fund reserves, U. S. Government securities, state and local government securities, corporate bonds, corporate stock, and other miscellaneous assets. The inclusion of corporate stock, which is evaluated at market value, noticeably affects the changes in the ratio of intermediary claims to total financial assets. The ratio of intermediary claims to financial assets other than corporate stock was only slightly lower in 1966 than in 1946.

total financial assets, remained fairly constant during the first four decades of this century (declining somewhat during the 1920s, increasing during the 1930s). In 1939 the ratio of intermediary claims to total financial assets was almost the same as during the 1900–20 period. The rapid wartime growth in claims increased this ratio above previous levels and set the stage for the postwar decline.

The postwar decline in intermediary claims relative to financial assets has been much less pronounced for households than for other sectors. In fact, Table 2 shows that, if life insurance and pension funds are treated as financial intermediaries, intermediary claims were more important in the financial asset portfolios of households in 1966 than 20 years earlier.

SHIFT AWAY FROM DEMAND DEPOSITS

One of the more important aspects of the public's behavior with regard to intermediary claims during the postwar period is the relative shift away from demand deposits. At the end of World War II, the public held around 58 percent of its intermediary claims in the form of demand deposits. By 1967, this ratio had been reduced to about 28 percent. (See Chart 1.)

This postwar decline in the relative position of demand deposits is not surprising. During the war, these assets accounted for a higher proportion of the public's intermediary claims than at any time for which data are available. During the first 30 years of this century, the public rearranged the composition of its portfolio of intermediary claims away from demand deposits and toward time claims. By 1929, demand deposits accounted for only 37 percent of total claims, compared with 54 percent in 1900. Total intermediary claims declined abruptly during the financial difficulties of the 1929–33 period, and, consistent with the trend of earlier years, demand deposits declined more in percentage terms than did time claims. However, this shift away from demand deposits was completely reversed in 1933, and by 1939 almost one half of total intermediary claims was in demand deposits. This reversal may be explained partly by the increased desire for liquidity due to experience during the 1929–33 period. It is true also that the yield on time claims was low and declining throughout the 1933–39 period. The financing of World War II resulted in very large increases in total claims. Due to the very low rates of return, there was little incentive to hold time claims; and the relative position of demand deposits continued to increase.

It may be that under "normal" conditions, as the volume of inter-

CHART 1 Distribution of Total Intermediary Claims Among Various Types, 1900-67

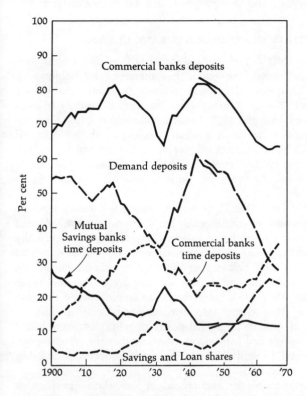

NOTE: Pre- and post-World War II data not stricly comparable.
SOURCE: Raymond Goldsmith, *A Study of Savings in the United States*, National Bureau of Economic Research, New York, (Princeton, N.J. Princeton University Press, 1955), Vol 1, and Board of Governors of the Federal Reserve System.

mediary claims increases, demand claims tend to occupy a less significant position in the public's portfolio of claims. Such a relationship generally held from the turn of the century until the 1930s. The relative attractiveness of demand deposits from 1933 through the war years may be explained by the unusual conditions of this period. From this perspective, the long-run continuous rearrangement of the public's portfolio of intermediary claims away from demand deposits was interrupted during the 1933–45 period and reappeared in the postwar years. This shift away from demand deposits has important implications for the competitive position of commercial banks—these banks must depend on time deposit growth to maintain a share of total intermediary claims. It also has implications for monetary theory and policy, which will be discussed later.

RELATIVE POSITION OF COMMERCIAL BANK CLAIMS

In line with the shift out of demand deposits into time claims during the postwar period, the public has increased its holdings of time deposits at commercial banks relative to total intermediary claims. However, the shift away from demand deposits has been more pronounced that the shift toward commercial bank time deposits, so that there has been a steady decline in the holdings of total commercial bank deposits relative to total intermediary claims. (See Chart 1.) In 1945, commercial bank claims accounted for 82 percent of the total. By 1967, this position had been reduced to 63 percent.

At the end of World War II, as was the case for demand deposits, the relative position of commercial bank deposits (demand plus time) in the public's portfolio of intermediary claims was unusually strong. Historically, holdings of commerical bank deposits increased more rapidly than total holdings of intermediary claims during the first two decades of this century but less rapidly during the 1920s and early 1930s. After 1933, commercial banks profited by the general shift out of time claims into demand deposits. This shift reduced the rate of growth of time deposits at mutual savings banks and shares at savings and loan associations, so that the relative position of commercial bank deposits in the public's portfolio of intermediary claims increased.

As this description of the fluctuations in the relative position of commercial bank deposits implies, there appears to be no long-run trend in this series. The relative position of commercial bank claims in 1967 was only slightly less than in 1900, and about the same as in 1933. (See Chart 1.) During most periods in which increases have occurred in the position of demand deposits relative to total intermediary claims, the relative position of time deposits at commercial banks has decreased and vice versa. These divergent movements have not always been completely offsetting, but, with important exceptions, the tendency has been evident.

RELATIVE HOLDINGS OF TIME CLAIMS

Although time deposits at commercial banks have increased more rapidly than total intermediary claims, these assets have increased

CHART 2 Distribution of Time Intermediary Claims Among Various Types, 1900-67

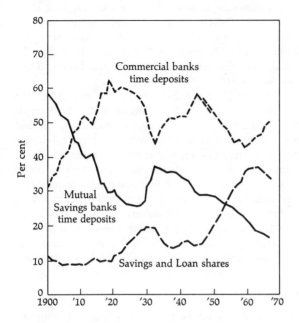

NOTE: Pre- and post-World War II data not strictly comparable.
SOURCE: See Chart 1.

considerably less rapidly during the postwar period than have time claims at all intermediaries (time deposits at commercial banks, time deposits at mutual savings banks, and shares at savings and loan associations). At the end of World War II, commercial bank time deposits accounted for around 57 percent of intermediary time claims. (See Chart 2.) From the end of the war until around 1960, the public steadily rearranged its portfolio of time claims away from time deposits at commercial banks; in 1960, time deposits at commercial banks accounted for only 42 percent of total intermediary time claims. Since 1960, however, time deposits at commercial banks have increased more rapidly than other time claims, and by 1967 accounted for 48 percent of the total. Historically, during the first decade of the century, time deposits at commercial banks increased much more rapidly than total time claims, but since about 1910, the percentage of total time claims accounted for by commercial bank time deposits has shown little trend.

The postwar decline in the relative position of commercial bank time deposits has been accompanied by a similar decline in the relative position of time deposits at mutual savings banks, and by a large gain in the position of shares at savings and loan associations. The relative position of time deposits at mutual savings banks has declined steadily throughout the postwar period. In fact, except for the 1929–33 period, this downward movement has been evident throughout this century.

Savings and loan shares increased from around 15 percent of the total at the end of World War II to 35 percent in 1967. These assets were relatively unimportant as a form of time claim during the first half of the century, accounting at all times for less of the total than either time deposits at mutual savings banks or at commercial banks. It was not until mid-1955 that the volume of shares first exceeded the volume of time deposits at mutual savings banks. It appeared for a time that savings and loan shares would eventually overtake time deposits at commercial banks. However, this movement was reversed around 1960, and since that time, the proportion of time claims held in the form of shares has declined slightly, while that held in the form of time deposits at commercial banks has increased.

CONCLUDING COMMENTS

From the point of view of monetary theory and policy, one of the more important of the postwar developments discussed here is the decline in the significance of demand deposits in the liability structure of commercial banks and in the public's portfolio of intermediary claims.

The importance of this development lies in its relation to the issue of the proper focus of monetary policy. Traditionally, monetary economists have argued that the focus should be the commercial banking system. This position may be supported in two different, but related, ways. One way relates to the supposed ability of commercial banks to alter the flow of investment funds in a way other financial institutions cannot. This ability is said to derive from the activities of banks as managers of the payments mechanism. Secondly, it may be argued that monetary policy should focus on the banking system because bank liabilities are used as a medium of exchange, or as money. The first variant leads to a focus on bank credit; the second leads to a focus on bank demand liabilities. To the extent that demand deposits constitute the major portion of bank liabilities, the practical effect of the two approaches is similar;

there is no need to choose between them. As demand deposits become less significant, a choice is forced.

There is one way to avoid the issue: redefine money in such a way that the correspondence between the special nature of bank credit and the unique nature of bank liabilities is preserved. That is, commercial bank time deposits may be included in the money supply. However, this creates problems for both variants of the traditional approach. The special nature of bank credit is said to arise from the fact that banks administer the payments mechanism. If a portion of bank credit corresponds to time liabilities not employed as a medium of exchange, what remains of the argument that bank credit is special? As for the money supply variant, it is difficult to justify including some assets not employed as a medium of exchange, such as time deposits at commercial banks, while excluding other assets, such as time deposits at mutual savings banks and shares at savings and loan associations. One possible partial solution to these problems is to shift the focus of attention from commercial banks to financial intermediaries (including, of course, commercial banks).[2]

However, a continued policy focus on commercial banks, even though the relative decline of demand deposits continues, may be justified on the basis of practicality. That is, given existing institutional and legal arrangements and accepted practices, the Federal Reserve has more control over the behavior of commercial banks than other financial intermediaries.

[2] This is the alternative suggested by John Gurley and Edward Shaw. Their work is summarized in *Money in a Theory of Finance*, The Brookings Institution, Washington, D. C. (Baltimore: The Lord Baltimore Press, 1960).

COMMERCIAL
BANKING

PART II

The selections in Part II concern two important subjects pertaining to commercial banking in the United States. The first five articles relate to the structure, competition, and control of commercial banks as business organizations. The last four selections deal with the asset management practices of banks and the consequent emergence of new markets to meet the changing requirements of loan demand and bank liquidity.

The article by the Federal Reserve Bank of Richmond introduces the problems of banks as business organizations by reviewing the history and major causes of bank failures in the United States. Since correspondent banking still plays a significant role in the activities of banking in the United States, the second brief article by the Federal Reserve Bank of Kansas City is included to expand understanding of interbank relations.

The brief article by Coldwell introduces the question of whether commercial banks are sufficiently different from other types of business organizations to require special regulation of their organizational arrangements. The articles by the Federal Reserve Bank of Chicago and Crosse carefully examine the more recent trends in bank competition (or lack of it) by examining several relevant indexes such as the number of banks, the number and types of branches, and bank mergers. All of these indexes have been used in arguments for and against more federal regulation of commercial banking as a means to ensure effective competition. The article by the Federal Reserve Bank of Chicago gives the flavor of this debate by presenting the relevant issues without making sweeping conclusions or recommendations with respect to regulation. Crosse presents the argument from the commercial banks' point of view, providing a view of this question from someone intimately involved in the diverse problems of banking.

After an introduction to the problem of how banks attempt to maintain liquidity provided by the presentation of the Federal Reserve Bank of Philadelphia, the last three articles discuss the theories and practices that banks have adopted to increase their liquidity while still remaining competitive in serving the credit needs of their customers. The two Woodworth articles not only examine banking theories of liquidity but also discuss thoroughly the sources and markets used for maintaining liquidity, with a complete discussion of the mechanics of the fascinating federal funds market provided in the second Woodworth selection. The last article of this part explores the impact of credit cards on commercial bank activities, particularly that of lending to consumers. The relatively recent but vigorous entry of commercial banks into the credit card business has resulted in a new and effective method of channeling consumer loan business to the banks. The wide acceptance of credit cards has some intriguing prospects for the future of our system of transactions, as demonstrated by the results of the study reported by the Federal Reserve Bank of Boston.

RECENT BANK
FAILURES—*WHY?*

5

For the first time in a generation, bank failures in the United States
have recently occupied a prominent place in the news. Fourteen
banks have failed in the past two years. Coming after a lengthy
period in which bank failures averaged only three or four per year,
the increase in the failure rate has attracted widespread attention.
Two Congressional committees have become sufficiently concerned
to institute investigations. A perspective on these recent failures,
however, should quickly dispel any fears for the soundness of the
banking system.

In contrast with the epidemic of bank suspensions in the 1920's
and 1930's, the recent closings do not involve a substantial fraction
of the banking industry and are not the result of weaknesses in the
economic environment. Each of the recent failures was due to conditions related primarily to the individual bank involved. They are
all traceable to one or more of four major factors: changes in ownership for ulterior motives, misuse of certificates of deposit, bad
loans, and bad checks or other uncollectable cash items. In almost
every case two or more of these factors were present.

CHANGES IN OWNERSHIP

Of the 14 recently failed banks, eight changed hands shortly before encountering difficulty, two of them twice within a few months. In another the ownership of the stock was not as represented in its charter
application. In each case, failure was directly related to the change
in ownership. Some of the new owners were inept in the field of
banking. Others apparently bought control of banks for the purpose
of deliberately milking them of their assets. Most of the banks involved were relatively small but large enough to make internal
looting attractive to the unscrupulous.

One bank with assets of $7 million had been operated in a very
conservative manner for years and was perfectly sound until two
persons with no previous experience in banking bought a majority
of the stock and took over early in 1963. Through a series of loans

Reprinted from "Recent Bank Failures—*Why?" Monthly Review* (September 1965), pp. 2–5, Federal Reserve Bank of Richmond.

and investments in their own interests, they drained the bank of over $1 million in less than six weeks. With some of the money they paid off indebtedness they had incurred to purchase the bank stock. Losses resulting from these transactions quickly exceeded the bank's capital and as a result it was placed in receivership.

In the same year the downfall of another bank with $30 million of assets was brought about in a similar manner. A group of amateur bankers acquired control through the purchase of controlling stock and directed bank funds to their own use. Some $900,000 of the bank's funds were used to repay loans with which the bank stock had been purchased. Within four months the new owners had expanded loans by $5 million. The diversion of bank funds for the benefit of the majority stockholders and their friends, relatives, and associates resulted in losses exceeding the bank's capital and it was closed in August of 1963.

A third small bank was exploited by two speculators in a somewhat more imaginative manner. These individuals first acquired control of the $2.5 million bank through relatively modest stock purchases, then hired money brokers to sell for the bank over $1 million in certificates of deposit. The certificates were sold to 23 savings and loan associations, each of which received a premium payment from the money brokers over and above the permissible interest rate. The two speculators then purchased $970,000 of inferior real estate mortgages at a sizable discount and sold them to the bank at only slightly less than the face value. Plans to market another $900,000 of questionable mortgages to the bank in a similar manner were thwarted by the closing of the bank.

Most of the banks which failed recently met their downfall at the hands of two or more get-rich-quick-partners, but one small midwestern bank was undermined solely by one man who purchased controlling interest and subsequently assumed the presidency despite the fact that he had no banking experience. Although the bank was an old one, it had assets of less than $1.5 million, which facilitated one-man control. The new president began paying checks drawn by other firms he controlled, without charging the drawers' accounts. The deficit was covered with forged notes. The president also caused the bank to extend questionable loans to his other corporate interests. When the directors objected, they were all replaced. He then marketed certificates of deposit in the amount of $100,000 through a money broker by paying a 1% bounty in excess of the maximum legal interest rate. Only $40,000 of the certificates of deposit were entered in the books of the bank as deposit liabilities, with the remaining $60,000 being used to eliminate from the books the loss items resulting from loans to his other businesses. These and similar actions quickly resulted in insolvency, and the bank was placed in receivership.

A much more complex series of events led to the failure of a West Coast bank with assets slightly over $2.5 million. In 1961, an out-of-town couple bought control of the bank, which had served the small town in which it was located for several decades. Under the new management, the bank's assets quickly mushroomed to more than five times their former level. Profits in 1962 were almost as great as total capital and surplus in 1961, although the economy of the community had not changed significantly. The bank's explosive growth was due to large deposits placed by a money order firm partially controlled by the new owners, and to lending operations outside the area.

The money order firm, operated on borrowed money, fell into difficulties and the bank was sold to help meet ensuing demands. Shortly thereafter, the money order firm was also sold, and most of the firm's deposits were withdrawn from the bank. The second new owner of the bank had expected to increase deposits still further by selling certificates of deposit to savings and loan associations through money brokers, but news of the bank's relationship with the defunct money order firm made new deposits difficult to obtain.

The bank paid as much as $2\frac{1}{2}\%$ above the legally permissible rate on time deposits to attract funds. Meanwhile, many of the bank's loans were going bad. In 1962 and 1963 the bank had written off 20% of its total loans outstanding, but in 1964 the situation was even worse, and in July 1964, the bank was found to be insolvent and the directors voted to place it in liquidation.

UNSOUND MANAGEMENT

Changes of ownership did not figure in six other bank failures of the past two years, but each of these cases involves serious errors of judgment or fraudulent practices on the part of existing management.

The largest of these banks, established in 1962, acquired assets of $54 million in less than three years of operation. Rapid growth was accomplished through a combination of deposits attracted by premiums above legal interest rates and questionable loans for which sizable fees were collected. At the time of closing the bank had over $20 million of certificates of deposit outstanding. Some of these deposits had been secured by the payment of additional compensation of as much as 3% above the maximum legal rate. Many of the loans were made to real estate speculators, who paid fees of as much as $120,000 for the privilege of borrowing. The bank encountered liquidity difficulties when many of its certificates of deposit matured within a short span of time and were not renewed. Those difficulties were dealt with for a time through borrowing at the District Federal Reserve Bank, but the true condition of the bank eventually was discovered and operations were suspended by the authorities.

A much smaller bank, with assets of slightly over $8 million at the time it was closed, apparently came to grief as a result of the company it kept and the gullibility of some of its officers. The management permitted three money order companies, purportedly owned by the same group, to draw on uncollected funds, and a junior officer of the bank entered credits in the amount of over $200,000 to partially cover the deficiencies. Substantial losses were also incurred through overdrafts, and through loans of approximately $2 million to borrowers who were not credit-worthy. Some of the funds used in these operations were raised through the issue of certificates of deposit at premiums above the maximum legal rate on time deposits.

Three other small banks were ruined by the misdeeds of individuals. The largest of these had resources of slightly over $7 million. The president of this bank acquired money to pay gambling debts by fraudulently advancing money to himself on notes signed by others. The second bank, with resources of $600,000, made the mistake of honoring a large number of worthless checks drawn by one of its customers. The third, with total resources of only $75,000, was declared insolvent when an unrecorded deposit liability of $380,000 was discovered.

Perhaps the most glaring example of bank manipulation was uncovered in the collapse of a $3 million bank only a few months old. A group of small businessmen, including the president of a bank in another town, joined together to acquire a Federal charter for the bank. They were to invest about $300,000 of their own money and borrow the rest of the initial capitalization of $500,000. But before the bank opened its doors in April of 1963, control had been taken over through the acquisition of 51% of the stock by another man who had not been one of the original charter applicants.

Most of the new capital was borrowed from a nearby bank with stock in the first bank pledged as collateral. Since the amount involved was several times the lending bank's legal limit, the loan could not legally be made directly to a single man. To meet this situation, the loan was divided among the majority stockholder, the president of the bank he was buying into, and three others, with an agreement that the new bank would maintain a compensating balance of $400,000 in the lending bank.

Of the newly-organized bank's capitalization of $500,000, only about $12,000 was unencumbered cash. Pressure to increase deposits led the organizers of the new bank to pay as much as 6% interest on certificates of deposit.

Early in the bank's brief history, $225,000 was withdrawn by the promoters through a complicated series of operations involving forged notes. These notes were then paid and additional money withdrawn through the use of seven new notes totaling $315,000 in the names of people who knew nothing about them or in fictitious names.

Shortly thereafter, the principals involved acquired control of another small bank through the use of additional doubtful notes. When they arranged to have $200,000 transferred to the first bank, an employee notified the State Banking Commissioner, who required return of the funds. But later, $400,000 was successfully transferred and most of it disbursed before it could be returned. Under pressure from the Commissioner, loans were tranferred to cover most of the losses.

The difficulties of the bank were compounded by the seizure of one million dollars of counterfeit securities by the FBI when the bank's president and principal stockholder attempted to market them. Some months after the seizure of these securities, the bank which had advanced funds to the promoters for the original capital foreclosed on the stock pledged as collateral and took over the bank. This led to investigations which resulted in the bank being declared insolvent by the FDIC, and one month later, it was ordered closed by the Comptroller of the Currency.

NEW LEGISLATION

All the recent failures had one thing in common. They were the result of efforts on the part of one or more individuals to use the assets, and in some instances, the money-raising potential, of commercial banks for personal gain. In a few cases, the individuals were from outside the banks involved, but all too often, they bought into the bank and undermined it from within. It is because of this, as evidenced by the cases described above, that Congress amended the Federal Deposit Insurance Act in late 1964 to require the chief executive officer of every insured bank to report to the appropriate Federal banking authority any change in ownership of the bank stock resulting in a change in control of the bank. The Act also requires all insured banks to report loans secured by 25% or more of the stock of any insured bank. After a change in control, the bank is required to report to the appropriate Federal banking

Bank Suspensions

| Capital Stock of: | 1921–1929 | | | | | | | | | | 1930–1932 | | | |
---	1921	1922	1923	1924	1925	1926	1927	1928	1929	Totals	1930	1931	1932	Totals
$25,000 and Less	301	217	446	511	376	628	413	302	382	3,576	767	1,058	737	2,562
$25,001 to $49,999	36	41	47	59	43	102	65	39	65	497	142	220	140	502
$50,000 to $99,999	83	56	92	124	131	167	121	96	120	990	219	457	294	970
$100,000 to $199,999	47	25	32	59	46	48	48	45	58	408	132	284	144	560
$200,000 to $999,999	16	15	16	16	18	15	15	11	20	142	70	227	126	423
$1,000,000 and Over	3	—	—	—	—	—	—	—	6	9	11	32	11	54
Not Available	19	13	13	6	4	16	7	6	8	92	11	16	4	31
Totals	505	367	646	775	618	976	669	499	659	5,714	1,352	2,294	1,456	5,102

SOURCE: Federal Reserve Board, Annual Report, 1932.

agency any changes in the chief executive officer or directors during the following year, and to provide a statement of the past and present business affiliations of the new chief executive officer or directors. This law does not eliminate the possibility of banks being taken over by unscrupulous operators, but it may discourage them, and certainly should alert the banking community to the danger.

Much attention has been focused recently on changes in capital-asset ratios and loan-to-deposit ratios, and on changes in the balance sheet structure of banks. Questions have been raised concerning the possible deterioration of loan quality and excessive liberality in lending. But all of this concern is with the possibility of marginal errors in judgment by bankers. In the banks that failed, there was no wide range of marginal error. Either the bank was deliberately looted from within or the banker took risks which were well outside the scope of prudent banking.

HISTORICAL PERSPECTIVE

The United States entered the decade of the 1920's with more banks than any country has ever had before or since. The nation's bank chartering policies over a long period had led to the establishment of a large number of small, weak banks. Many states had very liberal chartering provisions, some allowing new banks to be established with as little as $5,000 capital. Prior to the turn of the century, a Federal charter required a minimum of $50,000 capital, and in 1899, there were 10,283 state banks and only 3,617 national banks. But in 1900, national banking laws were revised to permit banks to be chartered by the Federal Government with a capital stock of as little as $25,000 in communities of 3,000 inhabitants or less. Passage of this Act was followed by a sharp increase in the issuance of both state and national charters. By 1921, there were 8,154 national and 22,658 state banks, a total of 30,812, or more than twice the number in operation today. Many of the new banks were small and weak, but due to the generally high level of prosperity, especially in agricultural areas, failures were relatively rare. In the two decades prior to 1921, about 85 banks per year closed their doors. Beginning in 1921, the failure rate increased sharply, and 5,714 banks suspended operations in the next nine years; most of them permanently.

Most of the suspended banks were small country banks with assets of less than $1 million. They had been chartered in a period of farm prosperity and rising land prices. Many of their loans were in the form of mortgages on farm real estate. Agriculture became overexpanded during World War I, and after the war, farm prices and the value of farm land fell sharply. With greatly reduced incomes, many farmers were unable to meet payments on bank loans. The accelerated movement of rural population to the cities further weakened banks in rural areas. Thousands of banks failed, but due perhaps to the general prosperity the failures caused no panic.

The panic came later when city banks began failing in even larger numbers. The banking collapse of the early 1930's had its roots in the 1920's. As non-agricultural prosperity increased, banks increased their loan-deposit ratios and made larger and larger numbers of demand and call loans secured by shares of stock. Banks assumed that these loans would provide liquidity, and in fact most of the open market call loans were repaid. But when the stocks with which the demand loans to individual customers were secured rapidly lost value during and after the crash of 1929, it was discovered that many of these loans were uncollectable. Borrowers who in other times might have shifted loans to another bank in order to repay the original lender found almost all banks attempting to call their loans simultaneously.

Today, a shortage of liquidity for the banking system as a whole could be countered by Federal Reserve action. Federal Reserve banks may provide additional reserves directly to banks through various kinds of advances, or indirectly through open market operations. But prior to 1932 this was not the case. Member banks could borrow from Federal Reserve banks only on collateral consisting of narrowly-defined "eligible" paper and open market operations were in a rudimentary stage of development. Thus, thousands of banks found themselves in an illiquid position and were unable to survive the waves of bank runs of the next few years. Between 1929 and

Number of Commercial Banks Closed Because of Financial Difficulties, 1933–1964

1933	4,000	1941	16	1949	9	1957	3
1934	61	1942	23	1950	5	1958	9
1935	32	1943	5	1951	5	1959	3
1936	72	1944	2	1952	4	1960	2
1937	83	1945	1	1953	5	1961	9
1938	79	1946	2	1954	4	1962	3
1939	71	1947	6	1955	5	1963	2
1940	49	1948	3	1956	3	1964	10

SOURCES: Federal Deposit Insurance Corporation, The Board of Governors of the Federal Reserve System.

1934, more than 9,000 banks closed their doors, and very few were able to reopen.

In today's economic environment, the general collapse of our financial structure seems impossible. The banking system is altogether different and much stronger than in the 1920's and early 1930's. There are fewer small, weak banks, mainly because capital requirements are higher and bank charters are more difficult to obtain. The average bank today is older and larger, and most bank deposits are insured by the Federal Deposit Insurance Corporation. Knowledge of that insurance prevents the sort of bank runs which closed many banks in the early 1930's.

There is still the possibility of additional failures due to dishonesty or ineptitude on the part of management. Out of more than 13,000 banks, it is not surprising that a handful should suffer management difficulties. By comparison with the failure rate among other firms of similar size, the bank failure rate is very low indeed. New legislation and renewed efforts of regulatory agencies may reduce the rate even further in the future.

FEDERAL RESERVE BANK OF KANSAS CITY

CORRESPONDENT BANKING

6

Commercial banks sell their services to individuals, businesses, and governmental units. Among the business customers of many banks are other commercial banks. As customers, commercial banks purchase the same general types of services—clearing, depository, credit advice and supply, etc.—as nonbank businesses and individuals. Like other customers, banks pay for these services by maintaining bal-

Reprinted from Stuart I. Greenbaum (unsigned), "Correspondent Banking," *Monthly Review* (March–April 1965), pp. 9–16, Federal Reserve Bank of Kansas City.

ances with the seller as well as by making explicit money payments. However, the relationship between banks as producers of services and other commercial banks as purchasers of bank output is thought to have special importance because of its possible implications for questions of banking structure as well as monetary policy.

Apart from its special importance, correspondent banking is highly complex. Small country banks commonly maintain correspondent relations with 5 or 6 banks, whereas larger banks may maintain balances with 30 or more banks. Flows of services are frequently reciprocal and at times quite circuitous. Nevertheless, the flow of correspondent services through the banking system traces a perceptible hierarchical structure of banks. Small country banks generally maintain balances with a series of larger banks in regional financial centers. Banks in regional financial centers maintain balances with other banks in regional financial centers, as well as with banks in New York and/or Chicago. New York and Chicago banks will, in turn, maintain balances with banks in the national financial centers and also with banks in various regional centers. The intricacy of this network indicates the degree of indirection and complexity that interbank service flows can assume.

PRODUCTION VERSUS PURCHASE OF BANK SERVICES

The basic reason for the flow of services among banks is that in some instances commercial banks find it either impossible or relatively costly to produce certain services required by their customers. When a profit-conscious bank finds it cheaper to purchase a service from another bank than to produce that service itself, it will resort to a correspondent. In determining which banks are to produce a given type of service and which are to purchase the service, bank size and location appear to be of paramount importance. These two factors, it may be noted, are not entirely independent of each other, since banks rarely grow to great size in sparsely populated or commercially remote areas.

The importance of bank location is, perhaps, best exemplified by clearing services. A bank receiving a check drawn on another bank must arrange for transportation of the check to either the paying bank's premises or to some location where the paying bank maintains an account. If a country bank regularly receives a substantial number of items drawn on a city bank, it may become convenient to maintain an account with the paying bank and use its clearing facilities. Since the volume of clearing flows between banks generally is influenced by the pattern of commerce in an area, the decision to maintain a correspondent relationship derives partly from the geographic location of participants.

Bank size, the second major element rationalizing the production of bank services, appears to have especially pervasive implications for the structure of correspondent relationships. The importance of bank size derives largely from the connection between size and division of labor. Because banks produce such diverse financial services, substantial size is necessary to permit the specialization required to gain expertise in all phases of the business. If the required volume of business is unattainable, it becomes cheaper for a bank to purchase services from other banks with more highly developed facilities. Correspondent banking thus may be viewed as a means of circumventing some of the disadvantages inherent in small size. In effect, the larger bank stands ready to sell or rent factors of production or services flowing from these factors to smaller banks in smaller amounts than are otherwise available.

The following cursory description of selected types of correspondent services is meant to convey an impression of the scope and variety of such services, but is not an exhaustive listing of types of correspondent services. Following the descriptive material are sections devoted to interpretation of the meaning and importance of correspondent banking. Most of the discussion is focused upon the relationship between the small country member bank and larger banks in regional financial centers; however, parts of the discussion are equally relevant to correspondent relationships among other types of banks. Correspondent services will be conveniently, albeit somewhat arbitrarily, grouped under three headings: clearing services, asset management services, and other miscellaneous services.

CLEARING SERVICES

It is significant that a sizable proportion of Federal Reserve member banks prefer to sustain the expense of clearing through correspondents, even though Federal Reserve Banks provide clearing services at no additional cost, once membership has been established. Banks in regional financial centers actively solicit this type of business with notable success. For example, less than one fourth of the member banks in the Tenth Federal Reserve District cleared directly through the Reserve Bank during 1964. It may be assumed that the remainder reply primarily on the facilities of correspondents. On the other hand, city correspondents will submit many of the items originating with their respondents to the Federal Reserve Bank. Thus, the practice of clearing through correspondents will not necessarily result in a material reduction in the volume of clearings handled by the Federal Reserve System, but an element of indirection is introduced into the clearing process.

The ability of city correspondents to sell clearing services to member banks is partly explained by the inclusion of these services as an integral part of a package of highly diverse services that comprise the typical correspondent relationship. However, it is also true that clearing services provided by correspondents are differentiated from those offered by Federal Reserve Banks. For example, the Federal Reserve Bank may require some sorting of items submitted for collection, whereas correspondents commonly accept clearing items unsorted. Federal Reserve Banks will not generally accept nonpar or foreign items, while correspondents do not usually impose such restrictions. In addition, correspondents frequently provide immediate credit for all cash items, whereas the Federal Reserve Bank gives immediate, 1-day, or 2-day credit depending upon the location of the paying bank. The point to be emphasized is that city correspondents augment the clearing services offered member banks by the Federal Reserve System.

ASSET MANAGEMENT SERVICES

With regard to portfolio management, the small bank faces two major problems. First, it does not generate sufficient expert information internally, and second, it is forced to trade in relatively small units. In helping the small bank circumvent these inherent disadvantages, the city correspondent promotes two socially useful ends. Inter-area capital mobility is enhanced and the dissemination of economically valuable informations is facilitated.

Expert information, purchased from a correspondent, may relate to problems as broad as the over-all structure of a bank's portfolio, or it may be confined to the merits of a specific municipal security. The intricacies of Treasury advance refundings and the creditworthiness of out-of-area loan applicants also serve as bases for exchanges of information. The city correspondent's highly specialized organization, as well as its numerous contacts with banks large and small, provide it with unique credentials as a purveyor of wide-ranging expertise.

The importance of trading units expresses itself in two ways. First, smaller banks occasionally are confronted by valued customers who wish to negotiate larger loans than these banks can legally or prudently make to any single borrower. These same banks, when in need of funds or outlets for the employment of idle funds, often find that the size of trading units in organized markets preclude their participation. The first type of contingency is often solved with a loan participation, whereby the city correspondent shares in the oversize loans originated by correspondents. The second type of problem may be dealt with by providing loans in which smaller banks may participate. In addition, correspondents may lend or borrow, using federal funds or other instruments, or they may buy or sell various types of earning assets. In effect, the city correspondent "makes a market" in various types of debt instruments designed to serve the needs of smaller banks. Depending on the needs and tastes of participants, the city correspondent may act as dealer, broker, or both. The importance of such a relationship is more fully appreciated by recognizing that assets flowing among banks are at times those for which there are no organized secondary markets.

MISCELLANEOUS SERVICES

In addition to the services already discussed, correspondents provide a group of miscellaneous services, some of which are used infrequently but remain crucial to the efficient operation of smaller banks. Examples of such services include trust and international banking, and consultation on management problems. Personnel problems of smaller, remotely situated banks are often particularly difficult. Correspondents commonly serve as a clearing house for higher level job applicants and openings at such banks. In addition, some smaller banks participate in the group insurance and retirement programs of city correspondents.

City correspondents also facilitate the exchange of equity in smaller banks by bringing together prospective buyers and sellers and by financing the purchase of stock. An indication of the importance of correspondents in financing equity transfers is suggested by a recent study done under the auspices of the House Committee on Banking and Currency. A questionnaire addressed to 6,200 member banks in 1962 revealed that 2,166 loans made by these banks were secured with 10 percent or more of the equity in other banks. The preponderant majority of these loans was made in areas with large concentrations of relatively small banks. For example, banks within the Tenth District had 470 loans outstanding that were secured by 10 percent or more of the stock of banks within the Kansas City District. Assuming no duplication, the banks whose stock served as collateral constituted more than one fourth of all commercial banks in the area. The purposes for which these loans were made were not disclosed, but it seems reasonable to expect that the borrowers had a wide variety of purposes. On the other hand, there is no reason to doubt that the acquisition of bank equity was one reason for borrowing.

The general acceptability of bank stock as collateral for bank loans has meaning beyond facilitating the transfer of equity. Since the market for the stock of small banks is not highly developed, owners may find it difficult to dispose of such assets on short notice without accepting sizable losses. So long as loans are readily available to those able to hypothecate bank stock, disposal of the stock on short notice becomes unnecessary. The ready availability of such loans may thus be viewed as enhancing the real rate of return on investments in bank stock.

Still other services commonly provided through correspondent relationships might be discussed in some detail. The provision of coin, electronic data processing services, and advice on building design and equipment are just a few. However, there is little point in trying to make this discussion exhaustive. The field is far too broad and simple enumeration of services conveys little insight.

AN INTERPRETATION OF CORRESPONDENT BANKING

The foregoing discussion suggested that the importance of correspondent banking results largely from economies of scale in the production of banking services. Since large banks can produce some types of bank output at lower cost than their smaller counterparts, the smaller bank can frequently purchase bank services at lower cost than it can produce them. Viewed in this way, interbank service flows become a type of "intermediate product," analogous to the semi-processed goods purchased by a manufacturer.

A measure of the importance of interbank service flows and a possible measure of economies of scale may be obtained by relating bank purchases of correspondent services to sales. Deriving such a measure is, however, complicated by a number of considerations. First, there are difficulties in measuring the volume of interbank service flows because payments for these services are made by explicit money transfers as well as by maintaining balances with the bank supplying services. The balances represent a type of payment "in kind" in which the medium of exchange is a factor of production, an ingredient used by the receiving bank in the further production of output. Surprisingly, "in kind" payments are easily estimated, but explicit interbank money payments are not. This stems from the fact that interbank balances are shown in Reports of

Condition, but interbank payments are not generally shown, as such, in Income and Dividend Reports. However, the inability to measure explicit interbank payments may not be a major problem since they are generally far less important than "in kind" payments.

A distinction must be made between Federal Reserve member and nonmember banks in the interpretation of their interbank balances. The correspondent bank receiving balances invests the funds, allowing for reserve requirements, and the earnings on such investments constitute the payment received from its respondent for services rendered. The *member* bank maintaining correspondent balances could alternatively withdraw these funds and purchase earning assets itself, thereby augmenting its income. Thus, interbank balances represent forgone income to the *member* bank maintaining them, as well as a source of income to the depository bank. These balances are maintained in consideration of services received and, provided respondents are profit conscious, the amount of income forgone by the member bank maintaining such balances should not tend to be greater than its estimate of the value of services provided by the depository bank.

In the case of nonmember banks, however, it is important to recognize that their correspondent balances may serve as legal reserves. A nonmember bank that is fully "loaned up"—without excess reserves—will not effectively have the option of withdrawing its correspondent balances for the purchase of earning assets. It is reasonable to assume that these deposits would be maintained even in the absence of services provided by the depository bank. Thus, the nonmember bank holding interbank balances for reserve purposes does not thereby sustain an opportunity cost in the same way as the member bank.[1] Of course, in choosing among possible depositories, the nonmember bank will attempt to select the bank making the most generous offer of correspondent services. However, there is no compelling reason to expect the value of these services to equal the forgone income, as measured by the member bank holding such balances, unless the sellers of bank services are in highly competitive markets.

If strong competition is absent, depository banks need not pay as much—in services—for the correspondent balances of nonmember banks as they would for the balances of member banks. Whether

[1] This argument is predicated on the assumption that the marginal return on vault cash is zero and that banks do not have the option of holding their reserves in the form of earning assets. In cases where these two assumptions are not satisfied, the distinction between member and nonmember banks can be weakened or nullified.

depository banks in fact pay more or less for these deposits is not known. However, it seems reasonable to assume that the earnings a member bank might have obtained by investing its interbank balances, again allowing for reserve requirements, may be used as a measure of the lower limit of the value of services the bank receives from correspondents. On the other hand, such an assumption does not appear warranted when applied to nonmember banks.

A second problem in deriving a measure of the relationship between sales and correspondent services purchased relates to the measurement of bank sales. The major difficulty encountered here relates to problems of asset valuation—the treatment of capital gains and losses. However, detailed discussion of this problem is beyond the scope of this article. Current operating revenue—mainly interest and service charge income—will be used as a measure of sales, while recognizing that the measure is not uniquely correct.

Chart 1 shows an estimated relationship between correspondent services purchased, or forgone income on interbank balances, and deposit size, for a sample of 602 country member banks in the Tenth Federal Reserve District. Banks in the sample ranged from approximately $0.5 million to $34.2 million in deposit size. The chart indicates that the smallest banks in the sample purchase about $1,400 per year in correspondent services. This value increases at a diminishing rate as deposits grow, and reaches a maximum of $38,500 for banks with deposits of $26.8 million. Thereafter, forgone income falls as deposits rise and at $34.2 million, the maximum deposit size in the sample, banks purchase approximately $35,600 worth of correspondent services per year. The remaining line in Chart 1 depicts the estimated relationship between sales—current operating revenue—and deposit size. (See Technical Note 2.) Sales rise at an increasing rate as bank deposits grow. A bank with $0.5 million in total deposits has estimated sales of $22,900 per year and banks of maximum deposit size—$34.2 million—show sales of $2.07 million.

Chart 2, which is derived from the equations depicted in Chart 1, shows forgone income and sales as a per cent of deposits, and forgone income is also shown as a per cent of sales. The chart indicates that forgone income declines as a per cent of deposits as bank size increases. For the smallest banks in the sample, forgone income on correspondent balances, or correspondent services purchased, amounts to 0.29 per cent of total deposits and for the largest banks the value is 0.10 per cent. In contrast, sales, as a per cent of deposits, rise consistently with bank growth, from a low of 4.6 per cent to a high of 6.1 per cent.

CHART 1 Sales and Correspondent Services Purchased Related to Total Deposits

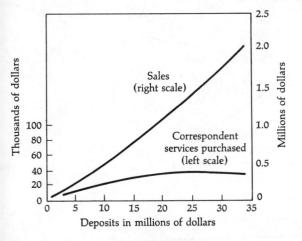

Deposits in millions of dollars

NOTE: The relationship between correspondent services purchased and total deposits was obtained in three steps. First, a statistical technique—least squares regression—was used to estimate the relationship between demand balances with correspondents and total deposits. The fitted equation was then multiplied by a constant—1 minus the legal reserve requirement against demand deposits for country member banks $(1.0 - 0.12 = 0.88)$—in order to transform the equation into a relationship between the investible portions of correspondent balances and deposit size. (Correspondent balances are treated as deductions from total demand deposits in the computation of required reserves.) The final step involved multiplying the resulting equation by a second constant—3.5 per cent—which was an assumed value for the rate of return on highly liquid bank investments. This multiplication further transformed the equation into a relationship between forgone income, or correspondent services purchased, and deposit size.

The line marked "correspondent services purchased/sales" is a lower limit estimate of the per cent of sales which are intermediate product—the resold output of other producers—for banks of varying deposit size. The equation underlying the charted relationship was obtained by dividing the correspondent services purchased relationship of Chart 1 by the sales relationship also shown in Chart 1. The resulting equation indicates that correspondent services become less important relative to sales as deposit size of banks increases. However, the ratio of forgone income to sales falls at a declining rate—there is a tendency for the line to flatten out—as deposits grow. For the smallest banks in the sample, 6.2 per cent of sales are intermediate product in the form of correspondent services, but only 1.7 per cent of sales of the largest banks are accounted for by

CHART 2   Relationships Derived from Equations Underlying Chart 1

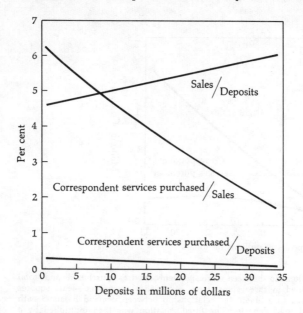

purchased correspondent services. This relationship provides tentative corroboration for the economies of scale explanation for the importance of correspondent banking. As banks become larger, they produce an ever greater percentage of their sales. The derived relationship is also significant in that it provides a measure of the quantitative importance of correspondent banking for small banks in a unit banking environment. On the other hand, it may be worth repeating that the measure of correspondent service flows covers only that portion of correspondent services which are paid for by the maintenance of interbank balances among the sample banks. In addition, the rate of return used in deriving the forgone income measure was selected somewhat arbitrarily, and the measure of sales is not entirely unambiguous. These shortcomings are, however, judged to be of relatively minor importance, and the contour of the derived relationship appears quite plausible.

EXPLICIT SERVICE CHARGES VERSUS THE MAINTENANCE OF BALANCES

To this point, the question of why banks apparently prefer to receive and/or make payments for correspondent services in the form of interbank balances has not been considered. If explicit and implicit payments were equal, banks might be expected to be indifferent to the form of payment. However, payment in the form of balances is rather general in banking. Services provided the U. S. Treasury are paid for by maintaining tax and loan account balances, and state and local governments commonly use the same means to compensate commercial banks. The role of compensating balance requirements in connection with loans is also analogous to the part played by interbank balances in connection with correspondent relationships. Thus any explanation of implicit payments in correspondent banking may be expected to have wider relevance.

Any one or a combination of three explanations may account for the use of implicit payments in correspondent relationships. First, the legal prohibition of interest payment on demand deposits exerts an important influence. Since deposits represent a productive input to the individual bank, banks seek to purchase them. Prohibition of interest payments precludes effecting such transactions in the conventional manner—through money payments—and thus banks remunerate their suppliers with services.

A second explanation, suggested by bankers, relates to the importance of deposits, apart from the considerations of short-run profit maximization. Some bankers argue that given the choice between implicit and explicit payments in equal amount, they would prefer implicit payment because it fosters deposit growth. The importance of deposit growth stems from its conventional use as a measure of management acumen. Its use as such may be rationalized by arguing that deposit growth provides a foundation for the future growth of earnings. Banks may even trade off current earnings to achieve a desirable rate of deposit growth, in which case the suppliers of deposits could benefit from the use of an implicit payment system. Correspondent services may be obtained at lower cost to the respondent than would be the case under a system of explicit payments. On the other hand, in the absence of the legal prohibition of interest payment on deposits, interest rates presumably would reflect the special value of deposits to banks.

A third reason for implicit payments may be found in bankers' preference for nonprice forms of competition. It has been argued that unbridled price competition imparts a destabilizing influence to the banking system, and thus has generally deleterious implications for the economy. Setting aside the question of the validity of such arguments, implicit payments can be explained by a general aversion to price competition. Although all three suggested explanations for implicit payments are potentially important, the first—the legal prohibition of interest payment on demand deposits—appears most compelling because of its obvious impact. The actual relevance of the other explanations is more open to question.

Consider the case of nonmember banks where the opportunity cost of maintaining interbank balances is zero, assuming such deposits are used to satisfy legal reserve requirements. If correspondents earn 4 per cent on such deposits, they will be able to provide services worth any amount between zero and 4 per cent of balances and both banks will find the relationship profitable. Assume, for the purpose of discussion, that the correspondent pays the respondent 2.5 per cent—in the form of services—on interbank balances. The respondent is thus earning 2.5 per cent on its legal reserves which, in effect, have no earning power in alternative uses. The correspondent also finds this arrangement advantageous in that it profits to the extent of the spread between the earning power of the deposits—4 per cent—and the cost of providing correspondent services—2.5 per cent—to its respondent. In highly competitive markets the value of correspondent services would be expected to approximate 4 per cent on balances, while in other circumstances some intermediate value might be arrived at through negotiation. In any case, the value of correspondent services might be expected to remain meaningfully above the zero floor because smaller state banks have the alternative of membership in the Federal Reserve.

The situation of member banks is altered in detail, but remains essentially the same. The difference stems from the fact that interbank balances of member banks serve as secondary reserves and the opportunity cost of maintaining interbank balances thus approaches the yield on highly liquid earning assets, say 3.5 per cent. This means the member respondent must receive services worth in excess of 3.5 per cent on balances to make the correspondent relationship attractive, whereas any nonzero return may satisfy the nonmember respondent. On the other hand, in highly competitive markets all respondents will be offered approximately 4 per cent—the assumed value of such balances to city correspondents—and the member-nonmember distinction will be inconsequential. But if such circumstances do not prevail and correspondents are able to treat different customers differently, the member bank may be able to command a somewhat higher return on its interbank balances.

CONCLUSION

The discussion presented thus far has touched many bases, several of them somewhat technical. In concluding, a few broad generalizations may be useful.

Many students of banking structure have argued the advantages of branch banking by alluding to economies of scale in the production of commercial bank services. Much of the foregoing discussion suggests that correspondent banking is a potentially effective means for circumventing these inherent disadvantages of small-size banking firms. To the extent that correspondent banking is an efficient system for the production and distribution of bank output, the advantages of branch banking attributable to economies of scale may be seriously weakened.

In serving commercial banks, correspondent banking mobilizes inter-area flows of capital, other factors of production, and information. It effectively integrates the banking system and in doing this it represents a cogent alternative to branch, group, or chain banking. On the other hand, there is reason to question the viability of unit banking in the absence of well-developed correspondent banking institutions.

PHILIP E. COLDWELL

IS BANKING UNIQUE?

7

Over the past five years and, in fact, as almost a hallmark of the decade of the 60's, there has been a major change of emphasis in structure and organization of businesses in the United States. Perhaps reflecting prior emphasis upon antitrust action to discourage monopolies, but also the rapid growth of small firms during the immediate postwar period, the recent trend may be a pendulum swing away from the small business and into the larger aggregation of capital control.

The forces bringing this about have been the pressure to develop laborsaving and improved technological equipment, the need to extend production to utilize fully the new methods and machines, the heavy capital requirements for both plant and equipment and work-

Reprinted from Philip E. Coldwell, "Is Banking Unique?" *Business Review* (October 1968), pp. 3–8, Federal Reserve Bank of Dallas.

ing capital purposes, and the desire to diversify companies which found their principal product and principal line of endeavor tied to only one segment of industry and, in a few cases, to a volatile defense connection. To some extent, the move toward larger aggregates also reflects the difficulties of obtaining qualified management, the need to innovate in an intensely competitive environment, and the very American characteristic of growth for the sake of bigness and enlargement of corporate influence. Perhaps even the emphasis of the United States tax laws, the possibilities of deferring capital gains and of growing without tax penalty by means of merger with noncomparable product companies, is a factor in the new move toward conglomerates. Some of the recent take-overs and mergers were probably originated to obtain new funds as an alternate to issuing corporate debt instruments or borrowing from banks. This impression is emphasized by the tendency of some companies to reach into the banking industry to obtain control of financial institutions for credit sources.

This quick overview of the recent changes in business corporate structure and diversification of product lines has obvious implications for the banking industry. The question we face today is one which we have faced many times, but perhaps in a slightly different fashion: "Is banking a business comparable to steelmaking, aircraft manufacturing, or a host of other industries; or is banking unique and to be treated in an entirely different way in the public interest?" Perhaps it would be well to begin our discussion of this matter by reviewing some of the same forces impacting upon banking structure that have developed in the business changes referred to above.

Certainly, banking has seen a marked change in its focus over the past 20 years. A large number of new units chartered into the banking industry have brought additional competition and intensified the hunt for capable leaders. Management has become a major problem to the banking industry, in both quantity and quality. The significant changes in methods of doing business, the advent of data processing, and the steady encroachment of internal and external banking system competitors have brought demands for management talent far exceeding those of banking even 20 years ago.

Concurrently, the customer mix has shifted markedly with heavier capital requirements and demands for materially longer and larger loans. Broadened service requirements and enlarged roles of banks in local financing needs, as well as the recent change in deposit mix toward larger proportions of time and savings deposits, have had a real impact upon bank lending and investing policies. These same factors, along with many others, are spurring bank considerations of mergers, consolidations, holding companies, and even product or service diversification.

The changes in banking and its responses to those changes focus our attention even more sharply upon the character of this industry and its relationship to the public interest which must be served. The fundamentals of the question regarding the character of this industry can be stated in a number of different ways. In the traditional sense, are the stockholders and purchasers of corporate debt instruments in a different position from the capital ownership and depositors of a commercial bank? Similarly, are the sources of funds available to banks markedly different from those available to business? Are the uses of these funds sufficiently different to require a distinctly different public policy? I submit that the changes over the post-war period have materially blurred some of the distinctions formerly made between banking and other types of business, though there remains a fundamental credit creation by banking which other industries cannot duplicate.

Banking today must draw upon funds for capital growth from markets which are tapped by other businesses as well and, in competition with those businesses, must provide a meaningful rate of return commensurate with risk sufficient to acquire the needed capital. In many ways banks with funds to make loans or investments are not wholly different from the corporations which use their funds in both the investment and working capital sense. Even the repayment requirements of banking and other industries are not materially different today, as business must make a return on its capital just as banks attempt to do for their stockholders, and business must repay its short- and long-term debt just as banks must be ready to repay CD holders and investors in debentures. Thus, in some areas banking is comparable to other businesses, but in the basic depositor relationships there is still something unique to the banking industry.

While the banking industry may have many elements in common with other businesses, there are still elements of confidence and trust required in handling the money supply of the Nation and an element of credit creation which distinguish this industry from its counterparts in other business pursuits. Demand deposit liabilities of banks are the major share of the Nation's money supply, and no other business has such liabilities. Moreover, only the banking system can multiply these deposits on a given base of excess reserves.

In the use of the lendable funds and the banking industry's competitive position, there has been a shift of positions which perhaps now should be recognized in the public mind and in governmental control and regulation of this industry. While banks provide a large share of the working funds for business operations and growth, the new world of business has found other sources and other techniques to meet these same requirements. Banking today is not the only source of funds and, in fact, in some areas is a declining source. The growth of Federal credit sources for agriculture and business, the growth of Euro-dollar financing, the substantial enlargement of the commercial paper market, and the heavy corporate financing issues may all be symptoms of the multiplicity of sources of funds competing with the traditional banking industry.

Even within the financial institutional structure there have been changes permitting savings and loan associations, insurance companies, credit unions, factoring groups, and even private investors to absorb larger and larger roles in the provision of funds for routine lending transactions. To meet the profit impact of this intense competition for their traditional role as lenders in the short run, banks have sought both to merge into larger units and to expand their influence into other industries by one-bank holding company relationships, ownership of equities through trust and investment accounts, and finally the creation of subsidiary corporations largely devoted to nonbank and even nonfinancial pursuits.

One of the central questions of today, then, is "Should this trend be permitted, encouraged, or discouraged in the public interest?" It has been a basic tenet of regulation in the banking industry that banks are supervised and regulated because the public interest requires regulation of an industry whose deposits serve as the money supply or savings of the people and because the depositor needs protection from unsound banking practices, mismanagement, and other similar problems of the past. Regulation has focused upon fostering competition among financial institutions and within the banking industry and yet preserving a protected position for banks.

The merger cases of today are replete with considerations of the competitive or anticompetitive factors impinging upon a particular situation. Public policy has encouraged new bank formations in specific situations and has broadened the authority of nonbank financial competitors. We must also recognize though that regulation has, to some extent, protected the banking industry, for entrance into this industry must be by charter, approved by a public body, and limits on the cost of the funds are similarly regulated to protect against the banker who seeks a quick profit despite the marginal cost of the funds.

Regulation is thus a two-way street for the banking industry, but probably few other industries are required to maintain as detailed records and reports to reflect developments which might impinge upon public policy requirements. Banking is unique in this respect and in respect to national monetary policy, although even here the events of the past 25 years now seem to dictate a much wider scope for policies to be set in the national interest to encompass more of those industries which provide capital and working funds, rather than just strictly the commercial banking industry.

Some observers have suggested that the fulcrum upon which monetary policy operates should be widened substantially to include all basic financial institutions, whether of a bank or nonbank character. Such a move, if ever accomplished, may be feasible only through the extension of reserve requirements to all banking institutions. The Nation expects an equitable and efficient monetary policy, but that policy must be effectuated in its primary impact only through the member commercial banks. Other observers have contended that in recent years, because of the small base from which monetary policy must be implemented, the actions of the monetary authorities have been accentuated perhaps beyond the needs of the moment in order to have the ramifying effects necessary in other segments of the economy.

Recent publicized discussions seem to imply that the nonmember bank responds to monetary restraint in the same way as the member bank and that extension of reserve requirements is, therefore, not needed. In fact, reference was made to the late summer of 1966 as an example demonstrating the overall effectiveness of monetary policy, even with its limited base. In my opinion, the heavy-handed restraint of that period demonstrates both the inequities and the effectiveness of monetary policy. If a much broader base were developed, policy moves might be somewhat more moderate, but broadening the base of monetary action will by no means guarantee perfect timing or results, nor perfect equity in application. Whether a broader base might moderate the excesses of tightness or ease in policy actions, the rapid and over-correcting swings in policy, or provide for quicker impact upon all elements has not yet been proven or accepted.

The broadening of authority in nonbank financial institutions, especially the savings and loan associations through the recently passed Housing Act will further intensify direct competition with the banking industry by institutions which are not subject to the same rules and regulations as banking and which do not have the responsibilities in the field of basic monetary policy implementation for the entire economy. One could say some of the same things about credit unions, insurance companies, mutual savings banks, factoring companies, and even some of the major corporations though the direct relationships to banking are much weaker. If monetary policy is to continue to accept the primary burden of stabilization control—and it would appear that this is a logical conclusion from the most recent difficulties of obtaining fiscal action —then I submit that monetary policy should be based as broadly as is needed for effective control, with equitable impacts on all elements of the economy and with as prompt reflection of action in these elements as can be achieved.

As can be seen by the matters heretofore mentioned, I believe there remains a unique character to the banking industry which requires more than usual public surveillance and even regulation in the public interest. Perhaps we should recapitulate the elements which set this industry apart from other businesses.

First, the banking industry operates in a manner which creates credit with a multiplier through lending and deposit creation. No other industry can achieve this, and the power to do this warrants careful attention. Secondly, the power of creation and the element of expansion through credit are fundamental to the well-being of the Nation's economy and must be closely controlled to avoid the excesses of expansion and contraction which are inherent in the system. Thirdly, banking represents a part of the financial structure of the Nation which, through its efforts, must retain the confidence of the people in the integrity and safety of their currency. Thus, it is in the public interest to regulate banking, supervise its operations, and require its adherence to both basic principles of conduct and rules to set the aggregate of credit use in the best interests of a sound and growing economy.

There still remains a debatable question of how many restraints are required, how much regulation is needed, and whether the principles and implementation of regulation are keeping pace with the changing economic and financial environment. We could spend hours discussing the need for each regulation or restriction and, similarly, many hours debating the merits of the present structure of regulatory agencies. I would rather discuss the last of these questions, for I believe it contains most of the elements which can answer the first two questions.

In a slightly different wording, then, I propose to look at the question of whether regulation is keeping pace or is unduly restricting the growth and diversification of banking. While I would insist upon the basic tenet that regulation is required, I am convinced that it need not be repressive and, in fact, should encourage sound expansion and better service to a steadily wider range of customers.

It seems to me that a wider range of opportunities could be opened to the banking industry, in keeping with some of those opportunities which other industries and corporations have developed in diversifying their sources of funds and possibilities for profit. The opportunities for diversification are apparent even in bank-related activities.

The overseas or foreign investment, lending, and servicing activities represent a broad field of endeavor which offers possibilities inherent in the Euro-dollar, Euro-bond, and other Euro-currency transactions, opportunities in financing foreign manufacturing and trade outlets, and increasing opportunities for export financing. These would appear to be a natural concomitant of domestic banking activities, and I would encourage the banks of this District to look toward such foreign connections, especially with our neighbors to the South. At present, of course, I must reserve my encouragement to those who can enter these fields through branches, Edge Act corporations, and equity ownership of foreign banks within the guidelines of the Voluntary Foreign Credit Restraint Program. Even within this program, however, there are elements of opportunity which only a few of you have started to explore.

Other opportunities in bank-related areas include the computer servicing of customer accounts, insurance relationships for loan accounts, the entire range of computer handling of billings, and the resultant closer ties to such industries as utilities, department stores, and oil companies. It does not seem unreasonable to me to permit banks to utilize fully the potentials of their computer installations in any way which retains an arm's-length dealing with customers. Even the on-line real-time applications and rentals look like possibilities where bank computer capacity exceeds that needed for routine operations. Certainly, the concentrations of bookkeeping and check handling are ideal uses for bank computers for both other banks and even nonbank financial institutions. In fact, I can visualize the central handling of checks as a step in the direction of direct funds transfers, either as an initial collecting point or as ultimate checkless operations. So much progress has been made along these lines that the mechanism for remittances has fallen out of step and needs updating to a modern automatic charge plan for all banks. We hope to introduce such a plan for District-wide use by early 1969.

The remaining point in our discussion of bank expansion and diversification concerns bank ownership or participation in nonfinancial enterprises in a manner similar to conglomerates.

Some qualified observers of the banking industry argue that if nonbank holding companies can purchase banks, then banks should be permitted equal rights in purchasing nonbank enterprises. This assumes that it is in the public interest to permit bank ownership by such holding companies. I suggest that there are at least a few undesirable elements to such ownership. If, as we contended previously, the banking industry retains a unique flavor by position, authorities, and operations, entry into this field must be carefully controlled. We do limit the establishment of new banks, but the transfer of ownership of existing banks is almost unregulated.

I have previously spoken about the abuses I see in the bank stock loan arrangements. There are similar potential abuses in the holding company purchases of banks. Let me hasten to say that I do not favor a legislative prohibition on such transfers, but merely regulation to limit the abuses and to keep the most dedicated, competent bank management free from stockholder pressures to accommodate loans which are questionable credits. Of course, we cannot indict all holding company ownership nor all owners who obtain bank stock loans, but there are sufficient evidences of abuse which appear to warrant some control.

Where does this leave us with regard to bank diversification into nonbank-related activities? Can we establish a significant difference between the bank as the parent versus the bank as the subsidiary? I am hard pressed to draw too fine a line of demarcation, but I believe there is a gray area within which it would still be in the public interest to permit bank expansion and diversification while limiting, in like fashion, bank take-overs by nonfinancial holding companies.

Stated in another way, I can see possibilities of bank investment and ownership of industries related to banking and industries which require the management talent and credit sources available at banking institutions; but I suggest that there are sufficiently unique characteristics in banking to limit the willingness of supervisors and legislators, to permit only a smaller and more restrictive range of acquisition of these outside corporations.

The apparent trend toward a department-store concept of financial institution which could offer the services of all present types suggests a reconsideration of the separation of banking and investment functions in our economy. In my opinion, we have already come a long way toward the blending of certain functions, though I will readily admit that the deposit creation powers of the banking system have not as yet been passed to the other, nonbank financial institutions. I am prepared to agree to a restudy of this relationship to see if the abuses and dangers which brought separation in the

1930's are still present in the environment of the 1960's. We have come a long way in modifying our financial structure in the past 30 years, and perhaps this separation is one of those carry-over restraints which need no longer exist. I do not know the answer but suggest that a reappraisal after 30 years is not unreasonable.

Another area in which change has outdated regulation is in the Federal Reserve discount window . . . A part of the new discount approach is to help the banks meet short-run adjustments and enable them to devote most of their lendable funds to helping their communities. Certainly, the banking community needs to grow with the commercial community, for if units of the banking industry do not keep pace with the size of their customers, then the servicing of these customers must be steadily concentrated into the hands of only a few very large banks. This would represent to me a greater hazard for competition and be farther away from the public interest than if banking were permitted to expand into other fields or, certainly, grow by mergers and holding companies. . . .

FEDERAL RESERVE BANK OF CHICAGO

COMPETITION IN BANKING: THE ISSUES

8

In an economy characterized by private property and production for profit, competition among buyers and sellers has long been considered a prime prerequisite of economic efficiency—efficiency in this context being construed to include both the maximizing of output for any given resource used and the allocation of resources among all possible uses such that total production is maximized.

So strong has been the American belief in impersonal market

Reprinted from "Competition in Banking: The Issues," *Business Conditions* (January 1967), pp. 8–16, Federal Reserve Bank of Chicago.

forces to set prices and guide production, as opposed to joint decisions among producers or the decrees of government boards, that our country early put on the books the strictest and most comprehensive antitrust legislation in the world. The basic statutes are the Sherman Act of 1890 and the Clayton and Federal Trade Commission Acts of 1914.

To be sure, it has long been recognized that the technologies of some industries preclude primary reliance upon competition to guide investment, production and pricing. In these so-called "natural monopolies," such as the production and distribution of electric power and other "public utilities," the discipline of the marketplace has been replaced by the deliberations of public regulatory agencies.

Still other industries, although not considered natural monopolies, have been acknowledged as greatly affecting the public interest and have been partially shielded from the impact of unrestrained competition. Put another way, the failure or other malfunctioning of an individual establishment in these industries has been deemed to have adverse effects on the economy over and beyond the injury accruing to the firm's stockholders. Consequently, public regulation has been imposed in order to assure that certain minimal operating and fiduciary standards are met. Of the industries accorded such treatment, commercial banking is probably the most prominent.

WHY BANKS ARE REGULATED

Demand deposits of commercial banks provide the primary means of payment and, hence, are the major component of the money supply. Widespread failures of banks and sharp declines in the money supply have been associated with economic crises in past years. Furthermore, banks, while presumed by the public to be safe depositories, typically have liabilities that are very large in proportion to their capital and consequently could provide an attractive temptation to gambling by reckless entrepreneurs. These conditions alone would suggest the desirability of regulation to assure the liquidity and solvency of commercial banks. In addition historical experience lends support to the view that permitting banks to engage in unrestrained competition may lead to disastrous results. The evils of the past—specifically, the chaos and instability that attended the era of "free banking" between 1837 and 1863, the large numbers of bank failures in the 1920s and the banking collapse and economic depression of the early 1930s—have sufficed to convince most people that some measure of Government intervention is not only desirable but an absolute necessity.

The Federal and state governments have responded to the apparent need by constructing over the years a highly detailed and extensive system of commercial bank regulation that includes specific lending and borrowing restrictions, usury laws, ceilings on rates that banks may pay on time deposits, the prohibition of interest on demand deposits, capital and management requirements for the establishment of new banks, geographical restrictions on branching, requirements for periodic publication of statements of condition and examinations by public officials.

WHY COMPETITION IN BANKING

Since official regulation imposes numerous limitations on the activities of banks, vigorous competition among banks may appear both superfluous and inconsistent. After all, one may ask, is not the public's interest in having quality services provided at reasonable prices protected in banking through public regulation, as it supposedly is for electric utilities and transportation? The answer, clearly, is in the negative.

Although commercial banks are subject to a great number of specific regulations limiting the scope of their activities, a broad range of discretion still remains open to them. As far as their lending and investment activities are concerned, banks retain the prerogative of emphasizing particular kinds of loans (for example, business, consumer, agriculture and mortgage loans) and of setting prices for these loans at whatever levels they choose, subject only to the ceilings on some types of loans established by state usury laws. Thus, there is ample room for the play of competitive forces to establish the actual levels of charges.

The scope for nonprice competition in banking is even wider. The services provided in conjunction with the bank's lending and deposit business provide a variety of opportunities for nonprice maneuvers designed to win new customers and retain old ones. It is the incomplete nature of regulation which, while imposing definite constraints on each bank's choice of alternative policies, nevertheless permits a wide latitude for the exercise of individual discretion that provides a meaningful role for competition in banking. This is the consideration that lay behind the Supreme Court's dictum in *U. S. vs. Philadelphia National Bank* that the regulated character of banking "makes the play of competition not less important but more so."

CHANGING VIEWS ON COMPETITION

Interest in banking competition has intensified in recent years. After virtually ignoring the commercial banking industry for many years, the Justice Department brought suit in the late 1950s in a number of cases involving clearinghouse agreements to set uniform service charges. In more recent years, despite a long and widely held belief to the contrary, the courts have ruled that the antitrust laws apply to acquisitions and mergers in banking as well as in other areas.

It may appear rather anomalous that the Federal Government, having established a superstructure of regulation designed at least in part for the purpose of limiting competition in banking, now undertakes to restrict banks' actions which might tend to reduce competition. The issue is further confused by the fact that the Office of the Comptroller of the Currency and the Department of Justice —two agencies of the Federal Government—have been on occasion cast in the roles of opposing parties in recent bank merger cases. It would be inaccurate to portray these events as reflecting merely a jurisdictional dispute between Federal agencies. Instead there appears to be a growing conviction on the part of public officials and bankers alike that a reevaluation and revision of policy may now be in order—though there is little agreement on specific issues.

Until recently students of banking were generally agreed that competition was not only less essential in banking than in most other industries but in many circumstances inherently destructive. However, new evidence and reexamination of old arguments now suggest that competition in banking may not have been the culprit it has been painted to be in bringing about the financial crises of earlier days. The banking troubles of the era before 1863 are now considered to have been the result of the absence of a uniform national currency as well as excessive competition and the lack of detailed controls over banking. This deficiency was remedied in part by the passage of the National Banking Act of 1863, which substituted national bank notes for the bewildering variety of state bank issues then in circulation.

Similarly, the periodic epidemics of bank failures of the late nineteenth and early twentieth centuries, as well as the striking and unprecedented attrition of banks in the decade following World War I, appear to have had their roots more in cyclical factors and secular changes in transportation and agriculture than in any inherent tendency toward destructive competition in banking. Even the banking debacle of the early 1930s is no longer uncritically viewed as the inevitable result of imprudent banking practices attributable largely to excessive competition for deposits. On the contrary, all of these instances of injury to the banking system—and in most cases, to the economy as well—are now generally agreed to have had their major cause in developments much broader than local competition and often far removed from the sphere of individual bank management.

Moreover, today there exist numerous safeguards against any widespread and self-reinforcing epidemic of bank failures. To the extent that violent cyclical fluctuations in aggregate economic activity may have been responsible for the waves of bank failures in the past, the announced readiness of the Federal Government and the Federal Reserve System to take whatever fiscal and monetary measures are required to maintain a high and growing level of income and employment serves as protection against similar future disturbances. To the extent that bank failures were the result of "runs" on banks occasioned by general fears on the part of the public of the inability by banks to redeem their deposits for currency, Federal Deposit Insurance and the readiness of the Federal Reserve to act as the lender of last resort appear to afford a sufficient remedy. These safeguards suggest that competition can play a more important role in banking than it has until recently without leading to undesirable consequences.

Regulation frequently has been unsuccessful in suppressing competition even where it has undertaken to do so. For example, the attempt to reduce interbank competition by erecting strict legal barriers to entry has been at least a major contributing cause to the rapid and continuing growth of such nonbank financial intermediaries as savings and loan associations, a growth that has brought with it increased interindustry competition.

The attempt to relieve effects of unduly severe competition among banks by prohibiting then from paying interest on demand deposits has been only partially successful at best. Far from eliminating competition, the prohibition simply caused banks to substitute less overt but nonetheless vigorous nonprice rivalry for the rate competition that previously existed. In effect, "interest" on demand deposits continues to be paid through an earnings credit offset to deposit service charges and numerous "free" services, all dependent largely on the size of the average balance and the number of transactions associated with each account. On the other hand, the depositor has been deprived of the option of being paid in cash.

CHANGES IN NUMBER OF BANKS

While much of the recent interest in competition in banking has been focused on the system of bank regulation as presently constituted, expressions of concern have also been voiced concerning the merging and branching activities of the banks themselves. Despite

**Increased Number of Branches More Than Offsets Decline in
Number of Banks**

State classification*	Change, 1946–1964					
	Banks		Branches		Banking offices	
	Num-ber	Per-cent	Num-ber	Per-cent	Num-ber	Per-cent
Branch banking						
Statewide	−323	−23	3,922	24	3,599	118
Limited	−979	−15	6,097	290	5,118	60
Unit banking	1,018	17	338†	148†	1,356	21
Total	−284	− 2	10,357	260	10,073	56

* Includes 50 states and District of Columbia.
† Includes offices that do not offer a full line of banking services. In addition, a few full service branches that were established before legal prohibitions of branching or after removal of such prohibitions are included.
SOURCE: U. S., Comptroller of the Currency, *Annual Report 1964* (Washington, D.C., 1965).

virtually uninterrupted prosperity and population growth in the postwar period, the number of commercial banks in the United States has been declining until very recently.

After a small immediate postwar rise from 14,011 in 1945 to 14,181 in 1947, the number declined steadily, reaching a low of 13,427 at the end of 1962. Since then the number of banks has increased slightly to 13,784 in November 1966. The net decrease of 227 banks since World War II—an average of about 10 a year —is small compared to the rate that prevailed throughout the generally prosperous 1920s when the average net annual attrition exceeded 700. However, in contrast to the earlier period when a significant part of the attrition resulted from bank failures and voluntary liquidations, virtually all the recent decline has been the result of mergers and acquisitions that have absorbed formerly independent banks.

NUMBERS AND COMPETITION

To many observers this decrease in the number of banks provides evidence that the availability of alternative sources of supply of banking services, and hence the vigor of competition, is undergoing a decline. This conclusion is based on the theory that the chances of collusion are less and the likelihood of independent rivalry greater when sellers are many than when they are few.

Number of Commercial Banks Rises in Recent Years Following Many Years of Decline

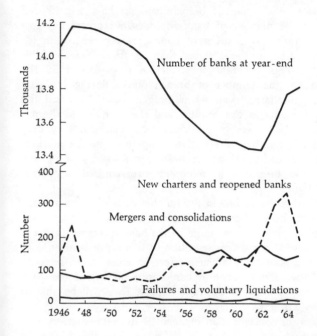

However, in evaluating the effect of the decline in the number of banks, it must be noted that all of the more than 13,000 banks in the United States do not compete in a single, nationwide market. A relatively few giant banks do operate in what is loosely referred to as the "national banking market"—the market for the loans and deposits of the largest corporations that have banking connections throughout the country.

But it is a widely acknowledged fact that, for most bank customers, the national market is segmented by the real and psychic cost of distance into relatively narrow regional and local submarkets. For this less mobile majority of customers, the most relevant consideration is the number of independent banks within the confined area in which their reputations are known and in which they find it practicable to seek accommodation. This number of banks, however, is not deducible from a knowledge of how many banks there are in some broader area, such as the state. Given the ability of banks to have branch offices in approximately two-thirds of the states, it is possible for the average number of individual banks competing in each local market to increase even though the number of banks in these states or in the nation overall is declining.

Although states which permit branch banking have experienced wide declines in the number of banks, it does not necessarily follow that significantly fewer different banks are represented in individual communities in these states than in those that prohibit branch banking. This apparent contradiction is explained by the great expansion in the number of branch offices during the past several decades. Similarly, even when mergers have decreased the total number of banks in the country and the number of alternatives available to customers in particular local markets, they may have added to the number of effective competitors in the markets serving large- and medium-sized corporate customers by permitting the merging banks to attain the minimum size required to operate in these markets.

Concomitant with the decline in the number of banks, the average size of bank and the percentage of banking resources concentrated in the hands of a relatively few large banks have increased in many broad areas of the country. Concentration in this sense is often considered to have a potentially adverse effect on competition because, however large the total number of banks in a market, if one or a few of them control most of the total supply, they will be able to influence prices strongly.

Available data on concentration of deposits in major metropolitan areas indicate that concentration levels were generally higher in the early 1960s than a decade earlier. On the other hand, they appear to have been lower than in the prewar year of 1939. Inasmuch as concentration and changes in concentration have significance for competition only in relation to specific product markets and particular groups of customers, it is necessary to take account of important interarea differences. For the period 1960–64 increases in concentration have been typical in metropolitan areas in states where statewide branching is prevalent (see table on page 108). In metropolitan areas where restricted branch banking is the rule, increases and decreases were about equally frequent. Decreases predominated in these areas where unit banking was the most common form of bank organization.

Some would interpret these figures as demonstrating that unit banking is more conducive to competition than branch banking. However, such a conclusion follows only if certain conditions are satisfied. Among these is the rather crucial assumption that metropolitan areas serve equally well as approximations to local banking markets under both branch and unit banking. To the extent that locational convenience serves to restrict the practicable range of alternatives of some customers to an area smaller than the whole metropolitan area, concentration in unit banking areas is understated by the measure used here. A more important qualification is that competition has not been shown to depend in any simple and reliable way on the degree of concentration in bank markets.[1]

PUBLIC POLICY TOWARD BANK MERGERS

In deciding whether to approve or disapprove a particular application to merge, the appropriate regulatory agency must arrive at a judgment concerning the probable effect of the merger on the public interest. The fundamental questions that must be answered include the justification of the consolidation in terms of economies of scale or the ability of a larger bank to render better, cheaper and more complete banking services and its effect, via changes in the number and size distribution of banks, on the competitive relations among the remaining firms. It is over answers to these questions that much of the interagency conflict has arisen.

For example, advantages in the form of lower operating costs have often been advanced as a major factor in bank mergers. Yet, available empirical studies tend to indicate that such economies may be quite modest—at least when the differences in output mix between large and small banks are taken into consideration, as they must be.

A second argument in support of mergers emphasizes the ability of a bank with greater resources to hire better management and to utilize more fully the services of a large number of specialists. This argument appears to have fairly general validity as indicated by both casual observation and a number of recent studies. Large banks generally do offer a broader variety of services than is obtainable at small banks in the same locality. However, whether this constitutes a net advantage is not immediately obvious. It must be determined whether a decrease in the number of alternative sources of banking services is adequately compensated by the availability of a number of special, but infrequently utilized, services that only large banks can supply.

BRANCH BANKING

Any discussion of the relative merits of large and small banks must include consideration of the arguments in support of and opposition to branch banking. One of the major advantages claimed for branch-

---

[1] These and other measures of the degree of competition are discussed in *Business Conditions*, December 1965, pp. 11–16.

**Metropolitan Areas in Statewide Branch Banking States Show
Greatest Increases in Concentration**

SMSAs including reserve cities*	Percent of total desposits held by three largest banks		
	1960	1962	1964
Branch banking			
Statewide			
Baltimore	59	73	72
Los Angeles	78	75	71
Portland, Ore.	87	90	89
San Francisco	60	79	77
Seattle	68	72	72
Limited			
Atlanta	72	75	74
Birmingham	93	93	97
Boston	79	83	83
Buffalo	77	93	95
Cincinnati	82	84	84
Cleveland	78	77	76
Columbus	88	87	93
Detroit	78	76	74
Indianapolis	97	96	96
Louisville	68	76	76
Memphis	93	93	93
Nashville	89	92	93
New Orleans	85	80	79
New York	49	53	54
Philadelphia	64	62	64
Pittsburgh	82	83	81
Richmond	80	78	73
Toledo	90	88	88
Washington, D. C.	74	75	73
Unit banking			
Chicago	48	53	52
Dallas	80	79	76
Denver	69	68	68
Fort Worth	77	76	73
Houston	60	59	64
Jacksonville	79	75	72
Kansas City, Mo.	63	61	58
Miami	41	43	40
Milwaukee	68	67	66
Minneapolis	60	62	60
Oklahoma City	70	72	71
Omaha	82	80	79
St. Louis	52	50	48
San Antonio	67	64	62
Tulsa	81	79	76

* Metropolitan areas of Reserve Cities having populations in excess of 400,000 as of April 1, 1960.   SOURCE: Federal Deposit Insurance Corporation.

ing is that it is often the quickest way a bank can grow to large size. Also, since the full resources and facilities of the bank can be made available to the customers of each branch, branch banking provides a means of bringing a fuller range of banking services and larger lending capacity to individual communities.

The advantages and disadvantages of branch banking constitute one of the oldest and most vitriolic controversies in American banking. The arguments involve questions both political and economic in character. Without evaluating the merits of the arguments, it may be noted that the unit-branch issue is an inseparable part of the larger public debate over competition in banking reviewed above.

The precise relationship between the branch banking and banking competition is a matter of dispute. A number of economists, bankers and public officials maintain that branching is an essentially procompetitive form of banking that facilitates the penetration of additional banking markets and brings to bear the force of potential competition on even the smallest and most isolated banking markets. On the other hand, many students of banking hold that branching is a monopolistic device whose prime purpose is the attenuation of competition. Which characterization is the more accurate may depend as much on what one understands by competition as on the objectively determinable facts of the case.

It is hardly open to serious doubt, for example, that some portion of the criticism of branch banking is of a protectionist nature, more concerned with preserving locally owned unit banks than with fostering vigorous interbank rivalry. Independent bankers frequently feel themselves threatened by the presence of a nearby office of a large branch bank.

On the other hand, it is not always easy to distinguish in practice between the protection of competitors and the preservation of competition. One reason is related to the difference between the incentives required to induce merger and those required to induce *de novo* establishment of a new bank or branch. It appears easier for two existing banks to come to terms on a merger agreement which has as one of its "fringe benefits" the elimination of competition than it is for a potential entrant into the banking field to obtain financing and run the regulatory gauntlet required to obtain a charter for a new bank. As was indicated above, it is in these areas where the possibility of operating an acquired bank as a branch maximizes the incentive to merge that the disappearance of banks and the concentration of banking have proceeded most rapidly. This pronounced asymmetry between merger and entry is the primary reason why branching via merger, which *ipso facto* involves the elimination of an independent source of supply, may have adverse and irreversible effects on competition. It is also one of the considerations that prompted Congress in 1950 to strengthen the Clayton Act and to pass the Bank Merger Acts of 1960 and 1966.

It might still be maintained, on the other hand, that *de novo* branching could have nothing but beneficial effects on competition. Its immediate effect is always to introduce a new competitive force into a banking market or submarket. When, for example, a branch bank sees a potentially profitable location for a banking office and opens a branch there—perhaps years in advance of the time when it would have been profitable to organize a new unit bank—it benefits the community to have banking facilities where none existed before or would otherwise have existed for a considerable period of time. Whether this is a net gain in the long term depends on the potential benefit to the local populace of having an independent source of supply of banking services when it would become feasible to open a new unit bank.

Where banks find it easy to establish branches within a local banking market they may—and often do—anticipate profitable locations and saturate entire areas with branches, thereby largely foreclosing future entry by competitors. In this they may be inadvertently aided and abetted by the regulatory agencies, which are frequently reluctant to grant a new charter that could conceivably result in "overbanking." Overbanking typically implies a situation in which insufficient banking business is considered to exist to support all of the banking institutions in the area and which must eventually result in the forced exit of one or more of them.

At a theoretical level a good case can be made for removing all geographic restrictions on branching, while simultaneously discouraging concentration in particular local banking markets. However, this would require a uniform national policy with respect to branching and the chartering of new banks, a development not now on the horizon. Legislation regarding branching traditionally has been left to the states. Nevertheless, the competitive environment created by state branching restrictions is clearly one of the many factors that must be taken into account in Federal Agency decisions governing mergers.

CONCLUSION

There exists a great deal of uncertainty at the present time as to what public policy would promote optimum competition in banking. Ideally, policy should undertake to attain a degree of interbank rivalry that assures that consumers will be provided bank services of high quality at minimum cost without sacrificing the private and public benefits of large-scale production or the regulatory aim of ensuring the liquidity and solvency of the banking system. The extent to which these goals can be realized simultaneously and even the direction in which policy should move to approach them as closely as possible is still imperfectly understood. However, a start toward collecting and interpreting the data that would permit a more objective basis for deciding these issues has been made. . . .

HOWARD D. CROSSE

BANKING STRUCTURE AND COMPETITION

9

. . . As a bank supervisor I come before you in the guise of a mystic: one to whom the Truth has been revealed—but who cannot prove it with statistics. I hope, in time, you will be able to demonstrate its validity.

I am reminded of an occasion many years ago when I rode from the Board building in Washington with a group of Reserve Bank economists who had apparently been discussing all day why excess reserves accumulate in country banks. They still could not understand this uneconomic behavior. The profit-minded economic man will seek to invest excess reserves! I listened for a while and finally asked, "Have any of you ever examined small country banks?" They hadn't, obviously, and I said, "Well, if you had you would understand perfectly why not only excess reserves, but back numbers of banking periodicals, and even instructions from the super-

Reprinted by permission of the American Finance Association and the author from Howard D. Crosse, "Banking Structure and Competition," *Journal of Finance*, Proceedings of the American Finance Association, Vol. XX (May 1965), pp. 349–357.

visor, pile up in country banks. You should see the desks of country bankers!"

One of our large branch banks recently acquired a small country bank through merger. They found the vault so cluttered with back numbers of the *Herald Tribune* and empty cigar boxes (sometimes useful repositories of cash) that there was no room for needed additional safe deposit boxes. How can you measure economies of scale in such circumstances?

I could regale you with many such stories. They underlie the mystic truths of experience I shall try to propound. But first let us establish some sort of logical framework for the many cross-currents that complicate the problems of banking structure and competition.

As a matter of public policy we want the best banking structure we can have. The big question is "The best for whom?" If it were only the bank stockholder, we could leave banking structure to market forces and the Department of Justice. But we are talking about money in which everybody has a vital interest. At some risk of oversimplification we can examine separately the interests of the depositor, the borrower, the stockholder and what I call for lack of a better term, the general public, my own particular boss.

The depositor is interested in the safety of his particular deposit; he is interested in compensation for the use of his money either in the form of interest or services. He is interested in the efficiency of his bank as reflected in the accuracy of the posting of entries to his account. And finally he is interested in an intangible quality which I shall call "recognition." He resents having a bank teller ask him whether he has an account in the bank. He wants to be known to *his* bank. Hodgman has shown that banks value "relationship."[1] So do customers.

The borrower from a bank (who of course may also be a depositor) wants availability of credit first, understanding of his business or credit needs second, and a competitive rate, somewhere down the line. He is less interested in the absolute rate than in knowing that his bank is not charging him any more than another bank would.

The stockholder, or management as his proxy, wants maximum profitability. If he is wise he is looking to maximize profits over time. He will recognize that the long-range success of the bank is intimately interwoven with the growth and prosperity of the com-

---

[1] Donald R. Hodgman, *Commercial Bank Loan and Investment Policies* (Champaign, Ill.: Bureau of Economic and Business Research, University of Illinois, 1963).

munity it serves; that maximum success is not possible, in short, without satisfying both depositors and borrowing customers.

The public interest is not much different, but is broader in scope. It is concerned less with individual banks than with the banking system. Deposit insurance and bank examination for example, are evidence of public concern with deposit safety.

The public concern is with an efficient payments system rather than the correct posting of an individual's pay check. The public can ignore or shore up an individual bank failure but regulates banks closely to prevent widespread failures. And the public is vitally concerned with competition: it wants enough to insure generally good service at reasonable prices to the broad aggregate of individual borrowers and depositors—but not so much as to threaten bank failures.

I am sure that we all recognize that this catalogue of objectives contains numerous contradictions. Nationwide branch banking, as in Canada, has proved to be more failure-resistant than our widely diffused system. But is it sufficiently competitive to assure adequate credit at reasonable prices? There is clearly much that we need to know before we can definitely answer such questions. That which we need to know is both the subject of your research and of our supervisory concern. It is important, as a minimum, that we do not start such research with a bundle of misconceptions or biases that can only confuse our thinking or lead us down blind alleys.

There can be little question but there are great pressures in the economy for a more concentrated banking structure. Without regulatory controls there would be a great many more mergers and a great many more new branches established. This trend represents the judgment of bank management representing the long-range interests of the stockholder. These are the views of management both in the acquiring banks and those that are acquired. It takes two to tango! It is clear that bankers believe sincerely that there are efficiencies of scale, if not economies. And I think they are right.

The revealed truth, to which I testify, is that these pressures are directly related to economic growth and to the changing needs for banking services which economic growth brings about. No two situations are ever exactly alike, but let us take as one typical example a bank in a suburban community such as the one in which I myself live. Twenty years ago the community's simple banking needs were more or less well-served by a small local bank operated in a very unimaginative fashion. Loans from this bank were hard to obtain but there was little demand for credit in the community. The bank was eminently safe. It was convenient, and everyone in the community was personally known to the tellers and officers. Most of the customers had lived in the community for years; had in fact grown up there, and their parents and often their grandparents had been equally well-known. This is a clear advantage if your reputation in the community is a good one.

Then came economic growth. During the past twenty years the population of the community more than doubled. Hundreds of new homes were built; most of them financed outside of the community. The town is now to a much greater extent the home of transient executives. New businesses have come into being to service the needs of the increased population. New credit demands came along with them. Management of the local bank was unable to accommodate itself to these changing condition. It didn't want to do business with strangers. It knew nothing about consumer credit. It couldn't understand the financial statements of the new businesses. It had no expertise in lending except against stock market collateral. It sat by frustrated and helpless watching a great deal of local business go to banks in neighboring towns.

At the same time the larger banks in the area eyed this growing community as a lucrative potential source of additional profitable business. With their well-developed consumer credit and mortgage departments, with their eager young commercial lending officers learning all about term loans and accounts receivable financing, they viewed themselves, and I think correctly, as much better able to serve the community's credit needs and able too, because of higher loan/deposit ratios to pay higher rates for savings deposits. To make a well-known story short, ten years ago the small banker sold out to the highest bidder—the largest bank in the county. He could not cope with the problems of growth and change.

The story is not much different in the rural areas where larger farms require larger credits and more lending expertise than small local banks are able to supply. And let me stress the expertise, for it is of even greater importance than lending limits. Any small bank can lend a customer whom it has known for years $1,000 to buy a new car. But this is a far cry from financing the retail paper of a local Ford dealer in a rapidly growing community, where half the borrowers are strangers, and especially if floor planning of inventory is also involved. Financing consumer credit in volume, if it is to be done safely, requires specialized skills and experience which small banks simply do not have. Nor do they have volume enough to justify developing these skills even if they could.

So, where permitted by law, we have more mergers, more branches, and less banking units. What are the results of this trend for the various public interests we have enumerated? George Benston has indicated some increase in the cost of doing business, and bankers generally recognize that theirs is becoming more and more a high volume and low profit margin business. Ted Flechsig has seen no important effect on lending rates as the result of concentration, and I agree with his findings. Don Jacobs has found a tendency for branch banks to concentrate on consumer lending, but I think that this is more a function of the markets branches serve than a question of structure. I cannot agree with his suspicion that large banks use the convenience of branches as a substitute for rate. In the Second Federal Reserve District, at least, the larger branch banks generally pay the highest rates on time and savings deposits. We must all agree, I think, that large branch banks, serving diversified areas, are safer and, because of their size and strength, can afford to take greater risks in individual credit situations. They can, and do make credit available where small unit banks do not.

More specifically, a number of things happen when a relatively small bank is merged into a large bank; happenings which, in fact, tend to confuse the statistics which have served as a basis for such studies as George Benston's and many others. The large bank immediately assumes what I have called the "prospective costs" which lead to bank mergers.[2] The first thing is a complete refurbishing of building and equipment at considerable expense. Then the employees of the small bank are brought into the salary program and pension plan of the larger bank which appreciably raises salary costs. Under most merger agreements, former management is retained, at least for a while, but the need for succession is met by bringing in an additional officer or two at the large bank's salary scale. The acquiring bank also usually pays the competitive rate on time and savings deposits which in many cases is more than the absorbed bank was paying. Thus the new branch starts off immediately with higher costs than the former unit bank. But it is *not* the same bank, either in appearance or in capacity for rendering banking services.

To recoup what it can of these additional costs, the large bank centralizes a number of functions. The investment account and money position are invariably transferred to the head office. The mortgage account and consumer loans are often centralized where they can be more efficiently handled in volume. Bookkeeping, at least for demand deposits, is consolidated. In these procedures I think there are evident economies of scale. They will become more

[2] Howard D. Crosse, *Management Policies for Commercial Banks* (Englewood Cliffs, N.J.: Prentice-Hall, 1962).

objectively measurable when increased participation of larger banks in the functional cost analysis program permits comparison of the processing costs of varying volumes of essentially similar items such as mortgages, consumer loans, et cetera.

The large bank also tends to impose higher (and I think more realistic) service charges on deposit accounts. One product of the functional cost studies used by George Benston was the clear demonstration that small banks generally recover a relatively smaller portion of their processing costs through service charges. The depositors' gain on this score is, in my opinion, at the cost of the better facilities and better management which, as I have pointed out above, the larger bank immediately sets out to supply.

Our experience also bears out the conclusion of several studies[3] that branch banks tend to be more aggressive lenders. In nearly every case the former unit bank increases the outstanding total of its loans, often dramatically. Again this increase is often difficult to measure statistically because of the transfer of mortgage and consumer credit loans to the head office controls. However, in one quite typical case where one of three relatively small banks in a community was acquired through merger, it increased its loans by 170 percent in the following five years, while the loans of the remaining unit banks increased only 63 and 64 percent respectively.

At the same time the larger bank brings not only greater expertness to its customer relations but frequently provides new services (investment advisory services for example) which were not previously available and which do not show up on the branch balance sheet.

In short, comparison of unit banks with branch banks (particularly the 8,000 or so unit banks with total resources of less than $5 million), when such comparisons do not take into account the upgrading of product, have the effect of comparing a Model A Ford with a Galaxie without reference to horsepower or chrome trim.

Not everything, of course, is pure gain. What may be lost is some measure of that personal relationship which I have called "recognition," a psychic benefit of considerable importance to many bank customers as well as some bank regulators and members of Congress. The large bank, despite its stepped-up public relations "program," tends to be more impersonal, although many large banks, recognizing this danger, have taken specific steps to alleviate it. I

[3] Irving Schweiger and John S. McGee, "Chicago Banking," *The Journal of Business* of the University of Chicago, July 1961.

read recently of a large branch organization which had created specialized departments for both "senior citizens" and young executives. The Franklin National Bank is planning an exclusive New York office which will provide highly personalized services in three languages to those who can afford it. Furthermore, I have never been able to determine to what extent the tendency to impersonalization is a result of branch banking or the natural concomitant of the suburbanization and economic growth which brought about the changes in banking structure. I'll leave that one to the sociologists.

One must admit too, that the results of these structural changes are themselves not uniform. The most important factor in the way an individual bank performs, whether it is a small bank or a large branch organization, is, and always will be, its management. Differences between individual banks of similar structure are often far greater than the differences between small banks and large, or branches and unit banks in general.

There are, for example, two large branch banks in the Second District with similar deposit totals and almost exactly the same number of branches. One bank formerly employed over 600 more people than the other. Despite a somewhat lower salary scale, its operations were clearly more costly and less efficient, with all the implications that that can have for staff morale and quality of services rendered. New management in this less efficient bank, addressing itself specifically to this problem, was able to reduce its staff by 125 people in less than a year. At which point in time is its performance typical of "large branch banks" of a certain size?

On the other hand, one of the most profitable banks by far in the Second Reserve District is a $16 million unit bank which last year had net current earnings of 3.1 percent of assets (three times the average) and salary expenses of 11 percent of gross income (half the average). These are the almost unbelievable results of unusually competent management regardless of size or structure. Somehow, as a supervisor, I have always been more interested in what well-managed banks *can* do than in what average banks actually accomplish.

Management also makes the difference with respect to the way small banks meet the challenge of a developing economy. The story of frustration and merger I related earlier may be typical but is far from inevitable. I am thinking of a bank in rapidly expanding Suffolk County, New York, which in 1955 (less than 10 years ago) had total resources of less than $3 million. Today, without benefit of any merger, it operates six branches, all established *de novo*, and has resources of $41 million. In this case, dynamic and effective management met the challenge of changing times.

Our supervisory knowledge of just how much difference the quality of management can make tends to make us suspect of generalizations based on statistics which do not take the quality of management into account. It is my deep conviction that, for all the various groups that are looking to our banking system for both economic and psychic benefits, management is a far more important factor than either size or structure. The real function of competition in banking, it seems to me, is to exert pressure for improved management. We see this pressure frequently being exerted by well-managed branches of large banks on the small bank which does not have the management capacity to adjust to economic changes. We have also seen it exerted by the small gadfly challenging the established giants with new ideas or highly developed specialties. To keep this challenge ever fresh, I am sure you will agree, we must preserve the "right of entry."

Academicians tend to think of entry almost exclusively in terms of new banks. They have often accused the supervisor of barring the way for many prospective entrants.[4] Donald Jacobs' presentation seemed to talk of entry restrictions as applying only to new banks. If we define entry, however, as the creation of a new competitive force in a local banking market, we must concede that the establishment of a branch, either *de novo* or by merger does intensify competition. In the community I mentioned earlier, for example, where one of three small local banks was acquired by a country-wide branch organization, the greater management ability of the larger and more aggressive bank immediately put pressures on the other local banks to improve their service to the community. One brought in new management—the other sought, itself, to merge with a larger bank. Entry by branching, in fact, is much more effective than entry through the formation of another bank because it brings into the community immediately the well-developed management techniques and capabilities of an established organization.

The real bars to "entry" are the bars to branching, including those laws in states which permit branching but prohibit the establishment of *de novo* branches in communities already served by other banks; the so-called "home office protection" laws. In New Jersey it is so bad that, except in a town served by its head office, a bank may not establish a branch in any municipality already served by an-

[4] Cf. David A. Alhadeff, "A Reconsideration of Restrictions on Bank Entry," *Quarterly Journal of Economics*, 76 (May 1962), pp. 246–263.

other branch, even one of its own! Laws which limit branching create an obvious bias in favor of new banks as the only available means of entry.

As a bank supervisor I am somewhat sensitive on the subject of new banks. I have never seen a charter denied where a proposed bank, by any stretch of the imagination, could have become a viable competitive force. I have seen many granted to banks which have never become viable. Needs and convenience, the criteria which Alhadeff found to be too strictly applied, are used by the chartering authorities as being broadly synonymous with "chances for success." The supervisory statement denying a charter may read in terms of needs and convenience, but more often than not, what will have been found lacking is management. No bank supervisor who wants to avoid suits for defamation of character can afford to announce publicly that he is denying a charter because he questions the business ethics of the organizers, or even express his doubts as to their credit-worthiness. He is going to find, publicly, a lack of need!

Alhadeff assumed that bank organizers know what they are doing. As one who has met with numerous would-be organizers over the years, I can testify that this just is not so. Most often they have little or no concept of the problems of running a bank successfully. I remember one attorney who discussed with me the organization of a bank to serve the peculiar credit needs of small diamond merchants. He was going to put the bank on the second floor of an obscure building in the knowledge that these borrowers would have no trouble finding it. I asked, "What about the depositors? Where are you going to get the money to lend?" He hadn't thought of that!

While this is an extreme example, let me assure you that few potentially viable banks have been denied charters. The rock on which most unsuccessful applicants founder is lack of responsible management (including directors). Many that were granted charters have had the same problem, unfortunately, and have had to be absorbed to bail them out of the difficulties poor management got them into.

On the other hand, when proposed new banks are sponsored by financially responsible and public-spirited organizers who engage competent operating management, the application is warmly welcomed by the supervisor.

To summarize, then, it has been my observation that banking structure and competition need to be studied more closely in terms of effective markets. For all but the larger corporations which have wide choices of alternatives, these are local markets. In all markets, it seems to me, the most dynamic competitive force is that of imaginative and effective (albeit prudent) management. Fortunately that kind of management is not the exclusive prerogative of any particular form of banking organization. Well-managed small banks are often more effective competitors in local markets than the branches of the largest banks.

While the right of entry of well-managed new banks should be zealously preserved, relaxation of branching restrictions will greatly intensify competition in many local markets, affording the user of bank services, both depositor and borrower, with a wider choice of expert service. I suspect that the banking public will do an increasing amount of its "shopping" in the "department stores" of banking as Don Jacobs calls them, but that there will always be a place for the well-run specialty shop and the delicatessen.

FEDERAL RESERVE BANK OF PHILADELPHIA

WHAT PRICE LIQUIDITY?

10

Did you ever sit down and figure the return on $1,000,000 at 6 per cent interest for one year? It comes to $60,000, and $60,000 pays a lot of wages, salaries, electric bills, and other expenses that bankers and other businessmen incur in the process of earning a profit.

Now suppose you just happen to have $1,000,000 lying around in a bank vault or elsewhere which you may not need in the form of ready cash or its equivalent. If you lend it out or invest it, you get the $60,000. If you don't, you don't. Interested? More and more bankers have been interested in the past decade for they have

Reprinted from "What Price Liquidity?" *Business Review* (September 1964), pp. 3–7, Federal Reserve Bank of Philadelphia.

steadily decreased the volume of cash assets they hold relative to the total assets they manage.[1]

EARNINGS VERSUS LIQUIDITY: THE BANKER'S AGE-OLD DILEMMA

In many respects a bank is much like any other business. It hires workers such as the tellers who stand at the front desk and accept deposits and pay out currency. It must buy or rent its business quarters and pay for heating, cooling, and lighting. It sells a "product" in the form of checking accounts, loans, and the like. Also, like any other business, a bank wants to maximize its revenues so it can meet its expenses and still turn a profit.

Unlike other businesses, however, a bank's primary stock in trade is the deposits of its customers which it uses to lend and invest. And a large proportion of these deposits, unlike the accounts payable of most businesses, must be paid out on demand.

The banker, for example, must stand ready on a moment's notice to pay out cash to his depositors and others. If he can't, he's in trouble. In the jargon of the trade, the banker must be "liquid." And here we have a seeming paradox. The most liquid asset—cash —provides no earnings. Assets which do provide earnings, on the other hand (loans and investments), are less liquid; they are more difficult to turn into ready cash.

How does the banker cope with this two-sided problem, with simultaneous need to be (a) liquid enough to meet cash demand and (b) invested and loaned enough to derive a good return? Answer: he keeps sufficient cash assets and near-cash assets to meet the cash demand he may reasonably expect, and then he invests and lends the rest. He thereby obtains both liquidity and earnings.

Yet in recent years, as shown in Chart 1, banks have reduced the proportion of their total assets held in the form of cash, this at the same time that holdings of short-term Governments have been falling and loan-deposit ratios have been rising.

In this article we take a look at the reasons why commercial bankers have decided they can do with less cash. We also examine some of the wider implications of a declining cash-asset ratio.

[1] In this article, the term "cash assets" is used to mean cash in vault, deposits with correspondents, required and excess reserves held with Federal Reserve Banks and cash items (checks and the like) in process of collection.

The term "managed cash assets" includes vault cash, deposits with correspondents, and excess reserves held with the Fed.

CHART 1   Cash Assets as a Percent of Total Assets, All Member Banks, United States

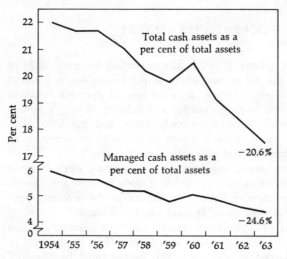

SOURCES: Board of Governors, Member Bank Call Reports. Data are averages of 4 call dates.

TO MARKET, TO MARKET

One reason why bankers have decided they can do with less in cash is simply that they can "buy" or borrow funds if they run short, often with little loss or delay. With such funds available, bankers have found that they need not keep cash on hand at all times in amounts large enough to meet peak cash drains.

The traditional methods of obtaining funds to meet immediate cash needs include the sale of near-cash assets such as Treasury bills, borrowing from other banks, and borrowing from the Federal Reserve Banks (a privilege which member banks may exercise in accordance with regulations specified by Federal Reserve authorities).

Another alternative which has become increasingly important in recent years (both in terms of the volume of funds changing hands and in numbers and sizes of participating banks) is the so-called "federal funds market." Through the federal funds market, banks with excess funds may lend to deficit banks who are temporarily deficient. The loan is usually of short duration, say, overnight or for one or two days. A typical transaction might go something like this: Bank A finds that a larger dollar volume of checks have been drawn against it than have been deposited with it, with the result that Bank A experiences a net drain of funds. Bank A contacts a federal funds dealer who puts him in touch with Bank B (Bank B having experienced a net inflow of funds in excess of its immediate needs). Bank A borrows the funds for one or two days then returns them with interest to Bank B.

The federal funds market has made possible the mobilization of excess funds among an ever-widening circle of both large and small banks. In the Third Federal Reserve District, for example, the large Philadelphia reserve city banks stand ready to buy or sell federal funds for the account of their smaller correspondents. They will buy or sell regardless of their own deficit or surplus position, using any excess funds, for example, to cover their own deficiency (if they happen to have a deficiency) or selling these funds to others if they should have a reserve surplus. The majority of transactions are consummated by direct debit or credit to the correspondent account at the prevailing federal funds rate. Typically, the reserve city banks will sell funds to correspondents in amounts of $100,000 or over and will purchase funds in amounts of $200,000 to $250,000 and over. A market for federal funds in such relatively small amounts opens the federal funds mechanism to a very wide range of smaller banks and thus a growing number of institutions feel they may safely decrease the volume of cash they hold.

But this is only one side of the earnings-liquidity coin. Institutional developments such as the federal funds market provide the *opportunity* to reduce cash holdings, but the opportunity might be passed over and indeed a federal funds market might never have developed if there were not some *inducement* to economize on cash holdings. The inducement has come from the earnings side of the coin.

THE PULL OF INTEREST RATES

Interest rates increased significantly in the 1950's from the low levels associated with wartime financing. This rise in interest rates, in effect, has made it more costly for banks to hold cash assets.

Whereas it cost banks only about $\frac{3}{8}$ of 1 per cent to hold cash instead of Treasury bills during the war (by holding cash, banks would give up the $\frac{3}{8}$ of 1 per cent they could otherwise have made by investing in Treasury bills), it now costs them around $3\frac{1}{2}$ per cent to hold cash instead of bills, and even more to hold cash instead of loans. Since banks are in business to make a profit, one

CHART 2   Changes in Cash Asset Holdings Appear to be Related to Changes in Interest Rates, in the Nation

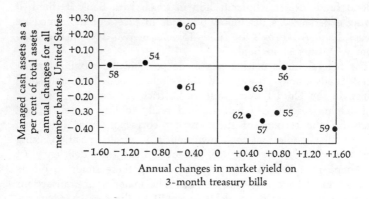

SOURCE: Board of Governors, Member Bank Call Reports.

might expect bankers to reduce their cash-asset ratios as interest rates rise (providing, of course, that bankers determine such action to be prudent and in keeping with liquidity needs).

In fact, changes in interest rates do appear to have influenced changes in cash-asset ratios. Charts 2 and 3 show that, more often than not in the 10-year period 1954–1963, bankers economized on

CHART 3   . . . and in the Third Federal Reserve District

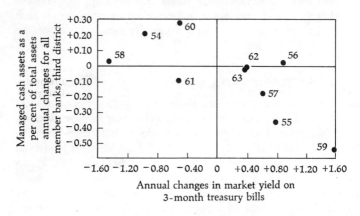

SOURCE: Federal Reserve Bank of Philadelphia, Member Bank Call Reports.

the cash assets which they can control or "manage" (vault cash, deposits with correspondents, and excess reserves held with the Fed)[2] in years when interest rates were rising and raised these same cash-asset ratios more often than not in years when interest rates fell.[3] Thus the pull of earnings reflected in the shifting attractiveness of interest rates does appear to provide an inducement for bankers to adjust their cash assets.

But earnings are a function both of revenues and of costs. We have seen that bankers apparently are influenced by the pull of revenues (interest rates) in managing their cash position; could they also be pushed by rising costs?

THE PUSH OF COSTS

Costs in banking, as for many industries, have risen significantly in the past decade. Wages, salaries, occupancy expenses have increased, and banks also have experienced rising costs in the form of higher interest rates which they must pay to compete effectively for time and savings deposits.

As can be seen in Charts 4 and 5, banks costs have risen both in terms of revenues and assets. For each dollar of revenues earned in 1954, member banks incurred operating expenses of about 62 cents. In 1963, operating expenses took about 71 cents of each dollar of revenue. Operating expenses per dollar of assets, on the other hand, rose from 1.8 cents in 1954 to over 3.1 cents in 1963. It would not be at all surprising if the reduction in cash-asset ratios were partially related to rising bank costs.

[2] The total of these items which can be "managed" or "controlled," (that is, which may more readily be converted from nonearning to earning assets) is actually less than their arithmetic sum at any one point in time. This is because correspondent balances, shifted into loans or investments, would then be subject on the liability side to reserve requirements. Since banks have been allowed to count vault cash as required reserves since 1960, vault cash too, is now less of a "manageable" asset.

[3] Despite the limited number of observations, the correlations observed are sufficiently high that they would seldom occur in sampling universes where no correlation existed.

	Number of Observations	Coefficient of Correlation	Correlation Significant at Level
Member banks, U.S.	10	−.67	.025
Member banks, Third District	10	−.72	.01

CHART 4   Total Expenses as a Percent of Total Revenue (*all member banks, United States and Third District*)

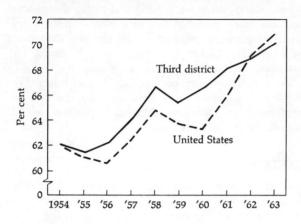

SOURCE: Board of Governors.

RESERVES HELD WITH THE FED: A SHARPER PENCIL

As already mentioned, one important component of a member bank's cash assets is its cash reserves held with Federal Reserve Banks. Today's banker who wishes to hold his cash assets at a minimum consistent with basic liquidity needs is aided in doing so by a basic improvement with respect to these reserves.

A portion of reserves held with the Fed is, of course, required. Country member banks, for example, must hold 12 per cent of their net demand deposits as required reserves and 4 per cent of their time deposits. The banker need not hold any *more* reserves than are required, however, and to the extent that the banker *does* keep a considerable sum in excess of required reserves, he bypasses loans and investments he might otherwise make and thereby earns less.

Question: how has the banker sharpened his pencil with respect to reserve balances?

Answer: he has become better informed of the day-to-day fluctuations in his reserves—whether he is about on the line with his requirements or whether he is building up a large deficit or surplus. If he is better informed, he is better able to minimize his reserve balances and thereby lend and invest more and improve his earnings.

The Philadelphia Federal Reserve Bank, for example, provides work sheets to member banks which aid them in computing, on a

CHART 5 Total Expenses as a Percent of Total Assets (*all member banks, United States and Third District*)

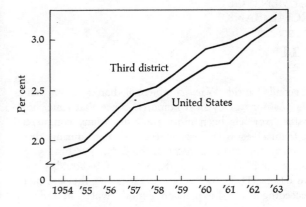

SOURCE: Board of Governors.

day-to-day basis, the reserves that they are *required* to hold at the Fed. Then, each day, the Philadelphia Fed sends each of its members a statement indicating reserves actually *maintained*. The difference between reserves maintained and reserves required gives the daily excess or deficiency. The member banker is thereby able to see each day if he is building up a considerable excess in his reserve position, and being thus informed, is able to take corrective action if he so desires. In effect, the Fed provides the member banker with a sharper pencil to manage his reserve position.

• • •

G. WALTER WOODWORTH

THEORIES OF CYCLICAL LIQUIDITY MANAGEMENT OF COMMERCIAL BANKS

11

Prior to the second World War, commercial banks often maintained excessive positions of cyclical liquidity. Since that time, however, the opposite error has been more common. Many commercial banks, finding themselves with large excess reserves during recessions, have reached for more current income by purchasing too many intermediate- and long-term bonds and too few liquidity (secondary) reserve assets. The penalty was paid during the last phase of all four succeeding cyclical-expansion periods when, in order to meet customer loan demands, investments were sold at substantial capital losses. These losses greatly exceeded the additional income from the longer-term as compared with shorter-term issues; consequently, net profits actually declined in most boom years even though net current earnings (before adjustments for capital gains and losses) recorded substantial increases.

It is the purpose of this paper to trace and analyze the various cyclical liquidity theories. Four different theories can be identified: (1) the commercial loan theory; (2) the shiftability theory; (3) the anticipated income theory; and (4) the liabilities management theory.

I. THE COMMERCIAL LOAN THEORY

The commercial loan theory had its origins in England during the 18th century,[1] and it prevailed in the United States until after the first World War. In fact, its philosophy permeated both the National Bank Act of 1864, as amended, and the Federal Reserve Act of 1913. In 1923, the Federal Reserve Board expounded a variant of

Reprinted from G. Walter Woodworth, "Theories of Cyclical Liquidity Management of Commercial Banks," *The National Banking Review*, Vol. IV (June 1967), pp. 377–395, Washington, D. C.: U. S. Treasury Department.

[1] See Adam Smith, *An Inquiry into the Nature and Causes of the Wealth of Nations* (Everyman's Library Edition), I, pp. 269, 272.

this theory, called a "system of productive credit,"[2] which was widely accepted throughout the 1930's.

According to the commercial loan theory, earning assets of banks should consist principally of short-term, self-liquidating loans to business firms for working capital purposes; that is, loans to finance the movement of goods through the successive stages of production, transportation, storage, distribution, and into consumption. Loans for long-term purposes—to finance plant, equipment, permanent working capital, real estate, consumer durables, and speculation—were not regarded as appropriate for commercial banks. The logical basis for the doctrine was that bank deposits are demand or near-demand liabilities, and should therefore be committed to obligations that are self-liquidating within a short period in the normal course of business operations.

Actually, the commercial loan theory was followed quite loosely in practice. This had to be the case since the theory did not fit the economic and financial environment of the United States. During the 19th century the economy was dominated by agriculture, and capital markets were in the early stages of development. Under these circumstances, intermediate- and long-term loans were essential to finance the purchase of land, houses and improvements, livestock, machinery and equipment, and other durables. In addition, loans were needed to finance the fixed-capital requirements of industry, trade, transportation, and public works. A large part of this credit was provided by the commercial banks, the only existing institutions in a position to do so. Frequently, the long-term nature of the credit was concealed by short-term loan contracts which were often renewed at maturity.

The theory was also deficient in other respects. A rigid restraint on the amount of bank assets would entail a similar stricture on deposits (and notes), and the banking system would be unable to provide a stock of money consistent with sustained full employment, healthy economic growth, and a stable level of prices. There was a failure to recognize the relative stability of the fund of deposits in the banking system and in the individual bank which justifies the holding in bank portfolios of long-term assets of high quality—despite the legal right of depositors to withdraw on short notice.

The liquidity of the individual bank was confused with the liquidity of the banking system. The fact that the liquidity of the banking system, irrespective of the maturity of bank loans, ulti-

[2] See Federal Reserve Board, *Tenth Annual Report*, 1923, pp. 33–34.

mately rests with the central bank was not recognized. Last, the commercial loan theory contemplated bank liquidity needs only in relation to the possibility of deposit withdrawals. No mention was made of liquidity requirements to meet the possibility of loan expansion. This aspect of the problem was not recognized until the 1950's.

II. THE SHIFTABILITY THEORY

Soon after establishment of the Federal Reserve System, some economists challenged the traditional commercial loan theory. They called attention to the wide divergence of actual commercial bank assets from those that qualified as automatically self-liquidating in a short period of time. In 1917, B. M. Anderson analyzed bank assets and concluded, "that the great bulk of banking credit in the United States, even of commercial banks, is not commercial credit. . . . Most of it, . . . represents advances to the permanent financing of corporate industry."[3] In another bank asset study in 1918, H. G. Moulton found that: "The statistics of all commercial banks show that something like 50 percent of all *loans* is devoted to investment uses; and that in the neighborhood of two-thirds of all the credit extended by commercial banks goes for fixed rather than working capital."[4]

The shiftability theory of bank liquidity, which Moulton originated, may be summarized as follows:

1. The greater part of business loans of banks supports permanent working capital and fixed capital needs. Such loans are not usually paid at maturity but are renewed to accommodate the customer. Only seasonal-type loans are paid at maturity, and the cash flow from them is not steady nor dependable, particularly in cyclical financial crises. ". . . the commercial paper of a bank's own customers is among the least reliable of all bank assets as a means of replenishing depleted reserves."[5]

2. Other loans of banks—largely secured by bonds, stocks, equipment, and real estate—represent principally fixed-capital financing, and do not provide an automatic cash inflow from maturities. However, loans secured by marketable stocks and bonds "are more reliable as a secondary reserve than commercial paper loans to customers."[6]

3. Recognizing the lack of liquidity of loans, banks in practice have

[3] B. M. Anderson, Jr., *The Value of Money*, 1926 ed. (New York: Macmillan, 1926), pp. 511–512.

[4] H. G. Moulton, "Commercial Banking and Capital Formation," *The Journal of Political Economy*, July 1918, p. 729.

[5] *Ibid.*, p. 709.

[6] *Ibid.*, p. 713.

long safeguarded their liquidity by other methods, principally by holding secondary reserves in the forms of open-market commercial paper and marketable notes and bonds which could be sold to replenish depleted reserves. " . . . the way to attain the minimum in the matter of reserves is not by relying on maturities but by maintaining a considerable quantity of assets that can be shifted to other banks before maturity as necessity may require. *Liquidity* is *tantamount to shiftability*."[7]

4. "Among the most shiftable, and hence among the most liquid, of assets are bonds and stocks, both as direct investments and as collateral. The development of the corporate form of enterprise has largely undermined the theory of commercial banking as elaborated to fit the conditions of early nineteenth-century England. They share and bond as claims to fixed capital have a ready transferability; indeed the active securities that are listed on the exchanges have in normal times an almost instantaneous convertibility into cash. The result is that securities are from the standpoint of any individual bank incomparably more liquid in ordinary times than commercial paper of customers—assuming that no special machinery, such as reserve banks, has been developed to permit the same shifting of commercial paper."[8]

5. Moulton also distinguished between the problem of liquidity in ordinary times and in times of cyclical strain or crisis: ". . . in time of crisis almost none of the assets of our banks are liquid in the sense that maturing obligations can be used to replenish reserves, and that so far as there is any liquidity at all it is the result of inter-bank accommodations. . . . A time of crisis reveals that the banks are tied up in a system; that the banks as a whole must carry business as a whole; and that when the strain on all banks is heavy, the additional reserve funds required can be secured only by attracting them from other countries or by the manufacture of new forms of reserve money."[9]

6. Finally, Moulton recognized the sharp difference between the individual bank and the banking system with respect to liquidity. He saw that under ordinary conditions the individual bank could repair deficient reserves by shifting (selling) marketable assets to other banks; he also understood that when bank expansion has fully utilized existing cash reserves, no earning assets—whether short-term or long-term—could be converted to cash to support further expansion. At this point, both the individual bank and the banking system could obtain additional liquidity only from the Federal Reserve banks or the Treasury.

The shiftability theory gained an increasing number of adherents

[7] *Ibid.*, p. 723 (italics supplied).
[8] *Ibid.*, p. 730.
[9] *Ibid.*, pp. 723, 730–731.

with the passage of time, but a traditional theory, even though out-moded, dies slowly and vestiges of the old commercial loan theory persisted through the 1930's.

III. THE ANTICIPATED INCOME THEORY

A new theory of commercial bank liquidity, designated "the an-ticipated income theory," was developed in 1949 by Herbert V. Prochnow. It grew out of a comprehensive study of bank term loans in which he found that:

> In every instance, regardless of the nature and character of the bor-rower's business, the banker planned liquidation of the term loan from the anticipated earnings of the borrower. . . . It (liquidation) is not by the sale of assets of the borrower as in the commercial credit or traditional theory of liquidity, nor by shifting the term loan to some other lender as in the shiftability theory of liquidity, but by the anticipated income of the borrower.[10]

Although Prochnow's study was primarily concerned with term loans, he noted that the anticipated income theory applied also to consumer loans.[11] He also recognized that: "In the event of wide-spread and large withdrawals in the entire banking system, ulti-mate liquidity is to be found in the central bank or Federal Reserve System."[12]

The early 1930's marked a new era in the terms of bank loan contracts, with highly significant consequences for the liquidity of bank loan portfolios. Loan officers began systematically to adapt loan repayment schedules to the anticipated income or cash receipts of the borrower. Under the new loan contracts with systematic repayment schedules, a continuous cash inflow could be expected from all types of amortized loans. In a growing economy, banks tend to experience cash outflows from their lending operations—from long-term growth in normal years, and from cyclical loan ex-pansion in prosperous years. But in periods of cyclical decline, loan repayments may exceed the amount of new loans with a resultant net cash inflow. Within limits, loan officers can control the net cash flow by policies with respect to (1) granting new loans, and (2) collection of outstanding loans. However, the net cash inflow under the anticipated income theory is not available to meet an increase

---

[10] Herbert V. Prochnow, *Term Loans and Theories of Bank Liquidity* (Englewood Cliffs, N. J.: Prentice-Hall, 1949), pp. 401–402.

[11] *Ibid.*, p. 408.

[12] *Ibid.*, p. 411.

in total loans during expansion periods, but only in economic contractions to meet possible shifts of deposits to other banks and withdrawals of currency.

It remains to mention that the anticipated income theory can be used to explain a degree of liquidity for the entire commercial banking system which is not implied in either the commercial loan theory or the shiftability theory. Since liquidity in this theory is expressly derived from the flow of income, total loans (and total deposits) may be reduced by savings from borrowers' incomes. This does not in itself increase total cash reserves of banks, but it releases required and working reserves needed to support deposits. In contrast, the commercial loan theory contemplates repayment of loans by the sale of the goods, rather than from income, and it implies the shifting of a repaid loan to another bank and another borrower. The shiftability theory also usually implies the sale of securities or the shifting of loans to other banks, perhaps including the Reserve banks, so that no reduction in total bank credit takes place. However, the exception should be noted that if the banks sell securities to individuals, business corporations, and other nonbank interests, a reduction of total bank loans and investments (and therefore of deposits) takes place. In this event, required reserves are released and the entire banking system becomes more liquid.

IV. THE LIABILITIES MANAGEMENT THEORY

During the 1960's, a new theory of cyclical bank liquidity emerged, which may be labelled the "liabilities management theory." According to this new doctrine, it is unnecessary to observe traditional standards in regard to self-liquidating loans and liquidity reserves, since reserve money can be borrowed or "bought" in the money market whenever a bank experiences a reserve deficiency. There are seven possible sources from which the individual bank may acquire reserves by the creation of additional liabilities: (1) acquisition of demand deposits; (2) issuance of time certificates of deposit; (3) purchase (borrowing) of Federal funds; (4) borrowing at the Federal Reserve; (5) issuance of short-term notes; (6) raising capital funds from the sale of capital notes, preferred stock, or common stock, or from retained earnings; and (7) the Eurodollar market.

A. Demand Deposits

The acquisition of demand deposits as a means of meeting cyclical liquidity needs might have been feasible before 1933, when banks were free to pay whatever rates they wished in bidding for such deposits. But the Banking Act of 1933 prohibited these interest payments. Moreover, there has been a definite tendency for total demand deposits to decline during the last half of cyclical expansion periods, largely in response to the tight rein of Federal Reserve policy. Banks must draw these deposits competitively from a smaller total reservoir by aggressive promotion and effective enforcement of balance requirements. Management cannot count on opening this valve whenever cyclical funds are needed.

B. Time Certificates of Deposit

The predominant liability source of reserve money for the individual bank since the early 1960's has been the issuance of time certificates of deposit, mainly in negotiable form. The negotiable certificate market was launched in early 1961 by the large money-market banks of New York City, mainly as a means of attracting deposits of large corporations. Prior to this time, New York City banks paid no interest on corporate time deposits as a matter of policy. But during the first quarter of 1961, they began to offer negotiable certificates with original maturities ranging between 90 days and one year at rates competitive with Treasury bills, commercial paper, bankers' acceptances, Federal agency securities, and other money market instruments. At the same time, the large bond dealers began to develop a secondary market in CD's which materially enhanced their liquidity features. Growth in the amount of CD's was meteoric, rising steadily from zero in early 1961 to $18.6 billion in August 1966—$7.4 billion in New York City and $11.2 billion in other cities.[13] With some time lag, the practice spread— first to the large banks outside New York, and later to intermediate-size banks throughout the country, although certificates of the latter were not ordinarily negotiable and did not reach the secondary market. A better idea of overall growth is conveyed by the fact that "other time deposits of individuals and businesses" (largely certificates) of all member banks increased from $7.1 billion in April 1961 to nearly $28.7 billion at the end of 1965.[14] Thus, a vigorous new segment of the money market, second only to short-term Treasury securities, grew to maturity in an incredibly short time.

The financial environment of those years provided fertile soil for

[13] *Federal Reserve Bulletin*, September 1966, p. 1369.
[14] Board of Governors of the Federal Reserve System, *Summary Reports of Assets and Liabilities of Member Banks*, April 12, 1961, p. 3; Dec. 31, 1965, p. 3.

growth of this new market. The period was one of rapid expansion in the economy accompanied by robust credit demands from businesses, consumers, and governments. These demands furnished the banks with unusual lending opportunities which supplied the incentive to compete strongly for deposits. At the same time, Federal Reserve policies were friendly toward the market's development. An easy monetary policy with relatively abundant bank reserves prevailed until the first quarter of 1965, after which the reins were gradually tightened, but not to the point of reducing the rate of expansion of member bank legal reserves until the second quarter of 1966. Also, the Federal Reserve Board raised the maximum rates which banks could pay on time deposits, so that the banks were not handicapped in bidding up rates to compete for funds.

In the banking system as a whole, the issuance of CD's involved a shift from demand to time deposits with a resultant release of required reserves. Table 1 indicates that in the period, 1961–1966, over four-fifths of the demand deposits created by the expansion of bank loans and investments were shifted to time deposits.

The relative ease with which the large city banks could buy reserve money by the issuance of CD's masked some of the limitations of this source under tight credit conditions. Such conditions almost invariably develop sometime during the last stage of a cyclical expansion, and in the current expansion they began to appear in the last half of 1965. Demands for bank credit continued their upsurge, and on the supply side the Federal Reserve tightened the credit reins another notch. Net free reserves of member banks,[15] which had shown a substantial surplus since the last quarter of 1960, moved

TABLE 1   Changes in Bank Deposits and Reserves, 1961 and 1966
(in billions of dollars)

Items	February 1961	September 1966	Amount of increase
Demand deposits*	112.1	132.6	20.5
Time deposits†	60.6	157.1	96.5
Total member bank reserves	18.9	23.5	4.6
Total loans and investments‡	199.3	313.8	114.5

* "Demand deposits adjusted" as a component of the money supply (seasonally adjusted).
† At all commercial banks.
‡ All commercial banks.
SOURCE: *Federal Reserve Bulletin*, June 1961, pp. 673 and 675; October 1966, pp. 1478 and 1480.

[15] Excess legal reserves less borrowing at Federal Reserve banks.

to a deficit position in the first quarter of 1965 and averaged about $150 million during the remainder of the year. Further restraint was applied in 1966, and by July net borrowed reserves exceeded $400 million. Meanwhile in December 1965, the Federal Reserve discount rate was raised from 4 to $4\frac{1}{2}$ percent. In this setting, open-market rates moved up sharply. The 3-month Treasury bill rate rose from 3.99 percent in August 1965 to 5.66 percent in September 1966, and the 4- to 6-month prime commercial paper rate increased in the same period from 4.58 percent to 6.26 percent.[16] In order to compete for money, the leading banks were forced to make corresponding increases in the rates offered on CD's—from 4.50 percent in August 1965 to 5.50 percent by midyear 1966 on certificates of 30 days and more.

This situation points up the first limitation on CD's as a dependable source of reserve money during boom conditions, namely, Federal Reserve control of maximum rates payable. If the structure of rates on competing money market instruments—principally Treasury bills, Federal agency securities, commercial paper, and repurchase agreements for Federal funds—rises above the ceilings on CD's set by the Federal Reserve, the banks can no longer sell them. And if this situation should persist, the amount of outstanding CD's would shrink as maturities occur. Since maturities of outstandings range from one day to one year or a little more, the drain on reserves of the individual bank would begin immediately and would continue until all interest-sensitive CD's were liquidated.

For the banking system as a whole, there would be a substantial increase in legal reserve requirements arising from the shift from time deposits back to demand deposits, although in fact it is likely that the Federal Reserve would soften the blow. It did so in December 1965, after some discomfort, when maximum rates payable were raised from $4\frac{1}{2}$ percent to $5\frac{1}{2}$ percent. But market rates soon closed the gap and rose above the ceiling, with the result that the amount of outstanding CD's declined almost $3 billion between August and November 1966.

Another limitation on CD's as a dependable source of reserves is the fact that the banks must compete strongly among themselves for existing reserve money in boom periods when it is scarce. The large money-market banks hold an advantage in this competition over the smaller banks, because of the wider acceptability of prime, large-denomination certificates, and of the lower rates at which they may be sold. This means that the penalty of excessive dependence

---

[16] Rates adjusted to comparable basis—actual yield on 360-day year.

on CD's is definitely heavier on intermediate- and small-size banks, since they reach the rate ceiling first. But the money-market banks also complete among themselves for reserves to a large extent, and so are not immune to difficulty.

A final limitation on CD's as a dependable source of reserves is the fact that the Federal Reserve authorities are almost certain to implement a monetary policy of restraint, thereby changing adversely the whole environment of the money market with respect to availability of business recession when the Federal Reserve is typically on the side of the banks in providing abundant reserves at low rates, it shifts to the opposing side sometime during the last stage of cyclical expansion. Witness 1952–1953, 1956–1957, 1959, and 1966—all periods of rising net borrowed reserves, and of sharply increasing money rates. In large part, these conditions were created, or at least validated, by Federal Reserve policies and actions—whether by sales of U.S. securities, by raising legal reserve requirements, by rationing advances and increasing the discount rate, or by some combination of these methods. Although this limiting factor affects all means of replenishing reserves, it applies uniquely to CD's because of Regulation Q. In contrast, a bank can always sell short-term U.S. securities to repair its reserve position; and if they are sold to non-commercial-bank investors, deposits decline correspondingly in the banking system and total required reserves are reduced.

In addition to the issuance of negotiable CD's to large corporations, a significant new development took place at the retail level in non-negotiable CD's and other time deposits, beginning in December 1965. On December 6, 1965, the Federal Reserve Board raised the maximum rates payable on time deposits with maturities of 30 days and over from $4\frac{1}{2}$ to $5\frac{1}{2}$ percent. This opened a new door through which commercial banks could compete for savings. Previously this door had been nearly closed by the rate ceilings, which were below rates paid by savings and loan associations and mutual savings banks, and below yields obtainable on open-market securities.

As indicated in Table 2, the banks aggressively entered this field with a variety of time deposit plans. Rates offered were soon bid up to the $5\frac{1}{2}$ percent maximum, which exceeded those paid by competing institutions and the 4 percent ceiling on passbook savings. "Other time deposits" increased $4,948 million during the first half of 1966, compared with only a $237 million increase in the last half of 1965. This gain represented largely the diversion of a greater proportion of savings to the banks. The savings and loan associations, which had enjoyed phenomenal growth since the second

TABLE 2   Time and Savings Deposits of Large Commercial Banks,
1965–1966 (in millions of dollars)

	July 7, 1965 (1)	Dec. 29, 1965‡ (2)	Change between (1) & (2) (3)	June 29, 1966 (4)	Change between (2) & (4)
Savings deposits	48,313	48,084	− 229	48,413	+ 329
CD's* Other time	15,587	17,063	+1,476	18,268	+1,205
deposits†	5,234	5,471	+ 237	10,419	+4,948

* Negotiable CD's issued in denominations over $100,000.
† Time deposits of individuals, partnerships and corporations.
‡ Estimated by raising old "Leading Cities" series by 6 percent.
SOURCE: Federal Reserve Bulletin, January 1966, p. 70; July 1966, p. 1008.

World War, suffered heavily. During the first seven months of 1966, their savings capital increased only $577 million compared with $3,758 million in the same period of 1965. Mutual savings banks were also hit hard, the respective gains in deposits during the same periods being $1,080 million and $1,995 million.[17]

The plight of these institutions and the associated threat to residential construction was so acute that the situation became one of considerable national concern. After extensive hearings, the House Banking Committee in late July 1966 approved a bill that would impose a $4\frac{1}{2}$ percent maximum until August 1, 1967 on all commercial bank time deposits of $100,000 and less, thus removing the existing discretionary authority of the Federal Reserve Board over maximum rates in this area.[18] However, the bill which became law on September 21, 1966 (Public Law 89-597) did not in the end set maximum rate ceilings, but granted more flexible authority to the Federal Reserve Board over maximum rates payable by member banks. Similar authority was given the Federal Deposit Insurance Corporation over nonmember banks, and the Federal Home Loan Bank Board over savings and loan associations.[19]

C. Federal Funds

The third source from which the individual bank may acquire reserve money by the creation of additional liabilities is the purchase

[17] Federal Reserve Bulletin, October 1966, pp. 1493–1494.
[18] Wall Street Journal, July 26, 1966, p. 3.
[19] Fderal Reserve Bulletin, October 1966, p. 1451.

(borrowing) of Federal funds. This is the market in which banks with deficient legal reserves borrow from other banks having excess reserves. Lenders and borrowers are brought together by two or three broker-dealers in New York City who receive reports by wire from banks all over the country in regard to bids and offers of funds, and by a few large money-market banks that act in part as dealers and in part as brokers and clearing centers of information. There are two principal methods of dealing in this market: (1) straight one-day loans; and (2) repurchase agreements. The great bulk of Federal funds is loaned on a one-day, unsecured basis, although a significant part is secured by U.S. securities. Banks also utilize repurchase agreements under which the borrowing bank actually sells U.S. securities under contract to buy them back in one or more days at a predetermined rate and price. Rates are very sensitive in response to changing currents of supply and demand. They are closely related competitively to other rates in the money market, and particularly to those on Treasury bills. Also, in ordinary times the Federal Reserve discount rate marks the upper limit of their fluctuations, since banks seldom choose to pay more when they can borrow at the discount rate. But in periods of strong loan demand and tight money, the Federal funds rate may rise well above the discount rate. This situation, which existed during the last half of 1965 and the first three quarters of 1966 developed from a combination of credit rationing by the Reserve banks, a relatively low discount rate, and exceptionally inviting loan and investment opportunities.

A more specific idea of the market's background is conveyed by the fact that in September 1966, total member bank legal reserves were $23,239 million while required reserves were $22,847 million, so that excess reserves were $392 million. The greater part of the excess reserves—$291 million—was held by the smaller country banks, with only $101 million in the large reserve-city banks, including New York City and Chicago.[20] It should be noted that the average size of excess reserves in the banking system materially understates the availability of Federal funds. This is true since the reserve position of each individual bank varies widely from day-to-day and within each day during the reserve computation periods— one week in reserve-city banks and two weeks in country banks. The lightning-like turnover of available Federal funds is indicated by the fact that combined purchases and sales of 46 major reserve-city banks during the first four weeks of September 1966 amounted to $19.7 billion—an annual rate of $1,022 billion.[21] More relevant

[20] *Federal Reserve Bulletin*, October 1966, p. 1468; preliminary figures.
[21] *Ibid.*, p. 1470.

to the present purpose, average borrowings of Federal funds by weekly-reporting large banks during September 1966 amounted to $5.8 billion—over two-fifths of their total legal reserve balances.[22]

The limitations of the Federal funds market as a dependable source of cyclical reserve money for the individual bank are similar in some respects to those of CD's, but there are also significant points of difference. A summary of the similarities will suffice. The first is that the banks must compete actively among themselves for existing reserve money when it is scarce during the last phase of business expansions. This may lead to a very high cost of funds, as illustrated between August and November 1966 when Federal funds typically traded at 6 percent while the Federal Reserve discount rate was $4\frac{1}{2}$ percent. The other similar limitation is the fact that a bank must face the high probability of a restrictive Federal Reserve policy in boom periods whether it expects to acquire reserves through CD's or Federal funds. This magnifies the degree of reserve scarcity.

There are three significant differences between Federal funds and CD's as dependable cyclical sources of reserve mony. First, the Federal fund rate is not subject to Federal Reserve regulation, nor is such regulation likely. On this count, Federal funds have a distinct advantage over CD's, which are subject to maximum rates under Regulation Q. However, the price may be too high to contemplate in practice when other alternatives to provide liquidity are considered, and under extreme conditions of restraint this source may nearly dry up at any price.

Second, there is no legal reserve requirement against the borrowing of Federal funds, whereas a reserve requirement of between 3 and 10 percent applies to time deposits. This difference has both a positive and negative aspect. On the positive side, the net cost of borrowing Federal funds is somewhat lower than the net cost of CD's when market rates are the same. But, on the other hand, there is no release of required legal reserves in the banking system when borrowings of Federal funds are increased.

Last, Federal funds are bought and sold by banks on a very short-term basis—predominantly for one day only, and seldom for more than one week, while original issues of CD's are for considerably longer periods. Most of them have maturities in the range of 3 to 12 months, although a significant part has maturities after one year and beyond two years.[23] The exceedingly short-term nature of Federal funds borrowing makes this source inconvenient and undependable for cyclical purposes.

[22] *Ibid.*, pp. 1486–1489.
[23] *Federal Reserve Bulletin*, April 1963, p. 465.

Closely related to Federal funds, is the borrowing of reserves by smaller banks from their large-city correspondent banks. A part of such loans is made according to the prevailing practices in the Federal funds market and may therefore be included in the funds market proper. But another part is made on a customer basis under prearranged lines of credit, and with maturities and other terms usually arranged to meet the needs of the smaller bank. However, liquidity pressures focus on the large city banks, and consequently they are likely to be least able to provide such loans when smaller banks face cyclical reserve deficiencies.

D. Borrowing at Federal Reserve Banks

The fourth source of reserves by creation of liabilities is borrowing from the Federal Reserve. In fact, the founders of the Federal Reserve Systm visualized the discount window as the principal pipeline through which high-powered reserve money would be released and withdrawn from commercial banks. The use of the term, "high-powered," calls attention to the profound difference between this source and those just discussed—CD's and Federal funds. When a member bank borrows from a Reserve bank it adds, other things being equal, to total bank reserves. This multiple expansion feature does not apply to either CD's or Federal funds, since these markets deal only with existing bank reserves and do not in themselves bring forth newly-created reserves. However, both markets do have a multiple-expansion effect insofar as they bring about a more complete utilization of existing legal reserves—that is, insofar as dealings through them reduce the amount of "excess legal reserves" in the banking system, or activate shifts of demand deposits to time deposits. This effect is a significant one during boom conditions when bank reserves become relatively scarce and money rates rise sharply. For example, excess reserves exceeded $700 million during the recession of 1960–1961, but as the economy recovered and interest rates rose they gradually declined, and during the first half of 1966 they were in the vicinity of $350 million.[24]

In practice, member bank borrowing at the Reserve banks predominantly takes the form of a renewable promissory note for 15 days or less secured by U.S. securities. Seldom utilized are other possible forms of borrowing, namely: (1) discounting of eligible customer notes with remaining maturities not in excess of 90 days;[25] and (2) a promissory note with a maximum maturity of four months

---

[24] *Federal Reserve Bulletin*, July 1966, p. 988.
[25] Nine months in the case of agricultural paper.

and secured by any satisfactory bank assets. However, in the latter case a penalty rate of ½ percent above the regular Federal Reserve discount rate applies.

Regardless of the method of borrowing, the Reserve banks observe certain guiding principles in the administration of discounts and advances. Federal Reserve credit is generally granted as a privilege rather than a right to meet day-to-day and seasonal liquidity needs of member banks. Under ordinary conditions, dependence on borrowing for longer-term purposes, including cyclical loan expansion, is not regarded as appropriate. Also, advances are not to be used in support of speculative activities in securities, commodities, or real estate. Only in unusual situations arising from national or local difficulties can a member bank count on borrowing continuously for longer periods.[26] In practice, a Reserve bank seldom refuses the first application for an advance to meet a purpose in line with the foregoing principles, but a large member bank which has borrowed continuously for three or four reserve-computation periods is likely to be called on the carpet.

Some idea of the extent to which member banks have depended on borrowings from the Reserve banks to meet liquidity needs at cyclical peaks may be gained from Table 3. It will be noted that this

TABLE 3   Member Bank Borrowings and Required Legal Reserves on Selected Dates, 1920–1926 (in millions of dollars)*

Dates	Member bank borrowing at F.R. Banks (1)	Required legal reserves (2)	Percentages, (1) to (2) (3)
October 1920	2,780	1,815†	153.2
July 1929	1,096	2,292	47.8
December 1952	1,593	20,457	7.8
April 1957	1,011	18,580	5.4
August 1959	1,007	18,141	5.6
September 1966‡	766	22,847	3.4

* Monthly averages of daily figures.
† Total legal reserves.
‡ Preliminary figures.
SOURCES: Board of Governors of the Federal Reserve System, *Banking and Monetary Statistics; Federal Reserve Bulletin*, various issues.

[26] Board of Governors of the Federal Reserve System, *Regulation A*, 1955 Revision, Foreword-General Principles.

dependence was very heavy in the 1920's. The record amount of borrowings occurred in October 1920, when they reached $2,780 million, or 153 percent of total legal reserves. At that time, total member bank deposits were $25.1 billion as compared with $271.2 billion in September 1966, so that a corresponding amount of borrowings in September 1966 would be $30 billion. A similar comparison with July 1929 would call for borrowings in September 1966 of $8.3 billion, in contrast with actual borrowings of $766 million. Since the second World War, Reserve bank borrowings have been modest even at cyclical peaks—never exceeding 8 percent of required legal reserves.

This marked decline in the relative importance of borrowings at the Reserve banks is largely attributable to (1) the profound change in the entire banking and financial environment, and (2) a change in Federal Reserve policy with respect to the release of reserve money through the discount window. In the 1920's, the financial environment did not provide liquidity alternatives to Reserve bank borrowing to anything like the degree that existed after the second World War. The short-term U.S. security market was relatively small, the Federal funds market had not yet developed, the negotiable CD market did not exist, the bankers' acceptance market was small and was dominated by the Reserve banks, the commercial paper market was likewise small, and there was not an active market in short-term obligations of states and political subdivisions, Federal agencies, and corporations. The large banks depended heavily on call loans to security brokers and dealers for asset liquidity. Such loans ordinarily served the purpose quite well when loans called by one bank could readily be shifted to other banks. But they became almost frozen in cyclical booms and financial crises when all banks needed additional reserves at the same time. The peak of borrowings in 1920 also reflected highly inflationary conditions superimposed upon the financing of the first World War when Treasury policy was to sell bonds directly to the public rather than to commercial banks. To support this program, banks were urged to lend to the public with U.S. securities as collateral, and the Reserve banks were encouraged to advance adequate amounts of reserve money to the banks.

In contrast with the 1920's, the short-term money markets developed enormously after the second World War. The U.S. securities market was, of course, predominant. At midyear 1947, marketable U.S. securities with maturities under one year totalled $51.2 billion, and those with maturities of one to five years amounted to $21.9 billion. By the end of August 1966 these categories were, respectively, $92.2 billion and $62.9 billion.[27] Also, significant growth took place in the bankers' acceptance market and the commercial paper market, and several new divisions of the money market developed: Federal funds, Federal agency securities, short-term municipal securities, and negotiable certificates of deposit. Thus, it is evident that commercial banks enjoyed materially wider alternatives in liquidity management after the second World War than during the 1920's. They were not so dependent for liquidity on borrowings from the Reserve banks.

The other main reason for the decline in relative importance of borrowings at the Reserve banks since the 1920's is a change in Federal Reserve policy in regard to discounts and advances to member banks. The Reserve banks have applied the rule of short-term borrowing rather assiduously, and this has apparently developed greater member-bank reluctance to borrow and to stay in debt. They have administered "discounts and advances" with a firm hand during cyclical booms when the banks have most needed reserves. They have preferred to release reserve money on their own initiative by purchasing U.S. securities in the open market and by reducing percentage reserve requirements from time to time. The best evidence of a firm policy of rationing reserve credit is the fact that Treasury bill yields have risen well above the Federal Reserve discount rate during the last phase of every cyclical expansion since the second World War, thus making it profitable to borrow. But despite the greater profit incentive, borrowings have remained at modest levels. Also, in 1965–1966, the Federal funds rate typically exceeded the discount rate by from one-half to 1 percentage point. In fact, Federal funds often traded at 6 percent during the period. August–November 1966, when the discount rate was $4\frac{1}{2}$ percent—a differential of $1\frac{1}{2}$ percent at a time when member bank borrowings averaged only about $750 million.

E. Short-term Notes

A fifth source from which the individual bank may acquire reserve money by the creation of additional liabilities is the issuance of unsubordinated, short-term, promissory notes. This new member of the money-market family was launched by the First National Bank of Boston in September 1964. The unsecured notes were offered in negotiable form with maturities to suit corporate and other large short-term investors. Shortly afterward, First Boston Corporation

[27] *Economic Report of the President*, January 1966, p. 275; *Federal Reserve Bulletin*, October 1966, p. 1499.

announced that it would make a market in the notes. Other large banks and security dealers followed suit, and with the blessing of the Comptroller of the Currency and the Federal Reserve Board the new market seemed to be off to a promising start.

There were significant advantages of such notes over CD's. Since they were not classified as deposits they were not subject to maximum-rate regulation (Regulation Q). For this reason, a bank could regard them as a more dependable reserve source because there was no obstacle in bidding up rates to attract or to retain funds. This constituted a special advantage for banks outside the circle of leading money-market banks. The smaller institutions had to offer somewhat higher rates on CD's to compete and whenever market rates approached the rate ceiling they tended to lose CD's to leading banks. Another advantage of the notes was that they were officially classified as borrowed funds and not as deposits. Consequently, they were not subject to either legal reserve requirements or to deposit-insurance assessments. This represented an annual cost saving at the time of about 0.2 percent.

The only apparent disadvantages of the notes were certain legal restrictions on borrowing. A national bank was prohibited from borrowing in excess of capital stock and 50 percent of surplus, and state-chartered banks were also restricted in this regard. In addition, the banking law of New York was interpreted to bar the issuance of such notes, whether negotiable or non-negotiable. Without a legal change, this would of course seriously limit growth of the market, since the great money-market banks in New York City were excluded. In August 1965, partial relief came to New York banks when the State Banking Department ruled that *non-negotiable* short-term notes, issued for specified periods in units of $1 million of more, were permissible. With this assurance, several large New York banks sold significant amounts of non-negotiable short-term notes to corporations and others.[28] However, the prohibition of negotiable notes in New York remained a major obstacle to development of an active secondary market, and to the potential growth of the new market. Pending a permissive change in the New York banking law, it seemed improbable that a major national market could be established in view of the predominance of New York City as a financial center.

Even if the New York banking law should be amended to permit issuance of negotiable notes, their future growth is called to question by restrictive measures taken in June 1966 by the Federal Reserve

[28] *The Wall Street Journal*, Sept. 3, 1965, p. 8.

Board. Effective September 1, 1966, short-term promissory notes of banks became subject to the regulations governing reserve requirements and payment of interest on deposits. The Board's purpose was, "to prevent future use of these instruments as a means of circumventing statutory and regulatory requirements applicable to bank deposits."[29] This action erased the advantages of such notes over CD's, except perhaps for use in individual situations. Moreover, in view of the limits on bank borrowings, the legal barrier to negotiable notes in New York, and the great head-start of the CD market, it now appears unlikely that a comparable new market in notes will develop.

Now that short-term promissory notes of banks have become subject to legal reserve requirements, the analysis of their effects on the money market becomes identical with that pertaining to CD's. That is, the individual bank may acquire liquidity through their issuance only by drawing existing reserves and deposits from *other* banks. The only difference is that the process involves a shift in the banking system from demand deposits or time deposits to note liabilities; whereas in the case of issuance of CD's there is a shift only from demand deposits to time deposits. In both cases, there is a reduction in the amount of required legal reserves when the shift is from demand deposits to a liability against which a materially lower percentage reserve requirement applies. The general conclusion is also the same as that with respect to CD's: Short-term notes are not a dependable source, except to a limited extent, to meet the liquidity needs of the individual bank during the last phase of cyclical periods of expansion.

F. Capital Funds

The sixth source from which the individual bank may acquire reserve money by the creation of liabilities is by raising capital funds in any one of several forms—sale of common stock, preferred stock, or capital notes, and retention of earnings. While these forms differ in character, the effect of their increase on the asset-liquidity position of the individual bank and the banking system is the same. When Bank A, having a legal reserve deficiency of $10 million, increases its capital funds by this amount, say by sale of common stock, its cash reserve is increased and so is its common stock account. Assuming that the stock is paid for by checks on other banks, total demand deposits of the banking system are immediately

[29] *Federal Reserve Bulletin*, July 1966, p. 979.

reduced by $10 million. At the same time, required legal reserves are reduced by $1.5 million when the reserve requirement is 15 percent. Given time, the released reserves provide the basis for loan and investment expansion (and therefore deposit expansion) of $10 million, so that the demand deposits initially extinguished may be recreated. Thus, the end result, assuming net free reserves of zero at the outset and full utilization of the released reserves, is no change in total demand deposits, an increase of $10 million in total capital accounts, and an equal increase in total loans and investments. It should also be noted that these transactions have made no change in total legal reserves of the banking system. Hence, the cash reserves that Bank A gained were drawn away from other banks which, collectively, are assumed to have excess reserves of $10 million—just enough to provide for Bank A's reserve deficiency. Thus, as a generalization, deposits are the immediate source of additional capital funds in the banking system, and an increase of capital funds of the individual bank causes a redistribution of existing cash reserves rather than an increase in total reserves.

Table 4 shows the changes in capital accounts of all member banks between 1961 and 1965. Over half the total increase of $6.3 billion came from retained earnings. Much dependence on this source does not seem practicable, since in periods of increased earnings stockholders expect higher rather than lower dividends. Issuance of preferred stock may also be dismissed in view of its insignificance in the banking field, and because of the depressed level of preferred stock prices during periods of high interest rates.

The sale of common stock likewise has a very small potential for this purpose. Bank stock prices are likely to be depressed by the high interest rates associated with boom conditions. For example, the index of bank stock prices reached a peak in the third quarter of 1964 and had declined one-fourth by June 1966, while Standard and Poor's index of industrial stock prices rose 8 percent during the same period.[30] In addition, banks are often reluctant to issue more common stock because of dilution of per-share equity, and because of control considerations.

One possibility for use of common stock in this connection would be issuance at an earlier stage of the business-expansion cycle when the price is favorable, as in 1964. Proceeds could be held in short-term U.S. securities and other liquidity reserves which then offer attractive yields. But the practicability of such a program is open to serious question. Success would depend on a higher degree of accu-

[30] M. A. Schapiro & Co., Inc., *Bank Stock Quarterly*, June 1966, p. 5.

TABLE 4 Capital Accounts of All Member Banks, 1961 and 1965 (in millions of dollars)*

	Dec. 30, 1961	Dec. 31, 1965	Increase	Percentage distribution
Common stock*	5,512	7,002	1,489	23.7
Capital notes and debentures	16	1,553	1,537	24.4
Preferred stock	7	32	25	0.4
Surplus and other capital accounts	13,102	16,341	3,238	51.4
Total	18,683	24,926	6,288	100.0

* An unknown part of the increase in common stock took place as a result of stock dividends which capitalize surplus or undivided profits. Hence, the table over-states to that extent the raising of new capital funds in this manner, and under-states retained earnings as a source of new funds. Any discrepancies in totals are the result of rounding.
SOURCE: Board of Governors of the Federal Reserve System, *Summary Report, December 30, 1961*, p. 3; Dec. 31, 1965, p. 3.

TABLE 5 Capital Accounts of Reserve City Member Banks, 1963 and 1965 (in millions of dollars)*

	Dec. 20, 1963	Dec. 31, 1965	Increase	Percentage distribution
Common stock	3,640.2	4,237.8	597.6	23.2
Capital notes and debentures	78.4	1,294.5	1,216.2	47.2
Surplus and other capital accounts	8,959.1	9,721.4	762.3	29.6
Total capital accounts	12,677.7	15,253.7	2,576.1	100.0

* Includes New York City and Chicago member banks. Any discrepancies in totals are the result of rounding.
SOURCE: Board of Governors of the Federal Reserve System, *Summary Report, December 20, 1963*, p. 3; Dec. 31, 1965, p. 3.

racy in business forecasting than past experience demonstrates, and also on timely action in accordance with the forecast. Although bank officers may wish to sell common stock as part of an over-all liquidity program, the uncertainties and limitations commit it to a minor role.

Capital notes have become a major source of capital funds since December 1962 when the Comptroller of the Currency approved their issuance if they were subordinated to deposits. As shown by Table 5, between 1963 and 1965, they represented 47 percent of the increase in total capital funds and over three-fourths of total capital raised in the investment market by reserve-city banks.[31] In New York City, the proportion of the increase in total capital funds represented by capital notes was appreciably higher during the same period—58 percent. Thus, it is evident that the banks eagerly grasped the opportunity to acquire liquid funds by this method during this phase of business expansion. It afforded the advantage of tax-free capital at a relatively low interest cost when customer loan demands were strong.

M. A. Schapiro & Company has reported that over 200 banks sold nearly $1.8 billion of capital notes between mid-1963 and mid-1966.[32] The average interest rate was 4.56 percent, and the average maturity was 24.3 years. Most of the issues (194) were nonconvertible, but a few were convertible into common stock. One aspect of the compilation has special significance for this study. During the first half of 1966, only 12 capital note issues totalling $43.7 million were sold. This compares with 100 issues in 1965 amounting to $863.9 million, and 82 issues in 1964 totalling $642.9 million. The principal explanation lies in the sharp tightening of the investment market in 1966—when the average rate on the issues was 5.31 percent compared with 4.60 percent in 1965. Understandably, the banks were reluctant to commit themselves to a high fixed-interest charge for period ranging from 15 to 30 years. This situation illustrates a serious limitation on capital notes as a method of acquiring liquidity during the last phase of cyclical expansions. However, the experience of the period, 1963–1965, does indicate that capital notes may be utilized during earlier stages of an economic expansion as part of an over-all cyclical liquidity program. Capital funds may then be raised on a favorable basis in larger amounts than currently needed, looking forward both to growth and the next

---

[31] Allowing for the fact that an appreciable part of the increase in capital stock occurred by transfer from surplus and undivided profits.
[32] *Bank Stock Quarterly*, June 1966, pp. 8–12.

cycle peak. Proceeds labelled for liquidity needs could be invested in liquidity reserves.

G. The Eurodollar Market

A final source of reserves for the large money-market banks is the Eurodollar market. This market deals in interest-bearing time deposits, denominated in dollars, on the books of large foreign banks— largely in London, but also in other European financial centers. Eurodollars originate when the holder (usually a foreign bank or firm) of a demand deposit in a U. S. bank transfers funds to a foreign bank with instructions to open a Eurodollar account. This transaction leaves the foreign bank with a new dollar liability in the form of a time deposit, and a counterpart demand deposit on the books of the U. S. bank. Thus, the foreign bank has become an intermediary between the original owner of the demand deposit and the U. S. bank. Having a claim on dollars, the foreign bank is then in position to make loans to others who wish to borrow dollars— whether they be foreign business firms and financial institutions, or U. S. banks and other interests.

While European banks accepted and tranferred deposits in dollars (and other foreign moneys) as far back as the post-World War I years, this market had its real beginnings in the mid-1950's and most of its development took place after 1958. According to estimates of the Bank for International Settlements, the gross Eurodollar deposit liabilities of the eight principal European countries[33] at mid-1966 were $11.5 billion and the net amount was $10 billion. The rest of the world, mainly Canada and Japan, accounted for another $1 billion.[34]

The reasons for the growth of this market, its complex features, functions, and outlook represent a long story which cannot be told here. Suffice it to say that one of its principal functions is to provide an international money market for the leading banks of all major nations—a market where they can place excess funds and where they can usually obtain needed liquid funds. This is the aspect which is relevant for the present purpose.

During 1965 and 1966, U.S. banks experienced growing liquidity pressures, largely from the upsurge in loan demands, outflows of currency and gold, and increasing restraint by the Federal Reserve.

[33] United Kingdom, Switzerland, Sweden and the five Common Market countries—Belgium, Netherlands, France, Italy, and West Germany.

[34] Milton Gilbert, "The Euro-Currency Market," Bank for International Settlements, H. S. 383, p. 4.

Individual banks met these pressures by tapping the various liquidity sources already discussed. In addition, according to official estimates, the large banks turned to the Eurodollar market—in the net amount of $2 billion during 1965 and the first quarter of 1966.[35] Such borrowings apparently continued to grow rapidly during the remainder of 1966, as indicated by the fact that short-term liabilities of U.S. banks to Europe increased by $3.2 billion between March and November 1966.[36]

In an immediate accounting sense, borrowing in the Eurodollar market by a U.S. bank does not represent a net addition to the reserves of the banking system. This follows from the fact that Eurodollars have demand deposit counterparts on the books of U.S. banks.[37] A change in ownership of a Eurodollar time deposit from one foreign owner to another brings about a corresponding shift of U.S. demand deposits, usually from one bank to another.

But, more basically, it is possible that borrowing in the Eurodollar market by U.S. banks may lead to an improvement of the reserve position of the domestic monetary and banking system. This would take place (1) if the Federal Reserve banks purchase foreign moneys by expanding their credit, such as in recent swap arrangements with foreign central banks; (2) if Federal Reserve credit is extended domestically in any manner; (3) if the Treasury borrows foreign moneys from the International Monetary Fund; and (4) if the Treasury or the private sector of the economy borrows more heavily abroad. Thus, it may be that increased borrowing by U.S. banks in the Eurodollar market will generate a train of circumstances leading to an increase in the total reserves of the banking system, and to an increase in the size of the Eurodollar market.

Dealings in the Eurodollar market are in wholesale lots with a minimum of $1 million, and with most single transactions in tens of millions. Direct access to this market is beyond the reach of small- and intermediate-size banks, and indirect access through correspondents involves uncertainties. But the Eurodollar market is, within limits, a potential source of cyclical liquidity for large money-market banks. International monetary conditions, however, are subject to unpredictable changes in larger measure than are domestic conditions. The supply of Eurodollars may shrink when needs are most imperative, and even if available their cost may become prohibitively

[35] Bank for International Settlements, *Thirty-Sixth Annual Report*, June 1966, p. 149.

[36] *Federal Reserve Bulletin*, April 1967, p. 668.

[37] In some cases, the Eurodollar counterpart is a loan payable to foreign banks by U.S. banks.

high. During 1965 and the first half of 1966, the three-month rate in London on Eurodollars averaged about ½ percentage point higher than that on CD's in New York, and on occasion the spread became as much as one percent.[38]

H. Summary and Conclusion

The potentialities of liabilities management as a source from which the individual bank may meet liquidity needs during the last phase of periods of cyclical expansion may be summarized as follows:

1. All sources with the exception of Federal Reserve borrowing have in common the fact that, assuming a fixed stock of legal reserves, the individual bank can acquire reserves only at the expense of other banks in the system.[39]

2. However, an individual bank may utilize any one of these sources as a means of capturing a larger share of total existing reserves.

3. The tight credit policy typically adopted by the Federal Reserve authorities during boom conditions strictly limits the availability of reserves, and may bring about an absolute reduction in total reserves. Therefore, the bank that needs more reserves at such a time is confronted with a highly-competitive situation in which other banks are also seeking more reserves.

4. The acquisition of demand deposits cannot be counted on as a source of cyclical liquidity because banks are prevented by law from paying interest on such deposits.

5. CD's and other time deposits are not dependable sources, except for short-term liquidity needs (including seasonal), to meet requirements in the first half (or even three-fourths) of a cyclical expansion period. The unique reason for this is the probability of maximum-rate regulation by the Federal Reserve Board.

6. The exceedingly short-term character of Federal funds, and

---

[38] Bank for International Settlements, *Thirty-Sixth Annual Rport*, June 1966, p. 150.

For more comprehensive treatments of the Eurodollar market, see G. Carroll Martenson, *The Euro-Dollar Market* (Boston: Bankers Publishing Co., 1964); Norris O. Johnson, *Eurodollars in the New International Money Market* (New York: First National City Bank, 1964); Bankers Trust Company, *The Euro-Dollar Market*, 1964; Ernest Bloch, "Eurodollars: An Emerging International Money Market," New York University, *The Bulletin*, No. 39, April 1966; Paul Einzig, *The Euro-Dollar System* (New York: St. Martin's Press, 1964).

[39] This generalization is subject to the qualification that issuance of CD's involves a shift from demand to time deposits and therefore releases required legal reserves.

their scarcity during boom conditions, largely restrict their employment to day-to-day, week-to-week, and seasonal adjustments of a bank's liquidity position.

7. Borrowing at the Federal Reserve has traditionally been reserved by law and policy for short-term and emergency purposes.

8. Rate regulation largely eliminates the sale of short-term notes as a dependable source of cyclical liquidity.

9. Common stock or capital notes may represent a source of cyclical liquidity if they are sold before the last phase of a cyclical expansion. The markets for both bank stock and capital notes are usually depressed during boom conditions by the sharp rise of interest rates. In view of the general reluctance of banks to sell additional common stock, the issuance of capital notes has a materially larger potential for this purpose.

10. The Eurodollar market merits a limited place in the cyclical liquidity program of a large money-market bank.

If the management of bank liabilities can make only a limited contribution to cyclical liquidity, by what methods can a bank provide for this essential need? Briefly, the answer lies in the management of asset liquidity. This may involve some loss of current income during the greater part of a cyclical expansion, but it is likely to avoid a far greater capital loss during the last phase of expansion. The essence of asset-liquidity management is to equate the probable earlier loss of income with the subsequent probable capital loss, taxes considered.

G. WALTER WOODWORTH

THE
FEDERAL-FUNDS
MARKET

12

The Federal-funds market is a distinctive outgrowth of both the central banking system and the unit banking system of the United States. With about 13,500 commercial banks in operation, there is real need for adequate markets and other facilities for efficient administration of liquid assets. The Federal-funds market provides part of this mechanism, along with short-term Treasury securities, bankers' acceptances, commercial paper, and borrowing at Federal Reserve Banks. In essence this market is in Reserve Bank deposits which are lent and borrowed, mainly overnight by large banks, at a specified rate of interest.

The market originated among major New York City banks in 1921 to satisfy a definite need. Some banks held sizable excess reserves while others were borrowing reserves from the Reserve Banks at between 5 and 7 percent. At the same time attractive lending and investing opportunities were not readily available. Under these circumstances the banks with excess reserves began lending them overnight to those with reserve deficiencies at rates below the Reserve Bank discount rate. This market developed rapidly in New York City and spread to other leading cities on a limited scale as the decade progressed. During 1925–1930, daily average volume of transactions ranged between $100 million and $250 million.[1] The market all but disappeared during the 1930s and 1940s, due to the presence of large excess reserves during the 1930s, and to continuation of abnormal liquidity during and following World War II. Revival of the Federal-funds market was an integral part of the new financial epoch ushered in by the Treasury-Federal Reserve Accord in the spring of 1951. From that point on Federal Reserve authorities tightened the rein on bank liquidity until many banks encountered temporary reserve deficiencies. This was an environment once again in which the Federal-funds market could breathe and grow.

Reprinted by permission of Harper & Row, Publishers, from G. Walter Woodworth, "The Federal-Funds Market," *The Money Market and Monetary Management*, pp. 52–65. Copyright © 1965 by G. Walter Woodworth.

[1] Board of Governors of the Federal Reserve System, *The Federal Funds Market* (Washington, D.C. 1959) p. 33.

NATURE OF FEDERAL FUNDS

Federal funds is a shorthand term for Federal Reserve Bank funds, or more precisely, for legal reserve balances of member banks on deposit with Federal Reserve Banks. Total legal reserve balances are composed chiefly of *required* reserves but a small part—between 3 and 4 percent—consists of *excess* reserves; that is, of reserves over and above requirements. For example in May, 1963 total reserve balances with Reserve Banks averaged $16.8 billion, of which $.5 billion were excess reserve.[2] It is the fund of excess reserves that constitutes the "stock in trade" of the Federal-funds market; required reserves are not free for trading but are in a sense frozen assets of member banks. In reality the stock in trade of the market is only a fractional part of total excess reserves, since most of them are held by relatively small banks throughout the nation. Referring again to May, 1963, only $86 million of excess reserves were in the hands of reserve city banks; the remaining $372 million were owned by banks in the "country" classification. Therefore, it is unlikely that the active stock in trade of Federal funds at that time exceeded $100 to $150 million. The remaining $300 to $350 million were probably beyond the practical reach of borrowers of Federal funds. They were owned by small banks where the tapping process would be either too costly or impossible.

The active stock in trade of Federal funds, say an average of $200 million in recent years, possesses attributes that elevate it to a key position at the heart of the money market. As the highest form of member-bank reserve money, Federal funds are somtimes referred to as the "cashiest cash." They are unsurpassed as a safe instrument for immediate payment throughout the country. When payment is required at once the Federal Reserve wire transfer system may be utilized to shift funds between debtors and creditors. When haste is not imperative, payments may take the form of checks drawn on Federal Reserve Banks. In any case creditors—whether they be banks, bond dealers, business corporations, or others—regard Federal funds as a preferred means of payment. Indeed, the advantages are such that important types of creditors, notably sellers of short-term Treasury securities, insist on settlement in Federal funds. The principal reason is to avoid loss of interest income on large sums. Payment by checks on commercial banks, known as "clearing-house

[2] For the present purpose it is assumed that all excess reserves exist in the form of reserve balances. This assumption is not unrealistic since member banks typically minimize holdings of currency.

funds," involves loss of interest for at least one day, even within New York City or Chicago, since today's checks are presented for payment at tomorrow's clearing. Moreover, the loss of interest may be for two or more days if the drawee bank is located in a distant city.

While Federal funds have increasingly been utilized for settlement of transactions in the money and capital markets, the great bulk of trading takes place among leading money-market banks. These institutions exercise great care, on the one hand, to avoid the penalty of deficient legal reserves, and on the other, to prevent loss of income on excess reserves. The Federal-funds market provides the most flexible and convenient facility for banks with excess reserves to lend them for a day at current rates to others whose reserves are temporarily deficient.

Up to this point, trading in Federal funds has been designated as lending and borrowing—terms which are accurately descriptive and doubtless most meaningful to the layman. But henceforth we must bow to the prevailing terminology of the market place, where a lender is known as a "seller" and a borrower as a "buyer" of funds.

STRUCTURE OF THE MARKET

Despite the enormous amount and number of transactions, the Federal-funds market has no formal organization. There is no physical meeting place such as the New York Stock Exchange, and there is no dealer group that stands ready to buy and sell at bid and asked prices, as in the United States security market. Lenders and borrowers are brought together by: (1) Garvin, Bantel & Co., a large New York stock brokerage firm; (2) a few large money-market banks that act in part as dealers and in part as brokers and clearing centers of information; and (3) the network of correspondent bank relationships through which information on rates and on potential borrowers and lenders is transmitted. United States security dealers are also sources of information as well as important participators.

Each morning Garvin, Bantel & Co. receives reports by telephone and wire from banks all over the country in regard to bids and offers of funds. On the basis of these reports the firm quotes rates, and matches lenders and borrowers who, after being brought together, proceed with transactions on their own. Thus, the firm does not buy and sell funds for its own account, but acts only as a broker. No specific commission is ordinarily charged for these services, but the firm hopes to be reimbursed by other security business from customers. If the volume of security business is inadequate, a supplementary service charge is made.

A number of leading money-market banks, mainly in New York City, serve as dealers in Federal funds, in addition to providing brokerage and informational services. One large New York City bank makes a two-way market continuously. It buys funds from all banks in appropriate amounts but sells only to banks whose loan lines have been established. The other major banks provide less extensive dealer services but buy and sell funds beyond their own reserve needs as an accommodation to correspondent banks. In fact this service is largely undertaken as an aggressive method of building up correspondent banking business. The leading banks that engage in it are sometimes called "accommodating" banks as opposed to others, known as "adjusting" banks, that deal in Federal funds only to adjust their own reserve positions. One other large bank, Irving Trust Company, is distinctive in that it has a separate brokerage department which arranges for active trading in Federal funds outside its money position. The operations of this department, which has over 150 regular banking contacts, resembles that of Garvin, Bantel & Co.

Beyond the orbit of accommodating banks, the network of relationships in the correspondent banking system facilitates transactions in Federal funds. Adjusting banks in leading cities disseminate market information to others in their trading areas, so that buying and selling banks are brought together. The largest regional market exists in San Francisco which is the clearing center for West Coast banks. A considerable part of this activity arises from the time lag compared with New York City where the market closes only a couple of hours after trading begins on the West Coast. The second largest regional market is the midwest with its focus in Chicago. But these regional markets are small in comparison with New York City which is the hub of the nation-wide market. Approximately one-half of total bank transactions take place there, and a large part of trading outside New York is arranged by New York banks and brokers. In addition the bulk of trading in Federal funds by United States security dealers centers in New York City.

Some conception of the huge volume of trading in Federal funds is conveyed by the fact that average daily volume of transactions during 1955–1957 was estimated to have ranged between $.8 and $1.1 billion. On an annual basis volume was between $200 and

$300 billion. Participation was concentrated in a relatively small number of banks—between 125 and 200—and 12 of these accounted for half of total volume. In 'addition, there were 18 participating United States security and bankers' acceptance dealers.[3] A rough estimate of average annual· volume in the early 1960s is $400 billion,[4] or about two-thirds of gross national product. As would be expected in such a market, the unit of trading is large, typically $1 million. Most transactions are in multiples of $1 million. Transactions of less than $1 million are made on occasion as an accommodation to small correspondent banks but these would seldom be less than $200,000.

Reasons for Buying Federal Funds

Large commercial banks, which account for the great bulk of transactions, use this market to maintain close adjustments of their legal reserve positions. The nature of their business is such that they experience unpredictable changes of considerable size in reserve position from hour to hour and from day to day. These changes take place for a variety of reasons associated with changes in loans, investments, seasonal and other deposit movements, correspondent bank balances, Treasury operations, Federal Reserve operations, float, foreign bank deposits, currency movements, and other factors. While large banks are permitted to meet legal reserve requirements on an average basis over their weekly settlement period, most of them follow the practice of running a moderate cumulative deficiency, but with rather close daily reserve adjustments. This avoids the possible embarrassment from encountering a sizable deficiency or investing a large surplus on the last settlement day (Wednesday). Consequently, even though reserve adjustment transactions reach a peak on Wednesday, they are in large measure spread throughout the week.

When a bank faces a reserve deficiency, it may make adjustment by deciding to (1) sell Treasury bills and other short-term secondary reserves; (2) borrow from the Reserve Bank; (3) buy Federal funds; (4) sell longer-term investments; (5) call dealers' or brokers' loans; and (6) curtail new loans. If the deficiency is diagnosed as temporary, the practical alternatives are usually limited to the first

[3] Board of Governors of the Federal Reserve System, *op. cit.*
[4] This estimate is in line with a Federal Reserve survey which found average daily purchases of Federal funds in November, 1960 to be $1.5 billion—an annual rate of $390 billion. See Federal Reserve Bank of San Francisco, "The Role of Twelfth District Banks in the Federal Funds Market," *Monthly Review*, June 1961, p. 108.

three, and many banks choose to buy Federal funds. Most of them are somewhat reluctant to borrow at the Reserve Bank, especially if they have been continuously in debt for several weeks. Moreover, even though they have not recently borrowed, they may prefer to save Reserve Bank borrowing for possible emergencies. Therefore, when Federal funds are available at a rate equal to or below the discount rate, most banks with reserve deficiencies buy them in preference to going to the Reserve Bank. However, this preference is not so firm that banks will pay more than the Reserve Bank discount rate for Federal funds, although this does occasionally happen.

There are several aspects to the choice between selling Treasury bills and buying Federal funds to repair a temporary reserve deficiency. The most important consideration is relative rates. When the rate on bills is $\frac{1}{2}$ percentage point or more below the cost of Federal funds most banks part with bills. But when the bill rate is equal to or higher, the typical procedure is to purchase funds which offer the advantages of freedom from interest rate risk and from the spread between bid and asked prices. Also, partly for these reasons, Federal funds provide a large measure of investment flexibility. For example assume that bills are sold instead of buying Federal funds when rates are the same; assume further that rates are lower the next day when excess reserves accumulate. Then in this event repurchase of bills could be executed only on a less favorable basis due to the lower rate and the dealer spread.

Reasons for Selling Federal Funds

On the other side, when a temporary surplus of bank reserves accumulates, the practical alternatives usually boil down to purchase of Treasury short-term securities, sale of Federal funds, or repayment of Reserve Bank borrowings. Most banks apply such a surplus to reduction of Reserve Bank borrowings, if they exist. In fact this step is often taken even though Treasury bill rates are higher than the discount rate. But when banks are free from debt to Reserve Banks, the choice narrows to bills versus Federal funds. The primary considerations in the decision are relative rates, risks, and flexibility of position. In meeting day-to-day adjustment, Federal funds are commonly superior on all three counts. While the yield on bills is sometimes higher, its average is appreciably below that on Federal funds. But even if the bill yield is somewhat higher, many banks still prefer Federal funds because of their freedom from interest rate risk and their greater flexibility. Bills are not well adapted to commitments for only a day or two in view of the dealer spread between bid and asked prices and the added risk that money rates may rise tomorrow or the next day. Such an unfavorable turn of events may, in case of the sale of bills by a bank to meet a reserve deficiency, reduce its net return well below the certain return on Federal funds. With these considerations in mind, most large banks sell Federal funds when temporary surplus reserves accumulate unless the rate is appreciably below rates on short-term United States securities.

Mechanics of Buying and Selling Federal Funds

While details of practice in buying and selling Federal funds vary flexibility to meet different circumstances, there are two principal methods of making these transactions: (1) straight one-day loans; and (2) repurchase agreements. Typical illustrations of each method follow in order to convey a more concrete understanding of operations.

As previously indicated, the Federal-funds market is principally an interbank affair. Banks account for between 80 and 90 percent of the total amount of transactions in the process of adjusting reserve positions from day to day, and even from hour to hour. Moreover, the predominant type of bank transaction is the straight, unsecured, one-day loan which may be illustrated, as follows: Assume that the First National Bank of Boston possesses $10 million of excess reserves which it wishes to sell in the Federal-funds market, and that the Cleveland Trust Company has at the same time a reserve deficiency of $10 million which it desires to repair by purchasing funds. Having been brought together by Garvin, Bantel & Co. or a large money-market bank, the two banks arrange a rate of 3 percent and other terms over the bank wire and confirm by telegraph or letter. The First National telephones the Federal Reserve Bank of Boston to make immediate transfer of $10 million from its reserve account to the reserve account of Cleveland Trust in the Federal Reserve Bank of Cleveland. The next day Cleveland Trust reverses the process by instructing the Federal Reserve Bank of Cleveland to transfer $10 million to the First National's reserve account at the Federal Reserve Bank of Boston. Since there is a charge for sending odd amounts by wire transfer, the interest for one day ($833.33) is settled by a check sent by mail. In the event that one bank has a balance with the other or that they have mutual balances, settlement of interest may conveniently be made by debiting or crediting the proper account.

While the great bulk of straight Federal-funds loans are unsecured, a small but significant part has been secured by short-term United States securities in recent years. Such loans are frequently used when New York City banks purchase Federal funds from smaller outside banks whose unsecured loan limit is 10 percent of capital and surplus. By a ruling of the Comptroller of the Currency in April, 1958, loans secured by United States securities with maturities of 18 months or less were exempted from the 10 percent limit. As a consequence the smaller banks, when secured, are often enabled to sell funds in large enough units to make purchases by money-market banks feasible. The securities are usually placed in custody in the trust department of the smaller bank's New York correspondent—often the fund-purchasing bank—and released the next day when the loan is repaid. Otherwise, the procedure is the same as for an unsecured loan. A new ruling of the Comptroller of the Currency on June 1, 1963 further liberalized restrictions on national bank transactions in Federal funds. Such transactions were interpreted to be sales and purchases, rather than lending and borrowing. As a consequence there is no longer a legal limit on the amount of unsecured sales (loans) of Federal funds. This should enable large city banks to be of much greater service to smaller national banks, since it is no longer necessary to secure purchases (borrowings) of Federal funds with United States securities. Also, the ruling means that the borrowing limit of a national bank of 100 percent of capital stock plus 50 percent of surplus no longer applied to Federal-funds transactions. The extent to which regulatory authorities will grant similar privileges to state-chartered banks remains to be seen, but it is likely that, in general, they will follow the Comptroller's lead.

The second principal method of buying and selling Federal funds is by repurchase agreements, or by a variant known as "buy-backs." The distinguishing feature of this method, as compared with straight loans, is that title to securities actually changes hands for the duration of the loan. The repurchase agreement may be illustrated as follows: Assume that the First National Bank of Kansas City has a $2 million reserve surplus which it desires to sell for a day and that the Irving Trust Company of New York wishes to purchase this amount; also assume that the Morgan Guaranty Trus Company is the New York City correspondent of First National. After reaching agreement on terms, First National sends $2 million by wire transfer to Morgan Guaranty and instructs the latter to pay this amount in Federal funds to Irving Trust upon receipt of securities which are to be held in custody. The agreement calls for sale of $2 million of United States securities by Irving Trust today and for repurchase from First National tomorrow at the same price plus interest at 3 percent. Accordingly on the next day Irving Trust draws a check on its Federal Reserve account for $2,000,166.67 payable to Morgan Guaranty, in return for which the securities are given back to Irving Trust. Thus, while the transaction takes the form of sale and repurchase of securities, in reality it is a loan of Federal funds for one day at the going rate.

In the foregoing illustration the operation would be known as a "buyback" if the agreement between Irving Trust and First National takes the form of two *separate* contracts: one covering the initial sale of securities by Irving Trust for Federal funds; the other providing for repurchase (and resale) on the next day. Buybacks are frequently used when discount-type securities, mainly Treasury bills, are sold and repurchased. One contract typically calls for sale at a given discount rate, e.g., 3 percent, with payment in Federal funds. The other contract provides for repurchase at the same rate of discount the next day. In this way the seller of Federal funds (initial buyer of securities) receives one day's interest at the agreed rate.

Repurchase agreements and buybacks are used extensively by non-bank United States security dealers in purchasing Federal funds from business corporations and smaller banks outside New York City. Large banks prefer the straight unsecured loan when possible, since this method avoids the considerable inconvenience and expense of handling and transferring title to securities. This disadvantage for money-market banks which predominantly engage in overnight transactions, loses much of its force for dealers who usually borrow for longer periods. Repurchase agreements also have the substantial advantages of eliminating credit risk for the seller of Federal funds, of removing the 10 percent loan limit of lending banks, and of enabling dealers to borrow up to market value of securities.

RATES ON FEDERAL FUNDS

Like other free-market prices, rates on Federal funds emerge from interaction of the forces of supply and demand, and tend toward a level at which these forces are equated. Since Federal funds occupy a key position at the heart of the money market, their rate reflects most of all the broad forces that govern the market as a whole. Nevertheless, the analyst must bear in mind that the Federal-funds market is highly specialized, and therefore mirrors most closely the state of its particular sector. In the main this is the market for overnight loans of funds by large banks to adjust reserve positions.

Federal-fund rates are quoted from hour to hour by Garvin, Bantel & Co. and by a few large money-market banks that serve as dealers and brokers. Quotations are based on a continuous flow of information from all parts of the nation with respect to amounts offered and demanded at various rates. Quotations reported daily in the press include opening, high, low, and closing rates as given by Garvin, Bantel & Co. The Federal Reserve Bank of New York also publishes the so-called "effective" rate which is the most common one at which transactions take place.

Relation to Other Rates

The Federal-funds rate bears a close relationship to all rates in the money market, since all are basically influenced by common causes. Also as indicated, the focal position of Federal funds often establishes this rate as the most sensitive indicator of money-market conditions. However, the Federal-funds rate is most closely related to the Federal Reserve Bank discount rate and the rate on shortest-term Treasury securities. This follows from the fact that these rates are the prices of the principal competitive alternatives in the reserve adjustment processes of large banks.

As a rule the Federal Reserve Bank discount rate sets the upper limit of the Federal-funds rate. Only under exceptional circumstances will banks pay more for Federal funds than the cost of borrowing at the Reserve Bank. The most notable exception occurred in the late 1920s when many banks were so heavily committed to stock exchange security loans that their ability to borrow at the Reserve Bank was impaired or exhausted. As a consequence during the tight-money period of 1928 to 1929 the funds rate moved appreciably above the discount rate. Also, during the recent firm periods of 1956 to 1957 and 1959, a few transactions in Federal funds took place at rates above the discount rate. They doubtless represented borrowing by banks unable or unwilling to borrow from Reserve Banks, and borrowing by bond dealers to carry inventories of United States and other securities. But despite they occasional exceptions the Reserve Bank discount rate almost always sets the upper limit, and during firm money periods the effective fund rate is typically identical with the discount rate.

At the other extreme when substantial surplus bank reserves accumulate, the Federal-funds rate commonly drops well below the Reserve Bank discount rate to a minimal level of $\frac{1}{8}$ to $\frac{1}{4}$ percent. Such a low rate barely covers the cost of transactions, so that banks reach a point of indifference whether they hold or lend excess reserves. Under these circumstances borrowings at Reserve Banks become very small, since individual banks with reserve deficiencies can obtain reserves more cheaply by purchasing Federal funds, or by selling short-term Treasury securities. This situation prevailed most of the time between 1934 and 1951, and reappeared in the recessions of 1954 and 1958.

Between the two extremes and especially in the zone of moderate ease to moderate tightness, the Federal-funds rate fluctuates responsively from day to day and week to week. At times it bumps the ceiling of the discount rate and sometimes it rests on the floor established by transactions costs. On the average it is appreciably below the discount rate. Most of the period, 1960 to 1964, fits this pattern.

Comparison of the shortest Treasury bill rate with the Federal-funds rate reveals a reasonably close competitive relationship. They usually rise and fall together except during tight conditions when the funds rate is at its ceiling. However, both rates exhibit individuality as reflected by independent movements. While bills are not a perfect substitute for Federal funds for reasons previously indicated, there is a definite tendency for banks to purchase bills when their rates are above Federal-fund rates. Such decisions of course have the equalizing effect of lowering bill rates and raising fund rates. Conversely, there is a disposition to sell Federal funds in preference to buying bills when fund rates are relatively high, again with an equalizing influence. The lower average rate on bills may be explained by the facts that bills are free from credit risk, enjoy world-wide investor familiarity, are legal investments for various purposes, and are more readily available to many investors. Independent variations in the two rates are to be excepted in view of different features of the instruments, individual conditions of supply and demand, and lack of perfect substitution. For example Treasury debt management policy may substantially increase or decrease the amount of bills outstanding. Or such factors as changes in Federal Reserve Bank holdings of securities, float, currency outside banks, and gold stock may materially increase or decrease the volume and distribution of excess reserves of banks.

Effects on the Money Market

The principal effect of the Federal-funds market is its contribution to efficient utilization of excess reserves in the banking system. This effect has several facets, including: (1) prompt transmission of Federal Reserve policies and operations throughout the country; (2) reduction of direct dependence of member banks on Reserve Bank borrowing as a method of repairing reserve deficiencies; (3) reduction of aggregate member-bank reserve balances; and (4) increase of earning power of commercial banks and bond dealers.

With some 13,500 commercial banks in the nation, most of them small, mobility of reserves is far from perfect. Pools of excess reserves accumulate in small- and medium-size banks, so that even in the presence of substantial member-bank borrowing at Reserve Banks, a hard core of $400 to $500 million in excess reserves exists. This amount would be much larger in the absence of Federal Reserve transfer facilities, the United States security market, the Federal-funds market, and other divisions of the money market which promote mobility. From the standpoint of effective monetary regulation, it is highly important that the effects of Federal Reserve open-market operations and other monetary actions be transmitted quickly throughout the country. The Federal-funds market tangibly contributes to effective monetary regulation by providing a ready facility for redistribution of bank reserves.

Closely associated with enhanced nation-wide mobility of bank reserves is their more efficient utilization, as excess reserves find their way through the Federal-fund market to banks with defficiencies. This has the effect of reducing member-bank dependence on Reserve Bank borrowing, since banks in need of reserves can more readily locate and borrow excess reserves. Another allied effect of the Federal-funds market is significant reduction in total member-bank reserve balances, and of aggregate Reserve Bank credit. This follows from the fact that less total reserve is needed to support the amount of money and the level of money rates that Federal Reserve authorities regard to be consistent with basic objectives.

Still a further incidental influence of the Federal-funds market is an increase in net earnings of banks and bond dealers. The market enables banks to maximize income from liquid assets by minimizing holdings of excess reserves. It also reduces expenses at times by reducing costs of borrowed reserves, and by avoiding penalties on reserve deficiencies. Bond dealers enjoy larger earnings as a result of increases in sales made possible by greater credit availability to carry more adequate inventories. In addition the funds market often enables dealers to reduce costs of borrowing.

POSTWAR PATTERN OF GROWTH

Analysis of postwar activity in Federal funds reveals both in a strong trend of growth and considerable cyclical variation. Several factors are responsible for this pattern of change.

Trend of the Market

A recent Federal Reserve study of the Federal-funds market finds that average daily volume of transactions more than doubled between the periods 1950–53 and 1955–57, from $350–$450 million to $800–$1,100 million.[5] This strong growth trend has since continued but at a considerably slower rate. While exact figures are not available, informed estimates place average daily volume during 1962 to 1964 in the vicinity of $1.5 billion, or an annual volume of $400 billion. Several factors have been responsible for this vigorous uptrend, the most important of which are the following: (1) A material expansion in the dollar size of the economy, as measured by gross national product, has taken place. Hence a considerable part of growth in funds transactions represents merely keeping pace with GNP. (2) Bank management has become increasingly sophisticated with respect to careful administration of liquid assets. This is in part a consequence of growing concentration in banking through mergers, branching, and holding companies; it is also a result of improved management techniques though education. (3) A marked increase in volume of trading in United States securities has taken place. This is associated with the increase in marketable federal debt, and particularly with the rapid expansion of short-term Treasury securities in which trading chiefly occurs. Settlement is largely made in Federal funds. (4) The practice of making settlements and payments in Federal funds has developed rapidly in New York City in recent years. Large creditors actively bargain for payment in such funds, rather than in clearing-house funds, in order to avoid loss of one day's interest. (5) The sizable increase in Reserve Bank float beginning in 1951 led to wider variations in day-to-day reserve positions of member banks with a consequent greater need for liquidity adjustments through Federal funds or otherwise. Float was increased when the maximum period before credit was given for checks in process of collection was reduced from three days to two days after receipt by a Reserve Bank. (6) Growth of the funds market has been promoted by improvements in trading facilities. A few large banks have assumed dealer functions in addition to serving as brokers and information centers. Also, more complete middleman services have been provided by Garvin, Bantel & Co., and improvements have been made in the Federal Reserve wire transfer system. Partly as a consequence, nonfinancial corporations and a layer of

[5] Board of Governors of the Federal Reserve System, *op. cit.*

medium-size banks have become important suppliers of Federal funds.

In addition to the foregoing factors, the Federal-funds market has expanded to fill a void in the money market created by reform legislation of the early 1930s which prohibited interest payments on demand deposits, and severely restricted call loans secured by stocks. The result was elimination of two of the principal methods by which banks previously adjusted reserve positions, i.e., by increasing or decreasing balances with correspondent banks, and by making and calling brokers' loans. Short-term Treasury securities do not fill this void in view of price changes and the spread between bid and asked prices. But Federal-fund purchases and sales do fill the gap in part by enabling banks and others to lend or borrow for a day at a specified rate and with no risk of price changes.

Cyclical Variations in Transactions

The volume of trading in Federal funds exhibits a fairly definite cyclical pattern. Cyclical bulges occur during periods of average to moderately easy-money conditions, such as 1954, 1958, and 1960–1961. On the supply side, a medium-size fund of mobile excess reserves becomes available and therefore for sale. On the demand side, sufficient credit stringencies exist in particular areas and banks to cause substantial needs for borrowed reserves. Also, credit demands of United States security dealers and of other bond dealers are usually high in view of favorable markets.

Cyclical troughs in fund transactions develop under extremely tight credit conditions, such as 1953, 1957, and 1959, and under extremely easy conditions, such as 1934 to 1940. When credit stringencies develop, the fund of mobile excess reserves shrinks so much that Federal funds are available, if at all, only in small amounts. Thus, even though demand for them is larger than usual, the amount of transactions materially declines. Under conditions of extreme credit ease trading volume also drops, but for quite different reasons. An abundance of mobile excess reserves exists so that Federal funds are readily available at very low rates. However, on the demand side few banks encounter even day-to-day reserve deficiencies, so that little need for borrowed reserves exists. These conditions characterized the entire period, 1934 to 1947.[6]

---

[6] In preparing this chapter the author has drawn heavily upon the comprehensive research study: Board of Governors of the Federal Reserve System, *The Federal Funds Market* (Washington, D.C., 1959).

IMPACT OF CREDIT
CARDS ON
COMMERCIAL BANKS

13

Bank credit cards have attracted more public attention than any other recent development in banking. They have become the center of much controversy. Some regard credit cards as an inappropriate activity for commercial banks and anticipate difficulties for consumers, the card issuing banks, and the entire financial system. Others see the card as the key to the future of banking. Credit card plans are thought to represent the first step on the long road to the checkless society—that promised land of instant money.

What impact have credit cards had on banks? Are they profitable? How do losses compare with those in other instalment loan programs? What are the implications of this new type of banking? To answer these and similar questions, an in-depth study was undertaken in 1967 of credit card operations in eight large commercial banks located in different areas of the country. The major findings of this study were subsequently confirmed by a nationwide Federal Reserve System survey made in the fall of 1967.

In the study of eight banks, three were early entries in the credit card field—one in 1953 and the other two in 1958–59. The remaining five banks started their plans in 1965 or 1966. The study revealed that the early plans are profitable today after incurring losses in earlier years. As expected, the credit card plans of the more recent entrants did not cover incremental costs in the first 2 years of operation. Credit quality of cardholders compares favorably with that of borrowers accepted for other types of consumer loans. The sample banks expect that the future development of credit card banking will have widespread effects on retail bank management. They anticipate that credit card outstandings will absorb much more of a bank's retail loan resources—probably at the expense of other instalment lending. In short, credit cards are viewed as an important vehicle for enabling banks to become lenders to individuals making retail purchases, rather than remaining secondary lenders through finance companies and department stores. While the sample banks

Reprinted from "Impact of Credit Cards on Commercial Banks," *New England Business Review* (August 1968), pp. 3–10, Federal Reserve Bank of Boston.

were all large with over $100 million in deposits, the growing availability of bank plans through correspondents, franchise arrangements, and nonprofit corporations suggests that size should not be a barrier to entry into credit card banking.

GROWTH OF BANK CREDIT CARDS

Credit cards for consumer purchases are hardly new. Major oil companies and large department stores have used them for handling credit sales since the ealy 1900's. After World War II an added impetus to the charge system arose from the development of the national travel and entertainment cards, such as Diners Club, Carte Blanche and American Express.

Some banks became interested in credit cards in the early 1950's. Over 60 plans were in operation at the beginning of 1953. Most, however, found the plans less profitable than anticipated and discontinued them. But at the end of the decade, a few large banks showed new interest and implemented credit card plans. Not until 1966 did a significant number of banks begin to enter the field.

According to the latest Federal Reserve System survey, 197 banks across the country are at present offering credit card plans. This number does not include banks that operate as local agents of large city correspondents. Almost two-thirds of the credit card banks entered the field in 1966. As of October 1967, total credit outstanding under credit card plans amounted to $640 million, a little less than 2 percent of total consumer instalment credit held by commercial banks.

CHARACTERISTICS OF CREDIT CARD PLAN AS A
NEW BANKING SERVICE

Credit card plans are differentiated from traditional banking services by three specific features. First, the credit card opens up a new relationship between the bank and the retail merchant. Prior to the credit card, banks were leery of lending to merchants against retail accounts receivable. It was considered a risky business. The bulk of the bank's business with the merchant had been in financing of large or big ticket items, while financing the accounts receivable was largely on an indirect basis. Now when a merchant agrees to honor a bank credit card, he must open an account at the bank if he does not already have one. With the deposit of his sales slips, he receives immediate credit (less a discount) in his bank deposit. Thus the bank takes over the financing of the merchant's accounts receivable. The bank issuing the credit card may obtain a new demand deposit account or increase balances maintained in existing accounts. In addition, the contact with the merchant through the bank credit card provides an opportunity for increased marketing of other bank services to both old and new retail customers. By the end of September 1967, 424,000 merchants had declared their intention of honoring bank credit cards. Most, however, tended to be concentrated in a few areas, with about half on the West Coast and another fourth in the Chicago area.

A second differentiating characteristic of credit card banking is the extension to individuals of a revolving line of credit without collateral. While the revolving credit aspects of the bank card are similar to the bank's traditional instalment lending activities, banks have discovered that the credit card is highly attractive to customers. Customers view the card as a convenient method of handling uneven expenditure patterns and of borrowing for emergencies. From the bank's standpoint, the revolving credit aspect becomes attractive because it provides an opportunity to increase its instalment loans and to handle small consumer loans more efficiently and profitably. Moreover, it offers an opportunity to tap new consumer markets. No prior banking relationship is necessary, a feature especially important to banks in states where branching is limited or prohibited entirely. As with the merchant, the possibilities of extending the market for other bank services is a key feature of the credit card.

The third distinguishing characteristic of bank credit card plans is that they represent a step in the direction of an electronic money transfer system. Most bankers believe that the future will bring about major changes in banking practices due to automation of the payments mechanism. The credit card operation is viewed as a method of providing the bank experience with the methods and equipment which will be used in tomorrow's banking. In addition, credit cards familiarize the bank and the cardholder with an automatic transfer system and with the use of a card for consumer identification. Thus, the desire to keep abreast of developments that may ultimately lead to the establishment of an electronic money transfer system has been one motivation in the development of bank credit card plans.

CARDHOLDER DISTRIBUTION POLICIES

Two major approaches were used by the sample banks to establish their cardholder groups. Most used mass mailing of credit cards; one provided credit cards only to selected customers of the merchants.

All the banks felt that competitive conditions at the present time made it essential to launch a plan with a mass issue of cards to establish a potential share of the market. The one sample bank which did not pursue this course first issued cards in 1953 when the threat of competition was insignificant. Moreover, to establish a profitable base of operations, the banks typically needed a large number of cardholders with high sales volume and outstandings to cover their operating expenses.

The mass issue banks used their own customer lists to provide names for sending out credit cards. The major criteria for an acceptable credit risk were the absence of any negative information, and evidence of a satisfactory balance in a checking or savings account. Other sources of names were such upper income groups as members of professions and country clubs, names provided by member merchants, and credit bureau lists. This last category, however, was generally regarded as less dependable and was used least. Because of the expense, the difficulties, and the time needed, detailed credit investigations of individuals were not usually made before the mass mailing.

MANAGEMENT OF CREDIT CARD PLANS

All the sample banks established new and separate organizations for the administration of their credit card programs. Most banks appointed plan managers who showed evidence of general management and promotional ability. Several banks suggested that the credit card field had to develop its own specialists because the average banker was not geared to credit card operating policies. The president of one bank put it this way:

> We started with a banker, but a banker doesn't know what he's doing in this area, and he isn't any good at it. A banker's approach is "pay us." This is no good because you have to have a retail merchant's approach, which is "come back to the store." To be successful, we feel very strongly, that you have to have a retail credit man from a retail store.

Interestingly, most of the banks felt strongly that credit card operations should be separated from their instalment loan departments. Even a bank instalment lending background was regarded as undesirable for officers associated with credit card departments. The consensus was that the traditional instalment lending practices would adversely affect the growth of credit card outstandings. Personnel trained in instalment lending would tend to be too strict in approving credits and in following up delinquent accounts. For these reasons, the banks felt it was desirable to establish a separate credit card group that would promote the development of the credit card actively. Still another consideration in setting up an independent department was that income and expenditures related to credit cards could be easily identified for accounting purposes.

CHARACTERISTICS OF CARDHOLDERS

Based on data from a few sample banks, the typical regular card user emerges as either a man or a woman in a family that earns between $5,000 and $10,000 a year, is between 25 and 55 years old, and has had a high school education or more. Even if grade-school educated persons held credit cards, they were much less likely to use their cards than those with more schooling. Most regular card users were white collar workers in professional, managerial, or sales and clerical occupations. Thus it appears that the bank credit card has had its greatest impact on a broad group of lower-middle income families in the age group where expenditures are at their peak, payment habits more flexible, and personal background indicating capacity for responsible borrowing behavior.

How often do cardholders actually use their cards? A comparison of cardholder usage experience in early and late entry banks shows that usage ratios tend to rise steadily over the first few years of a plan until they reach a plateau. By the fifth year between a third and a half of the outstanding accounts are active each month. The data also shows that each plan tends to develop a small group of regular users. These cardholders, representing less than 30 percent of the total accounts, tend to establish regular usage patterns early in their association with the plan.

These figures are similar to those reported in the Federal Reserve System survey. At the end of September 1967, the total number of credit card accounts was more than 14 million, but only about one-third were considered active. Moreover, they used, on the average, only about 12 percent of the authorized lines of credit.

CREDIT CARD PRICING POLICIES

The most important sources of revenue for the credit card plans were the interest charges paid by cardholders on balances outstanding in excess of 30 days and the discount paid by merchants on all credit card sales. The interest rates set by the sample banks were typically the maximums allowed by state laws and ranged between 1 and 1.5 percent a month. These figures were corroborated by the results of the nationwide Federal Reserve System survey of all credit card banks last fall which showed that as of September 1967 almost four-fifths of the credit card banks charged 1.5 percent.

In addition to the interest charge, the cardholder is also required to repay part of his outstanding balance each month. Most banks started out requiring $10 or 10 percent of the balance, whichever was higher, but under pressure to attract cardholders and generate outstandings, two banks later dropped their repayment terms to $10 or 5 percent of the balance, whichever was higher.

In contrast to the relative uniformity of cardholder charges, the sample banks showed considerable variation in their merchant discount rates, both in different banking markets and in methods used. The most common rates paid by member merchants were between 3.6 and 4.5 percent. The maximum charged by most banks was 6 percent, but one bank had a maximum merchant discount of only 3 percent. Three banks in the sample established separate rates for each type of business, volume of sales, and average size of ticket. The higher the size of the average purchase and the merchant's volume, the lower the assigned rate. For example, shoe stores as a category might be charged 4 percent while furniture stores could justify a rate of 3.25 percent. Some banks deducted the maximum from the deposited sales slips daily and then gave the merchants a quarterly rebate based on their average sales volume. One bank used an end of the month merchant settlement system based on average ticket size without daily discount deductions. One bank in a state where branching is prohibited split its discounts with correspondent banks in return for their aid in enrolling merchants. The wide diversity of merchant discount rates was also evident in the Federal Reserve System survey where rates ranged from a low of .5 to a high of 8 percent, with the average about 3.5 percent.

For most credit card plans in the sample banks, the largest source of income in 1966 was service charges paid by cardholders, accounting for 54 to 66 percent of total revenue. These charges generally tended to increase in importance as a source of credit card revenue over the life of the plan. Conversely, merchant discounts which provided between one-third and one-half of credit card revenue had generally declined in importance as a source of revenue.

FINANCIAL ANALYSIS

In general, the study showed that the proportion of bank loan funds absorbed by credit card plans has been minor. The largest percentage of loan resources used by credit card outstandings was 6 percent in the bank with the oldest plan studied. The majority of credit card plans had taken less than 2 percent of the issuing banks' total loan portfolio. Even when measured as a proportion of consumer instalment loans, credit card outstandings were small. In the nationwide survey of the Federal Reserve System, credit cards accounted for 7.4 percent of the instalment portfolio of credit card banks.

In analyzing the profit yield of credit cards, net operating profit—defined in this study as the difference between total revenue and direct costs—was measured as a percent of average outstandings. On that basis, the three older plans were currently profitable after losses in earlier years. Two plans with 12 percent net operating profit in 1966 were twice as profitable as the third plan. Data were not available to measure profit on a more sophisticated basis net of administrative overhead cost and the cost of money. As a result the profit performance of these plans could not be compared with the return on other loans in the bank portfolio. All the early entrants, however, regarded the credit card as important for long-term growth and as a valuable, although relatively small, contributor to the bank's earnings at the present time.

None of these credit plans had a positive net operating profit for its first or second year of activity. Typically, however, the banks expected some monthly profits toward the end of this period. In general, this profitability picture was corroborated by the Federal Reserve System's survey. That study suggests that after the initial start-up period, credit cards normally produce yields comparable with—if not higher than—those of other instalment lending operations in the bank. Moreover, to the extent that credit cards increase the sales of other bank services, even higher profits will be generated. It is also interesting to note that a number of small bank plans are very successful.

RELATIONS WITH CORRESPONDENT BANKS

The sample banks' credit card relations with their correspondents depended in part on the state branching laws. Two banks located in states permitting statewide branching had no credit card affiliations with correspondents because they believed their own branch systems gave them adequate access to the credit card market. The other six banks located in states that had limited branching or prohibited it entirely either had or were planning correspondent credit card policies. The effects of correspondent relationships were most significant in the states where branching was prohibited.

There 90 percent of the credit cards outstanding were issued through correspondents. One important implication for the future in such states is that if the major unit banks can achieve a fair share of retail borrowing through correspondent credit card outlets, their desire for new branches may be diminished.

Business terms for correspondent relationships varied somewhat. Because correspondents of the big city banks typically lacked the resources and the willingness to risk investment in cardholder balances, the arrangements usually provided that the major bank did most of the processing work, retained control over policy and received the bulk of the revenue. More "sweeteners" in the form of larger shares of merchant discounts and the specific identification of the correspondent bank were added in markets where it was necessary to attract correspondent cooperation.

INTERCHANGE SYSTEMS

To expand the acceptability of credit cards beyond local areas accessible to a particular bank, several interchange systems have been developed. Of the eight sample banks, six had joined one of three major interchange systems, thus effecting a new type of structural relationship. The development of national interchange systems is still in its early stages, however, and the volume and income effects of such interchanges on interstate banking relations are not yet significant.

Although every sample bank was in favor of some arrangement to make credit cards acceptable on a national and possibly an international basis, many problems remain to be solved. One difficulty is the distribution of revenue on interchange transactions. Because rates charged to merchants are not uniform, conceivably merchants might take advantage of lower charges and move their paper away from a local bank, although this is prohibited in some plans.

Another and more difficult problem is the relationship between the existing interchange systems. One of these, Bank Americard, grants franchises to its participants and receives royalties from them. Some arrangement would probably be necessary so that franchisee banks did not pay dual fees to a central association in addition to Bank Americard, if a single interchange system were established. Moreover, the antitrust legal issues of such a system would have to be clarified. To achieve a workable national interchange plan, the rates charged would probably have to be uniform thereby eliminating some competition among credit card systems. However, banks could still compete in signing up cardholders and merchants.

On the operational side, the most basic problem is the need for a system to clear merchant sales slips between member banks. Two main approaches could be considered. One might involve a series of clearing points set up by the member banks at central locations across the country. Another possibility might be the use of the Federal Reserve System's check clearing system. A step in this direction was indicated by the Fed's recent agreement to issue check transit numbers for credit cards. Standardized sales slips with special encoding would have to be developed to allow high speed handling. Finally, other problems such as auditing and fraud control would also have to be solved.

Still another important problem that may impede the overall growth of the credit card is the reluctance of large department stores to use them. So far these stores have found it profitable to conduct their own credit departments and are consequently unwilling to turn these operations over to banks.

BLUE SKY DEPARTMENT

If the credit card does succeed in becoming widely accepted, and if all the interchange problems can be ironed out so that a single national interchange system can be established, the nature of our banks and banking services could change considerably. The bank credit card might become the individual's principal financial instrument and means of identification. Most commercial banks would issue credit cards under these plans which would have five principal functions:

1. to obtain cash, either from banks or member merchants.
2. to purchase goods and services. Almost all retail establishments such as large department stores and supermarkets might participate. Also professional groups such as doctors, lawyers, dentists, and accountants might accept credit cards.
3. for automatic (pre-authorized) payment of regular bills, such as utilities, rent, and insurance.
4. as a consolidating point for all consumer lending. Larger loans including those for automobiles and home improvements might be included.
5. as a source of accounting information including the individual's checking account, transfers to savings accounts, etc.

These changes would have profound effects on retail stores. They will no longer need credit and collection departments. Thus, most of their bookkeeping functions will be taken over by banks, which will also provide sales analyses, inventory control data, payroll, and cash flow information.

The banks' economic relationships with cardholders and member merchants would also undergo changes. In general, the banks would pay customers for deposits and charge for loans and services. Merchants would pay a transaction fee based on the estimated cost of bookkeeping services and the value of money advanced by the bank.

CONCLUSION

Most of the sample banks believed that existing bank credit card programs are an interim and useful phase in the evolution of retail banking. They felt that credit cards could be used to prepare cardholders, retailers, and their own organizations for the implementation of an automated payment system in which checks would be used much less frequently than they are at present. Before such a system could begin to operate, the consumer has to become accustomed to substitute some form of money card for traditional payment practices. They felt that most commercial banks would issue credit cards to be in the strongest position to benefit from the funds transfer technology.

Although at present the total volume of credit card outstandings continues to be small as compared with other types of loans, credit card plans have produced important innovations in retail banking. These are primarily the new relationship between the bank and the retail merchant, the pre-approved revolving lines of credit, and a step toward an electronic money transfer system. On addition, these plans have been responsible for creating new methods for competition and developing new relationships between large city banks and their smaller correspondents.

INSTRUMENTS
OF MONETARY
MANAGEMENT

PART III

How exactly does the government attempt to control the supply of money and credit in the United States economy? Specifically, what are the tools that the Federal Reserve uses, and how do they work to restrict banking activities and, therefore, the level of the money stock in the hands of the public? Answers to these questions and an insight into the mechanics and environment of monetary policymaking are the major concerns of the articles in Part III. A complete analysis of the performance and objectives of monetary policy is provided by the articles in Part IV.

Horsefield's article introduces this section. It not only seeks an answer to the question posed in its title—an answer based on a general survey of central bank methods—but also indicates some of the major innovations in central banking. By way of introduction to the instruments of monetary policy, the Hastings and Robertson article provides an inside look at the sources of control within the system. The "Mysterious World of the Fed" describes a somewhat different structure of power than might seem to exist. Smith's article on the instruments of monetary management portrays the methods of coordination and the effects of all the major policy tools of monetary control. In addition, Smith appraises several recent proposals for reform of the existing manner in which these instruments are used by the Federal Reserve.

The article by the Federal Reserve Bank of Cleveland examines the market in which open-market operations are conducted and the strategy used by the Federal Reserve in conducting these operations. The manner in which the government securities market is operated by relatively few dealers is intriguing, but, more importantly, it gives a clear picture of the direct and indirect effects of open-market operations.

The last two articles in this part deal specifically with an instrument of policy which, until quite recently, has been largely ignored—Federal Reserve discount policy. Chandler not only explores the intricacies of changes in discount policy but also examines the importance of the privilege of banks' borrowing from the Federal Reserve as a source of liquidity. The last part of Chandler's presentation briefly appraises a few of the recent proposals for changing discount policy. This reappraisal of the discount policy is expanded in the last selection of this part, which is the statement of Mitchell (a member of the Board of Governors) before the Joint Economic Committee of Congress. This statement includes an explanation of the recommendations of a special Federal Reserve study reappraising the discount mechanism.

J. KEITH HORSEFIELD

WHY A CENTRAL BANK?

14

Why are central banks regarded as so indispensable? There are very few countries today that do not have a central bank—meaning a bank which deals less with private customers (if it has any at all) than with the government and the rest of the banking system. Most of the countries that do not have a central bank of their own share one with neighboring countries—as do, for example, the French-speaking West African countries that jointly own the Banque Centrale des Etats de l'Afrique de l'Ouest, and the second group that owns the Banque Centrale des Etats de l'Afrique Equatoriale et du Cameroun.[1] Furthermore, of the few countries that have neither a central bank of their own nor a share in one, almost all have joint currency authorities, which amount almost to the same thing.[2]

One curious feature about all this is that central banks are a relatively recent development. Like electric power and the automobile, they are to a large extent products of the twentieth century. Other kinds of banks have, of course, a much longer history. There have been state banks in existence for well over a thousand years, and some banks now functioning have records reaching back 300 years or so. But it was considerably less than 100 years ago that people began to have any clear idea of the work of a central banker, and even since 1930 there have been quite marked changes in the views of governments about what they should be doing.

CENTRAL BANKING FUNCTIONS

Nowadays it is customary to describe a central bank as one that (1) acts as banker and fiscal agent for the government, (2) holds part of the commercial banks' reserves, (3) holds or manages the country's gold and foreign exchange reserves, (4) has a monopoly of the banknote issue, and (5) can regulate credit. (These responsibilities are listed here not in order of importance but in the order

Reprinted from J. Keith Horsefield, "Why a Central Bank?" *The Fund and Bank Review: Finance and Development*, Vol. II (September 1965), pp. 159–166, Washington, D.C.: International Monetary Fund.
[1] These arrangements were explained in *Finance and Development*, Vol. I, No. 2, pp. 84–88.
[2] See the description of the East African Currency Board in *Finance and Development*, Vol. I, No. 3, p. 187.

in which they came to be exercised as central banking grew up.) In practice, not all central banks exercise all five functions, but in combination they represent what might be thought to be the job of the ideal central bank.

Central banking in this sense—as an activity separate from ordinary commercial banking—is generally considered to have emerged first in England. When the Bank of England was created in 1694, however, no one thought that it would have even one of the five responsibilities listed above. Its banking powers were, indeed, quite subsidiary; its main purpose was to lend £1,200,000 to the Government. It differed from other banks of the time only in being much larger than most, and in having its capital in the form of a semi-permanent government debt rather than in the personal resources of its partners.

The first central banking job (as we now think of it) that came the Bank of England's way was to act as fiscal agent for the Government. The Bank's close relations with the Government on the one hand and the City of London on the other made it easy and convenient for the Government to use it, from about 1700 onward, to circulate Treasury bills (short-term government securities), and later to handle the government debt generally. This in turn added to the Bank's reputation for stability, and encouraged other bankers to keep deposits with it. Because the Bank came to realize that the deposits of other bankers were more volatile than private deposits, it began, early in the nineteenth century, to hold a larger reserve of gold, in proportion to its liabilities, than other banks did; and this led to its third function, that of holding the gold (and later the foreign exchange) reserves of the country as a whole.

The acquisition by the Bank of England of the monopoly of bank-note issue (the fourth function listed above) was in a sense the result of a misunderstanding. In the 1830's it was thought that by controlling the note issue it would be possible to avoid the recurrence of financial crises, but it was not understood at the time that similar crises could be produced by the credit policies of banks whose demand obligations assumed the shape of deposits. Accordingly, steps were taken to concentrate note issuing powers in the Bank of England—though the process was not complete even in England until 1912, and still does not apply to Scotland.

This brings us to the fifth, and obviously the most significant, function of a central bank—the control of credit. For a long time the Bank of England was reluctant to accept responsibility for exercising any control over the other financial institutions, but it gradually learned to use appropriately the powers that it possessed.

By the time of World War I, the idea that such control was the proper function of a central bank was widely advocated. In 1920 it led the International Financial Conference, convened by the League of Nations at Brussels, to urge that every country should set up a central bank.

CENTRAL BANKS AND GOVERNMENTS

At this stage, however, emphasis was being laid on the independence of central banks. It was thought, to put it crudely, that governments always tended to be extravagant, and that central banks were necessary to prevent this extravagance from creating inflation and thus leading to financial crashes. Such a development could be prevented, it was believed, by central banks putting a squeeze on commercial banks' lending, thus offsetting any expansion of the money supply created by government deficits.

Very often the stability at which central banks were expected to aim was visualized as stability of prices. It is important, however, that rather less thought was given to the possibility of a central bank's keeping prices from falling, except by the indirect process of preventing a boom which could not be maintained. To support prices would, in any case, be a much more difficult thing for them to do. It was possible to prevent commercial banks from lending when prices were rising, but in the opposite situation it was not possible to make them lend more (at least in industrial countries), if only because borrowers would be reluctant to borrow if prices were tending to fall.

It was natural, therefore, that the notion that the primary duty of the independent central bank was to prevent inflation should be challenged first in primary producing countries, where, between the wars, price declines were disastrous. The changing attitude became apparent in the statutes of newly created central banks in the 1920's and early 1930's. Thus, in 1924 the Act creating the Central Bank of China laid upon it the following duties: "to develop industry, to stabilize commerce, to render financial help to the public, and to encourage international trade"—all positive activities, rather than the negative job of acting as a brake. Similar ideas were generalized in the preamble to the Bank of Canada Act in 1934, which set out that the Bank "is established to regulate credit and currency in the best interests of the economic life of the nation." But it was in New Zealand in 1936 that the most clear-cut break with former views on the independence of the central bank was achieved. The Reserve Bank Amendment Act of that year declared that "It shall be the general function of the Reserve Bank, within the limits of its powers, to give effect to the monetary policy of the Government, as communicated to the Bank from time to time by the Minister of Finance."

CENTRAL BANKING TODAY

Since then the predominant view has been that a central bank has independent responsibilities for the management of credit in its country, and as advisor to the government, but that it must in the last resort conform to the government's general line of policy. Lord Norman, who was Governor of the Bank of England from 1920 to 1944, put it this way: the Bank, he said, had "the unique right to offer advice, and to press such advice even to the point of nagging; but always of course subject to the supreme authority of the Government." If, therefore, the government thinks that expansion is essential to the development of the country, and the central bank cannot persuade the government otherwise, the bank will be expected to help the expansion, not to fight it. This change of view was clearly marked by the nationalization of the Bank of France in 1945 and of the Bank of England in 1946—the latter by an Act which enabled the Treasury to give such directions to the Bank as it believed to be necessary in the public interest.

All this has become much more important as the influence of governments over economic affairs has broadened. A hundred years or so ago, budgets were so small in relation to national incomes that government surpluses or deficits had comparatively little effect on the economy. But nowadays, when governments tend to spend (or at least to influence the spending) of perhaps one fourth of the national income, the impact of budgets has grown enormously; and the need for appropriate monetary policies as a counterweight to unbalanced budgets has grown with them. The logical outcome of this development has already been reached in some countries, such as Norway and Sweden, where two budgets are prepared—one, along conventional lines, for the government's accounts, and a second, called the National Budget, which reviews the whole of the economy and forecasts the inflationary or deflationary impact of the tendencies which its sees taking shape. Such a National Budget enables both fiscal policy and monetary policy to be appropriately planned. It is then up to the government on the one hand, through its fiscal policy, and the central bank on the other, through monetary policy, to try to keep the economy on an even keel.

So it is that a central bank has become far more than a prestige symbol: it is a complement to the government itself, taking responsibility for a separate area of economic policy, viz., the money supply. It can influence this either directly by varying the size of the note issue (if that is the main form of currency in circulation) or indirectly through its power over the commercial banks (if it is the latter that provide the main supply of purchasing power). In addition, a central bank can provide the government with expert assistance in quite a number of ways. Not only may it smooth out temporary inequalities between government revenues and expenditures; it also manages the government debt, it holds (or at least controls) the country's gold and foreign exchange reserves, it usually administers exchange controls and issues exchange licenses where exchange control is in force, and it often has a research department which can provide a useful complement to the resources of the government itself.

METHODS OF CENTRAL BANK CONTROL

All this remains true even though some countries' financial institutions are not sufficiently flexible to enable the central bank to wield the weapons that have been developed by central banks in the most advanced countries. Two of these weapons rely upon the fact that, as already mentioned, the ordinary banks customarily maintain deposits at the central bank, using these as part of their reserves. (A balance due from one bank to another is usually settled by a check drawn on the former's deposit at the central bank.) Moreover, the ordinary banks customarily borrow from the central bank, either directly or (as in England) indirectly. The central bank can therefore influence the activities of the ordinary banks by increasing or decreasing these banks' deposits in its hands.

One way by which it can do so is to sell some securities to an ordinary bank or a customer of that bank, which will force the bank to pay for them by drawing down its deposit at the central bank. This will contract the reserves of the paying bank, and so those of the banking system generally; there will not be so much room for expansion even if the banking system does not have actually to contract its liabilities. Since these liabilities are mainly the deposits of customers, which are in turn mainly created by loans to other customers, the effect is to necessitate a curtailment of the bank's loans.

A second method is for the central bank to raise its discount rate (the rate at which it will lend). This will discourage the other banks from borrowing from it, and thus tend to reduce their reserves, and hence (of necessity) their loans. The latter effect is reinforced by the close link which in many developed countries exists between the central bank's discount rate and interest rates generally; when the former is raised, interest rates generally rise, and business is discouraged from borrowing.

Of course, these methods of central bank control do not work only in one direction: if the central bank lowers its discount rate or buys securities, it will tend to encourage the other banks to expand their loans.

In less developed countries these particular techniques have only a limited usefulness. For instance, the sale or purchase of securities by the central bank ("open market operations") is practicable only where government securities are bought and sold so extensively that purchases and sales can readily be made by the central bank without having much effect on their prices. Such conditions rarely, if ever, exist in less developed countries, or, indeed, in quite a number of developed countries either. But this has not defeated central bankers; they have merely obtained legislative powers to use alternative methods of control. Two of these are worth a little discussion, because they illustrate clearly the responsibilities of central banks, as well as the way in which they are exercised.

The first of these is to issue direct injunctions to the ordinary banks, requiring them to restrict their loans to their customers. The injunctions may apply to individual banks, or to individual kinds of borrower (e.g., borrowers for hire-purchase transactions). They may apply to loans already made (requiring them to be reduced) or only to new loans (putting a ceiling on them). The prohibitions may be absolute, enforced by legal penalties, or qualified to the extent of allowing the banks to expand their loans if they charge unusually high rates of interest, or on payment of a penalty to the central bank. Again, the injunctions may relate the amount of the restriction to the size of the banks' existing loans, to the size of their capital, or to some other standard. Whatever the exact technique followed, the effect is the same; the amount of bank loans made is smaller than it would otherwise be.

The second of the new methods adopted by central banks somewhat resembles open market operations: it is to require the ordinary banks to maintain reserves (in the form of cash or deposits at the central bank) equivalent to a specified minimum proportion of their liabilities. This method is somewhat less arbitrary than a direct restriction on lending, in that it relates the impact to the resources of each bank; the banks are kept in step without the need to apply a specific restriction to each of them separately. By increasing the minimum required ratio the central bank can force the other banks to exercise caution in exactly the same way as it could do by selling securities. This would not, however, prevent a bank which is attracting an increasing share of the banking business of the country from expanding appropriately, whereas a more rigid restriction might do so.

Just as, in developed countries, changes in the discount rate or in open market operations can be used either to contract or to expand banking activities, so can restrictions on lending and minimum reserve ratios. The central bank can encourage the banking system to expand, if conditions warrant it, by lifting restrictions on new loans, and equally effectively by reducing the minimum reserve ratio required.

In some such ways as those just described, central banks have succeeded in achieving control over the banking systems even in countries where there are none of the facilities for the more traditional methods developed in European and North American countries. Moreover, in many less developed countries central banks have accepted a responsibility almost more important than that of control—to foster and develop financial institutions so that the economic life of these countries can be adequately supported.

So vital have these functions become that if there were no such things as central banks it would certainly be necessary to invent them. Governments seeking to ensure the stability of the price level in their countries can go a long way toward this by balancing the budget and by seeking to ensure that wages are related to productivity. But if the banking system is independent of any control, it may defeat the government's aims by lending freely to its customers. (There would, of course, be the risk that if it did so too lavishly, and mistrust of the system developed to the point that depositors sought to get their money back, the banks would have to close their doors. But that is not an alternative that governments can contemplate with comfort, since without banks the complicated economic systems in most countries could not be carried on at all.) Equally, of course, if a government is trying to lift a country out of a depression, it will rely on the banking system to help to finance recovery; but unless there is a central bank to which individual banks may turn in case of difficulty, none of them may be willing to take the risk of expanding their loans.

It is evident, therefore, that a central bank is able to offer considerable help to a government in any policy that it wishes to follow. Nor is this help necessarily confined to a single government. Central banks of a number of countries can cooperate successfully.

It is, however, important that the common policy of the group is a really comprehensive one. Only so long as the countries in the group are willing to coordinate their trade policies, to aim at similar stability (or similar rates of change) in prices, and generally to keep closely in step, can a central bank work harmoniously with the other members of the group. This subject will be further considered in a later article.

CENTRAL BANKS—PRO AND CON

The arguments for setting up a separate central bank in each country thus seem very strong. Indeed, as we have seen, they have received the support of a League of Nations Conference and have proved persuasive in very many countries. But it will not have been overlooked that there is an antithesis between the reasons given by the League of Nations Conference for promoting central banks and the reasons which have been developed in preceding paragraphs. The Conference advocated central banks for the purpose of restraining governments from unwise policies; but nowadays central banks are established principally to help governments to carry out the policies which they wish to pursue. This contrast was emphasized last November by Mr. Maurice Frère in the first lecture given under The Per Jacobsson Foundation.[3] It explains why some writers who previously supported the spread of central banking now tend to hesitate before recommending the creation of new central banks. For while a government's fiscal policy can readily produce inflationary symptoms in a country, a central bank committed to support that government's policy can easily make things worse by inflating purchasing power itself. A government which is anxious to avoid inflation, but is doubtful of its political ability to do so, might find a really independent central bank—such as an external currency authority—to be more of a help than a national central bank, which might equally be limited in its power to maintain stability. . . .

[3] Reported in *Finance and Development*, Vol. II, No. 1, p. 52.

DELBERT C. HASTINGS
ROSS M. ROBERTSON

THE MYSTERIOUS WORLD
OF THE FED

15

First-time visitors to the lovely Washington building that houses
the Board of Governors of the Federal Reserve System are invariably struck by its lofty tone. Federal Reserve personnel and guests
alike move decorously through marble halls and amber-lit, carpeted
rooms that epitomize the vast dignity of the monetary authority.
Highly placed staff members approach the offices of Board members
with deference; lesser functionaries enter with an obsequious respect that makes onlookers uncomfortable. Indeed, an almost religious aura pervades the place, and the uninitiated expect momentarily to catch a whiff of incense or the chant of choirboys not
far off.

The physical atmosphere is simply an extension of a carefully
nurtured public image of trustworthiness and high morality. Because of the technicality of its operations and the obscurity of its
statements of purpose, the Federal Reserve has avoided evaluation
and criticism of its actions by the public at large. Instead, explicit
comment has been left to academicians, highly placed financial managers, and a few Members of Congress. Thus, the public trusts the
Fed without fully understanding it; with the possible exception of
the Federal Bureau of Investigation, no other Government agency
enjoys such high repute and splendid public relations.

To be sure, much of the System's prestige is merited. It performs
its vast service roles—collector of checks, fiscal agent for the U.S.
Government, and issuer of currency—with accuracy and dispatch.
At both Board and bank levels, the Federal Reserve can boast a
research organization second to none. Yet it is by no means certain
that the Fed has managed the money supply better than the money
supply would have managed itself, nor is it clear that Federal Reserve
influence on growth, stability, and price levels has been as beneficial
as the Fed's reputation would suggest.

In a word, the Federal Reserve System has nobly performed its
service functions. On the other hand, it is by no means certain that

Reprinted from Delbert C. Hastings and Ross M. Robertson, "The
Mysterious World of the Fed," *The Federal Reserve System After Fifty
Years*, Vol. II, Committee on Banking and Currency, House of Represen-
tatives, 88th Cong., 2d Sess., 1964, pp. 1519–1531.

the control functions have been discharged with the imagination and vigor that modern central bank action requires. Painfully sensitive to criticism, which invariably evokes defense reactions, the monetary authority gives continual evidence of an eroding self-consciousness. Indeed, System acceptance of responsibility for stability of prices and output seems to vary from time to time. The Fed certainly wants no competitors; whenever it has been suggested that an administration economic policy group be formed, there is immediate central bank resistance to the proposal. Yet System authorities occasionally come close to admitting their inability to stabilize the economy, and, whenever the congressional heat is on, central bank spokesmen are at pains to explain that they can only nudge the economy in one direction or another, that there are too many variables to be controlled by any one institution. System attitude seems to be, "We will use the tools we choose in the way we choose, and if they don't do the job, we deny responsibility in the matter. But we don't want anyone else interfering." To understand the Fed, we must apprehend this deep-rooted instinct for self-preservation that manifests itself in insistence upon insulation from "political" interference.

The mysterious world of the Fed is really known only to its employees and its alumni—the insiders, as it were. No amount of examination, no amount of congressional testimony, no amount of study by scholars temporarily connected with the System can reveal the inner workings of Fed mentality. Only years of participation in the charismatic effort of central bank policy provide the sense of System motivation so essential to an interpretation of Fed dogma, facetiously referred to, internally, as the "party line." As alumni, now a decent interval away from System activity, we herewith set forth our observations about (1) the nodes of power in the System and (2) the tenuous lines of communication that carry power impulses from one node to another.

THE NODES OF POWER

Although its major structural outlines were laid down by the original Federal Reserve Act, the Federal Reserve System has evolved in a way clearly not foreseen by its founders. As in every organization that must act, there are important nodes of power within the System; the relative standing of these power centers depends somewhat on law, somewhat on custom, and somewhat on the economic facts of life, such as the size and wealth of the different Federal Reserve districts. In roughly descending order of power, the major nodes are as follows: (1) The Chairman of the Board of Governors; (2) the other Governors; (3) the staff of the Board, in particular the senior advisers; (4) the Federal Open Market Committee; (5) the trading desk of the New York Federal Reserve Bank; (6) the President of the New York Federal Reserve Bank; (7) other Federal Reserve bank Presidents; (8) boards of directors of the 12 banks; (9) System-wide committees, standing and ad hoc; and (10) the Federal Advisory Council.

This listing will doubtless raise eyebrows both inside and outside the System, but we consider it, nonetheless, a fair appraisal of the current order of power loci in the System. It is impossible to understand the operations of today's central bank without knowing the relative importance of these power centers.

It is common knowledge, of course, that the Banking Act of 1935 made a drastic switch in the seat of System power. Under the aegis of Benjamin Strong, fair-haired boy of J. Pierpont Morgan and the 1913 New York banking community, real authority in the System lodged in the hands of the chief executive officers of the several Reserve banks. Indeed, the quick seizure of the term "governor" by the executive heads of the 12 banks revealed their own assessment of their authority. Until Strong's death in 1928, the Federal Reserve Board made nearly futile efforts to seize the power it never had, and the terrible failure of the Federal Reserve to arrest the deflation of 1929–32 gave positive proof, if proof were needed, that Board authority had been emasculated in practice. The designation in the Banking Act of 1935 of the "Board of Governors" signified the intent of Congress to make it the "board of bosses."

Even so, no one could have foreseen a generation ago the gradual settling of vast power in the person of the Chairman of the Board. The tradition of Chairman domination was, of course, started during the reign of Marriner S. Eccles, but it has reached a new high under Chairman William McChesney Martin, Jr., able son of one-time Governor Martin of the St. Louis Reserve Bank.

This is not to say that other Board members are without authority. Yet the position of each one depends upon his intellectual quality and personal force. A Board member not deemed a contributor to the welfare of the System is likely to be shunted aside and given assignments that keep him away from inner councils. On the other hand, a particularly knowledgeable Governor may be given heavy responsibilities, especially if he has a bent for economic or legal analysis.

The fact remains that the Chairman of the Board is in a position to exercise a great measure of control over the Board and thus over the entire System. His is the final word on appointments at both Board and bank levels. He is the System spokesman in its relationships with Congress, other executive branches of the Government, the President, and even with foreign governments. Within the law, his powers are circumscribed only by the personal qualities of the other Governors and by the 5-year term of his appointment to the chair. When, as in the case of Martin, the Chairman possesses an uncommon singleness of purpose and great political ability, he will work by persuasion rather than by ukase. He nevertheless operates as a dominant political figure in the best and highest sense of the word.

The staff of the Board of Governors, particularly the senior advisers, are a frequently overlooked power center. To be sure, their influence is derived from that of the Governors. But their proximity to the Governors, their long service, and their familiarity with Fed history give them a more than considerable influence on policy matters. Old pros like Woodlief Thomas and Ralph A. Young command enormous prestige. Younger men like Guy E. Noyes, Director of Research and Statistics, exert their influence through control of research activities at both Board and bank levels; all publications of the several banks as well as reports of System-wide committees must receive the approval of the Board staff before release, and directives sent by staff members to the banks are accepted as bearing the authority of the Board of Governors.

Because it nominally determines the magnitude and direction of the most important monetary weapon—purchases and sales of Government securities—the Federal Open Market Committee is the next most powerful organization within the System. Since it is the official forum as well as the administrative body for monetary policy actions, the FOMC has a key place in System councils. As late as 1953, the Open Market Committee met only quarterly, with an executive committee meeting more frequently to perform the significant policymaking functions. Since that time, however, the full Committee has met at intervals of approximately three weeks. Although the official membership consists of the seven Governors and five of the 12 bank Presidents, all the Presidents try to attend regularly.[1]

Resisting the inexorable erosion of authority at the bank level, the Federal Reserve Bank of New York always poses something of

[1] The President of the Federal Reserve Bank of New York is a permanent member and Vice Chairman of the Committee. Membership rotates among the other bank Presidents as follows: Boston, Philadelphia, and Richmond; Chicago and Cleveland; St. Louis, Atlanta, and Dallas; and Minneapolis, Kansas City, and San Francisco.

a threat to Board authority in Washington. The trading desk, which administers the open market account upon receipt of FOMC directives, is the very nerve center of the System. Since, as we shall see, orders of the Open Market Committee are always ambiguous and often nebulous, the account manager, a Vice President of the New York Reserve Bank, must have great latitude in making judgments. And though he may have many masters, not excluding the senior staff member of the Board who advises with him each day, it goes without saying that the account manager's immediate boss, the President of the New York Reserve Bank, will not be without influence. Indeed, a strong New York President can be a source of great annoyance and even friction in Federal Reserve councils. It is no secret that many officers in the System heaved a collective sigh of relief when Allan Sproul, one-time chief officer of the New York bank and in some respects the most artistic of all American central bankers, went into retirement. But no matter what the attitude of a New York President toward Washington may be the counsels of that officer are bound to have weight as they reflect the opinions of the New York financial community.

It is no deprecation of the abilities and prestige of the other 11 bank Presidents to say that they rank well down the list of System power centers. The Presidents are in general gifted and articulate men, and their views will always be weighed by the Board and its Chairman. Nevertheless, the last remaining power of the banks vanished when the original tool of monetary management—changes in the discount rate—lost its money-market effectiveness. And since the appointments of Presidents and First Vice Presidents are subject to Board approval, really serious resistance to Board decisions is not to be expected at bank, to say nothing of branch, levels. It is probably not unfair to say that the boards of directors of the 12 banks have had their power reduced to that of nominating committees, which on occasion submit to the Board of Governors the names of possible President and First Vice President candidates. Like the boards of directors of the Reserve bank branches, their positions are largely honorific; and though the Board expresses public gratitude for the "economic intelligence" furnished by bank and branch directors, the plain fact is that their monthly meetings are simply genteel bull sessions.[2]

Indeed, it is probably a fair generalization that the Reserve banks,

[2] Branches of Federal Reserve banks are a historic anomaly, originally established to salve the feelings of citizens disappointed at their failure to get a Reserve bank in their city. For this story see Ross M. Robertson, "Branches of Federal Reserve Banks," *Monthly Review*, Federal Reserve Bank of St. Louis, XXXVIII (August 1956), pp. 90–97.

at least outside New York City, exert their remaining vestiges of influence by placing their talented officers and economists on System committees. Thus, a System Committee To Study Consumer Credit unquestionably affected Board and administration thinking with its multivolume 1957 report; more recently, a System committee has produced an influential report on the Federal funds market. Furthermore, articulate individuals like Robert V. Roosa and George Garvy of New York, Clay J. Anderson of Philadelphia, and Homer Jones of St. Louis, through their writings and oral presentations, are likely to have an earnest and respectful hearing by the policymakers in Washington. They are nevertheless a long way from the seat of power.[3]

The Conference of Presidents, once the vehicle of dominance over System policy, is now regarded largely as a forum for administrative and operating problems of the several banks. The Presidents advise with each other on such matters as check collection, currency and coin issue, agency functions for the Treasury, and personnel classifications. The Federal Advisory Council, never even ostensibly a part of the formal power structure, is clearly an honorific group. Although their advice is presumably weighed by the Board of Governors, council members, like directors of banks and branches, bring personal prestige and orthodox witness as their chief contribution.

TRANSMISSION LINES OF POWER

Few Federal Reserve insiders would make a major rearrangement of the order in which we have listed the nodes of power, but many would express the honest conviction that we have underestimated the democratic processes by which System decisions are made. A look at these procedures may be helpful to a clear comprehension of them.

As a prerequisite to understanding, we must divest ourselves of a good bit of textbook foolishness about how monetary policy is effected. Although it is customary to speak of the instruments of monetary control, there is really only one—the extension and absorption of central bank credit. The means by which central bank credit is manipulated are irrelevant. Changes in reserve requirements, though still employed, are an anachronistic inheritance from the excess reserve problem of the 1930's; any sensible person knows

[3] Mr. Roosa is presently Under Secretary of the Treasury for Monetary Affairs.

that required reserve ratios can be set at any level with consequent central bank and commercial bank adjustment to them. Changing the discount rate, though originally conceived to be the only weapon of monetary control, has long since lost its effectiveness; the discount rate is no longer a true money-market rate but serves simply as a Fed signal of reaffirmation of a policy in being or a change in monetary policy. In practice, the only demonstrable effect of the discount rate is to set an upper limit to the Federal funds rate; that is, the rate charged one bank by another for the short-term loan of deposits with a Reserve bank. So we are left with one important instrument of monetary control—open market operations. System intervention in the Government securities market is a day-to-day, hour-to-hour, minute-to-minute activity that intimately affects the lives of us all.

We have suggested that the Chairman of the Board of Governors is by all odds the most powerful person in the System. But power is synonymous with substantial control over Federal Reserve credit. How, then, does the Chairman exercise his great influence? Largely by being the mouthpiece and deciding vote of the Federal Open Market Committee.

In the conduct of FOMC meetings, a formality is observed that requires each Governor and President in attendance, whether currently a member of the Committee or not, to give a brief economic analysis and state his policy recommendations. By custom each member, together with the Board secretary, the senior advisers, and the Manager of the Open Market Account, occupies a fixed position around the great oval table in the Committee room. After a brief business and financial analysis by the senior staff members, the Account Manager reports on his activities since the last meeting. Next, the Governors and Presidents take turns in order of their seating at the table, the circuit being made in one direction at one meeting and in the opposite direction at the next. The Chairman speaks last, customarily framing his closing remarks in the form of a consensus of the preceding recommendations. Often, however, there is less than complete agreement among Committee members; less often, but not infrequently, the Chairman may wish to give stronger than usual direction to current policy. In such circumstances, the "Martin consensus" has emerged, this consensus being largely the view of the Chairman himself, whether or not it coincides with that of the majority. Rarely—if then—are policy recommendations put into a motion and voted upon.

The Account Manager listens to the discussion and at its conclusion is asked by the Chairman if he comprehends the wishes of the

Committee. He almost always answers in the affirmative. But though the Account Manager listens with great care, even tabulating the recommendations of each speaker, FOMC members frequently complain that they cannot communicate precisely with the Manager. This problem has several dimensions. First, each Committee member, being a rugged individualist, would probably be satisfied with little less than complete direction of current policy. Second, because the FOMC does not make a precise statement of its wishes, the Account Manager must consider 19 sets of recommendations, some of them rambling discourses on the state of the Union. Third, the three-week interval between meetings is long enough to require adaptations on the part of the Manager, and these cannot possibly coincide with all 19 Committee opinions. Fourth, policy recommendations of FOMC members are stated in terms that are at best ambiguous "a little tighter," or "about the same degree of ease," or "shoot for net free reserves between $500 and $600 million." Committee members frequently disavow the free reserves target, pointing out that it lacks sufficient connection with the complex of economic variables to be useful as a measure of the effectiveness of policy. It is little wonder then that communication between the FOMC and the trading desk is poor. Nor is it any wonder that Chairman Martin, for better or worse, must determine a consensus that would lead to endless argument if it were brought to a vote.

A more basic difficulty of communication arises from the unwillingness of the Committee to state its economic outlook in precise terms. There exists in the Federal Reserve System an unwritten rule against explicit forecasting of business conditions; even modest attempts at prognosis are blue-penciled if written and ignored if expressed verbally. Members of the FOMC often remark that "we are making policy only for the next three weeks," the implication being that inaction or wrong action can be reviewed or corrected at the next meeting. Now it is manifestly impossible to frame an intelligent monetary policy without at least implicit forecasting; and since a major objective of monetary policy is cyclical amelioration, the forecast period must be a major portion of a cycle. Fortunately, many FOMC members have their own unstated projections. But the emphasis on the short term, the avoidance of a solid, common forecast, and the frequency of FOMC meetings all lead to erratic action, lagged responses, and policy more often than not based on correction of past errors rather than on anticipation of future events.

But whatever the difficulties and ambiguities of communicating with the trading desk, transmissions are made and received. However, the man in charge of the desk, no matter how dedicated, has a rough, tough job. If, as is frequently true, the FOMC has set some range of free reserves as its most precise measure of policy direction, the Account Manager ideally tries to achieve this goal in his day-to-day operations. But the goal is elusive, simply because some of the money-market factors affecting reserves cannot be predicted at all and others can be estimated only with difficulty. (Actual figures may become available only two or three weeks later.) Actions taken by the desk on the basis of the daily predictions of the money-market factors frequently turn out to have been perverse —in the wrong direction. The chief upsetting factor, of course, is Federal Reserve float, which is extremely volatile and almost completely unpredictable on a daily basis. Float could be safely ignored on a daily basis and dealt with only on a weekly average basis, Federal Reserve studies having shown that commercial banks do not alter their short-term investment positions on the basis of changing float levels. Yet fear of commercial bank response ostensibly forms the basis for the frequency of a Fed's float-offsetting action, with consequent uncertainty in the money markets when desk action is in the wrong direction.

Another major influence on the administration of the trading desk is the solicitude of the Fed for the Government security dealers, particularly for the nonbank dealers. The basic premises of this solicitude are that a "broad, deep, and resilient" market for Government securities is necessary for successful Federal Reserve action and that such a market can be made only by financially impregnable dealers who can obtain financing on favorable terms. A "negative carry"—that is, a yield on any security held in inventory smaller than the rate paid on funds borrowed by the dealer—is taken as conclusive evidence that financing terms for the dealers are not favorable. The same concern is not felt for bank dealers, since they are assumed to have a ready internal source of funds to finance their positions.

Solicitude for the dealers is expressed in several ways. For example, the FOMC has approved and the desk has made frequent use of the repurchase agreement. Although this instrument is a means by which the desk can make bank reserves available for a short time with automatic withdrawal, it is also a means by which short-term credit is extended to a dealer.[4] The timing is usually to the advantage of the dealer, because the desk makes the privilege available when there is a real pinch in the money market. The re-

[4] Compare Robert V. Roosa, "Federal Reserve Operations in the Money and Government Securities Markets" (New York: Federal Reserve Bank of New York, 1956), esp. pp. 25–26 and 83–87.

purchase agreement is in reality a fully secured loan; the desk purchases securities (bills) from the dealer, who agrees to repurchase them within a definite period (maximum, 15 days). Interest is computed on the basis of amount and term of loan rather than by reckoning the difference between purchase and sale price of the bills, as would be true in the case of a true purchase and repurchase.

Fed concern for the Government securities dealer is further demonstrated by the expressed opinion that the money-market banks ought to favor the securities dealers in financing arrangements, particularly during tight-money periods. The money-market banks have protested that no group ought to be favored merely because of its function. Although the interest of the Fed authorities in maintaining a facilities market organization is understandable, it is doubtful that financing favoritism is essential to a strong dealer organization. A hands-off attitude, requiring dealers to stand the market test of services rendered, charges made, and competition for custom, seems more likely to achieve ultimate Federal Reserve aims.

Nor is arranging Fed intervention in the Government securities market to suit the convenience of nonbank dealers likely to inspire public confidence. Federal Reserve acceptance of the notion that System entry into the Government securities market should be in short issues, preferably bills, had its philosophical basis in a weird principle of "minimum effective interference," a mystical idea that the limitless authority of the central bank could somehow be softened by dealing in securities "closest to money" in the spectrum of financial assets. But a careful reading of the famed "Ad Hoc Subcommittee Report of 1952" makes it clear that strong support for the "bills only" dogma came from the dealers, who would avoid, for obvious reasons, "capricious" System purchases and sales throughout the maturity range of the Treasury list. Dealers with positions in bonds naturally want to be warned of fluctuations in bond prices by preliminary changes in the prices of bills.

RETURN TO REGIONALISM?

Knowledgeable men know perfectly well that the informal power structure of an institution—whether a Christian denomination, a great corporation, or a university—may well be more important than its formal one. So long as the distinction is clear, so long as people are aware of what is really going on, it makes little difference whether the formal or informal power centers are operative. But it makes a great deal of difference if the people in a democracy, un aware of the arbitrary nature of the actual decisionmaking, go on believing that the money power, like all other sovereign power, is responsive to democratic processes. For plainly it is not.

We do not for one moment question either the integrity or the sincerity of the money managers. If government at all levels were staffed by men of the competence and dedication of those found in the Federal Reserve System, the American political system would be upgraded tremendously.

We do believe, however, that a realistic appraisal of System structure in terms of its genuine power centers leads to only one conclusion—that the regional structure, adopted by the framers of the Federal Reserve Act two generations ago, is presently outmoded and has become an expensive anachronism. We may as well face up to the fact that Federal Reserve banks have become only operating offices with responsibility for service functions and not, in any real sense, for monetary policy.

In our view a workable regional system could be devised. A return to regional structure would require, as a very minimum, restoration of the discount rate as an instrument of monetary control. Such a restoration implies the rescinding of regulation A, the complex and meddlesome set of rules by which the 12 discount windows are presently administered. It further implies free access to discount windows at whatever rates the regional banks prescribe.

Ostensibly, the discount rates of the several banks are set by their boards of directors. In practice, they are raised and lowered at the wish of the board. When Chairman Martin senses the strategic moment has arrived for a discount rate change, he initiates action via a discreet telephone call to one or more bank Presidents out in the provinces. Once a Reserve bank President (at St. Louis, Kansas City, Atlanta, or Dallas, for example) has the word, it is up to him to get his Board of Directors, or the executive committee of his Board, to do what the Reserve Board wants. When the change is made, the business press ordinarily announces it as the simultaneous decision of two or more banks. Within 10 days or so, all the other banks fall in line—not by mere chance, you may be sure.

There is much to be said for operating the discount window on a rate basis rather than on an administered basis. To be sure, Federal Reserve credit must be injected partly with regard to grant strategic considerations, as determined by the board and the New York bank. But much of the hour-to-hour and day-to-day intervention by the trading desk could be avoided by letting the commercial banks tell the Fed when they need reserves. It sounds a little old-fashioned to suggest that the private banking community may on occasion know what's best for it, but we'd like to return some of the reserve-injection initiative to the commercial banks.

There are reasons why it may be impossible to go back to a regional system. For one thing, the American economy has lost most of the provincial characteristics that marked it as late as the eve of World War II. For another, our understanding of monetary (stabilization) theory has changed since the formulation of a geographically decentralized central bank, placing emphasis on unified control of the economy rather than on patchwork assistance to parts of it.

Yet there would be a demonstrable gain from making central bank control less authoritarian. Moreover, continued centralization of the money power leads logically to the ultimate in a centralized power structure—combination of the central bank and the Treasury under a single head. Those who feel that such an arrangement bodes no good would do well to reflect on the possibility of greater reliance on markets in the implementation of central bank policy.

WARREN L. SMITH

THE INSTRUMENTS
OF GENERAL
MONETARY CONTROL

16

I. INTRODUCTION

At present, the Federal Reserve System possesses three major instruments of general monetary control: the power to buy and sell securities in the open market; the power to fix discount rates and regulate other conditions of member bank borrowing; and the power to change within specified limits the reserve requirements of member banks. This paper deals with the relative usefulness of these

Reprinted from Warren L. Smith, "The Instruments of General Monetary Control," *The National Banking Review*, Vol. I (September 1963), pp. 47–76. Washington, D.C.: U.S. Treasury Department.

three credit-control instruments and with problems of their proper co-ordination.[1]

II. THE PRIMACY OF OPEN MARKET OPERATIONS

Nearly all students of American monetary affairs would probably agree that open market operations constitute the primary weapon of monetary policy. The initiative with respect to such operations lies firmly in the hands of the Federal Reserve System, and the weapon possesses great flexibility with respect to both timing and magnitude. That is, operations can be used to produce large or small changes in credit conditions, and the direction of operations can be changed almost instantaneously.

In addition to their use to control credit in the interest of economic stability and growth, open market operations are carried on continuously for the purpose of offsetting the short-run effects on member bank reserves resulting from factors outside the control of the Federal Reserve—changes in float, currency in circulation, gold stock, Treasury and foreign deposits at the Reserve banks, and so on. These operations, which have been increasingly perfected in recent years, serve the important function of maintaining an even keel in the central money market. They also act as a kind of camouflage which frequently makes it rather difficult to discern and interpret the longer-run objectives of System policy as reflected in open market operations. Thus, since open market operations are generally going on continuously and are directed at the accomplishment of a rather complex variety of objectives, they are relatively free from the psychological overtones (sometimes called "announcement effects") that frequently accompany changes in discount rates or in reserve requirements. For reasons that will be explained below, I believe this absence of psychological implications is a rather important advantage of open market operations.

To the extent of its net purchases or sales of Government securities, the Federal Reserve changes not only the supply of bank reserves but the amount of interest-bearing Federal debt held by the public. In addition, by varying its purchases and sales in various

---

[1] In addition to the three general credit control instruments, the System has from time to time employed selective controls, including the regulation of consumer and real estate credit. At the present time, however, the only important selective control power that the System has is the authority to regulate margin requirements applicable to loans for purchasing and carrying securities. This paper makes no effort to deal with the uses of selective controls or their coordination with general controls.

maturity sectors of the market, it can influence the maturity composition of the publicly-held debt and, to some extent at least, the
term-structure of interest rates. Thus, open market operations are a
form of debt management. They should be closely co-ordinated
with the Treasury's debt management decisions concerning the
maturities of securities to issue or retire in its cash borrowing,
refunding, and debt retirement operations.

For a period of about eight years beginning in March 1953, the
Federal Open Market Committee, which is responsible for the conduct of System open market operations, adhered to the so-called
"bills-only" policy, the key feature of which was that open market
operations for the purpose of effectuating stabilizing monetary
policy were confined to short-term securities, chiefly Treasury bills.
Early in 1961, this policy was altered to a more flexible one which
permitted operations in all maturity ranges of the U.S. Government
securities market.[2] The primary reason for the 1961 change in policy
was the emergence of a serious balance of payments deficit partly
caused by substantial outflows of short-term capital to foreign
money centers at a time when the domestic economy was suffering
from substantial unemployment and under-utilization of productive
capacity.

Although System open market purchases of longer-term securities
have actually been quite modest since early 1961, the greater flexibility of open market policy, together with associated shifts in the
conduct of Treasury debt management activities, has undoubtedly
helped to make it possible to maintain and even increase U.S.
short-term interest rates in line with those abroad, thus preventing
excessive outflows of short-term funds, while at the same time preventing increases in the long-term bond yields and mortgage interest
rates which influence plant and equipment expenditures, capital
outlays of State and local governments, and housing construction.[3]

[2] The changes were made at the meetings of the Federal Open Market
Committee on Feb. 7 and March 28, 1961. See the Record of Policy Actions
of the Federal Open Market Committee in the *Annual Report* of the Board
of Governors of the Federal Reserve System covering the year 1961, pp.
39–43 and 54–55.

[3] In addition to open market operations and debt management, other
policy actions have helped to "twist" the interest-rate structure; i.e., to
raise short-term rates while exerting as much downward pressure as possible on long-term rates. The increase in interest rate ceilings applicable
to time deposits by the Federal Reserve and the FDIC at the beginning of
1962 enabled U.S. commercial banks to compete more effectively with
foreign banks for deposits and also attracted an enlarged supply of funds
into time deposits—funds which were largely channelled into mortgages
and State and local government securities, thus bringing down yields on

Open market operations are firmly established as the fundamental weapon of monetary policy in the United States. Accordingly, the important questions concerning the proper co-ordination of monetary control instruments really have to do with the extent to which the other weapons—discount policy and reserve requirements policy —should be used to supplement (and perhaps in certain special circumstances to replace) open market operations. Let us begin by considering discount policy.

III. THE ROLE OF DISCOUNT POLICY

For many years prior to the Treasury-Federal Reserve Accord of March 1951, the amount of member bank borrowing from the Reserve banks was negligible. Throughout the later 1930's, the volume of excess reserves was continuously so large that it was seldom necessary for member banks to borrow. And during World War II, the Federal Reserve kept the banks amply supplied with reserves through open market operations so that there was little occasion for borrowing. The atrophied state of the discount mechanism is indicated by the fact that, for the entire period 1934 to 1943, member bank borrowing averaged less than one-tenth of one percent of total member bank reserves.

Since the Accord, the volume of borrowing has increased, especially during periods of credit restraint when the reserves of member banks have been under pressure. The Federal Reserve has encouraged this revival of the discount mechanism and has attempted to restore the discount rate to the important role it is supposed to have played in monetary policy prior to the 1930's.[4] But while member bank borrowing has increased in magnitude since the Accord, it is still very much less important as a source of reserves than it

---

such securities. And the reduction of reserve requirements on time deposits from 5 to 4 percent in October and November 1962, combined with action to sustain Treasury bill yields, undoubtedly also helped to some extent.

[4] In connection with the Accord itself, the Treasury and the Federal Reserve agreed upon the desirability of reviving the discount mechanism as a means for making adjustments in bank reserve positions. See the identical statements concerning the Accord by the Secretary of the Treasury and the Chairman of the Board of Governors in *Monetary Policy and Management of the Public Debt—Replies to Questions and Other Materials for the Use of the Subcommittee on General Credit Control and Debt Management*, Joint Committee on the Economic Report, 82d Cong., 2d Sess. (Washington, D.C.: U. S. Government Printing Office, 1952), Part I, pp. 74–76 and 349–351.

was in the 1920's. From 1951 to 1959, borrowing averaged 3.2 percent of total member bank reserves with average borrowings reaching peak levels of approximately 4½ per cent of total reserves in the years 1957 and 1959, when monetary policy was relatively tight. In contrast, during the period 1922 to 1929, borrowing averaged 30.0 percent of total reserves, with the ratio rising as high as 40 percent in 1923 and 1929.

A. The Discount Rate as a Cost Factor

It is possible to distinguish two main facets of Federal Reserve discount policy. In the first place, the discount rate represents the cost of borrowed reserves, and the rate is changed from time to time for the purpose of regulating member bank borrowing. Changes in the rate for this purpose should be coordinated as closely as possible with open market operations. In addition, however, the discount rate at times plays an independent role in monetary policy, serving as a signal to the economy of changes in Federal Reserve policy. Let us first consider the discount rate as a regulator of member bank borrowing.

1. Cost Versus "Reluctance" as a Regulator of Borrowing

Due to the organization of the banking and financial system in the United States, it has not been feasible to establish the discount rate as a "penalty rate" in the sense in which this has been the case in Britain. There a penalty rate has been possible because the discount houses rather than the banks have customarily done the borrowing from the Bank of England. Since the discount houses have made a practice of carrying quite homogeneous portfolios of commercial bills and, in recent years, Treasury bills, it has been feasible to keep the Bank rate above the yield on such bills, so that when the discount houses are "forced into the bank" (as the phrase goes), they lose money on their borrowings. Traditionally, this penalty rate has served to keep borrowing from the Bank of England to a minimum and to make the interest rate structure highly sensitive to monetary action carried out through the coordinated use of open market operations and the discount rate.[5]

In the United States, member banks borrow directly from the

[5] For a good recent discussion, see R. S. Sayers, *Modern Banking*, 4th ed. (Oxford: Clarendon Press, 1958), pp. 104–114. As indicated by Sayers, both the indirect nature of the relation between the commercial banks and the Bank of England and the penal Bank rate have become somewhat attenuated in recent years, as the Bank has developed the alternative practice of supplying funds to the discount houses and in some cases to

Reserve banks, and since there are very many member banks operating in numerous local and regional, as well as national, credit markets and investing in a great variety of earning assets bearing a wide range of yields, it is not feasible to maintain a true penalty rate.[6]

Since the 1920's, it has come to be widely accepted doctrine that use of the System's discount facilities is restrained by a tradition against borrowing on the part of member banks.[7] As evidence in support of this view, which has come to be known as the "reluctance theory," it was pointed out that in the 1920's open market interest rates were more closely related to the amount of outstanding member bank borrowing than they were to the discount rate, suggesting that member banks did not like to be in debt and, when they were, tended to liquidate secondary reserve assets in order to repay their borrowings, thus forcing up open market interest rates.[8]

Although the purposes for which banks borrow—to maintain their reserve positions in the face of customer withdrawals or clearing drains and to meet temporary (e.g., seasonal) increases in their customers' demands for loans—are commonly so pressing as probably to be quite cost-inelastic, it does not follow that member bank borrowing is insensitive to the discount rate. Banks have a choice of obtaining additional funds by borrowing at the Federal Reserve or by liquidating secondary reserves or other investment securities. Given a certain "reluctance to borrow," the major factor influencing the choice will presumably be the relevant cost of funds obtained by the various methods, and this depends chiefly on the relations between the discount rate and the yield on assets that the bank might liquidate. In principle, the relevant comparison is between the discount rate and the expected yield on the asset whose liquidation

---

the commercial banks themselves by purchasing Treasury bills at the market rate.

[6] In order to be a penalty rate with respect to a particular bank, the rate does not need to be higher than the expected return on all of the bank's earning assets. In fact, in a sense, it is a penalty rate if it is higher than the expected return on the lowest yielding assets in the bank's portfolio. However, the discount rate can be a penalty rate in this sense in relation to some banks and not others, due to differences in the composition of the banks' portfolios.

[7] This argument was advanced in W. W. Riefler, *Money Rates and Money Markets in the United States* (New York: Harper & Row, 1930), esp. chapter II. According to Riefler, the tradition against borrowing existed among commercial banks prior to the formation of the Federal Reserve System and was strengthened during the 1920's by the System's discouragement of borrowing for other than temporary purposes.

[8] *Ibid.*, pp. 25–28; also W. R. Burgess, *The Reserve Banks and the Money Market*, rev. ed. (New York: Harper, 1946), pp. 219–221.

is being considered over the period of time for which the funds will be needed, taking account of any capital gains or losses that may be involved. For instance, if interest rates are expected to fall during the period, the relevant interest rate for comparison with the discount rate may be higher than the current interest rate on the asset. This factor will be more important the longer the maturity of the asset.[9]

Thus, there is little doubt that commercial banks are "reluctant" to borrow in the sense that borrowing is felt to involve a form of disutility. However, the banks' reluctance can be overcome provided that the profits to be obtained from borrowing (as compared with other means of obtaining reserves) are sufficiently attractive—that is, banks balance the disutility of borrowing against the utility of further profits.[10] Moreover, not all banks are equally reluctant to borrow:[11] this is evidenced by the fact that the Federal Reserve has found it necessary to discourage "continuous borrowing" and to bolster the banks' reluctance in its regulations covering discounts and advances.[12] In addition, the System keeps the borrowing practices of individual member banks under constant surveillance and in this way attempts to reinforce the banks' reluctance to borrow. At the same time, the System apparently does not unequivocally refuse to lend to member banks, despite the fact that it has authority to do so under the Federal Reserve Act.[13]

[9] See W. L. Smith, "The Discount Rate as a Credit-Control Weapon", *Journal of Political Economy*, LXVI, April 1958, pp. 171–177; Ralph Young, "Tools and Processes of Monetary Policy," in N. H. Jacoby, *United States Monetary Policy* (The American Assembly, Columbia University, 1958), pp. 13–48, esp. pp. 26–27.

[10] For a systematic development of this point of view, together with some evidence to support it, see the interesting article by M. E. Polakoff, "Reluctance Elasticity, Least Cost, and Member-Bank Borrowing: A Suggested Integration," *Journal of Finance*, XV, March 1960, pp. 1–18.

[11] On this, see Lauchlin Currie, *The Supply and Control of Money in the United States* (Cambridge, Mass.: Harvard University Press, 1935), chapter VIII.

[12] See Regulation A of the Board of Governors regulating member bank borrowing as revised effective Feb. 15, 1955 (*Federal Reserve Bulletin*, January 1955, pp. 8–14). The Foreword to the revised Regulation contains a statement of "General Principles" (pp. 8–9) which attempts to delineate in a general way the purposes for which member banks should and should not use the System's discount facilities.

[13] On the subtleties of non-price rationing in the administration of the discount window, see C. R. Whittlesey, "Credit Policy at the Discount Window"; R. V. Roosa, "Credit Policy at the Discount Window: Comment"; and Whittlesey, "Reply," *Quarterly Journal of Economics*, LXXIII, May 1959, pp. 207–216, and 333–338.

2. Co-ordination of Open Market Operations and Discount Policy

It used to be said with reference to monetary policy in the 1920's that open market operations served the function of making the discount rate effective.[14] In order to implement a restrictive monetary policy, the Federal Reserve would sell Government securities in the open market; this would put pressure on member bank reserve positions and cause them to increase their borrowings. At this point the discount rate would be raised, and the increase in borrowings was supposed to help to insure that the discount rate increase would be transmitted through into an increase in other interest rates.[15]

In view of the primary role of open market operations under present conditions, it is better to look at the matter the other way around and to say that the discount rate can be used to support and strengthen the effectiveness of open market operations. Thus, when the System, for example, wishes to implement a restrictive policy during a period of inflation, it uses open market operations to keep down the supply of reserves in relation to the swelling demands for credit. As a result, interest rates rise and member banks, finding their reserve positions under increased pressure, tend to increase their borrowings from the Reserve banks. In order to discourage the creation of additional reserves through borrowing, the System can raise the discount rate in pace with the increase of other interest rates. Thus the discount rate can be used to supplement and strengthen open market operations. Conversely, when the System desires to ease credit conditions, it provides additional reserves through open market operations, and in order to discourage members banks from using a portion of the new reserves to repay indebtedness at the Reserve banks, the discount rate can be lowered.[16]

[14] Burgess, op. cit., p. 239.

[15] This is rather similar to the classical British practice of selling in the open market to reduce the cash reserves of the commercial banks. To replenish their cash reserves, the banks would call some of their loans to the discount houses. The discount houses, in turn, would be forced to borrow from the Bank of England at the (penalty) Bank rate, and as a result of the ensuing adjustments bill rates would be forced up. Thus, open market operations were said to have the function of "forcing the market into the Bank."

[16] See the statement of the Chairman of the Board of Governors concerning the relation between the discount rate and open market operations in United States Monetary Policy: Recent Thinking and Experience, Hearings before the Subcommittee on Economic Stabilization of the Joint Committee on the Economic Report, 83d Cong., 2d Sess. (Washington, D.C.: U. S. Government Printing Office, 1954), p. 11. A similar view is suggested in C. E. Walker, "Discount Policy in the Light of Recent Experience," Journal of Finance, XII, May 1957, pp. 223–237, esp. pp. 232–234.

A variant of this reasoning which stresses the reluctance of member banks rather than the discount rate has also been expressed by persons connected with the Federal Reserve System. According to this view, most member bank borrowing arises out of the fact that in a unit banking system such as ours with a very large number of banks, individual banks often find their reserve positions unexpectedly depleted as a result of unfavorable clearing balances associated with redistribution of reserves among the banks. Borrowing is a handy means of making temporary adjustments in reserve positions; if the depletion of a bank's reserve position lasts very long, the bank may later adjust by liquidating secondary reserves, using the proceeds to repay its borrowing at the Reserve bank.[17] The pressure on banks to make prompt adjustments in portfolios in order to repay borrowing depends on the level of the discount rate in relation to other interest rates.

At times when monetary policy is tight and the Federal Reserve is maintaining pressure on bank reserve positions in the interest of limiting excessive growth of bank credit, more banks will be managing their reserve positions closely, reserve deficiencies will occur more frequently, and member bank borrowing will increase.[18] Due to the fact that the banks are reluctant to borrow, the increase in borrowing causes them to adopt more cautious lending policies and to reduce the availability of credit. However, since banks balance the disutility of borrowing against the utility of increased profits, it is necessary to make successive upward adjustments in the discount rate as interest rates rise due to the effects of the restrictive policy, in order to stiffen the banks' reluctance to remain in debt and to encourage them to contract their loans and investments.

It may be noted, however, that short-term open market interest rates are subject to a considerable amount of random variation in the short run and that, under present arrangements, the discount rate is only changed at irregular and rather infrequent intervals.

---

[17] Roosa, *op. cit.*, p. 335.

[18] *Ibid.*, p. 336. A similar argument is presented by Young, *op. cit.*, who says (p. 34): "As a policy of monetary restraint continues or is accentuated, there will be more frequent and more widespread reserve drains among member banks. This will lead an increasing number of banks to borrow temporarily at the discount window of the Reserve Banks in order to maintain their legal reserve positions. For each bank, the borrowing will be temporary, but the repayment by one bank draws reserves from other banks, which in turn will have need to borrow at a Reserve Bank. Thus, restrictive monetary action leads to a larger volume of member bank borrowings, as more banks find their reserve positions under pressure more often."

CHART 1   Federal Reserve Discount Rates and Market Yield on Treasury Bills, 1953-1962

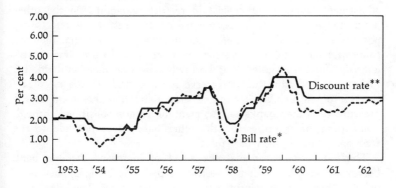

*Monthly average of daily yields on outstanding issues.
**Average of discount rates at all Federal Reserve banks.
SOURCE: Board of Governors of the Federal Reserve System.

For this reason, the differential between the discount rate and other interest rates varies rather erratically. This is apparent from Chart 1, which shows the movements of the discount rate and the yield on outstanding Treasury bills since 1953. As a result of the continuously shifting relation between the discount rate and other interest rates, the willingness of banks to borrow presumably undergoes considerable erratic variation.

3. Does Borrowing Reinforce or Offset Open Market Operations?

There has been some discussion as to whether the increase in member bank borrowing that occurs during a period of credit restriction is a factor which intensifies the restrictive effects or a loophole which weakens the effectiveness of monetary policy.[19] It is almost certainly true that as a result of the reluctance of member banks to borrow, banks tend to follow somewhat more restrictive and cautious policies as far as loans are concerned when they are in debt to the Reserve banks than when they are not in debt. However, the important thing to bear in mind is that if banks were constrained not to borrow when their reserve positions were impaired by a restrictive policy, they would have to adjust their reserve posi-

[19] Roosa seems to imply that it has an intensifying effect ("Credit Policy at the Discount Window," *op. cit.*). Whittlesey ("Credit Policy at the Discount Window," and "Reply" [to Roosa's comment], *op. cit.*) contends that it is an offset, although not, under present conditions, a very important one.

tions in some other way. This would ordinarily mean contraction of loans or investments.[20] Thus, in the absence of borrowing, the adjustment would itself *consist in* restricting credit. On the other hand, to the extent that borrowing occurs, restrictive effects are postponed and banks are merely put in such a position that they are somewhat more likely to restrict credit at some future time. Moreover, it should be noted that borrowing by one member bank for the purpose of adjusting its reserve position adds to the *aggregate* reserves of all member banks and thus indirectly takes some of the pressure off other banks. Adjustment of reserve positions through liquidations of securities, on the other hand, does not add to the reserves of the system of banks.[21]

Thus, it seems clear that the effect of increased member bank borrowing at a time when a restrictive policy is being applied is to offset rather than to reinforce the restrictive policy. The effect may not be very important in itself, since the induced increase in borrowing is not likely to be large enough to pose a serious problem for the authorities; it merely means that a somewhat more restrictive open market policy is required than would otherwise be necessary. However, there are a number of other offsetting reactions in the banking and financial system—such as shifts in the composition of bank portfolios from Government securities to loans, adjustments by financial intermediaries, and so on—and the addition of one more such reaction, even though not quantitatively very large, may not be wholly without significance.

Another point of view that has been expressed concerning the discount mechanism is that, while it has an offsetting effect, this effect is actually helpful to the monetary authorities, because it can be likened to a brake on an automobile. It is said that brakes, by making it pos-

[20] Another possibility is that banks might make greater use of the Federal funds market to adjust their reserves. Although use of this market has increased in recent years, the number of participating banks is still rather small, and there are technical impediments to a substantial increase. (See *The Federal Funds Market*, Washington, D.C.: Board of Governors of the Federal Reserve System, 1959). Increased use of the Federal funds market during periods when credit is being restricted economizes the use of existing reserves, reduces excess reserves, and thereby constitutes an offset to the initial restrictive action (see H. P. Minsky, "Central Banking and Money Market Changes," *Quarterly Journal of Economics*, LXXI, May 1957, pp. 171–187). Thus, resort to the Federal funds market has effects similar to member bank borrowing (as explained below).

[21] Smith, "The Discount Rate as a Credit-Control Weapon," *op. cit.*, pp. 172–173; also P. A. Samuelson, "Recent American Monetary Controversy," *Three Banks Review*, March 1956, pp. 10–11.

sible to control the car more effectively, permit one to drive at a higher rate of speed than would otherwise be possible.[22] Similarly, the discount mechanism, although seeming to weaken monetary controls, actually strengthens them by making it possible to use other controls (chiefly open market operations) more vigorously. However, this is not a proper analogy. If the automobile simile is retained, the discount mechanism is more like a defective clutch than a brake, and few would argue that a slipping clutch makes it possible to drive at a higher rate of speed.[23] A brake is a discretionary weapon and not a device that automatically operates more intensively, the harder one pushes on the accelerator.

4. A Critique of the Concept of "Free Reserves"

A by-product of the revival of the discount mechanism since the Accord is the emphasis that has been placed on the level of "free reserves" as an immediate guide to System policy. "Free reserves," of course, is simply the difference between aggregate member bank excess reserves and aggregate member bank borrowings. It appears that, increasingly in the last few years, the System has been setting its proximate goals of monetary policy in terms of "target" levels of free reserves. As can be seen from Chart 2, free reserves have been positive (excess reserves greater than borrowings) during periods of credit ease, as in 1953–54, 1958, and 1960–63, while during periods of credit restriction, free reserves have been negative (i.e., borrowings have been greater than excess reserves, or there have been "net borrowed reserves"). It has become commonplace to judge the objectives and direction of monetary policy to a considerable extent by the changes that take place in free reserves.[24]

The first thing to notice about free reserves is that the two components that compose it—excess reserves and borrowings—are distributed quite differently among member banks. Excess reserves tend to be heavily concentrated in the hands of country banks, while

[22] P. A. Samuelson, "Reflections on Monetary Policy," *Review of Economics and Statistics*, XLII, August 1960, p. 266.

[23] If the motor were too powerful for the car—e.g., if a Cadillac motor were mounted in a Volkswagen—I suppose a clutch that slipped might be helpful. But the proper analogy for the relation between monetary policy and the stability of the economy may well be just the reverse; i.e., monetary policy can be likened to a Volkswagen motor which has been assigned the task of operating a heavy Cadillac.

[24] No matter what the shortcomings of free reserves as a guide to monetary policy, it is appropriate for those who are attempting to judge the character of System policy to pay close attention to this magnitude simply because the System does seem to use it as a guide.

CHART 2   Free Reserves of Member Banks, 1953-1962

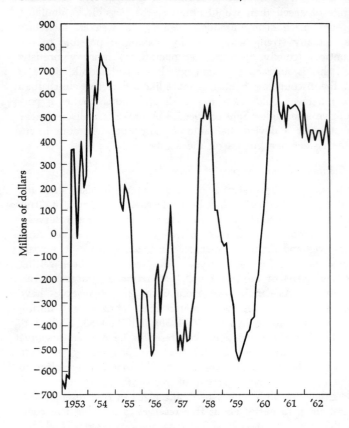

*Monthly averages of daily figures.
SOURCE: Board of Governors of the Federal Reserve System.

most of the borrowing is ordinarily done by reserve city banks. (See Charts 3 and 4.) Country banks tend to hold fairly substantial amounts of excess reserves most of the time, and are able to absorb pressure by drawing down such excess reserves. Reserve city banks, on the other hand, manage their reserve positions more closely, hold relatively small amounts of excess reserves, and borrow more frequently from the Federal Reserve when they are placed under pressure. Of course, these behavior patterns do not coincide exactly with the arbitrary classifications of banks for reserve requirement purposes—some reserve city banks, for example, undoubtedly hold large excess reserves, while some country banks manage their reserve

CHART 3 Excess Reserves of Member Banks by Reserve Requirements Classifications, 1953-1962*

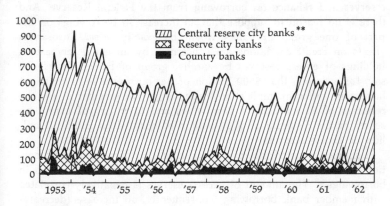

*Monthly averages of daily figures.
**Central Reserve City Classification terminated July 28, 1962.
SOURCE: Board of Governors of the Federal Reserve System.

CHART 4 Discounts and Advances of Member Banks by Reserve Requirements Classifications, 1953-1962*

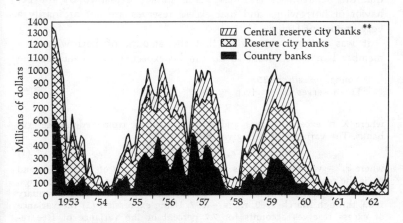

*Monthly averages of daily figures.
**Central Reserve City Classification terminated July 28, 1962.
SOURCE: Board of Governors of the Federal Reserve System.

positions closely. Nevertheless, it is quite clear that there are substantial differences among banks with respect to holdings of excess reserves and reliance on borrowing from the Federal Reserve. And there is no reason to suppose that an increase in borrowings on the part of one group of banks would be exactly offset, insofar as effects on credit conditions are concerned, by an equal increase in holdings of excess reserves by another group of banks. That is to say, for example, that $500 million of net borrowed reserves might have quite different implications depending upon whether it was the resultant of $1.5 billion of borrowings and $1 billion of excess reserves or the resultant of $700 million of borrowings and $200 million of excess reserves.

It should be noted, however, that in practice a very large proportion of the variation in free reserves is attributable to variation in borrowings.[25] The amount of excess reserves is negatively correlated with member bank borrowing; consequently, an increase (decrease) in free reserves is likely to be attributable partly to a decrease (increase) in borrowings and partly to an increase (decrease) in excess reserves. However, as a comparison of Charts 3 and 4 indicates, the variation in borrowings is much greater than the variation in excess reserves; in fact, the variance of borrowings accounts for about 62 percent of the variance of free reserves, whereas the variance of excess reserves accounts for only 7.7 percent, the remainder being attributable to the effects of the negative correlation that exists between borrowings and excess reserves.[26] This suggests that the behavior of free reserves is largely explained by the behavior of borrowings and that excess reserves are not ordinarily a very important factor.

It was pointed out earlier that the amount of borrowing that member banks will want to do can be expected to depend, among

[25] Young, op. cit., p. 35.

[26] Free reserves (R) is given by

$$R = X - B,$$

where X = excess reserves and B = borrowings from Federal Reserve banks. The variance of R is given by

$$\sigma_r^2 = \sigma_x^2 + \sigma_b^2 - 2r_{xb}\sigma_x\sigma_b, \tag{1}$$

where σ_x^2 = variance of excess reserves, σ_b^2 = variance of borrowings and r_{xb} is the coefficient of correlation between excess reserves and borrowings. Based on monthly data (averages of daily figures) for the period January 1953, through March 1960, r_{xb} is —.697. Using expression (1) the variance of excess reserves accounts for 7.7 percent of the variance of free reserves, the variance of borrowings accounts for 61.8 percent, and the remaining 30.5 percent is accounted for by the tendency for borrowings to vary inversely with excess reserves (as reflected in the term — $2r_{xb}\sigma_x\sigma_b$).

other things, on the relation between the discount rate and other interest rates, which can for our present purposes be represented by the Treasury bill rate. Since borrowing is the main element in free reserves, this suggests that the amount of free reserves member banks will desire to hold will vary inversely with the differences between the bill rate and the discount rate. As the bill rate rises relative to the discount rate, banks will tend to increase their borrowings and desired free reserves will fall; conversely, as the bill rate falls in relation to the discount rate, they will tend to repay existing indebtedness to the System, and desired free reserves will rise.[27]

Thus, during a period of credit restriction, as market interest rates rise with the discount rate lagging behind, desired free reserves will decline, and the banks will attempt to reduce actual free reserves. If the Federal Reserve attempts to hold free reserves constant, it will have to adjust its open-market policy to increase total reserves, thereby weakening the over-all restrictive effect of its policy. Conversely, when economic activity begins to level off in the late stages of an expansion, market interest rates may begin to fall. Under these circumstances, with a given or lagging discount rate, desired free reserves will increase, and if the Federal Reserve attempts to hold free reserves constant, it will have to tighten its open-market policy, and the over-all restrictive effect of monetary policy is likely to become stronger.[28]

This suggests that it is wrong to believe that a constant level of free reserves means a constant degree of credit tightness or ease. At the very least, it would be necessary to adjust the discount rate continuously to the changing level of market rates. Even if this were done, changes in other factors would mean that the effective degree of credit restriction could vary substantially while the level of free reserves was held constant.

Nor is an increase (decrease) in free reserves an unambiguous indication that credit has become easier (tighter). For example, if credit is tightened by raising the discount rate, the rise in the cost of borrowed reserves will cause the banks to reduce their borrowings, making offsetting adjustments in their reserve positions perhaps by selling Treasury bills. Total reserves will decline and interest rates will rise. But this tightening of credit will be accompanied by

---

[27] This is pointed out by Milton Friedman in *A Program for Monetary Stability* (New York: Fordham University Press, 1959), pp. 41–43. See also the excellent study by R. J. Meigs, *Free Reserves and the Money Supply* (Chicago: University of Chicago Press, 1962).

[28] Friedman, *op. cit.*, p. 42.

an increase in free reserves—indeed the increase in free reserves will be the means through which credit-tightening comes about.

On the other hand, if credit is tightened by open market sales of securities while the discount rate remains constant, the resulting rise in the bill rate (and other short-term open market interest rates) will make borrowing relatively more attractive as a means of obtaining reserves. The resulting increase in borrowing will reduce free reserves—thus, a tightening of credit will be associated with a decline in free reserves. But even in this case, the increased borrowing that is reflected in declining free reserves tends to increase total reserves and thereby to offset a portion of the restrictive effect of the initial open market sales.

"Free reserves" is an artificial construct, which has had the unfortunate effect of providing a spuriously exact guide to the monetary authorities—or at least has been so interpreted by persons outside the Federal Reserve System.[29] If the discount rate were regulated in such a way as to maintain a constant differential between it and the Treasury bill rate (a possibility that is discussed below), the amount of free reserves might perhaps become a somewhat better index of credit conditions than it is at present. Even in that case, however, it would commonly be a mistake to assume that a constant level of free reserves would necessarily mean a constant degree of credit tightness or ease. It would be better under most circumstances for the System to set its proximate goals in terms of interest rate behavior and growth of total reserves and to allow free reserves to seek the levels required to achieve these goals.

B. The Discount Rate as a Signal

Thus far, we have been considering changes in the discount rate as an adjunct to open market operations, the purpose of which is to serve as a partial governor of member bank indebtedness by regulating the cost of obtaining reserves by borrowing as compared with sales of secondary reserves.

To some extent, the discount rate also plays an independent role in monetary policy by serving as a signal of the intentions of the monetary authorities. Particularly at turning points in business con-

---

[29] The fact that the System officials are aware of the shortcomings of the free reserves concept is apparent from the criticisms directed at it by Ralph Young (op. cit., pp. 35–36). Young points out one defect not referred to above—the fact that the amount of free reserves is subject to considerable|day-to-day and week-to-week variations, due to unpredictable changes in factors outside the control of the Federal Reserve authorities.

ditions, a change in the discount rate is often the first clear indication of a basic alteration in monetary policy. Discount rate changes of this kind are said to have psychological effects or "announcement effects," which may influence business conditions by altering the expectations of businessmen and financial institutions.[30]

1. Difficulties of Interpreting Discount Rate Adjustments

It is commonly taken for granted that the announcement effects of discount rate changes are normally such as to strengthen the impact of monetary policy. However, those who advance the expectations argument have not explained in any detail the way in which the expectational effects are supposed to work. Actually, there are several different possible expectational effects, and in the case of each of them there is some uncertainty concerning even the direction (let alone the magnitude) of the effects.

One of the difficulties is that many changes in the discount rate are merely technical adjustments designed to restore or maintain an appropriate relationship between the discount rate and other rates of interest, as indicated above. Most of the periodic adjustments that are made during periods when interest rates are gradually rising or falling are of this nature. However, the interpretation placed on even these rather routine changes is sometimes unpredictable, because their timing may be affected by various considerations not directly related to stabilization policy. Sometimes, for example, discount rate adjustments may be accelerated in order to get the possible accompanying disruptive effects on the securities markets out of the way before an important Treasury debt management operation is scheduled. Or, on the other hand, action may be postponed until the repercussions of a forthcoming debt management operation are out of the way. Furthermore, the very fact that technical adjustments are sometimes interpreted by the public as having policy implications may affect System decisions concerning the timing of such adjustments. Such factors as these not only tend to make the interpretation of discount rate changes difficult, but are also partly responsible for the System's difficulties, referred to earlier, in adjusting the discount rate frequently enough to maintain a reasonably stable relation between that rate and other interest rates.[31]

[30] See, for example, Burgess, op. cit., 221–230.
[31] As Friedman puts it (op. cit., p. 40): "The discount rate is something that the Federal Reserve must continually change in order to keep the effect of its monetary policy unchanged. But changes in the rate are interpreted as if they meant changes in policy. Consequently, both the System and outsiders are led to misinterpret the System's actions and the System is led to follow policies different from those it intends to follow."

Partly as a result of erratic timing and partly due to the fact that the business situation is usually fraught with some uncertainty, discount rate changes that are in fact meant to be merely routine adjustments are sometimes endowed with importance as "straws in the wind" regarding System policy by the press and by students of financial and economic affairs. And sometimes even a *failure* to change the discount rate so as to maintain "normal" interest rate relationships is taken as a sign of a change of System policy. Moreover, it is quite common for different commentators to place different interpretations on System action—or even lack of action—with respect to the discount rate.

The truth is that changes in the discount rate constitute the crudest kind of sign language.[32] Why this Stone Age form of communication should be regarded as superior to ordinary English is really quite difficult to understand. And, in this particular case, the use of such crude signals is subject to a special disadavntage arising from the fact that the signal itself has an objective effect on the situation in addition to serving as a means of communication. That is, changes in the discount rate combine action and communication, and there may be times when it is proper to act and not speak and other times when it is proper to speak and not act.

It is possible that some of the disadvantages of discretionary discount rate changes could be overcome, if the changes that were made were accompanied, at least under some circumstances, by statements explaining the reason underlying the action. However, a change in the discount rate requires action by the boards of directors of the Federal Reserve banks and approval by the Board of Governors.[33] As a result, a very large number of persons are involved

[32] Some writers seem to show no realization of the difficulties involved in this peculiar form of communication. For example, Walker (*op. cit.*, pp. 229–230) says: "Discount policy—particularly with respect to changes in the rate—is a simple and easily understandable technique for informing the market of the monetary authorities' views on the economic and credit situation. Open-market operations, which are used to cushion the effects of seasonal influences as well as for cyclical and growth purposes, may at times be confusing to some observers because the System may be supplying funds to the market . . . when cyclical developments clearly dictate a restrictive monetary policy, or vice versa. The time-honored device of raising or lowering discount rates, however, can hardly be susceptible to misinterpretation by even the most uninformed observers."

[33] In this connection, see the interesting paper by H. C. Carr, "A Note on Regional Differences in Discount Rates," *Journal of Finance*, XV, March 1960, pp. 62–68, which uses differences in the timing of discount rate changes on the part of different Reserve banks as a means of classifying the banks as "leaders," "follow-the-leaders," "middle-of-the-roaders,"

and the reasons for the action may vary among the different participants—some of whom may not thoroughly approve of the action —thus making it difficult to agree upon a generally acceptable accompanying statement.[34] This raises an interesting question: how can the general public and the business community help but be confused in their interpretations of a change in the discount rate when the persons who are responsible for making the change are not themselves entirely clear about the reasons for it?

2. Announcement Effects of Discount Rate Adjustments

In addition to the confusion resulting from the fact that some discount rate adjustments are meant to be signals of a change in monetary policy while others are not, there is a further question whether the resulting announcement effects, even when they are intended, will help to stabilize the economy. Announcement effects work through expectations, and the relationships involved are quite complex. It is possible to break down expectational reactions into reactions of lenders, reactions of borrowers, and reactions of spenders.[35]

a. *Expectational effects on lenders and borrowers.* A discount rate change may cause shifts in lenders' supply curves of funds and/or in borrowers' demand curves, the nature of these shifts depending upon the kind of expectations prevailing among lenders and borrowers. If interest rate expectations are elastic, a rise (fall)

---

and "dissenters." By studying rate increases and rate decreases separately, he also tries to discern differences in the banks' attitudes toward inflation and deflation.

[34] This is pointed out by Burgess (*op. cit.*), who says: "No reasons for the action are ordinarily given out at the time, partly because the decision represents the views of many people, who have perhaps acted for somewhat diverse reasons, so that it would be an extremely difficult task to phrase a statement which would fairly represent the views of all the directors of the Reserve Bank concerned and the Washington Board; and partly because it would be equally difficult to make any statement which did not either exaggerate or minimize the importance of the change. Such a statement is always subject to misinterpretation, as has been repeatedly illustrated." This statement was written a number of years ago, but it probably still reflects rather accurately the problem involved and the attitudes of those responsible for the administration of the discount rate.

[35] Our approach follows that adopted in dealing with expectational effects of monetary policy in general by Assar Lindbeck in his study entitled *The "New" Theory of Credit Control in the United States*, Stockholm Economics Studies, Pamphlet Series, No. 1, Stockholm: Almquist & Wiksell, 1959, pp. 25–29, 38–39. To a considerable extent, borrowers and spenders are the same people, of course, but it is useful to consider the two activities separately.

in present interest rates creates expectations of an even larger proportionate rise (fall) in future interest rates, whereas, with inelastic expectations, a rise (fall) in present interest rates induces the expectation of a smaller proportionate rise (fall) in future interest rates.[36]

Let us take the case of a discount rate increase and suppose that initially it causes a rise in market interest rates. If lenders have elastic expectations, they may reduce their present commitments of funds in order to have more funds available to invest later on, when interest rates are expected to be relatively more favorable. Conversely, if lenders have inelastic expectations, they may increase the amounts of funds they are willing to supply at the present time. Borrowers, on the other hand, may postpone their borrowing if they have inelastic expectations and accelerate it if they have elastic expectations. For a reduction in the discount rate, all of these reactions are reversed.

According to this view, the announcement effects of a discount rate adjustment will be clearly of a stabilizing nature if lenders have elastic expectations and borrowers have inelastic expectations, since in this case an increase in the discount rate will reduce both the demand for and the supply of funds, while a reduction in the discount rate will increase both demand and supply. On the other hand, if lenders have inelastic and borrowers elastic expectations, the effects will be clearly destabilizing, while if both groups have elastic or both have inelastic expectations, the outcome is uncertain and will depend on the relative strengths of the two reactions.[37]

Thus, in order to get favorable reactions on both sides of the market, it is necessary for lenders and borrowers to have the op-

---

[36] We are using the Hicksian concept of the elasticity of expectations, defined as

$$N = \frac{r_2^{\,e} - r_1^{\,e}}{r_1^{\,e}} \Bigg/ \frac{r_2 - r_1}{r_1},$$

where r_1 and r_2 stand for the present interest rate before and after the change, $r_1^{\,e}$ and $r_2^{\,e}$ stand for the expected future interest rate before and after the change. Elastic expectations, as the term is used above, means $N > 1$, while inelastic expectations means $N < 1$. See J. R. Hicks, *Value and Capital*, 2d. (Oxford: Clarendon Press, 1946), chapter xvi.

[37] In the case of an increase in the discount rate, if both lenders and borrowers have elastic expectations, lenders will reduce their offerings of funds while borrowers will increase their demands. If both have inelastic expectations, lenders will increase their supplies and borrowers will reduce their demands. In each of these cases, the outcome will depend upon the relative magnitudes of the respective shifts of demand and supply, as well as on the interest elasticities of demand and of supply.

posite kinds of expectations—a phenomenon that does not seem very likely. However, the significance of all of these considerations is considerably reduced due to the fact that, in practice, their main effects may be confined to producing changes in the interest rate structure. That is, a lender who has elastic interest rate expectations is not very likely to reduce the total supply of funds offered in the market; rather, he is likely to reduce his supply of funds in the longer-term sectors of the market, putting the funds into the short-term sector, while he awaits the expected rise in yields. Or, if he has inelastic expectations, he may shift funds from the short- to the long-term sector. Conversely, a borrower who has elastic expectations may not accelerate his total borrowings, but instead merely increase the proportion of his borrowing in the long-term market. Or, if he has inelastic expectations, he may shift a portion of his borrowings from the long- to the short-term market.[38] With our present limited knowledge concerning the effects of changes in the structure of interest rates on the level of expenditures, it is impossible to judge the effects of such shifts in the supply and demand for funds between the long- and short-term markets. It does seem safe to conclude, however, that the effects would not be very important.

b. *Expectational effects on spenders.* A discount rate adjustment may affect not only interest rate expectations of lenders and borrowers but also the sales and price expectations of businessmen on which spending plans are based. However, it is not entirely clear what the nature of these effects would be or how they would

[38] If lenders have elastic and borrowers inelastic expectations, both demand and supply will tend to shift from the long- to the short-term market following a rise in the discount rate, and the shifts will tend to cancel each other out as far as their effects on the interest rate structure are concerned. It may be noted that the typical behavior of the interest rate structure is consistent with the hypothesis that both borrowers and lenders have inelastic expectations, since in this case (with a rise in the discount rate), demand would shift from the long- to the short-term market while supply would shift from the short- to the long-term market and these reactions would cause a rise in short-term interest rates relative to long-term rates. When rates are generally high, short-term rates actually do often tend to be higher than long-term rates. This is also consistent with the behavior postulated by the general expectational theory of the interest rate structure when expectations are inelastic, as set forth in Tibor Scitovsky, "A Study of Interest and Capital," *Economica*, VII, n.s., August 1940, pp. 293–317; see also F. A. Lutz, "The Structure of Interest Rates," *Quarterly Journal of Economics*, LV, November 1940, pp. 36–63, reprinted in W. Fellner and B. F. Haley (eds.), *Readings in the Theory of Income Distribution* (Philadelphia: Blakiston Co., 1946), pp. 499–529.

affect economic stability. Taking the case of an increase in the discount rate, two situations (doubtless there are many variants of these) may be distinguished to illustrate the possibilities.

First, if inflationary expectations were already widespread and quite firmly established, if the possibility of restrictive anti-inflationary action by the Federal Reserve had not adequately been taken into account in the formation of these expectations, and if there was widespread confidence that monetary policy was capable of bringing inflation promptly and firmly under control, then a rise in the discount rate heralding the onset of a vigorously anti-inflationary monetary policy might have a bearish effect on sales and price expectations and thereby cause cutbacks and cancellations of expenditure plans. In this case, the announcement effects would be helpful to the authorities.

Second, if the outlook was somewhat uncertain but shifting in an inflationary direction, if observers were aware of the Federal Reserve's concern about the situation and were waiting to see whether the System would act, and if—perhaps on the basis of past experience—it was felt that monetary policy (even though potentially effective) would take considerable time to be brought to bear effectively enough to check the inflation, then a rise in the discount rate might have a bullish effect by confirming the emerging view that the near-term outlook was inflationary. In this case the announcement effects would be destabilizing.

Similar alternative expectational reactions could be postulated in the case of a reduction in the discount rate for the purpose of stimulating business activity. Although it is difficult to generalize concerning such matters and the effects might differ considerably from one situation to another, the second of the possible patterns of reaction outlined above seems, in general, considerably more plausible than the first. That is, it seems likely that the announcement effects of discount rate changes on the expectations of businessmen may frequently be of such a nature as to weaken rather than strengthen the effectiveness of monetary policy. At the same time the actions of the Federal Reserve are only one of the factors—and ordinarily not a major one—on which business expectations are based, and it is therefore doubtful whether the announcement effects of discount rate changes are really very important one way or the other.

We may conclude that the "psychological" effects of discount rate changes on the domestic economy—like all expectational phenomena in economics—are highly uncertain and that the discount rate as a weapon of "psychological warfare" is of very dubious value to the Federal Reserve.

A change in the discount rate has traditionally been used as a "signal" by some countries in an entirely different connection. In time of balance of payments crisis, a sharp increase in the discount rate may be used to communicate to the rest of the world a country's determination to defend by whatever means may be necessary the external value of its currency. Britain has used discount rate changes for this purpose on occasion since World War II, and this was a major reason why Canada abandoned the "floating discount rate" system (discussed below) and raised the rate to 6 percent at the time of the Canadian balance of payments crisis in June 1962. While a long tradition has perhaps made discount rate increases a reasonably effective means of international communication in some situations of this kind, there are surely other equally satisfactory means available; e.g., English, French, Latin, or Zulu.

C. Conclusions Concerning Present Discount Policy

The above analysis suggests that the discount rate as presently handled is not a very effective element in Federal Reserve policy. At times when a restrictive policy is applied, the induced increase in member bank borrowing constitutes a minor "leakage" in the controls, since it permits member banks to postpone contraction of their loans and investments and also adds to the total supply of member bank reserves. For the purpose of controlling the amount of borrowing, the Federal Reserve relies on adjustments in the discount rate, together with a tradition against borrowing that prevails among member banks and System surveillance of the borrowing practices of the banks. Due to the fact that open market interest rates fluctuate continuously while the discount rate is changed only at somewhat unpredictable discrete intervals, the relation between the discount rate and open market rates (which largely determines the incentive to borrow) behaves in a very erratic fashion. The System relies on "free reserves" as an immediate short-run guide for monetary policy; however, the restrictive effect of a given amount of free reserves varies with (among other things) the relation between the discount rate and the yields on assets—especially Treasury bills—that banks might alternatively liquidate to adjust their reserve positions.

Discretionary changes in the discount rate may at times have rather unpredictable effects on the business and financial situation, partly because it is often uncertain whether such changes are meant to be passive adjustments to keep the discount rate in line with other interest rates or whether they represent independent moves to tighten or ease credit. To the extent that changes in the discount rate do influence business conditions directly, they do so chiefly through psychological or "announcement" effects, the nature of which depends upon the kinds of expectations held by lenders, borrowers, and spenders. Although these announcement effects are quite complex and probably not of great importance in most cases, it seems likely that on occasion they may tend to increase economic instability.

D. Possible Reforms in Discount Policy

A number of students of monetary affairs have expressed discontent with the present discount policy of the Federal Reserve, although some of them have not made specific suggestions for a change.[39] However, at least three fairly specific proposals for reform have been suggested. Two of these would de-emphasize discount policy —one by getting rid of the discount mechanism entirely and the other by tying the discount rate to market interest rates and thereby eliminating discretionary changes in it. The third would move in the opposite direction by trying to reform the discount mechanism in such a way as to make the discount rate a much more powerful weapon of credit control. We shall discuss each of these proposals in turn.

1. Abolition of the Discount Mechanism

The proposal has been advanced quite forcefully by Professor Milton Friedman that the discount mechanism should be abolished altogether.[40] Friedman argues that the legitimate function of the central bank is to control the stock of money and that the discount

[39] See, for example, E. C. Simmons, "A Note on the Revival of Federal Reserve Discount Policy," *Journal of Finance*, XI, December 1956, pp. 413–431.

[40] Friedman, *A Program for Monetary Stability, op. cit.*, pp. 35–45; see also his testimony in *Employment, Growth, and Price Levels*, Hearings before the Joint Economic Committee, Part 9A (Washington, D.C.: U. S. Government Printing Office, 1959), pp. 3019–3028. A. G. Hart also suggested the possibility of abolishing discounting a quarter of a century ago in connection with a discussion of the 100 percent reserve plan; see his "The 'Chicago' Plan of Banking Reform," *Review of Economic Studies*, II, February 1935, pp. 104–116, reprinted in F. A. Lutz and L. W. Mints, eds., *Readings in Monetary Theory* (Philadelphia: Blakiston Co., 1951), pp. 437–456.

rate is an ineffective instrument for this purpose. Many of his arguments are similar to the ones set forth above, and his analysis was
cited at several points in our discussion.

One difficulty with the complete elimination of discounting is
that the discount mechanism serves a useful function as a "safety
valve" by which banks are able to make adjustments in their reserve positions and the Federal Reserve is able to come to the aid
of the banking system—or individual banks—in case of a liquidity
crisis. In order to provide a means for individual banks to make
short-run adjustments in their reserve positions, Friedman proposes
the establishment of a fixed "fine" to be assessed on reserve deficiencies; the fine to be set high enough to be above likely levels of
market interest rates, in order to prevent the device from becoming
an indirect form of borrowing from the Federal Reserve.[41] As far
as liquidity crises are concerned, he contends that, due to the success of deposit insurance in practically eliminating bank failures,
such crises are now scarcely conceivable and that the "lender of
last resort" function of the Federal Reserve is now obsolete, so that
we need not worry about its elimination. It may be noted that if
the discount mechanism were eliminated, it would be possible to
use the repurchase agreement technique as a means of providing
emergency assistance to the banking system in times of crisis.[42]

2. Tying the Discount Rate to the Treasury Bill Rate

An alternative to the complete abolition of borrowing would be
to change the discount rate at frequent intervals in such a way
as to maintain an approximately constant relation between it and
some open market interest rate, such as the Treasury bill rate. For
example, each week as soon as the average rate of interest on Treasury bills at the Monday auction became known, the discount rate
could be adjusted so as to preserve a constant differential between
the two rates.[43]

[41] Friedman, A Program for Monetary Stability, op. cit., pp. 44–45.

[42] This possibility was mentioned by Hart in connection with his suggestion for the elimination of the discount mechanism (op. cit., p. 110 in
original, p. 447 in Readings in Monetary Theory).

[43] See Smith, "The Discount Rate as a Credit-Control Weapon," op. cit.
Friedman (A Program for Monetary Stability, op. cit., p. 45) refers to such
an arrangement as an alternative (albeit a less desirable one in his
opinion) to complete abolition of discounting. He points out, quite correctly, that if the differential between the discount rate and the bill rate
were made large enough, the plan would be equivalent to abolishing discounting. Professor J. M. Culbertson ("Timing Changes in Monetary Policy," Journal of Finance, XIV, May 1959, pp. 145–160, esp. 157–158) concludes with respect to discount policy that the Federal Reserve "should

Under this arrangement, the discount rate would no longer be a discretionary credit control weapon, and the unpredictable and often perverse announcement effects on the expectations of businessmen and financial institutions would be done away with. To the extent that the Federal Reserve wanted to influence expectations and felt that it could manage such effects so as to contribute to economic stability, it could implement these effects through the issuance of statements concerning its intentions, the economic outlook, and so on. While the present writer is rather dubious about the value of such activities, it is surely true that to the extent that they can contribute anything useful they can be handled better by verbal means than through reliance on such a crude signal as the discount rate.

The major question involved in the adoption of an arrangement for tying the discount rate to the bill rate would be the choice of the proper differential between the two. Obviously, the discount rate should be above the bill rate; beyond this the establishment of the differential is a matter of judgment. The larger the differential, the smaller would be (a) the average amount of borrowing and (b) the swings in borrowing that would occur as credit conditions changed. In view of the wide variations among individual banks with respect to both portfolio composition and expectations, the present writer feels that a fairly large differential of perhaps one percent would be desirable, in order to keep down the amount of borrowing, which, for reasons discussed earlier, represents a minor leakage in monetary controls. But there does not seem to be any analytical principle that provides a basis for selecting the proper differential. Doubtless the best procedure would be to experiment with various differentials, retaining each one long enough to observe its effectiveness.

Under this arrangement, in contrast to the complete elimination of discounting, the discount mechanism would continue to be available to serve as a means of making temporary adjustments in bank reserve positions and as a "safety valve" that could be used in times of crises. If this approach were adopted, it would probably be desirable to give up the efforts to rely on such an intangible and unreliable means of controlling discounting as the traditional "reluctance" of member banks and the so-called "surveillance" of the Federal Reserve, recognizing borrowing as a "right" rather than a

___
subordinate the discount rate by making adjustments in it routinely in response to changes in market rates and should seek a less ambiguous vehicle for such communication with the public as may be useful."

"privilege" of member banks, and relying entirely on the discount rate (in relation to the bill rate) as a means of controlling it.[44]

A procedure of the kind discussed above was employed in Canada from November 1956, to June 1962. During this period, the Bank of Canada adjusted its lending rate each week so as to keep it $\frac{1}{4}$ of 1 percent above the average rate on treasury bills at the most recent weekly auction. The reasons given for adopting such an arrangement in 1956 were similar to those set forth above.[45] The policy was abandoned at the time of the Canadian balance of payment crisis in June 1962, when, as part of a program for dealing with the crisis, the discount rate was raised to 6 percent as a signal to the rest of the world of Canada's determination to defend the external value of the Canadian dollar.[46] The traditional discretionary discount rate policy has been employed in Canada since that time.

3. Increasing the Effectiveness of the Discount Rate

A proposal for reform of the discount mechanism very different from the two discussed above has recently been advanced by Professor James Tobin.[47] Instead of dismantling the discount mechanism entirely or abolishing discretionary changes in the discount rate, Tobin would greatly increase the importance of the rate and turn it into a major weapon of credit control.

The Tobin proposal calls for two changes in present procedures:

1. The Federal Reserve would pay interest at the discount rate on member bank reserve balances in excess of requirements.
2. The prohibitions against payments of interest on demand deposits

---

[44] In this connection, Friedman (*A Program for Monetary Stability, op. cit.*) says: "If rediscounting is retained, it should be a right, not a privilege, freely available to all member banks on specified terms." It appears that Friedman exaggerates the amount of discretion exercised by the System with respect to lending to individual banks, although the views expressed by System officials, concerning the "administration of the discount window"—such as Roosa's attempt ("Credit Policy at the Discount Window: Comment," *op. cit.*, pp. 333–334) to draw a distinction between saying "No," and refusing to say "Yes"—are so ambiguous that it is very difficult to judge the amount of discretion employed.

[45] See Bank of Canada, *Annual Report of the Governor to the Minister of Finance*, 1956, pp. 45–46.

[46] See Bank of Canada, *Annual Report of the Governor to the Minister of Finance*, 1962, pp. 3–4 and 72–73.

[47] James Tobin, "Towards Improving the Efficiency of the Monetary Mechanism," *Review of Economics and Statistics*, XLII, August 1960, pp. 276–279.

and the ceilings on the payment of interest on time and savings deposits would be repealed.

These changes would greatly increase the leverage of the discount rate by making it an important consideration for banks that are not in debt to the Federal Reserve as well as for those that are. The opportunity cost to a bank of increasing its loans and investments would be the return it could earn by holding excess reserves, and this cost would be firmly under the control of the Federal Reserve. Moreover, the interest rate offered by the banks to holders of idle deposits would presumably be linked rather closely to the rate paid on excess reserves, since the bank could always earn a return on its deposits at least equal to one minus its reserve requirement times the discount rate. Thus, if the Federal Reserve wished to tighten credit, it could raise the discount rate, and this would increase the opportunity cost of lending for all of the member banks (whether they were in debt or not) and would, therefore, make them willing to lend only at higher interest rates than previously, while at the same time causing the banks to raise interest rates on deposits, thereby increasing the attractiveness of bank deposits relative to other assets on the part of the public.[48] The discount

---

[48] Allowing the banks to pay interest on deposits would have two related advantages. One is that it would probably reduce the propensity for the velocity of deposits to increase when a restrictive policy was applied, since the banks would be able to raise interest rates on deposits making them more attractive and weakening the tendency for rising interest rates on other claims to induce shifts of deposits into the hands of persons having a high propensity to spend. The other advantage is that it should reduce the amount of real resources devoted to the task of economizing the use of cash balances. Since the revival of flexible monetary policy, many large corporations, as well as state and local governments, have developed extensive facilities for handling short-term investments in order to minimize their holdings of sterile cash balances, and the amount of skilled personnel devoting its time to this kind of activity at present is certainly not trivial (see C. E. Silberman, "The Big Corporate Lenders," *Fortune*, August 1956, pp. 111–114, 162–170). Resources devoted to this purpose represent a form of economic waste, since the real cost of creating deposits is virtually zero so that there is no economic gain from exercising economy in their use. This is pointed out by Tobin and is emphasized even more strongly by Friedman (*A Program for Monetary Stability, op. cit.*, pp. 71–75). The two advantages (reducing destabilizing velocity changes and discouraging efforts to economize in the use of costless deposits) are related in the sense that the propensity to waste resources in economizing cash balances tends to increase during periods of credit restriction and rising interest rates, and this increased application of resources helps to permit a destabilizing rise in velocity.

rate could be used independently to control credit, or it could be combined with open market operations. It is not clear, however, what principle should govern the division of responsibility between the two weapons.

The proposal is ingenious and would certainly be practical and capable of being put in operation without causing disruption. And it might have the incidental advantage that the payment of interest on excess reserves might encourage more banks to become members of the Federal Reserve System. What is not clear, however, is why a flexible monetary policy could be implemented more effectively by means of the discount rate under this proposal than is now possible by means of open market operations. It is true that the proposal would presumably permit the Federal Reserve to control the cost of bank credit very effectively, but this can already be done—in principle at least—by open market operations. In part, the problems of monetary policy seem to stem from the fact that the demand for bank credit is not very sensitive to changes in interest rates and other monetary variables, so that it has proved to be difficult to operate forcefully enough to produce prompt changes of the degree necessary for effective stabilization. Perhaps it would be possible to bring the forces of monetary policy to bear more rapidly by means of the Tobin proposal, but this is by no means obvious. If the proposal merely provides another way of doing what is already possible, it hardly seems worthwhile.

The repeal of the existing restrictions relating to payment of interest on deposits is in no way dependent upon provision for the payment of interest on excess reserves, and there is much to be said for the repeal of these restrictions, even if the remainder of the Tobin proposal is not adopted.

4. Conclusions

Of the three proposals for reforming the discount mechanism, the present writer feels that the strongest case can be made for the procedure of changing the discount rate each week in such a way as to maintain a constant spread between the discount rate and the Treasury bill rate. This would be a less drastic reform than the complete elimination of discounting, would eliminate the unpredictable effects of discretionary changes in the discount rate, would preserve the discount mechanism as a safety valve, and would eliminate the effects on credit conditions that now result from erratic variations in the relation between the discount rate and open market rates. The Tobin proposal for increasing the potency of the discount rate as a credit-control weapon is worthy of careful study, but it is not yet clear that the proposal would greatly strengthen the hand of the Federal Reserve.

If the present system of making discretionary adjustments in the discount rate at irregular intervals is retained, it would be desirable to reform the administration of the discount mechanism, perhaps by shifting the authority for making changes in the rate from the individual Reserve banks to the Federal Open Market Committee. The purpose of such a change would be to reduce the number of persons involved in decisions regarding the discount rate so that it would be easier to agree on the reasons for making changes. This would facilitate the issuance of explanatory statements at the time changes are made, in order to eliminate the confusion that often results due to the varying interpretations that are frequently placed on rate changes in the absence of explanations. It should then be feasible to make more frequent technical adjustments in the rate with less need to worry about the danger of disruptive effects on the credit situation, thereby permitting closer coordination of the discount rate with open market operations.

IV. THE ROLE OF VARIABLE RESERVE REQUIREMENTS[49]

Since the accord with the Treasury in March 1951, the Federal Reserve has made no systematic anti-cyclical use of changes in member bank reserve requirements. Reductions in the reserve requirement percentages applicable to demand deposits were made in the recessions of 1953–54 (reductions in July 1953, and June–August 1954) and 1957–58 (reductions in February–April 1958). In the recession of 1960–61, reserves were released by permitting member banks to count vault cash as reserves—to a limited extent beginning in December 1959, and without limitation beginning in November, 1960. And, finally, reserve requirements applicable to time deposits were reduced from 5 to 4 percent in October–November 1962, at a time when output was expanding but unemployment remained high.

Under present provisions, the Board of Governors can change requirements on demand deposits between 10 and 22 percent for reserve city banks and between 7 and 14 percent for country banks, while it can change requirements on time deposits between 3 and 6

---

[49] Much of the discussion in this section is based upon the author's study entitled "Reserve Requirements in the American Monetary System," in *Monetary Management*, prepared for the Commission on Money and Credit (Englewood Cliffs, N. J.: Prentice-Hall, 1963), pp. 175–315.

percent; as this is written (July 1963) the requirements are 16½ percent and 12 percent for demand deposits at reserve city and country banks, respectively, and 4 percent for time deposits.[50] The Board may permit member banks to count all or part of their vault cash as required reserves; at the present time vault cash may be counted in full.

A. Variable Reserve Requirements as a Credit Control Weapon

A change in reserve requirements alters both the amount of excess reserves available and the credit expansion multiplier, which determines the amount of potential credit expansion per dollar of excess reserves. For relatively small changes in reserve requirements, the first of these effects is much more important than the second—with net demand deposits amounting to roughly $100 billion, a reduction of one percentage point in requirements releases approximately $1 billion of excess reserves.

However, changes in reserve requirements have harsh and rather indiscriminate effects, at least when the changes made amount to as much as one-half or one percentage point, as has been customary in recent years. This does not cause serious problems in the case of reductions in requirements, because, as explained below, excessive bank liquidity generated by such reductions can be—and in practice has been—sopped up by open market sales of securities. Increases in requirements, however, have troublesome side effects which are not quite so easily dealt with.

Increases in requirements affect all banks—or at least all the banks in a particular reserve requirement classification—including some banks that are plentifully supplied with liquid assets which permit them to make easy adjustments in their reserve positions, as well as banks whose liquidity positions are less comfortable. To the extent that banks are forced to carry out troublesome portfolio readjustments, they are able to see clearly that these adjustments were forced upon them by Federal Reserve action; whereas the adjustments resulting from open market operations are either voluntary or, to the extent that they are involuntary, appear to be the result of impersonal market forces. Thus, frequent reserve requirement increases are likely to cause resentment among member banks and, under present conditions, might even be a significant deterrent to

[50] Under legislation passed in July 1959, the "central reserve city" classification of member banks was eliminated effective July 28, 1962.

membership in the Federal Reserve System. Moreover, while the initial effect of reserve requirement increases is felt by all the banks, it is likely that there will be substantial secondary effects which will be concentrated on banks in the larger money centers as interior banks draw down correspondent balances and sell Government securities in the central money market in order to restore their reserve positions.

B. Co-ordination of Reserve Requirement Changes and Open Market Operations

To some extent, it is possible to soften the unduly harsh impact of changes in reserve requirements by proper coordination with open market operations. The open market operations associated with the mid-1954 reductions in reserve requirements, which were designed to encourage continuing recovery from the recession of 1953–54, provide a good example of this coordination. The reserve requirement reductions that were made resulted in the injection of what the Federal Reserve authorities felt was an unduly large amount of excess reserves within a short period of time.[51] Accordingly the Federal Reserve sold securities in the open market at about the same time the reserve requirement reductions were made, in order to absorb a portion of the released reserves: then, over a period of several months, it purchased securities in order to feed reserves back into the economy at times when additional reserves appeared to be needed in the interest of orderly recovery.[52] Thus, a skillful blending of reserve requirement changes and open market operations produced a smooth and gradual adjustment.

Similar recent examples of the use of open market operations to

[51] In a succession of changes in June, July, and August, 1954, demand deposit reserve requirements were reduced by 2 percentage points at central reserve city banks and 1 percentage point at reserve city and country banks, while time deposit reserve requirements were reduced by 1 percentage point at all classes of banks. These adjustments released about $1.5 billion of reserves.

[52] Between June and August 1954, the Federal Reserve reduced its holdings of Government securities (average of daily figures) by $1.0 billion, while the net effect of factors outside the control of the Federal Reserve was to reduce member bank reserves by another $200 million. Thus, total reserves declined by $1.2 billion, and required reserves fell by the same amount, leaving excess reserves unchanged. From August to December 1954, the Federal Reserve increased its portfolio of Government securities by $0.9 billion as it fed reserves back to the banking system to meet seasonal demands. (Calculations based on data from *Federal Reserve Bulletin*, February 1955, p. 149).

soften the impact of reserve requirement increases during periods of inflation are not available, since the Federal Reserve has not made use of reserve requirement increases since the Accord.[53] The blending of open market operations with reserve requirement adjustments would probably not result in quite such a smooth adjustment in this case, because the problem here is not only to prevent an unduly sharp impact on the total supply of money and credit, but to alleviate harsh impacts on individual banks. Since some banks which were squeezed especially hard might not possess securities of the maturities being purchased by the System, these banks might not be helped directly by open market operations.

If reserve requirement changes have important advantages as a means of controlling credit, the technical difficulties in making two-way adjustments could be greatly reduced by making smaller changes in the requirements than have been customary in the past and by smoothing the impact by means of open market operations. It has been suggested that more frequent and smaller changes be made, and there is no technical reason why this could not be done.[54] And if more frequent use of reserve requirement changes would clearly permit the Federal Reserve to conduct monetary policy more efficiently than would otherwise be possible, the fact that such adjustments might be somewhat unpopular with commercial bankers should not be taken too seriously. The real question is: What advantages do reserve requirement adjustments have in comparison with other credit-control weapons, especially open market operations? To this question we now turn.

---

[53] During the immediate postwar inflation in 1948 while the Federal Reserve was "pegging" the market for Government securities, reserve requirement increases were used on several occasions in an effort to implement a policy of credit restraint. In this situation, however, member banks were plentifully supplied with Government securities, which were saleable at virtually fixed prices. Consequently, the banks tended merely to sell more securities than they otherwise would have sold, and these securities had to be purchased by the System to prevent securities prices from falling. Thus, banks were able to replenish their reserves readily, and there was little effect on the cost or availability of credit. In this situation, open market purchases were, in effect, used to offset more or less permanently the effects of reserve requirement increases. Such operations did tend to reduce bank liquidity somewhat, since the banks were giving up liquid securities for less liquid required reserves; however, the operations were not on a sufficiently large scale to make this a significant factor.

[54] See C. R. Whittlesey, "Reserve Requirements and the Integration of Credit Policies," *Quarterly Journal of Economics*, LVIII, August 1944, pp. 553–570.

C. Possible Usefulness of Reserve Requirement Changes

Under most circumstances, the effects of (for example) expanding credit by lowering reserve requirements will almost surely be different in detail from those produced by the same amount of expansion (measured in terms of the increase in income-generating expenditures) produced by open market purchases. That is, the spending units which will be induced to increase their expenditures will be different in the two cases, as will the types of expenditures affected. Unfortunately, however, our knowledge of relative "incidence" of the two weapons is very poor, so that, while we may be sure that there are differences, there is very little that can be said about them. For this reason, we can scarcely even discuss intelligently the "mix" of the two that should be used to accomplish particular objectives. The best we can do is to indicate some rather general considerations which differentiate reserve requirement adjustments from open market operations and some special situations in which the reserve requirements weapon may be especially appropriate.

1. Neutrality

The Federal Reserve authorities in recent years have shown a strong antipathy toward selective credit controls and have taken the position that the central bank should confine its efforts to the control of the total supply of money and credit, leaving the task of allocating credit to market forces. This attitude has been reflected, for example, in the System's opposition to the establishment of consumer credit controls even on a stand-by basis. Although there are other considerations involved also, this philosophy seems to be one of the bases for the Federal Reserve's adherence to the "bills-only" policy between 1953 and 1961. During this period, the System carefully eschewed efforts to control the maturity structure of interest rates, leaving this to the determination of market forces.

If such a philosophy of "neutrality" were to be pushed to its logical conclusion, it would lead to reliance on reserve requirement adjustments as a means of monetary control. Even bill-only is not entirely neutral in its effects on the interest rate structure, since changes in the money stock produced by this method involve, as a by-product, changes in the stock of securities of a particular maturity (namely, Treasury bills) and have a special impact on short-term interest rates. Reserve requirement changes, on the other hand, have no direct effects on interest rates or on stocks of securities—

all such effects are produced by the decisions and activities of borrowers and lenders (including commercial banks).

The "neutrality" argument for reliance on reserve requirement changes would carry weight only with those who accept the "neutrality" philosophy. Moreover, its implementation would require that all monetary adjustment be accomplished by reserve requirement changes. This would include the day-to-day operations of the Federal Reserve designed to counteract the effect of uncontrollable factors (float, currency in circulation, etc.) affecting member bank reserves. These operations seem clearly to serve a useful, if not indispensable, function in keeping the money market on an even keel and are now quite efficiently carried out by means of open market operations. While it would undoubtedly be possible to make smaller and more frequent adjustments in reserve requirements than have been employed in the past, it would surely be wholly impracticable to employ reserve requirement changes on a day-to-day basis. For this, as well as other reasons, the "neutrality" argument for the use of reserve requirement adjustments appears to be purely academic and of no practical importance.

2. Announcement Effects

Like discount rate adjustments and unlike open market operations, changes in reserve requirement are overt actions of the Federal Reserve which are widely reported and commented upon in the press. As such, they are likely to have "announcement effects" through their influence on the expectations of businessmen and financial institutions. In fact, it seems quite likely that the reductions in reserve requirements that were made in 1953 and 1958 were motivated partly by a desire to convince the public that the System intended to take vigorous anti-recession action.

The question of announcement effects was discussed at some length in connection with discount rate changes, and the conclusion of that discussion was that such effects are uncertain and unpredictable. This conclusion seems to apply also to reserve requirement changes. For example, it seems at least as plausible to suppose that a dramatic reduction in reserve requirements in the early stages of a recession will strengthen the feeling that business conditions are worsening, as to suppose that it will make people optimistic by showing that the Federal Reserve is actively on the job trying to maintain stability.

I believe the fact that reserve requirement changes tend to have announcement effects is a disadvantage rather than an advantage.

The best way to produce announcement effects—if and when such effects seem likely to be desirable—is by means of carefully-worded public statements explaining the views or intentions of the authorities. Action and communication should, in general, be carefully separated rather than rigidly linked together.

3. Speed of Reactions

It has been argued that reserve requirements changes have more widely diffused effects than open market operations and therefore may effect economic conditions more promptly. The reasoning behind this argument is that open market operations are consummated in the central money market of the country in New York and therefore have their initial impact chiefly on the reserve positions of the money market banks. Effects are gradually diffused throughout the country, primarily by means of interregional flows of funds set in motion by the adjustments of these banks to the initial changes in their reserve positions—a process which takes some time to carry through. Reserve requirement changes, on the other hand, instantaneously affect the reserve positions of all banks and therefore produce more rapid effects on credit conditions outside the central money markets. Federal Reserve officials apparently accept this argument and think it is especially relevant with respect to anti-recession policies, since Chairman Martin of the Board of Governors has used it to explain why the System used reserve requirement reductions as a means of attacking the recessions of 1953–54 and 1957–58.[55]

One study covering the period from mid-1951 to mid-1953, when the Federal Reserve relied on open market operations to tighten credit rather gently at first and then with increasing intensity, suggests that the effects were felt first in New York and that there were noticeable lags in their transmission to the rest of the country.[56] The free reserve position of central reserve city banks appears to have been affected earlier and more strongly than that of other banks, and New York City banks showed an earlier and more pronounced tendency to shift the composition of their portfolios from investments to loans than did banks outside New York City. The author of this study suggests more frequent use of changes in reserve

[55] See Martin's testimony in *January 1960 Economic Report of the President*, Hearings before the Joint Economic Committee, 86th Cong., 2d Sess. (Washington, D.C.: U. S. Government Printing Office, 1960), pp. 163–212.
[56] I. O. Scott, Jr., "The Regional Impact of Monetary Policy," *Quarterly Journal of Economics*, LXIX, May 1955, pp. 269–284.

requirements, in order to shorten the lags in the regional transmission of monetary policy.

While this study is somewhat suggestive, it is not clearly convincing, since the statistical series involved are so ragged in their behavior as to be difficult to interpret, and because one cannot be sure that such differences in regional reactions as were present were not due to factors unrelated to monetary policy. There are several reasons for doubting whether the differenece in the reaction speeds of the two weapons is great enough to be an important consideration. In the first place, as noted above, while the initial impact of reserve requirement changes is widely diffused, adjustments of interior banks via changes in correspondent balances and security transactions are likely to pass a disproportionate share of it back to the central money markets. Furthermore, to the extent that the initial effects of open market operations are more concentrated, the fact that central money market banks are very sensitive to changes in their reserve positions and prompt in reacting thereto would suggest that the transmission of effects to other parts of the economy is likely to get under way quickly and proceed rapidly. And finally, the other lags in monetary policy appear to be so long that it is doubtful whether such differences as do exist between the two weapons are of appreciable importance in the overall picture. In fact, one cannot even be sure that there is not frequently some advantage in open market operations, because commercial banks all over the country adjust their reserves through sales of securities (which largely clear through the central money market) so that purchases (for example) of securities may have some tendency to direct the flow of new reserves to the points where they are most needed, instead of scattering them indiscriminately over the map.[57]

[57] Chairman Martin of the Board of Governors has stated his belief that an increase in reserve requirements would be the best way to offset the effects on member bank reserves of a substantial gold inflow, if circumstance required such offsetting (see his testimony in *January 1960 Economic Report of the President*, Hearings before the Joint Economic Committee, *op. cit.*, p. 187). Perhaps this would be true in some circumstances, but the present writer is inclined to believe that open market sales of securities might often be the more appropriate weapon for this purpose, since the funds resulting from the sale of gold to the Treasury by foreign governments are often likely to find their way to the central money market, so that the way to offset the effects of these flows with the minimum impact on domestic business activity might be through the sale of Treasury bills, which would, in the main, withdraw funds from the central money market.

4. National Emergencies

One circumstance in which the power to raise reserve requirements might be used to good purpose is in times of a war or major national defense emergency, which requires the expenditure of large amounts of borrowed funds by the Government during a period of full employment. Under such conditions, there is much to be said for the Treasury's obtaining such funds as it needs but cannot raise through taxation or through borrowing from the nonbank public by selling securities directly to the Federal Reserve, with the System raising reserve requirements to immobilize the excess reserves that are created when the Treasury spends the money. This process would avoid the accumulation of excessive liquidity in the hands of the commercial banks and the accompanying threat of post-emergency inflation and would save the Treasury some interest costs. It would, of course, require that the Federal Reserve be given virtually unlimited power to raise reserve requirements.

5. Conclusions

The upshot of the above discussion is that there appear to be few if any circumstances in normal times when reserve requirement changes are clearly superior to open market operations as a means of controlling credit. Reserve requirement changes have "announcement effects" while open market operations do not, but these may frequently turn out to be a nuisance rather than an aid to the Federal Reserve and, to the extent that they are desirable, can be produced more effectively by other methods. Conceivably, reserve requirement changes may affect business conditions more promptly than open market operations; however, this is not certain, and in any case the advantage is unlikely to be great enough to be of much significance. In view of the superior administrative efficiency of the open market operations, together with the unpopularity among commercial bankers of frequent two-way adjustments of reserve requirements, there is much to be said for relying exclusively on open market operations under normal circumstances.[58]

[58] Another issue that has come up recently relating to the choice between open market operations and reserve requirement changes is the differing effects that these two weapons have on the Treasury's interest costs and on the profits of commercial banks. For example, the creation of a given amount of additional money by open market purchases will result in lower costs to the Treasury and lower profits to the banking system than would the creation of the same amount of money by lowering reserve requirements. (For an extensive discussion, see Smith, "Reserve Requirements in the American Monetary System," *op. cit.*, pp. 216–

V. CONCLUDING COMMENTS

As they are used at the present time, open market policy, discount policy, and reserve requirements policy are three instruments of monetary control with essentially a single purpose—the regulation of the total supply of money and bank credit. Open market policy is powerful, effective, and administratively flexible; is it unquestionably the key weapon of general monetary control. Discount policy, as reflected in changes in the discount rate, has a weak and to some extent even perverse effect on the total supply of money and credit and is, at the same time, a rather inept and confusing device for waging "psychological warfare" against economic instability via the public's expectations. Reserve requirements policy is a powerful weapon but too cumbersome for frequent use and not clearly capable of accomplishing anything under ordinary circumstances that cannot be done at least as well by means of open market operations.

Doubtless the three weapons have somewhat different economic effects; however, detailed knowledge of the impact of monetary changes is inadequate to permit a meaningful differentiation. Consequently, it is not possible to specify the circumstances in which one of these weapons rather than the others should be used. They are all designed to serve the same purposes—one effectively and the other two rather ineptly.

Accordingly, I would favor placing complete reliance on open market operations, under ordinary circumstances, as the means of conducting general monetary policy. The best way of handling the discount rate would probably be to tie it to the Treasury bill rate as explained earlier in this paper. Reserve requirements should probably be fixed at an appropriate level and kept there.[59] I would also favor the elimination of the present threefold classification of banks for reserve requirement purposes and the establishment of uniform

---

249.) However, this matter is relevant chiefly in connection with long-term developments related to the choice between open market purchases and reserve requirement reductions as alternative means of providing reserves to support the secular growth of the money supply. It has little bearing on the relative merits of the two weapons as alternative means of producing two-way anti-cyclical changes in credit conditions.

[59] The question of what is the "appropriate" level of reserve requirements is beyond the scope of this paper and, in any case, is a matter of judgment. It is in connection with this question that the effects of reserve requirements on bank profits and Treasury interest costs referred to in footnote 58 become relevant.

reserve requirements for demand deposits at all banks, including nonmember banks. There does not appear to be any logical basis for differentiating among banks as far as reserve requirements are concerned, and uniform requirements would increase somewhat the precision of open market policy as a means of controlling the total supply of money and bank credit.[60]

There may be circumstances under which the Federal Reserve should try to affect economic activity by influencing the public's expectations, although this is clearly a tricky and possibly even dangerous form of activity. To the extent that it is employed, it should be divorced from actions designed to control bank reserves and should take advantage of the subtleties of everyday language. One of the advantages of open market operations is that they are necessarily being carried out continuously and are largely devoid of so-called "announcement effects."

One final question should perhaps be raised: Does not the situation of the last three years or so when monetary policy has had to be directed simultaneously at stimulation of the domestic economy and protection of the balance of payments against excessive outflows of short-term capital argue for the retention of all of the traditional credit control weapons, in order to maximize the flexibility of the monetary authorities? I do not believe so. It is true that, for example, by lowering reserve requirements and simultaneously selling enough Treasury bills to keep the bill rate from falling, the authorities could presumably stimulate the domestic economy to some extent without increasing outflows of short-term capital. But such a result could equally well be brought about by requisite purchases of longer-term securities combined with sales of bills. It is difficult to see that adjustments in reserve requirements and the discount rate give the authorities any ability to change the structure of interest rates and the total credit supply that could not equally well be accomplished by sufficiently flexible use of Federal Reserve open market and Treasury debt management operations.

[60] *Ibid.*, pp. 175–199.

FEDERAL RESERVE BANK
OF CLEVELAND

THE DEALER MARKET FOR
U. S. GOVERNMENT SECURITIES
AND MONETARY POLICY

17

In comparison to organized securities markets such as the New York or American Stock Exchange, the market for U. S. Government securities is certainly less widely known. Yet, in terms of activity as measured by the dollar volume of transactions, the U. S. Government securities market far surpass any of the well-known organized securities markets. For example, in 1966 the total volume of transactions (both sides, i.e., purchases and sales) by dealers in U. S. Government securities was valued at about $573 billion compared with the volume of stock transactions valued at $98.6 billion (one side) on the New York Stock Exchange and the $24.4 billion (one side) on all other registered securities exchanges in the country.

Even more importantly perhaps, the role of the U. S. Government securities market—and the dealers in that market—may be considered special in the sense that the market provides important (indeed essential) services to both private and public institutions. On the public side, both the U. S. Treasury and the Federal Reserve System make use of securities dealers to carry out their responsibilities—the Treasury in connection with marketing and refinancing the national debt and the Federal Reserve in connection with the conduct of open market operations. At the same time, private institutions such as commercial banks, insurance companies, savings and loan associations, and nonfinancial corporations, among others, rely on securities dealers for executing transactions in U. S. Government securities.

THE DEALER MARKET

Firms in the Market

At present, there are approximately 20 firms acting as primary dealers in U. S. Government securities. Some of these are special

Reprinted from "The Dealer Market for U.S. Government Securities and Monetary Policy," *Economic Review* (December 1967), pp. 3–12, Federal Reserve Bank of Cleveland.

departments of commercial banks and are accordingly classified as bank dealers, while the rest are essentially securities houses that are designated as non-bank dealers. In addition to handling U. S. Government securities, some of the dealers in the second category engage in other investment banking activities. Although the main offices of most dealer firms are located in New York City, branches are maintained by several in leading metropolitan areas throughout the country.

Formally speaking, the dealer market for U. S. Government securities is an "over-the-counter" market in which the bulk of transactions is conducted by telephone and teletype. That is to say, almost invariably, transactions are first contracted through telephone or teletype and then confirmed in writing.

The key to the organization and the functioning of a dealer firm is the trading room. It is there that markets in U. S. Government securities are in effect made. The terms at which securities can be bought and sold are set by individual traders in each firm. Terms are constantly readjusted as financial market conditions change, and news about business and financial developments is circulated. The terms traders quote for buying or selling securities are the market, and tend to reflect the desire of dealers to add to or reduce positions in light of their reading of current developments.

Transactions

Most dealer firms usually stand ready to execute transactions in some size in all maturity ranges of U. S. Government securities. Smaller firms, however, confine most of their business to short-term issues, primarily because they cannot afford the capital risk involved in longer maturities, preferring to concentrate in the most active sector in which risks are less.

Dealer quotations differ according to the maturity of the issue under consideration. Treasury bills are quoted on a yield basis. For example, Treasury bills maturing three months from now may be quoted at 4.90 "bid" and 4.80 "asked." This simply means that a dealer is willing to buy a block of these bills with a given maturity value at a price that would yield him 4.90 percent for the holding period, or is willing to sell the same bills at a price that would yield 4.80 percent to the buyer. In other words, the dealer's selling price is higher than his buying price. The difference, or spread, between the buying and selling price constitutes trading income for the dealer.

Trading spreads are also maintained on outstanding certificates, notes, and bonds. Dealer quotations on these issues are expressed in terms of prices rather than yields. For example, a bond issue bearing a coupon of $3\frac{1}{2}$ percent and maturing in 1980 may be quoted in the market at 83.24 bid and 84.8 asked. Since the figures after the decimal point are in thirty-seconds, the above quotation should be read as 83-24/32 bid and 84-8/32 asked which indicates that the dealer is willing either to pay $83.75 or to receive $84.25 for every $100 in maturity value of these bonds. A narrowing of spreads indicates greater willingness on the part of dealers to conduct transactions, i.e., to make a narrower market for U. S. Government securities, and reflects dealers' assessment of risk and their ability to turn over inventories.

The volume of securities transactions is often considered an indicator of performance. That is to say, a large and increasing volume may suggest the greater ability of the market to meet the varied needs of diversified groups of investors who wish to carry out transactions. Table I contains data on dealer transactions in the U. S. Government securities market during 1961–1967, and includes combined dealer purchases and sales as reported to the Federal Reserve Bank of New York. The data indicate that the level of market activity has risen fairly steadily during the 1960's, particularly in more recent years. The average daily volume of transactions for all maturity classes increased from $1,552 million in 1961 to $2,095 million in 1966. Average daily trading in issues maturing within one year has also shown consistent growth during the 1960's, rising from $1,203 million in 1961 to $1,706 million in 1966, in fact, accounting for virtually all of the increase in total transactions. In 1–5 year maturities, dealer transactions declined from an average daily level of $265 million in 1961 to $242 million in 1966. During the first nine months of 1967 of 1967, the average increased to $257 million. Dealer transactions in issues maturing after five years increased during 1962 and 1963, but then declined slightly during each of the next three years, and the first nine months of 1967. Nevertheless, average daily transactions in longer term issues during 1966 and 1967 were considerably higher than in 1961 (see Table I).

Positions

U. S. Government securities dealers do not act as mere middlemen for buyers and sellers, as is usually the case with brokers for registered stocks. Instead, dealers buy and sell securities for their own account, and in so doing act as principals rather than brokers. Consequently, dealer holdings of U. S. Government securities are subject

TABLE I   Dealer Transactions in U. S. Government Securities,
1961–1967, Par Value *(in millions of dollars)*

Year	All maturities	Within 1 year	1–5 years	After 5 years
1961	$1,552	$1,203	$265	$ 84
1962	1,786	1,401	228	158
1963	1,734	1,322	218	193
1964	1,770	1,382	220	168
1965	1,827	1,481	194	151
1966	2,095	1,706	242	146
1967*	2,087	1,733	257	96

* First nine months only.

NOTE: Data on transactions are averages of daily figures based on the number of trading days in the period. Transactions data represent combined totals of dealer purchases and sales as reported to the Federal Reserve Bank of New York. Excluded from the data are allotments and exchanges for new U.S. Government securities, redeemed securities before or at maturity, dealer security sales under the condition that they must be bought back by dealers, and dealer purchases that must be sold back to original owners.

SOURCE: Board of Governors of the Federal Reserve System, *Federal Reserve Bulletin* (various issues).

to capital gains and losses due to interest rate changes. For this reason, dealers' inventory positions are sometimes referred to as "positions of risk."

Technically, a dealer may take two types of positions—a long position and a short position. A dealer takes a long position when he buys securities outright for his own account. In a short position, the dealer sells securities that he does not have in his account but borrows the securities in order to deliver them to the purchaser. The dealer, of course, must buy back and return the borrowed securities at a later date. In addition, the dealer must put up securities that he owns as collateral for the borrowed securities. Not surprisingly, there are risks involved in both long and short positions. For example, if a dealer has taken a position and securities prices rise (interest rates fall), capital gains will be realized in the long position and capital losses in the short position. (In the latter case, the dealer will have to pay a price that is higher than his original selling price to buy back the borrowed securities.)

Obviously, the actual behavior of interest rates, as well as expectations about that behavior, will influence dealer position policy. If interest rates are expected to rise in the future (securities price fall), dealers will tend to decrease long positions and increase short positions. In the event that dealers expect interest rates to decline (securities prices rise), positions in securities will tend to be reversed. Dealers, of course, realize that expectations do not always materialize and to avoid the penalties or costs of mistaken expectations, dealers may hedge positions. That is to say, if dealers are not certain about the future course of interest rates, they can reduce or eliminate risk by covering long positions with short positions. In other words, dealers can sell a certain amount of securities short each time that the same amount of securities is taken into a long position.

Hedging also contributes to the improvement of the market by permitting the dealer to sell an issue that he does not hold against one that he does, and thereby satisfies a customer's need. In fact, many hedged positions result from security swaps with customers. In any event, from the standpoint of a well-functioning U. S. Government securities market, it is important to have dealers who are willing to take positions. Only in this way can the interests of individual investors be best served.

To a large extent, dealer willingness to take new positions is influenced by the size of actual positions already taken. Table II contains annual data on average daily positions during 1961–1967. It should be noted that the data represent "net" positions, i.e., short

TABLE II   Dealer Positions in U. S. Government Securities, 1961–1967, Par Value (*in millions of dollars*)

Year	All maturities	Within 1 year	1–5 years	After 5 years
1961	$2,748	$2,357	$338	$ 54
1962	3,320	2,922	276	122
1963	3,406	2,876	385	145
1964	3,423	2,901	313	217
1965	3,348	2,816	140	391
1966	2,476	2,262	142	76
1967*	3,469	2,911	415	143

* First nine months only.

NOTE: Data are averages of daily figures based on number of trading days in the period. Position figures are on "net" basis, i.e., short sales have been deducted from long positions. Securities sold by dealers under the condition that they must be repurchased at a later date (unless such sales are offset by equivalent amounts of securities purchased by dealers under the condition that they must be resold later to original owners) are included in long positions and therefore are reflected in net positions.

SOURCE: Board of Governors of the Federal Reserve System, *Federal Reserve Bulletin* (various issues).

positions have been deducted from long positions, so that net positions are in effect long positions "not hedged." Although Table II shows positive net positions on balance throughout the 1961–1967 period, net positions may have been negative for short time periods, in some maturity categories. Over longer time periods, however, long positions as a rule tend to be several times larger than short positions.

As shown in Table II, average daily positions in all maturities in 1961 were over $2.7 billion. Dealer positions rose to and remained at a level of around $3⅓ billion during the next four years. In 1966, the daily average of dealer positions fell appreciably, in fact, to almost $300 million less than the 1961 level, with a similar pattern emerging in positions classified by maturity. The decline in dealer positions in 1966 in large part can probably be ascribed to the marked and dramatic shifts that occurred in financial flows and financial markets, as well as in expectations. However, during the first nine months of 1967, when market conditions and expectations changed, dealer positions increased sharply in all maturity categories. Thus, on balance, the willingness of dealers to take positions in U. S. Government securities seems to have improved during the 1960's.

Financing

Dealer transactions, positions, and financing during 1960–1967 are illustrated in the chart. As the chart shows, dealer transactions, in general, tend to move in the same direction as dealer positions and financing, although the relationship between dealer positions and financing is certainly a closer one—indeed, the two series are conspicuously close. The latter relationship should not be surprising in that, although dealers act as principals in buying and selling securities, they use very little of their own funds. The bulk of dealer working capital is accounted for by borrowing. Securities dealers can usually borrow money from banks on a 2–5 percent margin of equity capital when making bond purchases and on virtually zero margin for bill purchases.

Dealers depend basically upon two types of loans to finance positions: bank loans (for which the securities purchased are used as collateral) and repurchase agreements (RPs). Bank loans as a rule carry a higher financing cost for the dealer than do RPs.[1] Accordingly, from the dealers' viewpoint, RPs constitute the preferred source of financing. Usually, a repurchase agreement involves a

[1] For a more complete discussion of the role of RPs in dealer financing, see *Money Market Instruments*, Federal Reserve Bank of Cleveland, 1965, pp. 19–30.

dealer's commitment to buy back securities that he has sold earlier. The interval from the time the dealer sells the securities to the time he buys them back may vary from one business day to several weeks, or even months. The relative amounts of dealer positions financed through collaterized bank loans and through repurchase agreements depend largely upon the general availability and distribution of funds in the money market. When interest rates are high and the availability of funds limited, the reliance on RPs for dealer financing tends to increase relatively.

U. S. Government securities dealers execute repurchase agreements with a number of institutions, including commercial banks, non-financial corporations, Federal Home Loan banks, and state and local governments. In addition, the Federal Reserve Bank of New York makes funds available under repurchase agreements to *non-bank* dealers. This, of course, is done at the initiative of the Federal Reserve Bank, when it is deemed desirable from the standpoint of open market operations.

Table III presents data on the major sources and extent of dealer borrowing during 1961–1967. As indicated earlier, the volume of dealer financing needs depends mainly upon the size of dealer positions. Throughout the 1960's, commercial banks have been the most important source of dealer borrowings, providing nearly half of dealer financing. Corporations have provided over 40 percent of dealer financing, while borrowings from other sources (including RPs from the Federal Reserve Bank of New York) have contributed over 10 percent during 1961–1967.

TABLE III   Financing of Dealers in U. S. Government Securities, 1961–1967, Par Value (in millions of dollars)

Year	All sources	Commercial banks	Corporations	All others
1961	$2,725	$1,289	$1,177	$259
1962	3,359	1,542	1,461	256
1963	3,559	1,705	1,465	389
1964	3,503	1,812	1,317	374
1965	3,546	1,738	1,336	471
1966	2,666	1,238	1,018	411
1967*	3,591	2,256	798	537

* First nine months only.
NOTE: Financing data are averages of daily figures based on the number of calendar (rather than trading) days in the period.
SOURCE: Board of Governors of the Federal Reserve System, *Federal Reserve Bulletin* (various issues).

Income

As noted earlier, the spread between dealers' selling and buying prices constitutes an important source of dealer income. Spreads vary according to the maturity of the issue. For example, the spread on U. S. Treasury bills is likely to be small. This is true first, because bills are not as susceptible as longer term issues to large capital losses, and second, because the volume of dealer transactions in bills is much greater than in coupon issues. Accordingly, the spread is usually much larger for longer term issues, which carry a greater risk of capital loss. Typically, spreads on 3-month bills average about 2-5 basis points, while spreads on long-term bonds average around 8-16 thirty-seconds, i.e., $0.25–$0.50 on a $100 bond.

A second source of dealer income arises from price changes in securities that dealers hold in position, which, of course, is not always positive. During periods of rising yields (falling securities prices), a dealer is likely to incur capital losses in his long positions and capital gains in his short positions. If long positions are larger than short (as is usually the case since dealers must maintain at least minimum trading positions), rising yields will tend to have a negative effect on dealer income. When interest rates are falling, the effect on income would be the reverse.

Finally, the difference between interest earned on securities in position and the interest cost of financing such securities constitutes another source of income for a dealer; usually referred to as "carry" income. Whether income from carry is positive depends mainly upon the composition of dealer long positions and the term structure of interest rates. For example, if a considerable portion of dealer long positions consists of coupon issues, and short-term interest rates are above long-term rates, the carry is likely to be negative. This could be the case because dealers finance positions through short-term funds and the interest cost would tend to be greater than the interest earned on long-term securities held in position.

Published data on dealers' income are not available for the period of the 1960's. In an earlier study, however, it was found that income of securities dealers varied widely during the 1948–1958 period, with net income before taxes ranging from a high of $38.8 million in 1958 to a low of − $1.9 million in 1955.[2]

---

[2] Allan H. Meltzer and Gert von der Linde, *A Study of the Dealer Market for Federal Securities*, Joint Economic Committee, 86th Cong., 2d Sess. (Washington, D. C.: U. S. Government Printing Office, 1960).

THE DEALER MARKET AND MONETARY POLICY

The Federal Reserve System, in carrying out its role in economic stabilization policy, relies mainly upon three instruments of monetary management: reserve requirement variation, discount rate changes, and open market operations. Of the three, open market operations are used most frequently. Open market policy is made by the Federal Open Market Committee, and in turn is executed at what is commonly known as the Trading Desk of the Federal Reserve Bank of New York, under the responsibility of the Manager of the Federal Open Market Account, who is an officer of the Federal Reserve Bank of New York.

Dealer services are essential in the process of implementing open market operations. In fact, the role of the dealers in this process may be construed as the first link in the series of events that transform actions taken by the Desk into financial and economic effects. Federal Reserve open market operations are initially reflected in the reserve position of commercial banks. Suppose, for example, that the Trading Desk sells securities to dealers. Bank dealers pay for the securities acquired from the Desk by drawing on their reserve accounts at the Federal Reserve Bank of New York. Nonbank dealers pay by using a check drawn on a commercial bank, which clears the transaction (the transaction is usually conducted in Federal funds, i.e., same day money); when this check is received, the Federal Reserve Bank of New York reduces the reserve account of the commercial bank. On the other hand, purchases by the Trading Desk lead to increases in member bank reserves. In this case, bank dealers are paid by credits to their accounts at the New York Federal Reserve Bank, as are eventually the banks with whom nonbank dealers do business.

In its approach to dealers, the Desk often employs a technique commonly known as a "go-around." This procedure begins when the Desk's traders contact securities dealers and ask for "firm" bids or offers, i.e., quotations that ordinarily cannot be changed or withdrawn within a stated time interval without the consent of the Desk. After all dealers have been contacted and their offerings tabulated and compared, the Desk chooses the offerings on a best price basis, while also taking into account several other considerations, for example, those affecting the System's portfolio. Dealers are then informed about the outcome of their offerings. The entire operation involved in a "go-around" is on average completed within 30 minutes time.

Types of Transactions

There are basically two types of transactions that the Desk may enter into with dealers. The Desk may buy or sell securities outright on behalf of the System's Account without any conditions attached. Alternatively, it may buy or sell while simultaneously contracting to resell (a repurchase agreement) or to repurchase (a matched sale-purchase transaction). All transactions are undertaken at the initiative of the Desk, which also determines the aggregate volume of transactions.

Only nonbank dealers are eligible for repurchase agreements (RPs), while matched sale-purchase transactions are carried out with all dealers. The length of time covered by the contract involving RPs between the Desk and dealers cannot be any longer than 15 days. At any time within the time interval of the contract, the agreement may be terminated by either party. RPs involve a repurchase price that affords a return to the System that is usually equal to the discount rate of the Federal Reserve Bank of New York. In matched sale-purchase transactions, the Desk offers to sell selected issues of Treasury bills at specified rates, with dealers competing at the rate at which they will sell the securities back within a stipulated time of several days. Contracts are concluded up to an amount the Desk wishes to do at the best rates available. Neither party can alter the terms of the transaction, once consummated.

Whether the Desk uses outright purchases or RPs depends, among other things, upon conditions in financial markets and the objectives of the Trading Desk and the Federal Open Market Committee. Outright transactions are usually undertaken when the System wishes to supply or withdraw bank reserves on a more permanent basis, whereas RPs or matched transactions are used to inject or withdraw reserves for a limited time only.

System Transactions, 1961–1967

The volume and nature of System transactions during 1961–1967 is shown in Table IV. Taken together, the volume of outright transactions and RPs increased from $24.6 billion during 1961 to $45.1 billion in 1966. The total of $41.0 billion of such transactions during the first nine months of 1967 suggests that System transactions in 1967 as a whole will surpass those of 1965 and 1966. The average volume of transactions during 1961–1966 was $34.7 billion per year. When total transactions are broken down into outright and repur-

TABLE IV   Federal Reserve System Open Market Transactions
(in millions of dollars)

Year	Outright (purchases plus sales)	Repurchase agreements (purchases plus sales)	Total transactions
1961	$15,162	$ 9,481	$24,643
1962	16,550	12,047	28,597
1963	13,322	18,121	31,443
1964	15,891	18,046	33,937
1965	14,115	30,094	44,209
1966	25,948	19,176	45,124
1967*	13,491	27,531	41,022
Annual Average 1961– 1966	$16,831	$17,827	$34,658

* First nine months only.
NOTE: Sales figures do not include redemptions.
SOURCE: Board of Governors of the Federal Reserve System.

chase agreements, it can be observed that, although the average RP volume of $17.8 billion was about $1.0 billion greater than that of outright transactions, the amounts of the two types of transactions varied from year to year. RPs exceeded outright transactions during 1963, 1964, 1965, and the first nine months of 1967.

Maturity Breakdown of Outright Transactions, 1961–1967

The bulk of outright transactions during 1961–1967 was conducted in Treasury bills (see Table V). System purchases during 1961–1966 amounted to $63.7 billion, of which $53.5 billion (84 percent) were in Treasury bills. The remainder of the purchases were in coupon issues varying in maturity from less than a year to over ten years.

System outright sales were even more concentrated in Treasury bills than were purchases. Of a total of $37.2 billion of securities sales, only $2.2 billion were in issues other than bills and almost all of these sales were in issues maturing within one year. The System did not undertake any sales of securities carrying maturities of five years or longer.

Although System transactions outside the Treasury bill area were

TABLE V Maturity Distribution of Federal Reserve System Outright Purchases and Sales (*in millions of dollars*)

	1961	1962	1963	1964	1965	1966	1967*	Annual average 1961–1966
Purchases								
Treasury bills	$5,794	$6,813	$7,280	$ 9,433	$8,958	$15,177	$ 8,959	$ 8,909
Other issues within 1 year	600	1,085	56	5	0	199	51	324
1–5 year issues	1,923	1,569	843	465	500	208	543	918
5–10 year issues	660	326	543	440	340	50	244	393
Over–10 year issues	128	37	68	111	90	17	133	75
Total	$9,105	$9,829	$8,790	$10,454	$9,888	$15,651	$ 9,940	$10,619
Sales								
Treasury bills	$4,486	$6,211	$4,429	$ 5,437	$4,227	$10,297	$ 3,555	$ 5,947
Other issues within 1 year	1,474	402	54	0	0	0	0	322
1–5 year issues	97	108	50	0	0	0	0	42
5–10 year issues	0	0	0	0	0	0	0	0
Over–10 year issues	0	0	0	0	0	0	0	0
Total	$6,057	$6,721	$4,533	$ 5,437	$4,227	$10,297	$ 3,555	$ 6,212

* First nine months only.
NOTE: Sales figures do not include redemptions.
SOURCE: Board of Governors of the Federal Reserve System.

small, they nevertheless constituted a departure from previous practice in that before 1961, System transactions were normally confined to Treasury bills. The Trading Desk bought and sold securities
with longer term maturities only in unusual circumstances, such as
disorderly conditions in the market for U. S. Government securities.
Beginning in February 1961, however, the Federal Open Market
Committee authorized transactions in longer term issues under
other circumstances. The Committee's decision was prompted in part
by the need to help protect the United States balance of payments
position at a time when domestic economic conditions dictated a
stimulative monetary policy. Under such conditions, there was some
feeling that open market purchases of longer term issues would help
the System to provide bank reserves without depressing short-term
interest rates—an approach that, it was believed, would tend to
reduce short-term capital outflow from the United States while at
the same time encouraging domestic economic activity.

SUMMARY

This article has attempted to describe the market for U. S. Government securities and its relationship to Federal Reserve open market
operations. In terms of number of firms, the dealer market is relatively small; only about 20 firms are responsible for all the business
in the market. Nevertheless, these firms occupy a key position in the
American financial system by virtue of the fact that they provide
important services to private as well as to public institutions.

It is, of course, not easy to find independent criteria upon which
the technical performance of the dealer market can be evaluated.
The data on the volume of dealer transactions and the size of
dealer positions, however, suggest a secular improvement in the
functioning of the market during the 1960's. For financing securities
positions, dealers largely upon borrowed funds, all of which are in
the form of short-term loans. The dealers have developed several
ingenious ways for tapping temporarily idle funds from financial and
nonfinancial institutions, with repurchase agreements a case in
point. During 1961–1967, commercial banks have been the largest
source of dealer borrowings, with business corporations running a
strong second.

From the standpoint of monetary policy, dealers are important
mainly because of their role in the execution of open market operations, which is the most frequently used method of influencing the
availability of credit. By standing ready to buy and sell securities
from the System's Open Market Account, the dealers constitute in

effect the principal channel through which the Federal Reserve ultimately influences the entire economy.

LESTER V. CHANDLER

SOME ISSUES IN FEDERAL RESERVE DISCOUNT POLICY

18

At the time of the Treasury–Federal Reserve Accord of March 1951, the Federal Reserve discount mechanism had lain largely unused for about seventeen years. From 1934 to 1942, thanks largely to huge gold inflows and some Treasury purchases of silver, member banks were flooded with excess reserves and had no need to borrow. During the nine years following March 1942 they had little need to borrow, because the Federal Reserve stood ready to purchase, passively and at relatively stable prices and yields, all United States government securities offered to it. Thus, at the time of the Accord many member banks had not borrowed for about seventeen years, and during the same period Federal Reserve officials had little experience in operating discount windows. In fact, there is little evidence that they had thought much about the future role of discount policy.

It was clear, however, that after the Accord, which relieved the Federal Reserve of the duty of pegging prices and yields on government securities, discounting and discount policy would again become of some importance. More banks would have to borrow more frequently to meet their liquidity needs. Yet there was not then agreement, nor is there now, as to what discount policy should be. What should be the relative roles of discounting, open market operations, and alteration of member-bank reserve requirements in

Reprinted by permission of Oxford University Press, London, from Lester V. Chandler, "Some Issues in Federal Reserve Discount Policy," *Essays in Money and Banking: In Honor of R. S. Sayers*, 1968, pp. 47–62.

supplying and regulating the reserves and liquidity position of the banking system? On what conditions and terms should an individual bank be permitted to borrow? On what types of collateral? To what extent should discounting be regulated by discount rates and to what extent by non-price methods? What should be the criteria and procedures for setting and changing discount rates? These are only some of the questions concerning discount policy that continue to be debated both within and outside the System.

For several reasons it was almost inevitable that discounting and discount policies would become less important, relative to open-market policies as instruments for general monetary management, than they were in the 1920s and early 1930s. For one thing, there had been marked changes in national objectives and in concepts of the responsibilities of the Federal Reserve. In the earlier period, when there was no national commitment to maintain continuously high levels of employment, many Federal Reserve officials and some economists believed that the System should supply funds primarily through discounting. It should provide 'elasticity' by responding to 'the needs of trade', as these needs were evidenced by business demands for credit from the banks and by bank applications for discounts to enable them to meet these demands—though not necessarily in full or at constant interest rates. To such officials, and others, open market operations undertaken on the initiative of the Federal Reserve were 'unnatural', 'artificial', and likely to lead to later trouble. The Federal Reserve should supply funds in response to demands, not force funds on the market or make forcible withdrawals from it. Ideas and attitudes such as these, rather than lack of power, were largely responsible for the failure of the Federal Reserve to make large open-market purchases earlier in the 1930s.

Ideas and attitudes had changed markedly by 1951. The nation had adopted the Full Employment Act of 1946 and Federal Reserve officials acknowledged their responsibility to contribute to its objective of promoting 'maximum employment production and purchasing power.' They believed that this required counter-cyclical actions taken on the Federal Reserve's own initiative and that open-market operations were more appropriate, powerful, and reliable than discount policy.

The elevation of open-market policy and relative decline of discount policy were also promoted by the increase of nearly $200 billion in the debt of the Federal Government during World War II. Early in 1951 the amount of Federal debt held outside the Treasury still amounted to nearly $218 billion. Of this, the Federal Reserve held about $21 billion and the commercial banks $62 billion; the remainder was widely distributed among all the principal types of financial intermediaries, non-financial corporations, and individuals. Moreover, the market for government securities was highly active and increasing in efficiency. These facts were relevant to Federal Reserve policy in several ways. The Federal Reserve, with its large holdings of governments, was in a position to absorb any likely accretion of unwanted reserve funds, and it could easily supply more funds by purchasing some of the large outstanding stock of government securities. The commercial banks, holding government securities equal to 47 percent of their total loans and securities and 40 percent of their total deposits, were in a highly liquid condition. Thus, it was reasonable to expect that they would meet their liquidity needs largely within their own resources, with little recourse to borrowing from the Federal Reserve.

It was under such conditions that the Board of Governors in 1955 issued Regulation A, which stated the principles governing member bank borrowing. This regulation stated that banks should borrow only to meet needs that could not reasonably be foreseen.

Federal Reserve credit is generally extended on a short-term basis to a member bank in order to enable it to adjust its asset position when necessary because of developments such as a sudden withdrawal of deposits or seasonal requirements for credit beyond those which can reasonably be met by use of the bank's own resources. Federal Reserve credit is also available for longer periods when necessary in order to assist member banks in meeting unusual situations, such as may result from national, regional, or local difficulties or from exceptional circumstances involving only particular member banks. Under ordinary conditions, the continuous use of Federal Reserve credit by a member bank over a considerable period of time is not regarded as appropriate.

Though these principles applied to borrowings by individual member banks, it was also clear that Federal Reserve officials did not want any considerable part of total bank reserves to be supplied by borrowing. In fact, during the entire period since World War II, discounts have provided a much smaller part of total bank reserves than in the 1920s. In the earlier period member bank borrowings were often equal to 20 percent, and at times even 40 percent, of total member bank reserves. However, in the post-war period borrowings have rarely exceeded 6 percent of total bank reserves, and they have usually been much smaller. This is not to say that fluctuations of borrowings between virtually zero and $1.5 billion are insignificant.

Several critics, primarily academic economists, believe that the Federal Reserve has not gone far enough in suppressing discounting.

Their most common complaint is that discounting constitutes a "slippage" or "escape hatch" in monetary management. This point of view has been stated most clearly by Milton Friedman. As is well known, he believes that the Federal Reserve's objective should be to increase the money supply at a uniform rate through time, and that for this purpose the System requires an accurate and precise control over the size of the reserve base. As he sees it, discounting weakens this control. Banks are tempted to borrow more in times of boom and to repay in times of recession, thus tending to make the money supply behave in a pro-cyclical manner. Moreover, the effects of Federal Reserve purchases and sales in the open market tend to be blunted by partially offsetting decreases and increases in bank borrowings. He therefore recommends that the Federal Reserve should abolish discounting altogether and levy fines on member banks if they fail to meet their reserve requirements. The fines would be set at such a high level as to make it unprofitable for banks to run reserve deficiencies.

This prescription has been criticized on at least two grounds. For one thing, it does not deal explicitly with discounting as a source of liquidity for individual banks. Friedman apparently believes that each bank should solve its liquidity problems by selling assets or borrowing from sources outside the Federal Reserve. His critics believe that these sources may at times be inadequate. This point will be discussed later. Some also deny that discounting, if properly regulated, is an undesirable "slippage" in general monetary management. Rather, it can provide a useful safety-valve or buffer which gives the Federal Reserve time to react to events, whether these events are its own actions or external shocks.[1] It is significant that most of those taking this position reject Friedman's contention that the behaviour of the money supply is a reliable guide to policy, and contend instead that the proper guide is the behaviour of interest rates, or more broadly the cost of capital, for it is through this channel that monetary policy influences aggregate demand. If discounting were abolished, interest rates might react rapidly and sharply to such events as increases or decreases in demands for credit and changes in the supply of reserves, whether because of open-market operations or for other reasons. Discounting serves as a shock-absorber which spreads the effects over time. It need not weaken control over interest rates or the money supply, for the Federal Reserve can achieve its desired results through appropriate

[1] I am indebted to James Tobin for interesting comments on these subjects, but he is not to be held responsible for my interpretations.

open-market operations and changes in discount rates. If it fails to do so the fault is not of the discount mechanism but of policy.

Another controversial question is: To what extent should the Federal Reserve regulate the volume and allocation of discounts through changes in discount rates, and to what extent by non-price rationing? In fact, the Reserve Banks rarely change their rates more than three times a year, and usually less frequently. Since open-market rates change frequently if not continuously, one result is a fluctuating relationship between discount rates and open-market rates. Control through the discount rate is supplemented by such Federal Reserve devices as emphasizing that borrowing is a "privilege and not a right," nurturing the "tradition against borrowing," admonitions, bringing pressure to bear on banks to reduce borrowings, and outright refusals of loans. Rationing through these methods rather than by price has been criticized on several grounds. For one thing, it may promote undesired changes in total discounts, for banks are likely to want to borrow more in boom periods and less in recession. To regulate discounting by some 6,200 member banks through non-price methods is difficult administratively. But even if changes in total discounts are appropriately offset through open-market operations, non-price rationing may lead to arbitrary and inefficient allocations of reserves and lending power among the banks. Reserves may go to those banks that are least heedful of Federal Reserve admonitions rather than to those whose customers can use loans most productively. Some conclude that reliance on non-price rationing of discounts should be abolished, or at least sharply reduced, greater reliance being placed on a more vigorous discount-rate policy. This would call for more frequent, and perhaps wider, changes of rates.

This leads to still other controversial questions: How should the discount rate be set and changed? How high should it be? As indicated earlier, the Federal Reserve promulgates specific discount rates and changes them only infrequently. Each rate change has at least two kinds of effects—effects on the cost of discounts, and "announcement" or "expectational" effects. Perhaps partly because rate changes are so infrequent, they are viewed by many as important indicators of Federal Reserve intentions or expectations with respect to future credit conditions. Rate increases are viewed as harbingers of future rates at least as high as those current, while rate decreases suggest the opposite. In earlier periods such announcement effects were considered to be, on the whole, beneficial to the effectiveness of monetary policy. More recently many economists have become more critical, contending that announcement effects are erratic and undependable in their strength, and even in their direction, and may be perverse. One reason for this is that a discount change is an ambiguous signal as to Federal Reserve intentions. For example, a rate increase may indeed be a part of a Federal Reserve policy of raising interest rates, or it may be only a "technical adjustment," an alignment of the discount rate with market rates, with no intention of allowing rates in general to rise. In the absence of any other announcement, the public may be misled. Rate changes, if they occur, may lead to undesirable effects on expectations, or the Federal Reserve, fearing such results, may be inhibited in changing rates.

A number of economists have proposed that the Federal Reserve should abandon the present system and adopt instead a "floating rate system," in which the discount rate would always be kept at some margin above a selected market rate. For example, it might be provided that the discount rate during any week would be equal to the average yield on 90-day Treasury bills during the preceding week plus one quarter of one percent. Two advantages over the present system are claimed. For one thing, this would virtually eliminate announcement effects, for rate changes would occur automatically every week and in accordance with a fixed formula. Also, by keeping the discount rate at a fixed height above the selected market rate, it would in a sense provide an unchanging penalty on borrowing. It would thus avoid the fluctuations in the size of the penalty which occur under the present system when the discount rate remains constant while market rates change.

Though a number of economists have come out in support of a floating rate system, others oppose it. Some of these favour more frequent changes in discount rates and less reliance on non-price rationing of discounts, but believe that for several reasons the Federal Reserve would be unwise to abandon discretionary control of discount rates. (1) The awkwardness and perversity of announcement effects have been exaggerated. Though discount-rate changes have at times been misinterpreted, the same is true of other policy actions, such as open-market operations. The lesson is not that the Federal Reserve should discard an instrument but that it should provide more specific information concerning its aims and intentions. (2) Announcement effects can be useful for domestic as well as international purposes. (3) A floating rate system, in which the discount rate would change automatically with every change in the selected market rate, would respond more radically to outside shocks—such as changes in demands for credit or in the supply of reserves—and would produce quicker and wider fluctuations of interest rates. On at least some occasions this might be undesirable;

it might be preferable for the Federal Reserve to absorb some part of the shock by lending more or less at an unchanged discount rate; with discretionary control of discount rates, it retains freedom of choice. (4) Advocates of a floating rate system have not given sufficient attention to the difficulties involved in selecting one out of many market rates to which the discount rate would be tied and in determining the appropriate margin above that rate. They might well discover that they had selected the "wrong" market rate or the "wrong" margin, or that a fixed margin would yield fluctuating and unexpected results. This leads us into a whole series of unresolved questions concerning "penalty rates."

From the beginning there has been strong support within the system for the idea that the discount rate should be a "penalty rate"—that in some sense it should penalize, not reward, borrowing. Yet the concept has never been clearly defined in operational terms by either Federal Reserve officials or economists. An earlier concept has long since been abandoned—that the appropriate discount rate is a rate somewhat higher than the yield on the particular type of paper offered for discount. For one thing, it has long been recognized that there need be no relationship between the type of paper discounted and the type of use to which the borrowed funds will be put. Also, the borrowing bank still bears the risk of loss on the paper discounted or pledged as collateral for advances. Though this concept has been abandoned, no satisfactory substitute has been found.

In deciding whether and how much to borrow from, or remain in debt to, the Federal Reserve, a rational banker presumably compares the marginal cost of borrowing and the marginal benefits accruing to him. The marginal cost of borrowing at a given discount rate may not be an unambiguous concept, especially if borrowing entails some danger of Federal Reserve displeasure. But to identify and quantify the marginal benefits of borrowing presents much more difficult problems. The benefits of borrowing are presumably the avoidance of alternatives that would otherwise have to be chosen—the sacrifice of yields on loans or investments that would otherwise have to be sold, the cost of borrowing from other sources, or forgoing returns on new loans or investments. To permit rational comparisons with the discount rate and the marginal cost of borrowing, the benefits of avoiding these alternatives to borrowing would have to be valued and stated in terms of an interest rate or yield. At any point of time, what do bankers consider to be the leading alternatives to borrowing? Is it to sell some of their earning assets? If so, which ones—Treasury bills, longer-term governments, or customer paper? Is the alternative to borrow outside the Federal Reserve? If so, what rates are considered most relevant—the rate on Federal funds, rates on repurchase agreements on government securities, or rates on inter-bank loans? Is the alternative to forgo acquiring new loans or investments? If so, what types—government securities, mortgages, or customers' loans? At any given time the explicit rates or yields represented by these alternatives differ widely, ranging all the way from the yield of the shortest term Treasury bills to rates on consumer instalment loans. This wide range of explicit yields would in itself make it difficult to define precisely a "penalty" discount rate.

However, this is not the end of the difficulties, for it seems unlikely that bankers make decision solely on the basis of comparisons of explicit market rates with the discount rate. For one thing, the rate expected by the banker may differ from the prevailing market rate. For example, the yield expected on a government security depends in part on expectations as to its price behaviour. And the yield expected on a loan to a customer may deviate significantly from the stated market rate because of such things as compensating balance requirements, the expected value to the bank of future business because the loan was made, and so on. Perhaps more important, other costs and benefits are also relevant to bankers' decision. These include marginal transactions costs of acquiring, holding, and disposing of assets, effects on the liquidity and safety of the bank, and so on. We still have much to learn about how bankers value such things or how their valuations change through time.

It might be thought that the discount rate is a penalty rate if it is above the yield on the lowest-yielding earning asset in a bank's portfolio, for the bank could get money by selling this asset. Thus, it has at times been argued that a discount rate above the yield on 90-day Treasury bills is a penalty rate, because for a bank the leading alternative to borrowing is to sell such bills. This is of doubtful general validity. It is clearly invalid for banks which do not hold such bills. Moreover, banks sometimes borrow at discount rates above yields on the Treasury bills that they continue to hold, and there are numerous instances in which banks sell longer term government securities with yields significantly above yields on the Treasury bills that they retain. Such behaviour may be quite rational, explicable by such things as marginal transactions costs, expectations relating to future prices and yields on assets, and effects on the liquidity and safety positions of banks.

The upshot of all this is that the concept of a "penalty rate" will continue to be ambiguous until we know much more about decision making in banks. It suggests some of the difficulties of a floating rate system—difficulties of selecting the rate to which the discount rate would be tied, and difficulties of determining an appropriate margin. A given system might well turn out to encourage borrowings at some times and discourage them at others, and there is no assurance that the fluctuations of borrowings would be counter-cyclical. It also suggests that if the Federal Reserve should abandon non-price rationing and rely solely on rationing through changes in the discount rate, it would have to rely heavily on trial and error changes in the rate, rather than on some fixed formula for a penalty rate.

The preceding sections have concentrated largely on discount policy as an instrument of general monetary management—as a means of regulating the reserves and liquidity of the banking system as a whole. We turn now to discounting as an instrument for supplying liquidity to individual banks or groups of banks within the system. Though these functions are closely related, they are separable. For example, the Federal Reserve might consider its function of providing liquidity to individual banks to be so important that it would provide discount facilities even if this did constitute a "slippage" in its general monetary management. The system might even look upon discounting not as an important instrument of general monetary management but as almost solely a device for allocating reserves among the banks and of meeting the liquidity needs of individual banks. It might rely upon open-market operations, and perhaps also changes in reserve requirements, to regulate the reserve and liquidity positions of the banking system as a whole but lend generously to those particular banks experiencing unusual deposit losses or unusually high demands for credit. In effect, it could secure funds by selling securities in the open market and reallocate these reserves by discounting. Few have argued that the Federal Reserve should do this on a large scale, but there remain wide differences of opinion concerning the responsibility of the system for meeting the liquidity needs of individual banks.

The American banking system is comprised of some 13,800 banks; a majority of these operate only a single office and virtually none operates branches outside its home state. This banking structure makes it possible and even probable that banks will experience widely differing behaviour of deposits and loan demands. Even when total deposits in the system are increasing, individual banks may suffer deposit drains, either temporary or more prolonged, this because of seasonal fluctuations in the receipts and expenditures of their depositors, local crop failures, depression of local industry, and so on; or most of the banks in a given region may suffer drains because of adverse changes in local industries. When this occurs there is a danger that legitimate local needs for credit will not be met. Banks may also experience widely differing behaviour of demands for loans, some facing large increases while demands in other areas remain low. There is no assurance that banks facing the largest demands will also experience the largest increases of deposits and lending power. There may also occur more prolonged credit shortages in regions where demands for credit are growing more rapidly than bank resources. This danger is alleviated to the extent that business in the area has access to distant banks or to the central capital and money markets, but regions in which small and medium sized businesses predominate may not have such access. It will be noted that in some of these cases a bank's need for liquidity is only temporary, but in other cases it is more prolonged.

Individual banks have, of course, many sources of liquidity other than recourse to borrowing from the Federal Reserve. For example, they can sell some of their Federal government securities in the highly organized and active market for these securities. There is also an organized, but less active, market for certain other bank assets, such as debt obligations of state and local governments and corporations. They can borrow in the Federal funds market, which has developed rapidly and in which increasing numbers of banks are participating, or from their correspondent banks, or even from nonfinancial corporations. In recent years many banks have also sought funds by bidding actively for time and savings deposits. Most spectacular has been the growth of negotiable time certificates of deposit. These have been most fruitful for the largest banks, though some smaller banks have also used them.

In the first part of the post-war period there was a widespread belief that such sources would by themselves be sufficient to provide adequate liquidity for individual banks and for adequate interregional flows of funds among banks, so that there would be little need for recourse to borrowings from the Federal Reserve. However, opinion has shifted somewhat in recent years. For this there appear to be several reasons. One is certainly the sharp decline of bank holdings of Federal government securities as a percentage of their total loans and investments and as a percentage of their deposit liabilities. As shown in Table 1, commercial bank holdings of Federal securities in mid 1951 were equal to 46.4 per cent of their total loans and securities. During the next fifteen years their loans increased 270 per cent and their holdings of other securities 271 per cent, while

TABLE I   Commercial Bank Loans and Investments: Seasonally
Adjusted Amounts *(in billions of dollars)*

June 30	Total loans and securities	Loans	U.S. government securities	Other securities	U.S. government securities as a percentage of total loans and investments
1951	126.5	55.0	58.8	12.7	46.4
1952	135.0	59.3	61.7	14.0	45.7
1953	138.5	64.9	59.4	14.2	42.8
1954	146.9	67.0	64.5	15.5	43.9
1955	155.6	74.3	64.5	16.8	41.4
1956	159.7	85.4	57.8	16.5	36.1
1957	164.6	91.1	56.8	16.8	34.5
1958	178.6	92.7	65.9	19.9	36.8
1959	184.6	101.7	62.3	20.6	33.7
1960	187.1	111.5	55.7	19.8	29.7
1961	201.3	115.8	63.4	22.0	31.4
1962	218.3	126.2	65.2	26.9	29.8
1963	237.2	141.0	63.9	32.3	26.9
1964	255.3	158.7	60.3	36.2	23.6
1965	281.7	181.4	58.2	42.1	20.6
1966	305.4	203.7	54.5	47.1	15.4

SOURCE: *Federal Reserve Bulletin,* July 1966, pp. 952–955.

their holdings of Treasury securities actually declined somewhat. The general pattern has been for banks to increase their holdings of governments during period of business recession and to decrease them during boom periods when credit demands rose. However, during the fifteen years ending in mid 1966 the percentage of bank holdings of governments to their total loans and securities fell from 46.4 per cent. to 15.4 per cent. Member-bank holdings of governments as a percentage of their total deposit liabilities fell from about 40 per cent. to 14.2 per cent. These statistics may overstate the extent and ease with which member banks could secure liquidity through their holdings of these securities. For one thing, some of these securities are pledged as collateral for government deposits, and thus are not available for sale or as collateral for borrowings at the Federal Reserve. Moreover, more than half of these securities have maturities in excess of a year, so that their sale, at times of unusually high interest rates, such as those reached in 1966, would entail book losses. There can be little doubt that the over-all liquidity of bank assets has diminished in recent years.

It also seems likely that in recent years banks have become subject to larger shifts of deposits, both shifts among banks and shifts between categories of deposits. This probably reflects both greater sensitivity of depositors to changes in relative yields on assets and also wider fluctuations in relative yields. The "Corporate Treasurers' Revolution" has been widely noted. Never before have managers of the financial assets of large and medium sized non-financial corporations been so sophisticated and willing to shift their holdings in response to changes in relative yields on such things as demand deposits, various classes of time deposits, government securities, repurchase agreements, acceptances, Federal funds, commercial paper, and even Eurodollars. Households, with increasing holdings of liquid assets, also seem to have have gained financial sophistication and readiness to shift response to changes in relative yields.

There have also been large changes in relative yields. Federal laws still prohibit payment of interest on demand deposits, and rates on time and savings deposits have varied widely. Up to 1957 the highest rate permitted by the Federal Reserve and Federal Deposit Insurance Corporation ceilings was $2\frac{1}{2}$ per cent., and the rates actually paid by many commercial banks were even lower. These were well below the rates at savings banks, savings and loan associations, and on some short-term direct securities. The result should have been predictable; time and savings deposits at commercial banks grew only slowly, while the public increased rapidly its holdings of higher yield assets. The situation has changed markedly since early 1957 and especially since early 1962. Ceiling rates have been raised in several steps, and banks in general have bid actively for these deposits, many paying the ceiling rates. The results have been several. One has been a very rapid growth of savings and time deposits, primarily the latter, at commercial banks, especially when their rates were high relative to rates at savings banks and savings and loan associations, and to yields on such open-market assets as short-term government securities. Another result is that many banks now have large amounts of deposit liabilities which they might lose quickly if their rates fell below competing rates. The potential dangers of this situation were widely discussed in 1965 and 1966 at times when yields on short-term government securities rose above the ceiling rates. Some even feared crises for banks heavily dependent on time deposits, especially those with large outstanding amounts of large denomination negotiable certificates of deposit. There was one obvious solution: to remove ceiling rates, or to raise them to such high levels that they would become ineffective and thus enable banks to compete freely for funds. However, the authorities were reluctant to do this, partly because of effects on competing institutions, especially savings and loan associations, and on supplies of funds for home-building. The danger of large shifts of deposits among banks, and from time to demand deposits, remains.

Such are some of the conditions which support the position that Federal Reserve discount policy should play a continuing, and perhaps increased, role in providing liquidity for individual banks or groups of banks: (1) The marked decline of bank holdings of Federal government securities in relation both to their total loans and securities and to their total deposit liabilities, and the decrease in the over-all liquidity of bank assets; and (2) the possibility of large shifts of deposits among banks and between the categories of demand and time deposits, a possibility which is enhanced if ceiling rates limit the freedom of banks to bid for funds as competing rates change. Many economists and others favour abolition of ceiling rates on time and savings deposits at commercial banks. However, it is doubtful that this view will prevail, or even that comparable ceilings will be imposed on rates paid by competing financial intermediaries.

Several proposals have been offered to change the discount mechanism. One is to amend the Federal Reserve Act to permit the Reserve Banks to lend at their regular discount rates on a wider range of bank assets. As the law now stands, only two types of paper are 'eligible' as collateral for loans at the regular discount rate: Federal government securities and certain short-term private paper of the "real bills" type. No one knows how many bank assets would meet these "eligibility requirements," but it is clear that a large part of them would not. Any Federal Reserve loan on other bank assets must be at a rate at least $\frac{1}{2}$ of 1 per cent. above the regular discount rate. In every year since 1962 the Board of Governors has recommended legislation which would permit member banks to borrow at the regular rate on any sound assets. This, it is believed, would both increase the ability of the Federal Reserve to provide liquidity and also encourage banks to meet the changing credit needs of the economy. Such a bill actually passed the Senate in August 1965, but the House took no action on it.

The Board of Governors has also recommended that insured non-member banks, as well as members, should be permitted to borrow from the Federal Reserve, but only if they are subjected to the same legal reserve requirements as those applicable to comparable member banks. One clear purpose of this two-part recommendation was to eliminate the discrimination against member banks in the form of legal reserve requirements more burdensome than those applying to most non-member banks. Federal Reserve officials complain that this is inequitable to member banks, that it has been a factor in accelerated withdrawals from membership of the System, and that withdrawals are 'fast reaching the point where System effectiveness in the implementation of monetary and credit policy may be impaired.'[2] Another purpose was to give the insured non-member banks, numbering about 7,300, direct access to the Federal Reserve discount window. Their lack of such access must on occasion impair their ability to serve their customer, and in time of crisis might weaken the entire banking system. The acid test of the 1930s showed that for many banks of these types their sources of liquidity outside the Federal Reserve were neither reliable nor adequate. The Congress has taken no action on this Board proposal, and history provides little basis for optimism.

Such have been some of the recent events and issues relating to Federal Reserve discount policies. They do not suggest that discount policy will again achieve the high position it enjoyed in the early years of the System. They do indicate, however, that earlier forecasts of a demise of discount policy were a bit premature.

[2] *Annual Report of the Board of Governors, 1965,* p. 236.

GEORGE W. MITCHELL

REAPPRAISAL OF FEDERAL RESERVE DISCOUNT POLICY

19

. . . The studies and research on which the Report[1] is based were undertaken to be sure our lending operations—properly called our discount mechanism—were appropriate to present-day banking institutions and environment. To be more effective in meeting changing

Reprinted from "Statement of Hon. George W. Mitchell," *Federal Reserve Discount Mechanism.* Hearings Before the Joint Economic Committee, 90th Cong., 2d Sess., Sept. 11 and 17, 1968, pp. 3–9.
[1] Report: *Reappraisal of the Federal Reserve Discount Mechanism.*

community credit needs, commercial banks need central bank assistance as well as supervision. We are pleased to discuss our findings with you.

The redesign suggested by the Report would represent the latest in a whole series of evolutionary changes in Federal Reserve lending policies and procedures. When first established by the Federal Reserve Act in 1913, the discount mechanism was expected to operate by member banks presenting certain types of short-term customer notes—termed "eligible paper"—as collateral for borrowing at the Reserve banks. During most of the first 20 years of Federal Reserve operation, member banks borrowed a sizable proportion of their total required reserves on the security of such customer notes.

After 1934, however, member banks accumulated large amounts of Government securities and other liquid assets; accordingly, they did very little borrowing from their Federal Reserve banks, and collateralized such borrowings as they did with Government securities. This marginal role for the discount window was formally recognized in a change in 1955 in the Board's regulation A covering loans to member banks; under that revision, bank borrowings from the Federal Reserve were to be limited to assistance over the peaks of temporary, seasonal, or emergency needs for funds that exceeded the dimensions that the banks could reasonably be expected to meet out of their own resources.

In the last decade or so, however, credit demands on banks have grown and loan-to-deposit ratios are much higher, rising from 47 percent to 60 percent. Moreover, at many banks portfolio management has pared liquidity positions substantially, and borrowings from sources other than the Federal Reserve have expanded enormously. In addition, a small but growing number of banks has also been led to withdraw from membership in the Federal Reserve System, chiefly in order to avoid reserve requirements and thus enable them to invest a greater portion of their resources in earning assets. In view of these developments, the proposed redesign of the discount mechanism is aimed at relating Federal Reserve lending more clearly and closely to the changing banking and community needs.

Before I outline the new proposals which have been made for our lending facilities, it might be well for me to mention three long-standing basic principles of Federal Reserve lending that were reaffirmed by our study.

First among these is that Federal Reserve credit is extended primarily to accommodate bank asset and liability adjustments over limited time periods and to meet essentially short-term fluctuations in member bank needs for funds.

In short, no continuous borrowing.

The second principle reaffirmed, however, is that Federal Reserve banks always stand ready to lend to any of their member banks caught in special regional or local adversities—such as droughts, drastic deposit drains, or other emergencies—for as long as reasonably needed for the bank to work out of these circumstances.

Thirdly, the Report recognizes that the Federal Reserve serves as "lender of last resort" to buttress the entire financial system in the event of widespread emergency. Within the limits of existing law, and lending primarily through member banks as intermediaries, the Federal Reserve is prepared to supply liquid funds to other types of financial institutions when such assistance is not available elsewhere and is necessary to avoid major economic disruption.

Along with these continuing principles, the Report suggests several modifications of lending operations to better serve emerging needs. Let me summarize the main new suggestions briefly, and then outline each one in somewhat greater detail.

To provide more clear-cut access to Federal Reserve lending facilities, the Report proposes that each soundly operated member bank be given a "basic borrowing privilege," enabling it to borrow up to a specified limit from its Reserve bank upon request in as much as half of its weekly reserve periods.

In addition, it is proposed that any member bank foreseeing large seasonal bulges in its needs for funds would be able to arrange for loans from its Reserve bank to meet such needs in excess of a specified minimum. This arrangement, more explicit and more liberal than currently provided, is termed the "seasonal borrowing privilege."

Member banks experiencing drains of funds that are not of a seasonal or emergency nature, but that are bigger or longer in duration that can be accommodated under the new "basic borrowing privilege," could also arrange for additional credit pending an expected and timely reversal of their fund outflows or an orderly adjustment of their assets and liabilities. Such borrowings would be subject to essentially the same kinds of administrative procedures now applied to similar situations.

A final innovation proposed by the Report is to make the discount rate—the interest rate charged by Federal Reserve banks on their loans to member banks—more flexible than heretofore. It is recommended in the Report that the discount rate be changed considerably more frequently and by smaller amounts, keeping it reasonably closely in line with the movements in other money market rates.

Turning now to some of the major features of these recommendations, the most commonly used of the new lending provisions for member banks in sound condition would undoubtedly be the basic borrowing privilege. The size of each bank's basic borrowing privilege would be established as a proportion of some base drawn from the bank's balance sheet; the current proposal suggests capital stock and surplus. Required reserves could also be used.

Frequency of use of the basic borrowing privilege would also be limited. This is necessary because Federal Reserve credit is not properly a long-term or permanent addition to the loanable funds of individual member banks. The aim is to make credit available over a long enough period to cushion the bulk of short-term fluctuations or portfolio adjustments and in most cases permit orderly adjustment to longer term movements of funds.

The proposed frequency limitation would allow assured and virtually automatic access to credit so long as the bank is indebted in no more than half the reserve periods in the specified interval.

Before the plan is finally made effective, choices will be made in the light of comments received as to the particular percentages which would apply to the amount and frequency limitations. The controlling considerations will be that individual credit access should not be so small or so infrequently available as to be insignificant to the member banks, nor should total access be so liberal as to interfere with Federal Reserve open-market operations aimed at carrying out national credit policy objectives.

Borrowing within the basic borrowing privilege limitations could, as noted, take place virtually upon request, unless the Reserve bank had notified the member bank that its overall condition was unsatisfactory as determined by such factors as adequacy of capital, liquidity, soundness, management, or noncompliance with law or regulation and that such unsatisfactory condition was not being corrected to the Reserve bank's satisfaction. The only other circumscription on the actions of a qualified borrowing bank would be the avoidance of net sales in the Federal funds market during the reserve periods in which it was borrowing from the Federal Reserve. This administrative rule, already in force, is retained in the new proposal in the interest of precluding retailing operations in Federal Reserve credit obtained through the discount window.

It is recognized that the basic borrowing privilege as I have been describing it would not be large enough to encompass every member bank's needs for funds in all instances that justify the use of discount credit. This is particularly true in cases of the larger banks which borrow infrequently but for rather large amounts, but it is also true in cases of smaller banks faced with sharp temporary drains of funds. Arrangements are therefore recognized as necessary to permit member bank borrowings outside the basic borrowing privilege up to the limits of appropriate needs on as convenient and understandable terms as possible. These arrangements, referred to in the Report as "other adjustment credit," would be available pending an expected and timely reversal of fund outflows or an orderly portfolio adjustment. Such borrowings would be subject to essentially the same kinds of administrative procedures and surveillance now applied to similar situations, with the precise timing and nature of administrative actions determined as at present by the circumstances surrounding individual cases. Close contact among the Federal Reserve Board staff and the Federal Reserve banks' discount officials will be maintained in the interest of dealing uniformly with similar cases.

The third general category of credit which would be available to member banks at the proposed discount window is called the "seasonal borrowing privilege." A reserve bank would be prepared to establish such a seasonal borrowing privilege for any member bank experiencing demonstrable seasonal pressures persisting for a period of at least four consecutive weeks and probably longer, and exceeding a minimum relative size. It is expected that this borrowing privilege would be of value principally to smaller unit banks in agricultural or resort areas in which seasonal swings have a substantial impact on the entire community and where access to the national money markets or other adjustment resources is not always readily available.

The existence of seasonal pressures would be judged on the basis of past years' patterns of loan and deposit fluctuations. The establishment of a qualifying seasonal swing in net availability of funds— defined as deposits minus loans to customers in the bank's market area—would ordinarily be fixed by negotiation once a year. Once the existence of a qualifying seasonal need was established, the reserve banks would agree to extend discount credit up to the qualifying amount and for the length of time the need was expected to persist, up to 90 days. The 90-day maximum is imposed by statute; however, should the need extend over a longer period than this, the reserve banks would regard renewals of credit as in accordance with the initial seasonal credit negotiation. Seasonal credit needs would normally be expected to last for several months, but in exceptional cases could range up to us much as 9 months, we believe.

Seasonal credit obtainable at a reserve bank would be limited to the amount of the borrowing bank's seasonal swing in excess of a specified percentage of its average deposits in the preceding year.

This "deductible" principle, requiring a bank to meet a part of its seasonal needs out of its own resources, is designed to encourage individual bank maintenance of some minimum level of liquidity for purposes of flexibility. It would also serve effectively to limit the aggregate amount of credit extended under the seasonal borrowing privilege to an amount consistent with overall monetary policy, while allowing the Federal Reserve to provide this assistance to all those member banks with relatively large seasonal needs.

The proposal redesign of the discount window would provide that the Federal Reserve continue to supply liberal help to its member banks in emergency situations. So long as the member bank is solvent and steps are being taken to find a solution to its problems, credit would be available on the same basis as it currently is, and, within the limits of the law, special and flexible arrangements would continue to be made where necessary. Assisting a bank in an emergency situation would generally require credit extension for periods longer than would normally be allowed at the window, but this would be expected and regarded as appropriate.

The Federal Reserve, in its role as lender of last resort to other sectors of the economy, may find it necessary to extend credit assistance to institutions other than member banks. This action would be taken only when other sources of credit have been exhausted and failure of the troubled institutions would have a significant impact on the economy's financial structure. When lending to nonmembers, the Federal Reserve would act in cooperation with the relevant supervisory authority to insure that steps are taken to find a solution to their problems. The Federal Reserve Act authorizes direct advances to nonmembers, but only if collateralized by U.S. Government securities. Since most nonmember institutions of the types apt to require emergency credit assistance do not have sizable holdings of this asset, credit would normally be extended through a conduit arrangement with a member bank. Most types of nonbank financial institutions have borrowing relationships with their commercial banks as a matter of course and, ideally, this indirect lending by the Federal Reserve could fit in with such business practice. Such credit would be provided at a higher rate than the basic discount rate.

The proposed discount window does not include the provisions of intermediate- or long-term credit to meet the needs of banks servicing credit-deficit areas or sectors—that is, areas or sectors where the opportunities for profitable investment continuously outstrip the savings generated locally. While this is recognized as a problem of some significance, it was concluded that its solution lies outside the proper scope of the discount window. The steering committee concluded that an appropriate and effective solution to this problem was most likely to be found in the improvement of secondary markets for bank assets and liabilities. Detailed studies of the feasibility of actions to promote such improvement are expected to begin in the near future.

I should emphasize that Federal Reserve open-market operations are still envisioned as the main tool of monetary policy. The proposed changes in discount operations, however, would alter to some degree the current relationship between these two methods of reserve injection, with the discount mechanism assuming a somewhat increased role. This would come about as a result of the accommodation of more of the day-to-day fluctuations of reserve needs at the window, the improved distribution of reserves brought about by injection of some reserves directly at the point of need, and more flexible and effective use of the discount rate as an influence on bank borrowing. The first and second of these benefits would entail a generally higher level of borrowing being done by a typically rotating group of member banks. But this is not conceived to mean a corresponding increase in total reserves or a loss of control in this area, since the Federal Reserve would retain the ability to bring about and maintain the desired level of overall credit availability, taking into account the relatively small increase expected in credit outstanding at the window, through purchases and sales of securities in the open market.

. . . I have avoided citing specific numbers, technical conditions, or underlying statistical evidence associated with the proposed changes in the discount mechanism. For your convenience, I have summarized these details in the . . . appendix table attached to my statement.

Summary of Proposal for Redesign of Discount Mechanism

	Basic borrowing privilege (1)	Other adjustment credit (2)	Seasonal borrowing privilege (3)	Emergency credit to member banks (4)	Emergency credit to others (5)
Definition	Member bank access to credit upon request, within precisely stated limits on amounts and frequency and on specified conditions.	Supplemental discount accommodation, subject to administrative procedures, to help a member bank meet temporary needs that prove either larger or longer in duration than could be covered by its basic borrowing privilege.	Member bank access to credit on a longer-term and, to the extent possible, prearranged basis to meet demonstrable seasonal pressures exeeding minimum duration and relative amount.	Credit extended to member banks in unusual or exigent circumstances.	Credit extended to institutions other than member banks in emergency circumstances in fulfilling role as lender of last resort of the economy.
Rate	Discount rate	Discount rate	Discount rate	Discount rate	Significant penalty above discount rate.
Quantity limitations	—(20 to 40) percent of 1st $1,000,000 capital stock and surplus plus —(10 to 20) percent of next $9,000,000 of plus —(10) percent of remainder.	None specified	Seasonal needs in excess of —(5 to 10) percent of average deposits subject to reserve requirements in preceding calendar year.	None specified	None specified.
Frequency or duration limitations .	—(6 to 13) of any —(13 to 26) consecutive reserve computation periods.	...do	Need and arrangement must be for more than 4 weeks. Maximum 9 consecutive months.	...do	Do.

Administrative procedures	None other than general discouragement of net selling of Federal funds by borrowing banks.	Appraisal and, where necessary, action broadly similar to procedures developed under existing discount arrangements.	Prearrangement involves discussion between discount officer and bank management concerning amount, duration, and seasonality of need. Administrative review maintained during borrowing to prevent abuse or misuse.	Continuous and thoroughgoing surveillance. Require that bank develop and pursue workable program for alleviating difficulties.	Continuous and thoroughgoing surveillance (may have to be through conduit). Require that institution develop and pursue workable program for alleviating difficulties.
Other restrictions ..	Must not have been found to be in unsatisfactory condition.	None specified	None specified	None specified	Required to use all other practicable sources of credit first.
Method of provision ..	Direct	Direct	Direct	Direct	(1) Through central agency; (2) direct; (3) conduit through member bank.

THE PROBLEMS AND CONTROVERSY OF MONETARY POLICY

PART IV

While in Part III the emphasis of the articles was primarily on the internal techniques of monetary management, the selections in Part IV concentrate on the external influences and controversies that have surrounded the performance of monetary policy. Most economists agree that the objectives of monetary policy are those stated in the Employment Act of 1946 —high levels of employment; price stability; steady growth; and, one receiving more attention recently, a favorable balance of payments. However, there is no consensus among economists as to the role or manner in which monetary policy should be conducted to attain these elusive goals. The authors of the articles presented in Part IV discuss (and debate) the efficiency of monetary policy in relation to these stated objectives.

The Anderson and Laird articles deal with the controversy and problems existing between the Federal Reserve and the Treasury. Anderson reviews the history of controversy between these two governmental organizations, with special emphasis on the World War II and post-World War II periods. Laird's article is specially directed at examining the problems of managing the large federal debt, the problems that consequently result between the Federal Reserve and the Treasury in managing this debt, and the changing atitudes of both central bankers and economists as to the use of debt management as a part of countercyclical policy.

As will be remembered, the last article in Part I described the relative growth and competition between commercial banks and nonbank financial intermediaries. The significance of the relative growth of nonbank financial intermediaries to monetary policy was briefly mentioned. In this section on monetary policy, however, three selections are presented that thoroughly analyze some of the differences in operation of these financial institutions and their implications for monetary policy. The Tobin article is presented first, although it was published more recently, because it presents in a concise manner the most relevant differences between the traditional money-creating activities (the old view) and the expanded analysis of the asset-creating activities of all financial intermediaries (the new view). Furthermore, Tobin does not actively enter the debate that is clearly presented in the Gurley-Shaw and Tussing articles. Gurley-Shaw argue for a more general analysis of all financial institutions' asset-creating activities rather than giving special and undue emphasis to the money-creating activities of commercial banks. Furthermore, they argue that since the monetary controls imposed on commercial banks do not extend to the flow of funds caused by other financial intermediaries, monetary policy is less effective.

In the last article in this subdivision on financial intermediaries and monetary policy, Tussing questions the effectiveness of monetary policy in influencing the availability of credit. Although the availability doctrine has its origins much earlier in history than the Gurley-Shaw thesis, credit availability arguments have been frequently used to challenge the Gurley-Shaw thesis. Tussing provides us with a perspective on these divergent criticisms.

The last subsection includes several selections on the question of rules versus authority in monetary policy. The more rigorous statement of the rule by Milton Friedman that the money supply should increase somewhere between 3 to 5 percent based on observed changes in the produce capacity of the economy has been maintained for over a decade. In an attempt to give the recent evolution and flavor of this important debate, several selections have been included that proceed from the earlier statements and analyses to the most recent statement of prominent economists at the hearings before the Joint Economic Committee in 1968.

It is important to recognize that many important questions (assumptions) underlie all of these analyses. Can the Federal Reserve effectively control the money supply? What is the appropriate definition of money? Is the velocity of money relatively stable in the long run? Is there a significantly large and variable lag in the effects of monetary actions on the level of economic activity? All of these questions will be encountered and closely examined in this subdivision, although the question of monetary and fiscal policy lags will be more thoroughly examined in Part V.

Cox introduces the debate by examining the origins and important differences in the analysis of both sides. The next selection is Friedman's statement of his position with some simplified but concise analysis of the underlying logic of his approach. Although Friedman has since made some refinements in his analysis to lend further support to this position, his basic argument is the same today.

Subsequent articles further analyze this debate. Although Samuelson's paper is not a direct response to Friedman's rule and clearly is much more comprehensive, it does give us an alternative analysis of the role and effects of monetary policy. The selection by Wallich argues against the rule proposed by the monetarists; but from a different perspective than that taken by Samuelson. Selden's statement, made at the same 1968 Joint Economic Committee hearings at which the Wallich statement was also given, supports the rule as proposed by Representative Reuss, but with important qualifications. In addition to reviewing some of the more familiar arguments for a rule similar to Friedman's, Selden discusses a fourth reason—the importance of lag in the effects of monetary operations. Selden recommends that the Federal Reserve adopt a flexible percentage change in the money supply and announce in advance the selected target percentage.

The last article in this subdivision, by Meltzer, also does not require a rule for monetary policy, but does recommend that long-run monetary policy objectives be based on a desired rate of growth of the money stock that is translated into the monetary base. He suggests that the manager of the open-market account should be instructed to conduct monetary operation based on some preselected desired monetary base. Meltzer offers recommendations that can be utilized within the existing monetary framework based on an analysis that avoids direct involvement in the abstract question of rules.

These selections offer the content and flavor of the debate on the efficacy and performance of monetary management. Hopefully, they will help you appraise the role and efficiency of monetary policy.

PART IV-B / / DEBT MANAGEMENT AND MONETARY POLICY

CLAY J. ANDERSON

FEDERAL RESERVE-TREASURY CONTROVERSIES

20

Large and habitual borrowers are not the best administrators of the fund to be lent. —*Nicholas Biddle*[1]

The proper relation between the central bank and the Government, especially the Treasury Department, has long been a subject of debate. For this reason, Federal Reserve experience with Treasury officials on questions of monetary policy during the past 50 years is of special interest. The purpose of this chapter is to explain the important differences that arose and the reasons for the divergent views.

It would be misleading should limiting the analysis to differences of opinion leave the impression that Federal Reserve-Treasury relations is one long period of controversy. Generally, there has been close cooperation to minimize disturbing effects of Treasury operations on the money market and to time Federal Reserve actions to avoid complicating the Treasury's financing problems. Since early in the history of the System, Federal Reserve and Treasury officials have worked closely together to smooth out the impact of Treasury receipts and disbursements on bank reserves and conditions in the money market. The Federal Reserve, as fiscal agent of the Treasury, has handled a growing volume of transactions involved in the issue, redemption, and exchange of U.S. Government securities. And as for monetary policy, System officials have long pursued an even keel during Treasury financing operations.

Reprinted from Clay J. Anderson, "Federal Reserve-Treasury Controversies," *A Half-Century of Federal Reserve Policymaking, 1914–1964*, pp. 140–154, *Federal Reserve Bank of Philadelphia, 1964.*
[1] President of the Second Bank of the United States.

FINANCING WORLD WAR I

Meeting the greatly enlarged Government expenditures incurred in the war, together with billions of dollars of credit extended to allied countries, required Treasury borrowing of unprecedented amounts. Treasury officials were concerned as to their ability to borrow such huge sums and were particularly anxious that the first few borrowing operations be an unqualified success. . . . Treasury officials decided in 1917 to issue Treasury securities at relatively low rates, and insisted that the discount rate be adjusted in harmony with these rates in order that credit would be readily available to bank and nonbank buyers of Treasury securities on reasonable terms.

Federal Reserve officials were opposed to some of the Treasury's debt management policies. The Secretary of the Treasury initially asked the Reserve Banks to buy short-term certificates at a low interest rate direct from the Treasury. The Reserve Banks did take practically all of the first $50 million issue at a $2\frac{1}{2}$ per cent rate; however, System officials were strongly opposed to direct purchases from the Treasury because of the dangerous inflationary implications. They were also opposed to the Treasury's low interest-rate policy, and were especially reluctant to establish the low discount rates requested by Treasury officials. Such low rates in time of war were considered inflationary. System authorities also stressed the need for greater reliance on taxation and borrowing from nonbank sources.

Federal Reserve authorities felt compelled to direct System policies toward facilitating war financing even though they did not agree with some Treasury policies.[2] Inasmuch as war financing was the responsibility of the Treasury and the Government, they believed it was the System's duty to help carry out the policies formulated by the Treasury.

POST-WORLD WAR I

Soon after the Armistice was signed in 1918, Federal Reserve officials turned their thoughts toward problems likely to be encountered in the postwar period: readjustments accompanying reconversion from war to civilian production; the large volume of credit built up on

[2] It appears that suggestions to Treasury officials soon came to have less and less influence. Reportedly, the Secretary of the Treasury (who was then an ex officio member of the Board) rarely attended meetings of the Board of Governors; instead, he conveyed his ideas on policy through an

Government securities as collateral; and the possible impact of the network of war-created foreign indebtedness and German reparation payments on international trade and finance. They thought the Federal Reserve should continue to assist the Treasury until the war-financing program was completed; however, they wanted to restore a more normal situation as soon as practicable, in which credit would be based on short-term commercial paper arising from production and distribution instead of Government securities.

Higher Rates

In the spring of 1919, discussion of a higher discount rate as one means of getting Government securities and Government-secured paper out of the banking system into the hands of investors brought immediate opposition from Treasury officials confronted with an uncompleted borrowing program and management of a large federal debt. They were vigorously opposed to any increase in discount rates or to removal of the preferential rate on advances collateralled by Government securities. In their opinion, termination of war contracts would result in a decline in Government expenditures and then loans would be liquidated regardless of the discount rate. Moreover, it was unrealistic to think the Treasury could borrow the large sums required from nonbank sources by offering higher rates. The only effective method was to appeal to patriotism.

The Treasury's opposition to using the discount rate to curb inflation is summarized in the following excerpts from a letter Secretary of the Treasury Carter Glass wrote to Chairman Harding of the Board of Governors:

The conditions under which changes in the Reserve Bank's rates of discount would operate effectively do not exist here today. . . . [An increase] will not result in a curtailment of the importation of goods nor in increasing our exports materially. In the present position of the international balances and of the foreign exchange and because of gold embargoes the Federal Reserve Bank rates cannot function internationally, and will operate solely upon the domestic situation. In that condition an important further increase in Federal Reserve Bank rates might have the effect of penalizing and discouraging the borrower for commercial and industrial purposes, thus curtailing production and distribution and increasing the shortage of goods, and consequently the price of them, and

---

Assistant Secretary or one of his own aides. Sometimes he would send for a Board member to come to his office in order to impress his views on the Board. See H. Parker Willis, *The Federal Reserve System* (New York, Ronald Press, 1923), pp. 1222–1224.

thus, in turn, stimulating speculation (An increase in rates . . . falls very lightly upon the borrower for speculative purposes, who figures a very large profit on the turnover in a day, a week, a month or some other short period.) It might have also a very grave effect upon the government's finances. . . .

Therefore, I believe it to be of prime importance that the Federal Reserve Board should insist upon and that the Governors of the banks should exercise a firm discrimination in making loans to prevent abuse of the facilities of the Federal Reserve System in support of the reckless speculation in stocks, land, cotton, clothing, foodstuffs and commodities generally.

We cannot trust to the copybook texts. Making credit more expensive will not suffice. . . . The Reserve Bank Governor must raise his mind above the language of the textbooks and face the situation which exists. He must have courage to act promptly and with confidence in his own integrity to prevent abuse of the facilities of the Federal Reserve System by the customers of the Federal Reserve Banks, however powerful or influential.

Speculation in stocks on the New York Stock Exchange is no more vicious in its effect upon the welfare of the people and upon our credit structure than speculation in cotton or in land or in commodities generally. But the New York Stock Exchange is the greatest single organized user of credit for speculative purposes.[3]

In short, Treasury opposition to any appreciable increase in the discount rate was based on the view that it would be ineffective in curbing use of credit for speculation, would have harmful effects on business, and might seriously interfere with the Treasury's financing and debt management programs. A selective approach in administering the discount window would be more effective—a view also held by some System officials, as previously explained. It was not until the early part of 1920 that Treasury officials thought their postwar debt management program had been sufficiently completed so that the discount rate no longer need be established for the purpose of facilitating Treasury financing.

A difference of opinion over discount rates arose in 1923. The Under Secretary of the Treasury proposed preferential discount rates on Treasury certificates and bankers acceptances—the discount rate on all other types of eligible paper, including other issues of Government securities, to be 1 per cent higher. Preferential rates would encourage development of a market for bankers acceptances which System officials had been trying to facilitate and would help broaden

[3] Letter dated Nov. 5, 1919. Proceedings of a Conference of the Federal Reserve Board with the Governors of the Federal Reserve Banks, Nov. 19–21, 1919, Vol. I, pp. 6–8.

the market for short-term Treasury certificates which the Treasury had been trying to develop. In addition, preferential rates on these instruments would encourage banks to adjust reserve positions in the market instead of by borrowing at the Reserve Banks.

System officials were strongly opposed. One Reserve Bank president stated: "We had our lesson once and I am amazed that the proposal should be seriously advanced again." Experience demonstrated that a preferential rate merely induced member banks to use paper carrying the lowest rate; the preferential rate becomes the effective discount rate.

Open Market Operations

The attitude of Treasury officials toward Reserve Bank purchases of Government securities apparently was based mainly on the interests and responsibilities of the Treasury. Occasionally, Treasury officials asked some of the Reserve Banks to buy Treasury certificates, but in general were opposed to the Reserve Banks buying Government securities in the open market. As already mentioned, the Reserve Banks began buying Government securities to bolster declining earnings as their earning assets were reduced by a decline in member-bank indebtedness in the depression of 1920–1921.

Early in 1922, Treasury officials expressed concern over the growing accumulation of Government securities in the Reserve Banks. They were afraid that large purchases by the Reserve Banks at times might push up the prices of Government securities temporarily, create an artificial market situation, and thus make it more difficult for the Treasury to select suitable terms on new issues. Once Reserve Bank purchases ceased, prices might decline. Should the terms on a new Treasury offering be established during a period of buoyancy created by Reserve Bank purchases, a subsequent decline might jeopardize success of the Treasury operation. Unrestricted Reserve Bank purchases to bolster earnings might also result in inflation and adverse effects on the economy.

System officials recognized that Reserve Bank purchases of Government securities might create difficulties for the Treasury. They took prompt action to minimize such undesirable effects. An even keel policy was suggested during periods of Treasury financing and in May, 1922, the Conference of Presidents of the Reserve Banks established a committee to centralize and coordinate Reserve Bank purchases of Government securities. . . .

There was strong opposition, however, to Treasury pressure to influence open market policy. One official stated that the Federal

Reserve Act put responsibility for credit control in the Federal Reserve System, not in the Treasury Department. The System should cooperate with the Treasury, but policy should not be formulated to conform to its views or interests, It should be determined on the basis of what is appropriate for the economy and the country as a whole.

FINANCING WORLD WAR II

Except for the usual differences of opinion to be expected in a free society, the next controversy between Federal Reserve and Treasury officials over monetary policy developed during and particularly following World War II. As in World War I, Federal Reserve officials were in agreement that policy should be directed primarily toward facilitating financing the war. System authorities agreed that this time it was desirable to maintain the pattern of interest rates for the duration. But there were differences over some secondary issues, such as short-term rates, types of securities, and the amount of excess reserves that should be maintained.

Short-Term Rates

Federal Reserve officials wanted to establish short-term rates considerably above the unusually low levels that had prevailed during much of the thirties, a period of economic stagnation and a huge volume of excess reserves. They thought a three-month Treasury bill rate of $\frac{3}{4}$ per cent or possibly higher, as compared to the existing rate of around $\frac{1}{4}$ per cent, would give a sounder rate pattern by making short-term issues more attractive investments, thereby enabling the Treasury to absorb more liquid funds of bank and nonbank investors. A narrower spread between short- and long-term rates would diminish the incentive to play the pattern of rates and would be less inflationary. They were confident that a rate pattern with the bill rate as high as $\frac{3}{4}$ or even 1 per cent could be maintained.

Treasury officials disagreed. They favored pegging the Treasury bill rate at about the prevailing level of $\frac{1}{4}$ per cent. In their opinion, maintenance of the $2\frac{1}{2}$ per cent long-term rate could be assured only by keeping short-term rates at about the same level they had been when the $2\frac{1}{2}$ per cent rate was established by market forces. Low short-term rates would not have any significant inflationary implications, in their opinion, because it would be necessary to rely on taxation and direct controls to combat inflation in wartime.

Even though Federal Reserve authorities felt strongly tha somewhat higher short-term rates were necessary, they recognized that primary responsibility for debt management policies rested with the Secretary of the Treasury. Consequently, they agreed to accept a directive from the Secretary as to the level of short-term rates provided he would take responsibility for the decision. The Secretary accepted the responsibility and asked the Federal Reserve to maintain the existing pattern of rates, except as he agreed to its subsequent modification.[4]

Excess Reserves

Closely related to the level of short-term rates was the volume of excess reserves that should be maintained. Treasury officials insisted on a large volume of excess reserves. Inasmuch as the interest-rate pattern was established when excess reserves were large, a substantial cushion of excess reserves was the only means of assuring that the pattern could be maintained. Furthermore, it was essential that reserves should be provided in anticipation of needs. Bankers limited their subscriptions for Treasury securities to the amount of excess reserves held. Hence waiting for reserve pressures to arise in the market during a period of Treasury financing before supplying reserves might have an unfavorable effect on subscriptions to new offerings. Consequently, Treasury officials wanted the Fed to supply, prior to a Treasury offering, the estimated amount of reserves that would be needed. They contended that large excess reserves would not be inflationary under war conditions because of direct controls.

Federal Reserve officials were opposed both to maintaining a large volume of excess reserves and to supplying reserves in anticipation of needs. They pointed out that the System could either maintain a certain volume of excess reserves with rates being determined by the market, or it could maintain a certain rate structure with the market determining the amount of reserves that would have to be created to do so. A large volume of excess reserves was not necessary inasmuch as System purchases to maintain the rate pattern would automatically create the necessary amount of reserves.

Neither was it necessary or desirable to supply reserves in anticipation of needs in order to promote the sale of Treasury securities. Banks make initial payment for subscriptions to new Treasury securities by crediting the Treasury's Tax and Loan Account; the drain on reserves comes as the Treasury transfers funds to the

[4] As explained later, a rate of 3/8 per cent was agreed on for Treasury bills.

Reserve Banks. Thus willingness to subscribe depends on ready availability of reserves, not on a large volume of excess reserves.

System officials also pointed out that maintaining a large volume of excess reserves was inconsistent with the policy of urging banks to keep fully invested. To the extent banks accepted this advice, it was impossible to keep large excess reserves outstanding. Attempting to do so resulted in a larger proportion of Government borrowing coming from commercial banks. Hence Federal Reserve authorities wanted to maintain a much lower level of excess reserves to help minimize bank purchases, but assure banks that adequate reserves would be readily available to facilitate Treasury financing.

The posted ⅜ per cent buying rate and repurchase option on Treasury bills agreed upon represented somewhat of a compromise between the Federal Reserve and Treasury positions on short-term rates. The posted rate also shifted some of the initiative over excess reserves to the Treasury. With banks and other investors less and less willing to hold low-yielding Treasury bills, an increase in the quantity of Treasury bills issued tended to result in Federal Reserve purchases and creation of reserves. As a result, Treasury officials generally favored a larger volume of bill issues than the Federal Reserve because of the resulting increase in reserve availability.

POST-WORLD WAR II

The period from the end of the war to the spring of 1951 was one of continuing controversy between the Federal Reserve and Treasury officials over modification of the rate pattern and, to a smaller extent, over issuing types of long-term Treasury securities that would require less support.

Federal Reserve authorities wanted to let short-term rates rise to gain more control over bank reserves and thus enable them to exert some restraint. But coordination of Federal Reserve policy with debt management policy was considered essential. If the Federal Reserve permitted market rates to rise without the Treasury raising the rates on its new short-term issues, System officials would be faced with either supporting the new issue and thereby creating more reserves or being held responsible for the issue's failure.

The initial move toward somewhat higher short-term rates was made in mid-1945 when Federal Reserve officials told the Secretary of the Treasury they were considering elimination of the preferential discount rate on loans collateralled by Government securities maturing or callable within one year. The preferential rate was adopted as a wartime measure and hence was no longer needed. Inasmuch as the Secretary had just tendered his resignation, he thought it more appropriate that the question be discussed with his successor. The new Secretary of the Treasury asked System officials to defer such action because of possible adverse effects on the Government securities market and because the action might be interpreted as signalling an end to the low interest-rate policy. The Federal Reserve acceded to his request and the preferential rate was not removed until the spring of 1946.

The real controversy over permitting short-term rates to rise began to develop in 1947.[5] Early in the year, System officials agreed that the 3/8 per cent posted buying rate on Treasury bills was no longer needed and should be terminated at a time when its removal would exert some restraining influence. Treasury officials were unwilling to agree to its removal unless some program could be worked out so that a large part of the increase in interest cost to the Treasury, resulting from higher rates, could be recaptured from earnings accruing to the Reserve Banks.

There was considerable sentiment within the System in favor of asking Congress to restore the former franchise tax on Federal Reserve Bank earnings. A serious drawback to this proposal, however, was uncertainty as to when or whether Congress would act on a recommendation to restore the franchise tax. The Board of Governors, after conferring with members of Congress more directly concerned with this type of legislation, decided to use its authority to levy an interest charge on Federal Reserve notes outstanding not covered by gold. The interest charge, which absorbs about 90 per cent of net earnings of the Federal Reserve Banks after dividends, is paid to the Treasury. In effect, it is the equivalent of the former franchise tax.

Treasury officials were still opposed to removal of the 3/8 per cent rate, however. They were afraid that any rise in short-term rates might cause some Treasury securities to fall below par. The 3/8 per cent rate was finally removed in July, 1947.

From the end of 1947 until early in 1951, desirability of permitting short-term rates to rise was an important topic of discussion at practically every meeting of the Open Market Committee and its

[5] In the President's January budget message to the Congress there was a passage to the effect that debt management policy is designed to hold interest rates at the present low level and to prevent undue fluctuations in the bond market. Included also was the sentence: "The Treasury and the Federal Reserve System will continue their effective control of interest rates." According to the Chairman of the Board of Governors, the Board had not been consulted about this statement on interest rates.

Executive Committee. There was general agreement that higher short-term rates were desirable as a means of regaining more control over reserve creation and the availability of credit. There was also agreement that the System's view should be communicated to the Treasury, usually by letter and personal conference between Federal Reserve and Treasury officials. System officials were also in general agreement until the latter part of the period that the Federal Reserve should not act unilaterally to raise rates without approval and cooperation of the Treasury. Treasury officials usually replied that the Federal Reserve's proposals would be taken under advisement but, often without further discussion with System officials, announced terms on new short-term securities at existing rates. This was the general procedure for many of the Treasury refundings during the period. Repeated efforts brought agreements for only minor increases in short-term rates.

The recession of 1948–1949, which convinced Federal Reserve officials that the support policy, was a handicap in dealing with economic slack as well as inflation, and the outbreak of hostilities in Korea in 1950 were significant events leading eventually to solution of the Federal Reserve-Treasury controversy.

The inflation threat arising from the outbreak of hostilities in Korea crystallized instead of softened policy differences between Federal Reserve and Treasury officials. The System felt a primary responsibility for curbing inflation because inflationary pressures were being fed largely by private credit expansion. This feeling of responsibility was intensified by a statement in the President's mid-year economic report in 1950 that in restraining inflation, major reliance should be placed on credit and fiscal policies. Under these circumstances, there was no real alternative to using available powers to restrict credit expansion. Federal Reserve authorities were convinced that effective restraint could not be applied while maintaining a rigid pattern of interest rates. They proposed to Treasury officials a more effective program to combat inflation, including higher short-term rates, an increase in reserve requirements, and a debt management program designed to attract nonbank funds with securities that would require less support.

Treasury officials disagreed with these proposals. Their position as to the ineffectiveness of higher short-term rates had not changed. They were unwilling to bring out a long-term bond to attract nonbank funds because their studies indicated such funds would not be available to the Treasury in any significant quantity. Therefore they would have to rely mainly on the banking system for new funds. In fact, Treasury officials, facing mounting financing requirements, were strongly opposed to any action that might unsettle the Government securities market and make their problems more difficult. The Secretary of the Treasury repeatedly stressed the importance of maintaining confidence in the credit of the Government and in doing everything possible to strengthen it. This required, first of all, avoiding any action that might inspire a belief that a significant change in the pattern of rates was under consideration. Referring to the Government securities market, the Secretary said that "every appraisal of the present situation indicates that the maintenance of stability should take priority over all other market considerations."

Meetings of the Open Market Committee and the Executive Committee in the latter part of 1950 and early 1951 were devoted largely to reviews of recent discussions with Treasury officials and, in view of Treasury opposition to Committee proposals, what the Federal Reserve could do to discharge its responsibility for credit regulation. Frequent discussions with Treasury officials and earnest efforts to reach agreement on monetary and debt management policies failed. It was only after prolonged efforts had failed and System officials were convinced that the Treasury would not agree to a program of credit restraint that they decided to act without Treasury approval. Eventually, others became involved in the controversy, including the President of the United States and some members of Congress.[6] Special meetings between representatives of the Treasury and the Federal Reserve, started in the latter part of February, led to agreement and the accord announced March 4, 1951.

CORE OF THE CONTROVERSIES

The fact that the major controversies between Federal Reserve and Treasury officials occurred in postwar periods affords a clue to the nature of the problem. During both world wars, Federal Reserve policy was directed primarily toward facilitating Treasury financing, despite the fact that System officials favored less inflationary

[6] For a chronological record of documents and events leading up to the accord see: U.S. Congress, *General Credit Control, Debt Management, and Economic Mobilization*, Materials Prepared for the Joint Committee on the Economic Report by the Committee Staff, 82d Cong., 1st Sess. (Washington, D.C.: U.S. Government Printing Office, 1951), pp. 50–74; U.S. Congress, *Monetary Policy and the Management of the Public Debt*, Hearings before the Subcommittee on General Credit Control and Debt Management of the Joint Committee on the Economic Report, 82d Cong., 2d Sess. (Washington, D.C. U.S. Government Printing Office, 1952), pp. 942–966.

Treasury borrowing programs. Debt management was the responsibility of the Treasury.

Financing the wars created serious postwar problems both for monetary policy and debt management. The Federal Reserve confronted a swollen money supply, vigorous private demand for credit, and strong inflationary pressures. The Treasury confronted large refunding operations to manage the vastly increased federal debt, and an environment in which investors were much less motivated by patriotism.

It was only natural that with the war over, each group of officials considered policies in terms of their own responsibilities. System officials, although cognizant of the Treasury's problems, felt an obligation to formulate policy more in terms of their responsibility for preventing inflation instead of facilitating Treasury financing. Treasury officials, even though aware of inflationary pressures, favored policies that would not interfere with debt management operations for which they were responsible.

With Federal Reserve and Treasury officials facing difficult problems in their own area of responsibility, and with monetary and debt management policies impinging on each other, it is not surprising that divergent views developed over monetary policy. The Federal Reserve's responsibility of regulating credit and the money supply to help maintain price and business stability called for a restrictive policy in both postwar periods. But effective restraint would result in a rise in interest rates from the artificially low wartime levels. As already explained, Federal Reserve authorities were persistent in their efforts following World War II to get Treasury agreement to more flexible short-term rates, the objective being to regain more control over bank reserves and the availability of credit.

Treasury officials vigorously opposed an increase in interest rates at the end of both wars, and for essentially the same reasons. Higher rates, in their opinion, would not be effective under the conditions that existed. They would not deter speculative demand believed to be widespread after World War I; "fractional increases" would have no perceptible effect on the demand for credit in the post-World War II environment. In other words, moderate increases would be ineffective in combatting inflation; increases sufficient to be effective would be too drastic in their impact on the economy. But higher interest rates would complicate debt management and increase the interest burden of the large federal debt. Treasury officials thus ruled out higher interest rates as a method of dealing with postwar inflation.

There is no simple rule or organizational structure that will prevent the type of controversy that has arisen in postwar periods. The controversy arises from the nature of the two functions—not the institution or agency performing them. With national economic goals of price stability and a reasonably full use of productive resources, the function of monetary policy in the environment prevailing after each war was to restrict credit expansion to avoid further inflation. On the other hand, managing a large war-created debt was easier and the interest cost less if interest rates remained low and the Government securities market strong. The necessity of choosing between these conflicting policies arises from the nature of the two functions; not because performance is lodged in separate institutions.

The volume of Treasury debt management operations has grown tremendously in the past half-century. The magnitude of these operations makes it essential that monetary and debt management policies be coordinated. An understanding or mandate that both are to be directed toward common national economic goals would be a step in this direction. Low rates on Treasury securities may appear warranted if the objective is a low carrying charge on the Government debt; they do not appear warranted in a period of strong inflationary pressures if the objectives are to help maintain business stability and a stable level of prices. Federal Reserve and Treasury officials with broad economic knowledge and an understanding of each other's problems and responsibilities also facilitate better coordination of policies. The period since the accord affords a demonstration that these officials cognizant of each other's responsibilities can, in a spirit of cooperation and good will, effectively coordinate their policies toward achieving common economic objectives.

WILLIAM E. LAIRD

THE CHANGING VIEWS
ON DEBT
MANAGEMENT

21

In the period before the Great Depression debt management was
not a topic of active controversy. There was virtual unanimity regarding the elements of "sound" debt management policy and very
little debt to manage. An interesting similarity of opinion was observed among academic economists and between the economists and
the Treasury.

The events of the 1930's and 1940's created problems for the
Treasury; the prolonged depression and the demands of war finance
resulted in a greatly expanded federal debt which led the Treasury
to retreat from its older and simpler precepts of debt management.
Some observers were concerned about the debt and the possibility
that it might permanently lay to rest independent and flexible monetary policy. Economists set about reconsidering their views on the
relationships of debt management, monetary policy, and economic
stabilization. The revision of Treasury policy did not coincide with
the advance of the newer doctrines. Academic economists disagreed
among themselves, and usually they disagreed with the Treasury.
Conflicting policy positions developed; proponents described them
as sound, and they were judged by various standards to contribute
to stability.

Currently there is some dispute about every major aspect of debt
management. This paper delineates the changing views on debt
management, contrasts the older views with the various newer concepts of policy, and points out the current, and very significant,
divergence of thought on debt policy.

OLDER VIEWS ON DEBT MANAGEMENT

In the pre-Keynesian, pre-fiscal policy era the benchmark of sound
finance was to be found in the concept, and practice, of funding
the debt. Short-term or floating debt was not looked upon with

Reprinted by permission of the publisher and the author from William
E. Laird, "The Changing Views on Debt Management," *Quarterly Review
of Economics and Business*, Vol. III (1963), pp. 7–17.

favor by the Treasury, and sound policy avoided excessive reliance on shorter-term securities. The objectives of debt policy were all related to these fundamental principles of debt management. Important advantages were seen to accrue from funding the debt and minimizing reliance on floating debt. A longer debt was less likely to expose the Treasury to the mercy of the market, since the Treasury would face fewer holders of maturing debt at any one time. The Treasury would not be tied so closely to the market, and shifts in the market would not be so serious from the Treasury's point of view. Refinancings could be smaller with longer debt. Also, a funded debt could more easily be adapted to plans for debt retirement, and debt retirement was considered a worthy endeavor.

Treasury policy was concerned with the interest burden of the debt, but the Treasury contemplated neither a program of inflation to cope with the debt nor extensive reliance on floating debt. Interest costs were to be kept down by retirement and by refinancing at lower rates.

Pre-Keynesian Treasury policy did not relate debt management to the cycle; neither did pre-Keynesian writers on public finance and debt management. One may observe the interesting similarity of academic view and Treasury policy. Shirras writes:

> It is therefore necessary to reduce the floating debt within manageable proportions, so that it can never be a source of great danger. It is better to borrow for a long time and to pay a higher rate of interest than to be perpetually at the mercy of holders of Treasury bills for repayment.[1]

C. F. Bastable's earlier statement is similar.

> As a general principle of finance it is unquestionable that the floating debt should be kept within the narrowest limits possible. . . . A growth of floating charges is at best a mark of weakness in the treatment of the state liabilities. . . . The great evil of a floating debt is its uncertainty.[2]

Others, including Henry C. Adams, had expressed similar views.[3]

Academic opinion favored debt retirement. It was judged to strengthen the national credit, to facilitate further borrowing should the need arise, and to increase the capital available for industrial

[1] G. Findlay Shirras, *Science of Public Finance*, Vol. 2, 3d ed. (London: Macmillan, 1936), p. 799.

[2] C. F. Bastable, *Public Finance*, 3d ed. (London: Macmillan, 1903), pp. 694–995.

[3] Henry C. Adams, *Public Debts, An Essay in the Science of Finance* (New York: Appleton, 1893), p. 148.

growth. Debt reduction increased confidence and gave a favorable tone to government finance.

THE GREAT DEPRESSION, WORLD WAR II, AND AFTER

The Great Depression intensified interest in economic stabilization. Full employment and stability became virtually synonymous, and as a policy goal full employment had no peer. While monetary policy, interpreted as interest rate policy, was relegated to a position of insignificance, fiscal policy emerged as the new and respected tool of analysis and policy. As the Depression lengthened, more attention was paid to this newly discovered weapon. Fiscal deficits became more than respectable. In certain groups deficits were considered the principal defense against secular stagnation.

As pump-priming shaded into compensatory finance, with deficits becoming more a rule than an exception, the growth of the debt appeared certain. Active compensatory finance had as its adjunct a growing federal debt, which would almost inevitably become a problem in its own right, as debt must be managed in some fashion. Since it was widely assumed that money was impotent, monetary policy would increasingly be directed toward "managing the debt." It was assumed that in any monetary policy-debt management conflict, debt would win.

It was World War II rather than the Depression which brought the monetary policy-debt management conflict to the surface, and for a while it appeared that the war debt had completely submerged the final traces of monetary policy. At the end of the war there seemed to be relatively little enthusiasm for ending the Federal Reserve's bond support program. Opinion within the Reserve System gradually solidified against the policy, and the Treasury reluctantly consented to ending the program.

About the time of the Accord, analysis had begun turning to a more sophisticated reinterpretation of classical and neoclassical economics and policy measures tended to reflect this development. Economic stability remained an important objective while discussion and analysis turned to the pressing question of means to attain that end.

It was difficult to ignore the role of liquidity in the postwar inflation and attention was turned to that vast conglomeration of liquid assets, the federal debt. In an era preoccupied with stabilization it is not surprising that any controllable sector in the economy that showed promise as a tool of policy came under consideration.

Post-Accord discussion pointed to the possibility of the debt contributing to the goal.

THE DEBT MANAGEMENT CONTROVERSY

The Countercyclical Approach

Post-Accord discussion relating debt management to economic stabilization, although a break with tradition, was not entirely without precedent. One version of stabilization via debt had been forcefully presented some years earlier by Henry Simons, at a time (1944) when few were prepared for such a view of the debt.[4]

STABILIZATION VIA COMPOSITION OF DEBT INCLUDING MONEY

Simons recognized the debt as exerting an influence on economic stability, and he believed the real danger of the debt to be inflation. Understanding the climate of opinion of the postwar years, he foresaw the inflation to come and stated quite specifically in 1946 that "we probably shall have, in the near future, no substantial protection against inflation save that which debt policy affords."[5]

In 1944, he had clearly linked debt policy to economic stabilization. Conceiving of debt to be either paper money or consols (having neither call nor maturity features), he prescribed a simple rule of action. "The rule for policy as to consols and currency, that is, the *composition* of the debt including money, is simply stabilization of the value of money."[6] The correct combination depends upon the particular circumstances of the time. "Converting money into consols is an anti-inflation measure; converting consols into money is a reflationary or anti-deflation measure. . . ."[7]

Should inflation be the problem, the appropriate action is to sell consol bonds—convert money into consols—which reduces liquidity in the economy, retards spending, and stabilizes the price level. With the economy under deflationary pressure the contrary action is appropriate. Simons assumed that actions taken to stabilize the price level work automatically toward stabilizing the economy. Thus,

[4] Henry C. Simons, "On Debt Policy," *Journal of Political Economy*, Vol. 52, No. 4 (December 1944).

[5] Henry C. Simons, "Debt Policy and Banking Policy," *Review of Economic Statistics*, Vol. 28, No. 2 (May 1946), pp. 85–89. Reprinted in his *Economic Policy for a Free Society* (Chicago: University of Chicago Press, 1948), p. 235.

[6] Henry C. Simons, "On Debt Policy," *op. cit.*, p. 223.

[7] *Ibid.*

price level stability provided a clear and serviceable criterion of performance.

Within his framework it is proper for the Treasury to pursue that policy indicated by the general condition of the economy regardless of interest cost. In fact, *within that framework* it is legitimate to say that the Treasury should pay as much interest as possible. Since transactions would take place in a competitive market and be subject to a price level stabilization rule, maximizing interest payments is equivalent to saying "pay only enough to achieve the goal."

Several comments about Simons' debt policy are in order. First of all, there is some logic to the position that Simons actually had no debt policy in the conventional sense, but rather merely translated his monetary policy into the language of the federal debt. His debt policy is contained in the opening sentence of "On Debt Policy." "I have never seen any sense in an elaborate structure of federal debt.[8] His debt policy per se consists of transforming all federal debt into pure consol bonds. His program is directed toward assuring that the proper quantity of money will be in circulation. He proposes countercyclical monetary policy couched in terms of the federal debt. It may be no more than simple semantic exercise to discuss his concept of countercyclical debt management, as he is actually taking the back door to a flexible monetary policy and merely emphasizing the point that the size of the debt is of secondary importance. A more conventional or "front door" approach would speak explicitly in terms of the money supply and its variations. At the time Simons wrote, fear of the large federal debt was effectively frustrating any real control of the money supply. By approaching the stabilization problem in this unusual fashion, he apparently was attempting to free monetary policy by abating fears of the federal debt. Essentially, he was expressing confidence that the federal debt would not crush the economy while warning that continued fear of the debt would lead to an inflation of the price level. He struck at the debt phobia then existing by posing the alternatives of inflation or interest payments.

STABILIZATION VIA CONVENTIONAL DEBT COMPOSITION (EXCLUDING MONEY)

In 1954 the Committee for Economic Development published a study entitled *Managing the Federal Debt*, which clearly related debt management to economic stabilization, as the following statement shows:

[8] *Ibid.*, p. 220.

Debt management is important primarily because it affects the economic stability of the country—whether we have high employment and economic growth and price stability, or inflation or depression. The main test of debt management is whether it contributes as much as it can to stability of employment and production at a high and rising level without inflation.[9]

According to the CED approach, the composition of the debt is to be varied in a generally countercyclical manner, with the Treasury operating in long-, intermediate-, and short-term debt. A great variety of debt is to be utilized, excluding money. The CED does not conceive of debt management influencing the *size* of the debt, nor the supply of money; those items are classified as "budget policy" and "monetary policy." Consistent with the current institutional arrangements, debt policy determines only the composition of the debt.

The Treasury is to sell long-term securities in boom periods in order to reduce liquidity in the economy, thus contributing to stability. Short-term highly liquid securities are to be sold during deflationary periods in order to increase the over-all liquidity of the economy. There is a minor qualification to the general policy. The CED retains some of the classical flavor in that it favors longer debt; lengthening the debt (at least in 1954), or selling long-term, gives a more "desirable debt structure."[10]

Interest costs would not be minimized, as higher-yielding long-term securities would be sold in larger quantities just at the times when these rates would tend to be highest. It is conceded that interest costs are important, "but reducing the interest cost of the debt is only a secondary objective, to be pursued insofar as it is consistent with a debt policy that conforms to the needs of economic stability."[11] The policy obviously breaks with the older views.

Debt policy is viewed as a potentially valuable supplement to conventional monetary and fiscal policies, not as a substitute for them. Ideally monetary, fiscal, and debt management policies would be coordinated. It is argued that debt policy can increase the flexibility and range of influence of fiscal and monetary policy.

It is worth stressing that the CED position is the antithesis of

[9] Committee for Economic Development, *Managing the Federal Debt* (New York: 1954), pp. 13–14.

[10] The CED thinks that debt can become "too short" and states that "every opportunity to lengthen the debt without seriously affecting economic stability should be taken." This longer debt "would contribute to stability." *Ibid.*, pp. 23–24.

[11] *Ibid*, p. 14.

Simons' policy position on the structure of the debt. Unlike Simons the CED pictures the *structure* of the debt changing in a counter-cyclical fashion but the *size* of the debt not changing so far as debt policy itself is concerned. Simons pictures the *structure* of the debt remaining unchanged during all phases of the cycle, but the absolute *size* of the debt varying in a countercyclical manner, being simply the reflection of flexible monetary policy. Simons carefully avoids the uncertainties associated with Treasury near-moneys, wheras the CED policy proposal is based on a flexible use of near-moneys in order to influence total spending. What Simons eliminates from consideration, the CED converts into a policy instrument. Whereas Simons views short- and intermediate-term government debt as creating intolerable monetary uncertainty and economic instability, the CED views such debt as an instrument of stabilization policy.

STABILIZATION VIA DEBT SIZE AND COMPOSITION

In 1957 Earl Rolph developed another system of countercyclical debt management.[12] His system in a sense combines the Simons and CED approaches in that it involves the manipulation of the size of the debt *as well* as the composition of the debt. He states:

> Our first main proposition is that an increase in the size of the net debt of a national government, given the debt composition, has the effect of *decreasing*, and a decrease in the net debt has the effect of *increasing* GNP expenditures. It is elementary that the sale of government securities by a central bank is a deflationary policy. We simply generalize this observation to sales of government debt by any official agency.
>
> The defense of this proposition is identical with the defense of monetary policy.
>
> *   *   *
>
> A shift in the composition of an outstanding public debt of a given size that reduces its average maturity increases private expenditures, and vice versa for increases in its average maturity. Like any empirical generalization, this proposition does not hold for all circumstances.[13]

[12] Earl Rolph, "Principles of Debt Management," *American Economic Review*, Vol. 47, No. 3 (June 1957), pp. 302–320.

[13] *Ibid.*, pp. 305–308. A very similar statement of policy is made by Richard A. Musgrave. "A given degree of restriction [stabilization] may be obtained through various combinations of public debt differing in composition and total amount. The problem, then, is to find that combination which secures the desired degree of restriction at least cost." *The Theory of Public Finance* (New York: McGraw-Hill, 1959), p. 601.

Debt policy is to operate in a countercyclical manner; during recession periods the size of the debt as well as its term may be reduced. Both of these debt operations would tend to increase the over-all liquidity of the economy. With inflationary pressures the size of the debt as well as its term might be increased.[14] Debt management may be viewed as the purchase of illiquidity.

Obviously such a policy is consistent with the debt growing either larger or smaller, and either longer or shorter, depending upon secular tendencies in the economy. Unlike the CED, Rolph does not appear to have any particular preference for longer-term debt. There is no single correct composition of the debt. What is correct depends on the circumstances of the economy; thus what is correct now may be mischievous at a later date.

In Rolph's system interest is minimized only in the sense that an efficient stabilization policy is pursued. For a given amount of stabilization the lowest cost combination of debt size and structure is chosen. Interest is minimized relative to the stabilization goal.

While the Rolph system of policy is a hybrid of sorts, it is worth while to point out briefly the contrast with the CED and Simons. Rolph would vary the *size* of the debt in the same manner as Simons, but he violates Simons' debt structure rule by using alleged near-moneys.

Thus three variations on the countercyclical debt management theme are found. These positions in part conflict with, and in part reinforce, one another. Yet they are only part of the debt management controversy. Two important positions remain to be discussed.

The Pro-Cyclical Approach to Stabilization

Most prominent among those taking the procyclical approach to stabilization are United States Treasury spokesmen. The Treasury position is of interest for two significant reasons. First, the Treasury is actually in charge of debt management operations. Second, Treasury policy is in sharp contrast with the countercyclical approaches just discussed.

Treasury experts believe that debt management can most effectively contribute to economic stabilization by following policies that will allow those directly charged with stabilization to pursue vig-

---

[14] As originally presented by Rolph, the scheme involved a unique solution to debt management policy and interest minimization. However, this involved a minor slip in logic and proved untrue. Multiple possibilities are present rather than one single solution. For purposes at hand this is of little significance and will not be pursued.

orous and appropriate countercyclical programs. The debt should
be managed so as to minimize interference with responsible monetary policy. Treasury spokesmen assert that the difficulties involved
in debt management make the debt best considered a problem in
itself, capable of generating substantial difficulties for the government and the market if not properly handled. Poor debt management operations are capable of creating instability in the economy.
They do not view countercyclical debt management favorably, believing that it would accentuate the stabilization problem through
a build-up of short-term debt over time and would greatly increase
costs.[15]

Treasury authorities do not contemplate debt management as influencing the money supply, but regard that as the proper power
of the Federal Reserve System. This view reflects the contemporary
division of existing powers and the Treasury's acceptance of this
institutional arrangement.

Treasury policy directly contradicts countercyclical debt management. The Treasury "tailors the debt to the market," which in practice has meant that longer-term issues have been offered during
periods of recession and shorter-term issues during prosperous
times. Obviously this results in liquidity restriction during periods
of recession and liquidity ease during more prosperous times. This
considered by itself is obviously pro-cyclical and antagonistic to the
previously discussed positions. However, spokesmen argue that this
policy is the most practical policy to follow in stabilizing the economy, because this allows the Treasury to maintain a longer debt
and thus lessen the danger of debt management interfering with
monetary policy. Absence of the Treasury from the market as much
as possible gives the Federal Reserve more latitude in executing its
policies. Treasury policy contributes "to the amount of free time
which the Federal Reserve has to take effective monetary action
without always having to be concerned with a new issue of securities which is still in the process of being lodged with the eventual
holders of the securities."[16] The Treasury's continued presence in

[15] A reasonably good statement of Treasury policy in recent years can
be found in U.S. Congress, Joint Economic Committee, *Employment,
Growth, and Price Levels,* Part 6C, *The Government's Management of Its
Monetary, Fiscal, and Debt Operations,* 86th Cong., 1st Sess., 1959.
[16] Remarks by Secretary of the Treasury Anderson, April 7, 1958, at
the opening of the "Share in America" savings bonds campaign, New
York City, New York. Reprinted in the *Annual Report of the Secretary
of the Treasury for the Fiscal Year Ended June 30, 1958* (Washington,
D.C.: U.S. Government Printing Office, 1959), p. 263.

the market might bias the Federal Reserve toward an easier monetary policy than it would otherwise follow.

The policy of tailoring new securities to the particular needs of the market enables the Treasury to secure necessary funds at lower cost than would otherwise be possible. The Treasury has a practical political interest in lowering the interest burden of the debt, and officials believe that countercyclical debt management would greatly increase interest costs. "Economical borrowing is an important goal of Treasury debt management."[17] This is not doctrinaire interest minimization. "The goal of holding down interest cost on the public debt, although important, does not take precedence over other major goals of debt management."[18] On the other hand, Treasury authorities assert that such policies as the CED recommends would significantly increase interest costs.

Thus, lengthening the debt and minimizing interest costs are both important goals of Treasury policy. These goals are reconciled in the Treasury's tailoring procedures. This tailoring is, in principle, destabilizing in its impact on the economy. Yet officials insist that this policy aids in stabilizing the economy because it lessens the danger of debt management disrupting monetary policy. They conclude that Treasury policy is in practice a program for economic stability and that the opposite policies in practice would be destabilizing, costly, and impractical.

It is apparent that on the policy level the Treasury spokesmen are in direct conflict with the proponents of countercyclical debt management, although both relate debt management to the cycle and to problems of economic stabilization. The policies border on being black and white contrasts, yet their proponents declare them both practical and stabilizing.

The Treasury has retreated somewhat from the simpler precepts of classical debt management. Policies have changed, but much of the old lies beneath the surface of the new. Older precepts did not relate debt operations to the cycle, and they laid greater stress on funding than does present Treasury policy. On the other hand, the current policy definitely retains a bias in favor of longer-term debt. Treasury policy has not departed entirely from the older views, but there has been a change in emphasis and mood. Some believe expediency has come to play a larger role.

Warren Smith develops a debt policy along unmistakably pro-

---

[17] U.S. Congress, Joint Economic Committee, *Employment, Growth, and Price Levels*, Part 6C, p. 1723.
[18] *Ibid.*, pp. 1723–1724.

cyclical lines,[19] thus, in effect, defending the essential aspects of Treasury policy: Long-term securities would be sold during recession periods to take maximum advantage of low interest rates. As interest rates rose during periods of expansion, the Treasury would gradually shift to the short-term market. The advantage is to minimize the interference of the Treasury's debt management operations with freedom of action by the Federal Reserve during periods of inflation and/or tight credit. Debt lengthening during recessions would reduce the frequency of the Treasury's presence in the market. Smith states that this approach would require a concomitant flexible monetary policy. If debt managers overshoot the mark in raising long-term funds during a recession, with the result that recovery is impeded, the Federal Reserve should be prepared for offsetting action.

Smith attacks countercyclical debt policy as "mystical." He argues that shifts in debt length do not significantly affect the liquidity of the debt and that "neither the interest rate nor the liquidity effects of marginal changes in the debt structure appear to be very important."[20] Treasury spokesmen often imply that such shifts are important. Smith opposes using liquidity shifts for stabilization and states that "to the extent that such changes do have a net effect on the public's aggregate spending, it would appear that similar effects could be produced by the use of monetary policy. For this reason, it is difficult to see what can be accomplished by contracyclical debt management policy that cannot be accomplished more efficiently by Federal Reserve monetary policy."[21] Further, such a policy would tend to maximize interest costs.

Smith explicitly recognizes the existing debt as an automatic stabilizer, whereas this is largely implicit in the Treasury position. He also clearly states that the benefits of maintaining the debt (rather than inflating it away) must be weighed against the cost of the debt. Treasury officials have said little about this.

Thus the Treasury is not alone in defending procyclical debt management. However, the Treasury's theorists and academic sup-

---

[19] Warren Smith, *Debt Management in the United States*, Study Paper No. 19 for U.S. Congress, Joint Economic Committee, Materials prepared in connections with the Study of Employment, Growth, and Price Levels, 86th Cong., 2d Sess., 1960. Herbert Stein also defends pro-cyclical policy. In doing so he clearly distinguishes between debt length and temporal structure and calls for careful control of the amount of debt coming due in any year. "Managing the Federal Debt," *Journal of Law and Economics*, Vol. 1 (October 1958).

[20] Smith, *op. cit.*, p. 8.

[21] *Ibid.*

porters appear subject to the criticism that there is no questioning of the Federal Reserve's ability (or willingness) to adapt monetary policy quickly and accurately to unmeasurable liquidity shifts within the debt. This is of particular interest in light of the apparently divergent assumptions regarding the importance of such shifts.

The advocates of pro-cyclical management in the Treasury and their academic supporters constitute another major division of the debt management controversy. They disagree with the proponents of countercyclical debt management, and the final faction in the controversy disagrees with both groups.

The third and most recent major group taking part in the debt management controversy sets forth a debt policy which is neither countercyclical nor pro-cyclical, but rather aims at "neutrality" and tends to stress the simplification of debt operations. This position divorces debt management policy from the cycle.

The Neutrality Doctrine

Milton Friedman, representative of the neutrality position, in 1959 published *A Program for Monetary Stability*. He set forth the view that our main need regarding debt management is "to simplify and streamline, in such a manner as to keep debt operations from themselves being a source of instability, and to ease the task of coordinating Treasury debt operations and [Federal] Reserve open market operations."[22] Debt operations should be "regular in timing, reasonably stable in amount, and predictable in form."[23] Friedman would reduce the variety of debt instruments, retaining the tap issues (savings bonds) plus two standard debt forms, a short-term (possibly 90-day) bill and a moderately long-term security (8 to 10 years). Both of these securities would be sold at regular and frequent intervals, and amounts would be kept reasonably stable as a policy goal.

Friedman is critical of the Treasury's tailoring, which he states has resulted in

a bewildering maze of securities of different maturies and terms, and lumpiness and discontinuity in debt operations, with refunding of major magnitude occurring on a few dates in the year. Instead of proceeding at a regular pace and in a standard way to which the market could adjust,

---

[22] Milton Friedman, *A Program for Monetary Stability* (New York: Fordham University Press, 1959), p. 60.
[23] *Ibid.*, p. 65.

debt management operations have been jerky, full of expedients and surprises, and unpredictable in their impact and outcome. As a result they have been a continuing source of monetary uncertainty and instability.[24]

Tailoring is also criticized on the grounds that in reality it does not lower costs and that it implies that the government is more efficient than the market in the conduct of a particular class of financial operations. Friedman rejects this notion.

He also points out that interest minimization is more complex than the Treasury assumes because "it is necessary to take into account not only interest-bearing debt but also non-interest-bearing debt—Treasury currency and Federal Reserve notes and Federal Reserve deposits."[25] If the debt is made longer and thereby less liquid, it can be reduced in size without inflationary pressures appearing.

It is difficult if not impossible in the present state of knowledge to predict whether one or another pattern of securities will involve or did involve lower costs, correctly interpreted; hence there is no real basis for judging or improving performance.[26]

Friedman takes the position that minor changes in the length of the debt have only slight influence on the demand for money; hence, changes in the length of the debt are not viewed as a promising tool of stabilization policy. He points out that "shifts in maturity add nothing to open market operations." Furthermore, open market operations seem "likely to be more consistent and predictable in . . . impact."[27] Thus debt management operations, in the strict sense, are not technically good instruments for economic stabilization activity. Countercyclical debt management is rejected.

Tilford C. Gaines develops a position similar in some respects to Friedman's, stating that neutrality should be the object of policy and that Treasury operations should be put on a more orderly basis. Debt operations should be on a routine basis, and the amount of securities offered at any time carefully controlled relative to the market's absorptive capacity. This policy would tend to stabilize the liquidity of the debt and introduce greater certainty into the market. Gaines argues that lengthening the debt "whenever possible" (tailoring) creates a great deal of uncertainty about Treasury operations and tends to disturb the market. Tailoring is a "massive

[24] Ibid., p. 60.
[25] Ibid., p. 62.
[26] Ibid.
[27] Ibid., p. 61.

source of instability in the capital market,"[28] and has probably involved added costs because of higher interest rates associated with uncertainty. Further, it tends to make debt operations work counter to monetary policy. Countercyclical debt policy is also rejected because of the inadequate present state of technical knowledge. It is not deemed feasible.

This analysis divorces debt management from the cycle and advocates leaving stabilization to monetary policy, which is judged technically better and more appropriate for that purpose. It argues that debt policy should be based upon simplicity, regularity, and predictability. Both procyclical and countercyclical policies are rejected as inappropriate. The neutrality approach conflicts with the other positions and differs from the classical precepts which stressed funding and interest minimization. It is reminiscent of the classical attitude, however, as debt management is not related to the cycle, and it has a tone of simplicity and certainty. Still, neutrality remains a distinct policy differing from the older and conflicting with the newer views.

CONCLUDING REMARKS

Before the Great Depression and World War II there was virtual unanimity regarding the elements of "sound" debt policy, and there could be observed a striking similarity of opinion among academic economists and between the economists and the Treasury. Events since that time have shattered this picture, and there is now much disagreement over what constitutes sound policy.

At the present time three general positions are recognizable, and there is some divergence of thought within each of the basic categories. These can be termed *countercyclical* (Simons, the CED, and Rolph), *precyclical* (the Treasury and Smith), and *neutral* (Friedman and Gaines). All of these positions diverge in some degree from, or conflict with, the older views.

The newer positions are clearly in basic conflict with one another and tend to rest on contradictory assumptions regarding the nature of the stabilization problem and the technical impact of debt operations. They reflect basic disagreement about (1) the importance of interest minimization, (2) the best way to secure lowest cost on debt operations, (3) the relevant sense in which interest is to be minimized, (4) what constitutes a desirable or sound temporal structure for the debt, (5) how frequently debt operations should be car-

[28] T. C. Gaines, *Techniques of Treasury Debt Management* (New York: The Free Press of Glencoe, 1962), p. 266. See especially chapter 8.

ried on, (6) how long the debt should be, and (7) the technical impact of changes in debt length.

There is even more disagreement than indicated here, because the topic of institutional reorganization has not been considered. There is disagreement regarding the necessity and/or desirability of changing our institutional framework, and of course a number of plans are suggested. Hence, there is even disagreement as to *who* should manage the debt.

It is obvious that the debt management controversy has many sides, and there seems to be some dispute regarding every major aspect of debt management at the present time. This controversy is one facet of the more general stabilization debate that arose in the 1930's and the 1940's. That debate continues today in a somewhat abated form, although the area of disagreement seems to have narrowed, and emphasis has again drifted toward classical and neoclassical interpretations. The debt controversy may yet follow the same pattern and work toward a more sophisticated reinterpretation of older doctrines. If that is the case, it is likely to mean the eventual triumph of the neutrality school of debt management. For that pattern of thought stressing simplicity and predictability and divorcing debt management from the cycle has much in common with earlier views, though it is more clearly and explicitly formulated and differs somewhat in emphasis. Its eventual impact may well be to bring the old views up to date on such topics as debt length, interest minimization, and debt structure.

PART IV-B // FINANCIAL INTERMEDIARIES AND THEIR EFFECTS ON BANKING AND MONETARY POLICY

JAMES TOBIN

COMMERCIAL BANKS AS CREATORS OF "MONEY"

22

I. THE OLD VIEW

Perhaps the greatest moment of triumph for the elementary economics teacher is his exposition of the multiple creation of bank credit and bank deposits. Before the admiring eyes of freshmen he puts to rout the practical banker who is so sure that he "lends only the money depositors entrust to him." The banker is shown to have a worm's-eye view, and his error stands as an introductory object lesson in the fallacy of composition. From the Olympian vantage of the teacher and the textbook it appears that the banker's dictum must be reversed: depositors entrust to bankers whatever amounts the bankers lend. To be sure, this is not true of a single bank; one bank's loan may wind up as another bank's deposit. But it is, as the arithmetic of successive rounds of deposit creation makes clear, true of the banking system as a whole. Whatever their other errors, a long line of financial heretics have been right in speaking of "fountain pen money"—money created by the stroke of the bank president's pen when he approves a loan and credits the proceeds to the borrower's checking account.

In this time-honored exposition two characteristics of commercial banks—both of which are alleged to differentiate them sharply from other financial intermediaries—are intertwined. One is that their liabilities—well, at least their demand deposit liabilities—serve as widely acceptable means of payment. Thus, they count, along with coin and currency in public circulation, as "money."

Reprinted by permission of Richard D. Irwin, Inc., from James Tobin, "Commercial Banks as Creators of 'Money'" Deane Carson (ed.), *Banking and Monetary Studies*, 1963, pp. 408–419.

The other is that the preferences of the public normally play no role in determining the total volume of deposits or the total quantity of money. For it is the beginning of wisdom in monetary economics to observe that money is like the "hot potato" of a children's game: one individual may pass it to another, but the group as a whole cannot get rid of it. If the economy and the supply of money are out of adjustment, it is the economy that must do the adjusting. This is as true, evidently, of money created by bankers' fountain pens as of money created by public printing presses. On the other hand, financial intermediaries other than banks do not create money, and the scale of their assets is limited by their liabilities, i.e., by the savings the public entrusts to them. They cannot count on receiving "deposits" to match every extension of their lending.

The commercial banks and only the commercial banks in other words, possess the widow's cruse. And because they possess this key to unlimited expansion, they have to be restrained by reserve requirements. Once this is done, determination of the aggregate volume of bank deposits is just a matter of accounting and arithmetic: simply divide the available supply of bank reserves by the required reserve ratio.

The foregoing is admittedly a caricature, but I believe it is not a great exaggeration of the impressions conveyed by economics teaching concerning the roles of commercial banks and other financial institutions in the monetary system. In conveying this mélange of propositions, economics has replaced the naive fallacy of composition of the banker with other half-truths perhaps equally misleading. These have their root in the mystique of "money"—the tradition of distinguishing sharply between those assets which are and those which are not "money," and accordingly between those institutions which emit "money" and those whose liabilities are not "money." The persistent strength of this tradition is remarkable given the uncertainty and controversy over where to draw the dividing line between money and other assets. Time was when only currency was regarded as money, and the use of bank deposits was regarded as a way of economizing currency and increasing the velocity of money. Today scholars and statisticians wonder and argue whether to count commercial bank time and savings deposits in the money supply. And if so, why not similar accounts in other institutions? Nevertheless, once the arbitrary line is drawn, assets on the money side of the line are assumed to possess to the full properties which assets on the other side completely lack. For example, an eminent monetary economist, more candid than many of his colleagues, admits that we don't really know what money is, but proceeds to argue that, whatever it is, its supply should grow regularly at a rate of the order of 3 to 4 percent per year.[1]

II. THE "NEW VIEW"

A more recent development in monetary economics tends to blur the sharp traditional distinctions between money and other assets and between commercial banks and other financial intermediaries; to focus on demands for and supplies of the whole spectrum of assets rather than on the quantity and velocity of "money"; and to regard the structure of interest rates, asset yields, and credit availabilities rather than the quantity of money as the linkage between monetary and financial institutions and policies on the one hand and the real economy on the other.[2] In this essay I propose to look briefly at the implications of this "new view" for the theory of deposit creation, of which I have above described or caricatured the traditional version. One of the incidental advantages of this theoretical development is to effect something of a reconciliation between the economics teacher and the practical banker.

According to the "new view," the essential function of financial intermediaries, including commercial banks, is to satisfy simultaneously the portfolio preferences of two types of individuals or firms.[3] On one side are borrowers, who wish to expand their holdings of real assets—inventories, residential real estate, productive plant and equipment, etc.—beyond the limits of their own net worth. On the other side are lenders, who wish to hold part or all of their net worth in assets of stable money value with negligible risk of default. The assets of financial intermediaries are obligations of the borrowers—promissory notes, bonds, mortgages. The lia-

[1] E. S. Shaw, "Money Supply and Stable Economic Growth," in *United States Monetary Policy* (New York: American Assembly, 1958), pp. 49–71.

[2] For a review of this development and for references to its protagonists, see Harry Johnson's survey article, "Monetary Theory and Policy," *American Economic Review*, Vol. LII (June 1962), pp. 335–384. I will confine myself to mentioning the importance, in originating and contributing to the "new view," of John Gurley and E. S. Shaw (yes, the very same Shaw cited in the previous footnote, but presumably in a different incarnation). Their viewpoint is summarized in *Money in a Theory of Finance* (Washington, D.C.: The Brookings Institution, 1960).

[3] This paragraph and the three following are adapted with minor changes from the author's paper with William Brainard, "Financial Intermediaries and the Effectiveness of Monetary Controls," *American Economic Review*, Vol. LIII (May 1963), pp. 384–386.

bilities of financial intermediaries are the assets of the lenders—
bank deposits, insurance policies, pension rights.

Financial intermediaries typically assume liabilities of smaller
default risk and greater predictability of value than their assets.
The principal kinds of institutions take on liabilities of greater liquidity too; thus, bank depositors can require payment on demand, while bank loans become due only on specified dates. The
reasons that the intermediation of financial institutions can accomplish these transformations between the nature of the obligation
of the borrower and the nature of the asset of the ultimate lender
are these: (1) administrative economy and expertise in negotiating,
accounting, appraising, and collecting; (2) reductions of risk per
dollar of lending by the pooling of independent risks, with respect
both to loan default and to deposit withdrawal; (3) governmental
guarantees of the liabilities of the institutions and other provisions
(bank examination, investment regulations, supervision of insurance
companies, last-resort lending) designed to assure the solvency and
liquidity of the institutions.

For these reasons, intermediation permits borrowers who wish
to expand their investments in real assets to be accommodated at
lower rates and easier terms than if they had to borrow directly
from the lenders. If the crediters of financial intermediaries had to
hold instead the kinds of obligations that private borrowers are
capable of providing, they would certainly insist on higher rates
and stricter terms. Therefore, any autonomous increase—for example, improvements in the efficiency of financial institutions or
the creation of new types of intermediaries—in the amount of financial intermediation in the economy can be expected to be, *ceteris
paribus*, an expansionary influence. This is true whether the growth
occurs in intermediaries with monetary liabilities—i.e., commercial
banks—or in other intermediaries.

Financial institutions fall fairly easily into distinct categories,
each industry or "intermediary" offering a differentiated product
to its customers, both lenders and borrowers. From the point of
view of lenders, the obligations of the various intermediaries are
more or less close, but not perfect, substitutes. For example, savings deposits share most of the attributes of demand deposits; but
they are not means of payment, and the institution has the right,
seldom exercised, to require notice of withdrawal. Similarly there
is differentiation in the kinds of credit offered borrowers. Each
intermediary has its specialty—e.g., the commercial loan for banks,
the real-estate mortgage for the savings and loan association. But
the borrowers' market is not completely compartmentalized. The

same credit instruments are handled by more than one intermediary, and many borrowers have flexibility in the type of debt they incur. Thus, there is some substitutability, in the demand for credit by borrowers, between the assets of the various intermediaries.[4]

The special attention given commercial banks in economic analysis is usually justified by the observation that, alone among intermediaries, banks "create" means of payment. This rationale is on its face far from convincing. The means-of-payment characteristic of demand deposits is indeed a feature differentiating bank liabilities from those of other intermediaries. Insurance against death is equally a feature differentiating life insurance policies from the obligations of other intermediaries, including banks. It is not obvious that one kind of differentiation should be singled out for special analytical treatment. Like other differentia, the means-of-payment attribute has its price. Savings deposits, for example, are perfect substitutes for demand deposits in every respect except as a medium of exchange. This advantage of checking accounts does not give banks absolute immunity from the competition of savings banks; it is a limited advantage that can be, at least in some part for many depositors, overcome by differences in yield. It follows that the community's demand for bank deposits is not indefinite, even though demand deposits do serve as means of payment.

III. THE WIDOW'S CRUSE

Neither individually nor collectively do commercial banks possess a widow's cruse. Quite apart from legal reserve requirements, commercial banks are limited in scale by the same kinds of economic processes that determine the aggregate size of other intermediaries.

One often cited difference between commercial banks and other intermediaries must be quickly dismissed as superficial and irrelevant. This is the fact that a bank can make a loan by "writing up" its deposit liabilities, while a savings and loan association, for example, cannot satisfy a mortgage borrower by crediting him with a share account. The association must transfer means of payment to the borrower; its total liabilities do not rise along with its assets. True enough, but neither do the bank's, for more than a fleeting

[4] These features of the market structure of intermediaries, and their implications for the supposed uniqueness of banks, have been emphasized by Gurley and Shaw, *op. cit.* An example of substitutability on the deposit side is analyzed by David and Charlotte Alhadeff, "The Struggle for Commercial Bank Savings," *Quarterly Journal of Economics*, Vol. LXXII (February 1958), pp. 1–22.

moment. Borrowers do not incur debt in order to hold idle deposits, any more than savings and loan shares. The borrower pays out the money, and there is of course no guarantee that any of it stays in the lending bank. Whether or not it stays in the banking system as a whole is another question, about to be discussed. But the answer clearly does not depend on the way the loan was initially made. It depends on whether somewhere in the chain of transactions initiated by the borrower's outlays are found depositors who wish to hold new deposits equal in amount to the new loan. Similarly, the outcome for the savings and loan industry depends on whether in the chain of transactions initiated by the mortgage are found individuals who wish to acquire additional savings and loan shares.

The banking system can expand its assets either (a) by purchasing, or lending against, existing assets; or (b) by lending to finance new private investment in inventories or capital goods, or buying government securities financing new public deficits. In case (a) no increase in private wealth occurs in conjunction with the banks' expansion. There is no new private saving and investment. In case (b), new private saving occurs, matching dollar for dollar the private investments or government deficits financed by the banking system. In neither case will there automatically be an increase in savers' demand for bank deposits equal to the expansion in bank assets.

In the second case, it is true, there is in increase in private wealth. But even if we assume a closed economy in order to abstract from leakages of capital abroad, the community will not ordinarily wish to put 100 percent of its new saving into bank deposits. Bank deposits are, after all, only about 15 percent of total private wealth in the United States; other things equal, savers cannot be expected greatly to exceed this proportion in allocating new saving. So, if *all* new savings is to take the form of bank deposits, other things cannot stay equal. Specifically, the yields and other advantages of the competing assets into which new saving would otherwise flow will have to fall enough so that savers prefer bank deposits.

This is *a fortiori* true in case (a) where there is no new saving and the generation of bank liabilities to match the assumed expansion of bank assets entails a reshufling of existing portfolios in favor of bank deposits. In effect the banking system has to induce the public to swap loans and securities for bank deposits. This can happen only if the price is right.

Clearly, then, there is at any moment a natural economic limit to the scale of the commercial banking industry. Given the wealth and the asset preference of the community, the demand for bank deposits can increase only if the yields of other assets fall. The fall in these yields is bound to restrict the profitable lending and investment opportunities available to the banks themselves. Eventually the marginal returns on lending and investing, account taken of the risks and administrative costs involved, will not exceed the marginal cost to the banks of attracting and holding additional deposits. At this point the widow's cruse has run dry.

IV. BANKS AND OTHER INTERMEDIARIES COMPARED

In this respect the commercial banking industry is not qualitatively different from any other financial intermediary system. The same process limits the collective expansion of savings and loan associations, or savings banks, or life insurance companies. At some point the returns from additional loans or security holdings are not worth the cost of obtaining the funds from the public.

There are of course some differences. First, it may well be true that commercial banks benefit from a larger share of additions to private savings than other intermediaries. Second, according to modern American legal practice, commercial banks are subject to ceilings on the rates payable to their depositors—zero in the case of demand deposits. Unlike competing financial industries, commercial banks cannot seek funds by raising rates. They can and do offer other inducements to depositors, but these substitutes for interest are imperfect and uneven in their incidence. In these circumstances the major readjustment of the interest rate structure necessary to increase the relative demand for bank deposits is a decline in other rates. Note that neither of these differences has to do with the quality of bank deposits as "money."

In a world without reserve requirements the preferences of depositors, as well as those of borrowers, would be very relevant in determining the volume of bank deposits. The volume of assets and liabilities of every intermediary, both nonbanks and banks, would be determined in a competitive equilibrium, where the rate of interest charged borrowers by each kind of institution just balances at the margin the rate of interest paid its creditors. Suppose that such an equilibrium is disturbed by a shift in savers' preferences. At prevailing rates they decide to hold more savings accounts and other nonbank liabilities and less demand deposits. They transfer demand deposits to the credit of nonbank financial institutions, providing these intermediaries with the means to seek additional earning assets. These institutions, finding themselves able to attract more funds from the public even with some reduction in the rates they pay, offer better terms to borrowers and bid up the prices of existing earning assets. Consequently commercial banks release some earning assets—they no longer yield enough to pay the going rate on the banks' deposit liabilities. Bank deposits decline with bank assets. In effect, the nonbank intermediaries favored by the shift in public preferences simply swap the deposits transferred to them for a corresponding quantity of bank assets.

V. FOUNDATION PENS AND PRINTING PRESSES

Evidently the fountain pens of commercial bankers are essentially different from the printing presses of governments. Confusion results from concluding that because bank deposits are like currency in one respect—both serve as media of exchange—they are like currency in every respect. Unlike governments, bankers cannot create means of payment to finance their own purchases of goods and services. Bank-created "money" is a liability, which must be matched on the other side of the balance sheet. And banks, as businesses, must earn money from their middleman's role. Once created, printing press money cannot be extinguished, except by reversal of the budget policies which led to its birth. The community cannot get rid of its currency supply; the economy must adjust until it is willingly absorbed. The "hot potato" analogy truly applies. For bank-created money, however, there is an economic mechanism of extinction as well as creation, contraction as well as expansion. If bank deposits are excessive relative to public preferences, they will tend to decline; otherwise banks will lose income. The burden of adaptation is not placed entirely on the rest of the economy.

VI. THE ROLE OF RESERVE REQUIREMENTS

Without reserve requirements, expansion of credit and deposits by the commercial banking system would be limited by the availability of assets at yields sufficient to compensate banks for the costs of attracting and holding the corresponding deposits. In a régime of reserve requirements, the limit which they impose normally cuts the expansion short of this competitive equilibrium. When reserve requirements and deposit interest rate ceilings are effective, the marginal yield of bank loans and investments exceeds the marginal cost of deposits to the banking system. In these circumstances additional reserves make it possible and profitable for banks to acquire additional earning assets. The expansion process lowers interest rates generally—enough to induce the public to hold additional deposits but ordinarily not enough to wipe out the banks' margin between the value and cost of additional deposits.

It is the existence of this margin—not the monetary nature of bank liabilities—which makes it possible for the economics teacher to say that additional loans permitted by new reserves will generate their own deposits. The same proposition would be true of any other system of financial institutions subject to similar reserve constraints and similar interest rate ceilings. In this sense it is more accurate to attribute the special place of banks among intermediaries to the legal restrictions to which banks alone are subjected than to attribute these restrictions to the special character of bank liabilities.

But the textbook description of multiple expansion of credit and deposits on a given reserve base is misleading even for a régime of reserve requirements. There is more to the determination of the volume of bank deposits than the arithmetic of reserve supplies and reserve ratios. The redundant reserves of the thirties are a dramatic reminder that economic opportunities sometimes prevail over reserve calculations. But the significance of that experience is not correctly appreciated if it is regarded simply as an aberration from a normal state of affairs in which banks are fully "loaned up" and total deposits are tightly linked to the volume of reserves. The thirties exemplify in extreme form a phenomenon which is always in some degree present: the use to which commercial banks put the reserves made available to the system is an economic variable depending on lending opportunities and interest rates.

An individual bank is not constrained by any fixed quantum of reserves. It can obtain additional reserves to meet requirements by borrowing from the Federal Reserve, by buying "Federal Funds" from other banks, by selling or "running off" short-term securities. In short, reserves are available at the discount window and in the money market, at a price. This cost the bank must compare with available yields on loans and investments. If those yields are low relative to the cost of reserves, the bank will seek to avoid borrowing reserves and perhaps hold excess reserves instead. If those yields are high relative to the cost of borrowing reserves, the bank will shun excess reserves and borrow reserves occasionally or even regularly. For the banking system as a whole the Federal Reserve's quantitative controls determine the supply of unborrowed reserves. But the extent to which this supply is left unused, or supplemented by borrowing at the discount window, depends on the economic circumstances confronting the banks—on available lending opportunities and on the whole structure of interest rates from the Fed's discount rate through the rates on mortgages and long-term securities.

The range of variation in net free reserves in recent years has been from −5 percent to +5 percent of required reserves. This indicates a much looser linkage between reserves and deposits than is suggested by the textbook exposition of multiple expansion for a system which is always precisely and fully "loaned up." (It does not mean, however, that actual monetary authorities have any less control than textbook monetary authorities. Indeed the net free reserve position is one of their more useful instruments and barometers. Anyway, they are after bigger game than the quantity of "money"!)

Two consequences of this analysis deserve special notice because of their relation to the issues raised earlier in this paper. First, an increase—of, say, a billion dollars—in the supply of unborrowed reserves will, in general, result in less than a billion-dollar increase in required reserves. Net free reserves will rise (algebraically) by some fraction of the billion dollars—a very large fraction in periods like the thirties, a much smaller one in tight money periods like those of the fifties. Loans and deposits will expand by less than their textbook multiples. The reason is simple. The open-market operations which bring about the increased supply of reserves tend to lower interest rates. So do the operations of the commercial banks in trying to invest their new reserves. The result is to diminish the incentives of banks to keep fully loaned up or to borrow reserves, and to make banks content to hold on the average higher excess reserves.

Second, depositor preferences do matter, even in a régime of fractional reserve banking. Suppose, for example, that the public decides to switch new or old savings from other assets and institutions into commercial banks. This switch makes earning assets available to banks at attractive yields—assets that otherwise would have been lodged either directly with the public or with the competing financial institutions previously favored with the public's savings. These improved opportunities for profitable lending and investing will make the banks content to hold smaller net free reserves. Both their deposits and their assets will rise as a result of this shift in public preferences, even though the base of unborrowed reserves remains unchanged. Something of this kind has occurred in recent years when commercial banks have been permitted to raise the interest rates they offer for time and savings deposits.

VII. CONCLUDING REMARKS

The implications of the "new view" may be summarized as follows:

1. The distinction between commercial banks and other financial intermediaries has been too sharply drawn. The differences are of degree, not of kind.

2. In particular, the differences which do exist have little intrinsically to do with the monetary nature of bank liabilities.

3. The differences are more importantly related to the special reserve requirements and interest rate ceilings to which banks are subject. Any other financial industry subject to the same kind of regulations would behave in much the same way.

4. Commercial banks do not possess, either individually or collectively, a widow's cruse which guarantees that any expansion of assets will generate a corresponding expansion of deposit liabilities. Certainly this happy state of affairs would not exist in an unregulated competitive financial world. Marshall's scissors of supply and demand apply to the "output" of the banking industry, no less than to other financial and nonfinancial industries.

5. Reserve requirements and interest ceilings give the widow's cruse myth somewhat greater plausibility. But even in these circumstances, the scale of bank deposits and assets is affected by depositor preferences and by the lending and investing opportunities available to banks.

I draw no policy morals from these observations. That is quite another story, to which analysis of the type presented here is only the preface. The reader will misunderstand my purpose if he jumps to attribute to me the conclusion that existing differences in the regulatory treatment of banks and competing intermediaries should be diminished, either by relaxing constraints on the one or by tightening controls on the other.

JOHN G. GURLEY
EDWARD S. SHAW

FINANCIAL INTERMEDIARIES
AND THE
SAVING-INVESTMENT PROCESS

23

It is fashionable these days to speak of the growing institutionalization of saving and investment. Rapid advances in recent years by pension funds, open-end investment companies, credit unions, and savings and loan associations, among others, have caught our eye. But the advance has been going on at least since the Civil War, and, as Raymond Goldsmith has recently shown, it was quite pronounced during the first three decades of this century. It is with these three decades that our paper is primarily concerned. Our method of analyzing financial data, however, requires explanation since it is based on unconventional theory. Accordingly, the first portions of the paper are largely theoretical. After that, we get down to brass tacks.

DEFICITS, SECURITY ISSUES, AND GNP

It is easy to imagine a world in which there is a high level of saving and investment, but in which there is an unfavorable climate for financial intermediaries. At the extreme, each of the economy's spending units—whether of the household, business, or government variety—would have a balanced budget on income and product account. For each spending unit, current income would equal the sum of current and capital expenditures. There could still be saving and investment, but each spending unit's saving would be precisely matched by its investment in tangible assets. In a world of balanced budgets, security issues by spending units would be zero, or very close to zero.[1] The same would be true of the accumulation of fi-

Reprinted by permission of the publisher from John G. Gurley and Edward S. Shaw, "Financial Intermediaries and the Saving-Investment Process," *Journal of Finance*, Vol. XI (May 1956), pp. 257–276.
[1] Securities might be issued by spending units to build up their financial assets or their holdings of existing real assets. However, in a world of balanced budgets, no spending unit would have a *net* accumulation of these assets, positive or negative.

nancial assets. Consequently, this world would be a highly uncongenial one for financial intermediaries; the saving-investment process would grind away without them.

Financial intermediaries are likely to thrive best in a world of deficits and surpluses, in a world in which there is a significant division of labor between savers and investors. In the ideal world for financial intermediaries, all current and capital expenditures would be made by spending units that received no current income, and all current income would be received by spending units that spent nothing. One group of spending units would have a deficit equal to its expenditures, and the other group would have a surplus equal to its income. And, of course, the *ex post* deficit would necessarily be equal to the *ex post* surplus. In this setting, the deficit group would tend to issue securities equal to its deficit, and the other group would tend to accumulate financial assets equal to its surplus. Security issues and financial-asset accumulations, therefore, would tend to approximate GNP or the aggregate of expenditures. No more congenial world than this could exist for financial intermediaries.

Unfortunately for these intermediaries, our own economy has been much closer to the first than to the second world. With some exceptions during the past half-century, the annual security issues of spending units over complete cycles have averaged somewhat below 10 per cent of GNP in current prices. These issues include government securities, corporate and foreign bonds, common and preferred stock, farm and non-farm mortgages, and consumer and other short-term debt. We shall call these primary security issues. Thus, at the turn of the century when GNP was around $20 billion, primary security issues ran a bit less than $2 billion per annum. In the late 1940's, with a GNP of approximately $250 billion, primary issues hovered around $20 billion per annum. Dividing the half-century into thirteen complete cycles, we find that the average annual ratio of primary issues to GNP was between 7 and 10 per cent in nine of the cycles. The exceptional cases include World War I, when the ratio reached 20 percent, the 1930's, when the ratio fell to 3 or 4 percent, and World War II, when it climbed to 25 percent. However, if we consider longer phases, 1897–1914, 1915–32, and 1933–49, the ratio was between 9 and 10 percent in each phase. There is sufficient strength, then, in the link between borrowing and GNP to make the relationship useful for financial analysis. And while the ratio lies closer to zero than to 100 percent, still it is high enough to permit financial intermediation to be a substantial business.

THE ROLE OF FINANCIAL INTERMEDIARIES

What is the business of financial intermediaries? They lend at one stratum of interest rates and borrow at a lower stratum. They relieve the market of some primary securities and substitute others—indirect securities or financial assets—whose qualities command a higher price. This margin between yields on primary and indirect securities is the intermediaries' compensation for the special services they supply.

The financial institutions that fit these specifications are savings and loan associations, insurance companies, mutual savings banks, Postal Savings banks, investment companies, common trust funds, pension funds, government lending agencies, and others. In addition, we count the monetary system, including commercial banks, as one among many intermediaries. It is a vitally important intermediary, in view of its functions and its size. But its elevated rank among intermediaries does not alter the principle that the monetary system, like other intermediaries, transmits loanable funds by issues of indirect financial assets to surplus units and purchases of primary securities from deficit units. The indirect financial assets, deposits and currency that it isssues or creates, are, like the indirect financial assets issued or created by other intermediaries, substitutes for primary securities in the portfolios of spending units. We shall return to this point in a few moments.

INTERNAL AND EXTERNAL FINANCE OF EXPENDITURES

In a world of balanced budgets, each spending unit's current and capital expenditures would be financed entirely from its current income. Thus, aggregate expenditures in the economy would be self-financed or internally financed. Internal finance would be equal to GNP.

In a world of deficits and surpluses, some expenditures would be financed externally. The extent of such financing is measured by the sum of the deficits (or surpluses) run by spending units. If at a GNP of $400 billion, the sum of all spending units' deficits as $40 billion, then 10 percent of GNP is financed externally and 90 percent is financed internally.

External finance may take two forms: direct finance and indirect finance. The distinction is based on the changes that occur in the financial accounts of surplus units' balance sheets. The finance is indirect if the surplus units acquire claims on financial intermediaries.[2] It is direct if surplus units acquire claims on debtors that are not financial intermediaries.[3]

While the proportion of GNP that is externally financed has not changed much over the past half-century, the proportion that is indirectly financed has risen and, of course, the proportion that is directly financed has fallen. In short, a growing share of primary issues has been sold to financial intermediaries.[4] But the relative gainers have been the non-monetary intermediaries and the relative loser has been the monetary system. Now, if we look at these trends from the standpoint of surplus spenders, we have the following picture: the surplus units have accumulated financial assets in annual amounts that, over long periods, have been a fairly steady percentage of GNP. However, these accumulations have been relatively more and more in the form of indirect financial assets, and relatively less and less in the form of primary securities. Moreover, the accumulations of indirect financial assets have swung toward the nonmonetary types and away from bank deposits and currency. Commercial banks and the monetary system have retrogressed relative to financial intermediaries generally.

A RECONSIDERATION OF BANKING THEORY

A traditional view of the monetary system is that it determines the supply of money: it determines its own size in terms of mone-

[2] In our empirical work, we exclude from indirect finance some kinds of claims on intermediaries, such as accrued expenses or even stockholder equities, that are essentially like debt issues of non-financial spending units.

[3] It may help to illustrate these financing arrangements. Suppose that at a GNP of $400 billion the sum of all spending units' deficits is $40 billion. Suppose further that $40 billion of primary securities, such as corporate bonds and mortgages, are issued to cover the deficits. The primary securities may be sold directly to surplus spending units whose aggregate surplus will also be equal to $40 billion, looking at it *ex post*. In this case direct finance will take place, with surplus spenders acquiring various types of primary securities. Alternatively, if the primary securities are sold to financial intermediaries, surplus spenders will accumulate claims on these intermediaries, indirect financial assets instead of primary securities. In this event we say that the expenditures represented by the primary securities have been indirectly financed. If indirect finance occurs through commercial banks, surplus spenders accumulate bank deposits; if through savings and loan associations, they acquire savings and loan shares; if through life insurance companies, policyholder equities; and so on.

[4] This growth has not been steady. Indeed, it is shown later that there was retrogression in intermediation from 1898 to 1921. The share of issues going to intermediaries rose in the 1920's, rose further in the 1930's, and remained high in the 1940's.

tary debt and of the assets that are counterparts of this debt on the system's balance sheet. Other financial intermediaries transfer to investors any part of this money supply that may be deposited with them by savers. Their size is determined by the public's choice of saving media.

As we see it, on the contrary, the monetary system is in some significant degree competitive with other financial intermediaries. The growth of these intermediaries in terms of indirect debt and of primary security portfolios is alternative to monetary growth and inhibits it. Their issues of indirect debt displace money, and the primary securities that they hold are in some large degree a loss of assets to the banks.

Bank deposits and currency are unique in one respect: they are means of payment, and holders of money balances have immediate access to the payments mechanism of the banking system. If money were in demand only for immediate spending or for holding in transactions balances, and if no other financial asset could be substituted as a means of payment or displace money in transactions balances, the monetary system would be a monopolistic supplier exempt from competition by other financial intermediaries.

But money is not in demand exclusively as a means of payment. It is in demand as a financial asset to hold. As a component of balances, money does encounter competition. Other financial assets can be accumulated preparatory to money payments, as a precaution against contingencies, or as an alternative to primary securities. For any level of money payments, various levels of money balances will do and, hence, various sizes of money supply and monetary system.

The more adequate the non-monetary financial assets are as substitutes for money in transactions, precautionary, speculative, and —as we shall see—diversification balances, the smaller may be the money supply for any designated level of national income. For any level of income, the money supply is indeterminate until one knows the degree of substitutability between money created by banks and financial assets created by other intermediaries. How big the monetary system is depends in part on the intensity of competition from savings banks, life insurance companies, pension funds, and other intermediaries.

Financial competition may inhibit the growth of the monetary system in a number of ways. Given the level of national income, a gain in attractiveness of, say, savings and loan shares vis-à-vis money balances must result in an excess supply of money. The monetary authority may choose to remove this excess. Then bank reserves, earning assets, money issues, and profits are contracted.

This implies that, at any level of income, the competition of non-monetary intermediaries may displace money balances, shift primary securities from banks to their competitors, and reduce the monetary system's requirement for reserves. In a trend context, bank reserves cannot be permitted to grow as rapidly as otherwise they might, if non-monetary intermediaries become more attractive channels for transmission of loanable funds.

Suppose that excess money balances, resulting from a shift in spending units' demand away from money balances to alternative forms of indirect financial assets, are not destroyed by central bank action. They may be used to repay bank loans or to buy other securities from banks, the result being excess bank reserves. At the prevailing level of security prices, spending units have rejected money balances. But cannot banks force these balances out again, resuming control of the money supply? They can do so by accepting a reduced margin between the yield of primary securities they buy and the cost to them of deposits and currency they create. But this option is not peculiar to banks: other intermediaries can stimulate demand for their debt if they stand ready to accept a reduced markup on the securities they create and sell relative to the securities they buy. The banks can restore the money supply, but the cost is both a decline in their status relative to other financial intermediaries and a reduction in earnings.

The banks may choose to live with excess reserves rather than pay higher prices on primary securities or higher yields on their own debt issues. In this case, as in the previous two a lower volume of reserves is needed to sustain a given level of national income. With their competitive situation improved, non-monetary intermediaries have stolen away from the banking system a share of responsibility for sustaining the flow of money payments. They hold a larger share of outstanding primary securities; they owe a larger share of indirect financial assets. They have reduced the size of the banking system at the given income level, both absolutely and relatively to their own size, and their gain is at the expense of bank profits.[5]

[5] We may mention a few additional issues in banking theory. As intermediaries, banks buy primary securities and issue, in payment for them, deposits and currency. As the payments mechanism, banks transfer title to means of payment on demand by customers. It has been pointed out before, especially by Henry Simons, that these two banking functions are at least incompatible. As managers of the payments mechanism, the banks cannot afford a shadow of insolvency. As intermediaries in a growing economy, the banks may rightly be tempted to wildcat. They must be

solvent or the community will suffer; they must dare insolvency or the community will fail to realize its potentialities for growth.

All too often in American history energetic intermediation by banks has culminated in collapse of the payments mechanism. During some periods, especially cautious regard for solvency has resulted in collapse of bank intermediation. Each occasion that has demonstrated the incompatibility of the two principal banking functions has touched off a flood of financial reform. These reforms on balance have tended to emphasize bank solvency and the viability of the payments mechanism at the expense of bank participation in financial growth. They have by no means gone to the extreme that Simons proposed, of divorcing the two functions altogether, but they have tended in that direction rather than toward indorsement of wildcat banking. This bias in financial reform has improved the opportunities for non-monetary intermediaries. The relative retrogression in American banking seems to have resulted in part from regulatory suppression of the intermediary function.

Turning to another matter, it has seemed to be a distinctive, even magic, characteristic of the monetary system that it can create money, erecting a "multiple expansion" of debt in the form of deposits and currency on a limited base of reserves. Other financial institutions, conventional doctrine tells us, are denied this creative or multiplicative faculty. They are merely middlemen or brokers, not manufacturers of credit. Our own view is different. There is no denying, of course, that the monetary system creates debt in the special form of money: the monetary system can borrow by issue of instruments that are means of payment. There is no denying, either, that non-monetary intermediaries cannot create this same form of debt. They would be monetary institutions if they could do so. It is granted, too, that non-monetary intermediaries receive money and pay it out, precisely as all of us do: they use the payments mechanism.

However, each kind of non-monetary intermediary can borrow, go into debt, issue its own characteristic obligations—in short, it can create credit, though not in monetary form. Moreover, the non-monetary intermediaries are less inhibited in their own style of credit creation than are the banks in creating money. Credit creation by non-monetary intermedaries is restricted by various qualitative rules. Aside from these, the main factor that limits credit creation is the profit calculus. Credit creation by banks also is subject to the profit condition. But the monetary system is subject not only to this restraint and to a complex of qualitative rules. It is committed to a policy restraint, of avoiding excessive expansion or contraction of credit for the community's welfare, that is not imposed explicitly on non-monetary intermediaries. It is also held in check by a system of reserve requirements. The legal reserve requirement on commercial banks is a "sharing ratio"; it apportions assets within the monetary system. The share of assets allocated to the commercial banks varies inversely with the reserve requirement. The proportion of the commercial banks' share to the share of the central bank and Treasury is the "multiple of expansion" for the commercial banking system. The "multiple of expansion" is a remarkable phenomenon not because of its inflationary implications but because it means that bank expansion is anchored, as other financial expansion is not, to a regulated base. If credit creation by banks is miraculous, creation of credit by other financial institutions is still more a cause for exclamation.

A RECONSIDERATION OF INTEREST THEORY

It is clear from the foregoing remarks that this way of looking at financial intermediaries leads to a reconsideration of interest theory. Yields on primary securities, the terms of borrowing available to deficit spenders, are influenced not only by the amount of primary securities in the monetary system—that is, by the supply of money —but also by the amount of these securities in non-monetary intermediaries—that is, by the supply of indirect financial assets created by these intermediaries. Suppose that savings and loan shares become more attractive relative to bank deposits, resulting in an excess supply of money. Now, if we suppose that the monetary system chooses and manages to keep the money supply constant under these circumstances, the excess supply of money will cause yields on primary securities to fall. The activities of non-monetary financial intermediaries, then, can affect primary yields. The same money supply and national income are compatible with various interest rate levels, depending upon the size of non-monetary intermediaries and upon the degree to which their issues are competitive with money.[6]

The analysis is only a bit more complicated when we allow for issues of primary securities and the growth of income. Let us take these one at a time. At any income level, some spending units will have deficits and others surpluses. During the income period, the deficit spenders will tend to issue primary securities in an amount equal to their aggregate deficits. Now, if the surplus spenders are willing to absorb all of the issues at current yields on these securities, there will be no tightening effect on security markets. Surplus spenders will accumulate financial assets, all in the form of primary

[6] We can reach the same conclusion by looking at the supply of and the demand for primary securities. The shift in demand to savings and loan shares reduces spending units' demand for bank deposits by, say, an equivalent amount. Consequently, the demand by spending units for primary securities is unchanged at current yields. Also, there is no change in this demand by the monetary system, since we have assumed the money supply constant. However, there is an increase in demand for primary securities by savings and loan associations. So, for the economy as a whole, there is an excess demand for primary securities at current yields, which is the counterpart of the excess supply of money.

Downward pressure on primary yields is exerted as long as the indirect debt of non-monetary intermediaries is to some degree competitive with money and as long as the additional demand for primary securities by these intermediaries is roughly equivalent to their creation of indirect debt.

securities, and financial intermediaries will purchase none of the issues.

But this is an unlikely outcome. Ordinarily, surplus spenders can be expected to reject some portion of the primary securities emerging at any level of income and demand indirect financial assets instead, unless their preference for the latter is suppressed by a fall in prices of primary securities and a corresponding rise in interest rates charged to deficit spenders. This incremental demand for indirect financial assets is in part a demand for portfolio diversification. The diversification demand exists because there is generally no feasible mixture of primary securities that provides adequately such distinctive qualities of indirect securities as stability of price and yield or divisibility. The incremental demand for indirect assets, however, reflects not only a negative response, a partial rejection of primary securities, but also a positive response, an attraction to the many services attached to indirect assets, such as insurance and pension services and convenience of accumulation. Part of the demand is linked to the flow of primary security issues, but another part is linked more closely to the level of income.

For these reasons, then, ordinarily some portion of the primary issues must be sold to financial intermediaries if present yields on these securities are to be defended. Assuming for the moment that the monetary system is the only financial intermediary, the increase in the money supply must be equal to the portion of primary issues that spending units choose not to accumulate at current yields. If the monetary system purchases less than this, spending units will accumulate the residual supply at rising interest rates to deficit spenders. The emergence of security issues and a diversification demand for money based on these issues means that the money supply must rise at a given income level to maintain current yields on primary securities.

Still retaining the assumption that the monetary system is the only financial intermediary, we now permit income to grow. As money income gains, spending units demand additions to their active or transactions balances of means of payment. An upward trend in money payments calls for an upward trend in balances too. The income effect also applies to contingency or precautionary balances. If spending units are increasingly prosperous in the present, they feel able to afford stronger defenses against the hazards of the future.[7]

[7] For periods longer than the Keynesian short run, it is hardly safe to assume that transactions and contingency demands for additional money balances are proportional to increments in the level of money income.

The combination of the income and diversification effects simply means that, when income is rising, a larger share of the issues must be purchased by the monetary system to prevent a rise in primary yields. The system must supply money for both diversification and transactions, including contingency, balances.

We may now introduce non-monetary intermediaries. The growth of these intermediaries will ordinarily, to some extent, reduce the required growth of the monetary system. We have already presented the reasons for this, so it suffices to say that primary yields may be held steady under growth conditions even with a monetary system that is barely growing, provided other intermediaries take up the slack.

In summary, primary security issues depend on aggregate deficits, and the latter in turn are related to the income level. At any income level, the diversification effect of these issues means that financial intermediaries must grow to hold primary yields steady. If income is rising, too, there is an incremental demand for money and perhaps for other indirect assets for transactions and contingency balances, requiring additional intermediary growth. To the extent that the issues of non-monetary intermediaries are competitive with money balances of whatever type, the required growth of the monetary system is reduced by the expansion of other intermediaries.

FINANCIAL ASPECTS OF OUTPUT GROWTH, 1898–1930

We turn now to the task of attaching empirical content to this theoretical structure.[8] Our period runs from about 1898 through 1930. It starts with an upturn in economic activity, following the depression of the 1890's. It then traces the especially high rate of growth in real output through 1906, the Panic of 1907 and the

---

They may be elastic to interest rates on such primary securities as Treasury bills and brokers' loans. For any increment in money income, they may rise with real income. As a larger share of national income involves market transactions, as population moves from farms to cities, as a dollar of income is generated with more or fewer dollars of intermediate payments, as credit practices change, as checks are collected more efficiently or as deposits cease to bear interest and bear service charges instead, one expects the marginal ratio of active balances to income to vary. And incremental demand for contingency balances must be sensitive not only to income, and perhaps to interest rates, but to the evolution of emergency credit facilities, to job security and social security, to an array of circumstances that is largely irrelevant in short-period analysis.

[8] Our empirical work was made possible by Raymond W. Goldsmith's significant contributions, especially his *A Study of Saving in the United States* (Princeton, N.J.: Princeton University Press, 1955).

ensuing depression, and the continuance of output growth, at a reduced pace, from 1909 to World War I. It covers the accelerated activity of the war and postwar years and the sharp downturn in 1920–21. Finally, the homestretch of the period is characterized by fairly steady output growth, with minor setbacks in 1924 and 1927. Over the entire period, GNP in current prices rose by more than 500 percent, while GNP in 1929 prices grew by almost 200 percent, at an average annual rate of about 3.5 percent.

Primary Security Issues

From 1898 to 1930, the annual ratio of primary security issues to GNP in current prices averaged just a bit more than 10 percent.[9] However, the range of fluctuation in the annual ratios was large, from about 2 to 20 percent. During years of rapid acceleration in GNP, the ratio was relatively high, and this was especially true during the war years. During years of retarded growth, the ratio dipped below its average value, but there was no year when primary security issues were negative.

A steadier picture, then, is obtained when the years are grouped into complete cycles, as Table 1 shows. Each of these subperiods,

TABLE 1 Primary Security Issues and GNP, 1898–1930, by Subperiods
(in millions of dollars; percentages)

	Total net issues*	GNP	Ratio of net issues to GNP	Alternative ratio†
1898–1900	4,731	50,812	9.3	9.3
1901–1904	8,603	86,174	10.0	10.0
1905–1908	10,117	110,141	9.2	9.2
1909–1911	9,126	98,081	9.3	9.3
1912–1914	9,557	109,170	8.8	8.8
1915–1921	67,595	479,394	14.1	14.1
1922–1924	17,197	244,207	7.0	7.1
1925–1927	26,497	282,652	9.4	9.5
1928–1930	23,196	291,878	7.9	8.2

* Unadjusted for mortgage write-downs and foreclosures.
† Net issues adjusted for mortgage write-downs and foreclosures.

[9] The flow of securities is measured in issue prices. The issues are net of retirements. The average for the full period is the cumulated flow of securities divided by cumulated GNP. For the entire period, this flow was about $180 billion. In 1898, the current value of outstanding primary securities was between $35 and $40 billion.

of which there are nine, commences with a recovery year and ends
with either a recession or a depression year. These subperiods are:
1898–1900, 1901–4, 1905–8, 1909–11, 1912–14, 1915–21, 1922–4,
1925–7, and 1928–30. In this way, nine ratios are obtained, each
of which is equal to the cumulated primary issues divided by cumulated GNP during a subperiod. Leaving aside the exceptional years
from 1915 to 1921, the ratios fall within the range of 7.1 percent
and 10.0 percent, with six of them between 8.8 percent and 10.0
percent. The "exceptional" ratio was 14.1 percent. All in all, the
series shows remarkable stability, with no evidence of an upward
or downward trend.[10]

Direct and Indirect Finance

The primary security issues were directly financed through spending units or indirectly financed through financial intermediaries. In
terms of the nine cycles, the indirect finance ratio—the ratio of
primary securities purchased by intermediaries to total primary
issues—commenced at 56 percent and then fell slowly and steadily,
with a single interruption, until it reached 36 percent in 1915–21. In
the next phase, 1922–24, the ratio leaped to almost 80 percent, and
then fell to 65 percent in 1925–27, and finally to 50 percent in
1928–30. There were two downward sweeps in the series. The first
covered the initial two decades of the period. The second, starting
from a fantastically high level, covered most of the third decade.
Because of this high starting-point, the indirect finance ratio was
unusually high, on the average, during most of the 1920's. From
1922 to 1929 for example, the ratio averaged about 65 percent. This
compares to 47 percent from 1898 to 1914, and 36 percent from
1915 to 1921.

[10] This is somewhat surprising in view of the large changes during the
period in the proportion of total issues represented by each of the several
types of issue. For example, at the turn of the century, mortgage issues
were about 10 per cent of total issues, but the proportion grew rapidly to
25 per cent a decade later, and then to 35 per cent at the end of the
period. On the other hand, consumer and other debt, mainly short-term
consumer and business borrowing, moved in exactly the opposite way,
from 35 per cent to about 10 per cent. United States government securities fluctuated widely as a percentage of total issues. Except for the first
subperiod, the ratio was negligible to 1914. It was 33 per cent from 1915 to
1921, and then averaged over minus 10 per cent for the remainder of the
period. Common and preferred stock issues, with two exceptions, were
either a bit below or above 20 per cent of total issues during each subperiod. In the 1915–21 phase, the proportion was about 12 per cent, and
it was 44 per cent from 1928 to 1930. State and local government securi-

TABLE 2 Direct and Indirect Finance Ratios, 1898–1930, by Subperiods
(*in percentages*)

	Direct finance ratios			Indirect finance ratios		
	I*	II†	III‡	I*	II†	III‡
1898–1900	43.7	43.7	45.2	56.3	56.3	54.8
1901–1904	46.0	46.0	45.9	54.0	54.0	54.1
1905–1908	56.7	56.7	55.0	43.3	43.3	45.0
1909–1911	53.5	53.5	49.7	46.5	46.5	50.3
1912–1914	58.5	58.5	58.3	41.5	41.5	41.7
1915–1921	63.5	63.5	64.5	36.5	36.5	35.5
1922–1924	20.7	21.2	18.8	79.3	78.8	81.2
1925–1927	35.1	35.3	34.5	64.9	64.7	65.5
1928–1930	49.7	49.4	47.5	50.3	50.6	52.5

* Unadjusted for mortgage write-downs and foreclosures.
† Adjusted for mortgage write-downs and foreclosures.
‡ Above adjustment plus adjustment for foreign purchases of primary securities.

The direct finance ratio—the proportion of total issues purchased by non-financial spending units—naturally behaved in the opposite fashion. In 1898–1900 it began a long upward sweep, which carried to the subperiod 1915–21. In the following cycle, it fell to an extremely low level, and then rose during the remainder of the period. Table 2 records these trends.

The significant finding here is the steady retrogression of financial intermediation during the first two decades and its resurgence during the 1920's. The counterpart of the retrogression was the growing share of primary issues absorbed by spending units, and the counterpart of the resurgence was the relatively low share of issues absorbed by spending units.

Indirect Finance and Financial Intermediaries

The principal intermediary during the period was the monetary system, including Federal Reserve Banks after 1914. Up to World War I, life insurance companies, mutual savings banks, and savings and loan associations dominated the non-monetary intermediary group. After the war, land banks, management investment companies, and federal agencies and trust funds became important.

The main responsibility for the retrogression of financial inter-

ties gained relative to the others during the period while corporate and foreign bonds, if anything, lost some ground.

mediation during the first two decades, or at least up to 1915, must be laid at the door of the monetary system, that is, commercial banks. In 1898–1900, the system absorbed over 40 percent of the primary issues. By 1912–14, it was purchasing less than 25 percent of the issues. This relatively low share was not raised during the subperiod 1915–21, even with the addition of the Federal Reserve Banks to the monetary system. However, this perhaps is not surprising in view of the abnormally heavy issues of securities during these years. But the performance of the system did not improve from 1922 to 1930, on the average, when security issues were normal relative to GNP. In fact, during these years, the average annual share of issues taken by the system fell to 21 percent.[11]

The group of non-monetary intermediaries purchased 15 percent of total issues in 1898–1900. The share rose very slowly to 17 percent just before the war, and then fell to 11 percent in the face of the heavy issues of the war period. After that, the activity of these intermediaries was phenomenal. During 1922–24, their share jumped to 40 percent, remained at about this level in the following subperiod, and then hit 50 percent during the final three years of the period. The high indirect finance ratio during most of the 1920's, therefore, was due principally to the growth of non-monetary intermediation. These and the monetary trends are shown in Table 3.

In short, the monetary system retrogressed up to World War I and it participated very little in the resurgence of intermediation after that date.

Direct Finance Ratios and Long-Term Yields

Our theoretical framework suggests that there should be a positive relationship between the direct finance ratio and changes in interest rates on primary securities. We should expect interest rates to rise whenever a large share of primary issues is absorbed by spending units; in the opposite case, when intermediation is heavy, we should expect falling rates.

The direct finance ratio may be a crude indicator of changes in primary yields. This may be most easily seen in terms of a simple financial growth model. Assuming that non-monetary indirect assets are competitive only with money, spending units' incremental de-

---

[11] The share was a great deal higher than this, though from 1922 to 1924 and somewhat higher from 1925 to 1927. The system purchased only 0.2 percent of the issues from 1928 to 1930. However, excluding the "bad" years of 1929 and 1930, the system purchased only 29 percent of the issues (from 1922 through 1928), which is much lower than its share from 1898 to 1904.

TABLE 3 Indirect Finance Ratios of Selected Intermediaries, 1898-1930, by Subperiods (*in percentages*)

	Monetary system*	Life insurance companies	Mutual savings banks	Savings and loan associations	Management investment companies	All others
1898–1900	41.3	6.7	7.7	−0.8	—	1.4
1901–1904	38.3	8.1	5.3	0.5	—	1.8
1905–1908	25.6	9.7	4.2	1.6	—	2.2
1909–1911	28.0	8.0	5.5	2.2	—	2.8
1912–1914	24.4	8.2	4.0	2.7	—	2.2
1915–1921	24.5	4.3	2.7	1.9	0.1	3.0
1922–1924	39.3	12.8	7.8	8.0	0.1	11.3
1925–1927	26.3	13.6	6.2	7.7	1.8	9.3
1928–1930	0.2	17.2	5.0	4.7	17.1	6.1

* Includes Federal Reserve banks after 1914.

mand for primary securities is: $e(abY - tdY)$. abY is primary security issues, where e is the ratio of issues to aggregate deficits of spending units, b is the ratio of deficits to GNP in current prices, and Y is GNP in current prices. tdY expresses spending units' incremental demand for transactions and contingency balances. At given interest rates, spending units will desire to purchase the proportion, e, of the residual supply of primary securities. The remainder of the issues, $1 - e$, they will want sold to financial intermediaries so that an equivalent amount of indirect assets for diversification balances may be accumulated. Thus, $e(abY - tdY)$ is the desired incremental demand of spending units for primary securities. Interest rates will remain steady if the incremental realized supply of the securities to spending units is equal to this demand.

Now, dividing through by abY, we have:

$$\text{Realized Direct Finance Ratio} = \text{Desired Direct Finance Ratio} = e - g \ (et/ab),$$

where g is the annual growth rate of GNP. When the realized exceeds the desired ratio, interest rates will rise. When the desired ratio is the larger, interest rates will fall. If we assume that the desired ratio moves within relatively narrow limits, a high realized ratio will generally indicate upward pressure on yields, and a low realized ratio will generally mean downward pressure on yields. With this assumption, then, we can compare the realized ratio to changes in interest rates.

Before doing this, though, we should take a moment to comment on the last assumption. Is it likely that the desired ratio will move within narrow limits? The answer is almost certainly "no" when we are dealing with annual data. To begin with, as we have seen, ab fluctuated between 2 percent and 20 percent during the period. Second, the annual growth rate of GNP was highly unstable.[12] Third, speculative demand, reflected in e, was undoubtedly quite high in some years and quite low in others. Finally, even annual t may have been unstable. Consequently, a high realized ratio, for example, may not indicate upward pressure on interest rates because the desired ratio may be just as high or higher.

But, in some large degree, these problems disappear when we work with annual averages during complete cycles. We have previously observed that, in these terms, ab was remarkably stable. In addition, fluctuations in speculative demand are likely to be smoothed out when annual data are averaged over a cycle. Moreover, the growth rate of GNP is less unstable when it is expressed as an average annual rate during a cycle, and the same is probably true of t. The assumption, then, that the desired ratio fluctuates within relatively narrow limits would appear to be reasonable, provided that annual averages for our subperiods are used. Nevertheless, there is nothing to prevent the desired ratio from showing an upward or downward drift over long periods of time. Our results should be checked against this possibility.

There is one more problem to straighten out. The interest rate used in this paper is the long-term yield on high-grade corporate bonds. This series, extending from 1900 to 1950, was recently compiled by W. Braddock Hickman.[13] For our period, it is probably the best series available. However, we have experimented with other long-term yields and with unweighted averages of several, and the results are substantially the same in every case. On the other hand, our results are much less satisfactory when short-term rates are used. There are some obvious reasons for this, and probably others not so obvious, but there is no time to explore them here.

We may now return to the heart of the matter. We have seen that the (realized) direct finance ratio,[14] starting at 44 percent, rose

[12] The first two factors may partly cancel. When g is high, ab tends to be high, too, and the reverse is also true.

[13] W. Braddock Hickman, *Trends and Cycles in Corporate Bond Financing*, National Bureau of Economic Research, Occasional Paper 37 (1952), pp. 34–35. The use of the series carries a disadvantage, since our initial subperiod, 1898–1900, cannot be used in the correlation analysis.

[14] The ratio used here is corrected for net foreign purchases of primary securities (see Table 2, ratio III).

TABLE 4

1901–1904	+0.017	1915–1921	+0.189
1905–1908	+0.068	1922–1924	−0.313
1909–1911	−0.037	1925–1927	−0.143
1912–1914	+0.073	1928–1930	+0.040

almost without interruption through the sixth subperiod, 1915–21, at which time it was 64 percent. It then fell sharply to 20 percent, moved up to the still relatively low level of 35 percent, and ended the period a little below 50 percent. On the basis of these movements, we should expect growing upward (or diminishing downward) pressures on the long rate lasting through the phase 1915–21. We should then expect the rate to fall sharply in 1922–24, fall again but less sharply in 1925–27, and perhaps rise a little (or fall a little) in 1928–30.

In a way it is embarrassing to find that the actual world is almost identical to this mental image of it. The average yearly changes in the long rate during the eight subperiods were as shown in Table 4. The sole interruption to the rise in the direct finance ratio during the first two decades came in the phase 1909–11. Over the same period, the only interruption to the upward trend of interest rates also came in this phase. With this exception, each increase in rates up to the 1920's was larger than the preceding one. This conforms exactly to movements in the direct finance ratio. The sharpest fall in rates came in 1922–24, and the next sharpest in the following subperiod. Again, this is in conformity with the ratio. Finally, there was a small upward movement in yields, as we would expect, during the final years of the period.

Using the direct finance ratio as the independent variable and the average annual change in bond yield as the dependent one, the coefficient of correlation is 97.5 percent, with a standard error of about one-tenth of 1 percent. A direct finance ratio of 48 percent was sufficient to hold the yield almost constant. Anything higher raised it, and anything lower reduced it. A change in the ratio of 5 percentage points changed the yield by 0.05[15] (see Chart I).

Some Alternative Models

An alternative model frequently used is that which relates the income velocity of the money supply to interest rates. Aside from

[15] The estimating equation is: average annual change in bond yield = −0.50 +1.04049 (direct finance ratio).

CHART I

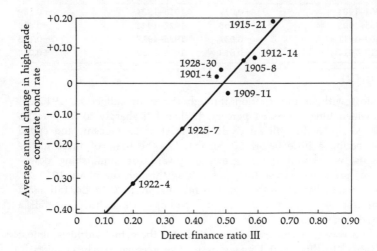

some basic difficulties with this model, which we have discussed elsewhere, it is not likely to be useful under growth conditions, especially when non-monetary intermediation is important. For one thing, under ordinary circumstances, the money supply has to grow relative to national income to keep interest rates stable. This is because primary security issues tend to force rates up unless a portion of the issues is sold to the monetary system. Moreover, the money supply growth required to stabilize interest rates depends on the growth of other indirect assets that are competitive with money. If non-monetary intermediaries are growing rapidly, it is perfectly possible for money supply growth to lag behind income growth without any adverse effects on security markets.

There is a good example of this in our period, from 1922 to 1929 or 1930. In the subperiod, 1922–24, income velocity averaged 3.63. It was 3.67 in the next phase, and 3.74 from 1928 to 1930. Over these years, income velocity was higher than it was during any other phase of the full period with the exception of the war years. And yet these high and rising velocities were compatible with downward trends in interest rates over most of this decade. The reason is simply that non-monetary intermediaries grew so rapidly that the required growth of the monetary system was sharply reduced. Financial analysis cannot stop with the money supply when other indirect assets are of growing importance.

Nevertheless, as other investigators have discovered, there was a fairly good relationship between income velocity and interest rates

CHART II

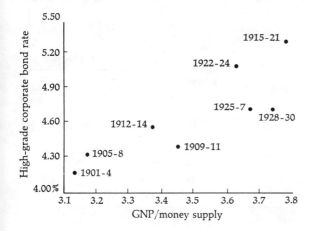

CHART III

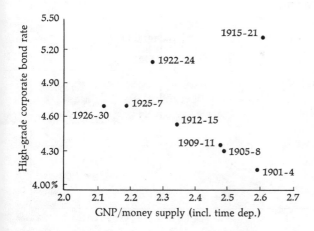

during the period 1900 to 1930, in spite of the negative correlation between the two variables during most of the 1920's. But the relationship is much less impressive than the one presented above, especially when one views the 1920's as the crucial decade, the decade of rapid growth in non-monetary intermediation (see Chart II).

CHART IV

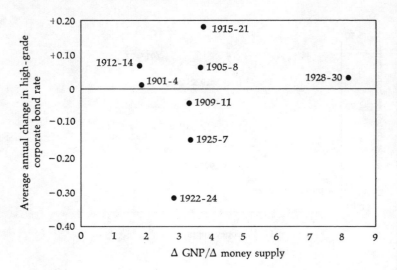

CHART V

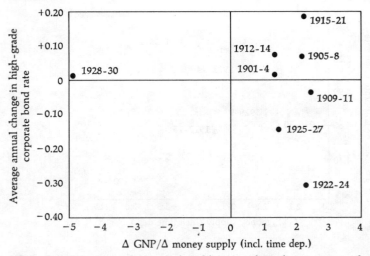

The link between velocity and yields is weakened, moreover, when time deposits are included in the money supply. In fact, in this case, a negative correlation for most of the period is evident (see Chart III). Finally, the relationship between marginal velocity and the change in yields is not very close, whether time deposits are included in or excluded from the money supply (see Charts IV and V).

Briefly, then. we have obtained the best results when account is taken of primary security issues and the growth of all intermediaries, including the monetary system. The two familiar variables, the money supply and national income, form only a part of the total picture.

A. DALE TUSSING

CAN MONETARY POLICY INFLUENCE THE AVAILABILITY OF CREDIT?

24

Over the past decade and a half, it has become increasingly accepted that orthodox central bank policy exercises an influence over something called "the availability of credit." In the 1950's, this idea was actively promoted by the Federal Reserve, first to support their position that the post-war interest-rate "pegging" program should be discontinued and flexible monetary policy revived,[1] and then later to buttress the official Federal Reserve position of the middle and late 'fifties that interest rates were set by market forces and not by design of the Federal Reserve—monetary policy then being seen as primarily a matter of regulating the volume of commercial bank assets through controlling the amount of reserves owned by the banks.[2]

With the "revival of monetary policy" the "pegging" controversy

Reprinted by permission of the publisher from A. Dale Tussing, "Can Monetary Policy Influence the Availability of Credit?" *The Journal of Finance*, Vol. XXI (March 1966), pp. 1–13.

[1] The view that the "availability doctrine" of the 1950's was originally offered primarily as an argument to end the pegging program has appeared in many places, . . .

[2] This official view was associated with the practice which became known as the "bills only" policy.

is a thing of the past; and concern over interest rates (and a Federal Reserve confession of control over them), has been forced by the worsening U.S. international payments situation. Thus the factors leading to official central bank advocacy of an "availability-of-credit" interpretation of the influence of monetary policy have all but disappeared. Moreover, the empirical foundations of Robert V. Roosa's "availability doctrine," on which much of the Federal Reserve's position had been based, have been effectively undermined.[3]

Nonetheless, the notion persists that monetary policy, besides (or instead of) influencing aggregate demand *via* the quantity of money and/or interest rates, does so through influencing the availability of credit. In a survey of contemporary monetary thinking, H. G. Johnson in 1962 reviewed the availability doctrine, noting the theoretical and empirical shortcomings which had been discovered in it during its brief life. "Nevertheless," Johnson added, "the doctrine and discussion of it have helped to popularize the concept of 'availability of credit' as one of the main variables on which monetary policy operates."

Unfortunately, it has never been very clear what is meant by the availability of credit, especially as a variable subject to the influence of monetary policy, separate and distinguishable from the quantity of money and the interest rate, and nonetheless significant in its influence on aggregate effective demand. The virtually complete rejection of the availability doctrine has complicated, rather than simplified, the situation; we are left with a "popularized concept" (to use Johnson's words somewhat out of context) without either a definition or a theory.[4]

---

[3] See below, footnote 10.

[4] One element of the availability doctrine of the 1950's which has stood the test of time has been the concept of nonprice rationing of credit—an idea, however, neither original with nor rigorously developed in the doctrine. Recent theorizing points to the development of a theory of the bank as a firm, with particular attention to the portfolio selection and credit rationing problems. . . . Unlike the availability doctrine of the 1950's, the developing credit rationing theory does not concern itself, except in a minor way, with implications for the effectiveness of monetary policy. The main thrust of the availability doctrine was that there were credit effects of tight-money policies which supplemented or substituted for interest-rate and stock-of-money effects in limiting aggregate demand. It is these aspects of the doctrine on which this paper concentrates. Credit-rationing theory, which is not treated in this article, is concerned primarily with the question, "Should a rational profit-maximizing banker or even a rational utility-maximizing banker practice credit rationing, or should the amount he is willing to lend be an increasing function of the interest rate the borrower is willing to pay . . ."

This paper has the modest objectives of setting forth a definition of the availability of credit and indicating, in general terms, what must be done to make it a variable "on which monetary policy operates." The definition must (1) be consistent with the most common doctrines offered in the name of availability, (2) show that the availability of credit is a variable distinguishable from the stock of money and the interest rate, and (3) relate the availability of credit to effective aggregate demand. Though this objective can be called "modest," inasmuch as it is clearly only a preliminary step in the formulation of a rigorous availability-of-credit theory, it is nonetheless an objective neither sought nor obtained by any of the economists, central bankers, and others who have contributed to the formulation or the criticism of the availability concept over the past fifteen years. This is especially true with respect to the third point, above: no one has bothered to indicate why, if control over the availability of credit is possible, it makes any difference.

I. TWO AVAILABILITY APPROACHES

The two approaches to monetary policy most commonly offered in the name of credit availability are (a) the availability doctrine and (b) the credit-creation doctrine. The former is associated with the names of Robert V. Roosa and others then at the Federal Reserve Bank of New York,[5] though in one sense it can be said that the availability doctrine has no real author at all. There is no internal or external evidence that those to whom the doctrine is ordinarily attributed intended to propose it as a new theory of credit control; and neither Roosa's article nor the subsequent "official" statements of the doctrine by the Board of Governors[6] was sufficiently integrated, precise, or operational that it would normally be accepted as a theory. The most (or only) clear-cut exposition of the doctrine was in professional economists' journal accounts of it; but these

[5] At the time of the publication of Roosa's important article he was vice president, Federal Reserve Bank of New York. The article appeared in a volume dedicated to John Henry Williams, also an F.R.B.N.Y. vice president; and Roosa gives Williams major credit, "largely through an oral medium, without benefit of a published written record" for development of the availability approach. In the same volume, Allan Sproul, president of the F.R.B.N.Y., offers strikingly similar views on monetary policy.

[6] The official Federal Reserve statement first appeared in Congressional testimony. The statement was explicitly an official Federal Reserve statement on its theory or how monetary policy operates.

economists cannot be credited with (or blamed for) proposing the doctrine, as their purpose was commonly to bury the doctrine, not to praise it. Moreover, and more oddly yet, the economists' journal accounts of the doctrine frequently contained elements found neither in the Roosa article nor in the official Board of Governors statement.[7]

The authorship of the credit-creation doctrine is only slightly less clouded than that of the availability doctrine. This second view is the commonly held one that central bank control over the assets of commercial banks is important because of the ability of banks to "create credit": only commercial banks, goes the doctrine, can be a source of expansional instability, because only they, of all lenders, can lend without there being a prior voluntary deposit by (presumably) a saver, an ability derived from commercial banks' money-creating ability. While many economists will agree that this doctrine has become an orthodox one, it is difficult to cite clear-cut statements of it. It is rather more often the underlying premise of published statements on monetary policy than it is their substance.

Fortunately (for purposes of this paper), two events of the past decade did elicit such substantive statements. One was the attempt of the Federal Reserve, already referred to, to play down the role of monetary policy in influencing interest rates, and correspondingly to play up its influence on commercial bank lending capacity. The other was the appearance of the "Gurley-Shaw thesis," the responses to which ordinarily relied heavily on the credit-creation doctrine. It was not the Gurley-Shaw theory, as such, which elicited the strongest objections, but instead the two authors' conceptual framework, in which commercial banks were seen to play a role not fundamentally different from that played by other deposit-account finan-

[7] For instance, Tobin reviews what he calls the "new theory of monetary control" developed "under the leadership of Robert V. Roosa." His review of that new theory depends on the official Federal Reserve version; indeed, the article cited is a review of the published record of the Congressional hearings in which that version first appeared. Yet Tobin includes a theoretical point—substitution of government for private debt in institutional portfolios, motivated by rising yields on the former and rigid yields on the latter, and an accompanying pattern of credit rationing—not explicitly found in that version. In doing so, he does not cite any particular page or statement in the official version; he cites only P. Samuelson's testimony criticizing such a theoretical point. Samuelson, in turn, does not attribute the theoretical point to either the Roosa or the Federal Reserve versions, nor in fact to anyone. In Kareken's critique of the doctrine the same point is included, but Kareken relies for support only on Tobin's earlier article. In his answer to Kareken, Hodgman includes the same point, but cites only Kareken.

cial intermediaries. That commercial banks are fundamentally different from other intermediaries is, of course, of the essence in the credit-creation doctrine.

Both doctrines will be reviewed briefly, with their shortcoming noted.

The Availability Doctrine

The propositions of the availability doctrine are many, some of them resting on complex assumptions concerning expectational patterns. It is fair to say, however, that the doctrine's central proposition was the so-called "lock-in" effect: the argument that a tightening of monetary policy, with rising interest rates, would induce institutional holders of government securities to hold onto them, and perhaps even to increase them, thereby preventing them from financing new private loans through the sale of securities. This effect was to proceed from a number of causes: rising long-term rates, by reducing the current market values of long-term securities, would, it was thought, inhibit sales of these securities, through institutional lenders' unwillingness to realize capital losses; rising rates would also reduce the liquidity of lenders' portfolios, and encourage them to maintain or increase their short-term holdings; and rising rates on marketable securities would not be matched, at least at first, by increases in loan rates, because the latter, as "administered prices," adjust to new equilibrium levels only with some lag.[8] It is not really worth while exploring this reasoning in detail, since the lock-in effect has been shown to be theoretically defective,[9] and experience of the 1950's shows the lock-in effect to be empirically false, especially with respect to commercial banks, who have engaged in heavy sales of government securities in each tight-money period, replenishing them during the subsequent monetary ease of recessions.[10]

[8] Not all the above propositions were stated in such a clear-cut manner in the original sources; but the present writer is confident that all were originaly, or later became, part of the availability doctrine, as that doctrine was understood by economists.

[9] In addition to the works already cited, see Robertson, Lindbeck, and the more recent study by Kane and Malkiel, which shows strong rational economic motives for bankers to shift from securities into loans in periods of high loan demand and tight money, even where the return on the former exceeds that on the latter.

[10] Between October, 1954, and October, 1956, commercial bank holdings of U.S. government securities declined by approximately $13 billion, remaining at their low level until November, 1957 (close to a monetary-policy turning point), at which time they recovered by $10 billion within the space of seven months. Between January, 1959, and April, 1960, the banks disposed of approximately $10 billion worth of government secu

Proposals are made from time to time to enforce a lock-in effect through security-reserve requirements and similar devices. It is thus not idle to raise the question of what difference it would make if the doctrine on this point were both valid and true. Certain inferences can be drawn, but the doctrine itself was never explicit on the question. "General tightening of credit," begins the official Federal Reserve version of the doctrine, "restricts most directly the amount of spending which can be done with borrowed funds." The theory implied by the proposition of the lock-in effect is that where banks change the *composition* of their assets, reducing security holdings and increasing loans, a contribution is made to aggregate effective demand. Why central bankers would argue that this is so is puzzling, in light of orthodox banking theory, for in engaging in such transactions commercial banks lose the special and unique characteristics which distinguish them from other institutional lenders. If they finance loan expansion through security sales, they do not create demand deposits; functionally, such transactions are little different from the operations of, say, savings and loans associations, which must finance lending operations through sale of share accounts.

Did the proponents of the doctrine, virtually all of them central bankers, join with and even lead those who have held nonmonetary financial intermediaries to be potentially destabilizing in their day-to-day activities? Apparently so, for the availability doctrine also included, as subsidiary arguments, the following two propositions:

1. Conventional monetary policy also has an impact on nonbank lenders. Open-market purchases and sales, when dealings are with nonbank lenders, increase and reduce, respectively, the funds available to these institutions for lending. The lock-in effect is also explicitly extended to nonbank lenders.

2. Underwriters also respond to tightening credit conditions, discouraging new private security issues during periods of rising rates in order to avoid market losses on their own holdings.

What these two points must be taken to mean, considered together with the lock-in effect, is that conventional monetary policy restricts the ability of potential borrowers to make financial arrangements, through intermediaries and market institutions, with households and businesses which, cash in hand, are ready to acquire interest-earning

---

rities. During both 1954–1957 and 1958–1960 tight-money periods, commercial bank business loans rose at a rate exceeding their post–Accord trend value. Life insurance companies' holdings show a similar pattern. Mutual savings banks and mutual savings and loan asociations showed less regular behavior, but were clearly not "locked in" with respect to government security holdings.

assets. Regardless of the empirical truth or falsity of the doctrine, it represented a radical revision in the official *modus operandi* of monetary policy.

The Credit-Creation Doctrine

Commercial banks, according to this second availability approach to the effects of monetary policy, "create credit": that is, by virtue of their ability to pay for new assets with newly issued demand deposit liabilities (i.e., their ability to "create money"), commercial banks can lend (or acquire marketable financial assets) with no prior act of voluntary saving on the part of any other economic unit. This means that commercial banks can permit an excess of planned investment, for instance, over planned saving.

Most adherents to this view overstate their case. Not content to argue that commercial banks, in the sense defined, can create credit, they often argue (a) that commercial banks *always* create credit when they acquire additional assets, and (b) that *only* commercial banks can create credit, so that only commercial banks can lend to borrowers or acquire additional financial assets without a prior "act of saving" on the part of some other economic unit. Both these extreme statements of the doctrine are false. Commercial banks can also finance the purchase of "old" securities by creating demand deposits, thus creating money without creating credit. Other lenders, including households, can lend by running down money balances, thus in effect "creating credit" with no concurrent *ex ante* saving.[11]

[11] For an example of the overstated version of the credit-creation doctrine, see W. W. Riefler's statement to the Radcliffe Committee, in which (since Riefler was testifying in behalf of the Federal Reserve) the doctrine was made official Federal Reserve theory. For similar statements, see also Aschheim, Culbertson, and Thomas. Gurley and Shaw show that the error in this version of the doctrine derives from an erroneous definition of saving, which identifies saving with the payment of money for a non-money asset, an act which may signify, but is not the same as, *ex ante* saving. A number of writers make a careful though erroneous distinction between money acquisition and saving, and an equally careful association between acquisition of non-money assets and saving. Thus Thomas writes that for stability, "the bulk of credit needs must be met out of saving, not by the creation of additional money," thus implying a clear-cut distinction between the two. And Culbertson writes, ". . . The usual banking theory would call for social accounting definitions representing creation of loan funds as involved in both of two types of actions; that of the banking system in acquiring additional debt by creating demand deposits (and the government in adding to currency in circulation) and that of other economic units in increasing their net holdings of nonmonetary debt." The latter type of action is described as an "act of saving." In fairness, it should be noted that those advocating the credit-creation view

The fact that the doctrine is usually overstated does not mean that it is false. It is true that commercial bank finance *can*, and probably frequently does, account for an excess of *ex post* over *ex ante* saving, though the relationship is far from one of identity.

Even when stated in this more modest way, however, the credit-creation doctrine is unacceptable as a theory of the effect of monetary policy on aggregate demand. Clearly, all it tells us is that bank finance *can permit* an excess of *ex post* over *ex ante* saving. It does not explain why there must be such an excess. It does not, in short, present us with a theory of aggregate demand. By contrast, the quantity theory of money, for instance, argues that an increase in the stock of money *induces* more demand; the interest-rate approach argues that increases in the money supply relative to the demand for money reduce interest rates, thereby increasing investment demand and, perhaps, consumer demand (by reducing the propensity to save). But the credit-creation doctrine is not a theory of demand. It only says that *if* there is excess aggregate demand that excess can be financed through the banking system (and in extreme form, only through the banking system). This point provides a useful clue to the meaning of credit availability, and will be dealt with further momentarily.

II. THE FRAMEWORK FOR AN AVAILABILITY THEORY

One matter on which virtually all widely accepted macroeconomic theories of instability find consensus is that the problem is in essence a financial one. Thus modern quantity-of-money theory stresses the search, by household and firm, for an optimum balance of assets, both real and financial, and argues that changes in the stock of money alter this balance, a correction being sought through acquisition of additional real assets. Thus income-expenditure theory stresses the investment-saving relationship (a financial relationship), and further usually stresses the role of changes in the money stock (*via* interest-rate changes) in influencing investment behavior. And thus, too, the availability theses, as seen, stress financial institutions and processes themselves. Indeed, the common characteristic which separates these macroeconomic theories from those structural and distributive theories emphasizing costs, wages, profit margins, etc., is that the former are financial theories, even though they may not

---

described may be asserting (but not demonstrating) an empirical proposition rather than a doctrine: that only commercial bank finance *does* (rather than *can*) account for an excess of *ex post* over *ex ante* saving.

be expressed in financial terms. The framework employed here is explicitly financial.

The framework is borrowed from the initial joint work of J. G. Gurley and E. S. Shaw. The fundamental behavior units of the economy are "spending units"—households, business firms, individual government units, and miscellaneous other units such as churches, universities, and trade unions. These units are classified according to their "budget"[12] positions: those having balanced budgets, i.e., whose ordinary receipts, received as transfers, factor income (for households), sales receipts (for business firms), or taxes (for government units) exactly meet their transfer payments, factor payments, payments for product, and payment of taxes; those having deficit budgets, whose payments exceed their receipts; and those having surplus budgets, whose receipts exceed their payments. For simplicity, a closed economy is assumed, though no particular difficulty would be created by including the rest of the world as a surplus or deficit sector.

It is only a truism that the total net surpluses of surplus-budget spending units must equal the total net deficits of deficit-budget units. This is the same as saying that, in a closed economy, the economy as a whole is a balanced-budget unit—that factor payments equal factor receipts, product sales equal product purchases, tax payments equal tax receipts, etc.

While there is an *ex post* identity between net deficits of deficit-budget spending units and net surpluses of surplus unit, there is no necessary reason for *ex ante* equality. Different spending units may respond to different inducements, and have conflicting intentions. The possibility for conflicting intentions is at the heart of conventional aggregate demand theory of instability, since that type of theory is, either explicitly or implicitly, a theory of the relative sizes of aggregate *ex ante* deficits and *ex ante* surpluses. This emphasis is most explicit in Keynesian income-expenditure theory, where concentration is on planned deficits of the private business sector (investment) and planned surpluses of the household sector (saving).

Expressing the stabilization problem in explicitly financial terms underlines the fact that there are two distinct but interrelated types of questions with which theory and policy legitimately may become concerned:

1. There are behavioral questions concerning the determinants of planned deficits and planned surpluses, especially with respect to

---

[12] "Budget," a word borrowed from the Gurley-Shaw nomenclature, is probably a misnomer, since it implies a planned or *ex ante* character, a connotation which is not here intended unless specifically so noted.

the inducements to invest and to save. Modern macroeconomic theory of instability has consisted in large part of a search for dependable behavior relationships which would permit an explanation of what changes in independent variables induce spending units to desire changed deficits or surpluses. Thus quantity-of-money doctrine can be described as concentrating on the motives of spending units to increase their intended expenditures, relative to their saving.[13] An increase in the quantity of money purportedly induces an increase in desired deficits, then, relative to surpluses. Similarly, income-expenditures theory ordinarily revolves around the influence of the interest rate on motives to invest (and, in some cases, on motives to save). In any event, there is typically a theory relating demand behavior to some variable subject to the influence of monetary policy.

2. There are also questions—again, behavioral questions—concerning the institutional processes through which destabilizing changes in deficits and/or surpluses can be achieved; i.e., there are questions concerning whether *ex ante* deficits in excess of *ex ante* surpluses can in fact be financed. Availability-of-credit theories concentrate on this second type of question. This is a point worth emphasizing: Neither the availability doctrine nor the credit-creation doctrine deals with the motives or behavior of ultimate lender (surplus-budget spending unit, or "saver") or ultimate borrower (investor or other deficit-budget spending unit). The concentration of both these doctrines is on financial processes and on institutions *relating* ultimate borrower and ultimate lender. This point is explicit in the availability doctrine, where much is made of the point that monetary policy operates through its effects on lenders, meaning in all cases institutional lenders and not households or other "ultimate" lenders. Though not explicit in the credit-creation doctrine, the point nonetheless applies there as well; as noted earlier, there is nothing in that doctrine to explain *why* borrowers want to borrow. The doctrine concentrates on their ability to do so, in the absence of "prior saving," when they borrow from commercial banks.

Hence availability-of-credit theories, in general, are those theories which deal exclusively with the financial mechanism rather than with the variables which influence demand. Influencing the availability of credit has to do with influencing deficit units' *access* to

[13] Though a modern quantity theorist might not put it that way. Perhaps preferable would be a statement that an increase in the stock of money inuces spending units to increase their demand for real as opposed to financial assets, in order to bring into an optimal arrangement the flow of benefits from all types of assets.

financing, as distinct from influencing their desire to borrow or the desire of savers to save.

The best definition of the availability of credit, then, is probably the "supply side" of the loanable funds equation: saving (*ex ante*), plus reduction of money balances by money-holders, plus new money creation.[14] But it is not the definition of availability of credit which is the significant characteristic of availability-of-credit theory distinguishing it from other types of theory: it is instead the new type of theory's concentration on the financial process, rather than the determinants of demand behavior by spending units, that marks it as a new approach.

This distinction between demand-behavior theories on the one hand, and availability-of-credit theories on the other, makes clear that a number of theories commonly grouped under the latter heading actually belong under the former. For instance, theories purporting to show an influence of monetary policy on the desire to borrow, *via* changes in such non-interest lending terms as compensating balances and loan discounts, are not really "availability" theories at all; they are essentially extensions of the interest-rate approach. Under them, the effectiveness of monetary policy depends on the response ("elasticity") of potential borrowers to changes in non-interest terms.[15] Similarly, as has already been noted by Musgrave, the concept of credit availability does not apply when imperfection in credit markets "arises because of heterogeneity of product, so factors of risk and diversification enter," so long as the volume of lending in each market (determined by the lender, according to the characteristics of the borrower) depends on the interest-elasticity of loan demand in *that* market. The Gurley-Shaw thesis has

[14] But availability-of-credit theories are not otherwise related to the loanable funds theory. The latter is a theory of interest rate determination, and belongs under the "demand behavior" heading (number one, above), rather than availability of credit.

[15] See J. Guttentag, who proposes that the expression "availability of credit" be used to describe non-interest lending terms. He makes clear that his use of the term "availability" is quite different from that of Roosa, *et al.* though Guttentag was then an economist for the Federal Reserve Bank of New York when he writes: "One possible source of confusion between availability and supply is the emphasis given in the literature to the operations of lenders. It is frequently stated that the older monetary theory emphasized the borrower whereas the availability doctrine emphasizes the lender. Of course the fact that the lenders administer terms does not mean that the basic forces underlying changes in availability originate on the supply side of the market. On the contrary, it would appear that for the most part changes in availability originate on the demand side."

achieved note as an assault upon orthodoxy because it argues for a major role in the stability problem for financial intermediaries other than commercial banks; but Gurley and Shaw assign this major role to these institutions not because of their role in financing deficits, but because their liabilities can substitute for money for asset purposes, thus lowering interest rates, other things being equal, and inducing more investment. Even the Gurley-Shaw thesis, then, despite its concern with present-day financing institutions, must be classified as demand-behavior and not an availability-of-credit theory. This is a point missed by most Gurley-Shaw critics, who concern themselves, as already noted, with commercial banks' ability to create credit.

Conventional aggregate-demand theory, where concern is exclusively with the determinants of demand (i.e., of *ex ante* budget positions), ordinarily leaves the method of financing various budget positions an unexplored matter. Their tacit assumption must be that, whatever the economy's financial institutions, they are inevitably adequate to the task of financing whatever deficits and surpluses they are called upon to finance. The financing institutions have a wholly passive role, responding to decisions made by ultimate lenders and ultimate borrowers. Financial processes can be taken for granted. Acceptance of this type of theory implies employing stabilization policy directed at influencing the demand behavior of spending units (including the possibility, when the policy-maker is a spending unit, as is the Federal government, of it adjusting its own budget position in accordance wtih stabilization objectives).[16] This presumption on the part of conventional theory that financial processes may be taken for granted may help explain why such theory, which is at heart financial theory, can so often be presented in entirely non-financial terms[17]—in terms of "leakages," "injections," etc.

Where conventional theory has concentrated on the determinants of *ex ante* budget positions and taken adequate financing for granted, availability-of-credit theories have concentrated on financing processes and taken the existence of excess demand (excess of *ex ante* deficits over *ex ante* surpluses) for granted. Thus there is no availability-of-credit theory of instability, but only an availability-of-credit approach to stabilization policy. Instability derives from

[16] Even though this type of theory can "take for granted" financial processes, an important role may nonetheless be given by them to the behavior of financial institutions, insofar as it influences *ex ante* budget positions, without altering the exclusively demand-behavior nature of the theories.

[17] Even, oddly enough, in money and banking textbooks. Usually the "theory section" is the only non-financial section.

the existence of excess aggregate demand; the objective of policy, under this approach, is to frustrate, rather than to dissuade, those who intend to incur deficit positions.

The search for an availability theory on which policy could be based would seem likely to stem from two environmental conditions: (1) the existence of excess aggregate demand; and (2) an inability to deal directly, within the institutional constraints imposed on policy, with the determinants of demand. For instance, it might be held that planned deficits are sensitive to interest-rate changes, but that a significant reduction in planned deficits could only be achieved by means of an interest-rate increase exceeding institutional maxima imposed by convention, by the existence of a large public debt whose market value is sensitive to interest rate changes, or by the possibility that marked changes in the money supply and in commercial-bank-owned reserves that would be incident to an interest-rate increase might endanger the viability of parts of the financial system.

The fact that availability-of-credit theories can take for granted the existence of excessive aggregate demand may be the feature of these theories which explains why they are incompletely formulated, though a reading of the availability literature suggests that its authors simply did not recognize the important distinction between influencing ultimate demand and influencing the financial process.

III. PROLEGOMENON TO ANY FUTURE AVAILABILITY THEORY

It is not the purpose of this paper to present a full-fledged theory of credit availability. Indeed, it is not certain at all whether this is possible. The purpose is to indicate the meaning of credit availability as "one of the main variables on which monetary policy operates." It is possible here only to suggest some elements any such theory will have to contain, elements policy-makers will have to take immediate account of, if they do indeed operate on the assumption that they are influencing the availability of credit.

It adds little to knowledge to point out that *ex ante* deficits in excess of *ex ante* surpluses can be financed through money creation plus attempts at reduction of money balances by money-holders. To control the availability of credit sufficiently so that no excess demand can be financed would seem to require influencing both these two types of financing operations. Thus the credit-creation doctrine, in the more modest interpretation of it set forth above, must be a part of an overall availability-of-credit theory. Unfortunately, it is only a part, and a small part at that. The volume of money-creation in the United States each year (even assuming all of it to be associated with credit-creation) is small by comparison with the volume of money-transferring financial transactions, a great many (but an uncountable number) of which do not involve *ex ante* surpluses but merely the substitution of income-earning assets (both real and financial) for money assets. All the indicators we have—income velocity of money, volume of trade credit, commercial bank sales of government securities, etc.—suggest that in boom periods, money goes "where the action is," i.e., to deficit-budget spending units.

There is no doubt about the ability of the monetary authorities, using conventional techniques, to control money-creation. There is considerably more doubt about their ability to control the transfer of money from money-holders to deficit units (either directly or through intermediaries) in exchange for newly created nonmoney financial instruments. The availability doctrine is best interpreted, to be consistent with the view taken in this paper of the availability of credit, as an allegation that the volume of such transactions is limited as a byproduct of the exercise of conventional monetary techniques. If, for instance, commercial banks were to find money-holders willing to buy government securities, the lending capacity of banks would be enhanced, and banks, without "creating credit" in the conventional sense could nonetheless finance deficits unmatched by a corresponding volume of *ex ante* surpluses. But if the banks were to be locked in, some potential borrowers would be frustrated.

As noted, this major proposition of the availability doctrine has proved to be empirically false. Of course, this does not remove the problem the lock-in effect was intended to solve. Indeed, it points up the fact that monetary policy may have perverse effects on the availability of credit. For instance, it has often been noted that the same tight-money policies of the central bank which limit the ability of commercial banks to "create credit" may, though the inducement of higher interest rates, bring money-holders to desire to hold interest-earning assets instead of money, thereby permitting the achievement of deficits in excess of *ex ante* surpluses. This is not done solely through institutional lenders' sale of government securities; in the United States, there is a vast, complex, and highly efficient financial system well geared to satisfying the needs of deficit-budget units, whatever the circumstance.

When the matter of controlling the availability of credit is defined in terms of "clogging up" this financial process, rather than attempting to act upon motives to save, borrow, spend, etc., it becomes clear that many proposals have already been made to strengthen the hand of the Federal Reserve in controlling credit availability. The old secondary-security-reserve proposal, originally offered to "insulate" the public debt from interest-rate changes so as to permit resumption, in the immediate post-war period, of flexible monetary policy, has recently been revived as a means to limit credit availability. A similar proposal has been to require commercial banks to hold, in place of long-term coupon-bearing government securities a special, nonmarketable issue. There have been several proposals for limiting the assets of noncommercial-bank financial intermediaries, usually through a reserve requirement. One proposal which deserves more attention than it has received is for the payment of a variable interest rate on demand deposits, "to tighten the Federal Reserve's control over the opportunity cost that bank depositors charge against any alternative investment of funds."[18]

Before any proposal be taken seriously, one thing should be carefully noted. An excess of *ex ante* deficits over *ex ante* surpluses is a disequilibrium situation. If the excess of deficits simply cannot be financed, the disequilibrium exists in financial markets. If they can be financed, the disequilibrium is transferred into product markets in the form of excess aggregate demand for output and, under capacity-output conditions, inflation. Conventional policy has as its objective preventing both types of disequilibrium by acting on the motives of spending units, encouraging smaller deficits and/or larger surpluses. To restrict the availability of credit, as defined here, means to prevent product market disequilibria by *maintaining* a disequilibrium condition in credit markets; as noted already, the objective is to frustrate, rather than to dissuade, those planning deficits.

Since an attempt to restrict the availability of credit means an attempt to maintain a disequilibrium, it shares some of the disabilities and disadvantages of direct controls. One suspects that, regardless of the techniques employed, ways will be found around the particular controls and techniques used. The objective of maintaining indefinitely a disequilibrium situation seems extremely ambitious; but that and nothing less is what is meant by limiting the availability of credit.

---

[18] Commercial banks are now prohibited from paying interest on demand deposits. The rationale for this restriction has to do with supervisory control over bank performance rather than with monetary policy *per se*; and it appears that economists concerned with bank performance are in increasing numbers endorsing repeal of this prohibition.

PART IV-C // THE QUESTION OF RULES VERSUS AUTHORITY IN MONETARY POLICY

WILLIAM N. COX III

THE MONEY SUPPLY CONTROVERSY

25

The present controversy over the importance of money and monetary policy is by no means unprecedented—economists have pondered and argued about money for decades. There is nevertheless a new element in the current controversy over the money supply: The debate has heated up substantially enough to move from the professional economic journals into the popular press. Fundamentally at issue is the influence of money on spending, prices, employment, and economic growth—matters that certainly concern us all.

This article cannot pretend to describe the money supply debate comprehensively, since the arguments involved are numerous, extensive, and in some cases quite technical. Fortunately, however, the basic positions in the debate are straight-forward enough to permit a simplified description that captures the flavor of the controversy between the "Keynesians" and the "Monetarists." The following synopsis presents an idea of what the money supply controversy is all about.

HISTORICAL PERSPECTIVE

Some notion of history will help us place the current money dispute in perspective, and the period just before the Depression is a good place to begin. At that time, many economists thought the quantity of money (currency plus private demand deposits) had a strong impact on prices, but had little or no influence on jobs or business activity. In its crudest form, the pre-Depression theory was simple:

Reprinted from William N. Cox III, "The Money Supply Controversy," *Monthly Review* (June 1969), pp. 70–75, Federal Reserve Bank of Atlanta.

The amount of money, in relation to the supply of goods and services produced, determined prices. An increase in the money supply encouraged spending and raised prices; a decrease in the money supply lowered prices. A crude form of the quantity-of-money theory predicted that a 50-percent increase in the money supply would raise prices by 50 percent as long as there were no changes in the physical quantity of goods available. The amount of goods produced and number of jobs available, on the other hand, were expected to be untouched by changes in the quantity of money since the economy's productive resources—labor and nonlabor alike —were assumed to be fully employed, guided by the unseen hand of market forces.

In the more refined versions of pre-Depression quantity-of-money theory, the velocity, or turnover of money (the speed at which money circulates through the economy), was also recognized as an important determinant of the price level. But velocity, like the physical amount of goods produced, was thought to be relatively stable, so these more refined theories also concluded that changes in the quantity of money were primarily a cause of price changes, and of little else.

This is not to say that every economist writing before the Depression looked at the world in quite this way. But our generalizations still form a reasonably accurate description of pre-Depression economic views: automatic full employment together with a price level set by the quantity of money. Not too surprisingly, this approach produced few debates about what the Federal Reserve System should do to stabilize spending and production, for the economy was expected to take care of itself automatically.

THE KEYNESIAN VIEW

Then came the Depression, bringing serious questions about the prevailing economic doctrines and shaking the pre-Depression assumption of automatic full employment. Controversy flared as millions of people remained out of work and output fell far below the economy's capacity to produce. Something obviously was wrong, but pre-Depression economic theory was unable to explain what it was.

Keynesian Economics

The basic difficulty of the Depression was obvious: Why were people eager to work and spend but unable to find jobs when businessmen were eager to produce but unable to find customers? The English economist John Maynard Keynes offered both an explanation and a remedy. The problem, he said, was that the amount of goods and services demanded by consumers, investors, and the Government was not sufficient to keep the economy producing at full capacity. Businessmen could not be expected to produce what they could not sell. If private demand was not strong enough to pull the economy out of depression, then the Government should step in and stimulate spending enough to provide buyers for the nation's full-capacity output. This was the essence of the "Keynesian" prescription and the beginning of the broad concept of Government responsibility for economic stabilization which was eventually written into the Employment Act of 1946.

Fiscal Policy

Most Keynesians believed that fiscal policy—the use of the Government's power to spend and tax—offered the best way to bridge the gap between insufficient spending and full-capacity output. The Government, by increasing its own spending, could contribute directly to the total demand for goods and services. Alternatively, it could reduce taxes, giving the private sector more disposable income to spend. Although Keynesians disagreed on the dosage of fiscal policy and on the details of how it should be operated their confidence in fiscal action was virtually universal.

Many Keynesians, recommending the use of fiscal policy, doubted whether monetary policy could do much by itself to stimulate spending and economic activity. Still, monetary action did occupy a prominent place in the Keynesian theoretical scheme, which described how an increase in the money supply might lower interest rates and thereby induce businessmen to spend more for plant and equipment. Unlike the pre-Depression economists, then, the Keynesians did think monetary action might affect employment and production as well as prices. But in practice they were afraid that bank reserves pumped into the economy by the Federal Reserve System would pile up unused instead of generating new spending. A favorite homily of the forties and early fifties, "You can't push on a string," succinctly captured the prevalent scepticism about the effectiveness of monetary policy.

By the late 1950's, the Keynesian fiscal policy prescription had won the acceptance of most economists, and of many policymakers as well. Congress enacted a tax cut in 1964 for the specific purpose of stimulating the economy, and subsequently passed the tax increase of 1968 with a restrictive objective in mind. Although the effectiveness of these fiscal actions is still in dispute, their existence illustrates how much the Keynesian view has been accepted.

Monetary Policy Becomes More Appealing

But even as fiscal policy came to be deliberately administered in the sixties, fresh controversy arose about its superiority over monetary policy as a tool of economic stabilization. Monetary policy began to look increasingly appealing. One reason is that enactment of fiscal legislation takes time—it took 18 months to pass the 1968 tax surcharge. Monetary policy decisions can be implemented much more quickly.

A changed economic environment also helped to bring monetary policy back into favor. Monetary economics is a pragmatic business, one where researchers are prone to concentrate on current policy problems. In the thirties and forties, when the main problem of unemployment clearly called for stimulative action, theorists focused on the problem of economic stimulation. But the 1950's brought an additional headache—inflation—and the 1960's brought unprecedented difficulties in our balance of payments. These new problems both called for policy measures that were restrictive, not expansionary. Consequently, many Keynesians who had said "you can't *push* on a string" began to take the position that monetary policy could indeed *pull* on the string—could pull down total spending. Monetary policy offered a method of restricting spending that was easy to implement, even if it could not stimulate spending.

Policy Mix

For these and other reasons, most Keynesians today believe stabilization of the economy requires an appropriate "mix" of both fiscal and monetary actions. The recommended policy mix is likely to be one in which flexible monetary actions by the Federal Reserve are combined with occasional but more massive shifts in fiscal policy.

Keynesian economists still disagree on exactly how the Federal Reserve exerts its influence on aggregate spending. Generally speaking, they say changes in bank reserves initiated by the Federal Reserve affect the prices (interest rates) of diverse financial assets such as money market instruments and bonds. These price changes then produce adjustments in financial portfolios and changes in spending. Elaborate statistical models are now being used to trace responses to monetary actions through specific financial markets. The basic thesis underlying these studies is that Federal Reserve actions operate through the cost and availability of credit.

THE MONETARIST VIEW

While Keynesians stress the importance of both fiscal and monetary policy, other modern economists take a quite different position. These so-called Monetarists believe that changes in the money supply are the crucial determinants not only of prices, but also of spending, production, and employment. They downgrade the importance of Keynesian fiscal policy and are decidedly unsympathetic to the notion of "fine-tuning" the economy.

Just as Keynesian economics is associated with Keynes, Monetarist economics is often linked to Professor Milton Friedman of the University of Chicago. The contemporary money supply controversy now raging in the popular press is essentially a debate between the Keynesians and the Monetarists.

Though the Monetarists are not of one mind, they agree that money exercises a dominant influence on business activity, and they go on to draw definite policy recommendations from this thesis. Monetarists feel the economy is inherently stable, tending toward full employment and sustainable growth. In these circumstances, the best thing the Government can do to help the economy realize its full-employment potential is to allow the money supply to grow at the same rate as the economy's capacity to produce (roughly 3 to 5 percent annually). This is the "money supply rule."

The Federal reserve has the power to stabilize the economy, or at least to let the economy stabilize itself, through its ability to control bank reserves and the money supply. Unfortunately, say the Monetarists, this power has been misused. They feel Keynesians have intensified rather than mitigated business fluctuations with their well-meaning attempts to manage the economy. Money supply growth, as a consequence of discretionary efforts to stabilize the economy, has fluctuated. A boom has followed whenever the Federal Reserve System has quickened the rate of money growth. Recessions, they allege, have resulted when money growth has slowed.

Empirical Support

Considerable empirical work has been presented to support the Monetarist opinion. Most prominent is a study by Milton Friedman and Anna Schwartz, in which they analyzed data on the behavior of money in the United States all the way back to the Civil War.[1] Changes in money supply growth have been very closely associated with changes in income, economic activity, and prices, they found. From their analysis, they and other Monetarists conclude that changes in the money supply *cause* swings in the business cycle.

Monetarist Theory

Monetarists base their arguments on theory as well as history, describing the way in which they think changes in the money supply produce adjustments affecting output, employment, and prices. The amount of money people wish to have is tied closely to the level of income, they say. If the supply of money expands faster than the amount people wish to have, they will try to spend away the unwanted portion of their money balances. Inflation results. If the money supply expands more slowly than income, rising less rapidly than the amount of money people want to have, people will try to build up their money balances by cutting back their spending. In this case, the result is unemployment, according to the Monetarist theory.

We should point out that the Monetarists do not regard the cause-and-effect relationship between money and income as absolutely tight. Monetarists recognize, just as Keynesians do, that the economy will always be subject to unexpected shocks from changes in expectations and from adjustments to imperfections and structural changes in our economy. They also realize that the Federal Reserve's control over the money supply is not perfect. Monetarists do not argue that adherence to the money supply rule would produce perfect economic stabilization; they simply say that it would yield much better results than the flexible policy mix approach now in vogue.

Monetarists, incidentally, take a non-Keynesian view of interest rates, doubting that they exert much influence on total spending and business activity. Monetarists are inclined to feel instead that interest rate changes result from the allocation of funds by market forces. Changes in both spending and interest rates, they feel, are mutual responses to changes in the money supply.

SHORTCOMINGS

The Monetarists offer a persuasive case for their prescription, and efforts to promote their view have won varying degrees of support.

[1] *A Monetary History of the United States—1867–1960* (Princeton, N.J.: National Bureau of Economic Research, Princeton University Press, 1963).

The money supply controversy received extensive hearings before the Joint Economic Committee of Congress last year. The hearings culminated in a recommendation by the JEC that the Monetarist prescription of steady money supply growth be followed—with qualifications.

Yet, a great many economists still have reservations about the Monetarist scheme. These reservations involve fundamental disagreements about monetary theory. Whereas Monetarists think the influence of money supply on economic activity is important enough to neglect virtually everything else, other economists feel such neglect would be unwarranted and dangerous.

Is Money All That Matters?

The issue is whether money is nearly all that matters, or merely one of many things that matter, as far as stabilization policy is concerned. Spending, and hence production and incomes, may change when businessmen alter their expenditures for plant and equipment because of inflationary expectations. Consumers may decide to cut back their spending and increase their saving for reasons unrelated to the money supply—such as in anticipation of higher taxes. Shifts in Government spending may affect total spending. Strikes may interrupt the course of business activity. Such things may be equally important as changes in the money supply, or even more important.

Do changes in money *cause* changes in income and production? Probably. But the causal influence may run the other way too. An increase in spending and business activity may itself stimulate additional demands for money which, if accommodated by the Federal Reserve, result in an increased money supply. An increase in spending calls for greater amounts of money for use in the channels of trade. When this happens, a change in the money supply is a response to, rather than a cause of, a change in business activity. To the extent that this happens, the Monetarists have the tail wagging the dog.

Velocity

Another unresolved aspect of the controversy is the question of velocity. Velocity, the ratio of income to money, describes the speed with which money changes hands as it flows through the economy. Increases in velocity may affect spending decisions, because spenders then have more money available than they want to hold—not because there is more of it, but because it is circulating faster.

Although Monetarists think velocity is relatively stable, this remains an unsettled question. If velocity is not stable, then a reduction in the money supply would not reduce spending, since the money already in the economy would change hands more quickly. The decrease in money might be offset substantially by an increase in velocity. Whether this happens or not is an open question.

What Is Money?

Generally rising interest rates in the postwar period have made interest-bearing financial assets, such as certificates of deposit, more attractive than they used to be relative to money. Corporations in particular have economized on their money balances, substituting interest-bearing assets for demand deposits. As these kinds of substitutes for conventionally defined money have become more and more appealing, considerable controversy has developed about the proper definition of "money."

Professor Friedman, for instance, prefers to include time deposits at commercial banks in his definition, along with currency and private demand deposits. His historical investigation mentioned earlier suggested to him that changes in time deposits have much the same influence on income as do changes in demand deposits and currency. Yet the period Friedman examined in his study preceded the evolution of the large denomination certificate of deposit, a unique financial instrument that now comprises an important part of time deposit balances. Today's time deposits, in other words, are different from the time deposits Friedman studied. For this and other reasons, Friedman himself agrees that this is not an ideal measure of money since there is actually a spectrum of financial assets possessing varying degrees of "moneyness."

The basic problem is that the significance of changes in any particular group of financial assets can be deceptive. Movements may simply represent investor substitution between, say, time deposits and marketable securities such as Treasury bills. Many other financial assets, such as accounts at savings and loan associations, may be close substitutes for demand deposits. Is it proper to include one kind of financial asset in the all-important definition of money while excluding other close substitutes? This definitional question has not been satisfactorily resolved.

Problems of Aggregation

One further important shortcoming of the Monetarist view deserves our attention. Monetarists are prone to take an aggregated view of the economy, and to leave the distribution of money and income to competitive forces. Such an aggregated approach seems unsatisfactory, partly because it neglects the disproportionate impact of monetary actions. A case in point is the homebuilding industry where market imperfections have at times impeded the flow of funds through savings institutions into home mortgages. Monetary policy must recognize and adapt to situations like this.

CONCLUDING COMMENTS

It would be nice if we could project ourselves 20 years into the future and look back to see how the money supply controversy had been resolved. Perhaps we could also see what new controversies had moved into the spotlight by that time. But since this is impossible, we shall conclude instead with several comments on the present status of the money supply debate.

The arguments are heated, but the fervor of the parties involved should not obscure the substantial amount of agreement that exists. Almost all economists today share the goals of high employment, orderly economic growth, stable price levels, and long-run balance in our international payments. They generally agree, too, that the Government should do what it can to influence total spending in such a way as to achieve these goals. The basic question is not *if*, but *how*, these things can best be accomplished.

At first glance, the Monetarists argue persuasively that money is the crucial determinant of economic activity. But as we have examined the Monetarist scheme more closely, we have noted a number of serious shortcomings.

Even aside from these, the Monetarist theme, by attaching so much importance to the behavior of a single economic variable, tends to downgrade the complexity of our economy. Monetarists are less inclined to appreciate the consequences of this complexity, partly because they have assumed them away in their theorizing. But acceptance of the Monetarist arguments, in the sense of basing policy on them, requires a reasonable acceptance of the assumptions on which their arguments are based. This is a strong requirement. Our economy's wages, prices, and interest rates, for instance, do not allocate labor services, products, and credit nearly as neatly as the Monetarists hope they do and, therefore, may be incapable of acceptably providing "automatic" economic stability. Whether balance of payments problems might be solved by allowing the exchange rates between currencies to move freely, as the Monetarists suggest, is debatable.

Is a simple monetary rule the final answer? Economists have

long sought to find such a simple answer. Some, for example, thought fiscal policy was a panacea, but disillusion followed. We have to be prepared to admit that a simple answer does not exist. But even if a simple rule could be found, discretionary policy would still offer an important advantage that could not be matched by rigid adherence to a rule. Flexible policy permits learning from mistakes, offering a built-in capability for improving the efficiency of policy actions. Policy performance can continue to adapt and improve by preserving its flexibility.

Judging from the way in which other economic controversies have been resolved in the past, we can expect a synthesis to emerge. Indeed, there are already some signs of this. Monetarist attacks have caused Keynesians to pay much more attention than they previously did to the behavior of money. Monetarists, on the other side, are increasingly recognizing that the economy deviates from their theoretical assumptions, and are consequently qualifying the rigidity of their money supply rule. When we look back on the money supply controversy 20 years from now, we shall probably find that these synthesizing tendencies have produced considerably more agreement than now exists in the controversy over the money supply.

MILTON FRIEDMAN

RULES VERSUS AUTHORITY IN MONETARY POLICY

26

. . . Unless we can achieve both a reasonably stable economy in the short run and a reasonably stable price level in the long run, our free enterprise economy is unlikely to be permitted to survive. And without a predominantly free enterprise economy, we shall

Reprinted from "Statement of Milton Friedman," *Employment, Growth, and Price Levels*, Part 4—The Influence on Prices of Changes in the Effective Supply of Money, Hearings Before the Joint Economic Committee, 86th Cong., 1st Sess., May 25, 1959, pp. 605–612.

neither preserve political freedom nor attain healthy economic growth, which in a free society means the possibility for individuals to use their resources effectively to promote their own aspirations.

. . .

The past three decades have seen first a sweeping revolution against previously accepted economic thought about the role of monetary factors in economic change and then a counterrevolution that is still incomplete but promises to be no less sweeping. As with any successful counterrevolution, the result has not been simply to restore the status quo ante. In the process, views initially held rather uncritically have been reexamined and improved, and some elements of the revolutionary interlude absorbed.

Before the great depression of the early 1930's, accepted economic doctrine attached great importance to the stock of money as a determinant of the level of money income and of the price level. This view rested on experience covering centuries in time and spanning the globe in space. On numerous occasions, substantial increases in the stock of money relative to output had been associated with substantial increases in prices, and substantial decreases in the stock of money relative to output with substantial decreases in prices. And there were no known cases in which substantial changes in either money or prices had occurred without a similar change in the other magnitude.

The theoretical relation suggested by this experience was generally termed "the quantity theory of money." Like most established orthodoxies, it became unduly rigid in form and structure and thereby gave rise to expectations that were bound to be disappointed. In particular, in the 1920's, it was a major element in the widespread belief that the Federal Reserve System could and, what is even more extreme, would succeed in producing for an indefinitely prolonged period a high degree of economic stability, itself a major ingredient in the belief in a new era.

The great depression spawned a revolution in views. Though on a restrospective examination the depression is a tragic testimonial to the potency of monetary factors—the stock of money fell by a third from 1929 to 1933—the failure of the monetary authorities to stem the depression was taken as evidence that they could not have done so. And in any event, the obvious disorders in the economy and the urgent need for a remedy made the world in general and the economic profession in particular receptive to new ideas.

John Maynard Keynes was the chief architect of the subsequent intellectual revolution. He shifted emphasis from the relation between the stock of money and the flow of income which was at the heart of the quantity theory to the relation between different flows, in particular between the flow of capital expenditures and the flow of income. He regarded changes in the stock of money as of minor importance in times of unemployment, and as exercising a significant influence only in times of full employment. His disciples, as disciples will, went much farther than the master. The view became widespread that "money does not matter," that the stock of money was a purely passive concomitant of economic change and played no independent part except as it might affect interest rates, and that hence the only role for monetary policy was the minor one of keeping interest rates low so as to avoid interfering with the investment regarded as needed to offset the secular stagnation that was confidently expected to be the major problem for the future.

Two forces combined to produce a counterrevolution in ideas. One was strictly academic. Scholarly criticism and analysis of Keynes' ideas demonstrated a logical fallacy in one of his central propositions; namely, the proposition that, for a given stock of money, there might, even in principle, exist no price and wage level consistent with full employment; or, to put the proposition differently, that even in the economist's never-never land of the long run, and even if all prices and wages were perfectly flexible, a free market system might have no inherent tendency to full employment.

It has turned out on analysis that Keynes' proposition involved an error of omission. He neglected to take account of the effect of different levels of prices on the real value attached by the community to its wealth relative to its income, and of the effect of changes in this ratio, in its turn, on consumption expenditures. When this effect is taken into account, there is always in principle a price and wage level consistent with full employment, though of course frictions or other disturbances may prevent the economy from attaining such a position at any point in time. Unemployment, that is, cannot be attributed to an inherent "flaw in the price system;" it requires explanation in terms of such other forces as rigidities in adjustments, external disturbances, and the like.

The second, and more obvious, though perhaps not more important, factor that produced a counterrevolution was the brute force of events. Many countries in the postwar period, including the United States, pursued cheap-money policies, partly under the influence of the ideas derived from Keynes that I have so briefly sketched. Every such country experienced either open inflation or a network of partly effective, partly ineffective, controls designed to suppress the inflationary pressure. In every case, the stock of money rose as a result of the cheap-money policies and so did prices, either openly or in whatever disguise was most effective in circumventing the controls. No country succeeded in stemming inflation without adopting measures that made it possible to restrain the growth in the stock of money. And every country that did hold down the growth in the stock of money succeeded in checking the price rise.

Western Germany's "economic miracle" after the monetary reform of 1948 was the most dramatic episode, but the experiences of Italy, of Great Britain, and of the United States differed only in detail. And French experience, prior to the monetary reforms at the turn of this year, is equally striking testimony by its contrast in both policy and outcome.

These developments in the world of scholarship and of affairs have produced a rebirth of interest in monetary changes. It is by now clear, and widely accepted, that money does matter and matters very much. There has been an increasing amount of research by economists during recent years on just how monetary forces operate, on what the relation is between monetary changes and other economic changes, and on the structure and operation of our financial system. I venture to predict that this trend will continue.

The modern version of the quantity theory that has been developed as a result of this work is more sophisticated and subtle than the earlier version. Like that earlier version, however, it attaches great importance to the quantity of money as a determinant of prices and like it, also, it is consistent with centuries of experience.

An examination of the role of money must distinguish sharply between the arithmetic and the economics of the relation between money and other magnitudes.

As a matter of arithmetic, we can always express national income in two different ways:

First, as the product of the amount of money and its velocity of circulation.

Second, as the product of an index of the quantity of goods and services produced and an index of the average price of these goods and services.

The two products are always equal, which gives the famous quantity equation: $MV = Py$, in its income form, where M is the stock of money at any time; V, the income velocity of circulation of money; P, the price level, and y, the rate of flow of real income.

As it stands, this equation is simply a definition of velocity; for any values of the price level, real income, and the stock of money, all of which can be observed directly, we can compute the value of V that will make it true. It says nothing about the factors that might produce a change in the stock of money or about the effect of such a change. Conceivably, such a change might be absorbed entirely in V, without affecting prices or output at all—this is the result implicit in the views of the extreme and rigid disciples of Keynes. Or the change in M, the stock of money, might be entirely absorbed by prices, without affecting velocity or output at all—this is the result predicted by the extreme and rigid quantity theorists. Or the change in money might be partly offset by a change in velocity, and the remainder reflected partly in prices, partly in output—this is the result experienced in the United States in the longer period movements of the past century. Or the change in money might be reinforced by a change in velocity in the same direction, the combined effect being reflected in both prices and output, but in widely varying proportions, depending on circumstances—this is the result experienced in the United States during the shorter period movements, the so-called business cycles, of the past centuries. And still other combinations are possible.

The economic issue concerns the circumstances under which one or another of these outcomes is likely to occur and the process whereby it does occur. This in turn depends on the factors that determine the quantity of money, the problem of the supply of money; the factors that determine the amount of money people want to hold, the demand for money; and the factors that determine the process whereby the amount of money people want to hold is adapted to the amount available, the adjustment between demand and supply.

Under present conditions in the United States, the Federal Reserve System essentially determines the total quantity of money; that is to say, the number of dollars of currency and deposits available for the public to hold. Within very wide limits, it can make this total anything it wants it to be. Of course, it cannot do so instantaneously or to the precise dollar, and it frequently expresses its proximate objectives in terms of other magnitudes, letting the quantity of money be whatever is consistent with these other objectives. But there is no doubt that, if it wanted to, it has both the formal power and the actual technical capacity to control the total stock of money with a timelag measured in weeks and to a degree of precision measured in tenths of 1 percent.

Broadly speaking, therefore, the public cannot by itself affect the total number of dollars available to be held. For any one individual separately, it both appears to be true and is true that he can control the amount of cash that he holds. He can increase his cash balances by selling some assets for cash or spending less than he receives from other sources. He can reduce his cash balances by spending on assets or for other purposes more than he receives. For all individuals combined, however, the appearance that they can control their cash balances is an optical illusion. One individual can reduce or increase his cash balance only because another individual or several others are induced to increase or reduce theirs; that is, to do the opposite of what he does. If individuals as a whole were to try to reduce the number of dollars they held, they could not all do so, they would simply be playing a game of musical chairs. In trying to do so, however, they would raise the flow of expenditures and of money income since each would be trying to spend more than he receives; in the process adding to someone else's receipts, and, reciprocally, finding his own higher than anticipated because of the attempt by still others to spend more than they receive. In the process, prices would tend to rise, which would reduce the real value of cash balances; that is, the quantity of goods and services that the cash balances will buy.

While individuals are thus frustrated in their attempt to reduce the number of dollars they hold, they succeed in achieving an .equivalent change in their position, for the rise in money income and in prices reduces the ratio of these balances to their income and also the real value of these balances. The process will continue until this ratio and this real value are in accord with their desires.

Conversely, if individuals were to try to increase the number of dollars they held, they could not do so if the Federal Reserve System did not increase the number available to be held. But in their attempt to do so, individuals would try to spend less than they received, which would lower the flow of spending and reduce the level of money income and of prices. This would raise the ratio of cash balances to income and the real value of cash balances.

This essential difference between the situation as it appears to the individual, who can determine his own cash balances but must take prices and money income as beyond his control, and the situation as it is to all individuals together, whose total cash balances are outside their control but who can determine prices and money income, is perhaps the most important proposition in monetary theory and certainly the source of greatest confusion to the layman.

It follows from this analysis that if the nominal stock of money changes, but the public at large wants to hold the same real stock of money, the monetary change will be reflected fully and proportionately in prices after adjustment has been made to the change. In the interim, the effect on prices might be less or more and real income might also be affected. However, systematic discrepancies over any period between movements in prices and in the stock of money must reflect changes in the real stock of money that the public at large wishes to hold.

It is pointed out in greater detail in the technical papers that have been submitted that the main factors affecting the real stock of money the public wishes to hold are:

(1) The level of income

(2) The cost of holding money

The level of real income affects desired real cash balances in two ways:

In the first place, a change in real income affects the total volume of transactions to be effected; that is, the amount of work, as it were, for money to do. This effect would lead to a change in the desired real stock of money in roughly the same proportion as in output.

In the second place, if there is a change not only in total real income but also in per capita income, it means that people are at a higher or a lower level of living. With such a change in the level of living, they may want to increase their stock of money more or less than proportionately, just as an increase in level of living means a less than proportionate incraese in expenditures on bread but a more than proportionate increase in the stock of durable consumer goods. It turns out empirically that in this respect money is like durable consumer goods rather than like bread, so that an increase in real level of living is on the average associated with a more than proportionate increase in the real stock of money.

A very recent and rather novel finding is that the income to which cash balances are adjusted is the longer term level of income that can be expected, rather than the income currently being received. This finding goes far to explain much that has hitherto been puzzling in the cyclical behavior of the stock of money relative to income.

The cost of holding cash balances depends mainly on two factors: The rate of interest that can be earned on alternative assets, and the expected rate of change of prices.

If a Government bond, for example, yields 4 percent, it costs an individual $4 a year to hold $100 in cash instead of in the form of a bond. If prices are rising at the rate of 4 percent per year, for example, it will take $104 in cash to buy at the end of the year as much as $100 at the beginning, so that it costs an individual $4 a year to hold $100 in cash instead of in goods initially worth $100. In consequence, the higher are interest rates and the higher is the expected rate of change in prices, the greater is the incentive for individuals to economize on cash balances, and conversely.

Empirical evidence suggests that interest rates have a systematic effect in the expected direction but that the effect is not large in magnitude. The experienced rate of change in prices has no discernible effect in ordinary times, when prices are not expected to change by much. On the other hand, the rate of change in prices has a clearly discernible and major effect when price change is rapid and long continued, as during extreme inflations and deflations.

In recent years, both interest rates and the expected rate of change in prices have been working in the same direction in the United States. Expectations of inflation have become more and more widespread and, partly for that reason, interest rates have risen. These changes doubtless help to explain the recent tendency for the ratio of the stock of money to income to decline despite a rise in real income per capita.

Of course, even after allowance is made for changes in real income per capita and in the cost of holding money, the ratio of cash balances to income is not perfectly steady. But the remaining fluctuations are minor, certainly far smaller than those that occur in the stock of money itself.

In concluding this statement, I should like to emphasize two points that seem to me of central importance in fashioning a wise national monetary policy.

The first is the closeness, regularity, and predictability of the relation among the stock of money, the level of price, and the level of output over any considerable period of years.

The second is our present inability to predict at all accurately this same relation over very short periods, from month to month, quarter to quarter, even year to year.

The first proposition means that in order to attain a reasonably stable price level over the long pull, we must adopt measures that will lead to a growth in the stock of money at a fairly steady rate roughly equal to or slightly higher than the average rate of growth of output.

The second proposition means that in the present state of our knowledge we cannot hope to use monetary policy as a precision instrument to offset other short-run forces making for instability. The attempt to do so is likely merely to introduce additional instability into the economy, to make the economy less rather than more stable.

It should be emphasized that this conclusion about short-run changes is valid not only for monetary policy but also for fiscal or other policies. All these policies operate with a long lag and with a lag that varies widely from time to time. We know too little about either these lags or about what the economic situation will be months or years hence when the chickens we release come home to roost, to be able to be effective in offsetting the myriad of factors making for minor fluctuations in economic activity. This is one of those cases in which the best can be the enemy of the good.

As I examine the past record of stability in the United States, I am impressed by the number of occasions on which major fluctuations have been a consequence of changing and at times erratic governmental policies with respect to money. This record offers much support for the view that, if the monetary framework were stable, our private enterprise economy is sufficiently adaptable to the other changes that occur to yield a high degree of economic stability in the short run as well as the long run.

For this reason, the urgent need, I believe—and here I am venturing farthest from any academic ivory tower—is to keep monetary changes from being a destabilizing force, as they have been through much of our history. In my view, this can best be done by assigning the monetary authorities the task of keeping the stock of money growing at a regular and steady rate, month in and month out. This would at one and the same time provide a stable monetary background for short-run adjustments and assure long-run adjustments and assure long-run stability in the purchasing power of the dollar.

The elimination of monetary uncertainty would promote healthy economic growth by providing a stabler environment for both individual planning and social action. But it would be no panacea. The springs of economic progress are to be found elsewhere; in the qualities of the people, their inventiveness, thrift, and responsibility, in public policies that give a free field for private initiative and promote competition and free trade at home and abroad. Mistakes in monetary policy can render these forces impotent. A stable monetary environment can give them an opportunity to be effective; it cannot create them.

PAUL SAMUELSON

REFLECTIONS ON
CENTRAL BANKING[1]

27

Contrary to the opinions of many contemporary economists (and to some of my own earlier views), I believe that monetary and credit policies have great potency to stimulate, stabilize, or depress a modern economy. This belief is based on my evaluation of the tremendous amount of empirical data given by (1) history, (2) current statistics, and (3) case studies of business behavior. These data are diverse, conflicting, and often inconclusive, and therefore have to be interpreted with the help of all the tools of economic analysis inherited from the past and developed by the present generation of scholars.

In thus differing from the pessimists, I want to make clear that I am *not* agreeing with that much smaller group of older economists who think that monetary policy by itself is the sole or principal mechanism for controlling the aggregative behavior of a modern economy. I believe such a view to be factually wrong or irrelevant; and would add that, even if monetary policies truly had this exaggerated degree of potency, I would not deem it optimal social policy to rely exclusively or primarily upon that weapon alone.

Today all experts dismiss the ancient view that *laissez-faire* can properly hold in the field of money and banking. "Money will not manage itself." Banking institutions are not perfectly-competitive self-regulating enterprises that can be free from strict governmental regulations and controls. They are "public utilities vested with public interest" and the same is true in equal or lesser degree of various financial intermediaries, such as savings institutions, finance companies, and insurance concerns. Let me make clear that all this is stated from the standpoint of one who philosophically values individual freedoms. A person who cheerfully accepts the idea of direct price, wage, and production controls can afford to give a relatively large measure of freedom to credit institutions; but one who

Reprinted from Paul Samuelson, "Reflections on Central Banking," *The National Banking Review*, Vol. I (September 1963), pp. 15–28. Washington, D.C.: U.S. Department of the Treasury.

[1] This article is based upon the author's previously unpublished testimony before the Canadian Royal Commission on Banking and Finance in October, 1962.

wishes to minimize (except in emergency periods) the use of such direct controls will realize that we maximize total freedom in a society by limiting it in the areas which crucially determine the aggregate of effective demand.

I must firmly disassociate myself from the small but important group of writers who, agreeing that money will not run itself, go on to argue that it ought to be determined permanently by certain automatic formulas. Sometimes this is put in the fancy language of "rules versus authorities," or "laws versus men," or "automaticity versus discretionary action." Of course, no one, myself included, will admit to favoring arbitrary caprice of bungling rulers over the even-handed justice of well-formulated rules. If every form of explicit cooperative action set up by men is bound to be completely nearsighted, venal, and blundering, then recourse to astrological rules might pragmatically be defended—although no wise man could have any secure belief that such bungling human beings would ever bind themselves and stay bound to such arbitrary mechanisms. The vicissitudes of ancient coin standards—which were at the mercy of the accidental discovery of precious metals in Latin America, Australia, California, Alaska, South Africa, and now Soviet Russia—would certainly be preferable to some forms of "managed money."

In practice, however, there have always been—for both good and evil—substantial departures from any automatic coin, bullion or other kind of gold standard. In principle, the choice has never been between discretionary and non-discretionary action: for when men set up a definitive mechanism which is to run forever afterward by itself, that involves a single act of discretion which transcends, in both its arrogance and its capacity for potential harm, any repeated acts of foolish discretion that can be imagined. Since I have argued elsewhere the philosophical principles involved in this choice and have never seen any written refutation of these arguments by adherents of the "automaticity" school, I shall merely state here that the relevant choices have to be made pragmatically in terms of the goodness or badness of behavior patterns that result from various kinds of discretionary action.

Specifically, consider the suggestion of a money supply which is to grow at exactly 3 per cent per year, a policy advocated by some who think no other actions would then be required. Suppose this had been enacted in the United States in a random recent year, without knowledge of the balance-of-payments problems just ahead, and without knowledge of the massive shift to time deposits such as we have been experiencing as a result of both raised interest-rate ceilings on such deposits and the natural shift to such deposits as interest rates generally rise. The results could have been quite bad in comparison with what actually happened; and if the balance-of-payments situation had, for unpredictable reasons, been a great deal worse, the results could have been disastrous. I realize the adherents of such proposals will argue that such dire results might have been avoided if there had been floating exchange rates, perfectly flexible wage rates, and never, never any interest-rate or other ceilings. But since we do not and shall not live in such a never-never land, legislating part of the package would surely do more harm than good.

I. THE QUANTITY THEORY AND MONETARY POLICY

There are many reasons why any automatic gadget can be improved upon by decision-makers, even by fallible decision makers. This statement will be denied by those who are firm believers in the ancient Quantity Theory of Money. If it were true *in a causal sense* that there is an invariant relationship between, on the one hand, total dollar income and spending, and, on the other, the supply of money defined in such a way as to be capable of predetermination by the central bank, then an autogyro which kept total money supply growing smoothly would, by hypothesis, keep total money income growing smoothly. While I know that some modern scholars have tried by historical studies to establish an empirical concomitance between money supply and aggregate income, let me simply state here that I find the implied proof of a simple, controllable, causal proportionality relationship unconvincing.

It is the easiest sport in the world to shoot down any crude formulation of the Quantity Theory. But I think it quite illegitimate to conclude from this what the Radcliffe Committee and many modern scholars have stated: namely, if total money supply, M, does not invariably create an exactly proportional total income and product because the income velocity of circulation of money, V, is not a constant—it follows that we should turn our attention away from conventional central bank controls and rely instead upon some global concept of "liquidity." As will become evident, I attach considerable importance to various concepts of liquidity.

But I think it wrong to believe that recognizing such concepts should undermine the belief that conventional central bank operations of open-market purchase and sale of securities, discount lending, and reserve-ratio changing are likely to have important effects upon the total of investment and consumption spending. Emphasizing "liquidity" quite properly serves to debunk a crude quantity theory, and it thereby scores a fatal point against advocates of simple automaticity gadgets. But it leaves the position I am here expounding unscathed, and it is for this reason that a number of reviewers have criticized the Radcliffe Report.[2]

Because of the human temptation to deify any concept that has been defined and to tend to regard, as approximately constant, the last variable that one has defined, I do not find the velocity variable, V, a very useful one. But older economists did, and some younger ones are beginning to again. So I shall restate the heart of the matter in such terms.

If the requisite V were a strict constant, $P \times Q$ would, by hypothesis, be exactly proportional to the requisite definition of money, M. Experience shows that V is not a constant: it shows certain historical trends in the long run; in the course of the business cycle, it has generally shown fluctuations that are sympathetic with the cycle itself, rising in good times and falling in bad. After more studies have been made, I believe V will also show certain fluctuations with interest rate and other conditions, tending, other things equal, to rise when interest rates are high and the opportunity cost of cash balances is great, and tending to fall when short term investment opportunities all have a very low yield.

The behavior of V will also be quite sensitively affected by the particular concept of the money supply that is adopted, being quite different if currency alone is considered (as with the nineteenth century Currency School and Edwin Cannan in the 1920's) than if demand deposits are included and various categories of time deposits and close money substitutes are, or are not, included in the definition of money. Some of the movements of V will be erratic and relatively unpredictable; others will be in some measure predictable. In particular, although they are operationally hard to identify in the empirical record, certain changes can always be expected in V that are themselves induced by the change in M itself and, certain other things being held constant, are part and parcel of such a change in M. Some sensible probability statements can be made about these induced changes in V at various phases of the business cycle and at various time points in history.

Now, if it were the case that recognition of the importance of money substitutes and various concepts of liquidity were to imply that changes of M in one direction could be expected to be followed systematically by opposite changes in V just large enough to offset

[2] See John Gurley, "The Radcliffe Report and Evidence," *American Economic Review* (September 1960).

any resulting induced changes in $MV = PQ$, then the casual reader of the Radcliffe Report would be right in thinking that central banks are unable to affect significantly aggregate spending by conventional open-market and lending operations. But none of the testimony or arguments in connection with the Radcliffe Committee succeed, in my judgment, in establishing a presumption in favor of this doctrine of induced-velocity-changes-that-just-offset-money changes.

Not only is this not demonstrated in the historical record, but, in addition, such a finding is not in accordance with that type of analysis which is thought to have displaced the old Quantity Theory. For, in the various Keynesian models, there is generally a presumption that an increase in M engineered by the central bank will cause such a reduction in interest rates and such increases in credit availability as to generate an increase in investment and total spending just large enough to create an extra level of income which would absorb in transaction balances the new increment of money created. While the mechanism just described holds for the most primitive Keynesian model, the same conclusion is found to be valid for more sophisticated models, which pay explicit attention to wealth and other stock effects and which distinguish a long chain of assets that range from being very near to money (like short-term government bonds) to being very illiquid and difficult to sell or evaluate (like built-in machinery that is highly specific to a particular location and owner). And the qualitative nature of the conclusion—that the central bank can expand spending by expansive open-market, lending, and reserve-ratio fixing operations—will still hold, even after we have admitted the existence of relatively less-controlled financial intermediaries such as savings banks, finance companies, insurance companies, mutual or unit-trust funds, and various forms of equity and loan participants.

With his permission, I will refer briefly to an interesting demonstration by Professor James Tobin of Yale in an unpublished manuscript[3] privately circulated several years ago. Suppose that we have a chain of substitutes, which instead of being called tea, coffee and cocoa are called bank money, short-term bonds, long-term bonds, insurance assets, and so forth; call them M_1, M_2,—and suppose that their respective prices are N_1, N_2, ... If the central bank could decrease all of the M totals together by operations and fiats that apply to insurance companies as well as to banks and to all financial intermediaries, then no one doubts that the total of "liquidity," however measured, would go down and that this would,

[3] Cowles Commission Study Paper #63.

other things equal, tend to have a depressing effect on aggregate spending and general inflationary pressures. Specifically, with every M_1 decreasing because of direct central bank action, the unweighted or weighted sum of the M's and every other recommended measure of "liquidity" would also go down. But now suppose that the central bank can only decrease directly M_1, having no direct controls on the reserve-ratios or totals of any other sectoral M_1. A reader of the whole of the Radcliffe Report and Hearings might be forgiven for inferring that in this case nothing positive could be said about the ability of the central bank to affect total liquidity, as measured by some kind of total of the M's or weighted-sum of the M's or other measure of liquidity; and hence, that we should abandon the simple notion that a modern central bank can by its conventional operations push aggregate spending in a desired direction. Tobin, however, in his unpublished memo, has shown that, provided the M's are all *substitutes* (in the sense that the excess demand for each M_1 decreases when its own N_1 price rises but increases when some other M_1's N_1 goes up—as, for example, that an isolated increase in the price of short-term bonds should cause less of them to be demanded and more of long-term bonds to be substituted for them), then the central bank can cause *every* M_1 to go down by simply depressing M_1! (The theorem is like the Leontief one which says that raising the consumption requirements for hats must raise gross output of every good in a well-behaved input-output system, and like the Metzler-Keynes theorem that an increase in domestic investment in one country must to some degree raise outputs everywhere in a well-behaved many-sector multiplier model.) This important Tobin result accords well with intuition. Oné should not push it beyond its actual statement: each indirect effect is, generally speaking, weaker than each direct effect, *and* the central bank may have to push undesirably harder on M_1 to get the same change in overall M's than it would have to do if it were given direct powers to affect financial intermediaries.[4] Later I shall have to point out some important limiting cases where the potency of central bank action becomes quantitatively zero or almost zero.

It has often been said that monetary policy is more effective in contracting an economy than in getting it to expand. There is an

---

[4] This corresponds to a theorem that, in appropriate units, $\partial N_1/\partial M_1 > \partial N_1/\partial M_1 > 0$ for certain systems of Leontief, Metzler, and Mosak-Hicks type, as has been recognized by diverse writers, such as Hicks, H. Johnson, Morishima, and others. It does not deny that in certain limiting cases of perfect substitution these effects will be equal, or that in certain limiting cases one or both may be zero.

important grain of truth in this observation. Thus, when the bank rate or the discount rate is six or seven percent and the commercial banks' excess reserves are at a minimum and the business community is heavily dependent upon bank borrowings for its current investments in inventories and other items, then further restrictive action by the central bank can, by a variety of channels, cut deeply into the aggregate of investment and total spending.

On the other hand, in a period like the 1930's, when the market yield on short-term government securities has already been driven down to a fraction of one percent, and when banks have copious excess reserves and business firms are regretting their past investing and regarding the marginal profitability rate on all further investments as negative, there would be little potency indeed in conventional central bank operations. (Buying short-term bonds in the open market would then merely take from the community a very close money substitute and replace it by money itself.) This would not have much further depressing influence on the interest rate structure and would not make credit more readily available to borrowers (who are in any case virtually nonexistent and automatically regarded as suspiciously risky chaps, if they should come forward with a loan application).

From the technical fact that monetary policy works more effectively at high than at low interest rates, no one should make the mistake of concluding that the goal of policy should be to avoid low rates. Forks must be made to fit fingers, not fingers, forks: when an economy will suffer from tight markets and the technician will benefit, it is of course the technician who must properly give way.

This last case then is one where an induced change in velocity can be expected to wipe out almost completely any contrived change in money narrowly defined. It is the case often referred to as the Depression-Keynes model, where (1) there is a liquidity trap near to a zero rate of pure interest, at which the Keynesian liquidity preference schedule is practically infinite in elasticity so that the system will absorb great amounts of M at practically the same interest rate and credit-availability; and/or where (2) the rate of investment spending is almost completely inelastic with respect to changes in the interest cost and availability of credit.

I believe, in the face of some doubters, that such a depression model has occasional empirical validity—certainly in the short run and possibly for a vexingly long time. Moreover, bitter experience in the United States of the last few years leads one to suspect that it is not always so easy to engineer a deepening of capital by conventional central bank operations, even when one is not in a deep-depression liquidity trap: for, even when gilt-edge rates are lowered farther and farther, the effective profit rates that businessmen must anticipate to get them to make somewhat risky investments may remain quite high—say 15 per cent before corporate taxes or 8 per cent after taxes. Thus, even massive open-market purchase of government bonds may not be able to push the system down through a high-profit floor that acts rather like the older Keynes liquidity trap interest floor in keeping investment resistant to expansion.

I know it can be argued that the central bank, provided it is ready to abandon notions of feasibility and force the market rates of interest up to 40 percent in boom times and down to zero or, for that matter, down to negative rates of interest, can control the amount of total money and spending activity to any desired levels, regardless of adverse fiscal policies and adverse behavior propensities on the part of business and the public. Personally, I consider it irrelevant to talk about 40 percent bank rates, and in any case undesirable to put the burden of such extreme adjustments on the narrow sectors most affected by monetary actions. And as far as forcing extremely low interest rates is concerned, it is simply not true that lending money to people at negative interest rates is guaranteed to result in any desired expansion in spending: making gifts might, but if these are loans that have to be paid back, it would be rational for people to borrow at negative interest rates and just hold the proceeds in safety lock boxes, thereby earning a handsome yield. The total of something called M might rise, but that does not mean that the requisite MV can be achieved in any short period by *conventional* central bank operations.

My purpose here is not to score a point against some extreme Quantity Theory formulation, but to call attention to the fact that in many social situations a well-running democracy will want its central bank to engage in *unconventional* activities. (Examples: in the 1930's Federal Reserve Banks made loans directly to certain small businesses: in a future balance of payments crisis, the central bank might want to provide certain guarantees and investment insurance to desired domestic investments, while keeping up the yields on short-term government bills; and the day could come when the central bank would want to make loans at negative interest rates to applicants who satisfied certain requirements, such as a guaranteeing that the proceeds would go into resource-using investment; if *laissez-faire* conditions should prove to choke off deepening of capital when profits rates are still as high as 10 per cent and conventional credit operations proved not able to overcome this, the intrinsic logic of central banking requires recourse to new unconventional programs.)

Finally, I once felt it necessary to point out a minor flaw in certain descriptions of the asymmetry of monetary policy's potency. It is not correct to say that monetary policy can contract an economy more easily than it can expand it. In buoyant times when interest rates are already high and credit already tight, monetary policy is quite potent enough to *both* expand and contract the system from its previous situation; in slack times when interest rates are near the floor and the system is swimming in liquidity, monetary policy is quite impotent with respect to contraction and expansion of the system from its previous level. Thus, the true asymmetry is not that depicted by a corner in the schedule relating general activity and central bank activity, with the slope for an up movement being greatly different from the slope for a down movement; the asymmetry merely refers to the putative difference in slope at any given point in a slack as against a tight credit market.

Central Bankers abhor a situation which they feel is not closely responsive to their control. So they naturally dislike being so expansive as to create a "sloppy market." As shown above, the consequences of this abhorrence may not be too costly in the short run; yet they should often brave the displeasure of commercial bankers (who abhor sloppy markets for the good commercial reasons that such markets are hard on bank earnings) and flood the market with a view to the longer-run stimulus in investment that may come from gradual penetration of alleged liquidity-trap floors. One has no right to assume away such longer-run benefits from a policy of "over-ease." The central banker will tend to feel that the cost of such a policy will be the danger that in the subsequent recovery period the redundant credit, which had previously done no harm and precious little good, will come to life and create the possibility of an over-fast expansion and of undue inflationary pressures. This is just another aspect of his reluctance to let the money market get out of his immediate control.

While recognizing some merit in this view, I would point out that the goal of policy is not to minimize the unease of central bankers; they are supposed to suffer psychic pain when that is in a good cause. Moreover, some quickening in their contractionary actions early in the recovery may serve to undo much of the harm to be expected from an earlier policy of over-ease, and such a quickening would in many cases be a worthwhile price to pay for improving the slump situation. What I am saying here would not be so important if the only thing to fear were a regular cycle involving a recession known to be short-lived. But when an economy moves into an epoch when profit rates are sluggish (having been competed down by the plentifulness of capital stock relative to labor, and the nature and speed of contemporaneous technical change) and investment is hard to coax out at still lower profit rates, the best policy for conventional central banking operations is to keep the money market flooded with reserves, with a view to eroding gradually resistant long-term interest rates and the profit-rate floors that businessmen insist upon getting, if they are to make resources-employing investments. Specifically, in the U. S. environment of the 1930's, it was right to have great excess reserves and minimal short-term rates: the slow, too-slow, drop in long-term interest rates was thereby encouraged. With due regard to future international payments considerations, the same strategy will be needed in certain future times; and American central bankers are wrong to reproach themselves for over-ease in the 1953–4 and 1957–8 recessions.

Zealots for monetary policy are, somewhat pardonably, infuriated by a related asymmetry that used to be argued by critics. These critics would say in one breath, "Monetary action is practically impotent," and in the next breath they would add, "But using monetary policy determinedly will plunge the system into a crisis and major depression." This argument is thought to involve almost a self-contradiction. How can a thing be simultaneously both weak and strong? Formally, this can be saved from being utter nonsense by modifying it to say, "For a small exercise of monetary policy, the results will be not only small but disappointingly small; for a really large exercise, the results will be disastrously large." To this, defenders of the view that M can take care of everything will naturally reply, "Aha then, it is really only a matter of using the right (intermediate) dosage."

On the whole, I have to agree with this defense of monetary policy, particularly in the historical context of the postwar U. S. debates as to whether letting War Bonds fall below par would entail uncontrollable disaster. But in terms of the logic of all the situations that could possibly arise, two qualifications ought to be made. (1) If the response to a control lever satisfies a function that changes suddenly from a low slope to a high one, and at an unknown spot, then a correct dosage is extremely hard to reckon or to work out experimentally; so in some, perhaps rare and unrealistic, situations the asymmetry arguments of the pessimists might have a measure of validity. (2) There is a second complication that may have been envisaged by users of this asymmetry argument; namely, the possibility that in certain situations market expectations are important, with investment demand depending on the bond prices that the central bank engineers and also on the *rate of change of prices*; given differential equation relationships of the form $F(I,P,dp/dt, M \ldots) = 0$, there could result discontinuities in the solution. An example would be the case where shovelling a little snow up hill may, at an unknown and quite unpredictable point, set off an avalanche of snow. To say in such a situation, "It is only a question of the right intermediate dosage," is to miss the point.

II. EFFECTS OF MONETARY POLICY ON PRICE AND OUTPUT

It was once widely believed, and some central bank authorities still believe it, that the central bank operates to control money, or M, and that M operates directly to control the price level, P. In the old days the quantity of output, Q, was not thought to need determining by any particular agency, since something like full employment was more or less taken for granted. In more recent decades, holders of the present view have been prone to think of government *fiscal* policy as somehow having the ability to control Q, with monetary policy controlling P. The point I want to make is a purely mechanical one and has nothing to do with subjective value judgments. It is simply untrue that money and credit programs have any way of peculiarly affecting the P or price factor: successful monetary expansion will, as I have shown above, have some favorable effect on the dollar value of total output $P \times Q$, and so will expansionary fiscal policy. The resulting change in $P \times Q$ will get distributed between expansion in Q as against expansion in P, depending upon how much or how little labor and capital remains unused to be drawn on, and upon how strong or weak are the cost-push upward pressures that come from the institutional supply conditions of organized and unorganized labor, of oligopolistic price administrators and more perfectly-competitive enterprises.

No one has been able to establish any presumption that either monetary policy or fiscal policy has some special impact upon the price as against the output factor. Indeed, one cannot too often correct the view widespread among noneconomists, that a "natural" upswing in consumption or investment spending is less inflationary than an equivalent upswing in aggregate spending, $P \times Q$, brought about by deliberate public policies. (It is true that one expects a somewhat different mix of expenditures to result from new investment spending induced by credit policy than from new consumption spending induced by tax rate reduction. Likewise, a private inventory boom will encounter price rises from bottleneck pressures different from those of a private equipment boom or those of a defense boom. But there is no differential price-level presumption associated in general with deficit, credit, or private stimulation.)

I have been carefully to state the Quantity Theory of Money in terms of proportionality between M and $P \times Q$, rather than in the older terms of proportionality between M and P. The first of these formulations has the advantage that it allows real output to increase considerably from an underemployment situation without there having to be much price rise up to the time that bottlenecks and resource scarcities appear. It allows also for the occurrence of "sellers' inflation," in which there may be an upward push on prices from the wage, profit, and raw material cost side. Since V and Q both tend to rise with the business cycle, Irving Fisher and older writers thought that the ratio of P to M might be approximately constant; however, the facts of the last 40 years do not accord well with such an hypothesis.

Facts aside, there is one model or case in which the older Quantity Theory would indeed be true. Imagine a new situation in which *every* price and every value magnitude has exactly doubled or halved, so that *all* price ratios and real quantities are absolutely unchanged. The essence of money—be it shells, or gold, or bits of paper (and in contrast to drinkable coffee or any good where consumption gives psychic satisfaction)—is that we want it only for its ultimate indirect utility in getting goods that can give direct utility. Basically, we want to hold money only in order to be able to spend it some day in exchange for something directly useful. Therefore, when all prices have exactly doubled or halved while all real magnitudes and exchange ratios and interest rates have stayed exactly constant, the desired amount of money holding can be thought of as exactly doubling or halving.

In this sense and situation, there is an underlying truth in a strict Quantity Theory that makes P and M exactly proportional. (Technically, economists describe this by saying that all real qauntity relations are homogeneous of degree zero in *all* absolute prices and all value magnitudes like $p_i \times q_i$ are homogeneous of degree one in terms of all p's; hence the needed amount of money—the number of wampum beads or ounces of gold or items or paper currency— is a homogeneous function of degree one in all the prices when expressed in terms of that unit. Note that whenever a substance used as money also has a direct utility—as in the case of gold for teeth or of beaver skins for coats—this strict Quantity Theory no longer applies: double the amount of beaver skins by central bank or other activity and the price of wool will not double even if the

384 RULES VERSUS AUTHORITY IN MONETARY POLICY

price of mousetraps should. From this formulation it will be evident that, along with the total of any useless M stuff, be it shells or metal or fiat paper money that represent non-interest-bearing I.O.U's of the government, we should also take account of any interest bearing I.O.U's of the government (which people think of as an asset but fail to think of as involving a personal liability for future taxes).

The strict Quantity Theory now says, double fiat M and fiat government bonds and you will exactly double all prices and value in a classical model that has all its real magnitudes and relative prices unchanged. These fiat bonds are important without regard to the fact that they are useable directly for exchanges or are close money substitutes. As will be seen shortly, some conventional credit operations that involve the same change in M will differ markedly in their "Pigou effects" and potency, a fact ignored by simple-minded theorists. Note too that this version of a quantity theory would hold even if the real part of the model were different from the classical one involving full employment, as in the case of some of the deep-depression Keynesian models of underemployment where so-called Pigou-effects were deemed not to operate. If the economist stipulates a real model that lacks unique equilibrium, then a change in absolute price levels might jar the system from one admissible equilibrium to another, thereby jeopardizing the "neutrality" of money.

III. PRICE CHANGES AND DISTRIBUTION EFFECTS

Simple models do great good in clarifying issues. They can also do great harm if carelessly applied to real life in all its complexity. History does not record nicely balanced changes in all prices that are as neutral with respect to real effects as would be a dimensional transformation in which one chooses to reckon in terms of cents rather than dollars, or in terms of dozens of eggs rather than single ones. And what is more relevant, when the central bank increases one or another measure of the money supply by 10 per cent, this will not, and cannot, result in a nicely balanced change in all prices and values. It literally cannot do so because all past contracts and past prices are already determined: as a debtor your real position is altered by this new change in M, just as my position as a creditor is altered. Nor is there the slightest guarantee that what I gain you will lose, since there is no law of conservation of total well-being under such a change. Indeed, since the time of David Hume, it has been generally thought that mild *unexpected* price rises tend to expand the degree of utilization of resources and to channel resources into the hands of the more active entrepreneurial elements at the expense of more inert classes. During periods of mild or severe inflations, certain *changes in relative prices* have been considered to be characteristic.

While the conditions for a strict Quantity Theory to be valid are unrealistic, they probably become somewhat less so in the long run. I suspect that after more research has been done we shall learn that many of the systematic changes in *relative* prices induced by transitional inflations are not so great as has been believed; for, it seems odd that continuing price rises should keep coming as a surprise to people. Moreover, the longer the run, the less important will be the effects of past contracts and remembrance of lower levels of past prices. The past is, one supposes, as long as the future. But well-behaved and stable price systems tend to have the property of gradually "forgetting" the past. If that were not so, the way that the War of the Roses was financed would be as important for 1962 behavior as the sliding-scale wage contracts of 1961. So a once-and-for-all doubling of money will eventually imply that the distortion inherent in the fact that past prices certainly have not doubled will become less and less relevant. The simpler minded Quantity Theory is thus seen to have its greatest measure of empirical validity in the longest run.

Having emphasized this kernel of truth, I must quickly add the warning that it is precisely in the long run that other things will not have remained equal: exogenous and endogenous shifts in the relations determining equilibrium will certainly have taken place, thereby vitiating any simply price-scale change as an interpretation of the empirical facts. Even if one could rule out purely exogenous disturbances, real economic life does not consist of a return to the same predetermined real equilibrium after a transient change in money supply. I live but once and, if an inflation wipes out my real net worth, that is an irreversible fact. The distribution of income and corporate power was never (including the position of Hugo Stinnes) quite the same after the 1920–23 German inflation: even if a Lorenz curve depicting the inequality of distribution of income or wealth begins to revert toward its earlier form, the class ownership of wealth could be permanently different. Even the same Lorenz curve will not imply the same people in the background and the same behavior propensities. Capitalism, as we know it today, probably would have been systematically different if Columbus had never discovered the New World with its vast areas of gold and silver. All that I have just been saying is rather hypothetical. But there can be no doubt that if Canada and the United States had followed policies which prevented the Great Depression of the 1930's, today we would have an entirely different stock of capital goods. And it is wrong to argue that this means merely that we arrive today at the state we would have otherwise reached in 1953 or 1945: to have arrived at our present "capital abundance" prior to knowing the discoveries of *recent* science would imply a qualitatively and quantitatively different pattern of economic history. (Technically, the theorist describes all this by saying that every economic equilibrium displays important *hysteresis* effects; where the very location of the equilibrium position depends upon the actual historical path of the system, and thus, there can never be truly neutral changes in the absolute price level. As a craftsman, I could wish that reality corresponded to the mechanics of a system without hysteresis, because this would make my task of analyzing economic reality so much more pleasant and simple. But just as the purpose of evolution has not been to give central bankers an easy life, neither has it been to give theorists restful nights and plenty of time to play golf or chess.

While my examples have been primarily taken from price rises, the hysteresis effects from price declines are greater still because of price and wage rigidities which persist even in the long run. The attempt after World War I to roll back the price rises by reverting to 1913 gold parities has aptly been compared to the act of running over a man and then backing up over him a second time to undo the first effects. The corpse would recognize hysteresis effects even if many of the best economists of that day did not.

All this may seem abstract, and admittedly it is expressed in technical language. Yet it does have fundamental economic implications. Simple believers in M as the determinant of total effective demand do not feel the need to distinguish between, say, an increase in M that comes from the Treasury's (or central bank's) printing new dollar bills and (1) sending them to all family heads, or (2) lending them at interest to investors, or (3) spending them on subsidies to investors, or (4) buying back Treasury bills with them. The same increase in M leads, they allege, to the same change in $P \times Q$ (and by strict "homogeneity" reasoning to the same real magnitudes). This is, of course, patent nonsense in the short run, as they concede when challenged. Under (1) consumption is presumably stimulated and interest rates, if anything, raised; under (2) interest rate falls, and presumably V too, depending upon how much investment rises. Only in the longest run, if then, can one assume that the new M gets distributed "ergodically" (i.e., independently of its original point of entry): I say, *if then*, because, at best, the stock of capital is permanently different. Note that (4) is without direct

Pigou effects and hence is presumably permanently different.

Gustav Cassel's famous purchasing-power-parity theory of war-dislocated foreign exchange rates was, prior to its reformulation by Keynes and others as a mere condition of spatial price equilibrium, based originally upon precisely the homogeneity assumption I have just described. It could be precisely applied only to balanced inflation—a situation which did not exist around the time of World War I. As a matter of fact, in such an hypothetical balanced inflation resulting from a mere change in the absolute amount of an essentially neutral money, we would not bet any predictive power from the purchasing-power-parity formulation, since in such a world of perfect flexibility the exchange rates would already be at their equilibrium; but to this Cassel would no doubt reply that his theory would have predictive powers in cases where there are only short-term transient departures from balanced inflation and deflation, and during such times his theory would point to the longer-run equilibrium. Eclectic defenders of the usefulness of the reasoning that underlies the strict Quantity Theory and purchasing-power-parity doctrines will gladly jettison the notion that a trillion-fold increase in 1920 German marks will result in an exactly trillion-fold change in domestic prices and foreign exchange rates: it is enough for their purpose, and mine, to stress that such massive changes in M and related magnitudes will inevitably be associated with massive changes in price levels; and that such massive changes in price levels cannot take place if the total of currency, bank deposits, and related magnitudes are kept fairly constant.

IV. THE TIMING OF MONETARY POLICY

The effects of monetary policy are not instantaneous. This is not surprising, since there are no effects in nature that are secured instantaneously. Even when I turn my key in the lock, the fact that there are no perfectly rigid metals means that a slight twisting and delay is inevitably involved. But the intrinsic delays involved in effectuating monetary policy are much longer than this. It is widely believed that monetary policy delays are considerably less than those involved in fiscal policy actions—such as public works. And this is considered to be one of the great advantages of monetary policy. Actually, however, not a great deal is known in this area, and the empirical researches performed so far are only a beginning. (I find it interesting that Lord Cobbold of the Bank of England in his testimony to The Royal Commission on Banking and Finance of Canada referred to his experience of a six-months lag in monetary policy.) I merely want to point out that the inevitable lags both underscore the lack of perfection to be expected from monetary control and condition the procedures to be followed in making optimal decisions.

If monetary policy acted almost instantaneously and were subject to easy cancellations,[5] the central bank would find its task a much easier one: thus it might not have to take *anticipatory* action prior to a turn down of business activity from a full-employment level; for many purposes it would be sufficient to recognize a turn after it had already happened, which would be a procedure relatively immune from the false forecasts of turns which always plague practical forecasters. But once we recognize that lags of some considerable number of months are involved in securing the effect of new actions, there may be grave harm in a policy which tries to offset a new movement only after enough months have passed to make the direction of that movement terribly obvious. "Don't try to look over hills or beyond valleys" is the sage advice often given by those leery of our ability to forecast. This can be very bad advice, and, in fact, one has to be very arrogant concerning his understanding of the exact degree of a government's ability to forecast, in order to be able to set down this rule or any other specific rule concerning the sluggishness with which an adapting mechanism is to adjust and react to the information input available. If an airplane follows a relatively smooth path with moderate random errors superimposed on it, the electrical engineer knows he should set up a target computer which is based on considerable extrapolation of previous trajectory. If the statistical properties to be expected of the airplane are quite different—for example, involving almost completely random and unpredictable movements—the optimal servomechanism should be a much more sluggish one.

So, few *a priori* rules can be stipulated in advance and certainly none by those who profess to be nihilistic about man's ability to forecast at all. We must get the best guidance possible from experience itself. I'm quite sure that economic historians will feel that the Federal Reserve system was not premature intaking anticipatory action to ease the money market in the Spring of 1960, which was prior to the May turning point and which definitely involved looking over hills and not waiting to find out exactly which way the

---

[5] This inability to cancel out previous action without delay is the one valid argument, which I referred to in an earlier section, for not relying upon the flooding of the money market in time of presumably short recession; note, however, the need to be able to forecast correctly the shortness of the recession.

wind was blowing in order to lean against it. It is precisely the consideration that optimal stabilization policy must vary with the probability pattern of the system to be stabilized, which makes it rather ridiculous to specify in advance and for all times that some particular gadget like three-per-cent-money-increase-per-year should be adhered to, in season and out of season. Where the cold war suddenly to end, imagine the avoidable evil consequences that would follow from such a pre-determined policy.

V. EVOLUTION OF CENTRAL BANKING GOALS

Anyone who has studied carefully the evolution of Central Banking will have noted the steady broadening of its functions and goals. In the beginning, most central banks, being first among equals and merely endowed with certain special privileges and duties, were hardly distinguishable from a commercial bank. Long-run profit maximization was their proper criterion of action. Gradually the profit motive became subordinate, and today it should be of no consequence at all. (The various money creation privileges given by the government to the central bank usually have implied more than enough profits anyway; and in a modern economy the accumulated earnings beyond a nominal minimum must be thought of as reverting, eventually or continuously, to the government—and note that I did not write the Treasury, since that is merely an administrative subdivision.) Profit maximizing is at least a definite task and its disappearance makes the job of decision-making all the more ambiguous and difficult.

After central banks had been recognized as quasi-public institutions, there continued to be an evolutionary broadening of their functions and goals. And I ought to say that these purely factual trends are regarded by most economic experts as desirable developments. The same cannot always be said about the attitude of bankers. And even central bankers are not to be regarded as reliable authorities on the proper role of the modern central bank. Governor Strong of the New York Federal Reserve Bank and Montague Norman of the Bank of England agreed on many things; from beyond the grave they undoubtedly would disapprove of most changes in central banking which are not even matters of controverse today. If Canada appoints another Royal Commission to look into this matter 25 years from now, the witnesses before it will take for granted many changes that would shock the present generation of central bankers. I suspect that the direction of many such changes can be fairly confidently predicted today. I should add that these developments impress me as being, for the most part, salutary moves in the battle to improve the performance of non-totalitarian mixed-enterprise systems.

HENRY C. WALLICH

RULES VERSUS
AUTHORITY IN
MONETARY POLICY

28

STANDARDS FOR GUIDING MONETARY ACTION

Among the numerous standards of monetary policy that have been suggested, such as money supply, credit, interest rates, and bank reserves, one has attracted particular attention: a rule for a stable increase in the money supply. This proposal, associated principally with the name of Professor Milton Friedman of the University of Chicago, is embodied in recommendations made by this Committee. It was supported, as early as 1930, by Carl Snyder of the Federal Reserve Bank of New York. A detailed specification has been offered by Representative Henry Reuss, in this Committee's Report on the February 1968 Economic Report. My comments will be principally concerned with the fixed money growth rule.

Rationale of the Rule

The rule rests upon the theoretical and statistical finding, not universally accepted, that the *rate of growth* of money supply and the *level* of economic activity are closely related. A downturn in the rate of money growth, even when it does not lead to a positive shrinkage of the money supply, tends to be followed by a decline in the level,

Reprinted from Henry C. Wallich, "Prepared Statement of Henry C. Wallich," *Standards for Guiding Monetary Action*, Hearings Before the Joint Economic Committee, 90th Cong., 2d Sess., May 8, 1968, pp. 17–23.

rather than the rate of growth, of economic activity. The same applies to troughs in the two series. It is argued that the behavior of money, because it precedes movements in the economy, causes the latter. The effect takes place with a long and variable lag, however. Hence, while those controlling the money supply have great power over the economy, the long and unstable lag makes it difficult to apply monetary policy on a discretionary basis for stabilization purposes. Monetary policy has so often been wrong that it seems preferable to deprive it of discretion and subject it to a fixed rule. It is not claimed that the fixed rule will produce perfect policy. But it will produce better policy than discretion is likely to do.

The main burden of my argument will be that this reasoning is fallacious. Before proceeding with the argument, I would like to point out, however, that while the rule at times is likely to have very bad results, it will probably have better results than alternative fixed rules that have sometimes been proposed. For instance, a rule that fixes the rate of growth of money supply is vastly superior to a rule fixing the interest rate. The fixed money growth rule may at times lead to wrong action. It may also have bad side effects through instability in the capital markets and in the balance of payments. But so long as the money supply is kept growing at a stable rate, roughly commensurate with the growth rate of the economy, cumulative instability is unlikely to develop. Short run fluctuations may be wider than under a competent discretionary policy. But in the long run money and income will move broadly hand in hand, with at most a moderate rate of inflation or deflation, and moderate changes in the foreign exchange value of the dollar.

A rule pegging the interest rate, on the other hand, for which some time ago there was widespread support, would be cumulatively destabilizing. If, for instance, interest rates were pegged below their equilibrium values, i.e., below the level consistent with stable prices or a stable rate of inflation, the open market purchases required to keep rates at the pegged level will sharply increase the money supply. Inflation would start or accelerate. This would raise the equilibrium rate of interest, which must be higher, in nominal terms, the faster the rate of inflation. This in turn would widen the gap between the equilibrium rate and pegged rates. The scale of open market operations, and the growth in the money supply, would then have to be stepped up. The process would lead to accelerating inflation. In the unlikely case that the pegged rates should be above equilibrium rates, an accelerating deflation would follow.

The same is true with respect to a rule that would try to peg the level of unemployment. In the long run, there is only one level of unemployment consistent with stable prices: the unemployment at which real wage increases are equal to nationwide productivity gain. At a lower level of unemployment, labor demands, and business is willing to grant, higher money wage increases than are consistent with productivity gains. This leads to price increases. These reduce nominal wage increases to less than what labor and business had anticipated. In the following bargaining round, therefore, the existing rate of inflation will be taken into account; nominal wage increases will be higher. Then the process repeats itself, the bargaining parties always vainly trying, by higher nominal settlements, to achieve a rate of real wage increase that, because it is in excess of productivity gains, the economy cannot provide. A policy rule seeking to peg the level of unemployment above or, more likely, below its equilibrium value will lead to increasing deflation or inflation. In this it resembles a fixed interest rate policy, both contrasting with a fixed money growth rule. This, however, does not show that a fixed money growth rule is superior to discretionary monetary policy. I shall argue the case by pointing to the difficulties that a fixed money growth rule is likely to encounter. Obviously this does not prove that discretionary policy is bound to be better. Discretionary policy *can* be worse. All that can be done is to compare the probable defects of the two systems. In doing so, I shall draw on some findings in a study I recently completed ("Quantity Theory and Quantity Policy," in *Ten Economic Studies in the Tradition of Irving Fisher*, John Wiley & Sons, Inc., 1967).

1. Can the Money Supply Be Controlled?

The fixed money growth rule takes for granted that the central bank can make the money supply anything it pleases. That assumption is made also, of course, by all those who argue for a discretionary money supply target. The process of money creation encounters leakages, however. These may slow down attainment of the desired money volume. In the extreme case, they may prevent it altogether. At the level of the banking system, changes in excess reserves and in rediscounts can temporarily prevent the central bank from achieving its objective. The tendency of banks, after a period of great stringency, to rebuild liquidity by paying off rediscounts rather than purchasing assets is familiar. The central bank can overcome these obstacles, by operating on a scale sufficiently large to make its objective prevail. This involves some danger, of course, of overshooting if the banking system later makes fuller use of the reserves supplied.

At the level of the money holding public, shifts from demand deposits into time deposits may frustrate the central bank's effort to increase the money supply. Again, operations on a sufficiently large scale will overcome the resistance of the public, again with some danger of overshooting later. Because the relative expansiveness of an added dollar of demand deposits and of time deposits, respectively, is not known, the ultimate effects of a monetary expansion that increases time deposits along with demand deposits are difficult to estimate. The same applies in the case of relative or absolute contraction.

In the longer run, however, the most serious leakage is that via the balance of payments. A monetary policy that generates either interest rates much below foreign rates, or prices much above foreign prices, will produce a deficit on capital or current account, or both. This deficit reduces the money supply. If the central bank increases the scales of its expansive operations to compensate, it will increase the leakage. In the United States, the desired money supply may prove attainable most of the time despite this leakage. In a smaller economy, where the balance of payments leakage is proportionately larger, it is quite obvious that the central bank cannot put the money supply at any level it pleases so long as the currency is to be kept stable and convertible.

For all these reasons, control over the money supply on the part of the central bank is less than complete.

2. A Fixed Rule Requires Flexible Exchange Rates

Let us assume that the Federal Reserve achieves its money supply objective. This may, however, lead to large international reserve losses if the money supply objective leads to outflows on current or capital account. In time the outflows will exhaust exchange reserves. Thereafter, unless payments controls are introduced, the dollar would be on a floating exchange rate. If the money growth rule continues to be overly expansive, this would result, not in a deficit, but in a continuously declining exchange rate for the dollar. Academic discussions of a money growth rule generally recognize that floating exchange rates are its logical and necessary counterpart. This has not been the case, so far as I know, in congressional discussions. If a flexible exchange rate is not acceptable, then the money growth rule will have to be modified from time to time to prevent reserves from being exhausted. Related considerations apply to the case where a fixed money growth rule would produce a continuing balance of payments surplus. To avoid draining the world of its reserves, the dollar would have to be allowed to appreciate, or the fixed rule would have to be abandoned.

3. Balance-of-Payments Objectives

If an internationally stable dollar and an equilibrated balance of payments are desired, any money supply target, whether based on a rule or on discretion, is inferior to a monetary policy using interest rates as a target. An important part of the balance of payments is determined by flows of short and long term capital, so long as these are not subject to controls. These flows reflect interest rate differentials between the United States and abroad. They can best be controlled, therefore, by a monetary policy using an interest rate target.

That an interest rate target, pursued without regard to domestic equilibrium, can be much more disruptive than a money supply target, whether based on rule or discretion, has already been pointed out. Nevertheless, monetary policy, in one form or another, is the appropriate weapon for balance of payments management. It is superior, in this regard, to fiscal policy. If the objectives of domestic and external stability should conflict, as they sometimes do, it is best to pursue domestic stability by means of fiscal policy, balance of payments equilibrium by means of monetary policy. The reason for this is that while both fiscal and monetary policy affect domestic activity and thereby also the level of imports, monetary policy additionally affects the balance of payments via capital movements. Thus, monetary policy has a "comparative advantage" in dealing with the balance of payments. To implement this advantage, an interest rate target is superior to a money supply target or rule.

4. Stable Money Growth—Unstable Interest Rates

If the volume of money were rigidly fixed from day to day, interest rates probably would jump about within a wide range. The exact amount of money demanded by the economy varies from day to day. It depends on the payments that firms and households have to make, subject to weekly, monthly, quarterly and annual "seasonals," and also to purely random fluctuations. The normal policy of central banks is to stabilize interest rates in the short run by allowing bank reserves and the money supply to vary. The Federal Reserve's policy of maintaining "net free reserves" roughly constant over short periods has the same effect. Any change in the economy's demand for money is thus validated by a change in the supply of reserves and of money. Without this flexibility in the money supply, those in need of money would have to sell short term securities, thereby unsettling interest rates.

A fixed money growth rule would put an end to this accommodating central bank behavior. The ensuing instability of interest rates would probably be moderated, in the course of time, by the market itself. Speculators and arbitragers would buy short term securities when they seemed depressed by transitory factors and sell them when they have risen because of temporary excess liquidity. This smoothing activity of the market would not be perfect, however, nor costless.

Unstable interest rates are not an intolerable calamity. They are painful mainly to participants in the financial markets. They would damage the real sector of the economy only if instability was transmitted to it, or if uncertainty in financial markets leads to a reduction in the flow and an increase in the cost of capital for investment. Some cost increase probably would result, since market participants would have to protect themselves against interest instability by charging higher risk premia.

Unstable interest rates might destablize international capital flows. It is true that these international flows would help to limit the amplitude of domestic interest rate fluctuations. They would also, however, destablize foreign capital and exchange markets. Foreign countries might reasonably complain about an American monetary policy that interfered with their own stability.

5. What Definition of Money?

Reference was made above to the leakage from the money supply through the creation of time deposits. The problem goes deeper, however. All near-monies are substitutes for money in some degree. The exact equivalents are unknown. No doubt they vary from time to time and from holder to holder. The historical evidence seems to say that it does not matter greatly whether a fixed money growth rule is based upon money supply narrowly or broadly defined, i.e. including or excluding time deposits. For the broad definition, a higher rate of growth would be needed than for the narrower, since time deposits have grown more rapidly. But recent gyrations of time deposits and other near-monies make clear this much: either the conditions that in the past made the two types of rules equivalent have changed, or else that equivalence and hence the precision of the monetary growth rule itself was of a very rough sort. The rules specified by Representative Reuss have tried to take unstable behavior of near-monies into account. But they do not provide for quantitatively precise adjustment. In the present state of knowledge, not even a discretionary policy can take erratic behavior of near-monies adequately into account. To allow for it accurately in a fixed money growth rule would be even more difficult.

6. The Relation of Money to Income

Less than twenty years ago, it was fashionable to argue that money had no influence on income. Monetary policy was considered powerless by a great majority of economists in and out of government. Today we are in danger of overshooting in the opposite direction. The existence of an effect running from money to economic activity seems well documented. Its mechanics and its timing are only imperfectly understood.

That the relationship should be between the rate of money *growth* and the *level* of economic activity, for one thing, is not untuitively obvious. One would expect more likely a relationship between the *level* of money supply and the *level* of economic activity, or else between their respective rates of growth. The principal reason why some investigators have chosen the rate of growth rather than the level of money supply seems to be that historically the money supply has declined much less frequently than the level of economic activity. Thus, the level of money and the level of activity have at times moved in opposite directions, casting doubt on the relationship. On the other hand, a relationship between a rate of growth and a level may well be meaningless. It is true of any time series moving in a cyclical, i.e. wave-like pattern, that its rate of growth must decline before the absolute value of the series can decline. Thus, to the extent that money and economic activity are in fact correlated, the rate of money growth is bound to decline before the level of activity, without this implying any causal relationship.

Furthermore, while there is good reason to think that money influences activity, it is obvious also that activity can influence money. It does so by stimulating the demand for bank credit. The banks can meet this demand by using their excess reserves and by borrowing from the central bank. Moreover, if the central bank is interested in maintaining reasonably stable interest rates, it will supply the banks with reserves needed to meet a stronger loan demand. Alternatively, if the central bank is determined to curb an expansion, the appearance of incremental loan demand may cause it to tighten the financial markets even more than the incremental demand itself would. Thus, an incipient change in the level of economic activity may very well cast its shadow ahead, in the form of a prior change in the demand for credit and in the rate of growth of money.

To the extent that money does determine income, the mechanics of this influence remain only partly resolved. There is wide agreement that interest rates play a key role. But if interest rates are the mechanism that transmits impulses from money to the real economy, why look at money instead of at interest rates?

One possible answer to this question is that there is a "direct effect," running from money to income and bypassing interest rates. An increase in money may raise aggregate demand, not because money holders buy securities and drive down interest rates, but because they use their excess money holdings to buy goods directly. This is the manner in which the "quantity theory" often is explained: "when people have more money than they want, they spend it and drive up prices."

But the "direct effect" is less plausible than appears. Households presumably make a decision how much to consume and how much to save. If they accumulate cash, it is by virtue of a prior saving decision. It seems unlikely that, having just decided to save this money, they should then turn around and spend it on consumer goods. The most likely use of excess money saved would seem to be for financial assets, for residential housing, and conceivably for durable consumer goods, if these are regarded as assets. In the case of households, therefore, a "direct effect" seems to be precluded except in the narrow areas of housing and durables.

For firms, saving means to retain profits. The resulting cash balances can be spent on any of the assets that firms acquire—receivables, inventories, fixed assets—or for debt repayment. Here the range for a "direct effect" is wider.

Any demand for physical assets—plant and equipment, inventories, homes—will stimulate economic activity. This demand may be influenced by the liquidity of households and firms. Very importantly, this demand will depend, however, on the rate of return that the assets yield, and on the rate of return that potential asset holders want to obtain. Anything that raises the return on assets, e.g., technological improvements, or reduces the return that asset holders expect, e.g., a fall in rates of return on financial assets—will increase the demand for physical assets and stimulate economic activity. The rate of money growth will affect economic activity insofar, directly or indirectly, it affects these key elements. This is considerably more complex a process than one described by the statement "more money means more demand."

For the setting of a precise rule it is important to know whether money tends to grow faster, as fast, or more slowly than real income. This decisive question unfortunately remains unsolved. According to one theory, money is a luxury good. It follows that the demand for it should expand more rapidly than per capita income, i.e. the velocity of circulation tends to fall. According to a second theory, there are economies of scale in the use of money that allow larger transactors to operate with relatively smaller balance, i.e. velocity tends to rise. The historical evidence shows that there have been long periods of declining velocity of money, which would seem to confirm the "luxury good" theory. Since World War II, however, velocity of money has greatly increased. This change has been accompanied by a rise in interest rates, by a growing expectation that inflation will be a permanent condition, and by various technological improvements that permit economies in the holding of balances.

Another factor that may possibly influence the velocity of money is the proportion of the money supply based upon government debt and international assets ("outside money"). According to the findings of my recent study, which must be considered highly tentative, a decline in this proportion tends to increase velocity. In the United States, this proportion has in fact declined substantially in the post-war period.

Some progress has been made in estimating the quantitative impact upon velocity of these various determinants. But even if we Schwartz has shown that the lag between peaks in money growth rule, which is premature, it would remain necessary to estimate future levels of the determinants. It would be necessary, that is to say, to forecast such factors as interest rates and inflationary expectation as would prevail given any proposed rate of money growth. Only then would we know what the appropriate rate of money growth should be. To set a fixed rate of money growth without knowing these determinants is hazardous in the extreme. In the post-war period, for instance, a rule based on money growth during the interwar period would have been highly inflationary.

The manner in which money is created may also count, especially in the short run. Money created through bank loans and therefore spent immediately may have a more stimulating effect than money created through banks' purchase from investors of highly liquid short-term assets.

Likewise, the phase of the business cycle may affect the appropriate rate of money growth. Historically, velocity has increased during periods of cyclical expansion, even during epochs when the long run trend of velocity was downwards. The same money growth rule may not, therefore, be equally appropriate for all cyclical phases, assuming that even under a fixed money growth rule some cyclical fluctuations will remain.

Finally, it is necessary to point out that all these relationships are highly aggegative. Households with different income levels and firms with different kinds of cash flows have different individual velocities. National velocity is an average. Changes in the mix of households and firms almost certainly would alter average velocity and hence the appropriate growth rate of money.

7. Lags

Research performed by Professor Milton Friedman and Mrs. Anna Schwartz has shown that the lag between peaks in money growth and in economic activity has ranged from 6 to 29 months. The lag from the trough in money growth to the trough in economic activity has ranged from 3 to 22 months. This great variability has been interpreted as demonstrating the uncertainty of monetary policy. It is argued that an action taken, say, to curb an expansion may achieve its main effects only in the succeeding recession.

This reasoning seems unconvincing. The peak rates of monetary growth rarely can be interpreted as indicating a deliberate stance of monetary policy. Monetary policy has not been guided by money growth. Certainly one cannot assume that the start of a decline in money growth marks the moment when the monetary authority decided to put on the brakes. Accordingly, the lag from the peak in money growth to the peak in economic activity is not indicative of the lag of monetary policy. The same applies to the troughs of money growth and economic activity.

A better test of the lag in monetary policy can be derived from observing its effect on the occasion of drastic shifts in policy. Such a shift occurred in 1966. It took only four months to move from reasonable liquidity in the financial markets in April to a serious crunch in August. It took little time to convert a crunch into expectations of recession, and only another four months to move from the crunch to a positive halt in the growth of industrial production in November. Mild monetary measures are another thing—their effect may well be long delayed, since they are not intended to produce abrupt changes in economic activity.

At a more theoretical level, the lead-lag relationships exhibited by money growth and the level of income, respectively, have been examined, as well as some properties of models embodying a fixed money rule.[1] These analyses show that the nature of the leads and lags depends heavily on what factor is assumed to be "driving" a cyclical fluctuation, and what causal relationships are assumed to

[1] James Tobin and William C. Brainard, "Pitfalls in Financial Model-Building," paper presented at the December 1967 meeting of the American Economic Association; Richard Marcotulli, "Lags Under a Fixed Rule and Under Discretionary Monetary Policy," unpublished manuscript.

exist among the various factors. It is even possible to show that money growth may lead income in a model where, by assumption, money has no influence on income at all. Under different assumptions, the rate of money growth, or the level of money supply, may lag changes in income, yet by assumption have a causal effect upon income. The length of time over which a system, once thrown out of balance, returns to equilibrium tends to be, in general, longer under a fixed rule than under a reasonable discretionary policy. While these models cannot form a basis for policy, they serve to show that observed relationships, such as the lead of money growth over income levels, do not unambiguously point to any particular casual mechanism. They also show that a fixed rule may be a costly substitute for sensible discretionary policy. To use a simple analogy, a fall in the barometer usually—not always—precedes rain. No conclusions as to causality can be drawn.

8. Comparison of Results of a Fixed Rule and of Actual Policy Measures

Studies have been made seeking to compare the performance of variously specified money growth rules with actual performance. Usually this involves specifying what policy would have been optimal at any given time, and examining the degree to which the rule and actual policy, respectively, have conformed to this optimum. The cyclical behavior of the economy makes specification of optimum policy rather uncertain. For instance, it depends entirely on the lags with which monetary policy is assumed to work, how soon during a cyclical expansion monetary policy should shift from stimulation to restraint, and whether it should shift back again from restraint to stimulation ahead of the upper turning point. Analogous problems arise on the downside. Again, the relative weight given to full employment, price stability and the balance of payments, respectively, will influence what is considered optimal policy. There is also the question of defining "policy." Policy may not look the same in terms of a money supply standard, a credit expansion standard, or an interest rate standard. Thus the attempt to compare policy by rule and by discretion against an optimal policy is in any event questionable.

The comparison becomes virtually invalid, however, when another circumstance is taken into account. The cyclical and other conditions of the economy, in terms of which optimal policy is defined, are those brought about, at least in part, by the actual policies pursued. They are never the conditions that would have prevailed had policy been guided by a fixed money growth rule. But if the money growth rule, under certain circumstances, destabilizes the economy, then the proper test for it would be how it performs in correcting a disequilibrium of its own making. To such a disequilibrium, a discretionary policy could react flexibly. The fixed rule can respond only by doing more of the same. For a while, at least, that may increase the disequilibrium.

For example, if a fixed rule should lead to inadequate growth of the money supply, as it might have in 1967, and cause or contribute to a recession, nothing can be done under the rule to turn the economy around quickly. The same would be true in case of an inflation, or of a balance of payments deficit. Conceivably, very extreme conditions might develop before the economy returns to equilibrium. Discretionary policy, whatever its defects, usually has succeeded in preventing the occurrence of such extreme conditions, with a few lamentable exceptions. Thus a comparison of a rule and an actual policy, employing the actual historical record, gives the rule the wholly unjustified advantage of always starting from a situation that discretionary policy has kept from going to an extreme. Put in simplest terms, a rule could get us into a big mess, yet the tests rarely confront the rule with such a mess.

9. Will the Rule Be Sustained?

No Congress, no President can bind a successor. Short of being anchored in the Constitution, any money growth rule can altered or dropped. What are the chances that a rule, whether simple or complex, whether enacted into law or adopted voluntarily by the Federal Reserve, will be broken?

I believe the chances are excellent the first time the rule deviates substantially from what discretionary policy would counsel. In a recession, when the Federal Reserve would be inclined to generate liquidity rapidly, would the Congress, the public, and the Federal Reserve itself be satisfied with money being pumped out slowly? In an inflation, when money growth should be slowed sharply, would we be satisfied to see the Federal Reserve continuing to feed the process? In a balance of payments crisis, would we sacrifice a large volume of reserves instead of adopting the monetary policy that would stop the drain? In simplest terms, if the car is going off the road and one wheel is over the ditch, will we keep turning slowly because we have made a rule never to jerk the wheel?

In addition to the prospect of major breaches, there is the probability that minor adjustments in the rule will be demanded from time to time, unless the rule is very broadly defined. Evolving circumstances will show that any single percentage growth rate, or narrow range, is not the right one. If the range is wide, and if full discretion is given to the Federal Reserve within that range, the policy will not differ greatly from a discretionary one. In the end therefore, even if a rule were adopted, discretion probably would be reestablished soon in one way or another. I would regard that outcome as fortunate.

RICHARD D. SELDEN

RULES VERSUS
AUTHORITY IN
MONETARY POLICY

29

The quest for monetary guidelines goes back at least to the famous controversy of the 1940's in England between the currency school and the banking school. In the 1920's in this country, there was lively discussion of proposals to direct the Federal Reserve to attempt to stabilize an index of commodity prices. In 1936 Prof. Henry Simons published an article titled "Rules versus Authorities in Monetary Policy" in which, after surveying a variety of monetary rules, he concluded that the selection of a particular guideline, such as stabilization of the price level or of the volume of money, was less important than acceptance of the principle that some rule should be adopted and announced to the public.

Simons saw three main advantages to the adoption of a monetary rule. First, it would tend to stabilize business expectations. According to Simons, the major source of the uncertainties that plague business planning and lead to fluctuations in investment spending is government itself—and especially the monetary authority. The announcement of a simple rule that would be adhered to steadfastly would create a stable environment within which rational decision-

Reprinted from Richard D. Selden, "Statement of Richard D. Selden," *Standards for Guiding Monetary Action*, Hearings Before the Joint Economic Committee, 90th Cong., 2d Sess., May 8, 1968, pp. 95–100.

making could proceed with comparative calm. Second, Simons was disturbed by the antidemocratic implications of vesting great power in the hands of a quasi-independent agency such as the Federal Reserve Board. Congress, he felt, should retain closer control over this important area. However, the only feasible way of establishing firm congressional control over money would be for it to lay down guidelines within which the Federal Reserve would have to operate. Third, adherence to a rule would prevent the monetary authority from following perverse policies. The case that usually is cited is the 1929–32 period when the volume of money fell by about 25 percent during one of the most severe business contractions the country has ever known. It is generally agreed that a policy of maintaining a constant money stock—assuming this could have been achieved, and I have no doubt at all that it could have been—would have been far preferable to the one actually followed by the Federal Reserve, and it is plausible to suppose that instead of suffering through a great depression the economy would have experienced something more closely resembling our mild postwar recessions after 1929. This point of view received empirical support from the work of Dr. Clark Warburton, former chief economist for the Federal Deposit Insurance Corporation, who found that every business cycle peak during the interwar period was preceded by a lapse of monetary growth from its "normal" upward trend of 5 percent per year. Warburton concluded that the Federal Reserve should aim at at a growth rule that would prevent such lapses—as well as inflationary excesses—in the future.

It is probably fair to say that the contemporary phase of the guidelines debate grows out of Prof. Milton Friedman's work on lags in the effect of monetary policy, which has provided a fourth reason for adoption of a monetary rule. While by no means rejecting the arguments of Simons and Warburton, Friedman has argued that a flexible: that is, discretionary, monetary policy is likely to intensify business fluctuations rather than moderate them. The reason is that policy changes influence the economy only after very substantial time-lags. The policy initiated in May 1968 may not reach its maximum impact until, say, July 1969. But neither the Federal Reserve nor anyone else possesses dependable means of forecasting the state of the economy a year or more in advance; hence there is every likelihood that today's policy will turn out to be inappropriate by the time it matures. And to compound difficulties, Friedman believes that monetary lags are highly variable, and unpredictably so. Hence even if we could foresee the state of the economy a year or two from now there would be no assurance that the policy changes initiated today would blossom forth precisely when intended.

Friedman's doctrine of long and variable monetary lags has not gone unchallenged, of course. Critics have disagreed with his statistical methods and his choice of variables for timing comparisons. It has been pointed out that the effects of monetary policy are likely to be spread out over lengthy time spans and that a significant portion of the effects will be felt fairly soon. However, work by others, including Prof. Thomas Mayer and Prof. John Kareken and Robert Solow and even the Federal Reserve Board's own staff, has established rather definitive the reality of monetary lags. Moreover, Friedman readily admits that some of the effects of policy changes will be felt quite quickly; what is vital to his position is that a substantial portion of the effects are not felt until long after they are needed, and his critics have not been able to fault him so far on this point.

While nearly everyone now accepts long monetary lags as a fact of life, most students of monetary policy remain unconvinced about the wisdom of setting guidelines for the Federal Reserve. This is particularly true of the policymakers themselves.

Failure of the pro- and anti-guidelines advocates to reach agreement can be attributed largely to disagreements on the following three points. First, the advocates of discretion seem to have different objectives of monetary policy in mind than do the advocates of guidelines. Second, there is disagreement on the theory of monetary policy, that is, on the channels through which policy changes influence the economy's ultimate goals. Third, although this is something of a red herring, it is contended by the advocates of discretion that the best rule for the 1960's may be wholly inappropriate for the 1970's or some later period; rules inevitably become obsolete. I shall offer a few comments on each of these sources of disagreement.

It is commonplace to observe that the ultimate goals of economic policy, including monetary policy, are to maintain (1) high levels of employment of the economy's resources, (2) a stable price level for goods and services, (3) equilibrium in the balance of payments, (4) efficient patterns of resource use, and (5) an adequate rate of economic progress, whatever that may be. The Federal Reserve authorities, of course, affirm these objectives like everyone else. Yet at least three other objectives seem to play a role in the Fed's determination of proper policy. One such objective is to aid the Treasury in its task of managing the Federal debt. A second objective is to avoid making membership in the system unattractive to member banks. This unspoken objective appears to be the major explanation of the Fed's forthcoming liberalization of policy at the discount window. A third implicit objective, often lost sight of by academic critics of the Federal Reserve, is protection of the money market against the random shocks that continually buffet it. One gets the impression from reading their commentaries that Federal Reserve officials regard the money market as a delicate plant that needs constant attention in order to survive.

It should be noted that lags probably do not interfere significantly with the Fed's attainment of these three "lesser" objectives—in sharp contrast to the ultimate goals discussed earlier. On the contrary, adoption of simple monetary guidelines such as Friedman's 4 percent growth rule or mandatory stabilization of a price index would require abandonment of at least some of these special Federal Reserve objectives, especially that of protecting the money market.

My own view is that these are unworthy objectives that should be rejected in any event. Although I cannot pose as an expert on the money market, I am inclined to think that the Fed has an exaggerated view of the value of the role it is playing in the market. Furthermore, I see no justification for constraining monetary policy in order to accommodate the Treasury's borrowing plans. Finally, I believe that Congress should make all insured banks, whether members of the system or not, subject to the same reserve requirements.

A much more important source of disagreement on the advisability of establishing guidelines is the lack of consensus on the way in which monetary policy influences economic activity. Typically monetary, fiscal, debt management, and other policy changes take place simultaneously, along with a multitude of "exogenous" nonpolicy changes—all of which influence the economy with varying lags. At any moment it is impossible to say with certainty just what the contribution of monetary policy has been to the end result. It is possible, therefore, for competent economists to hold rather different views about the relative importance of the money stock (variously defined), bank credit, total unborrowed reserves, the monetary base, etc., as factors influencing the ultimate goals. Even if the general idea of guidelines is accepted, there may be disagreement over the selection of an appropriate target. There may also be disagreement about the ability of the Fed to hit whatever target is selected, although I certainly agree with Professor Dewald that there is not a whole lot of room for disagreement on that point. But one should not exaggerate the extent of our ignorance of monetary economics. In my judgment adoption of target growth rates for any of the variables just listed would probably give better results than we have been getting from monetary policy in recent years.

This leads us to the third source of disagreement—the likely obsolescence of any monetary rule. I have called this a red herring because those advocating guidelines have always recognized the desirability of continuous appraisal of results and the possibility of occasional modifications when the results turn out to be negative. Several years ago I suggested a mechanical device for imparting some flexibility into the monetary growth rule by making the growth rate of money depend on a moving average (say over a 15-year period) of past growth rates in real output and in the velocity of circulation of money. Perhaps a more sensible procedure would simply be an annual review of the guidelines to determine whether they need revision. Of course, the spirit of the whole guideline approach would be violated by sudden revisions of a substantial magnitude but this would in no way preclude a high degree of flexibility in the long run.

I turn now to Representative Reuss' suggestion that the Fed keep monetary growth (money defined narrowly) within guidelines of 3 to 5 percent per year. I think this is a reasonable suggestion and one that would achieve better results over the long haul than those we have attained in the last decade or so.

My only criticism is of the loopholes Representative Reuss has created by design. I have no quarrel with the idea of allowing for changes in the relative importance of time deposits and other liquid assets so long as this is restricted to taking account of what seem to be longrun trends. However, if we are convinced that the demand for money is highly sensitive to variations in yields on these assets, then the solution would be to expand the scope of our monetary target to include them. Similarly, I am skeptical of the value of Representative Reuss' second and third qualifications, which would permit suspension of the guidelines during slack and inflationary periods and during periods when businesses "are making exceptionally heavy demands on credit" in order to replenish liquidity. What we know about lags in the effect of monetary policy suggests that these deviations from the guideline would be ill advised.

The next three qualifications seem to be especially questionable. The fourth, relating to the accommodation of cost-plus inflation, would guarantee a secular rise in the price level. The basic reason why cost-plus inflation has been such a minor problem in the U.S. economy has been the unwillingness of the Fed to underwrite "excessive" wage increases through monetary expansion. With respect to the accommodation of the Treasury, I see no reason why the Federal debt should be managed in such a way that large indigestible blocks of debt must from time to time be refunded, with the tacit cooperation of the Fed. A more even spacing of maturities over a long time span would obviate any special function for the Fed in aiding debt management. With respect to the balance of payments, I certainly share Mr. Reuss' dislike for subjecting the domestic economy to monetary change because of balance of payments problems. However, I believe he is much too optimistic about what can be accomplished through strategies such as "Operation Twist." Ultimately it will turn out that monetary policy can ignore the balance of payments only if exchange rate variations are used as an equilibrating device. This is an expedient I am quite content to see us follow, especially if "exchange variability" means a regime of floating rates.

Finally, I think it would be most unwise for the Fed to engage in open market operations in obligations of the FNMA and the FHLB's. Down this path, it seems to me, there is a real danger lurking—that gradually the Fed will be drawn into all sorts of overt interferences with the free market in order to "improve" the allocation of resources. The Fed already has too many responsibilities— for example, regulation of bank holding companies and administration of "voluntary guidelines" for bank loans to foreigners—to permit devotion of its best efforts toward achievement of our ultimate goal; it should not be encumbered with this additional duty. Moreover, in my judgment the difficulties that beset savings institutions and the housing industry in 1966 were in part unique events that are not apt to be repeated and in part the result of the absence of monetary rules in 1965 and 1966 of the very sort Mr. Reuss is proposing. In my opinion the credit crunch was a result mainly of excessive monetary growth, well above 5 percent per year, during the 18 months or so prior to the summer of 1966.

I should like to close by making a few observations on the Federal Reserve Board staff comments on Representative Reuss' proposed guidelines. At the top of page 2 it is stated that "the Federal Reserve should be chary of rules that seek to specify, once and for all, what growth of money over the long run is appropriate." Of course, but that is hardly the issue. The problem that the guidelines are aimed at is excessive *short-run* variations in money, as in 1965–67. The guidelines could be adjusted gradually to take care of long-run changes in the demand for money.

The illustration of dire consequences that may result from adoption of a monetary rule given on pages 2–3 of the comment also is not very convincing. One can always select time periods that are congenial to a particular point of view; calculation of growth trends in money over the period 1947–67 is highly misleading. Suppose, for example, that the Fed staff had taken 30-year trends instead of 20 years. I have not bothered to make the computations but it is clear that a rather different picture would emerge. And as stated in the preceding paragraph, there is no reason why the guideline could not be adjusted gradually to conform more accurately to the growth trends in output and velocity.

The Fed staff has rightly criticized Mr. Reuss' recommendation that monetary growth be accelerated during periods of cost-plus inflation. Identifying such periods is an extremely tricky business and certainly could not be done quickly enough to assure reasonable results, even in the absence of significant monetary lags.

Most of the remainder of the Federal Reserve Board staff comment deals with the specific qualifications that Mr. Reuss has built into his proposed guidelines. In general I find myself in agreement with the positions taken by the staff.

In summary, I would like to state my recommendations with respect to the guidelines issue. I certainly would oppose any attempt to set up a rigid x percent per year guideline for all future monetary growth. At the same time I feel strongly that the U.S. economy has been subjected to excessive fluctuations in the growth of money and bank credit, in the recent as well as more distant past, and I would welcome adoption by the Fed of a 3 to 5 percent per year guideline—without the loopholes contained in Mr. Reuss' proposal. In addition I would like to see a willingness on the part of the Federal Open Market Committee to announce exact growth goals in the money stock within the 3- to 5-percent band—for example, 4.6 percent—these targets to be sought over periods of 2 or 3 months. There would, of course, be random weekly deviatons from the desired trend but the public would not mistakenly interpret these as harbingers of change. The targets could be adjusted at any time, preferably in small steps, and a public announcement to this effect would be made. Hopefully, however, the FOMC would resist the temptation to attempt a fine tuning of the economy as in 1965–67.

ALLAN H. MELTZER

CONTROLLING MONEY

30

Three questions recur frequently in current discussions of monetary policy: (1) Can the Federal Reserve control the stock of money if it chooses to do so? (2) What are some main consequences of choosing the stock of money as opposed to some other variable as the focus of control? (3) Which stock of money can be controlled best; or stated in another way, how should we define and measure the stock of money that is to be controlled?

These questions are distinct from the larger question: Should the stock of money, somehow defined, receive the main attention of policymakers when they seek to translate some broad national or international objective, or combination of objectives—such as balance-of-payments equilibrium, reduced inflation, high level employment of resources—into an operating monetary policy? Although I do not bypass this question completely, in most of my discussion I assume that the larger question has been answered affirmatively and that there is general agreement on the following four propositions.

First, the stock of money is a main—indeed *the* main—objective of monetary policy operations. This statement means either that directives are written or monetary policy actions are judged in terms of some level, change or rate of change of one or another monetary aggregate.

Second, control of the stock of "money" is a means and not an end. Given our limited and uncertain knowledge of the timing and magnitude of the effects of policy changes, the growth rate of the stock of money is used to indicate the effects that are likely to be achieved, at some sequence of dates in the future, as a result of monetary policy operations that have been taken up to the present.

Third, monetary policy is not the only means of achieving the broad national or international objectives mentioned above, although it may be the most important means. Other policy operations (tax and spending decisions or changes in the size of the government deficit, and changes in tastes and opportunities for example) have

Reprinted from Allan H. Meltzer, "Controlling Money," *Review* (May 1969), pp. 16–24, Federal Reserve Bank of St. Louis.

short- or long-term effects on output, employment, prices and interest rates that are independent of the effects on these variables of changes in one or another measure of the stock of money.

Fourth, "money" is used to assess the relative and not the absolute effects of monetary policy. A maintained increase in the growth rate of money is interpreted as a more expansive action; a maintained decrease is interpreted as contractive. The terms "expansive" and "contractive," however, compare the size of monetary changes to the changes that have gone before and not to some absolute or ideal rate of monetary expansion.

The questions posed at the outset, though more narrow and technical, are no less important than the larger question. If the term "money" cannot be defined, money cannot be controlled. Even if there is an acceptable or accepted definition, the decision to control money is said to have unacceptable consequences. Two types of objections to controlling money are generally raised, one broad, the other more narrow and technical. Separating the two permits a far more meaningful discussion of the short-term consequences of monetary policy and gives more precision to the role that money can play and the various ways in which the stock of money can be used as an instrument of monetary policy. In the next section, I comment on several of the issues briefly. Then I discuss some of the more technical problems and in the process, define money and suggest an appropriate role.

SORTING OUT THE ISSUES

Many, if not most, of the criticisms of assigning money a more important role either rest on a misconception or attack a "straw man." The misconception is that any decision to assign a larger role to money means that discretionary monetary policy must be abandoned and replaced by a monetary rule. The attack on the monetary rule—a law of constant monetary growth—is an attack on a straw man because the critics of the rule generally fail to deal with any of the relevant issues. Choices need not be limited to decisions between extreme points. Abandoning the present policy of high variability does not require a move to the other extreme: a constant growth rate.

In this section, I distinguish three separable issues. One is the role assigned to money. A second is the ability to control the stock of money. A third is the ever-important, but often neglected, distinction between nominal and real changes in money and interest rates.

The Role of Money in Monetary Policy

Money may be used as an *indicator*, as a *target*, or as both *indicator* and *target*. Broadly speaking, when money is used as an indicator, changes in the growth rate of the stock of money become the principal means of deciding whether monetary policy is more or less expansive. When money is used as a target, policy decisions are directed toward providing a particular stock or growth rate of money, or perhaps maintaining the growth rate of money within certain limits. The limits within which such policies may be carried out are set by the extent to which money or its growth rate can be controlled. For short-term movements, the degree of control depends very much on the definition of money.

The same problem exists, of course, for any variable chosen as a target. Neither the level of free reserves nor the Treasury bill rate are now controlled completely. The relevant issues here are not whether money or some other variable can be completely controlled, but whether the degree of control exercised by the Federal Reserve is increased or decreased, and the effectiveness of monetary policy in carrying out its assigned tasks enhanced or weakened, by the substitution of some money stock target for some money market target. I return to this subject in a later section, where I suggest an appropriate target and discuss the degree of control.

The use of money as an *indicator* of monetary policy does not presuppose and does not require *any* reduction in the variability of the growth rate of money. In principal and in practice, money can be used as an indicator while the Manager of the System Open Market Account conducts his daily operations in precisely the same way he does now. He can continue to use free reserves, interest rates or money market conditions as his targets. He can offset, or fail to offset, any of the changes in float, currency, or Treasury deposits, that he wishes. Discussion of the appropriate amount of variability in the growth rate of money can and should be separated from the decision to accept money as a reliable indicator of changes in the size of policy operations and of the future effect of policy. Here, the relevant choice is not between a rule and complete discretion but between various indicators that provide more rather than less accurate information about the future effects of policy.

The reason that choosing money as an indicator has no necessary consequence for the variability of the stock of money is recognized in the distinction between so-called defensive and dynamic operations. The Manager can continue to offset money market changes, conduct defensive operations while the Open Market Committee or its staff uses some monetary aggregate to judge the direction in which monetary policy has changed and the future effects of policy operations. If the Open Market Committee decides to make policy less inflationary, the growth rate of the stock of money is reduced. While carrying out the defensive operations, the Manager sells more on balance, and both the Committee and the Manager determine how much to sell by comparing the maintained and desired average growth rates of money.

The question arises as to whether this minimal step is feasible. Can money be used as an indicator even if daily operations are conducted with as much variability as in the recent past? The answer seems obvious. Those who used money as an indicator in recent years correctly predicted the inflation of 1966, the slowing of economic activity in 1967, the renewed inflation in 1967 and the increased rate of inflation in 1968. Despite the high variability of the monetary growth rate, it was possible to predict the longer-term consequences of monetary policy with reasonable accuracy. Since some of the predictions were made at meetings with the Board of Governors and rejected, it seems reasonable to conclude that the Open Market Committee and its staff relied on less accurate indicators. It is hard to avoid the conclusion that monetary policy would have achieved more of the policymakers' announced and frequently repeated aims, if changes in the maintained growth rate of money had been used as an indicator in recent years and in earlier periods as well.

The Ability to Control Money

Critics of the use of money as an indicator of monetary policy delight in pointing out that there is less than unanimous agreement on the most appropriate definition of money. The critics hardly ever mention that there are very few times when it would have made much difference whether one or another of the commonly accepted definitions had been used. The maintained growth rates of currency plus demand deposits and currency plus total deposits—the most common definitions—are almost always in the same direction, and changes in the growth rates generally occur at about the same time. There are very few periods in which the qualitative judgment reached about the future effect of monetary policy depended importantly on the definition chosen. Among the exceptions are several recent periods in which changes in market rates relative to Regulation Q ceiling rates caused large, temporary changes in time deposits and in the relative growth rates of time and demand deposits. In these periods, I believe the narrower definition—currency and demand deposits—generally provided the more accurate indicator.

If policy operations retain their short-term focus and some measure of money replaces market rates or free reserves as a target of the Manager's operations, it becomes important to choose between the various measures. One difficulty in using money (currency and demand deposits) or money plus time deposits as a target of monetary policy is that reliable information is not available daily or even weekly. Another difficulty is that when information becomes available, it is imprecise.

Both of these objections apply to the use of money as a target of monetary policy; neither applies with much force to the use of money as an indicator. Both objections are overcome by choosing the monetary base as a target. The monetary base can be measured, weekly, with greater reliability than some of the operating targets now in use, such as the level of free reserves. Weekly data on the base are now available from the Federal Reserve Bank of St. Louis. If the Manager of the Open Market Committee wishes to combine control of money with defensive operations, the directives written to the Manager should specify a desired change or level of the monetary base.[1]

Evidence from past periods suggests that the monetary base is the most important determinant of the money supply and that there is a high degree of association between the base and the money stock. The degree of association and the extent to which money can be controlled by controlling the base varies with the length of the period. Our analysis suggests that even if policy retains its short-term focus, month to month changes in money can still be kept within a very narrow range. In the past, 85 per cent of the variance of the monthly change in money—currency and demand deposits—resulted from changes in the monetary base and changes in Treasury deposits at commercial banks in the current and previous month. Even in periods of substantial variability in the growth rate of money and sizable defensive operations, monthly changes in money were dominated by current and past changes in the base. The relation between monthly changes in the monetary base and money plus time deposits is not as good. Nevertheless, more than 75 per cent of the variance of the monthly changes in this mone-

[1] In a later section and in Table II, I compare the information required to control the monetary base to the information now collected daily at the Federal Reserve Bank of New York.

TABLE I   Correlations Between Monthly Changes in "Money" and Some Explanatory Variables

Time period	Definition of money	Explanatory variables and their coefficients (constant term omitted)	R^2
March 1947 to March 1965	ΔM_1	$2.38\ \Delta B_t - .85\ \Delta D_t$ $(24.6) \qquad (-18.0)$	.80
	ΔM_1	$2.23\ \Delta B_t - .74\ \Delta D_t + .78\ \Delta B_{t-1} - .02\ \Delta D_t$ $(26.0) \qquad (-17.3) \qquad (8.84) \qquad (-.58)$	.86
	ΔM_2	$2.15\ \Delta B_t - .82\ \Delta D_t$ $(17.7) \qquad (-14.2)$	.70
	ΔM_2	$1.98\ \Delta B_t - .70\ \Delta D_t + .91\ \Delta B_{t-1} - .05\ \Delta D_{t-1}$ $(18.3) \qquad (-13.0) \qquad (8.15) \qquad (-.86)$	.77
Feb. 1947 to Dec. 1964	ΔM_1	$1.39\ \Delta B_t$ and 11 dummy variables to (5.88) adjust for seasonal variation	.80

Explanation of symbols
ΔM_1 = Monthly Change in Currency and Demand Deposits.
ΔM_2 = Monthly Change in Currency and Total Deposits.
ΔB_t = Monthly Change in Monetary Base.
ΔD_t = Monthly Change in Deposits of the Treasury at Commercial Banks.
NOTE: "t" statistics are in parentheses. None of the data were seasonally adjusted.

tary aggregate can be controlled by using the base as a target and estimating Treasury deposits as accurately as in the past. Table I shows some of the evidence on which these conclusions are based, giving the correlations between money and some explanatory variables.

A related but very different argument raised against the use of any monetary aggregate is that, even if these variables can be measured accurately and promptly, they cannot be controlled. Changes in the composition of deposits between demand and time account, changes in the composition of money between currency and deposits, gold flows and changes in the proportion of deposits held by foreigners are cited as sources of changes in the monetary base or the stock of money that are not controlled and are said to be outside the control of the Federal Reserve. Since the evidence cited above (and a substantial body of additional evidence) makes clear that if the Federal Reserve controls the size of changes in the monetary base, it controls by far the larger portion of the changes in the stock of money, I shall discuss this argument with reference to the monetary base and compare the degree of control over the base to the control of short-term market rates or free reserves.

To a very large extent, arguments suggesting that the base cannot be controlled are a play on the use of the word "control" that fail to separate short- and long-term changes and do not distinguish between the sources and the uses of the base. The problem of controlling short-term changes arise whether the Committee uses free reserves or the monetary base (or almost any variable worth mentioning) as the target of monetary policy. The reason is that monthly or weekly changes in both free reserves and the monetary base are the result of (1) actions taken by the Manager, for example, purchases and sales of securities (2) changes resulting from market forces that the Manager observes, but chooses not to offset, and (3) changes that are unforseen because of errors in reporting or errors of measurement. I see no point in describing the changes that the Manager makes as "controlled" and the changes he permits as "uncontrolled." The more relevant question is the extent to which the Manager has more accurate and reliable information, within a given time span following the change, about one target variable rather than another. As I indicated, the weekly change in the monetary base can be known more reliably than the weekly change in free reserves. This is one important reason for choosing the base as a target. I return to this point below.

Whether the target variable is the level of free reserves, the short-term market interest rate or the monetary base, changes in the target during any period are the result of both current and past policy and nonpolicy changes. Suppose a policy of reducing the rate of inflation is translated into a policy target of forcing or permitting higher market interest rates or a lower growth rate of the monetary base. If the policy is maintained and begins to take effect, weeks or months after the policy is initiated the inflow of gold or foreign exchange rises, and with fixed ceiling rates of interest paid on time deposits, time deposits decline relative to demand deposits. Gold is a source of base money, so the inflow of gold raises the base and lowers market interest rates; the redistribution of deposits from time to demand accounts raises the weighted average reserve requirement ratio, lowers the base, and raises interest rates. There is no reason to expect these effects to occur at the same time, to be offsetting on any particular day or over any particular span, or to cancel the effects of changes in tastes, opportunities, and actual or expected rates of inflation. Nor is cancellation essential for the conduct of monetary policy.

The Committee and the Manager require: (1) an accurate estimate of the size of the current change in the target variable (the base or interest rates, or free reserves); (2) a clear idea of the desired value of the target variable; and (3) an ability to translate the longer-term goals of monetary policy into a desired current value of the target and to translate changes in the target into changes in the rate of inflation, level of employment, or balance of payments.

The crucial problem in the example, as in practice, is not one of measuring the so-called noncontrolled changes in the target but of deciding how large the change in the target should be to achieve longer-term objectives. The Federal Reserve can observe and record current changes in the base, free reserves, or short-term interest rates shortly after they occur. If they could translate these changes into future levels of employment and rates of inflation, they could decide how much to buy or sell to achieve the level of interest rates, free reserves or base that are consistent with the long-term aims of economic policy. The difficult problem is not the measurement of short-term changes but the interpretation of these changes—for example, knowing whether a given level or change in market interest rates is too low or too high, too large or too small, to prevent inflation or unemployment.

I see no way of resolving this problem, given the present or forseeable future state of knowledge, other than by choosing a reliable and readily available *indicator* of the future effect of policy. The reason is well known: the effect of current changes in policy on output, prices and the balance of payments are not observable for months and in some cases are not recognized for years. Equally important, errors generally cannot be offset or reversed without forcing large and sudden changes in policy that have destabilizing effects. There is, perhaps, little reason to dwell on this point. Too many of the current problems of monetary policy are now recognized as the result of errors in judging the expected effects of past policies or justifiable fears of the consequences of suddenly reversing previous policies.

The above discussion should not suggest that the choice of the target is a subsidiary and unimportant matter. The choice depends very much on the information reliably possessed and the ability to measure, control and interpret short-term changes. My remarks are misread if they appear to downgrade the problem or to suggest that one target is as useful as another. They should be read instead as an attempt to sort out some of the meanings of "controlling money."

In discussing the meaning of "control," I found it useful to make three distinctions. One is the degree to which monetary aggregates can be measured and manipulated during a particular time span. The monetary base can be controlled weekly and perhaps daily with as much accuracy as other variables now used as targets. In the past, we have found that most of the monthly changes in money can be controlled by controlling the monetary base. The base is, therefore, a more useful target than the stock of money (or other monetary aggregates) if policy retains its short-term focus. A second distinction is between controlled and noncontrolled changes in a target variable (such as the base) and the degree to which controlled changes can be used to offset the changes resulting from past policy and nonpolicy decisions. A third is the distinction between measuring the change in a target variable and interpreting the change. By controlling the growth rate of the base the Federal Reserve can contain the short-term growth rate of money within narrow limits. Since the stock of money is a useful and reliable indicator of changes in the thrust of monetary policy, I believe the Federal Reserve should use the stock of money—currency and demand deposits—as an indicator.

To this point, I have discussed the ability of the central bank to use monetary aggregates as useful targets and reliable indicators of monetary policy and to offset the effects of past policy changes and noncontrolled changes on current nominal values of the monetary base, money, market interest rates or free reserves. The Federal Reserve, and any other modern central bank, can offset and hence control the size of current changes in free reserves, short-term market interest rates or the monetary base, and to a very large extent can determine the size of changes in money if it chooses to do so. However, there is a very important sense in which a central bank cannot control either money or interest rates. To discuss this meaning of control, we need an additional distinction—the distinction between nominal and real changes in money and interest rates.

Nominal and Real Changes

Perhaps the oldest and best established proposition in monetary theory states that the government or central bank controls the nominal stock of money while the public decides on the price level at which it willingly holds the nominal stock. In our day, the nominal stock is the amount of currency and demand deposits issued by commercial banks and Federal Reserve banks. The real stock of money is the nominal amount deflated by some representative index of prices.

The distinction between nominal and real applies with equal force to every monetary aggregate and to interest rates as well. To compute the real rate of interest from the norminal or market rate, we have to subtract the *anticipated* rate of price change. One major problem in interpreting changes in market interest rates and using levels or changes in market rates as indicators of monetary policy is separating the effects of anticipations from other forces affecting market rates. Without reliable estimates of the anticipated rate of price change, it is impossible to interpret changes in market rates or to use market rates as indicators of monetary policy. Recent monetary history suggests the type of error that is likely to be made if high or rising market interest rates are interpreted as a sign of restrictive, anti-inflationary policy. The same or opposite error has been repeated throughout monetary history.

Just as the Federal Reserve cannot control the value of real money balances, it cannot control the long-run market rate of interest. A brief description of some links between money, interest rates, actual and anticipated price changes may explain the reasons.

Let the Federal Reserve increase the growth rate of the nominal stock of money. Initially market interest rates fall, but the initial reduction is temporary and is followed by a rise in market interest rates as consumers and business attempt to borrow more so as to accumulate inventories and increase expenditures. The Federal Reserve can, if it chooses, increase the amount of open market purchases and more than offset the rise in market rates resulting from the increased demand for loans and increased expenditures. However, with technology and real resources fixed or changing more slowly than the quantity of money, the continued expansion in the public's expenditures causes prices to rise.

If the higher growth rate of money is maintained, eventually consumers and businessmen are confronted with frequent announcements of price increases. They are led to examine the prices they charge for the goods or services they sell and to consider whether their prices should be adjusted upward. Gradually, they learn to anticipate price increases.

Individuals and businessmen attempt to protect themselves against the consequences of inflation or to profit from those consequences. They sell bonds and spend money to reduce their holdings of claims fixed in nominal value. They seek to borrow to increase liabilities with fixed nominal values. They switch, at the margin, from assets with fixed nominal value to assets that rise in price during inflation.

All these responses can be summarized by saying that if the Federal Reserve maintains the higher rate of increase in the nominal stock of money, markey interest rates rise with the spreading anticipation of future inflation. To maintain the previously prevailing market rate, the Federal Reserve must supply an ever-increasing amount of base money and permit the money supply to increase at an increasing rate. Attempts to lower or maintain the market rate however, implant the anticipation of inflation more firmly and force still higher actual and anticipated rates of inflation.

The process I have described as an adjustment of nominal rates could be described just as well as an attempt by moneyholders to reduce the amount of money they hold. As before, the attempt causes prices to rise and, as prices rise, the real amount of money corresponding to any nominal stock falls. Attempts to maintain the higher growth rate of money eventually produce a higher actual and anticipated rate of inflation and a higner market rate of interest. If tastes and productive opportunities reman unchanged, equilibrium is restored when the public is willing to hold an unchanged real amount of money at the higher market rate of interest.

One frequently repeated form of the argument just made confuses the Federal Reserve's inability to control the long-run real value of the stock of money with an inability to control the nominal amount of money if exchange rates are fixed. This line of reasoning starts by showing that among the consequences of the inflationary increase in the nominal stock of money (or reduction in market interest rates) are increases in imports and declines in exports, an increased deficit in the balance of payments. The (increased) deficit on current account causes an outflow of gold that reduces the nominal stock of money and raises market interest rates. This portion of the argument is correct. However, the Federal Reserve can offset or more than offset the effect of the gold outflow on money and interest rates, if it chooses to do so. In the past decade, we have elected to raise the growth rate of the stock of money in an attempt to hold market interest rates below the level they would have reached in the absence of inflationary monetary policies. Gold outflows have not prevented the Federal Reserve from maintaining one of the highest rates of monetary expansion in United States history.

If foreign countries inflate at a slower rate than the U. S., one ultimate consequence of our higher rate of inflation is a change in the dollar price of gold or in the fixed exchange rate system. Neither these consequences nor the outflow of gold should suggest that the Federal Reserve is unable to control the nominal stock of money. On the contrary, inflation and the balance of payments deficit are consequences of the system of fixed exchange rates and of an over-production of nominal money—production of more nominal money than the public is willing to absorb at the anticipated rate of price change. The public's ability to reduce its holdings of real money balances, not the inability of the Federal Reserve to control the nominal stock, should be seen as the means by which excessive expansion of nominal money is translated into inflation and a balance-of-payments deficit.

A related argument is used to suggest that the stock of money cannot be controlled because an increase in money or its growth rate reduces interest rates and causes a short-term capital outflow. I have dealt with one part of the argument above and suggested that the Account Manager can observe the outflow and offset the effect on interest rates or money, if the Committee desires to do so. Public policy may dictate that open market operations be used to offset the gold outflow or prevent it. The latter decision should not be confused, however, with an inability to control the nominal stock of money since the identical problem arises whether the Federal Reserve uses money, interest rates or some other variable as an indicator or target of monetary policy. The core of the problem is a conflict between a relatively high rate of inflation (or deflation) and a fixed exchange rate. At the present time, conflicts of this kind are of little practical importance, since policies designed to reduce the rate of inflation would help to maintain the prevailing exchange rate.

TECHNICALITIES AND TECHNIQUES

Several of the arguments I discussed in the previous section reflect a lack of understanding of the means by which the monetary base can be manipulated to control the stock of money. In this section, I first discuss the sources and uses of the base, pointing out the information available to the Manager and comparing the available information on sources of the base to the information now collected on the sources of free reserves. Then I discuss, briefly, the validity of some of the criticisms of the use of money in monetary control.

Data on Sources and Uses

The data for computing the monetary base is obtained from the table "Member Bank Reserves, Reserve Bank Credit, and Related Items" in the Federal Reserve *Bulletin*. The table also serves as the basis for computing free reserves and other reserve measures. There is, therefore, a similarity about the basic input data used for the computation of the base and other measures of reserves. Many of the computational differences result from the way items are grouped or classified. Table II compares the components of the base to the components of free reserves.

TABLE II   Sources and Uses of Free Reserves and the Monetary Base
(*illustrative calculation—in billions of dollars*)

SOURCES	Monetary base	Free reserves
Factors supplying sources		
Reserve bank credit net of discounts and advances	55.0	55.0
Reserve adjustment (cumulated sum of reserves liberated by reserve requirement changes)	4.8	—
Discounts and advances	0.8	—
Gold stock	10.4	10.4
Treasury currency outstanding	6.8	6.8
Total factors supplying sources	77.8	72.2
Factors absorbing sources		
Treasury cash	0.8	0.8
Treasury deposits at Federal Reserve	0.6	0.6
Foreign and other deposits	0.6	0.6
Other Federal Reserve accounts	−0.8	−0.9
Required reserves	—	27.1
Currency in circulation	—	49.2
Less currency held as reserve	—	−4.6
Total factors absorbing sources	1.2	72.8
Total sources (factors supplying sources minus factors absorbing sources)	76.6	−0.6
USES		
Reserve adjustment (cumulated sum of reserves liberated by reserve requirement changes)	4.8	—
Total reserves	22.6	—
Currency in circulation	49.2	—
Excess reserves	—	0.2
Less discounts and advances	—	−0.8
Total uses	76.6	−0.6

The *uses* of the base are bank reserves plus total currency held by the public and by nonmember banks plus the amount of reserves liberated or impounded by changes in reserve requirements or redistributions of deposits between classes of banks. Accurate weekly estimates of each of these uses are not available directly. A more reliable method is to compute the sum of the *sources* of base money;

the sum of the sources is, of course, equal to the uses and can be computed daily or weekly from the information now collected at the Federal Reserve Bank of New York. As Table II shows, there are two main differences between the computations now prepared and the data required to compute the base. One is the way in which the items are combined. The other is that the estimates of a few items such as excess reserves and vault cash held by banks are not required for the computation of the base. Computation of these two important sources of error can be eliminated.

Instability of Interest Rates

One of the main arguments against controlling the stock of money is that variability of interest rates would increase—that interest rates would be "unstable." This is not a necessary consequence of the use of money as an indicator or the use of the monetary base as a target. As I noted earlier, the use of money as an indicator of monetary policy and the use of the base as a target should not be confused with acceptance of a monetary rule.

There are several strands to the argument and I attempt to deal with the most common versions. One version concerns the usefulness of defensive operations. This is an issue that is best resolved by measuring, or attempting to assess, the cost and benefits of more rather than less variability in money. However, the decision about variability is independent of the decision to control money. Any of the defensive operations that the Manager now undertakes to smooth market interest rates can be carried out just as effectively if the base is the target and the stock of money is the indicator.[2]

A second version concerns the level around which interest rates fluctuate. Again, this has little to do with the decision to control money rather than interest rates. The level of market interest rates, or the average around which rates fluctuate during any three- or six-month period, is determined—in the one case as in the other—by a combination of market forces and policy decisions.

However, there is one important reason to expect a change in the average level of market interest rates if money replaces interest rates as an indicator of monetary policy. Since money is a more accurate

---

[2] This leaves aside the desirability of these operations or the desirability of these operations or the desirability of institutional changes that would remove some of the sources of instability. Recent practice has been to make institutional arrangements more complex and thus adds to the variability.

indicator, the Federal Reserve obtains a more accurate assessment of the thrust of current policy. It avoids misinterpretations of policy that cause acceleration or deceleration of prices and eventually large changes in the anticipated rate of inflation or deflation. Recent policy provides an example. The highest rates in a century are in part a result of misinterpreting the trust of monetary policy. If money had been used as an indicator, policy—guided by this indicator— would have been less inflationary; the high rates would have been avoided; the average market rate would have been lower, and monetary policy would have contributed more to economic stability and less to inflation.

A basic error lies behind the notion that the average level of interest rates would change if money replaced interest rates as the indicator. The source of the error is the belief that the Federal Reserve is able to control market interest rates, and the cause of the error is the neglect of the role of changes in the actual and anticipated rate of price change in the determination of market interest rates. There is no reason to doubt the Federal Reserve's ability to reduce or increase the level market interest rates temporarily. However, there is also no reason to believe that the Federal Reserve can maintain rates above or below their equilibrium level, if it is unwilling to produce an ever-increasing rate of inflation or deflation. As before, it is important to recognize the roles of anticipations in the determination of market rates and to separate nominal and real changes.

A third issue requires a distinction between the size of interest rate changes and the time rate of change. Many of the fears of market participants and Treasury department officials reflect concern about the size of cyclical or monthly changes in interest rates. On closer examination, the focus of the concern is on the effects of large changes in interest rates during periods of Treasury (or private) financing.

As before, there is incompatibility between the use of money as an indicator, the use of the monetary base as a target, and the maintenance of defensive operations. The critical question is whether defensive operations and so-called "even keel" policies designed to assist the Treasury to sell debt issues should be permitted to interfere with the attainment of longer-term aims of monetary policy. In the recent past, the base money supplied during periods of even keel has remained in the system and has been used to produce the increases in money that have maintained or increased the rate of inflation.

CONCLUSION

The main practical issues about controlling money concern the role or roles assigned to money, the speed with which information on monetary aggregates becomes available, the degree to which unforeseen or unanticipated changes in monetary aggregates can be offset and the extent to which monetary aggregates can be controlled during short and longer time spans. By discussing these issues and avoiding the more abstract discussion of rules, I was able to compare some operating consequences of controlling money to the results of present policies which are based on control of interest rates and money market variables.

As in previous work with Karl Brunner, I distinguished between the role of money as an indicator, or measure of the thrust of monetary policy, and as a target of monetary operations. As an indicator, money provides a relatively accurate measure of changes in the degree to which monetary policy has become more or less expansive. Used as a target, money becomes the variable that the Manager attempts to control when carrying out the policies agreed upon by the Open Market Committee. Unlike previous work and despite my own predilections, I assumed, throughout, that defensive operations would be retained, that the short-term focus of policy operations would continue, and that the principal difference between future and past policies would be the use of monetary aggregates in place of free reserves and interest rates.

My main recommendations can be summarized succinctly. The Federal Reserve should translate the longer-term goals of monetary policy into a desired growth rate of money, defined as currency and demand deposits. The growth rate of the stock of money is then used as the indicator of monetary policy. The desired growth rate of money is translated in turn into a desired growth rate of the monetary base and a desired weekly or daily change in the monetary base. The Manager is instructed to obtain the target change or rate of change of the base.

The Committee is able to audit the Manager's performance by observing the change or rate of change in the base. More importantly, the Committee is able to assess the extent to which monetary policy is too expansive or too contractive by observing the size of changes in the indicator, the growth rate of money, and can change the degree to which monetary policy is expansive by changing the rate of change of the base. Nothing in the proposal requires the Federal Reserve to adopt a rule as a condition of controlling money.

The desirable size and frequency of changes in money can and should be separated from the use of money as an indicator.

Since the Manager can control changes in the base more accurately than he now controls money market variables such as free reserves, there is no difficulty in using the base as a target. Data from past periods suggest that by controlling changes in the base and obtaining estimates of the change in Treasury deposits at commercial banks, the Federal Reserve is able to control more than 85 percent of the monthly changes in money.

Past policy errors were very often the result of misinterpretations of the effect of policy and reliance on misleading indicators. Acceptance of a more reliable indicator and more appropriate target can go a long way toward improving the conduct of monetary policy and avoiding some of the more serious errors of the past.

MONETARY
AND
FISCAL
STABILIZATION
POLICY

PART V

The knowledge gained in Parts III and IV concerning instruments, problems, and controversies of monetary policy can be applied now to monetary and fiscal stabilization policy. That is the purpose of the readings in Part V. The selections are subdivided into two classes: Section A embraces articles primarily devoted to explaining and analyzing the meaning, characteristics, economic implications of inflation and unemployment, and the trade-off (Phillips curve relationship) between price-level stability and unemployment. Section B is comprised of four articles examining the method, relative effectiveness, and appropriate monetary-fiscal policy mix for achieving the economic goals of full employment, reasonable price level stability, and optimum economic growth.

Wallich, in the first article, discusses the objectives of the Employment Act of 1946 (which he interprets to include full employment, reasonable price level stability, optimum economic growth, and balance of payments equilibrium). He pays particular attention to the possibility that some of these objectives may be incompatible. If measures designed to promote one goal impede the attainment of another, a trade-off between the two becomes necessary.

The next article, by Stahl, looks at some measures of price-level instability; that is, measures of inflation and deflation. It explains the nature and recent behavior of the Consumer Price Index (CPI), Wholesale Price Index (WPI), and Implicit Price Index (IPI). The article pointedly illustrates that these indexes do not always move in the same direction nor by the same magnitude; thus, one measure may indicate inflation and another not. Or, what is more likely, one may indicate a higher degree of inflation than another. It is, therefore, a matter of importance which measure the monetary authorities use as their referent of inflation.

Economic effects and types of inflation are examined in the next two articles. An excerpt from the *Staff Report on Employment, Growth, and Price Levels* manifests the effects of inflation on the distribution of income and wealth, and, gives a brief description of various theories of the inflationary process. Martin builds on this foundation with an analysis of cost-push inflation and demand-shift (structural) inflation, and their implications for the effectiveness of monetary policy. The last article, by Spencer, investigates the relationship between inflation and unemployment. He present two views of this relationship, one being the short-run thesis hypothesizing a trade-off between inflation and unemployment. The other view maintains that in the long run the two objectives basically are compatible. He then briefly discusses the policy implications of both views.

Section B contains four articles dealing with the relative effectiveness and appropriate mix of monetary and fiscal policy. Anderson enlarges on the optimum mix of monetary and fiscal policy for economic stabilization. Specifically, he discusses the major considerations involved in the choice of a particular fiscal-monetary mix and the mechanics, problems, and limitations on the effectiveness of changing the policy mix. Like Anderson, Smith is concerned with the relative effectiveness and optimum combination of monetary and fiscal policy. Smith, however, relates his discussion of these points not only to stabilization policy per se, but also to growth policy and the U.S. balance of payments problem. The optimum policy mix for achieving the economic objectives is an important consideration and, as such, deserves much attention. (The nature and problems of the U.S. payments imbalance will be considered in depth in Part VI, International Monetary Relations. At this point it is only necessary to recognize that the appropriate mix of monetary and fiscal policy will be determined partly by the state of a nation's balance of payments.)

Willes investigates another important aspect of government economic policy, the lags in monetary and fiscal policy. He divides the total lag into three parts: a recognition lag, action lag, and lag in effect on economic activity. Willes summarizes various estimates of these lags, then considers the implications they have for public policy. The last article, and one of the more difficult ones in this book, is by Andersen and Jordan, both of the Federal Reserve Bank of St. Louis. They tested the relative importance of monetary and fiscal policies in economic stabilization. The tests were designed to establish whether economic activity responds (1) to a greater degree, (2) more predictably, and/or (3) faster to fiscal policy or to monetary policy. The authors present the results of their tests, then discuss the implications of those results for the relative importance of monetary and fiscal policy in stabilizing the economy.

In this Part, attention is focused on the use of monetary and fiscal policy for domestic stabilization, that is, for achieving full employment, reasonable price level stability, and optimum economic growth. The next Part shifts attention from domestic to international banking and monetary policy. It becomes apparent that, in the present international banking and monetary system, both internal and external stability must be sought actively. Domestic measures must be consistent with external equilibrium.

HENRY C. WALLICH

THE EMPLOYMENT
ACT OBJECTIVES—
AFTER 20 YEARS

31

. . . It is a tribute to a law and to the law's sponsors when 20 years after its passage no voice is raised deploring that event. It is an even greater tribute when, because it has worked well, there is widespread sentiment for strengthening that law. Both kinds of tribute, I believe, the Nation today pays to the Employment Act and those who conceived it.

Credit is due also to American political institutions and processes, and to the men who operate with and through them, for making the Employment Act work. The founding fathers of the act had the wisdom to make it a flexible instrument. The Members of the Congress and successive administrations have taken advantage of that flexibility to adapt the act to ever-changing conditions.

The experience of these changing conditions must be our principal guide to any extension of the act that we may want to contemplate. But before entering upon an analysis of that experience, I would like to examine briefly the elements of flexibility built into the act that have permitted its creative adaptation to changing conditions.

They are to be found in the marching orders of section 2 of the act: "The Congress declares that it is the continuing policy and responsibility of the Federal Government. . . ." The passwords to prosperity there used are "maximum employment, production, and purchasing power." These are not the terms an academic economist might have chosen. Employment and production are largely, though

Reprinted from Henry C. Wallich, "The Employment Act Objectives— After 20 Years," *Twentieth Anniversary of the Employment Act of 1946: An Economic Symposium*, Hearings Before the Joint Economic Committee, 89th Cong., 2d Sess., Feb. 23, 1966, pp. 12–19.

not altogether, coextensive. "Purchasing power" is not a well-defined term. A maximum of three different variables is something at which a mathematician would wince—one cannot stand on three hilltops at once. These three goals, moreover, are tied to the preceding part of the sentence in a manner that leaves uncertain whether the "continuing policy and responsibility of the Federal Government" is to promote the three goals, unqualifiedly, or whether the Government's policy and responsibility is

to use all practicable means, consistent with its needs and obligations and with other essential considerations of national policy . . . to promote maximum employment, production, and purchasing power.

What I believe to read in this language is a desire of the legislator to see the Government play a larger role in the pursuit of national economic goals. The nature and content of these goals, however, was to some extent left flexible.

Experience has shown the wisdom of this decision. The Government's "needs and obligations and other considerations of national policy . . ." have changed repeatedly since the passage of the act. In 1946, fear of a great postwar depression was the dominant concern. This probably is the reason why price stability, which later became a serious problem, was not specifically mentioned among the objectives. As the avoidance of large-scale unemployment came to be taken for granted, national interest shifted to economic growth. This objective, too, was not mentioned in the act.

Nevertheless, it became customary to integrate the new concerns of price stability and growth into the act by identifying "maximum production" with growth and "maximum purchasing power" with price stability. Employment remained employment. When the economy developed a persistent large balance of payments deficit, the possibility of which had not been anticipated in the days of massive dollar shortage, the policies appropriate for dealing with that problem, too, could be accommodated under "other essential considerations of national policy."

As of today, then, I would say that the specific content that experience has given to the goals of the Employment Act is full employment, growth, price stability, and payments equilibrium. Experience has also taught us something about the compatibility of these goals, and has forced us to decide on priorities.

We cannot have a maximum of everything at once. We therefore must try to establish the tradeoffs among goals; that is, how much of one must be sacrificed to gain a little more of another. This is an empirical question to which objective answers ought to be possible, within reason. We must also ask ourselves, each for himself, how much of one goal is worth sacrificing to get the obtainable amount of another. This is a value judgment on which agreement is unlikely.

Employment and growth are generally judged broadly compatible. Employment could be raised at the expense of growth, to be sure, by inhibiting automation and other productivity advances. But by raising the rate of growth it is always possible to raise also employment, and that is the sensible way to deal with automation.

The principal conflict occurs between employment and growth on one side and price stability and, in some circumstances, payments balance on the other. Economists' efforts to measure the tradeoff involved in trying to reduce unemployment at the expense of inflation have been embodied in the so-called Phillips curve. Estimates made for the American economy are not as firm as those available for the United Kingdom. They seem to show that it would take unemployment well in excess of 4 percent to achieve full stability of the consumer price index or the GNP deflator. The experience of the last few years seems to confirm this.

Personally I am skeptical of the durability of this approach. It seems to rest on the assumption that people will never learn to discount inflation. If labor really continues to believe that a 6 percent wage increase accompanied by 3 percent inflation is more than a 3 percent increase with no inflation, if businessmen continue to believe that the former increase is more costly to give than the latter, then unemployment can be permanently reduced by accepting more inflation. I doubt that people are incurably afflicted with this kind of money illusion.

If inflation can be predicted, it can be discounted. Labor, business, consumers, investors will think in "real" terms; that is, in terms of constant purchasing power. To achieve the same employment effect, inflation would have to be accelerated beyond the expected rate, and when that new rate became expected, more acceleration would be needed. Few people believe that constantly accelerating inflation is a feasible policy. I conclude that the possibility of raising employment by accepting inflation exists only in the short run, until people have caught onto the game. If that is true, the cost of price stability in terms of unemployment is very much lower than is commonly thought. Just how large the level of unemployment compatible with price stability is, and what can be done to lower it, is an important matter to which I shall return presently.

Next, let us contemplate the likewise much publicized conflict between price stability and economic growth. Some see a conflict because they equate growth with pushing employment to very high levels. That is a palpable misinterpretation of the meaning of growth, although a frequent one. Raising the rate at which existing productive capacity is utilized is not growth. True growth consists in increasing productive capacity itself. But a little reflection will show that growth in productive capacity is not closely dependent upon the rate of unemployment.

The principal factors through which a free market promotes growth are investment in plant and equipment, and research leading to technological advance. These are importantly influenced by the rate of growth of demand, by the pressure of demand upon plant and equipment capacity, and by the level of profits, both as incentive and as source of funds. Among these three stimulants to investment and research, the rate of growth of demand and the operating rate of equipment are not dependent upon the level of unemployment. GNP can be rising rapidly at lower as well as at higher rates of unemployment. Demand can press closely on plant and equipment capacity without pressing equally hard on labor capacity. Only profits may be dependent upon the level of unemployment—they are likely to be higher when there is some amount of inflation. But if inflation is of the cost push variety, even that ceases to be probable.

It is clear that heavy unemployment would act as a disincentive to investment and research in many ways. But the issue is not whether heavy unemployment should be tolerated—it obviously should not. The issue is whether growth could be promoted by reducing unemployment to the point where significant inflation occurs. The facts I have cited suggest that growth would benefit little from such policy.

Growth would suffer if inflationary pressures are combated mainly by high interest rates instead of by fiscal restraint. Proper fiscal policy can take us off the horns of this dilemma. I conclude that the conflict of price stability and growth is no deeper, and perhaps less so, than that between price stability and full employment.

Similar conclusions follow when we examine the frequently mentioned antagonism between balance-of-payments equilibrium on one side and full employment and growth on the other. Payments balance requires, broadly speaking, that the United States inflate no faster than other countries. Advocates of high inflation tolerance believe this competition-imposed quasi-stability may be a drag on full employment and growth. Many, therefore, propose flexible exchange rates. My own view, which I would like to note parenthetically, is that flexible rates would get us from the frying pan of payments imbalance into the fire of trade wars, exchange speculation, and accelerated inflation. But, in any event, the dilemma that flexible exchange rates supposedly would solve is itself more apparent than real. If price stability is not, in the long run, severely at odds with full employment and growth, neither is payments equilibrium. Moreover, the price restraint that needs to be applied in order to end a payments deficit is nonrecurring: once domestic prices have become more competitive, we can live happily ever after with a strong balance of payments.

Growth could be hurt by balance-of-payment policies that take the form of high interest rates to restrain capital outflows instead of fundamental improvement in competitiveness. Defensively high interest rates must remain a temporary measure. Aside from this, I believe in the longrun compatibility of payments balance with employment and growth.

It may be surprising to arrive at this happy conclusion about the possibility of peaceful coexistence among our goals, at least in the long run. It should not be. Truly competing objectives are those that make demands upon resources—more investment for growth versus more output for current consumption, moonshot versus poverty programs, public versus private use of resources. Full employment, growth, and price stability are not of this sort. Each moves in a different dimension. A rational society should have no permanent difficulty in reconciling them, though the learning period may be painful.

I have tried to show how the flexibility which the founding fathers introduced into the Employment Act has permitted a reinterpretation of its goals in the light of contemporary needs. Beyond that, I have argued that while there are serious shortrun conflicts among some of the goals that we now read into the act, these conflicts diminish in the long run. Next, I shall proceed to raise questions about the present explicit and implicit goals. Are they adequate as statements of our purposes, or should the act be amended, be it by making implicit goals explicit, or by defining targets more precisely, or by adding new goals?

In undertaking this assessment, I should like first to raise some general questions about the propriety of setting national goals in a democratic society.

There are pitfalls that the goal setter must avoid. First, the goal setter must bear in mind clearly that the Nation is nothing but the sum of its citizens, and that a nation's goals cannot be anything but the totality of their enlightened self-interest. To argue differently is to place democracy itself in jeopardy. For if the citizens' goals do not exhaust the national interest, then there must be somebody who knows better than the citizens what decisions to make. Totalitarian governments exalt the state and its goals against those of its people. A democracy cannot.

Second, the goal setter must remember that his activity involves certain logical perplexities that have never been satisfactorily resolved. It seems fair to demand that the process of democratic decisionmaking meet certain criteria of reasonableness. Yet it has been shown that the process often cannot meet these criteria. In other words, public decisionmaking may either violate democratic standards, or fail to demonstrate that it makes even the majority of voters better off. To illustrate, if three Members of the Congress were to rank the priorities of spending an added $1 billion on the poverty program, the moonshot, and defense, each in different order, there would turn out to be a majority of 2 to 1 favoring the poverty program over the moonshot, the moonshot over defense, and defense over the poverty program.

Finally, even when it is clear that a majority is made better off by implementing a public goal, there is a question how far it can properly go in imposing its will upon the minority. In our system of checks and balances, this question is less serious than in a parliamentary system where even a small majority wields great power while it remains in office. In our system a narrow majority rarely can impose anything very serious upon the minority. The latter can usually bid away enough votes from the other side to block a proposal. Nevertheless, it should give the goal setter pause to think that, as broad goals are reduced to specific decisions, what makes the majority better off makes the minority worse off.

These thoughts, abstract as they are, counsel caution in setting national goals. The need for caution is underscored by the experience of the Employment Act goals. If the goals of maximum employment, production, and purchasing power were taken literally, they would long be out of date. They would have failed to anticipate the problem of inflation, the problem of growth as contrasted with mere "production," and the problem of the balance of payments. Interpreted in this sense, the lesson of experience is that goals date very quickly and that, raised to a high legal pedestal, they will be bypassed by the future. If the goals of the Employment Act are understood symbolically, as I have argued they should be, they demonstrate the virtue of flexibility. The lesson of experience, then, is that this flexibility should be preserved. We should not, by crystallizing the lessons of 20 years, try to freeze the wave of the future.

In addition to these warning signals, however, the lessons of the last 20 years also contain many positive hints. Economic experience does not necessarily lead to economic agnosticism. We have learned much about the goals that are explicit in the act, and about those that are implicit.

About employment we now know, what we did not know in 1946, that it can readily reach a 96-percent level and, what few would have believed then, can reach this level quite possibly without massive budget deficits. There is every reason to think that enough aggregate demand can push unemployment still lower. The experience of continental Europe, if not our own, shows that peace-time economies can achieve less than 1 percent unemployment, although differences in definitions may enter here.

At the same time we have observed, in the course of the past year, that below 5 percent unemployment significant price and wage pressures develop. "Full employment" seems to lie somewhere in the 4- to 5-percent range. As I have argued earlier, the relation between unemployment and prices probably is not a stable one. A small stable rate of inflation will help to keep unemployment down only so long as labor, business, and investors have not learned to discount it. But before this discounting becomes general, there is a trade-off between unemployment and inflation, and we are now discovering what it is.

To improve this trade-off is an urgent policy goal. Two approaches are available: to match the skill structure of the labor force to the skill structure of jobs, by education and retraining, and to modify wage and price setting habits of labor and business through the guideposts or some other form of incomes policy. The subject of policy tools, however, I must leave to other speakers.

In time, we must succeed in reducing the level of "full employment unemployment" well below the 4- to 5-percent range. The experience of 1965 has shown that we cannot do it yet. With our employment goals thus in a state of flux, I conclude that it would not be advisable to write a precise employment target into the Employment Act.

The last 20 years also have taught us something about economic growth. We now know that the rate that has prevailed in the United States for so long as we have data is not easy to speed up. We did not know this during the first fine flurry of growth enthusiasm during the late fifties, when the sky was just an interim goal. We also have learned that we are still quite uncertain about the quantitative effect of particular actions to strengthen investment, research, and education. We know enough to be able to say that measures in these areas will accelerate growth. It would seem entirely reasonable for the voters and the Congress to decide that, in the light of international and domestic needs, we should accelerate growth. We can then adopt particular measures and see how far they take us. But the lessons of experience provide no basis for writing a particular growth rate into the law. We do not know the measures required to reach that rate, and we might not like them once we did know.

On the subject of price stability, the last 20 years have taught us that perfect stability is very hard to achieve. We have also learned that inflation, once it exceeds the 1- to 2-percent rate and becomes widely expected, can be kept from accelerating and reduced to a slower rate only at great cost. Even so, I am unable to share the view that a low rate of inflation, of 1 to 2 percent, is only a minor nuisance and a cheap price to pay for gains in employment and growth that, to boot, I believe to be transitory. A good monetary system is part of our social fabric, like our system of laws. Lack of trust in stable money means lack of trust in all economic relations. It has been well said that an inflationary economy is like a country where nobody speaks the truth.

A government that inflates while professing to aim at stability, thus denying its people the opportunity to anticipate inflation correctly, may be acting in their interest in terms of employment and growth. But if such benevolent deceit is justified in economic matters, why not also in matters of war and peace, or any other? I prefer truth.

Our balance-of-payments experience of the last 8 years has taught us another lesson about inflation. If the international value of the dollar is to be maintained, and all that goes with it economically, politically, and militarily, we must keep our international payments in balance and hence inflation under control.

Payments equilibrium has become a major objective of policy in its own right. I see no escape from it through flexible rates. It is the only objective where a fairly precise target must be achieved. We can choose our way of achieving balance, beyond the deficit justified by amount of dollars the world wants, by exporting more, or investing less, or by borrowing abroad. But we cannot afford to run out of international reserves.

Since stable prices as a goal can be found in the Employment Act only by interpretation, and payments balance only under the catchall "needs and obligations and other essential considerations of national policy," there is a good case for writing both into the act. I would favor this amendment. However, I doubt that, up to the present, inflation and the payments deficit would have been fought any less energetically had the two new goals always been set forth clearly in the act. To amend the act, therefore, would not mean much without a new resolve on the part of the people and the Congress to hold the line hereafter.

Inclusion of price stability and payments balance would advance the Employment Act in a direction that strikes me as desirable: toward more qualitative goals. I use the term not in contrast to target goals, but as focusing on the content rather than the amount of things. The basic English of the Employment Act is heavily quantitative: a maximum of everything. But employment, too, has qualitative aspects. A job is not only a source of income, but the foundation of human dignity. Stability and balance, which a poet once equated, are qualitative concepts. As we become richer, it seems increasingly appropriate to concern ourselves not only with "how much?" but also with "how good?" The Great Society programs are designed largely to improve our life qualitatively as well as quantitatively—through medicare, education, the ending of poverty, pollution control, a more beautiful America. In time, I expect, our goals will become more social and less purely economic. As new aspirations acquire the status of national goals, they should be given greater force by embodiment in the Employment Act. Legislative pronouncements will have to reflect a broadly felt need, however, if they are to amount to more than economic New Year's resolutions.

Economists can play an important role in the evolution of our goals. Economics is a discipline that seeks to trace farflung interdependencies, remote often in point of impact as well as in time. If these lead to conclusions sometimes beyond the borders of economics, they are nevertheless worth following up. There are no disciplinary boundaries in national legislation.

Economists can render the best service to the evolution of our goals if we take advantage of these potentialities of our discipline. This means to emphasize more strongly the long-run effects of our recommendations. The short-run effects usually are sufficiently obvious to be visible without benefit of economic advice. We need not be dismayed by the retort that in the long run we are all dead, or that the long run unfortunately is a succession of short runs. It is equally true that most short-run problems are the long-run consequence of something that was done years ago.

Knowing that in economics everything depends on everything else, we should beware of the simple solutions to which human sympathies make us prone. We ought to know better than to say "there ought to be a law" in the face of every malfunctioning of markets and institutions. The cost of simple and direct solutions through government intervention may be felt in complex and indirect ways. The malfunctioning that arouses us often is the consequence of the simple and direct solution given to some other problem. And as representatives of a discipline that once prided itself upon having pulled away the "veil of money" that obscures real economic relationships, perhaps we should be more hesitant in proposing the creation of a little more money as the standard solution for all problems.

The first 20 years of the Employment Act have given economists an unprecedented opportunity to place themselves at the service of the community. The experience, I believe, has been mutually beneficial, as transactions in free markets are supposed to be. Both sides can do even better during the next twenty.

SHELDON W. STAHL

A LOOK AT
SOME MEASURES
OF INFLATION

32

Inflation is a term which has been, and continues to be, subject to a variety of interpretations. Even a casual observer of the current economic advance since it got underway early in 1961 would have seen or heard numerous references made to one or another kind of inflation. A considerable segment of the literature devoted to an appraisal of the economic outlook stresses the danger of growing "cost-push" inflation as a consequence of diminished productivity gains combined with aggressive wage demands. Coming at a time when the forward pace of the economy has slowed perceptibly, this is in contrast to "demand-pull" inflationary pressures generated when the level of aggregate demand exceeds the real output capabilities of the economy. However, in both instances the causative dimensions of inflation, rather than inflation itself, have been described. Inflation is the result of demand and/or cost pressures which force the general level of prices to rise. It is inflation in this

Reprinted from Sheldon W. Stahl, "A Look at Some Measures of Inflation," *Monthly Review* (March-April 1967), pp. 11–18, Federal Reserve Bank of Kansas City.

latter sense—price inflation—that is the focal point of concern in this article.

To be sure, while a rise in the general level of prices is necessary to define the existence of inflation, it is not necessarily a sufficient condition to identify or label inflation. Not even the pervasiveness of price increases should, at all times, warrant concern that every upward movement in the price level is evidence of inflation. For example, it is not uncommon for widespread price increases to occur during the recovery phase of a business cycle. However, the mere reversal of earlier cyclical price declines is not generally thought of as a manifestation of inflation. The current economic advance witnessed substantial increases in the prices of certain nonferrous metals, livestock, hides, and skins. In each of these instances, the increases were of sufficient magnitude to yield a rise in the general level of prices, yet the forces which triggered these price increases stemmed from limitations on supply or strong export demand which frequently were unrelated to cyclical factors or to the prevailing level of economic activity.

Despite these precautionary remarks regarding judgments on the presence or absence of inflation, there is some basis for concern over the problem of inflation. The recovery phase of this expansion is far behind and the current economic advance has entered its seventh year. Resource utilization rates are at relatively high levels and the general rise in prices which occurred in 1966 cannot be dismissed simply as an aberration. This concern was expressed in the 1967 *Economic Report of the President*[1] which stressed the importance of restoring price stability through such means as prudent fiscal and monetary policies, by governmental action to relieve key pressure points on prices, and by responsible action on the part of both business and labor in arriving at wage and price decisions.

The courses of action noted above are an integral part of what may be termed economic policy. Such policy—private or public—depends for its success upon the quality, comprehensiveness, and timeliness of the data used in its formulation. In attempting to deal with inflation, perhaps no series of data is of greater importance than the indexes used to measure price changes and price trends. Probably the three major indexes used for this purpose are the Consumer Price Index (CPI), the Wholesale Price Index (WPI), and the Implicit Price Index (IPI)—also known as the Gross National Product Deflator.

Chart 1 traces the course of these indexes from 1958 through

[1] *Economic Report of the President* (Washington, D.C.: U. S. Government Printing Office, 1967).

CHART 1   Major Measures of Price Change

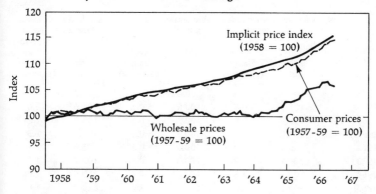

SOURCE: U.S. Department of Labor, Bureau of Labor Statistics; and U.S. Department of Commerce.

1966. It can be seen that the evidence of inflation—at least from 1958 through 1964—is far from uniform, while developments during 1965 and 1966 still leave a number of questions regarding inflation unresolved. The behavior of the WPI during the 1958–64 period would provide very little corroboration for the charge of inflation; however, both the CPI and IPI were marked by persistent rises throughout those 7 years. Thus, the relevant evidence of inflation for this period would depend on the particular index chosen— even if one ignored the matter of what rate of annual price increase constituted inflation.

Table 1 quantifies the index changes shown in Chart 1 and, additionally, separates the 1958–66 period into two subperiods. During 1958–64, the WPI advanced only .1 per cent, and the index actually recorded declines in 1961 and 1963. In contrast, the CPI and IPI showed aggregate increases of 7.3 per cent and 8.9 per cent, respectively. The average annual increase in the CPI was 1.2 per cent, while the IPI rose at an average rate of 1.4 per cent. For the period 1964–66, however, all three indexes not only moved in the same direction, but the WPI outpaced both the CPI and the IPI. The aggregate gain in wholesale prices was 5.3 per cent, versus 4.6 per cent and 4.9 per cent, respectively, for the other two indexes. During this same period, the annual rate of increase in consumer prices doubled and that of the IPI increased by about two thirds.

In face of the nearly parallel over-all performance by the three major price indexes in 1965 and 1966, it might seem moot to consider the question of whether the United States recently has been

TABLE 1   Major Price Index Changes, 1958–1966

	Consumer price index (all items)		Wholesale price index (all commodities)		Implicit price index (for total GNP)	
	1957-59= 100	Year-to-year change (per cent)	1957-59= 100	Year-to-year change (per cent)	1958= 100	Year-to-year change (per cent)
1958	100.7	—	100.4	—	100.0	—
1959	101.5	0.8	100.6	0.2	101.6	1.6
1960	103.1	1.6	100.7	0.1	103.3	1.7
1961	104.2	1.1	100.3	−0.4	104.6	1.3
1962	105.4	1.2	100.6	0.3	105.8	1.1
1963	106.7	1.2	100.3	−0.3	107.2	1.3
1964	108.1	1.3	100.5	0.2	108.9	1.6
1965	109.9	1.7	102.5	2.0	110.9	1.8
1966	113.1	2.9	105.8 p	3.2	114.2	3.0
Percentage change:						
1958–66	12.3*	1.5†	5.4*	0.7†	14.2*	1.7†
1958–64	7.3	1.2†	0.1	(‡)	8.9	1.4†
1964–66	4.6	2.3†	5.3	2.6†	4.9	2.4†

p Preliminary.
* Components may not add to total due to rounding.
† Average annual rate.
‡ Less than .5 per cent.
SOURCES: U. S. Department of Labor, Bureau of Labor Statistics; and U. S. Department of Commerce.

subjected to price inflation. However, the matter of which index best measures inflation still would remain unresolved, even if there were general agreement on the notion that upward movements in all three major indexes are indicative of inflation. Public or private economic policy decisions made during the period 1958–64, for example, might vary depending upon whether the measure used to gauge price changes was the WPI (which showed no trend) or either the CPI or the IPI (both of which exhibited persistent annual increases averaging from 1 to 1.5 per cent, respectively). Similarly, policy actions or prescriptions during 1965 and 1966 also might differ if one attached greater significance to the dramatic advance in the level of wholesale prices following many years of no change, rather than to the acceleration in the rate of price advance which was evidenced in both the CPI and IPI. In this important matter of formulating policy to cope with inflation, the key role of the major price indexes should be evident. Nonetheless, the appropriate interpretation of the signals given by them must rest on an understanding of precisely what is, or is not, being measured by each of the indexes, as well as on the collateral issue of the usefulness or validity of the various measures of price change in attempting to gauge the incidence of inflation. In the following analysis, the three major price indexes will be examined more closely, in order to better appraise them as measures of inflation.

THE CONSUMER PRICE INDEX

The Consumer Price Index or, as it is officially called, the Consumer Price Index for Urban Wage Earners and Clerical Workers, is a statistical measure of changes in prices of goods and services purchased by urban wage earners and clerical workers, including families and, since the January 1964 revision, single persons living alone. The coverage of the index, according to the Bureau of Labor Statistics (BLS), includes:

. . . prices of everything people buy for living—food, clothing, automobiles, homes, house-furnishings, household supplies, fuel, drugs, and recreational goods; fees to doctors, lawyers, beauty shops; rent, repair costs, transportation fares, public utility rates, etc. It deals with prices actually charged to consumers, including sales and excise taxes. It also includes real estate taxes on owned homes, but it does not include income or personal property taxes.[2]

CHART 2   Consumer Prices. 1957-59=100

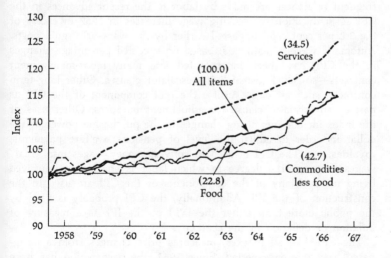

SOURCE: U.S. Department of Labor, Bureau of Labor Statistics.

[2] U. S. Department of Labor, Bureau of Labor Statistics, *The Consumer Price Index*, revised January 1964 (Washington, D.C.: U. S. Government Printing Office, September 1964), p. 1.

To be sure, the above list is not all-inclusive, as the "market basket" used for pricing purposes since January 1964 contains nearly 400 items. Nonetheless, it does help to give a reasonably good idea of the wide range of goods and services which are included in the calculation of the over-all index. Chart 2 shows the performance of the over-all CPI and major groupings (relative weights shown in parentheses) during the period 1958–66.

The CPI probably is the most familiar of the three major price indexes discussed in this article. Its lineage may be traced to World War I, when it was referred to as the Cost-of-Living Index, a term which still is frequently, although erroneously, applied to the CPI. Initially formulated as an aid in wage negotiations, the index has undergone a series of revisions, the most recent occurring in 1964, as noted above. The revisions have encompassed the goods and services priced in the index, the list of survey cities used, as well as the weights assigned to the various index components. Emphasis has shifted over time, as a basis for assigning weights, from the expenditures of wage-earner families to the outlays of middle-income wage and salary workers.

As indicated earlier, the CPI was initially used to aid in wage negotiations. It still is used extensively in collective bargaining negotiations—especially during periods of rising prices. Currently, frequent references are made by labor to the recent advances in the CPI as justification for seeking wage increases in 1967 in excess of the 3.2 per cent rate suggested earlier by the wage-price guideposts. Automatic wage adjustments, based on specified percentage changes in the CPI, have been incorporated into many labor-management contracts—so-called cost-of-living escalator clauses. Other long-term contracts, such as leases, utilize the rent component of the CPI as part of an escalator clause for adjustment purposes. Other uses of the index include measuring changes in the purchasing power of the dollar in order to adjust the level of pensions, welfare payments, royalties, etc. The CPI is used to convert money wages into "real" wages to gauge the degree to which labor is sharing in improved living levels. Many of the components of the CPI are used in the construction of the IPI. Additionally, the CPI probably is used by the public more than either the WPI or the IPI as a measure of inflation or deflation in the economy.

The CPI, like all indexes, measures price changes from a designated base reference period. Since 1962, the base period has been 1957–59 equals 100. Thus, an index level of 113 means that prices have risen by 13 per cent from the base period. Conversely, an index level of less than 100 would mean that prices have fallen. It is important to remember, however, that what is being measured is the change in the amount of money required as prices change—with all other things, such as income, being held constant—to buy a fixed combination of goods and services (the market basket). The market basket is regarded as being representative of all goods and services purchased by consumers in the particular period used to derive both index weights and pricing samples. The fact that the market basket of the base period is held fixed, until the next weight revision, means that the CPI maintains the pattern of expenditures of the base period in measuring subsequent price changes. This sort of index makes no allowance between weight revisions for the adjustment or alteration of spending patterns by consumers so as to maximize the purchasing power of their incomes as prices change. However, in a true cost-of-living index, the level of living, welfare, or utility would be held constant, while the consumer would be permitted to alter his pattern of expenditures (the market basket would no longer be fixed) as prices changed. For this reason, despite the fact that the CPI measures changes in many of the key items which enter the cost of living, it is not a cost-of-living index *per se*.

From the standpoint of practicality, it is not reasonable to expect a monthly index, such as the CPI, to serve as a measure of changes in the cost of living. However, in order to make the index more representative of shifting patterns of consumer expenditures, the BLS utilizes the results of consumer expenditures studies to periodically change the relative importance of the major components of the CPI. Such changes are shown in Table 2. At such times, changes in the index would, of course, more closely reflect changes in the cost of living. The lengthy intervals between such revisions, however, mean that the farther away one moves from the revision date, the less will price changes, as measured by the CPI, reflect actual changes in the cost of living.

The data in Table 2 largely reflect the influence of rising income levels over time on spending patterns. The dramatic decline in the proportion of total income expended on food, and the relative stability of spending on clothing and housing, stands in sharp contrast with the marked rise in the proportions of what may be termed discretionary spending on the other groups shown in Table 2. In addition, each of the groups has been marked by changes, in varying degrees, in the kinds of goods and services priced by the index, with the addition of new products and/or the replacement of older ones. The current market basket undoubtedly represents a higher level of living than formerly. In the light of these developments, it becomes quite difficult to assess the over-all inflationary implications

TABLE 2   Relative Importance of Consumer Price Index Major
Groups, Selected Periods of Expenditures Studies (in percent)

	1917–19	1934–36	December 1952	December 1963
All items	100.0	100.0	100.0	100.0
Food	40.7	33.5	29.6	22.4
Housing	26.6	32.0	32.5	33.2
Apparel	17.7	10.6	9.2	10.6
Transportation	3.1	8.3	11.3	13.9
Medical care	4.7	3.9	5.1	5.7
Personal care	1.0	2.0	2.0	2.8
Reading and recreation	3.7	5.9	5.3	5.9
Other goods and services	2.5	3.8	5.0	5.4

SOURCE: Table II-1 in "Inflation and Price Indexes," *Materials Submitted to the Subcommittee on Economic Statistics of the Joint Economic Committee, Congress of the United States* Washington, D.C.: U. S. Government Printing Office, July 1966), p. 18.

of increases in the CPI over time. It may be worth reflecting further on the suggestion advanced in 1961 by the National Bureau of Economic Research Price Statistics Review Committee that ". . . it is quite possible that the cost of maintaining a fixed standard of living has fallen despite the fact that the price of a fixed market basket has risen."[3]

THE WHOLESALE PRICE INDEX

The purpose of the WPI is to measure average price changes in commodities sold in primary markets of the United States. The base reference period, as in the case of the CPI, is 1957–59 = 100. The WPI, or its components, is used for a variety of purposes, including economic forecasting and the escalation or scaling down of long-term industrial purchase and sales contracts, in much the same way as the CPI is used in making cost-of-living adjustments. Again, as was true of the CPI, components of the WPI are used in estimating the IPI.

The BLS has compiled an index of wholesale prices dating back to 1890. It should be noted that the term "wholesale," as used in the

[3] U. S., Congress, Joint Economic Committee, *Government Price Statistics, Hearing . . . January 24, 1961*, 87th Cong., 1st Sess., 1961, p. 51.

CHART 3   Wholesale Prices, 1957–59=100

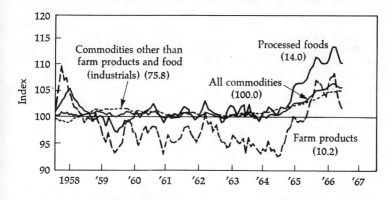

SOURCE: U.S. Department of Labor, Bureau of Labor Statistics.

title of the index, does not refer to prices received by jobbers, whole-
salers, or distributors, but simply to sales in quantities. The coverage
of the WPI does not include price movements of retail transactions
or transactions for services (except gas and electricity), construction,
real estate, transportation, or securities. Similarly, the prices of
products entering into international trade are excluded from the
WPI. Chart 3 shows the performance of the over-all WPI and the
major commodity groups (relative weights shown in parentheses)
during the period 1958–66.

According to the BLS, the prices used in the construction of the
WPI:

. . . are those which apply as nearly as possible to the first significant
commercial transaction in the United States. Later transactions for the
same item at other stages in the distribution cycle are not included. However, as raw materials are transformed into semifinished and finished
goods, the resulting products are represented according to their importance in primary markets.[4]

The price quotations used in compiling the WPI are obtained from
respondents by mail. It is important to note that the prices received
by the BLS are from the sellers of good, not the buyers. Although
the sellers are requested to provide actual prices charged to their
customers, including all discounts from list prices, the response has
not been uniform and the BLS, at times, receives only list prices.

[4] *Wholesale Prices and Price Indexes, 1963*, U. S. Department of Labor,
Bureau of Labor Statistics, Bulletin No. 1513 (Washington, D.C.: U. S.
Government Printing Office, June 1966), p. 9.

TABLE 3   Relative Importance of Commodities in the Wholesale Price
Index and Number of Commodities at Selected Dates (in percent)

	1890	1918	1929	1947	1960
All commodities	100.00	100.00	100.00	100.00	100.00
Farm products	29.04	27.11	19.01	14.59	10.59
Processed foods	25.54	25.80	18.36	15.87	14.04
Nonfarm, nonfood (industrial)	45.42	47.09	62.63	69.54	75.37
Number of commodities	199	534	784	1,819	2,161

SOURCE: U. S. Department of Labor, Bureau of Labor Statistics.

At times, when list prices and transactions prices tend to diverge,
the WPI fails to reflect the actual price changes which occur. To the
extent that this kind of bias is symmetrical in periods of both rising
and falling price levels, it would tend to cancel out over time. However, at critical phases of a business cycle, the short-term sensitivity
of the WPI to actual price changes may be less than desired.

The WPI has gone through several comprehensive revisions since
1890. The weights used in the index are revised at approximately
5-year intervals, as data from industrial censuses become available.
Coverage of the index has grown from less than 200 commodities
in 1890 to nearly 2,200 in 1960. Table 3 illustrates this extended
coverage and also shows very clearly the marked changes in the relative importance of the major commodity groups over a 70-year
period. The relative weight changes shown reflect the transition of
the economy from a largely rural and agrarian society into a much
more urban and highly industrialized society.

The growing importance of industrial prices in the WPI probably
has served to make the index more stable, since industrial prices
tend to fluctuate less widely than those of either farm products or
processed foods. Nonetheless, the element of duplication in the WPI,
owing to the inclusion of products at different stages of production,
can result in a dramatic impact on the entire index, when the price
of a key item changes. A notable example of this is the decline in
the supply of livestock in 1965, which triggered off substantial increases in the prices of farm products, processed foods, and hides
and skins. Yet, this same element of duplication has its merits, since
price increases can be traced through successive stages of production
—from the raw material to the finished product. By providing evidence of the pervasiness of price increases at differing points in the
production process, the behavior of the components of the WPI may

be of help in assessing more correctly the movement in the over-all index. Because the WPI tends to reflect price pressures at the earliest stages of the production-distribution process, it may well be the best indicator of future price trends in the over-all economy.

THE IMPLICIT PRICE INDEX

The Implicit Price Index is the newest, and probably the least familiar, of the three major indexes discussed in this article. It was first published in 1951 and is compiled and published quarterly by the Office of Business Economics (OBE) of the U. S. Department of Commerce, using the reference base 1958 = 100. It is the most comprehensive of the three major price indexes, in that it attempts to measure the general price level of all final goods and services produced by the economy during a given period. However, the IPI is not derived by means of direct price collection, as is the case with the CPI and the WPI. That is, in its efforts to determine the level of real (constant dollar) GNP, the OBE generates the IPI as a by-product. It is derived by taking the ratio between current dollars gross national product (GNP) and constant dollar GNP and multiplying it by 100.

It should be pointed out that current dollar GNP may increase, either as a consequence of an increase in the physical volume of goods and services produced or merely through an increase in prices with no change in physical production. The determination of the real growth in output involves removing the effect of price increases by use of deflation procedures. The OBE deflation process entails dividing the current dollar value of each component of GNP by some appropriate price index and summing the deflated components to arrive at the level of real GNP. When the deflated GNP data are divided into the current dollar GNP figure, the resulting ratio represents an implied average price relationship.

Both the CPI and the WPI are fixed weight indexes in which the expenditure weights and the contents of the respective market baskets being priced are fixed between revision dates. The theoretical design of these indexes is such that price changes of the same, or essentially similar, items can be measured directly over time. The IPI, on the other hand, is not a fixed weight index. The weights used in estimating the IPI are the proportions in which the different components of GNP are entered in the national income accounts from year to year. Any change in the yearly pattern of spending on the components of GNP automatically will result in a change in weights. Thus, because the IPI cannot directly measure price changes

TABLE 4   Relative Importance of Price Deflators for Total Gross
National Product in the Implicit Price Index

	Percent importance in terms of base year (1958) weights of:					
Implicit price deflator	BLS Consumer prices	BLS Wholesale prices	USDA Agricultural prices	Other prices*	Implicit prices	Earnings indexes†
100.0	45.6	12.3	6.8	13.5	9.3	12.5

* Other prices refer to price data collected by Government agencies other than the BLS and USDA and by private organizations.
† Includes implicit earnings indexes for Government compensation.
SOURCE: U. S. Department of Commerce, Office of Business Economics.

when the composition of output changes, the quality of the index rests heavily upon the choice or appropriateness of the various price deflators employed in estimating real GNP.

Table 4 shows the relative importance of the six different classes of price and wage data used to deflate total GNP. The components of the CPI and the WPI account for nearly 60 per cent of all GNP deflators used in the IPI. Thus, much of the accuracy of the IPI rests upon two measures of price change which are, themselves, subject to qualifications in their use. With the added exception of agricultural prices, which are collected by the U. S. Department of Agriculture (USDA), the remaining deflators in Table 4 are supplied either by Government agencies other than the BLS and the USDA, by private organizations, or are arrived at indirectly. In this connection, one of the major criticisms of the IPI involves the use of price deflators in the private sector which are not strictly comparable —and, therefore, unsuitable—to the dollar totals to which they are applied. The failure to allow for increases in output per man-hour in deflating the construction sector and Government services also has been cited by many observers as a prime factor which introduces a significant element of distortion into the IPI, and thereby over-states the magnitude of price inflation and understates the increase in real GNP. It can be seen, then, that the method of computing the IPI compounds the probabilities of error or bias which are an inherent part of the construction of any price index.

A FINAL NOTE

Price statistics are an important component of our total body of economic knowledge. In conjunction with other kinds of economic intelligence, they play a key role, not only in the evaluation of the performance of the economy but, additionally, in the formulation of public and private economic policy. The three price indexes discussed in this article frequently are relied on as measures of inflation. Each of them can help shed some added light on that complex phenomenon. Their usefulness in this capacity is directly related to a better understanding of what they measure, as well as a recognition of their limitations. The growing burden of public and private policy formulation being placed upon measures of price change indicates the increasing need for more and better price statistics, and a correspondingly greater effort at understanding and interpreting their meaning.

STAFF REPORT OF
JOINT ECONOMIC COMMITTEE

THE GAINS AND LOSSES
FROM INFLATION

33

To most individuals and families in society, inflation is much more than a distant and impersonal phenomenon. Its effects can be seen daily in the prices they must pay for the goods and services they buy. The severest effects of inflation, however are found in the great burden it imposes on those persons whose incomes, for various reasons, do not rise in step with the increasing prices of the things they need. Among the groups who are most hurt are the aged, the sick, and those who must live on fixed incomes or on past savings. In effect, inflation robs these groups of their share in the distribution of income and reduces the real value of their wealth. In the following discussion, therefore, we will be concerned with the

Reprinted from Staff Report on Employment, Growth, and Price Levels, "The Gains and Losses from Inflation," *Employment, Growth, and Price Levels*, Joint Economic Committee, 86th Cong., 1st Sess., Dec. 24, 1959, pp. 110–117.

effects of the postwar inflation (1) on the distribution of income and (2) on the ownership of wealth.[1]

THE DISTRIBUTION OF INCOME

As a payment for productive services rendered by their labor or their capital, people in society receive incomes in the form of wages, salaries, profits, interest, or rent. These people are then able in turn to utilize these incomes to purchase the goods they need or want from others. In this way, goods and services are continually being exchanged for money, and vice versa, in a never-ending flow.

Clearly, the ability of any individual to command a share of the goods produced will depend upon the price of his productive service (including the quantity of it he can sell) relative to the prices of the goods he wishes to buy. If inflation develops, so that all prices rise, the effects of that inflation on each individual's share of the income produced—i.e., on the distribution of income—will depend upon whether his income (price) rises more or less rapidly than prices he pays. And this, in turn, will depend upon a number of other considerations including the presence or absence of long-term contractual commitments, the mobility of the suppliers of services, the degree to which custom plays a role in price setting, etc.

On this basis, it has usually been presumed that the major group which benefits from inflation is the profit recipient, since costs tend to lag behind prices during an upswing. Wage earners may also often gain since their payments are more flexible upward than those of fixed-income recipients. At the other extreme are those who earn interest and rent, whose payments are often fixed at contractual levels for long periods of time. Finally, there is a broad group of salaried workers, many of whose incomes are quite "sticky"— teachers, nurses, white-collar groups, etc.—and begin to move upward only with a considerable lag. If the inflation continues for long, however, even the fixed and sticky incomes are renegotiated and the continuing redistribution effects of the inflation tend to become considerably less.

These expectations have been only partially supported by the

[1] This discussion draws heavily on several papers written in conjuction with the present study, particularly S. E. Harris, "The Incidence of Inflation: or Who Gets Hurt," Study Paper No. 7; A. H. Conrad, "The Share of Wages and Salaries in Manufacturing Incomes, 1947–56." Study Paper No. 9: and G. L. Bach, "How Important Is Price Stability in Stable Economic Growth," in "The Relationship of Prices to Economic Stability and Growth," a compendium of papers submitted to the Joint Economic Committee, March 31, 1958.

actual distribution of income trends during the postwar inflation. These trends, of course, may have been affected by other factors than the inflation. The major shifts in income shares since 1946 have been the following:

1. The share of national income going to all employees—a heterogeneous category which includes all types of wage and salaried workers, from a corporation's president to its janitor and from a schoolteacher to a lathe operator—rose from about 65 to 69 percent. It is very probable that a portion of this increase was due to a change in the "product-mix," particularly the shift away from agriculture into services (which would shift many people out of the category of unincorporated businessmen into employees). This possibility is given support by the fact that within the manufacturing sector only, the wage and salary share remained quite stable throughout the period. A further portion is explained by the shift in the relative importance of Government employment, since income originating in this sector is 100 percent labor income.

2. By far the greatest loss has been suffered by unincorporated business, whose share was cut by almost 50 percent from 1947 to 1957. Here, again, however, a large portion of this decline was a reflection of the drastic reduction in total farm income, due in part to the declining level of agricultural prices and in part to a sharp decline in the number of persons in agriculture.

3. For the entire period, the share of corporate profits before taxes declined very slightly. During the period, however, this share rose at the beginning of each inflationary upswing in 1947–48 and 1950–51. After the initial upsurge, the share again declined. Within the manufacturing sector alone, the corporate share remained quite stable.

In evaluating these trends in corporate profits, it must be noted that they are net of depreciation. If depreciation charges are included in the returns to corporations, their share shows no decline. To the extent that depreciation charges are based on historical rather than replacement costs, however, this share will be overstated.

4. The interest share rose slightly, while the rent share remained about the same. However, both of these shares had already declined very markedly during the war years and even in the late 1930's, largely as a result of Government monetary policies and wartime controls. The minor recovery of the postwar decade, therefore, is not surprising, and does not indicate that these shares did not suffer markedly. In fact, it is largely as a result of the declining share going to interest that the older people in society have suffered the most, since they are no longer in a position to provide a labor serv-

ice and are dependent primarily on fixed incomes from savings accumulated in the past.

5. Within the broad employee group mentioned under item 1, above, various subgroups were affected very diversely. The most important lagging income groups were employees of governments, educational institutions, and religious and charitable organizations. In some instances, salaries of these groups lagged so greatly that their real incomes have actually declined over the past two decades.

Of greater importance as a measure of the unequal burden of inflation on individuals is the fact that it is primarily the incomes of older retired persons which have been most unresponsive to a rising price level. This arises, of course, from the fact that it is this group more than any other which must depend upon interest income, pensions, life insurance annuities, or other types of fixed income payments. Furthermore, older persons have little or no capacity or opportunity to supplement their incomes by active employment. By the same token, older persons who depend upon social security payments for their major source of support have been able to avoid serious reductions in their real standard of living only because of numerous upward revisions in the tax and benefit programs. *Continuing revisions of this type are essential if the burden of inflation on these groups is not to become severe.* The same is true, of course, for other recipients of social security benefits through unemployment insurance, workmen's compensation, etc.

TABLE 1   How Family Income Was Shared by Income 5ths and by the Top 5 Percent, 1935–36, 1944, 1954, 1957 *(percent shares)*

Quintile	1935–36	Before tax 1944	1954	1957 Before tax	After tax	Average income after tax[1]
Lowest	4.1	4.9	4.8	4.8	5.1	$1,428
2d	9.2	10.9	11.1	11.3	11.8	3,290
3d	14.1	16.2	16.4	16.3	16.8	4,690
4th	20.9	22.2	22.5	22.3	22.7	6,326
Highest	51.7	45.8	45.2	45.3	43.6	12,154
Total	100.0	100.0	100.0	100.0	100.0	
Top 5 percent	26.5	20.7	20.3	20.2	18.2	20,279

[1] Federal individual income tax.

SOURCES: Survey of Current Business, June 1956 and April 1959, and earlier studies of the staff of the National Income Division of the U.S. Department of Commerce.

Nor does the available evidence indicate that the period of inflation has seen any improvement in the share of income going to those families at the bottom end of the income scale. According to Lampman,[2] "the lowest fifth of income receivers now get 5 percent of all income. It received 5 percent of income in 1947. It apparently received about 5 percent of income in the 1930's." Lampman also points out, however, that the income share of the top 5 percent of income receivers has been lowered considerably at the expense of a gain in the share of the upper middle income group. It is not clear, however, whether this redistribution is attributable solely, or even primarily, to the inflation. Data on the distribution of income by families are given in Table 1.

THE DISTRIBUTION OF WEALTH

In addition to its effects on the distribution of current income, inflation brings about a redistribution in the ownership of wealth, measured by the net worth (the market value of assets less liabilities) of different households, business enterprises, or governments. As in the case of income, this redistribution is due to differences in price movements of various assets during and under the influence of inflation. While the dollar value of monetary assets such as bank deposits, saving and loan shares, mortgages, Government and corporate bonds, life insurance contracts and claims under most pension and social insurance contracts remains unchanged, inflation commonly increases the price of equities and tangible assets such as common stock, real estate, producer and consumer durables and inventories. Obviously individual economic units or groups of them will profit to the extent that they hold price-sensitive rather than monetary assets; that the price-sensitive assets they hold increase in price; and that the assets they hold have been financed by borrowing which is payable in dollars. Because the share of price-sensitive assets in total assets held by different groups, the extent to which their price-sensitive assets increase in value, and their debt-to-asset ratios vary, they are differently affected by inflation.

From the end of 1939 to the end of 1959, the price of common stock has increased by about 350 percent. That of real estate, for which our information is much more deficient, has advanced by 200 to 250 percent. On the other hand, the cost of living has advanced during the same period only by approximately 110 percent. A household without debt holding all its assets in monetary form

[2] Robert J. Lampman, "The Low Income Population and Economic Growth," Study Paper No. 12.

would therefore have suffered a decline of a little more than 50 percent in the purchasing power of its net worth, as the result of inflation. On the other hand, a household that had divided all its assets between real estate and common stock and had at the beginning of the period financed one-half of its total assets by borrowing, would at the end of the 20-year period not only have preserved intact the purchasing power of its net worth, but would actually have increased it by 60 percent.

The available statistics, defective as they are, indicate that for most of the major sectors in the economy, monetary assets were either less than debt or not much in excess of debt, so that the purchasing power of their net worth has been little if at all damaged by inflation. This is the case, for instance, for nonfarm households, farmers, unincorporated business enterprises, corporate business, and State and local governments. All these sectors have owned enough assets that have advanced in price and have been sufficiently in debt to offset the losses in purchasing power suffered on their monetary assets. The Federal Government has on balance profited from the inflation since the purchasing power of its debt has been substantially reduced by the rise in prices.

While the inflation of the last two decades thus has not impaired the net worth of the major sectors of the economy or sharply changed the distribution of national wealth among them, there undoubtedly have been substantial groups of households, and also some groups of businesses, that have suffered an impairment in net worth as a result of inflation, though there are others who have benefited. On the basis of our information about the character of assets held by different groups of households, business, and governmental units, and about their debt-to-asset ratios, it is known, or at least it is very likely, that the main groups of households whose net worth has been impaired by inflation have been people in the older age groups and of modest income and wealth, particularly those that did not own their home. On the other hand, households with heads in their twenties or thirties, who often acquire homes and consumer durables on credit, and individuals in the upper wealth groups concentrating their assets in common stock, have actually seen the purchasing power of their net worth increased by the differential price movements accompanying the inflation of the last 20 years. Such increases have been particularly marked during the last 6 years during which the level of stock prices more than doubled while the cost of living increased by less than 10 percent.

The statistics available now are not sufficient to show in detail the effect that inflation has had on the purchasing power of the net worth of different groups of households, business enterprises, and governmental units, and on the distribution of total national wealth among them. They do suffice to show, however, that at least among individuals, the postwar inflation has increased the inequality in the distribution of wealth. It is estimated[3] that the share of the top percentile of wealthholders, that is, the one percent of individuals ranking highest if measured by total assets, which had fallen from 32 percent to 21 percent between 1922 and 1949, increased to 24 percent in 1953 and to 26 percent in 1956, the latest data for which such estimates can be made. Because of the further sharp advance in stock prices in the last few years, it is likely that the share of the top one percent of wealthholders has increased and by the end of 1959 may not be far from its level of 1922, if the calculation is made on the basis not of individuals but of families. Thus the postwar inflation appears to have reversed, at least for the time being, the trend toward a more equal distribution of personal wealth and to have restored inequality to approximately the level of the early 1920's.

The Volume of Real Output and Its Rate of Growth

Inflation may affect not only the distribution of output, but also the total available to be distributed. Inflation may lead to waste, to less saving, to a poor allocation of resources, etc. Conversely, a rising price level can raise investment and facilitate readjustments within the economy. In the United States there has been no clear relationship between output and prices; we have experienced rising output in periods of both rising prices and declining prices; the precise relationship between them, therefore, is far from clear.

THEORIES OF THE INFLATIONARY PROCESS

Before proceeding with a brief discussion of the alternative explanations of how and why inflation arises, an important distinction must be stressed. The term "inflation" is usually used to mean a general rise in the price level; contrariwise, the methods of prevention of inflation normally center on policies designed to hold the general price level reasonably stable. Price *level* stability, however, should in no sense be identified with the stabilization of any *particular* price. It is the very essence of a free enterprise economy that the

---

[3] R. J. Lampman, "Review of Economics and Statistics," XLI (1959).

prices of *individual* products and services be free to adjust to changing market conditions. A change in price in response to changes in market demand or natural changes in supply conditions is essential to induce particular industries or firms to expand while others contract. To achieve price *level* stability by requiring that *particular* prices remain stable, therefore, may well create more problems than it solves. In fact, as will be seen, it may well be that price level stability can be more readily achieved by making individual prices more flexible.

Demand-Pull Inflation

Despite a vast outpouring of writings in the past decade or more concerning the nature of the inflationary process, the basic theoretical frame of reference is still essentially quite simple. The traditional economic theory of inflation—commonly called a "pure demand-pull"—has long held that the primary cause is to be found in an excess of available purchasing power (demand) competing for a relatively limited quantity of available goods (supply), resulting in a rise in prices. The limitation on supply is due to the fact that available resources are being fully utilized—i.e., *that there is full employment in the economy*—so that the excess purchasing power can only bring about a higher price level. Assuming no further increases in aggregate purchasing power, the competitive pressures of buyers will cease once prices have risen to the point where total money demand is just adequate to purchase the available (full employment) flow of goods.[4]

Furthermore, this equilibrium will not be seriously affected by shifts in the composition of a given total demand. For while such shifts will result in price increases in the sectors where demand is rising, purchases in other sectors must decline correspondingly and prices in those sectors will drop. On balance, no net upward movement will follow.

The "demand-pull" theory of inflation presumes that the prices of productive services and of goods are determined in the market by the impersonal competitive forces of supply and demand. Prices are reasonably flexible both upward and downward; by the same token,

---

[4] If purchasing power rises as well, as part of the inflationary process, there will be further price increases. The process may or may not come to an end, depending on the extent of feedbacks. A strong and progresive tax system or an unwillingness of the central bank to increase the money supply would ultimately halt the process.

monopolistic considerations are sufficiently minor that they do not significantly affect the final outcome.

The policy implication of a demand-pull inflation are likewise quite clear. Since the basic cause is an excess of aggregate purchasing power, policy must be directed toward reducing that purchasing power by aggregate fiscal and monetary policies. And since markets are competitive and wages and prices flexible, this result can be achieved without developing any serious unemployment.

Market Power Inflation

An alternative theory of the inflationary process which has been increasingly stressed during the postwar period has been variously referred to as a "cost-push," an "administered-price," or a "sellers" inflation. In the following discussion, we will use the term "market power" inflation to denote this type of theory. The term "market power" is extremely difficult to define precisely. *Conceptually*, it refers to the ability of any groups of sellers (or in the case of industry, the ability of a monopolist) to establish a price for its product or service which differs from the "competitive" level. This ability is usually, in turn, the result of some type of group action, which may be quite open, as in the case of labor unions, or quite tacit, as in the case of "accepted" practices in industries with a few relatively large firms. Thus no collusion or concerted action is necessarily implied. *Operationally*, the exercise of such market power would usually be most clearly identified by an increase in wage rates not associated with the existence of a relatively tight labor market or by a rise in price not associated either with pressures on capacity or with rising costs. It may also be that *downward rigidity* of wages and prices in the face of declining employment and sales is also a reflection of the exercise of market power; this is, however, a weaker case, which will be discussed in more detail in a subsequent section.

If an important degree of "market power" inflation exists, two major policy approaches have been suggested. One, perhaps paradoxically, is identical to that proposed to deal with a pure demand-pull, viz, to restrict *aggregate* demand by stringent monetary and fiscal policies. This approach is based upon the fact that a market power inflation cannot—unless extreme assumptions are made—continue for long unless accompanied by a continually rising aggregate demand. For if demand is held constant, continually rising wages and/or prices will result in continually rising unemployment of both labor and capital. *At some point*, the depressing effects of these developments will weaken market power sufficiently that the inflationary pressures will cease. Some proponents of this view believe that the level of unemployment necessary to achieve this stability is low enough to be socially tolerable; others feel that price stability is of such overriding importance that the problems of unemployment associated with achieving price stability are secondary.

The second approach is designed to deal with the problem by reducing, directly or indirectly, the power to set prices by the groups involved. The variations on this theme are extensive. Some proposals call for Government participation in wage and price setting in the key sectors of the economy in which market power is considered excessive. Other proposals call for much stronger application of antitrust legislation in both the labor and product markets in order to restore the constraints imposed by a more competitive market.

Structural Inflation

A third approach to inflation, largely developed within the past 2 or 3 years, presents the view that inflation can arise from *structural* adjustments in the economy, in the absence of either excess aggregate demand or concentrations of market power. The most recent and comprehensive statement of this theory is that of Schultze,[5] who develops the proposition that an initial upward thrust of prices and wages can occur in particular sectors of the economy because of substantial and rapid *shifts* in demand toward those sectors, though aggregate demand in the economy is not excessive. A *net* inflationary movement can result, however, partly because of the immobility of factors of production—which prevents supply from adjusting quickly to the shifts in demand—but more importantly, because of the *lack of downward flexibility* of prices and wages in those sectors in which demand has declined.

The inflationary impact of structural imbalances becomes further accentuated by secondary effects of the original demand-pull in the favored sector. To the extent that the price increases result in higher input costs for other industries, other prices will rise. If the cost of living rises, wage rates in other industries may rise, even though no tightness exists in the labor market; also wage increases in the areas where demand is expanding may establish a "pattern" for equivalent adjustments where unemployment is still substantial. The final result of this process of interaction can be continuing infla-

[5] Charles L. Schultze, "Recent Inflation in the United States," Study Paper No. 1.

tionary pressures even after the initiating forces have disappeared.

The problems of dealing with the downward inflexibilities and interpendencies of structural inflation from a public policy point of view are extremely difficult. It is clear that the use of aggregative monetary and fiscal controls will result primarily in lowered output and employment with only small effects on the level of wages or prices. If attempts are made by selective controls of some sort to halt the price rise in the particular sectors where demand pressures exist, there is danger that additional resources of labor and capital, which should be attracted into those sectors, will not be; in the long run, the allocating function of the pricing mechanism will be seriously impaired. Conceptually, the most appropriate policy would be to reduce the degree of downward inflexibility in the labor and product markets. How this can be done without sacrificing other desirable objectives, however, is a most difficult question.

The Complex Real World

To this point, we have been concerned with the various ways in which an inflationary process *can* occur. Any actual inflation, however, may be made up of several interrelated factors, reflecting some elements of all of these "theories." An inflation which is initiated by a condition of excess demand may be accentuated by the use of market power; conversely, an inflation initiated by autonomous increases in wages and/or prices through market power cannot long continue without an increase in aggregate demand financed by an expansion in the money supply. Or, in the case of "structural inflation," sectoral increases in demand and employment may pull up wages; these wage increases may establish a pattern, however, which unions in other industries follow despite poor demand and employment conditions. Finally, it may simply be that at the same time, demand forces are strong in some industries while market power is strong in others. Prices and/or wages may rise in both cases quite independently of each other.

It is essential to recognize, therefore, that the real world is varied and interrelated, and that no one "theory" is likely to provide a complete explanation of an actual inflation. Nevertheless, if we are to formulate an improved public policy in this area, we must do what we can to identify and, so far as possible, isolate the *dominant* factors involved at various times and in various industries.

. . .

WILLIAM MC CHESNEY MARTIN

COST AND DEMAND INFLATION: IMPLICATIONS FOR MONETARY POLICY

34

NATURE OF COST-PUSH AND DEMAND-SHIFT EXPLANATIONS

Controversy over causes of postwar inflation has focused mainly on developments since 1954. On the causes and nature of the episodes of inflation in the earlier postwar years, there appears to be widespread agreement. World War II left a legacy of accumulated demands for goods of all kinds, and methods employed in financing the war resulted in highly liquid financial positions. When wartime price controls were removed, effective demands at current prices were considerably in excess of supplies in virtually every market.

When the Korean War began in mid-1950, memories of war-induced shortages and price increases provoked protective buying by consumers and businesses, here and abroad. In both periods of inflation, costs as well as prices rose and there were large shifts in the composition of demands, but the influence of strong demands in originating and sustaining price advances was by far the predominant one.

In the 1954–57 inflation, demands were not strong in all markets simultaneously, and the advance in prices was moderate in comparison with the war-related experiences. In view of these circumstances, several interpretations of the period since 1954 have emphasized the independent nature of costs. Another interpretation has stressed rapid changes in the composition of demands. What is common to these interpretations is that they have attributed primary importance to rigidities or to autonomous elements in markets for goods and services and have given little or no weight to the role of aggregate demands. From these theses, further interpretation is drawn that use of general instruments of restraint on aggregate demands in order to check such price increases would be ineffective or would incur unacceptable social costs in terms of unemployment of human and material resources.

The "cost-push" approach to the explanation of price inflation

Reprinted from William McChesney Martin, *1967 Economic Report of the President*, Part II, Hearings Before the Joint Economic Committee, 90th Cong., 1st Sess., 1967, pp. 434–440.

seems fundamentally to assume that costs are more or less independently determined by market power and, therefore, little can be done about them. Prices are set by administrative decisions to cover all costs, including a satisfactory margin of profit, without regard to current or prospective demand conditions. Production is scheduled to conform to sales at these prices.

In such circumstances, it is said, Government policies—monetary and/or fiscal—must operate to provide demand sufficient to assure maximum output and full employment at the wages that are the result of labor-management agreements and at the prices businessmen—and, sometimes, public agencies—deem necessary. Otherwise, output and employment will be held or reduced below attainable levels, but there will be no appreciable restraint on advances in price levels and labor or other costs.

In practice, however, the extent to which the price of a product can be raised is limited by actual or potential competition from other products or from imports; these checks are strengthened by Government policies that operate to restrain demands and prevent ebullient expectations from developing. Competitive constraints on prices strengthen resistance to increases in costs and at times may exert downward pressures as businessmen attempt to maintain or increase profit margins. The influence on costs may take such forms as programs to raise productivity, various efforts to economize on the use of materials, control of administrative and other types of salaried employment, or resistance to increases in wage rates and fringe benefits.

The "demand-shift" explanation of the type of inflation experienced in the 1954–57 business expansion rests on a combination of factors. Inflation, it is said, originates in the general excess demands which temporarily emerge as the economy passes from recession to full employment, and from the excess demands in specific sectors that often remain after the aggregate excess has been eliminated. Inflation is perpetuated and spread throughout the economy, the argument proceeds, by the influence of costs in wage and price determination and by the relative insensitivity of prices and costs to decreases in demands.

In this view, particularly as it relates to the 1954–57 business expansion, demands increase and full employment is reached without generating upward price and cost pressures. Then, a rapid shift in the composition of demands is reflected in excess demands in some sectors and insufficient demands in others. Because prices are more sensitive to increases than to contractions in demands, a general rise results as prices advance in those sectors where demands are increasing rapidly and decline by smaller amounts or not at all in those sectors where demands are decreasing. General monetary and fiscal policies appropriate to combat an inflation arising out of excess aggregate demand are not suitable, it is contended, to combat an inflation arising out of excess demands in particular sectors of the economy.

The composition of demands relative to the composition of available resources has an important bearing on developments in business expansions. The problems of inflationary pressures, however, are likely to arise well before demands and output reach the limits of capacity, partly because the use of marginal production facilities raises costs. Problems of inflation certainly arise before output reaches capacity in all major sectors because resources are not highly mobile. In 1955 and 1956, for example, output was well below capacity in the basic textile industries but very close to capacity in the basic metals industries. As E. A. Goldenweiser wrote in 1941:

It should be mentioned . . . that there is no clear-cut line at which an increasing number of bottleneck advances in prices passes over into a general inflation. The development of a number of bottlenecks in many leading commodities may be the introductory phase of a general inflation. It can occur long before the entire country is operating at full capacity, because neither plant capacity nor labor supply is completely mobile. The existence of unused capacity in some industries may not prevent great shortages of capacity in others, and the presence of large numbers of unskilled workers without jobs may not prevent grave shortages in many skilled lines. So long as these instances of shortages are scattered and relatively few the situation is not properly described as inflation and can be handled by nonmonetary remedies. But it may become general long before full capacity is achieved. It should be kept in mind that it is the available supply of goods and not the theoretically possible supply that must meet a growing demand in order to prevent inflation.[1]

The demand-shift approach treats the milder, peacetime inflations of the sort experienced in 1954–57 as something different in kind from the type often associated with wars, whereas the difference appears rather to be one of degree. The immobility of resources is more obvious in the former cases, but it is not confined to them. In the more severe inflations, immobility of resources also limits shifts to areas of strongest demands, but its existence and influence are concealed by the general excess of demands.

In an economy with high and rising standards of living and many

[1] E. A. Goldenweiser, "Inflation," Federal Reserve *Bulletin*, April 1941, p. 292.

other features fostering change, demands are not likely to expand in such a way that their composition is always in balance with the location and types of existing plant and other resources. In business expansions, imbalances are likely to exist, and they are not likely to be precisely the same from one expansion to the next. Such imbalances operate to attract the newly available resources (and savings) into the sectors of strongest demand pressures.

PATTERNS OF PRICE AND COST CHANGES IN BUSINESS FLUCTUATIONS

Prices are determined by the interaction of a number of factors functioning continuously in many different types of markets, and there is an unending process of market adaptation to changes in the various factors. While business fluctuations differ from one another in important respects, they all have features in common with regard to the interactions of demands, output, costs, prices, and profits. Reviewing the process of change during postwar business expansions and contractions in this country, certain relationships and patterns of behavior are discernible.

Periods of Expansion

Early in expansions of business activity, prices usually are rising in markets for "sensitive" industrial material—that is, the materials whose prices are most responsive to short-run changes in demand. For rubber, hides, and some other sensitive materials, world production cannot be increased much (if at all) in the short run in response to rising demands. As a result, increases in demands are rather promptly reflected in price advances and may alter the international flows of commodities.

Production or supply can be increased in the short run for other sensitive materials, such as scrap metals, wastepaper, copper, lead, zinc, and lumber. Because increases in output are accompanied by rising costs per unit of output or because of other conditions of supply, expansion in demands is reflected in price rises which provoke increases in supply. Price trends for a group of these sensitive materials often suggest the direction and strength of demands before other types of data for the same time period become available.

Many foods and foodstuffs—including livestock, poultry, and some crops—also conform to the type of market behavior described for sensitive industrial materials. For these, however, the response of domestic demands to cyclical and secular income changes is slight (the income elasticity of demand is low). Substantial changes in output may occur, however, mainly because of variations in weather, swings in the hog and cattle cycles, or rising productivity. Consequently, price fluctuations for these commodities usually reflect changes in supplies to a greater extent than they reflect shifts in demands.

Agricultural commodities subject to Federal support programs are largely protected from the price-depressing influence of large increases in production. At the same time, the existence of stocks previously accumulated in the process of supporting prices has limited in recent years the response of prices to a crop failure or other events that reduce production and supply.

For most industrial materials other than those described as sensitive, supply is expansible in the short run until some relatively high rate of capacity utilization is reached. This is true for steel mill products, paper products, many chemicals, cement, brick, and other materials. In the early stages of expansion, variable costs per unit of output are not likely to rise as increases in output are accompanied by gains in productivity and wage rates do not rise much. Fixed costs per unit and average costs per unit decline, and profit margins as well as total profits rise. Expansion in demands for these materials is accompanied for a time by rising output and supply without widespread advances in list prices. Absorption of freight and other concessions from list prices which had developed during the previous recession tend to be reduced during the early stages of expansion. These changes in actual prices are not reflected in the established price indexes, which are based mainly on manufacturers' published price lists.

The behavior of wholesale or manufacturers' prices of most finished industrial products in the early stages of expansion is much like that described for the second group of industrial materials—for similar reasons. Therefore, increases in their prices early in expansions are likely to be restricted in scope.

Continued expansion of demands eventually generates upward pressures of costs on prices of industrial materials in the second or nonsensitive group and on prices of finished products. The upturn in costs is primarily a consequence of higher levels of output in relation to available manpower and material resources.

Contrary to the suggestion sometimes made that pressures of demand against resources available to produce specific products cannot possibly contribute to increases in their prices and costs until operations are at 100 percent of capacity, costs of production often begin to rise before output approaches such high levels. The plant and equipment existing in an industry at any time is of varying age and efficiency. As demands expand, less efficient facilities must be used if output is to be increased to fill the rising volume of orders. Partly because these marginal facilities have to be activated, over-all productivity advance slows and may actually cease or be reversed. This contributes, along with increasing wage rates, premium payments for overtime, and advances in prices of some materials consumed in the industry, to rising costs per unit of output.

Price- and cost-raising pressures of demands in specific industries, furthermore, may become widespread enough to constitute a general problem before output reaches high rates in relation to capacity in all major industries. Usually, some industries are growing while others are not, and some regions are gaining while others are losing business. A number of important bottlenecks may develop even while unused capacity exists elsewhere. These developments also contribute to a higher level of frictional unemployment of labor than might exist otherwise. A judgment that output in the whole economy is at a high rate relative to plant capacity does not require that there be no margins of unused capacity, any more than "full employment" means that there are no persons looking for jobs.

Given variations in the timing and intensity of demand and cost pressures among industries, Governmental policies to further expand aggregate demands in order to raise demands and output in those industries where capacity is not being intensively utilized would intensify demand pressures on those industries where output is already close enough to capacity to result in rising costs and higher prices. Consequently, while a higher level of aggregate demand might increase total output somewhat, it would also accentuate upward pressures of demand on prices.

An additional and important aspect of these developments and relationships is that an expansion of capital outlays is likely to be stimulated well in advance of full utilization of plant capacity. Business enterprises always have some capital replacement needs, and additional capital expenditures in most cases reduce costs or increase sales potentials. Incentives to undertake new commitments for expansion as well as for replacement are intensified if business managers expect higher levels of demand for their products from both secular growth and cyclical expansion. Since it ordinarily takes many months before new facilities can be acquired and efficiently integrated into the production process, business managers must plan expenditures to increase capacity well before output reaches the limits of their ability to produce.

Among the elements of cost, attention in recent years has been focused on changes in labor costs, partly because wage rates have risen persistently and labor costs are an important part of total variable costs. In major industries, where changes in wage rates tend to be industry-wide, such changes occur at a particular moment in time and they usually are widely publicized. On the other hand, changes in productivity, which operate in the direction of offsetting the effect of wage rate increases on labor costs per unit of output, occur over a period of time. Also, the advances are likely to vary considerably from plant to plant and from one producer to another.

For many industries, average measures of productivity show more cyclical variability than wage rates, rising in the early stages of expansion, leveling off as output approaches capacity, and declining in the early stages of recession. This pattern of change is probably accentuated by the short duration of the business fluctuations of postwar experience. Many new facilities are put in place late in expansion—or in the early months of recession—and there is some time lag between installation and their efficient operation. When there is such a lag, the resulting productivity gains may appear late in recession and early in expansion.

Partly for this reason, unit labor costs tend to decline in the early stages of expansion when productivity gains generally exceed increases in wages. As expansion develops, unit costs turn up because productivity advance slows and the rise in wages continues and possibly accelerates. In recession also, unit labor costs typically rise in certain industries as output per manhour declines.

Meanwhile, capital consumption and other relatively fixed costs—by definition—do not vary with the level of output. On a per unit of output basis, therefore, they show an inverse correlation with output, decreasing when output is rising and increasing when output is falling.

Cyclical variations in costs per unit of output, which result in considerable part from swings in production, are not accompanied by similar variations in prices. Consequently, profit margins fluctuate more widely than labor and other costs per unit of output, generally moving in the opposite direction. In the early stages of expansion, profit margins rise sharply; in later stages, they level off or decline; in recession, they decline decidedly.

The preceding review of price and cost influences indicates that in early stages of economic expansion, production and employment are likely to advance without generating widespread price and cost pressures. While wage rates and prices of certain materials increase, margins of profits over costs widen and are likely to approach their cyclical peaks. After expansion has progressed for a time, however, upward price and cost pressures build up, primarily because output in some industries has reached high levels in relation to capacity and unemployment has been reduced. As described earlier, less efficient plant facilities must be used and productivity advance slows or is reversed. At the same time, reduced unemployment and enlarged profit margins intensify pressures for increases in employee compensation.

With demands strong and output in some industries already at high levels in relation to capacity, the subsequent behavior of prices and costs is strongly influenced by the rate at which over-all activity has been expanding and by expectations. If the pace of expansion has been moderate, competitive conditions are maintained within most industries, between industries serving common markets, and between domestic goods and goods produced abroad. In these circumstances, increases in prices and costs are likely to be confined to a relatively few markets and are unlikely to be very large.

On the other hand, if demands have been expanding rapidly and assessments of prospects are highly optimistic, increases in wage rates and fringe benefits are likely to be large and price advances extensive. Increases in wages will be propagated throughout industry and may directly cause further expansion in demands for goods and services. Price advances may indirectly contribute to expanding demands by generating expectations of additional advances.

Increases in the price indexes will further contribute to cost increases through escalator provisions of labor, rent, and other contracts. Some State and local taxes and fees may be raised to cover the rising costs of current services and higher costs of school, highway and other construction. These taxes are also reflected in the consumer price index used for escalation purposes. And thus an interacting inflationary process of demands, prices, and costs can get in full operation.

Implicit in this description of price behavior for industrial commodities is the fact that relatively few markets conform to an ideal competitive model. In the competitive model, prices are determined by the interaction of buyers' bids and sellers' asking prices in the market; the individual seller has no significant influence on total supply and therefore has no discretion except with regard to his acceptance or rejection of the going price or how much he will supply at that price. This type of market behavior is approached most closely in markets for livestock, some other agricultural commodities, and the industrial materials earlier described as sensitive.

Markets for industrial commodities, on the contrary, are generally characterized by "imperfect" or "monopolistic" competition. Prices in these markets often are described as "administered." In such industries, a producer must make decisions regarding the pricing of the product—including all the price-related decisions associated with quality, design, and selling techniques. These pricing decisions are based on judgments of what sales would be at different levels of prices, on calculations of what costs per unit would be at various levels of production, and on the behavior of competing producers and products. Thus pricing decisions take into account, in addition to demand, the range of forces affecting production and costs, just as sales, production, and costs are influenced by pricing decisions. Producers must attempt to find a price that is in harmony with all the relevant short- and long-term demand and cost considerations, but without knowing precisely what will most effectively accomplish this aim.

The fact that prices are set by the decisions of producers implies a degree of market power—stemming from the nature of the product and the nature of the production process—but it does not connote full monopoly power. On the contrary, market forces—including competition within the industry and from other domestic or foreign products or alternative sources of satisfaction—are constantly working to alter past price decisions.

Rates for utilities, freight, public transportation, insurance, and postage are also administered prices, as are rates for many other business and consumer services. Both the cost and demand conditions encountered in the service industries vary widely. Some services are produced under conditions affording opportunities for basic technological improvement and productivity advance while for others such opportunities are limited. Some are primarily labor while others have a higher commodity content. Prices of some services are very responsive to local labor market and related economic conditions while others are subject more to nationwide forces. Some are regulated by public commissions and still others are stipulated fees for public services. In particular instances, service prices follow trends in wage rates fairly closely.

The result of most of these influences is that inflationary pressures in the economy are transmitted to services via increases in costs. For the regulated prices, advances may lag considerably behind the initiating causes and may occur in many instances even after business expansion has given way to recession.

Periods of Recession

During contractions in demands and activity, changes in prices and costs and in relationship between them are determined mainly by the duration of the contraction and by developments in the preceding expansion. In a prolonged and severe depression, accompanied by distress sales and substantial decreases in prices of existing assets, strong downward pressures develop on prices of currently produced goods and on wage rates and other elements of production costs. Since a contraction of this severity has not occurred since World War II, attention may be confined to the milder recessions experienced since then.

In recession, prices of sensitive industrial materials generally decline. Contraction in domestic demands and decreases in prices may reduce domestic supply by altering international commodity flows and/or by making marginal operations unprofitable. For the nonsensitive materials, analysis is complicated by the tendency of producers to change prices by varying concessions and discounts from unchanged list prices. While it is known that net or actual prices fluctuate more widely than list prices, little information is available to show the degree of change in actual prices.

List prices tend to be maintained in the early stages of contraction and if the recession proves to be brief, recovery in activity begins before many list-price cuts have been made. When it becomes clear that demands are reviving, the list price for a product on occasion is lowered to conform to actual transactions prices—because the operation of new facilities or some other development causes demand-cost relationships to be fundamentally different from those on which producers had been basing their decisions.

In describing the behavior of nonsensitive materials during business expansion, it was emphasized that producers' price decisions are based largely on calculations of costs at various possible levels of output as well as on judgments about demand. When demands contract and production is reduced, many elements of costs do not decline. Wage rates, for example, are maintained—or may actually increase in some lines owing to the terms of long-run labor agreements. The tendency of wage rates to be maintained was characteristic also of the mild recessions of prewar years.

Even in an administered price market, individual producers, faced with declining demands, have an incentive to reduce prices in order to increase sales, if they think competing producers will not also reduce prices. This goes far to explain the preference of producers for unpublicized price cuts—for price cuts brought about through concessions rather than through reductions in list prices. In certain situations, however, there may be incentives to publicize price reductions by cutting list prices: a cyclical contraction in demand for a particular material may be accompanied by competition from a new and lower cost source of supply or a new substitute material, or it may be accompanied by a change in the methods of production that appreciably reduces costs.

The recession behavior of manufacturers' prices of most finished industrial products is similar to that of the nonsensitive materials. To the extent that prices of materials decline, however, downward pressures on prices of finished goods are intensified. Prices of services tend to resist forces of decline in recession. In many cases, they rise further because of the increases authorized by regulatory agencies on the basis of earlier increases in costs, but the rate of rise in average prices of services slows down.

To summarize, prices of many sensitive materials typically decline in recession. These commodities have little weight in broad price indexes, however, and their influence currently is much less than in the indexes available for prewar years. Declines in prices of some other commodities are likely to be concealed in concessions from stable list prices. Still other prices, however, may resist any downward adjustment to declines in aggregate demand in moderate recessions.

If the previous expansion was accompanied by inflationary developments and appreciable increases in levels of prices, the increases are not likely to be fully erased during mild business recessions, giving rise to what has been called the "ratchet effect." If, however, price increases in the previous expansion were small, they may be subsequently offset as the competitive pressures that develop during recession, domestic and foreign, strengthen incentives to cut costs and to reflect these reductions in the form of lower prices. This emphasizes the importance of containing growth in credit and in demands for goods and services during periods of economic expansion and of preventing a climate of expectations conducive to large and widespread advances in prices and costs.

SUMMARY

Business fluctuations in the United States since World War II, while differing from one another in many ways, have had features in common with respect to the interactions of demands, output, costs, prices, and profits. The description of these relationships provided above indicates that the problems of inflationary pressures arise during the expansion phase of the business fluctuations characteristic of industrial economies, when demands are expanding. In the early stages of a business expansion, production and employment are likely to increase without generating widespread upward pressures on prices and costs. Continued expansion in demands eventually generates upward pressures on prices and costs as output in some industries reaches high levels in relation to capacity and unemployment is reduced. If the pace of expansion is moderate and competitive conditions are maintained, increases in prices and costs are likely to be confined to a relatively few markets. On the other hand, if demands expand rapidly and expectations are ebullient, increases in prices and costs are likely to become widespread.

With respect to the second of the two questions raised, once the process of inflation is under way, it is usually not possible to determine whether the dominant influence on prices stems from "cost push" or "demand shift." Since prices of goods and services represent costs to someone, increases in costs are one of the ways by which inflationary pressures are transmitted through the economy. At the same time, increases in some costs are promptly reflected in income payments and thus exert an influence on demands. Through this interaction of demands, prices, and costs, the inflationary process is initiated, and once in operation, the demand and cost elements interact in such a manner that they cannot be disentangled as separate and distinct forces.

In the chain-reaction process of demands, prices, and costs, the most direct influence that monetary policy can exert is on demands for goods and services. Through its influence on credit availability and on liquidity, monetary policy endeavors to maintain a climate of demands and expectations during business upswings that is conducive to a high rate of utilization of available resources without widespread upward pressures on prices and costs. Should upward pressures nevertheless develop, monetary policy can help to restrain them. Appropriate monetary policy can limit the funds that may be made available through bank credit to finance the expansion in demands stimulated by the income effects of price and cost increases, by expectations, and by other forces.

When business activity is high, prices generally are advancing, and the community expects continuing advances in prices, a monetary policy that restrains the use of bank credit is an appropriate and necessary tool. Whatever the causes or the means of propagating inflation, expansion of bank credit would influence both spending and expectations and so would provide additional impetus to the price-cost spiral. Under these conditions, individual and group efforts to hedge against inflation or to protect against it by tying contractual arrangements to price indexes would tend to aggravate inflationary forces.

In appraising the effectiveness of monetary policy, a number of factors must be considered. The formation of policy, first of all, depends on current assessments of developing business and financial conditions and, despite improvements in economic intelligence over the years, it is not possible always to judge accurately the strength of the forces developing. Other activities of the Federal Government, furthermore, have an impact on levels of production, employment, and income, and thus they influence needs for greater or lesser degrees of monetary ease or restraint. These policies, consequently, may complicate or simplify the task and they may inhibit or enhance the performance of monetary policy. Government policies that affect the functioning of markets and those that directly affect prices—such as import duties and quotas and antitrust policies— also bear on the effectiveness and results of monetary policy. The degree of market power exercised by private groups also may affect the sensitivity of markets to current and prospective demands. If monopoly power were widespread, it could have an influence on the effectiveness of both monetary and fiscal policies in pursuing their goals.

ROGER W. SPENCER

THE RELATION BETWEEN PRICES AND EMPLOYMENT: TWO VIEWS

35

Monetary and fiscal authorities are currently confronted with the task of simultaneously slowing price increases and maintaining employment growth. Policies directed toward the achievement of both objectives are affected by the policymakers' understanding of the underlying factors influencing prices and employment (or unemployment). Two principal views on this issue have emerged in the past decade. One stresses the short-run "trade-off" between prices and

Reprinted from Roger W. Spencer, "The Relation Between Prices and Employment: Two Views," *Review* (March 1969) pp. 15–21, Federal Reserve Bank of St. Louis.

unemployment, and the other emphasizes the absence of a stable long-run relationship between varying rates of anticipated price changes and the level of unemployment. The short-run, for purposes of this analysis, is a period in which the relevant economic factors do not fully adjust to expectations, while the long-run is a period in which the values of actual and anticipated variables coincide.

This article discusses these two views of the relation between prices and employment without delving excessively into the theoretical complexities of the relation. For expositional purposes, the two views are discussed separately, because the literature tends to be divided into these two groups. The purpose of the article, however, is to demonstrate that the differences between the two views stem primarily from the emphasis on short-run vs. long-run considerations rather than from diametrically opposing theories or models. Whether the short run or the long run is emphasized has substantially different implications for stabilization policy. These different implications are discussed in the concluding section of the article.

THE SHORT-RUN TRADE-OFF VIEW

High levels of unemployment in this country have generally been associated with slowly changing price levels, while low levels of unemployment have usually been accompanied by rapidly rising prices. These observed relationships have prompted attempts to explain price variations through changes in unemployment relative to the labor force. The Trade-Off View does not focus on unemployment as a determinant of prices directly, however. It holds that unemployment and the rate of change of unemployment influence money wages, and wage changes, in turn, bring about changes in the level of prices.

A. W. Phillips' study of the relation between wages and unemployment in England is generally considered the point of departure for most recent investigations into the trade-off controversy.[1] Phillips constructed a "trade-off curve" between the unemployment rate and wage changes, which indicated that wages in Great Britain rose rapidly when unemployment was declining and slowly when unemployment was rising. The "Phillips curve" was drawn to reflect a relationship between wages and unemployment, but other analysts

[1] A. W. Phillips, "The Relationship Between Unemployment and the Rate of Change of Money Wage Rates in the United Kingdom, 1861–1957," *Economica*, Vol. XXV (November 1958), pp. 283–299.

have maintained that a similar relationship holds between prices and unemployment.[2] They have assumed or observed that the factors which influence wages similarly influence other prices, or that wages are a principal independent determinant of prices.

Those analysts who follow Phillips in stressing a trade-off between wages or other prices and unemployment have found several factors besides employment pressures which apparently determine wage changes. Factors most often included in this group are profits, productivity, and the cost-of-living. Employment pressures, however, remain the primary explanatory variable.

Factors Influencing Wage-Price Changes

The unemployment rate reflects the state of the demand for labor, a demand which is derived from the demand for goods and services. In a period of rising labor demand, employers attempt to attract workers from one another, thus bidding up wage rates. Additional labor may be obtained by attracting, through higher pay, such "secondary" or "reserve" workers as housewives, students, retired persons, or those already holding one job. The ability of workers to obtain large wage gains may be increased in periods of rising demand for goods and services when employers are especially anxious to avoid strikes. Profits are usually higher and inventories are often at lower levels when demand is high; consequently, employers probably exhibit less resistance to wage demands at such times.

A state of falling demand for goods and services and labor is reflected in a higher unemployment rate. According to Phillips, ". . . it appears that workers are reluctant to offer their services at less than the prevailing rates when the demand for labour is low and unemployment is high so that wage rates fall only very slowly."[3]

Changes in both profits and consumer prices are positively associated with changes in wages in the Trade-Off View. Workers often use high earnings reports and cost-of-living advances to improve their bargaining position. Some labor groups have cost-of-living escalator clauses written into their wage contracts.

No general agreement relating productivity and wage changes can be found among those who favor the Trade-Off View. Statis-

[2] See, for example, George L. Perry, *Unemployment, Money Wage Rates, and Inflation* (Cambridge: The M.I.T. Press, 1966), p. 107. Perry states that "the factors affecting wage changes have been analyzed on the assumption that the wage relation is central to an understanding of the inflation problem."

[3] Phillips, p. 283.

tical studies have produced conflicting results.[4] Analysts have found insignificant, significantly positive, and significantly negative relationships between productivity and wage changes. Consequently, for purposes of analysis, productivity is generally assumed to increase at some constant rate. Analysts then can focus on the effects of changes in other variables, particularly unemployment, on wage rates.

Most observers who emphasize the Trade-Off View relate money (nominal) wage changes to the above explanatory variables through regression analysis. If all but one of the explanatory factors are held constant, a relationship between one variable—usually the unemployment rate—and wages can be depicted graphically. The resulting curve slopes downward from left to right, and is usually shaped similar to the rounded "L" determined by Phillips. (See Figures 1 and 2). The non-linear shape suggests the existence of a critical high-employment range. According to Levy, "That price inflation, rather than reduced unemployment, is the main result of any expansionary policy after the economy has reached a *critical high employment range*, is a basic inference from traditional economics which is rarely questioned."[5]

The critical high-employment range may be defined as that range in which the number of employment vacancies are approximately equal to the number of workers seeking employment.[6] By this definition, excess demand in the labor market exists when the number of vacancies exceeds the number of job seekers, and there is an excess supply of labor when the number of workers seeking employment exceeds the number of vacancies. Excess demand causes wage rates to rise rapidly in the former case, and excess supply in the latter case tends to slow the rate of wage increase. Labor demand and supply factors may vary from sector to sector, but there is some evidence that a close tie exists between the ". . . aggregate unemployment rate and unemployment among various subgroups in the population."[7]

[4] See Ronald G. Bodkin, *The-Wage-Price-Productivity Nexus* (Philadelphia: University of Pennsylvania Press, 1966), pp. 143–151, for a discussion of such studies as well as Bodkin's own regression results.

[5] Michael E. Levy, "Full Employment Without Inflation," *The Conference Board Record*, Vol. IV (November 1967), p. 36.

[6] Edmund S. Phelps points out that labor union behavior and the existence of "unemployables" may partially account for the fact that excess demand in the labor market seldom appears to exist, that is, ". . . vacancies almost never exceed unemployment." See "Money-Wage Dynamics and Labor-Market Equilibrium," *The Journal of Political Economy*, Vol. LXXVI (July/August 1968), p. 686.

[7] Perry, p. 25.

FIGURE 1 Rates of Change of Manufacturing Wages and Rates of Labor Unemployment *(Curve has been arbitrarily fitted to 1961-1968 data; data shown are in percentages)*

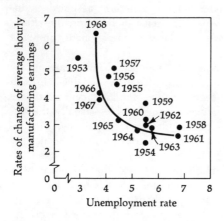

The Stability of the Phillips Curve

An issue of particular importance to policymakers is the stability of the prices (wages)-employment relationship. Most Trade-Off View studies, by holding constant those factors other than unemployment which determine wages, do not stress fluctuations within a Phillips curve, shifts of the curve itself, or changes in the critical high-employment range. These studies, which rely heavily on regression analysis, often imply that the economy is operating on a single curve, and stabilization actions directed toward guiding the economy to some point off the curve may prove unsuccessful. Such studies, strictly interpreted, indicate that the Phillips curve is a stable relationship.[8] This implication is refuted by Michael Levy, who found that "during the post-war years, the basic (Phillips curve) relationship for the U.S. economy between wage rate advances on the one hand, and the unemployment rate, the corporate profit rate, and cost-of-living increases on the other, has been highly unstable."[9] [Italics omitted.]

Although the relationship may be technically unstable, a plotting of the wage and price changes and the unemployment rate reveals that Phillips' hypothesis—regarding the association of declining un-

[8] Stability exists, technically, when the parameters computed for various time periods appear to be drawn from the same underlying population.

[9] Levy, p. 37. Levy's conclusion is based on a statistical technique ("the Chow test") designed to test the degree of stability among relationships.

employment with rapidly rising wages (prices), and rising unemploy-ment with slowly changing wages (prices)—has been generally ob-servable over the past sixteen years. A simple correlation between two variables, as given here by a plotting of points on a two-dimensional graph, does not demonstrate causality, however. The relationship between the rate of change of manufacturing wages and the unemployment rate for the 1953–1968 period is plotted in Figure 1. The curve, which is similar in shape to the curve deter-mined by Phillips, has been arbitrarily drawn to fit the data from 1961 to 1968, a period of uninterrupted economic expansion.[10] The shape of the curve would be altered to some extent if fitted to the 1953–1960 period. For the sixteen-year period, the curve would be shifted slightly to the right.

Graphical trade-off analysis usually focuses on the wages-unem-ployment relationship, but it has also been extended to the prices-unemployment relationship as has been done in Figure 2. The overall fit for the sixteen-year period would not be as satisfactory as in the previous chart, but there is a close parallel for the past eight years. In some earlier years, sharp price increases occurred at vary-ing rates of unemployment. Unemployment averaged slightly above 4 per cent of the labor force in the 1955 to 1957 period, more than 5 per cent from 1959 to 1960, and a little less than 4 per cent in the 1965 to 1968 period. This evidence suggests that the critical high-employment range has varied, perhaps reflecting the changing nature of the labor force in particular and the economy in general.

Phillips curves derived from regression analysis are based on rather specific assumptions, and the shape can vary substantially when minor modifications of the behavioral assumptions are made, as illustrated by the two following examples. A basic curve derived by George Perry relating consumer prices and unemployment was

---

[10] The 1961 to 1968 curve for the United States mirrors more closely the relationship found by Phillips than do other possible subsets of the sixteen observations. Moreover, the fitting of the curve to the last eight years emphasizes the present position on the "low unemployment-rising wages" portion of the curve. Annual data were used in keeping with Phillips' original work. The problems inherent in using annual data in the Phillips curve relationship are well known. ". . . we regard the construc-tion of a plausible Phillips curve from annual data for a long period as a tour de force somewhat comparable to writing the Lord's Prayer on the head of a pin, rather than as a guide to policy. This is because it is highly probable that the relationship has changed during the period . . . and because of the large changes in some of the variables that take place during the course of a calendar year and are blurred in the annual data." Albert Rees and Mary T. Hamilton, "The Wage-Price-Productivity Perplex," *Journal of Political Economy*, Vol. LXXV (February 1967), p. 70.

FIGURE 2   Rates of Change of Consumer Prices and Rates of Labor Unemployment (*Curve has been arbitrarily fitted to 1961-1968 data; data shown are in percentages*)

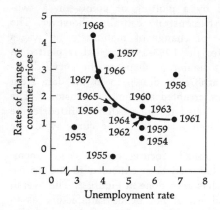

constructed from an equation in which prices were allowed to respond freely to market pressures. By assuming instead that half of the price increases were autonomous, Perry found that the curve, fairly steeply sloped in the first instance, became relatively flat. In fact, the slope of the curve was less than half of that calculated originally.[11]

Ronald Bodkin[12] determined a near-horizontal linear relation between wages and unemployment. Rees and Hamilton,[13] utilizing the same data and nearly the same assumptions as Bodkin, found a much steeper curve. Their results precipitated the remark:

> Our final caution is that we have been astounded by how many very different Phillips curves can be constructed on reasonable assumptions from the same body of data. The nature of the relationship between wage changes and unemployment is highly sensitive to the exact choice of the other variables that enter the regression and to the forms of all the variables. For this reason, the authors of Phillips curves would do well to label them conspicuously *"Unstable. Apply with extreme care."*

This conclusion implies that the usefulness of such statements as ". . . 4 per cent unemployment is consistent with a 2 per cent rate of inflation if profit rates are at 11.6 per cent . . . ."[14] is limited by the validity of the assumptions which underlie the model.

[11] Perry, p. 68.
[12] Bodkin, p. 279.
[13] Rees and Hamilton, p. 70.
[14] Perry, pp. 108–109.

Characteristics of the Trade-Off View

The chief characteristics of the Trade-Off View might be summarized as:
1) The relation between money wages and unemployment is stressed, rather than the prices-unemployment relation.
2) Money wage changes are assumed to be a primary, if not the primary, determinant of changes in prices of final goods; consequently, changes in prices of final goods follow wage changes.
3) The relevant variables are specified in nominal rather than real (or price-deflated) terms.
4) The basic relationships are established by the use of regression analysis using observed data.
5) The relation between rates of wage or price changes and the unemployment rate may be represented by a line which curves downward on a graph from left to right.
6) The rationale behind movements along the Phillips curve, rather than shifts of the curve itself, is stressed. The policymakers attempt to attain the point on the curve which seems least undesirable.
7) The time units and period covered by the analysis are specified in terms of months, quarters, or years. Phrases such as "the length of time required for the factors to reach their long-run values" are not found in the Trade-Off View.

THE LONG-RUN EQUILIBRIUM VIEW

The Long-Run Equilibrium View considers the trade-offs between wages or prices and unemployment as transitory phenomena, and that no such trade-off exists after factors have completely adjusted to the trend of spending growth. In the short-run there can be a discrepancy between expectations and actual price or wage changes, but not in the long-run. After the discrepancies between expected and actual values have worked themselves out, the only relevant magnitudes are "real," or price-deflated ones.

To illustrate the view, consider the following hypothesized sequence of events in the upswing of a business cycle, beginning with an initial condition of significant unemployment. Monetary or fiscal actions may start an upturn of business activity. Spending occurs in anticipation of a continuation of the price levels which had prevailed in the downswing. Employers begin actively seeking workers to accommodate the rising demand, but wages increase only moderately since a large number of unemployed are seeking jobs. Output and employment rise more rapidly than wages or prices. The remainder of the scenario is outlined by Milton Friedman:

Because selling prices of products typically respond to an unanticipated rise in nominal demand faster than prices of factors of production, real wages received have gone down—though real wages anticipated by employees went up, since employees implicitly evaluated the wages offered at the earlier price level. Indeed, the simultaneous fall *ex post* in real wages to employers and rise *ex ante* in real wages to employees is what enabled employment to increase. [The non-technical reader may wish to substitute "anticipated" for "*ex ante*" and "actual" for "*ex post.*"] But the decline *ex post* in real wages will soon come to affect anticipations. Employees will start to reckon on rising prices of the things they buy and to demand higher nominal wages for the future. "Market" unemployment is below the "natural" level. There is an excess demand for labor so real wages will tend to rise toward their initial level.[15]

As real wages approach their original level, employers are no longer motivated to hire workers as rapidly or bid up wages so much as in the earlier portion of the upswing. Moreover, rising wages may encourage employers to utilize more labor-saving equipment and relatively fewer workers. As the growth of demand for labor slows, the unemployment rate declines to its "natural" level. Economic units come to anticipate the rate of inflation, and are no longer misled by increases in money income—the so-called "money illusion." The unexpected price increases which accompanied the original expansion of total demand and production caused a temporary reduction of unemployment below the long-run equilibrium level. Only accelerating inflation—a situation in which actual price rises continue to exceed anticipated rises—can keep the actual unemployment rate below the "natural" rate.[16]

Inflation has not been allowed to rise uncontrolled for sustained periods in this country, so little empirical evidence can be amassed to support the contentions that no permanent trade-off exists. In other countries such as Brazil, however, it has been found that sustained inflation does not generate continuous employment gains; in fact, recessions and high unemployment rates have occurred as secular inflation continued. Unanticipated price increases have, in

[15] Milton Friedman, "The Role of Monetary Policy," *The American Economic Review,* Vol. LVIII. (March 1968), p. 10.

[16] Phelps, pp. 682–683, provides a comprehensive listing of several authors and their variations of the "anticipated inflation" thesis. Also, see: Charles C. Holt, "Improving the Labor Market Tradeoff Between Inflation and Unemployment" (Working Paper P-69-1, The Urban Institute, Washington, D.C., Feb. 20, 1969).

those countries as well as in the United States, generated increased temporary employment, just as unanticipated declines in the rate of price increase have caused temporary rises in unemployment. But if inflation is "fully and instantaneously discounted, the Phillips curve becomes a vertical line over the point of 'equilibrium unemployment.' This is the rate of unemployment where wage increases equal productivity gains plus changes in income shares. The unemployment-price stability trade-off is gone."[17] In other words, there is no particular rate of price change related to a particular rate of unemployment when the price changes are fully anticipated. Unemployment shifts to its equilibrium value and is consistent with any rate of change of prices. A low rate of unemployment can no longer be "traded-off" against rapidly rising prices, nor can a high unemployment rate be "traded-off" against slowly changing prices.

Costs of Information

A modified version of the Long-Run Equilibrium View is framed in terms of costs of obtaining information about job opportunities. When the demand for labor is low, the costs to a worker of discovering the state of labor demand are relatively high because employers are not actively seeking workers by publicizing extensive lists of vacancies. Employers are not as likely to absorb job training and transfer costs as they are when aggregate demand is rising. When labor demand rises and employers begin bidding up wage rates to attract additional labor, the costs of information, training and transferring are lowered to employees. The lower costs mean that employees will not have to search as long for acceptable employment, and the shorter the search time, the lower the rate of unemployment. Rising wages are accompanied by a declining unemployment rate.[18]

A reversal of stimulative policies will generate declining demand for labor. Some workers will accept smaller wage increases or reduced wages, but others will prefer to leave their jobs to seek em-

[17] Henry C. Wallich, "The American Council of Economic Advisers and the German *Sachverstaendigenrat:* A Study in the Economics of Advice," *The Quarterly Journal of Economics,* August 1968, pp. 356–357.

[18] The cost of information analysis is derived from studies by George J. Stigler, "Information in the Labor Market," *Journal of Political Economy,* Vol. LXX (Supplement: October 1962), pp. 94–105; and Armen A. Alchian and William R. Allen, *University Economics,* 2d ed., chapter 25 (Belmont, Calif.: Wadsworth Publishing Company, Inc., 1967). Also see Armen A. Alchian, "Information Costs, Pricing, and Resource Unemployment" in a forthcoming issue of the *Western Economic Journal.*

ployment at their former money wage rates. They expect prices and wages will remain at their earlier, higher levels. Prices and output will have fallen, however, and the high real wage rate will have stimulated employers to lower the quantity of labor demanded, thereby raising search costs to those workers who leave their jobs to seek employment elsewhere.[19] Higher search costs and lower money wage rates will be accompanied by rising unemployment. When workers realize that demand and price increases have slowed, they will be willing to accept the lower money wage rates and unemployment will stabilize at the "natural" level. For the stabilization to occur, however, no money illusion can exist. Anticipated wage (or price) changes must equal actual wage (or price) changes.

The costs-of-information approach combines the two factors determining the equilibrium rate of unemployment—the structure of real wage rates as determined by labor demand and supply, and "imperfections" within the labor market.[20] Bottlenecks, labor and product market monopolies, positive costs of information, training and transfers create "imperfections" in the labor market. In other words, all markets are not cleared instantaneously and without cost. At any point in time the degree of the so-called "imperfection" within the labor market will vary, depending on transactions and information costs; correspondingly, the "natural" rate of unemployment will vary.

Enactment of policies oriented toward eliminating or reducing market imperfections (adjustment costs) will cause the short-run Phillips curve to shift to the left and down. Policies which increase these costs move the short-run Phillips curve upward and to the

[19] The Committee for Economic Development points out that "slow adjustment to unexpected price increases may increase employment as prices accelerate, but this slow adjustment may also cause an increase in unemployment as the rate of price inflation slows. The temporary trade-off is a double-edged sword." *Fiscal and Monetary Policies for Steady Economic Growth*, a statement on National Policy by the Research and Policy Committee of the Committee for Economic Development, January 1969, p. 40.

[20] The Equilibrium View maintains no monopoly over discusssions of the relevance of labor market structure; indeed, Lipsey's rigorous reformulation of Phillips' original view was predicated to a large extent on the importance of unemployment among different sectors of the economy. See R. G. Lipsey, "The Relation between Unemployment and the Rate of Change of Money Wage Rates in the United Kingdom, 1862–1957: A Further Analysis," *Economica*, Vol. XXVII (February 1969), pp. 1–31. On the whole, however, it seems that the Equilibrium View, which stresses the reasons for the changing nature of the short-run Phillips curves—varying expectations and cost-of-information—is the view in which structural considerations should be discussed.

FIGURE 3   Hypothetical Relationships Between Prices and Unemployment

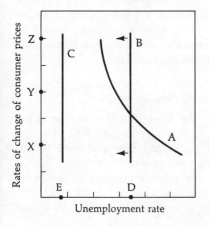

Curve "A" is a short-run prices-unemployment relationship.
Vertical line "B" is the long-run relationship between prices (fully anticipated regardless of the rate of change) and the "natural" rate of unemployment, "D", before reduction of market "imperfections."
Vertical line "C" is a similar long-run relationship between prices and unemployment after assumed reduction of labor and product market imperfections.

right. Different forces are at work at different times, causing the curve to shift frequently. Expectations of higher prices will cause the curve to shift upward, and expectations of lower prices move the curve in the opposite direction. The optimal stabilization policies, therefore, would be those which would reduce market adjustment costs and expectations of higher prices. Enactment of such policies would at first move the short-run Phillips curve to the left and downward, and in time, as expectations are fully realized, cause the curve to become a vertical line over the "natural" rate of unemployment.

A hypothetical, long-run relationship between prices and unemployment is presented in Figure 3. Point D represents the "natural," or equilibrium rate of unemployment before market imperfections or adjustment costs are reduced. Curve A represents one of many possible short-run Phillips curves that exist before price changes are fully anticipated. After the rate of inflation becomes fully discounted, the unemployment rate will shift from some point beneath curve A to point D, regardless of whether prices are rising at some slow rate, X, or a rapid rate, Z. The shift may occur along any of an infinite number of Phillips curves. The vertical line above point D indicates that no economic units—workers or employers, sellers or consumers, borrowers or lenders—are surprised by price changes. If programs to reduce labor and product market imperfections are implemented, vertical line B will shift, after a transitory period, to the left. Vertical line C represents the new long-run relationship between prices and employment above point E.

Characteristics of the Long-Run Equilibrium View

The principal characteristics of the Long-Run Equilibrium View might be summarized as:

1) The relationship between all prices and unemployment is emphasized, rather than the wages-unemployment relation.
2) Changes in selling prices usually precede changes in the prices of productive agents.
3) The relevant economic factors are specified in real rather than nominal terms.
4) Because of the lack of data on accelerating inflations, expectations of price changes, and the "natural" rate of unemployment, the analysis is generally accomplished through abstract reasoning rather than empirical testing.
5) The relation between the long-run rate of price or wage changes and the unemployment rate is a vertical line over the equilibrium rate of unemployment.
6) The long-run relationship and reasons for observed shifts of the Phillips curve are stressed. The authorities do not have to choose as a target some fixed relationship between prices and unemployment on a Phillips curve, but can attempt to move the economy off a short-run curve. In the long-run, they can seek any trend in prices desired without a sacrifice in terms of foregone employment or production.
7) The time period of the analysis is not specified. In the long-run, the actual values of the relevant economic variables equal the expected values, while in the short-run, they do not.

POLICY IMPLICATIONS OF THE TWO VIEWS

Unemployment declined from 5.2 per cent of the labor force in 1964 to 3.5 per cent in 1968. The annual rate of increase in consumer prices rose from 1.3 per cent to 4.2 per cent for corresponding years. These data indicate, according to the Trade-Off View, that stabilization authorities must decide to accept either high rates of price increases in order to maintain low unemployment rates, or adopt deflationary measures and accept relatively high levels of unemployment. Only significant reductions of imperfections within the product and labor markets could prevent employment declines in the face of deflationary policies.

Proponents of the Long-Run Equilibrium View point out that even in the absence of structural improvements, monetary and fiscal policies need not be limited by a short-run trade-off between prices and employment. Continuation of expansionary developments will generate either (1) a high, steady rate of inflation which will eventually become fully anticipated and confer no net additional employment benefits (unemployment will gradually return to its "natural" rate), or (2) an accelerating rate of inflation which will permit unemployment to remain below the "natural" rate. Neither expansionary policy alternative appears economically or politically desirable. Deflationary actions would produce increased unemployment (as expectations of price changes are slowly revised) but only temporarily, according to the Equilibrium View. As soon as a new price trend becomes stabilized and fully anticipated, nominal and real wages will coincide, and unemployment will fall to its "natural" rate. An inflationary policy is neither a necessary nor a sufficient condition for the attainment of high levels of employment. Since price expectations seem to change only slowly, actions to reduce the rate of inflation should probably be applied gradually to minimize the transition cost in terms of reduced output and increased unemployment.

Both views recognize the merits of structural measures in complementing monetary and fiscal actions. Policies which reduce the costs of obtaining employment information, improve labor mobility and skills, and eliminate product and labor market monopolies will lower the optimal level of unemployment. Adoption of such policies would improve the short-run dilemma faced by monetary and fiscal authorities and enable them to shift their long-run unemployment target to a lower level.

PART V-B / / MONETARY AND FISCAL POLICY: OPTIMUM MIX AND EFFECTIVENESS

CLAY J. ANDERSON

FISCAL-MONETARY POLICIES: WHAT MIX?

36

Fiscal policy is too easy; monetary policy is too tight. This is a view frequently expressed in recent months. The emphasis is on a different mix, not on a general increase in restraint.

The need for coordinating fiscal and monetary policies in order that one would not tend to offset the other has long been recognized. But varying the blend better to achieve economic goals is of fairly recent origin.

This article deals briefly with some of the principal considerations involved in using the fiscal-monetary mix as a tool of economic stabilization: the mechanics of fiscal and monetary policies; problems of implementation; suggested mixes to achieve certain objectives; and limitations on the effectiveness of varying the mix.

MECHANICS OF FISCAL POLICY

The Federal Government has become big business. It is the largest spender, the largest taxer, the largest borrower, and the largest buyer of our total output of goods and services.

That operations of such magnitude have important effects on the economy is not debatable. The crucial question is whether we use fiscal operations to help achieve our economic objectives.

General Effects

Treasury operations have far-reaching effects. Over 50 million people and hundreds of thousands of corporations make income-tax

Reprinted from Clay J. Anderson, "Fiscal-Monetary Policies: What Mix?" *Business Review* (January 1967), pp. 3–12, Federal Reserve Bank of Philadelphia.

payments to the Treasury. Millions of individuals and business firms are recipients of funds paid out by the Treasury in its purchases of goods, services, and in social welfare benefits. Thus Treasury operations affect the spendable income of millions of consumers and business firms. It is useful to distinguish two types of effects: the direct impact, and secondary reactions initiated by the original transactions.

Direct

Treasury receipts transfer funds from taxpayers to the Government. Personal and corporate income taxes now run around $100 billion a year. The immediate effect is apparent—the Government will have that much more to spend, and individuals and corporations less.

Government cash payments put additional funds in the hands of the public; they directly add to disposable income. Moreover, the Federal Government is our largest buyer. It takes about 10 per cent of our total output of goods and services. Government purchases are a strong prop under total demand.

With the Treasury siphoning in and paying out many billions of dollars, the net over-all effect depends on the relative magnitude of receipts and payments. If the Treasury takes in more than it pays out, the net direct effect is a reduction in funds at the disposal of the public. With less money to spend, total demand for goods and services should be less. If the Treasury pays out more than it takes in, the public has more to spend. Thus a surplus tends to reduce spendable funds and total demand; a deficit tends to increase them.

Actual results, however, may differ from the immediate impact. The final effect depends on disposition of the surplus or how a deficit is financed.

A surplus will have little, if any, restrictive effect if the excess receipts are returned to the public or replaced by the creation of new funds. Using a surplus to redeem Government securities held by the public shifts funds from taxpayers to holders of the securities. There is likely to be a redistribution of funds available for spending but there is no change in the total. Redeeming securities held by commercial banks results in a decrease in deposits and bank holdings of Government securities. But it also frees reserves, and may result in somewhat lower market rates; banks have sufficient reserves to expand loans and restore deposits to the former level. There is a net reduction in deposits and spendable funds only if the reserves released are held as excess (which is unlikely), used to repay indebtedness to the Reserve Banks, or absorbed through Federal Reserve action. Redemption of securities held by Federal Reserve

Banks exerts the greatest restraint because the net result is a reduction in both bank reserves and deposits.

A fiscal surplus is not necessarily restrictive. It is not restrictive
if Congress is induced to authorize a corresponding increase in expenditures. It is not restrictive if the surplus is used to redeem Government securities held by nonbank owners.[1] And it is not restrictive if used to retire bank-held securities unless monetary policy
prevents use of the released reserves for additional loans and investments. In short, a surplus is likely to bring a net reduction in
disposable income and total demand below what it would have been
only when accompanied by some monetary restraint.

It is equally important to note that the stimulating effect of a
deficit depends on how it is financed. If financed by additional taxes
or by selling securities to nonbank buyers, there is a shift of funds
but no change in the public's disposable income. The deficit results
in an increase in total spendable funds only if the borrowing results in creation of new funds; i.e., if purchased directly or indirectly by the Federal Reserve and commercial banks; or if it activates
funds which otherwise would have been idle. If purchased by commercial banks, more reserves would be required to support the newly
created deposits; less reserves would be available for extending
credit to other borrowers. Therefore, for a deficit to have a stimulating effect the support of monetary policy is also required.

Secondary

The direct effects are only the initial impact of the Government's
financial operations on disposable income and aggregate demand.
The initial rise in income would touch off more spending. Improved
sales swell the flow of new orders to manufacturers. Manufacturers
buy more supplies and use more labor. Higher levels of production
and employment generate more income, which in turn touches off
another rise in total demand and business activity. A reduction in
disposable income would set in motion a contraction in demand and
output.

The chain reaction to an initial rise or fall in disposable income
does not continue forever. There are leakages, so that the secondary
effects are similar to the waves created by throwing a rock into a
pond—they spread in ever-widening circles but with diminishing
intensity. Some of the increase in income, for example, may be used
to repay outstanding debt; taxes will siphon some back to the Trea-

---

[1] There could be some net reduction in total demand if holders of the
redeemed securities were less eager spenders than the taxpayers.

sury; and a part may be offset by reduced unemployment benefits. As leakages divert funds from the income-spending stream, secondary effects gradually fade away.

The secondary response of consumer expenditures to an initial increase in disposable income is fairly prompt and predictable. The ratio of consumer spending to disposable income has moved within a narrow range of 92 to 95 per cent for almost two decades. Some have estimated that the major part of the effect on consumer expenditures occurs within the first quarter following the initial impact on disposable income.

Business investment is likely to be more sensitive to economic conditions. Rising retail sales may be met for a while out of top-heavy inventories. If so, only after inventories have been reduced to desired levels will the larger flow of new orders be matched by a rise in production. Likewise, rising production may be met for a while by using existing productive facilities. Excess capacity, profit expectations, and availability and cost of financing are among the factors that will influence the secondary effect on investment.

Selective Effects

Fiscal policy has considerable potential for influencing the composition as well as the aggregate demand for goods and services. The direct impact can be varied somewhat by altering the tax structure and composition of federal expenditures.

Tax Structure

Tax changes can be designed so as to put most of the direct effect on consumption or investment.

The direct impact of raising or lowering the personal income tax will fall mainly on consumer income and expenditures. The effect on consumption may be greater if tax changes are concentrated in the lower income brackets. People with lower incomes are likely to spend a larger proportion on consumer goods and services. There are limitations, however. Those with a taxable income of less than $5,000 account for about one-third of total individual tax returns but less than 10 percent of total personal income tax receipts. Individuals with taxable incomes under $10,000 account for less than one-half of total receipts.

Tax changes can also be formulated to concentrate the direct effect on investment. Changes in the corporate income tax affect net earnings and the supply of internal funds available for investment. They also alter net profit margins and incentive to invest.

Changing individual tax rates on high- instead of low-bracket incomes is more likely to affect the flow of personal savings into investment. Investment tax credits and depreciation allowances are other methods of altering the inducement to invest.

Only the initial impact of a tax change can be directed toward certain parts of the economy. Once new dollars injected by fiscal policy get into the hands of consumers and businessmen they lose their identity. They will be spent like any other dollar. The secondary effects, therefore, will reflect consumer and investor preferences —not necessarily those of fiscal authorities.

Composition of Expenditures

Projects can be selected so that payments will go mainly to lower-income groups. For example, old-age and retirement benefits, unemployment benefits, public assistance and relief, and housing subsidies are likely to go mostly to people with below-average incomes. In effect, such payments redistribute income from higher to lower income groups. But it should be noted that expenditures of this type are usually determined largely by considerations other than cyclical stabilization.

Some types of expenditures are more closely related to business investment. Government expenditures for research and development may well create opportunities for private investment. Expenditures for education and job training improve the quality and skill of the labor force. Investment in human resources, as well as plant and equipment, tends to increase productivity.

Taxes Versus Spending

Effectiveness in achieving selective effects is one important consideration in choosing between taxes and spending. Another factor that should not be overlooked is the allocation of resources between private and public use.

The restrictive effect of a surplus can be achieved either by a reduction in Government spending or an increase in taxes or both. A reduction in Government spending tends to divert resources from public to private use. A larger portion of total output goes to satisfy private wants and preferences, unless the surplus results in a proportionate decline in private output. Raising taxes to create a surplus does the opposite. It diverts resources from private to Government use. The choice at stake is how much of our income we want to spend ourselves and how much we want the Government to spend for us.

MECHANICS OF MONETARY POLICY

Tax and expenditure changes directly enlarge or reduce disposable income; monetary policy influences use of credit to supplement current income.

Credit is a means of drawing on future income to pay for today's purchases. The effect on total demand depends mainly on whether borrowing results in the creation of new funds. If the lender advances to the borrower funds collected from savers, as in the case of savings institutions, the net effect is a transfer from saver to borrower. There is no increase in total amount of spendable funds. Total demand is not increased unless some borrowed funds would have been held idle otherwise. If the lender puts newly created funds at the disposal of the borrower, as in the case of commercial banks, there is a net increase in checkbook money.

Monetary policy impinges directly on bank reserves and the capacity of commercial banks to create new deposits. Open market operations supply or withdraw reserves; a change in the discount rate makes it more or less expensive for banks to borrow additional reserves; and a change in reserve requirements alters the amount of reserves banks are required to hold against deposits. In short, Federal Reserve tools enable the System to alter the cost and supply of reserves, which in turn affects both ability and willingness of commercial banks to create new deposits by making loans and investments. The Federal Reserve can restrict deposit creation by making reserves less readily available and more expensive; it encourages credit and deposit expansion by increasing the supply of reserves and making borrowed reserves less expensive.

The impact of monetary policy extends beyond bank credit and money supply. Monetary restraint may cause banks to sell securities and compete more aggressively for new deposits. Declining securities prices and possibly a reduced inflow of savings may cause nonbank as well as bank lenders to be more cautious and selective in extending credit. Rising interest costs and less favorable terms discourage borrowing. Thus monetary policy, by altering the cost, supply, and availability of credit, may encourage or discourage borrowing for consumer and investment expenditures.

Federal Reserve actions, except for authority to establish margin requirements on stock market credit, influence the total quantity of credit and spendable funds. Even though general monetary instruments may have an uneven impact, monetary authorities can do little to regulate how funds are allocated among competing borrowers. The impact is usually greater, however, where cost and availability of credit are more important in spending decisions. Housing and business fixed investment, for which financing is usually long-term, are likely to be more sensitive to interest rates and monetary policy.

In short, the operation of monetary policy has several significant features. First, Federal Reserve actions operate mainly on use of credit to supplement current income. They do not directly affect the level of *existing* income available for expenditure; however, unfavorable credit terms may encourage borrowers to use current income to repay outstanding indebtedness instead of to purchase goods and services. Second, the Federal Reserve can make additional reserves and deposits available in a period of economic slack, but there is no increase in total demand unless someone is willing to spend. Third, the instruments of monetary policy primarily affect the price of credit and total supply of spendable funds. The possibility of using existing general monetary tools to attain certain selective effects is limited; however, such use should be explored more fully.

PROBLEMS OF IMPLEMENTATION

Successful use and blending of fiscal and monetary policies require enough flexibility so that actions can be adapted to changing economic conditions. Federal Reserve authorities can take action promptly once the need is recognized. One of the advantages of monetary policy is its flexibility.

Inflexibility is a serious weakness of fiscal policy. It is one of the main reasons this potentially powerful and useful stabilization tool has been used little in actual practice. Whether the problem can be solved or at least mitigated will have an important bearing on successful use of the fiscal-monetary mix.

Inflexibility of Fiscal Policy

Preparation and enactment of the federal budget is currently a time-consuming process. Formulation of the budget for the fiscal year beginning July 1, 1967, for example, has been under way several months. The President submits his budget recommendations to Congress in the latter part of January. Congressional committees conduct hearings and then the budget recommendations are debated on the floors of the House and Senate. Action on all budget items is usually not completed until shortly before the beginning of the new fiscal year.

When the budget is being formulated and considered by Congress no one can tell what economic conditions will be during the coming fiscal year. It is impossible to determine so far in advance whether the budget will or should show a surplus or a deficit, much less how large a surplus or deficit should be. At present we cannot approach the forecasting accuracy required much of the time so that enactment of the budget may include such changes as are needed for purposes of economic stabilization.

The time required for fiscal actions, once taken, to affect disposable income and the flow of federal expenditures varies. An income-tax change that does not alter collection procedures may affect disposable income in a short time. This is especially true for withheld taxes. There is usually a considerable time lag between Congressional action on expenditure projects and the flow of payments to the public. The time lag is less for actions altering expenditures such as social security and unemployment benefits. It is likely to be much longer for major defense and public works projects. Preliminary planning and awarding of contracts may consume considerable time before new orders are placed. For heavy durables and large construction projects, several more months may elapse before payments start to flow in substantial volume.

The time lag between monetary actions and the impact on spending and demand also varies according to economic conditions; however, it is likely to be several months before the bulk of the impact is felt.

Automatic Stabilizers

Inflexibility inherent in the budget process has long been recognized. A partial solution is to build into the budget, items that automatically respond to changes in production and employment.

Progressive income-tax rates and employment taxes exercise a stabilizing influence on disposable income. A decline in total income and employment results in more than a proportionate decrease in income and employment tax receipts. The declining tax bite cushions the effect of a recession on disposable income. In periods of expansion, rising business activity and income bring more than a proportionate increase in tax receipts. The slower rise in disposable income acts as a drag on business expansion.

Some Government expenditures also respond automatically in a stabilizing manner. Unemployment benefit payments, for example, rise as employment declines; they decrease as business activity and employment expand.

Automatic stabilizers, although helpful, are only part of a solution to the problem of implementing an effective fiscal policy. Some have estimated that currently automatic stabilizers offset about 30 cents of each dollar rise or fall in G.N.P.

Strengthening the automatic stabilizing effects, however, would create other problems. Built-in stabilizers become restrictive as soon as an upturn in business activity begins. They tend to choke off expansion long before manpower and other productive resources are being fully utilized. More potent automatic stabilizers would increase the fiscal drag on expansion and growth.

More Flexible Discretionary Action

Built-in stabilizers are only a partial solution to the problem of better timing of fiscal policy. Greater flexibility in discretionary actions is also needed.

On the tax side, a recent proposal is that Congress give the President stanby authority to make tax changes of limited amount. For example, the authority might be limited to a 5 per cent across-the-board increase or decrease in individual and corporate income taxes. Congress would retain complete control over tax reform. Even with such safeguards, however, Congress seems reluctant to delegate limited standby authority to the President.

Another proposal that would avoid delegation of authority is for Congress to plan in advance so that a tax change could be enacted more promptly. In anticipation that tax action might soon become desirable, a bill could be drafted and hearings held by the appropriate Congressional committees. If possible, agreement should be raeched on the type and perhaps the amount of a tax change so that only a joint resolution of Congress would be required to put the change into effect. Such advance legislative preparation would enable Congress to act promptly once the need for a tax change became reasonably clear. There is a natural reluctance, however, to spend time preparing legislation for some presumed future need of uncertain magnitude.

It is also difficult to achieve much flexibility on the expenditure side of the budget. A major part of total expenditures is determined largely by non-economic objectives. For instance, defense expenditures, interest on the debt, and veterans' benefits can hardly be deferred or expanded in order to exert a stimulating or restrictive effect on the economy. For various reasons, only a small portion of the total is amenable to variation in accordance with changing economic conditions. And even this small part may not be flexible as to timing.

WHAT KIND OF MIX?

Different features and a close interrelationship offer opportunities to employ a varying fiscal-monetary mix in order better to meet the needs of a particular economic situation. A few of the more common recent proposals are used to illustrate both the advantages and limitations of altering the fiscal-monetary mix.

Selective Effects

In recent months, there has been considerable discussion of a tax increase which would make possible a less restrictive monetary policy. The intention is a change in mix, not in the over-all degree of restraint. Monetary restraint in the face of vigorous credit demands helped lift interest rates to levels that had not been reached for many years. High rates and reduced availability of credit hit certain sectors of the economy, such as housing, especially hard. A tax increase combined with less monetary restraint would ease some of the pressure on these sectors and possibly spread the impact more evenly over the economy.

The fiscal-monetary mix has often been suggested as a method of altering distribution of expenditures and resources between consumption and investment. In an inflationary situation powered mainly by strong consumer demand with only a sluggish rise in fixed investment, a relatively heavy dose of fiscal restraint on consumer income and expenditures could be combined with monetary policy and possibly some fiscal actions, designed to encourage a more rapid rise in investment and in productive capacity. If, on the other hand, an investment boom is threatening to create excess capacity, corporate tax changes could be coordinated with a more restrictive monetary policy to curb the rise in investment expenditures.

In periods of recession and economic slack, the mix could be heavily weighted toward fiscal action to lift the level of private disposable income. A rise in consumer income and spending would, by absorbing unused resources, help create an environment more favorable to an increase in investment. Fiscal policy, as we have seen, can directly increase consumer disposable income both by personal income-tax reduction and carefully selected increases in Government expenditures. The stimulative effect is likely to be considerably greater than making credit more readily available at low rates. Consumers and business firms are reluctant to borrow as long as employment and profit prospects are uncertain. As consumer expenditures and business activity rise, excess capacity will be reduced. With improving profit prospects and a dwindling margin of unused resources, policies designed to encourage investment will be more fruitful. As recovery proceeds, and especially, if investment lags, the mix could gradually be shifted more toward stimulating investment.

A mix heavily weighted toward fiscal action to stimulate consumption is also especially suitable for recession when a country is confronted with a balance-of-payments problems. Fiscal action to swell disposable income probably puts less downward pressure on short-term rates and hence is less likely to stimulate an outflow of short-term capital. Financing a deficit primarily by issuing short-term securities would tend to increase the market supply and help keep short-term rates up.

Limitations on Selective Use

There is a wide range of combinations in which monetary and fiscal policies conceivably could be employed. We should recognize, however, that there are limitations on what can be accomplished by changing the policy mix. For instance, combining fiscal restraint and monetary ease in such a way as to divert resources from consumption to investment may be hard to accomplish in practice.

First, because of the mobility of funds and close interrelation between fiscal and monetary policies, it is difficult to effect a restrictive fiscal policy with monetary ease. In theory a fiscal policy directed toward curbing consumer expenditures will release resources, and an easy money policy will encourage their use in investment. But in practice these results may not be achieved.

A fiscal surplus is not necessarily restrictive, as we have seen. To be restrictive, the surplus must be employed in such a way that excess receipts are not returned to the public or replaced by new funds created by credit expansion. If used to redeem securities held largely by commercial banks, an easy money policy would permit banks to use the reserves released to extend credit and bring deposits up to the former level. There is no net reduction in funds available for expenditure unless monetary policy is restrictive enough to prevent creation of new funds to replace the excess receipts siphoned from taxpayers.

Second, curbing consumer demand sufficiently to release resources for the production of additional capital goods may weaken the incentive to invest. A slump in consumer spending is soon felt by merchants and manufacturers. Adverse effects on current and prospective profits would make them less willing to invest. Curbing consumer demand might diminish inducement to invest as much as or more than an easy money policy would increase it.

A third limitation is that only the direct effects of either fiscal or monetary policy can be slanted toward a certain type of economic activity such as consumption or investment. Dollars injected either by fiscal policy or monetary policy are just like any other dollars to those who receive them. The secondary response initiated by the direct effects cannot be regulated. Policies designed to alter the proportion of total income used for consumption and investment are unlikely to be successful unless accompanied by a corresponding shirt in preferences between consumption, and saving and investment.

Short Versus Long-Run Stabilization

Hazards involved in forecasting together with the inflexibility of fiscal policy have led to proposals that we should rely primarily on automatic stabilizers and monetary policy to smooth out short-term fluctuations in business activity. Automatic stabilizers, which respond promptly to changes in production and income, exert considerable cushioning effect. Monetary policy, which can be quite flexible as to timing, could be used to supplement automatic stabilizers.

Discretionary fiscal actions could then be directed toward longer-run stability and sustained growth. Such actions would be taken mainly to help keep total demand in balance with expanding productive capacity instead of being directed mainly toward counteracting business fluctuations.

Two guides have been developed in recent years to facilitate implementing this type of fiscal policy. The "high or full employment surplus" represents the excess of receipts over expenditures that the existing tax structure would yield with the economy operating at capacity. The "production gap" is the difference between actual G.N.P. and G.N.P. at full employment.

The production gap shows how far below potential capacity the economy is actually operating. It serves as a useful guide as to how much additional stimulus may be needed. The surplus that would be produced at full employment is a useful indicator of whether the current tax structure is likely to be too restrictive or too expansionary. A large surplus means the tax structure becomes restrictive before full employment is reached. There is fiscal drag on continued expansion and sustained growth. A sizable deficit, on the other hand, means the tax structure would continue to provide a stimulus even after full employment is reached. A tax increase would likely be needed as the economy approached full employment to avoid excess demand and rising prices.

A semi-automatic, long-range budget policy was suggested a few years ago by the Committee for Economic Development. Government expenditures, which determine allocation of resources between public and private use, should be established at the level society prefers. The tax structure should then be adjusted as necessary so as to yield a moderate surplus when productive capacity and resources are being fully utilized. It was believed that over a span of years such a policy would provide some net surplus for debt retirement.

This longer-range type of fiscal policy was expected to contribute to stability and growth with only limited discretionary action. The policy would also retain some of the discipline imposed by the goal of an annually balanced budget. New expenditures would require additional taxes in order to maintain the planned surplus at full employment.

It seems likely, however, that considerable discretionary action would still be needed to maintain the desired surplus at full employment. The tax structure required would vary with changing conditions and could not be accurately determined far in advance. Changes in the level and composition of income, for example, would affect income-tax yields. Population growth and innovations might create a need for more Government services and a higher level of expenditures than anticipated. War and international tension might require large increases in Government expenditures.

CONCLUDING COMMENTS

It would be a marked step forward if both fiscal and monetary policies could be timed and coordinated toward our general economic goals of full employment, sustained growth, and price stability. Both tools, impersonal and indirect in their operation, are especially suitable in a democratic free enterprise society.

Greater flexibility is a prerequisite for more effective use of fiscal policy. Proposals to improve flexibility have some disadvantages, but these are small compared with the loss arising from not being able to time fiscal actions properly.

The next step, once we have improved flexibility, is use of fiscal policy to help curb inflationary pressures as well as to stimulate expansion in periods of economic slack. Coordinated fiscal-monetary actions to curb excessive demand and rising prices are more effective than either used alone and probably result in a more even distribution of the burden among sectors of the economy.

Altering the fiscal-monetary mix in order to meet more effectively the needs of a particular situation is a further refinement in implementation. But the results that can be achieved are limited. This refinement is of considerably less importance than overcoming the more fundamental weaknesses of inflexibility and failure to use fiscal policy as an instrument of restraint.

WARREN L. SMITH

MONETARY
VERSUS
FISCAL POLICY

37

INTRODUCTION

Most economists are now in agreement that both monetary and fiscal policy are capable of exerting independent effects on the aggregate demand for goods and services.[1] To be sure, the two kinds of policy have quite different impacts on the economy. Monetary

Reprinted from Warren L. Smith, "Monetary Versus Fiscal Policy," Harry L. Johnson and Ernest W. Walker (eds.) *Monetary Issues of the 1960's*, Bureau of Business Research, University of Texas, 1968, pp. 13–37.

[1] There is some disagreement with this view; the most prominent dissenter being Professor Milton Friedman, who appears to believe that fiscal measures unsupported by monetary action are incapable of producing significant effects on aggregate demand. An increase in government expenditures (unaccompanied by an increase in taxes) would lead to a rise in interest rates as a consequence of government borrowing to finance the resulting budget deficit—unless, of course, the supply of money was expanded to accommodate the increased demand for funds. Friedman believes that this rise in interest rates would be great enough to depress private spending by about as much as government spending would be increased; as a result, there would be no significant net effect on aggre-

policy works by inducing changes in the composition of the public's financial assets and liabilities, and the associated changes in yields alter the public's desired holdings of real assets, thereby changing the demand for goods and services. Fiscal policy, on the other hand, affects expenditures or disposable income and net worth directly. Thus, the effects of monetary policy are more indirect and subtle than those of fiscal policy and therefore somewhat more difficulty to identify and measure. However, the very fact that the two kinds of policy work through different channels means that they have different effects on the composition of demand, making it important that they be suitably coordinated. In this paper, the relative usefulness and proper coordination of monetary policy and fiscal policy will be discussed under three headings: stabilization policy, growth policy, and the balance-of-payments problem.

STABILIZATION POLICY

The productive capacity of the economy—defined as the total output that can be produced under conditions of full employment—increases with the passage of time as a result of the growth of the labor force, the improvement in labor skills through education and training, the accumulation of capital, and the advancement of technology. The objective of stabilization policy is to maintain full employment by keeping aggregate demand growing in pace with productive capacity. The objective of growth policy is to influence the rate of growth of productive capacity by altering one or more of the determinants of capacity growth referred to above.[2]

---

gate spending. [M. Friedman, *Capitalism and Freedom* (Chicago: University of Chicago Press, 1962), pp. 81–84.] This view, of course, is quite consistent with Friedman's finding ["The Demand for Money: Some Theoretical and Empirical Results," *Journal of Political Economy*, LXVII (August 1959), pp. 327–351] that the demand for money depends almost entirely on (permanent) income and bears only a negligible relation to interest rates.

Nearly all other investigators have concluded that the demand for money does depend significantly on interest rates. This dependence breaks the rigid link between money and income and permits fiscal policy to exert an independent effect. [J. Tobin, "The Monetary Interpretation of History: A Review Article," *American Economic Review*, LV (June 1965), pp. 464–485.]

[2] While stabilization policy and growth policy can be distinguished in this way, the distinction is in some cases a little blurred. For example, if output, for some reason, falls substantially below capacity so that unemployment rises above desired levels, as was the case when the Kennedy Administration came into office in 1961, the task of stabilization policy is to increase aggregate demand in order to bring actual output up to

In order to arrive at a determination of productive capacity, it is necessary to define full employment. There is a good deal of evidence that, over a considerable range, the economy of the United States is characterized by an inverse relationship between inflation and unemployment. That is, the further the unemployment rate is reduced by policies designed to increase aggregate demand, the greater is the tendency for the price level to rise.[3] There are three important reasons for this relationship:

1. An increase in aggregate demand shifts the balance of power in collective bargaining away from business and toward organized labor. Reduced unemployment appears to increase the willingness of unions to undergo strikes if necessary to secure wage increases, and increased sales and profits reduce the willingness of business to accept interruptions of production. The rise in profits that normally occurs, as unemployment declines and capacity is more fully utilized, also strengthens the bargaining position of labor. Wage settlements in a few key industries may set patterns that are transmitted to others. To the extent that wage increases exceed increases in output per worker, labor costs are raised, and prices are likely to be pushd up.[4]

---

productive capacity and reduce unemployment to target levels. Under these conditions, rising profit rates and increased rates of capacity utilization are likely to stimulate investment, leading to more rapid capital accumulation and increased growth of capacity itself. Indeed, this seems clearly to have happened during the post-1961 expansion. Nevertheless, the indicated distinction between stabilization policy and growth policy is a useful one.

[3] A. W. Phillips, "The Relation Between Unemployment and the Rate of Change of Money Wages in the United Kingdom, 1861–1957," *Economica*, XXV (November 1958), pp. 283–299, and P. A. Samuelson and R. M. Solow, "Analytical Aspects of Anti-Inflation Policy," *American Economic Review*, L (May 1960), 177–194. For a recent quantitative appraisal of the trade-off between inflation and unemployment in the United States, see G. L. Perry, "The Determinants of Wage-Rate Changes and the Inflation-Unemployment Trade-Off for the United States," *Review of Economic Studies*, XXXI (October 1964), pp. 287–308.

[4] There is considerable evidence that, as unemployment declines sharply during periods of recovery from recession, output per worker (i.e., labor productivity) rises unusually fast. As unemployment is reduced, however, the rate of increase in output per worker declines toward more normal levels. As a result, generous wage settlements in key industries in the early stages of a period of recovery, although not putting immediate upward pressure on costs and prices because productivity is increasing rapidly, may nevertheless cause trouble by setting patterns which affect wage settlements in other industries in later phases of recovery when productivity increases are smaller. This seems to have happened, for example, in the 1954–1957 recovery.

2. When output and employment expand under the impetus of increasing aggregate demand, the pressure is not likely to be spread evenly over all segments of the labor market. Excess demand for labor and upward pressure on wages can be expected to be felt in some labor sub-markets while the overall unemployment rate is still relatively high. As the general level of unemployment declines, the number of particular labor sub-markets experiencing excess demand is likely to increase. To the extent that increases in money wages in these particular labor sub-markets exceed the corresponding increases in output per worker, labor costs per unit of output will increase, thereby putting upward pressure on product prices. Large increases in money wage rates in these sub-markets also may have some tendency to produce sympathetic increases in wages in other markets not experiencing labor shortages, and the products—whose price rise as a result of excessive wage increases—may enter as inputs in the production of other products, thereby pushing up their costs and prices. Through processes such as this, excessive wage increases in particular labor sub-markets experiencing excess demand will fan out through the economy and raise the general price level.

3. As aggregate demand increases, bottlenecks may occur in some industries as a result of inadequate plant capacity at a time when the over-all level of unemployments is still relatively high. These bottlenecks may result in price increases which may spread to other sectors of the economy, as the products whose prices have been raised enter as inputs in other industries. Bottlenecks in specific industries would not result in overall inflation if prices were equally flexible in both directions, because, in that case, price declines in industries with excess capacity would roughly counterbalance price increases in industries suffering from capital shortages, thereby keeping the overall price level from increasing significantly until the overall unemployment rate reached a low level. However, due to the existence of market power and oligopolistic rigidities, it is quite clear that, in the United States economy, prices are more flexible in the upward direction than in the downward direction.[5]

As a consequence of these relationships, the makers of economic policy may be faced with a trade-off between inflation and unemployment, such as that depicted by AA' in Figure 1. According to this particular trade-off, in order to achieve complete price stability,

[5] The way in which changes in the composition of demand can cause inflation when prices are more flexible upward than downward is explained in detail in C. L. Schultze, *Recent Inflation in the United States* (Study Paper No. 1; Joint Economic Committee, 1959), pp. 1–77.

FIGURE 1 Relation Between Unemployment Rate and Rate of Change of Price Level

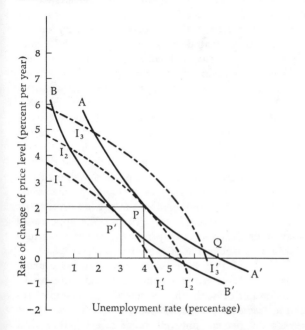

it would be necessary to accept an unemployment rate of 7.0 percent (at point Q). On the other hand, to achieve an unemployment rate of 4.0 percent, it would be necessary to accept a rate of inflation of 2.0 percent per year (at point P). In order to arrive at a rational decision, policy-makers would have to weigh the disadvantages of inflation against those of unemployment. The views of the policy-makers might be thought of as being reflected in a social welfare function, portions of which are depicted in Figure 1 by the indifference curves $I_1I'_1$, $I_2I'_2$, and $I_3I'_3$. Each indifference curve includes combinations of unemployment and inflation which would be equally acceptable to the authorities. Indifference curves that are closer to the origin include combinations that are superior to those included on curves lying further out. Thus, all combinations on $I_1I'_1$ are superior to those on $I_2I'_2$, because any given level of unemployment is associated with a lower rate of inflation on the former curve than on the latter. The approach of the authorities should be to select from the attainable price-employment combinations (those lying on AA') the one that lies on the highest indifference curve. Thus, in the case depicted in Figure 1, the authorities would presumably select as their target the combination designated by point P—an unemployment rate of 4.0 percent and an associated increase of 2.0 percent per year in the price level. Capacity output would thereby be defined as that level of Gross National Product (GNP), valued at constant prices, that could be produced by the economy at an unemployment rate of 4.0 percent.

The price-employment target of the authorities may change from time to time for either of two reasons. First, the trade-off function (curve AA') may shift as the price-wage responses of the economy change, and such shifts in the trade-off presumably will require adjustments in the target. Second, the attitude of the authorities toward inflation versus unemployment (as depicted by the indifference curves) may also change. Such alterations in the social welfare function may occur for various reasons, such as a change in the presidency from one political party to the other or the occurrence of changes in the economic environment—for example, the appearance of a balance-of-payments deficit that may necessitate greater attention to price stability as an objective of economic policy.

There are some kinds of policy measures that may be capable of changing the trade-off between unemployment and inflation in a favorable way. Adoption of such policies might, for example, result in a shift of the trade-off function from AA' to BB', making it possible to achieve a 3.0 percent unemployment rate together with a rate of inflation of 1.5 percent per year (at point P'), a combination more favorable than could have been achieved with the original trade-off function. Policies that might be capable of improving the trade-off include so-called "incomes policies" (represented in this country by the Kennedy-Johnson wage-price guideposts), policies for training or retraining members of the labor force or increasing their mobility in order to deal with labor shortages in particular sub-markets. In principle, it might be possible to make rather sophisticated use of monetary and fiscal policies to influence the composition of demand in such a way as to avoid the occurrence of bottlenecks in particular industries. As a practical matter, however, it hardly seems feasible to use monetary and fiscal policy in such a subtle and sophisticated manner except perhaps under certain rather special circumstances. As a general rule, it seems fair to say that monetary policy and fiscal policy must operate within the constraint of a price-employment trade-off that is determined by the structure of the economy, influenced to some degree perhaps by other policies which might affect the functioning of the labor and product markets.

Prospects for Stabilization Policy

The period from early 1961 to mid-1965, especially after tax cut was enacted in early 1964, was one in which there was increasingly widespread public acceptance of what has been called the new economics. While economists at the Council of Economic Advisers during the Kennedy Administration did develop a conceptual apparatus, involving such notions as the gap between actual and potential output and the full employment budget surplus, which was helpful in formulating policy and particularly helpful in explaining it to the public,[6] the only thing really new about the economics involved was the effort to apply it systematically to the U.S. economy. All of the essential ideas were developed in Keynes's *General Theory*, which was written a quarter of a century earlier in 1936. There is no doubt whatever concerning either the validity or the great importance of the doctrines set forth by Keynes and refined by a succeeding generation of economists. There has been a tendency, however, especially apparent after the tax cut of 1964, to view the Keynesian doctrines as a panacea, acceptance of which would almost automatically bring a new era of continuous stable economic growth.

The period beginning in early 1961 was one in which the problems facing the makers of economic policy were basically simple. There could be no real doubt that the economy was operating at an excessive rate of unemployment and with a very large gap between actual and potential output.[7] Thus, an expansionary fiscal and monetary policy was clearly called for, and there was little danger, particularly given the political constraints inhibiting the vigorous use of fiscal policy, that the stimulus would be so large as to overshoot the mark and generate inflationary pressures. Economists, both in and out of the government, therefore, could feel perfectly safe in using all of their influence to support the adoption of the maximum feasible dosage of expansionary policy. When the economy did begin to move vigorously toward the coveted 4.0 percent unemployment rate after the 1964 tax cut, the economists who had espoused expansionary fiscal policy looked like heroes, and the

[6] See, particularly, *Annual Report of the Council of Economic Advisers* (January 1962), chapter 1.

[7] The Council of Economic Advisers estimated the gap between actual and potential output at roughly $50 billion in the first quarter of 1961 (*ibid.*, pp. 51–53).

doctrines of the new economics were regarded by a wide segment of the public as having been completely substantiated.

This was all to the good, as far as it went. However, modern Keynesianism is a good deal more subtle and sophisticated than its application in the special circumstances of the post-1961 period might suggest. The Keynesian prescription for an economy operating as far below capacity as that of the United States in 1961 is perfectly obvious and not very difficult to explain to the untutored. However, when the economy is operating approximately at the target level of employment, as has been the case recently, the problems faced by policy-makers are much more difficult and complex. Even though the vagaries of individual spending behavior average out to a considerable extent due to the operation of the law of large numbers, aggregate spending is nevertheless far from fully predictable despite the extensive economic research of recent years. Moreover, there can be no doubt that the economy contains a number of inherently destabilizing elements of the accelerator type which influence expenditures on durable goods of various kinds by both business and consumers. As a result, there is unquestionably an inherent tendency toward instability in the economy, and it is normally the major task of monetary and fiscal policy to offset these destabilizing forces. This, however, is a very tricky and difficult task when the economy is operating in the neighborhood of target levels, (a) because the precise magnitude and timing of the effects of the policy measures that might be taken to offset prospective fluctuations are not yet fully understood, (b) because there is always considerable uncertainty about the strength—and in some instances even the direction—of the destabilizing forces that policy must attempt to offset, and (c) because there is inevitably an element of ambiguity in the selection of the targets themselves—for example, the prospective trade-off between inflation and unemployment referred to above is subject to some uncertainty, and there is often considerable dispute about the weights to be attached to price stability versus unemployment.

The significance of these considerations is that they put a premium on flexibility as a criterion for effective discretionary fiscal and monetary policies. If such polices are to be effective in stabilizing the economy, they must be administered in such a way that adjustments can be made quickly as the prospective economic outlook unfolds. One implication of this need for policy flexibility is that discretionary changes in government expenditures are of limited usefulness as an instrument of stabilization policy. This is a matter of expediency rather than of principle. There are reasons for believing that the marginal net benefits of additional government spending vary relative to those of additional private spending over the business cycle in such a way as to suggest the propriety in principle of countercyclical changes in government expenditures.[8] However, administrative difficulties in the rapid activation of public works projects and the long lags that often intervene between the activation of such projects and the production of the desired economic effects constitute a severe impediment to the effective use of such projects as a countercyclical device. Of course, during times when the economy is operating with a very large margin of excess capacity, as was the case in 1961, so that there is little danger that expansionary measures will be too large in magnitude, increases in government expenditures may be a useful component of an expansionary policy. Moreover, to the extent that considerations of efficient resources use permit, it is desirable to avoid ill-timed changes in government expenditures that may precipitate fluctuations or accentuate instability arising from variations in the strength of private demand. Indeed, to the extent that it is consistent with appropriate allocation of resources between the public and the private sectors, a reasonably steady and predictable growth in public expenditures from year to year will add a stable component of aggregate demand that will simplify the task of maintaining stability. And, finally, any substantial reductions in government expenditures —such as might be permitted by a relaxation of world tensions leading to a program of disarmament—should be timed to coincide with offsetting measures in the form of increases in other types of government expenditures or reductions in tax rates.

If, as is being suggested, systematic changes in government expenditures normally cannot be used effectively as an instrument of stabilization policy, the instruments of monetary policy and tax policy remain. It seems that the great administrative flexibility of monetary policy, which permits it to be changed frequently in either direction and by relatively small amounts, makes it inevitably the first line of defense among discretionary instruments in combating instability on occasions when the balance-of-payments situation permits its vigorous use. This last qualification, however, is of considerable importance. Under present conditions, for example, the

[8] P. A. Samuelson, "Principles and Rules in Modern Fiscal Policy: A Neo-Classical Reformulation," in *Money, Trade, and Economic Growth: In Honor of John Henry Williams* (New York: Macmillan, 1951), pp. 157–176.

balance-of-payments deficit would make it impossible for the United States to follow a vigorous easy-money policy if recessionary tendencies were to appear. The balance-of-payments problem will be discussed further in a later section of this paper. However, there are more difficulties concerning monetary policy that arise from the fact that, as indicated earlier, its impacts are more subtle, sophisticated, and indirect and therefore more difficult to predict than those produced by fiscal policy. Most of the evidence now available suggests that the effects of monetary policy occur only after substantial—and perhaps quite variable—lags which add substantially to its awkwardness as a stabilization device.[9]

The most feasible tax adjustments to make for countercyclical purposes are changes in individual income tax rates. I would favor some reform—perhaps along the lines suggested by the Council of Economic Advisors in its 1962 *Annual Report* or by the Commission on Money and Credit in 1961—for simplifying the administrative procedures to be used in making changes in personal income tax rates for countercyclical purposes.[10] Under present arrangements, any change in tax rates must be acted upon by Congress through the regular legislative procedure. Legislation is likely to (a) take considerable time, (b) make the subject of tax adjustment a major political issue, and (c) make it difficult to distinguish as sharply as would be desirable between a simple change in rates as a means of influencing consumer demand and the controversial issues of structural tax reform. As a consequence, tax adjustments as a means of regulating demand are likely to be postponed or even avoided entirely, thereby placing an undue burden on monetary policy.

Even if a streamlined administrative procedure for changing individual income tax rates was put into effect, some problems would

[9] M. Friedman, "The Supply of Money and Changes in Prices and Output," in *The Relationship of Prices to Economic Stability and Growth*, compendium of papers submitted by panelists appearing before the Joint Economic Committee (Washington, D.C.: Government Printing Office, 1958), pp. 241–256; M. Friedman, "The Lag in Effect of Monetary Policy," *Journal of Political Economy*, LXIX (October 1961), pp. 447–466; J. M. Culbertson, "The Lag in Effect of Monetary Policy: Reply," *Journal of Political Economy*, LXIX (October 1961), pp. 467–477; T. Hayer, "The Inflexibility of Monetary Policy," *Review of Economics and Statistics*, XL (November 1958), pp. 565–587; and A. Ando, E. C. Brown, R. M. Solow, and J. Kareken, "Lags in Fiscal and Monetary Policy," in *Stabilization Policies* (Englewood Cliffs, N.J.: Prentice-Hall, 1963), pp. 1–96.

[10] *Annual Report of the Council of Economic Advisers* (January 1962), pp. 74–76; *Money and Credit: Their Influence on Jobs, Prices, and Growth. The Report of the Commission on Money and Credit* (Englewood Cliffs, N.J.: Prentice-Hall, 1961) pp. 133–137.

remain. While it is quite clear that the tax cut of 1964 provided a powerful stimulus to economic expansion,[11] it should be remembered that the Revenue Act of 1964 was represented as making a permanent reduction in income tax rates, accompanied by fairly substantial structural reforms in the tax system. Experience with rates. If Professor Friedman's permanent income hypothesis is cor- that tax measure does not provide very much evidence concerning the effectiveness of temporary countercyclical adjustments in tax rect, temporary changes in individual income taxes could be expected to have a relatively weak effect on consumer demand— although it must be remembered that Friedman includes consumer durable goods in saving rather than in consumption, and a considerable increase in the demand for durable goods is entirely consistent with his hypothesis.[12]

Although the evidence is by no means conclusive and probably will not be until there has been some experience with temporary tax adjustments, most students of fiscal policy probably would agree that a dollar of temporary income tax change is likely to have substantially less effect on aggregate demand than a dollar of permanent change. Furthermore, there is a possibility that, if tax rates are changed too frequently, consumers will have a tendency to disregard these temporary changes and base their decisions on some concept of the normal tax rates that they expect to prevail on the average, thereby reducing substantially the responsiveness of consumer expenditures to temporary tax changes. It seems clear that, since it would be unwise—and if balance-of-payments problems are serious, virtually impossible—to saddle monetary policy with the primary responsibility for economic stabilization, some steps will have to be taken to increase the flexibility of tax rate adjustments.

If experience shows that the problems relating to temporary changes in individual income tax rates referred to above are quite serious, the possibility of adopting an expenditure tax as a component of the federal revenue system might be considered. While an expenditure tax would introduce a regressive element into the tax system, temporary changes in the expenditure tax rate should be a particularly effective instrument for influencing consumer demand, since the changes would provide a powerful incentive for consumers to make substitutions between present and future expenditures.

[11] A forthcoming study by George Katona and Eva Mueller of the Survey Research Center of the University of Michigan will assess the effects of the 1964 tax cut on consumer expenditures.

[12] M. Friedman, *A Theory of the Consumption Function* (Princeton, N.J.: Princeton University Press, 1957).

Structural Aspects of Stabilization Policy

If an effective job of economic stabilization is to be done, the regulation of aggregate demand will not be enough. It will be necessary also to maintain a reasonable balance among major components of demand. The main problem is to moderate the excessive fluctuations in business investment in plant and equipment which have been a major source of instability in the U.S. economy. The situation that existed at the time this paper was written is a good case in point. During the early stages of the long expansion that began in the first quarter of 1961, an important characteristic was the balance that was achieved in the growth rates of the major components of aggregate demand. It seems likely that the balanced nature of the expansion was one of the reasons that it was possible to achieve a steady reduction in unemployment and at the same time maintain remarkable stability in the general level of prices. As the expansion continued, however, a tendency for business plant and equipment expenditures to rise at an increasingly rapid rate developd. This tendency has continued in 1966, and, according to the Department of Commerce and McGraw-Hill surveys of investment intentions, the acceleration of investment can be expected to continue at least into 1967.

Some observers view the current investment boom with equanimity or even with satisfaction. They argue that a high investment ratio is favorable to long-run economic growth and tends to increase labor productivity, thereby perhaps putting some downward pressure on costs and prices. But, while a high investment ratio is favorable in this respect, a rapidly rising ratio—a situation in which investment is rising much more rapidly than GNP—is likely to be a source of trouble. First, it can put pressure on productive capacity in the capital goods industries, thereby causing prices in this sector to rise. Since prices are more flexible upward than downward, these price increases in the capital goods sector are unlikely to be balanced by price declines in other sectors, and the result will be inflation of the structural or bottleneck variety. Second, if investment increases at a much more rapid rate than overall aggregate demand, the result, in the course of time, is very likely to be the development of excess capacity in some industries, which will eventually lead to a sharp decline in investment spending which may make a recession difficult to avoid. A case in point is the 1955–1957 period. At that time, a rapid acceleration of plant and equipment expenditures appears to have been an important cause both of the 1956–1957 inflation and of the 1957–1958 recession.

In order to be able to deal with problems of this kind, it is important that those responsible for policy have at their disposal some weapon that can be used to dampen an excessively rapid rise of business investment in plant and equipment. The classic weapon used for this purpose is, of course, monetary restriction. However, tight monetary policy seems to have its major effects on components of spending other than business investment. Experience with restrictive monetary policy in the United States in the 1950's suggested that the major impact fell on residential construction, and this conclusion clearly seems to be borne out by the responses induced by restrictive monetary policy in 1965 and 1966. It seems very doubtful whether a reasonable degree of monetary restraint is capable of checking a powerful investment boom, without producing unduly drastic effects on other components of aggregate demand, particularly residential construction, and without putting heavy strains on the financial system.

In view of the importance of wide fluctuations in business investment as a source of instability and the inadequacies of monetary policy as a means of offsetting these fluctuations, it is important that other means be devised for exerting some moderating effects on investment. This suggests that provisions be made for temporary reductions or suspensions of the 7-percent investment tax credit that was adopted in 1962 as a means of stimulating growth.[13] The incentive effects of a suspension of the tax credit would be equivalent to those of a very large change in interest rates. For example, for an investment having a life of ten years, suspension of the credit would lower the prospective yield by roughly one and one-half percentage points.[14] Since interest is deductible

---

[13] The credit applies to machinery and equipment but not to buildings. The rate is 7 percent for eligible assets having a life of eight years or more, with lower rates of $4\frac{2}{3}$ percent and $2\frac{1}{3}$ percent for assets having useful lives of six to eight years and four to six years, respectively. Lower rates of 3 percent, 2 percent, and 1 percent for the three classes of eligible lives are applied to purchases of machinery and equipment by public utilities. The credit can be used against the first $25,000 of tax plus 25 percent of any tax over $25,000. Originally the taxpayer was required to deduct the credit from the base to be used in depreciating the asset, but this provision was repealed by the Revenue Act of 1964.

[14] Assuming straight-line economic-life depreciation, the yield (i) on an asset subject to a tax credit not deductible from the depreciation base can be calculated by use of the expression,

$$1 - k = \left[\frac{E}{C} - t \left(\frac{E}{C} - \frac{1}{n}\right) \right] \frac{1 - (1 + i)^{-n}}{i}$$

where C is the cost of the asset, E is the expected return per year before depreciation and interest, t is the tax rate, n is the life of the asset in for federal income tax purposes and the present corporate income tax rate is 48 percent, suspension of the tax credit would be roughly equal to the effect of a rise of three percentage points in the rate of interest. Needless to say, a monetary policy sufficiently drastic to produce changes of this magnitude is literally unheard of. In addition to the incentive effects, suspension of the credit would increase corporate tax liabilities by roughly \$2 billion a year under present conditions, thereby producing an equivalent reduction in the volume of internally generated funds available for financing investment.

In recent months, a number of economists have suggested temporary suspension of the tax credit as a means of checking the investment boom. Two major arguments have been advanced by the opponents of such a step. First, it was argued that the tax credit was sold to the public, and particularly to the business community, at the time of its original enactment as a structural reform in the tax system designed to stimulate economic growth, and that it would be inconsistent with the position originally taken by the Kennedy Administration to vary the tax credit for countercyclical purposes. This is essentially a political argument, but it may be noted that a policy of temporary suspension would mean that the credit would be operative under normal conditions and would, therefore, continue to serve its original purpose of stimulating long-run growth.

The second objection was related to the fact that the credit becomes available at the time equipment is installed rather than at the time orders for equipment are placed. If the credit was suddenly suspended, some persons feel that businessmen, who had placed orders for equipment and undertaken investment projects in the belief that they would receive the tax credit, would be treated unfairly. In principle, however, the problem seems to be similar to that which arises in connection with any increase in tax liabilities. Many taxpayers make decisions based on the assumption of a continuation of present tax provisions, and an increase in taxes is likely to upset some of their calculations. This is the normal risk that taxpayers take, and it is difficult to see that the inequities associated

---

years, and k is the rate of tax credit. If $E/C = 0.15$, $t = 0.48$, and $n = 10$, i is 4.44 percent when $k = O$ (i.e., when there is no tax credit), while i is 5.94 percent when $k = 0.07$. That is, the yield would be reduced by about one and one-half percentage points by the removal of a 7 percent tax credit. It may be noted that the tax credit discriminates in favor of short-term investments; therefore, its suspension would reduce the yields on short-term investments more than those on longer term investments.

with suspension of the tax credit would be different from those connected with any other increase in taxes. Moreover, the adverse effects on profits would be considerably softened, because of the fact that suspension of the tax credit likely would occur only at times when business conditions are exceptionally prosperous and the general level of profits high. It also has been contended that the effects of suspension of the credit would be felt only with a considerable lag, because projects already under way would be affected little by the suspension. This contention, however, is a problem that would be present with any device—including monetary policy—that might be used to influence business investment. It is impossible to tell how strongly and how promptly a suspension of the tax credit would affect investment spending until some experience has been accumulated through the use of the instrument. The fact that the suspension would be temporary, with the prospect that the tax credit would be restored at a later time, would be likely to increase the potency of the suspension in affecting investment spending. While there are admitted difficulties with temporary suspension of the credit as a means of regulating investment, it does appear to be a potentially useful instrument for dealing with an important problem and is worthy of a trial.[15]

One final point may be worth noting. While in the present situation, in which the U.S. balance-of-payments is in deficit and a tightening of monetary policy as a means of checking inflation will, if anything, have a favorable effect on the external payments position of the country, it seems fair to suppose that, in future inflationary situations, this always will not be the case. If, at some future time, the country should suffer from inflation at a time when the balance-of-payments was in surplus, a tightening of monetary policy would be a decidedly inappropriate anti-inflationary device since it would tend to magnify the problems of deficit countries. Under such conditions, suspension of the tax credit might be an especially useful substitute for restrictive monetary policy as a means of exerting some moderating effect on investment.

ECONOMIC GROWTH

The task of stabilization policy is to keep actual output growing in pace with productive capacity, defined in terms of the criteria

[15] As this paper was prepared for publication (early September 1966), President Johnson submitted to Congress a recommendation that the 7 percent tax credit be suspended for a period of sixteen months as a means of dampening the investment boom.

of unemployment and price stability. Growth policy, on the other hand, involves the use of monetary, fiscal, and other instruments at the disposal of the government to influence the growth of productive capacity itself. In addition to rate of growth of the labor, force, the growth of capacity depends upon (a) the rate of improvement in labor skills resulting from education and training, (b) the rate of technological progress, and (c) the rate of capital accumulation in both the private and public sectors of the economy. Since the last three of these factors are affected inevitably by government activity, the authorities hardly can avoid influencing economic growth, whether or not they intend to do so. Moreover, a convincing case can be made that the government should concern itself with long-term growth and not leave it to be determined entirely by private saving and investment decision.[16] Therefore, the federal government should choose an appropriate target for long-term economic growth and attempt to use the various policy instruments at its disposal to achieve this target.

Acceleration of economic growth involves the foregoing of current consumption in order to achieve a higher level of consumption in the future. In making decisions concerning the extent to which policy should be oriented toward the acceleration of growth, the authorities should be guided by their judgment regarding the extent to which the public is willing to sacrifice current consumption for future consumption. In the present state of knowledge, however, the criteria for growth policy necessarily must be somewhat vague. Empirical research on economic growth has not reached the point yet where the authorities can be very sure of the terms on which it is possible to trade current consumption for future consumption through the use of public policies to stimulate growth. There are, however, pretty good ideas concerning the kinds of policies which are conducive to growth, even though the quantitative magnitudes of the contributions these policies are capable of making are not fully known.

One method of accelerating growth would be to alter the mix of monetary and fiscal policies. Under full employment conditions, an easing of monetary policy to stimulate private investment, accompanied by an off-setting increase in individual income taxes to reduce consumption, would increase the fraction of national resources devoted to capital formation, thereby speeding up the growth of capacity.[17] In this case, the posture of public policy in a long-term

[16] J. Tobin, "Economic Growth as an Objective of Government Policy," *American Economic Review*, LIV (May 1964), pp. 1–20.

[17] The *equilibrium* rate of growth of capital and income may be independent of the fraction of income saved and invested. For example, sup-

or secular context is being considered in contrast with the discussion in the previous section which dealt with countercyclical policy adjustments. Translated into the earlier context, a growth conducive policy would mean somewhat easier monetary policy and somewhat tighter fiscal policy over the entire course of the business cycle. Of course, stabilization policy also would have to be adapted to growth policy. During the course of time, a policy that might be successful in bringing about more rapid growth of capacity would have to be accompanied by adjustments to permit total demand to grow more rapidly in order to achieve desired employment targets.[18]

---

pose the growth of output is governed by an aggregate production function of the Cobb-Douglas variety with neutral technological change and constant returns to scale—i.e.,

$$Y = Ae^{gt}K^{\alpha}L^{1-\alpha}$$

where Y is net output, g is the rate of technical change, K is the stock of capital, and L is the labor force. Differentiating logarithmically with respect to t,

$$\frac{\dot{Y}}{Y} = g + \alpha\frac{\dot{K}}{K} + (1 - \alpha)\frac{\dot{L}}{L}$$

can be obtained. If the rate of growth of the labor force ($\dot{L}/L$ is a constant equal to n, and if the rate of growth of capital ($\dot{K}/K$) is equal to the rate of growth of income ($\dot{Y}/Y$), this reduces to

$$\frac{\dot{Y}}{Y} = \frac{g}{1 - \alpha} + n$$

If the fraction of income saved and invested is denoted by s, note that s does not appear in (1)—i.e., the equilibrium rate of growth of income is independent of s. Since capital grows at the same rate as income and since sY is the amount of net saving and investment, the rate of growth of capital is sY/K. Setting this equal to the rate of growth given by (1), the following expression for the equilibrium capital-output ratio is obtained:

$$\frac{K}{Y} = \frac{s(1 - \alpha)}{g + n(1 - \alpha)}$$

An increase in the saving ratio will put the economy onto a higher growth path with an associated increase in the capital-output ratio, but the equilibrium *rate* of growth is the same on all paths. However, movement from one growth path to another as a result of an increase in s is an asymptotic process, so that, as a practical matter, an increase in s will result in an increase in the rate of growth for an indefinitely long period as the economy climbs gradually toward the new higher equilibrium path.

[18] For a discussion of adjustments to be made in monetary and fiscal policy to influence the growth of capacity and at the same time to keep demand growing in pace with capacity, see W. L. Smith, "Monetary-Fiscal Policy and Economic Growth," *Quarterly Journal of Economics*, LXXI (February 1957), pp. 36–55.

Instead of relying on an easing of monetary policy to stimulate investment, structural adjustments in the tax system might be used for this purpose. For example, lower business tax rates, provisions for more rapid depreciation of capital assets, or liberal tax credits for business investment could be employed. Indeed, several changes in the federal tax system have been made in the last few years that were designed expressly to stimulate private capital formation to accelerate the growth of capacity. These measures include (a) the liberalization of tax depreciation guidelines, (b) the enactment of the 7 percent investment tax credit in 1962, and (c) the reduction in the corporate income tax rate enacted in the Revenue Act of 1964. The tax credit device is an especially appropriate instrument to use to encourage private investments, since it is precisely aimed at that particular objective. Moreover, as indicated above, the enactment of a tax credit, that is in effect under normal conditions but which is subject to suspension (or reduction) at times when some restraint on the excessive growth of private investment is needed for stabilization purposes, represents a quite satisfactory means of separating the secular growth and countercyclical stabilization aspects of public policy with respect to private investment.

In addition to measures designed to stimulate private investment, public policy can spur economic growth through (a) government expenditures on education and training to improve the quality of the labor force, (b) government programs to stimulate research and development, (c) programs for the improvement of natural resources, and (d) investment in highways and other public facilities. Presumably, an optimum policy for stimulating economic growth would involve combinations of (a) measures to stimulate private investment, (b) increases in government programs of education and training, (c) stimulation of research and development, (d) and public investment. However, in the present state of knowledge, it is impossible to estimate with any precision the way in which these programs should be combined in order to achieve the maximum increase in future productive capacity for each dollar of current consumption foregone.

There are other kinds of policies, such as measures to increase labor mobility and to improve the efficiency of labor and product markets, which may be capable of making a permanent addition to productive capacity by improving the terms of trade between employment and price stability. For example, if measures of this kind enabled the authorities to adopt more expansionary policies which succeeded in reducing the rate of unemployment from 4 percent to 3 percent without any increase in the rate of increase of the price level, the result would be a redrawing of the entire growth curve of productive capacity at a higher level than previously drawn.

Under conditions of full employment, any increase in private or public investment (broadly defined) for the purpose of accelerating growth necessarily must be accompanied by a corresponding increase in national saving in order to keep aggregate demand from rising above the full-employment level. Such an increase in saving may be accomplished either by measures designed to stimulate private saving by individuals or business enterprises or by increased public saving through the federal government budget brought about by increased taxation or reduced government noninvestment spending. Various tax incentive devices designed to stimulate private saving may be feasible, but probably the most reliable way to accomplish a substantial increase in national saving is by an increase in taxes. A federal budget surplus, under conditions of full employment, represents an addition to national saving which, if offset by appropriate measures to stimulate investment, will quicken the pace of economic growth. In popular discussions, it is often suggested that those who advocate the active use of fiscal policy contend that budget deficits are favorable to growth. However, in the context of the refinements of post-Keynesian economics, this is precisely the opposite of the truth. It is surpluses, not deficits, that promote growth, provided it is possible to stimulate additional investment to neutralize the deflationary effects of the surpluses and keep the economy operating at full employment. Growth policy does have its dangers. If additional saving is generated under conditions of full employment, but measures designed to increase investment are unsuccessful, the result may be unemployment and underutilization of productive capacity rather than more rapid growth.

As a final note on growth policy, under the present tax system, assuming a growth rate about equal to recent performance, full-employment tax receipts tend to rise at a rate of about $7 billion per year with GNP in the neighborhood of current levels. Unless tax rates are reduced, government expenditures are increased, or the economy experiences an extraordinary ebullience of private demand, this growth in federal revenues can exert a market depressing effect on economic activity. Normally, some measures must be taken from time to time to offset the "fiscal drag" resulting from growing tax revenues. If the stimulation of more rapid growth is desired, the automatic increase in tax revenues that occurs from year to year without any increase in tax rates may provide a valuable opportunity. If tax revenues at full employment rise more rapidly than government expenditures, it may be possible to stimulate more rapid growth through the use of measures, such as easy monetary policy or fiscal stimuli of various kinds, to generate additional investment to offset such automatic increases in the full-employment surplus.

THE BALANCE-OF-PAYMENTS PROBLEM

A good deal of the previous discussion would have been accepted by many, though not all, economists prior to the advent of the problems of the U.S. balance-of-payments deficit around 1960. Since that time, the need to be concerned about external stability under a regime of convertible currencies, fixed exchange rates, and relative freedom of international trade and capital movements has inintroduced serious complications. In addition to the goals of high employment, price stability, and a suitable rate of growth, the United States must now manage its affairs in such a way as to avoid large and protracted balance-of-payments deficits which impose drains on its gold reserves. As a result of a series of historical accidents, for many years prior to 1960, the United States, unlike most other countries, was in the fortunate position of being able to largely disregard its balance-of-payments position and to formulate monetary and fiscal policies primarily with a view toward achieving domestic goals. Under present conditions, however, the balance-of-payments may impose important constraints on the freedom to make use of monetary and fiscal policy.

The most serious constraint is that a country having a recession and a balance-of-payments deficit—such as the United States during the last five years—cannot freely employ expansionary monetary policy. The resulting fall in interest rates would be likely to cause a large outflow of capital that would aggravate the deficit. For this reason, it is appropriate for a country in this position to rely primarily upon expansionary fiscal policy as a means of inducing domestic recovery. Indeed, it might even be appropriate for a country in such a position to adopt a tighter monetary policy involving higher interest rates in order to attract an inflow of capital to cover a portion of its deficit, while, at the same time, adopting a sufficiently expansionary fiscal policy to offset the domestic effects of tighter money and also to provide the desired expansionary stimulus.[19]

The opposite situation may arise when a country is simultaneously

[19] R. A. Mundell, "The Appropriate use of Monetary and Fiscal Policy for Internal and External Stability," *International Monetary Fund Staff Papers*, IX (March 1962), pp. 70–79.

experiencing inflation and a balance-of-payments surplus. In such a situation, it would be inappropriate for the country to rely on tighter monetary policy as a means of checking inflation. The resulting higher interest rates would attract an inflow of capital which would magnify the country's surplus, the counterpart of which must be a deficit in the international accounts of some other countries. Under these conditions, a tighter fiscal policy would be the appropriate weapon for dealing with domestic inflation; indeed, it might even be appropriate for the country to ease its monetary policy to some degree as the means of reducing its balance-of-payments surplus.

It may be noted that the constraint is not as severe in this case as it is in the situation in which the country is suffering simultaneously from excessive unemployment and a balance-of-payments deficit. The existence of a limited supply of international reserves generally places a fairly definite limit on the magnitude of the cumulative deficit that can be financed, whereas there is no corresponding limit on the amount of reserves that can be accumulated as a result of continuing balance-of-payments surpluses. However, since one country's surplus is necessarily another country's deficit, responsible participation in the international monetary system requires that surplus countries take appropriate action to correct their surpluses so that the entire burden of adjustment does not fall on deficit countries.

Under some circumstances, the requirements of internal and external stability both call for the same type of monetary action. If a country is suffering from inflation and a balance-of-payments deficit, a restrictive monetary policy is appropriate as a means of dealing with both problems. Similarly, if a country has a balance-of-payments surplus and excessive unemployment, an expansionary monetary policy will help to correct both defects. However, circumstances in which the internal and external criteria for monetary policy are in conflict are likely to occur rather frequently. Even if both internal and external considerations call for the same kind of monetary policy in the beginning, it is very likely that internal equilibrium will be achieved before external equilibrium, or vice versa, and, once this has happened, a conflict situation will arise.[20]

To a limited extent, it is possible to use monetary policy to serve both internal and external objectives at times when the two are in conflict. An example of this is the so-called "Operation Twist" that was attempted in the United States during the early stages of the

[20] J. E. Meade, *The Balance of Payments* (London, England: Oxford University Press, 1951), chapter X.

recovery that began in 1961. The Federal Reserve and the Treasury attempted to use their monetary and debt management powers to hold up short-term interest rates in line with those abroad in an effort to minimize outflows of short-term capital, while, at the same time, maintaining downward pressure on long-term bond yields and mortgage interest rates which were judged to be especially important in stimulating domestic recovery.

Although there are some statistical difficulties in interpreting the evidence, it appears that some success was achieved with Operation Twist.[21] However, there is some empirical evidence to suggest that the term structure of interest rates is determined primarily by investor expectations and that monetary and debt management actions are capable of having only a relatively minor effect.[22] Efforts of this kind may be of some use under circumstances in which political considerations prevent the effective use of fiscal policy—as was the case in the United States in 1961–1964. However, the use of monetary policy to serve the two masters of internal and external equilibrium simultaneously can at best be only a palliative. Situations of conflict between internal and external objectives can be dealt with effectively only by the vigorous combined use of monetary and fiscal policy.

The experience of the United States in grappling with a serious unemployment problem while, at the same time, trying to correct a sizeable and chronic balance-of-payments deficit suggests the need for several changes in the approach to economic policy. First, it sug-

[21] For an appraisal of the effectiveness of Operation Twist, see F. Modigliani and R. Sutch, "Innovations in Interest Rate Policy," *American Economic Review*, LVI (May 1966), pp. 178–197. The conclusion of this article is that the most effective measures in implementing Operation Twist were the increases that were made in ceiling interest rates on time deposits under Regulation Q. These increases put some upward pressure on short-term interest rates while attracting funds into time deposits which the banks then invested in long-term debt, thereby lowering long-term interest rates. The article concludes that changes in the maturity composition of the publicly-held debt resulting from Treasury debt management and Federal Reserve open-market operations had negligible effects on the structure of interest rates.

[22] There has recently been a considerable amount of empirical research on the determinants of the term-structure of interest rates. See, especially, *ibid.*; A. M. Okun, "Monetary Policy, Debt Management and Interest Rates: A Quantitative Appraisal," in *Stabilization Policies* (Englewood Cliffs, N.J.: Prentice-Hall, 1963), pp. 331–380; and D. Meiselman, *The Term Structure of Interest Rates* (Englewood Cliffs, N.J.: Prentice-Hall, 1962). These studies provide fairly strong evidence that changes in the composition of the publicly-held debt have very little effect on the structure of interest rates.

gests the need for much greater administrative flexibility in the use of fiscal policy—especially tax policy—and greater public acceptance of its vigorous use, not only in the United States but in the Western European countries as well. Second, it suggests that, contrary to the views of some economists who attach great importance to changes in the money supply, interest rates must be regarded increasingly as the primary indicator of monetary policy. It seems doubtful, as long as the present international monetary system continues to exist, that the more or less complete freedom to use monetary policy as the primary instrument of domestic stabilization that existed in the United States for many years prior to 1960 ever will be achieved again. To a considerable extent and under many circumstances, monetary policy will need to be tailored primarily to the requirements of the international payments position, relying primarily on fiscal policy to regulate domestic demand. This indicates the importance of the development of arrangements for international cooperation with respect to interest rate policies. It is easy to imagine a situation in which one set of countries is raising interest rates to deal with balance-of-payments deficits, while another set of countries (having balance-of-payments surpluses) is raising interest rates to check domestic inflation. Such a competitive race to raise interest rates, even if offset by fiscal adjustments to sustain aggregate demand, might have very undesirable effects on investment and the long-term growth of the world economy. Some progress has already been made in the coordination of the monetary policies of the United States, Canada, Japan, and the Western European countries through discussions in Working Party Three of OECD and in the IMF, as well as through informal consultations among central banks. Further effort needs to be made through these and other channels to develop appropriate "rules of the game" for the coordination of monetary policies under the present international monetary system. And, finally, recent experience suggests the need for international monetary reform to provide more adequate liquidity in order to relax the policy squeeze that is felt primarily by deficit countries under the present system.

It may be noted that, if monetary policy must be oriented primarily toward the achievement of reasonable equilibrium of the balance-of-payments, it will not be possible to use the monetary-fiscal mix for the purpose of achieving target levels of private investment for economic growth, as was suggested earlier in this paper. Accordingly, if such investment targets are to be achieved, more emphasis will need to be placed on tax incentive devices of various kinds to exert an influence on investment levels. It may be noted that, in principle at least, it is possible to achieve various levels of private investment, at any specific level of interest rates, by using tax incentive devices to shift the marginal efficiency of investment schedule to the right or to the left as the situation seems to require. It may be noted also that, if a balance-of-payments deficit requires the maintenance of high interest rates to control capital movements, these high interest rates may deter investment unless they are offset by appropriate tax incentive devices. This may be particularly undesirable for a country suffering from a chronic balance-of-payments deficit, because the achievement of a basic solution to the deficit problem may be dependent upon bringing about increases in productivity which will make the country's exports more competitive in world markets.

CONCLUDING COMMENTS

The major problems involved in the coordination of monetary and fiscal policy have been discussed in this paper. All of the factors discussed under the headings of stabilization policy, growth policy, and the balance-of-payments problem must be taken into account in the administration of monetary and fiscal policy. Moreover, as a matter of actual practice, nearly all of the considerations discussed have, in fact, entered at one time or another into the decisions that have been made regarding U.S. monetary and fiscal policy in the last five years or so. In conclusion, while the knowledge of the responses of the economy to various kinds of policy stimuli has increased substantially in recent years and can be expected to increase still further as a result of economic research in the years ahead, there still is, and will continue to be for the foreseeable future, a substantial degree of uncertainty regarding these responses. Accordingly, while it is probably fair to say that the formulation of economic policy has become more sophisticated in the last few years, it is still by no means fully scientific. Personal judgment still plays a prominent role, and administrative arrangements that permit a prompt and flexible response to changing circumstances are of primary importance.

MARK H. WILLES

LAGS IN MONETARY AND FISCAL POLICY

38

WHY POLICY EFFECTS LAG

Lags of monetary and fiscal policy can be traced to several causes, as shown in Figure 1.

Recognition Lag

It takes time to recognize that the economy has changed in such a way as to require a change in policy. Assume, for example, that a business decline should be offset by an easing of policy. Although such a decline actually begins at point t_0 in Figure 1, it will be some time before reports evidencing the decline will be received by various Government agencies. More time will pass while these reports are aggregated and analyzed. Most analysts will not be content with one piece of information; they will want supporting evidence from several economic series over some period of time before they will be ready to conclude that they are confronting a general decline in

FIGURE 1 Schematic of the Lags of Monetary and Fiscal Policy

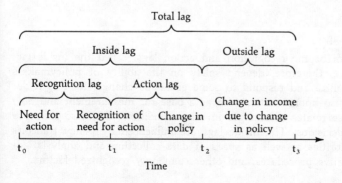

Reprinted from Mark H. Willes, "Lags in Monetary and Fiscal Policy," *Business Review*, Federal Reserve Bank of Philadelphia (March 1968), pp. 3–10.

business rather than simply a transient fluctuation in one statistic. Time elapsing between the start of the decline (t_0) and when this decline is recognized (t_1) has been dubbed by economists as the recognition lag.

Action Lag

Once the need for a policy change is recognized, it takes decision-makers time to alter policy. This lag is shown in Figure 1 as the period between points t_1 and t_2. Action lags can be caused by several things. First, not all those with policy responsibilities may be convinced of the need for change; this may delay action. Second, it may take time to work out details of the change and to go through the administrative exercises necessary to implement them. Finally, there might be political or other economic objectives which lead policymakers to put off any policy change. For example, a change in monetary policy might be delayed if such action would hamper current or prospective Treasury financing operation. Or, an easing of policy to stimulate business might be put off because it would conflict with a desire to protect the balance of payments.

Responsiveness to more than one objective need not always extend the length of the action lag, however. It could cause policymakers to change policy before they recognized a general movement in business, thus producing a *negative* action lag. This could happen, for example, if a decline in the money supply or an increase in unemployment led to an easing in monetary policy even though a downturn in general business conditions was not yet evident.

Inside Lag

The sum of the recognition and action lags, called the inside lag, does not, therefore, depend solely on the ability of policymakers to recognize and respond to some economic change. Its length depends also upon what is used as a base for measurement and how this base relates to changes in other conditions that also influence policy decisions. The inside lags are influenced by policy tradeoffs and priorities as well as speed of data collection and analysis, administrative procedures, and other commonly recognized factors.

Outside Lags

After policy is changed, it takes time for the effects of the change to work their way through the economy and alter spending. This outside lag is shown as the space between points t_2 and t_3 in Figure 1.

Causes of outside lags are difficult to analyze because they involve complex aspects of the way the economy works. Economists have incomplete knowledge of all the relationships involved. Some of the main factors can be discussed in a general way, however. The outside lag associated with income tax changes, for example, depends on the time required to alter the disposable income of individuals and corporations and their spending. Adjustments by corporations probably tend to be more sluggish than those by individuals. Corporate cash positions generally are not affected so quickly as are those of individuals, corporate planning and spending tend to be longer, and so on. These differences between individuals and corporations likely diminish as corporate tax payment schedules are accelerated.

Changes in Government expenditure policies may influence the pace of economic activity quickly. In some cases, placement or cancellation of orders for goods can cause changes in production and income before any actual alteration in Government spending takes place. Even without this, release of additional funds to an ongoing project often will stimulate spending immediately, while a cutback in actual expenditures generally will have immediate depressing effects on national income. Similarly, changes in transfer payments (like unemployment benefits) or purchase of services usually will cause an almost immediate alteration in disposable income and spending. On the other hand, newly appropriated funds for projects involving considerable planning or organization may begin to find their way into the spending stream only after some months. Similarly, reduced appropriations may not produce an immediate cut in spending if unused previous appropriations exist.

The link between changes in monetary policy and spending is not so direct as in the case of fiscal policy. Economists are still debating exactly what the channels are. Some think monetary policy is linked to the real sectors of the economy primarily through interest rates. An increase in rates inhibits investment and perhaps consumption and thereby causes a reduction in the rate of growth of income. Other economists view the monetary mechanism as involving primarily the quantity rather than the cost of money. As individuals and corporations adjust to changes in their actual and desired holdings of money, they change their expenditures on goods and services, thus altering the level of national income. Still other economists focus on availability of credit, arguing that a change in monetary conditions alters banks' willingness to lend. Bank lending behavior, in turn, influences the amount of investment and consumption expenditures that can be financed and therefore the level of income.

The first step in each of these theories is the response of banks to changes in monetary policy. Banks may or may not adjust quickly to changes in monetary policy depending on their current reserve position, loan demand, interest rate expectations, and so on. The longer banks delay in making adjustments, the longer the outside lags of monetary policy.

Proponents of interest-rate theories acknowledge that interest costs are often only a small fraction of the cost of a good or service, so a change in the rate may exert little influence on many spending decisions. Even in those cases where interest costs do matter, it may take time for them to affect aggregate spending. Some projects may already be under way. The cost of curtailing them may be greater than the cost of continuing under more expensive financing conditions. On the other side, it takes time to plan and carry out investment and other projects. A decline in interest costs may lead to increased spending, but only after a long start-up period.

Changes in the quantity of money also may affect spending totals only after a lag. Alterations in spending may be more closely associated with long-run than short-run changes in the money supply. In the short run, individuals and businesses may try to use their existing money balances more or less intensively, thereby avoiding the need to make significant spending adjustments.

HOW LONG ARE THE LAGS?

On the basis of what economists know about how the economy works, they have attempted to get some idea of how long these lags are.

Inside Lags

The Federal Reserve generally has been able to recognize cyclical changes in economic activity within three months of their occurrence [8].[1] Since there is no reason to believe that analysts in the executive and legislative branches of the Government are not equally good in recognizing shifts in the economy, this suggests that the recognition lag for monetary and fiscal policy is probably about three months.

In the postwar period, the action lag of monetary policy as mea-

[1] Numbers in brackets refer to references listed at the end of this article.

sured in relation to cyclical turning points usually has been zero. At times, however, it has been negative as the monetary authorities responded to factors that preceded cyclical declines in the economy [8].

In monetary policy, the decisionmaking group is relatively small and homogeneous. It can and does act quickly. In contrast, fiscal policy decisions are made by Congress and the President. The larger number of people involved increases the likelihood of diversity of opinion and objectives, slowing down the decisionmaking process. In addition, the administrative machinery is complex. As a result, while fiscal policy decisions have at times been made in less than a month, on some occasions many months have passed before agreement has been reached on a course of action. The fate of the 1966 tax increase proposal is a case in point. More than a year has passed since the President first suggested the increase, and it has been over seven months since the 10 per cent surcharge proposal went before Congress. Lags in planning and appropriations have also meant delays in making changes in Government expenditures.

Consequently, while it is difficult to make precise statements about the action lags of fiscal policy, it is clear that many months can pass before a policy change is made. This compares with the zero or negative action lags of monetary policy and goes far to explain the preference of many for the use of monetary rather than fiscal policy for stabilizing the economy in the short run.

Outside Lags[2]

Outside lags of fiscal policy are often relatively short. Changes in personal income taxes generally produce significant changes in disposable income and consumption spending within a month or two [1]. Changes in corporate tax rates take longer to have an effect. One study has suggested three or four months [1]. Similarly, if action is taken directly on Government expenditures, income can be affected within a few months. A broad range of expenditure and income tax policies, therefore, can have a significant effect on na-

---

[2] The discussion might seem to imply that the outside lag is some discrete time period. Action is taken, and the impacts are registered on the economy at some single point in the future. Actually, it is more likely that the effects of a given policy change will be distributed over a period of time. A significant proportion of these effects may be clustered within a short interval, but then perhaps not. Generally the term "outside lag" is used to denote the time it takes for a policy change to have a "significant" effect (often difficult to define) on the economy, or the time it takes for a policy change to have its peak effect.

tional income within a period of one to three months. This is one estimate of the range of outside lags of fiscal policy.

For monetary policy the situation is more complicated. As noted earlier, estimates of outside lags depend partly on what is viewed as the most important short-run link between monetary policy and the real sectors of the economy.

The one element common to most theories of the relationship between monetary policy and economic activity is the process of adjustment by banks. Recent evidence suggests that banks make adjustments to monetary changes quickly—within a month or two. [2, 5, 7]. This type of evidence leads those who focus on credit availability to conclude that changes in monetary policy are quickly felt by bank borrowers and depositors and that income changes follow shortly thereafter.

Actions of the monetary authorities and banks produce changes in the money supply. Quantity theorists start with this change in money supply to measure what they consider the most significant part of the outside lag of monetary policy. The best-known study of this lag found that changes in income lagged changes in the quantity of money by an average of about fourteen months using one type of formulation, and by about five months using another method of comparison [3]. Other studies obtained similar results.[3]

Most investigators have used a change in interest rates as the starting point to measure the major component of the outside lag of monetary policy. Their estimates vary widely, but the minimum lag found has been about three months, with many estimates ranging up to eighteen months and more.[4] There is little concentration of estimates at any point in the three- to eighteen-month range, so that on the surface an estimate of almost any length within this range seems equally likely.

LAGS AND PUBLIC POLICY

Table 1 presents a range of estimates for the various components of the lags of monetary and fiscal policy suggested in the previous section. While these ranges are not all-inclusive, they do include the thinking and findings of most economists.

Table 1 suggests several conclusions which have important implications for public policy:

1. Estimates of the lags of monetary and fiscal policy differ widely.
2. Monetary and fiscal authorities are doing a relatively good job in recognizing changes in the economy.

[3] See [6] for a summary of some of these studies.
[4] For summaries of some of these studies see [4].

TABLE 1 Range of Estimates of the Average Lags of Monetary and Fiscal Policy *(in months)*

| | Inside lags | | | |
	Recognition lags (1)	Action lags (2)	Outside lags (3)	Total lags (4)
Monetary policy	3	0	1–20	4–23
Fiscal policy	3	1–15	1–3	5–21

3. Monetary authorities generally act promptly but the effects of action may take considerable time to be felt.
4. Fiscal authorities often act slowly but the effects are usually felt fairly quickly.

Inasmuch as changes in policy—especially monetary policy—take time to be effective, it is necessary to anticipate. Given the objective of trying to reduce fluctuations in economic activity, monetary and fiscal policy should have a stimulative effect when the economy is declining and a restraining effect when it is increasing. If outside lags are very long, a change of policy initiated at the beginning of a change in the economy may not begin to have any substantial effect until the need is past. Instead, it may have its greatest effect when the direction of the economy has reversed and the opposite policy is called for. In such case, changes in monetary and fiscal policy would aggravate fluctuations in the economy. The shorter the outside lags, the less likely is a distortion of this kind and the more effective are the policies in reducing undesired fluctuations in economic activity. Policy changes, therefore, sometimes need to be out of step with current fluctuations in the economy, coming *before* the need arises so that their effects will be felt at the appropriate time.

This puts a premium on business forecasting. Good forecasts, by "recognizing" a change before it occurs, in effect make the recognition lag negative and greatly improve the timing of monetary and fiscal policy by compensating for the other lags. If the outside or action lags are very long, good forecasting is essential for monetary and fiscal policy to be effective in helping the nation achieve its economic objectives. Even if the outside or action lags are not long, good forecasting can contribute significantly to the timeliness of policy actions.

Another way to reduce the over-all lags of monetary policy is to reduce the action lag. For fiscal policy there is considerable room for movement. Most proposals involve giving the President authority to make changes in taxes or expenditures without waiting for the full process of Congressional review and determination. There may be ways to speed up Congressional action as well.

The length of the outside lags of monetary and fiscal policy is determined by responses to policy changes of many individuals and businesses. It is not known whether or not anything can be done about this reaction time. Perhaps research will reveal possibilities of influencing the outside lags of monetary and fiscal policy by changing the types or mix of tools employed.

Some economists, convinced that the lags of monetary and fiscal policy are long, have suggested that the Government get out of the stabilization business. They advocate replacing current reliance on discretionary policies with a set of rules that would hold the monetary and fiscal environment stable rather than try to have it counter short-run fluctuations in economic activity. This would not reduce cyclical fluctuations but, it is argued, would keep them from being aggravated by well-intentioned but inappropriate Government policies.

Many economists do not go this far. They think the lags are at the short- rather than the long-end of the ranges given in Table 1 or they are confident that lags can be reduced. They see discretionary monetary and fiscal policy helping in a significant and positive way to reduce undesired fluctuations in the economy.

Much has been done toward understanding lags and in dealing with them, but much more remains. One thing is certain. Policy decisions and actions must be made and interpreted with the problem of lags clearly in mind. Policymakers and the public must look to the future if they are to obtain the conditions they desire in the present.

TECHNICAL APPENDIX—MEASUREMENTS OF THE LAGS

Measurement of lags of monetary and fiscal policy is difficult. Notions of the exact nature of the lags are not completely developed and the methodological and statistical problems involved are formidable. These factors account, at least in part, for a wide divergence of opinions and estimates of the length of the lags.

Inside Lags

Conceptually, measurement of the inside lags is fairly straightforward but in practice is often complicated by lack of suitable data and difficulties in interpreting available data. What is required is an indication of when those with policy responsibilities recognize changes in the economy and when they *decide* to change policy. Since these lags generally relate to unannounced judgments and intentions of policymakers, currently available time series will not do. These series may well be influenced by other factors and give a misleading impression of the length of the recognition and action lags.

Consequently, in [8] the official minutes and staff memoranda of the Federal Open Market Committee for the years 1952–1960 were used to see how long it took the monetary authorities to recognize cyclical turning points in general economic activity (NBER reference dates were used as a benchmark). It was assumed that this would be a good indication of the length of time it takes the monetary authorities to recognize significant changes in any target economic variable. These records, reflecting policy decisions as well as statements on the conomic outlook of policymakers, were also used to measure the action lag of monetary policy.

Comparable data are not available for the fiscal authorities, so an assumption was made that the recognition lag was the same for fiscal as for monetary policy. Also, no formal attempt was made to estimate the action lag of fiscal policy. The record of explicit attempts to take countercyclical fiscal action, especially on the tax side, is relatively short. This makes it difficult to say anything definite about the action lag of fiscal policy. Experiences of the 1962 and 1967 tax proposals suggest that the action lag may easily be a year or more. On the other hand, some excise tax legislation, the speed-up or slow-down of some Government procurements and expenditures, and other fiscal measures have been handled by the Congress or the President relatively quickly. In short, the nature of political and legislative processes gives little meaning to the idea of an average action lag for fiscal policy. A range rather than a point estimate gives a better indication of the length of this lag, and experience may be too limited to set a definite upper bound on this range.

Outside Lags

Measurement of outside lags of monetary and fiscal policy is plagued by conceptual as well as methodological and statistical problems. It was noted in the accompanying article that the outside lag is not a discrete phenomenon. Rather, the effects of a policy change are *distributed* over a number of subsequent periods. Economic theory provides little help in deducing the precise shape of this distribution. It may well vary from one economic sector to another, and different policy actions might result in different distributions as well.

Some investigators assume a policy change has limited immediate effects on the economy but that these effects build up as time passes, reach a peak in some future time period and then subside. Others assume that a policy change has its greatest effect initially, and that these effects then become smaller in each subsequent period. Still other assumptions are possible. Depending on the assumption used and the statistical formulations employed, the shape of lag distributions can vary widely. Since the term "outside lag" is generally interpreted as meaning the time it takes for a policy action to achieve a certain percentage of its total effects, or to reach its peak effect, these different distributions can imply greatly different estimates of the outside lags of monetary and fiscal policy.

Numerous statistical formulations and techniques are used to try to estimate the distributed lags associated with policy changes. In [2], an adjustment coefficient for banks that can be converted into a lag distribution is estimated by correlating (in a multiple regression) changes in excess reserves (dependent variable) with the stock of excess reserves at the beginning of each period (independent variable). In [7], the distributed lag in bank adjustments is estimated by regressing deposit changes (dependent variable) against current and lagged changes in unborrowed reserves (independent variables). Coefficients of the independent variables describe the lag structure.

Lag distributions describing relationships between changes in interest rates or income and various types of expenditures have been estimated by the use of a variety of functional forms and statistical methods. Generally they involve including as independent variables in a multiple regression equation lagged observations of the dependent variable (e.g., plant and equipment expenditures) or lagged observations of the independent variable (e.g., interest rates or income). The resulting coefficients and lag distribution depend significantly on the functional form used, the constraints imposed on the coefficients, and the statistical estimating procedures followed. These factors account in part for the different estimates of the outside lag of monetary policy recorded in [4]. The results for fiscal policy contained in [1] reflect similar considerations.

Those who focus on the quantity of money as the main link between monetary policy and the economy generally do not actually estimate the shape of the entire lag distribution. Instead, they compare turning points in income with turning points in the money stock to see how long the former lags the latter [3], or they correlate lagged changes in the money stock with income or changes in income [6]. The assumption is that these procedures yield an estimate of the weighted average interval between action and effects. The entire lag distribution is compressed into one number.

Economists are not agreed on the best way to estimate the outside lags of monetary and fiscal policy. Much progress has been made in recent years, but much is yet to be learned. A real concern of many, especially in the case of monetary policy, is that in spite of the sophisticated techniques used, we have still been unable to isolate the effects of policy changes from all of the other things which influence the pace of economic activity. This separation is essential if the lags are to be measured correctly.

REFERENCES

1. Ando, Albert, and E. Cary Brown, "Lags in Fiscal Policy," *Stabilization Policies* (Englewood Cliffs, N.J.: Prentice-Hall, 1963), pp. 7–13, 97–163.
2. Bryan, William R., "Bank Adjustments to Monetary Policy: Alternative Estimates of the Lag," *American Economic Review*, September 1967, pp. 855–864.
3. Friedman, Milton, "The Lag in the Effect of Monetary Policy," *Journal of Political Economy*, October 1961, pp. 447–466.
4. Hamburger, Michael J. "The Impact of Monetary Variables: A Selected Survey of the Recent Empirical Literature," *Staff Economic Study Number 34*, Board of Governors of the Federal Reserve System, July 1967.
5. Horwich, George, "Elements of Timing and Response in the Balance Sheet of Banking, 1953–55," *Journal of Finance*, May 1957, pp. 238–255.
6. Mayer, Thomas, "The Lag in Effect of Monetary Policy: Some Criticisms," *Western Economic Journal*, September 1967, pp. 324–342.
7. Rangarajan, C., and Alan K. Severn, "The Response of Banks to Changes in Aggregate Reserves," *Journal of Finance*, December 1965, pp. 651–664.
8. Willes, Mark H., "The Inside Lags of Monetary Policy: 1952–1960," *Journal of Finance*, December 1967, pp. 591–593.

LEONALL C. ANDERSEN
JERRY L. JORDAN

MONETARY AND
FISCAL ACTIONS:
A TEST OF THEIR
RELATIVE IMPORTANCE
IN ECONOMIC STABILIZATION

39

High employment, rising output of goods and services, and relatively stable prices are three widely accepted national economic goals. Responsibility for economic stabilization actions to meet these goals has been assigned to monetary and fiscal authorities. The Federal Reserve System has the major responsibility for monetary management. Fiscal actions involve Federal Government spending plans and taxing provisions. Governmental units involved in fiscal actions are the Congress and the Administration, including the Treasury, the Bureau of the Budget, and the Council of Economic Advisers.

This article reports the results of recent research which tested three commonly held propositions concerning the relative importance of monetary and fiscal actions in implementing economic stabilization policy. These propositions are: The response of economic activity to fiscal actions relative to that of monetary actions is (I) greater, (II) more predictable, and (III) faster. Specific meanings, for the purposes of this article, of the broad terms used in these propositions are presented later.

This article does not attempt to test rival economic theories of the mechanism by which monetary and fiscal actions influence economic activity. Neither is it intended to develop evidence bearing directly on any causal relationships implied by such theories. More elaborate procedures than those used here would be required in order to test any theories underlying the familiar statements regarding results expected from monetary and fiscal actions. However, empirical relationships are developed between frequently used measures of stabilization actions and economic activity. These relationships are consistent with the implications of some theories of sta-

Reprinted from Leonall C. Andersen and Jerry L. Jordan, "Monetary and Fiscal Actions: A Test of Their Relative Importance in Economic Stabilization," *Review* (November 1968), pp. 11–23, Federal Reserve Bank of St. Louis.

bilization policy and are inconsistent with others, as will be pointed out.

A brief discussion of the forces influencing economic activity is presented first. Next, with this theory as a background, specific measures of economic activity, fiscal actions, and monetary actions are selected. The results of testing the three propositions noted above, together with other statements concerning the response of economic activity to monetary and fiscal forces, are then presented. Finally, some implications for the conduct of stabilization policy are drawn from the results of these tests.

A THEORETICAL VIEW OF ECONOMIC ACTIVITY

Our economic system consists of many markets. Every commodity, service, and financial asset is viewed as constituting an individual market in which a particular item is traded and a price is determined. All of these markets are linked together in varying degrees, since prices in one market influence decisions made in other markets.

About a century ago, Leon Walras outlined a framework for analyzing a complex market economy. Such an analysis includes a demand and a supply relationship for every commodity and for each factor of production. Trading in the markets results in prices being established which clear all markets, i.e., the amount offered in a market equals the amount taken from the market. According to this analysis, outside occurrences reflected in shifts in demand and supply relationships cause changes in market prices and in quantities traded. These outside events include changes in preferences of market participants, in resource endowments, and in technology. Financial assets were not viewed as providing utility or satisfaction to their holders and were therefore excluded from the analysis.

Later developments in economic theory have viewed financial assets as providing flows of services which also provided utility or satisfaction to holders. For example, a holder of a commercial bank time deposit receives liquidity service (ease of conversion into the medium of exchange), store of value service (ability to make a future purchase), risk avoidance service (little risk of loss), and a financial yield. According to this later view, economic entities incorporate choices among goods, services, *and* financial assets into their decision-making processes.

The fact that economic entities make choices in both markets for goods and services and markets for financial assets requires the addition of demand and supply relationships for every financial asset.

Market interest rates (prices of financial assets) and changes in the stocks outstanding of most financial assets are determined by the market process along with prices and quantities of goods and services.

These theoretical developments have enlarged the number of independent forces which are regarded as influencing market-determined prices, interest rates, quantities produced of commodities, and stocks outstanding of financial assets. Government and monetary authorities are viewed as exerting independent influences in the market system. These influences are called fiscal and monetary policies or actions. Random events, such as the outbreak of war, strikes in key industries, and prolonged drought, exert other market influences. Growth in world trade and changes in foreign prices and interest rates, relative to our own, influence exports and therefore are largely an outside influence on domestic markets.

Market expectations have also been assigned a significant factor in markets, but these are not viewed as a distinctly independent

EXHIBIT I   Classification of Market Variables

Dependent variables
  Prices and quantities of goods and services.
  Prices and quantities of factors of production.
  Prices (interest rates) and quantities of financial assets.
  Expectations based on:
    a. movements in dependent variables.
    b. expected results of random events.
    c. expected changes in fiscal and monetary policy.
Independent variables
  Slowly changing factors:
    a. preferences.
    b. technology.
    c. resources.
    d. institutional and legal framework.
  Events outside the domestic economy:
    a. change in total world trade.
    b. movements in foreign prices and interest rates.
  Random events:
    a. outbreak of war.
    b. major strikes.
    c. weather.
  Forces subject to control by:
    a. fiscal actions.
    b. monetary actions.

force. Expectations result from market participants basing their decisions on movements in market-determined variables, or they are derived from market responses to the expected results of random events, such as the outbreak of a war or the anticipation of changes in fiscal or monetary policy.

These dependent and independent market variables are summarized in Exhibit I. The dependent variables are determined by the interplay of market forces which results from changes in the independent variables. Market-determined variables include prices and quantities of goods and services, prices and quantities of factors of production, prices (interest rates) and quantities of financial assets, and expectations. Independent variables consist of slowly changing factors, forces from outside our economy, random events, and forces subject to control by fiscal and monetary authorities. A change in an independent variable (for example, a fiscal or a monetary action) causes changes in many of the market-determined (dependent) variables.

MEASURES OF ECONOMIC ACTIVITY AND OF MONETARY AND FISCAL ACTIONS

Three theoretical approaches have been advanced by economists for analyzing the influence of monetary and fiscal actions on economic activity. These approaches are the textbook Keynesian analysis derived from economic thought of the late 1930's to the early 1950's, the portfolio approach developed over the last two decades, and the modern quantity theory of money. Each of these theories has led to popular and familiar statements regarding the direction, amount, and timing of fiscal and monetary influences on economic activity. As noted earlier, these theories and their linkages will not be tested directly, but the validity of some of the statements which purport to represent the implications of these theories will be examined. For this purpose, frequently used measures of economic activity, monetary actions and fiscal actions are selected.

Economic Activity

Total spending for goods and services (gross national product at current prices) is used in this article as the measure of economic activity. It consists of total spending on final goods and services by households, businesses, and governments plus net foreign investment. Real output of goods and services is limited by resource endowments and technology, with the actual level of output, within this constraint, determined by the level of total spending and other factors.

Monetary Actions

Monetary actions involve primarily decisions of the Treasury and the Federal Reserve System. Treasury monetary actions consist of variations in its cash holdings, deposits at Federal Reserve banks, and issuance of Treasury currency. Federal Reserve monetary actions include changes in its portfolio of Government securities, variations in member bank reserve requirements, and changes in the Federal Reserve discount rate. Banks and the public also engage in a form of monetary actions. Commercial bank decisions to hold excess reserves constitute a monetary action. Also, because of differential reserve requirements, the public's decisions to hold varying amounts of time deposits at commercial banks or currency relative to demand deposits are a form of monetary action, but are not viewed as stabilization actions. However they are taken into consideration by stabilization authorities in forming their own actions. Exhibit II summarizes the various sources of monetary actions related to economic stabilization.

The monetary base[1] is considered by both the portfolio and the modern quantity theory schools to be a strategic monetary variable. The monetary base is under direct control of the monetary authorities, with major control exerted by the Federal Reserve System. Both of these schools consider an increase in the monetary base, other forces constant, to be an expansionary influence on economic activity and a decrease to be a restrictive influence.

The portfolio school holds that a change in the monetary base affects investment spending, and thereby aggregate spending, through changes in market interest rates relative to the supply price of capital (real rate of return on capital). The modern quantity theory holds that the influence of the monetary base works through changes in the money stock which in turn affect prices, interest

---

[1] The monetary base is derived from a consolidated monetary balance sheet of the Federal Reserve and the Treasury. See Leonall C. Andersen and Jerry L. Jordan, "The Monetary Base: Explanation and Analytical Use," in the August 1968 issue of this *Review*. Since the uses of the base are bank reserves plus currency held by the public, it is often called "demand debt of the Government." See James Tobin, "An Essay on Principles of Debt Management," in *Fiscal and Debt Management Policies*, The Commission on Money and Credit (Englewood Cliffs, N.J.: Prentice-Hall, 1963). In some analyses, Tobin includes short-term Government debt outstanding in the monetary base.

EXHIBIT II   Stabilization Actions and Their Measurement

Stabilization actions	Frequently used measurements of actions

1. Monetary actions
Federal Reserve System
  a. open market transactions.
  b. discount rate changes.
  c. reserve requirement changes.
Treasury
  a. changes in cash holdings.
  b. changes in deposits at Reserve banks.
  c. changes in deposits at commercial banks.
  d. changes in Treasury currency outstanding.
 	
2. Fiscal actions
Government spending programs.
Government taxing provisions.
	1. Monetary actions
	Monetary base*
	Money stock, narrowly defined*
	Money plus time deposits
	Commercial bank credit
	Private demand deposits
	
	2. Fiscal actions
	High-employment expenditures.*
	High-employment receipts.*
	High-employment surplus.*
	Weighted high-employment expenditures.
	Weighted high-employment receipts.
	Weighted high-employment surplus.
	National income account expenditures.
	National income account receipts.
	Autonomous changes in Government tax rates.
	Net Government debt outside of agencies and trust funds.

*Tests based on these measures are reported in this article. The remaining measures were used in additional tests. These results are available on request.

rates, and spending on goods and services. Increases in the base are reflected in increases in the money stock which in turn result directly and indirectly in increased expenditures on a whole spectrum of capital and consumer goods. Both prices of goods and interest rates form the transmission mechanism in the modern quantity theory.

The money stock is also used as a strategic monetary variable in each of the approaches to stabilization policies, as the above discussion has implied. The simple Keynesian approach postulates that a change in the stock of money relative to its demand results in a change in interest rates. It also postulates that investment spending decisions depend on interest rates, and that growth in aggregate spending depends in turn on these investment decisions. Similarly, in the portfolio school of thought changes in the money stock lead to changes in interest rates, which are followed by substitutions in asset portfolios; then finally, total spending is affected. Interest rates, according to this latter school, are the key part of the transmission mechanism, influencing decisions to hold money versus alternative financial assets as well as decisions to invest in real assets. The influence of changes in the money stock on economic activity, within the modern quantity theory framework, has already been discussed in the previous paragraph.[2]

The monetary base, as noted, plays an important role in both the portfolio and the modern quantity theory approaches to monetary theory. However, there remains considerable controversy regarding the role of money in determining economic activity, ranging from "money does not matter" to "money is the dominant factor." In recent years there has been a general acceptance that money, among many other influences, is important. Thomas Mayer, in a recent book, summarizes this controversy. He concludes:

All in all, much recent evidence supports the view that the stock of money and, therefore, monetary policy, has a substantial effect. Note, however, that this reading of the evidence is by no means acceptable to all economists. Some, Professor Friedman and Dr. Warburton for example, argue that changes in the stock of money do have a dominant effect on income, at least in the long run, while others such as Professor Hansen

---

[2] Also see Leonall C. Andersen and Jerry L. Jordan, "Money in a Modern Quantity Theory Framework" in the December 1967 issue of this *Review*. For an excellent analysis of these three monetary views see David I. Fand, "Keynesian Monetary Theories, Stabilization Policy and the Recent Inflation," a paper presented to the Conference of University Professors, Ditchley Park, Oxfordshire, England, Sept. 13, 1968.

believe that changes in the stock of money are largely offset by opposite changes in velocity.[3]

The theories aside, changes in the monetary base and changes in the money stock are frequently used as measures of monetary actions. This article, in part, tests the use of these variables for this purpose. Money is narrowly defined as the nonbank public's holdings of demand deposits plus currency. Changes in the money stock mainly reflect movements in the monetary base; however, they also reflect decisions of commercial banks to hold excess reserves, of the nonbank public to hold currency and time deposits, and of the Treasury to hold demand deposits at commercial banks. The monetary base reflects monetary actions of the Federal Reserve, and to a lesser extent, those of the Treasury and gold flows. But changes in the base have been found to be dominated by actions of the Federal Reserve.[4]

Other aggregate measures, such as money plus time deposits, bank credit, and private demand deposits, are frequently used as monetary indicators (Exhibit II). Tests using these indicators were also made. The results of these tests did not change the conclusions reached in this article; these results are available on request. Market interest rates are not used in this article as strategic monetary variables since they reflect, to a great extent, fiscal actions, expectations and other factors which cannot properly be called monetary actions.

Fiscal Actions

The influence of fiscal actions on economic activity is frequently measured by Federal Government spending, changes in Federal tax rates, or Federal budget deficits and surpluses. The textbook Keynesian view has been reflected in many popular discussions of fiscal influence. The portfolio approach and the modern quantity theory suggest alternative analyses of fiscal influence.

The elementary textbook Keynesian view concentrates almost exclusively on the direct influence of fiscal actions on total spending. Government spending is a direct demand for goods and services. Tax rates affect disposable income, a major determinant of consumer spending, and profits of businesses, a major determinant of invest-

[3] Thomas Mayer, *Monetary Policy in the United States*, (New York: Random House, 1968), pp. 148–149.
[4] For a discussion of these points, see: Karl Brunner, "The Role of Money and Monetary Policy," in the July 1968 issue of this *Review*.

ment spending. Budget surpluses and deficits are used as a measure of the net direct influence of spending and taxing on economic activity. More advanced textbooks also include an indirect influence of fiscal actions on economic activity through changes in market interest rates. In either case, little consideration is generally given to the method of financing expenditures.

The portfolio approach as developed by Tobin attributes to fiscal actions both a direct influence on economic activity and an indirect influence. Both influences take into consideration the financing of Government expenditures.[5] Financing of expenditures by issuance of demand debt of monetary authorities (the monetary base) results in the full Keynesian multiplier effect. Financing by either taxes or borrowing from the public has a smaller multiplier effect on spending. Tobin views this direct influence as temporary.

The indirect influence of fiscal actions, according to Tobin, results from the manner of financing the Government debt, that is, variations in the relative amounts of demand debt, short-term debt, and long-term debt. For example, an expansionary move would be a shift from long-term to short-term debt or a shift from short-term to demand debt. A restrictive action would result from a shift in the opposite direction. As in the case of monetary actions, market interest rates on financial assets and their influence on investment spending make up the transmission mechanism.

The modern quantity theory also suggests that the influence of fiscal actions depends on the method of financing Government expenditures. This approach maintains that financing expenditures by either taxing or borrowing from the public involves a transfer of command over resources from the public to the Government. However, the net influence on total spending resulting from interest rate and wealth changes is ambiguous. Only a deficit financed by the monetary system is necessarily expansionary.[6]

High-employment budget concepts have been developed as meas-

[5] Tobin, pp. 143–213.

[6] The importance of not overlooking the financial aspects of fiscal policy is emphasized by Carl F. Christ in "A Simple Macroeconomic Model with a Government Budget Restraint," *Journal of Political Economy*, Vol. 76, No. 1, January/February 1968, pp. 53–67. Christ summarizes (pages 53 and 54) that "the multiplier effect of a change in government purchases cannot be defined until it is decided how to finance the purchases, and the value of the multiplier given by the generally accepted analysis [which ignores the government budget restraint] is in general incorrect . . . (the) multiplier effect of government purchases may be greater or less than the value obtained by ignoring the budget restraint, depending on whether the method of financing is mainly by printing money or mainly by taxation."

ures of the influence of fiscal actions on economic activity.[7] In these budget concepts, expenditures include both those for goods and services and those for transfer payments, adjusted for the influence of economic activity. Receipts, similarly adjusted, primarily reflect legislated changes in Federal Government tax rates, including Social Security taxes. The net of receipts and expenditures is used as a net measure of changes in expenditure provisions and in tax rates. These high-employment concepts are used in this article as measures of fiscal actions (Exhibit II). Tests were also made alternatively using national income account Government expenditures and receipts, a series measuring autonomous changes in Government tax rates, a weighted high-employment expenditure and receipt series, and a series of U. S. Government debt held by the public plus Federal Reserve holdings of U. S. Government securities. These tests did not change the conclusions reached in this article. Results of these tests are available on request.

Other Influences

Measures of other independent forces which influence economic activity are not used in this article. Yet this should not be construed to imply that these forces are not important. It is accepted by all economists that the nonmonetary and nonfiscal forces listed in Exhibit I have an important influence on economic activity. However, recognition of the existence of these "other forces" does not preclude the testing of propositions relating to the relative importance of monetary and fiscal forces. The analysis presented in this study provides indirect evidence bearing on these "other forces." The interested reader is encouraged to read the technical note presented in the Appendix to this article before proceding.

TESTING THE PROPOSITIONS

This section reports the results of testing the three propositions under consideration. First, the concept of testing a hypothesis is briefly

---

[7] See Keith M. Carlson, "Estimates of the High-Employment Budget: 1947–1967," in the June 1967 issue of this *Review*. The high-employment budget concept was used in the *Annual Report of the Council of Economic Advisors* from 1962 to 1966. For a recent analysis using the high-employment budget, see "Federal Fiscal Policy in the 1960's," *Federal Reserve Bulletin*, September 1968, pp. 701–718. According to this article, "the concept does provide a more meaningful measure of the Federal budgetary impact than the published measures of actual Federal surplus or deficit taken by themselves."

discussed. Next, the results of regression analyses which relate the measures of fiscal and monetary actions to total spending are reported. Finally, statistics developed from the regression analyses are used to test the specific propositions.

The Concept of Testing a Hypothesis

In scientific methodology, testing a hypothesis consists of the statement of the hypothesis, deriving by means of logic testable consequences expected from it, and then taking observations from past experience which show the presence or absence of the expected consequences. If the expected consequences do not occur, then the hypothesis is said to be "not confirmed" by the evidence. If, on the other hand, the expected consequences occur, the hypothesis is said to be "confirmed."

It is important to keep the following point in mind. In scientific testing, a hypothesis (or conjecture) may be found "not confirmed" and therefore refuted as the explanation of the relationship under examination. However, if it is found to be "confirmed," the hypothesis cannot be said to have been proven true. In the latter case, however, the hypothesis remains an acceptable proposition of a real world relationship as long as it is found to be "confirmed" in future tests.[8]

The results presented in this study all bear on what is commonly called a "reduced form" in economics. A reduced-form equation is a derivable consequence of a system of equations which may be hypothesized to represent the structure of the economy (i.e., a so-called structural model). In other words, all of the factors and causal relations which determine total spending (GNP) are "summarized" in one equation. This reduced-form equation postulates a certain relationship over time between the independent variables and the dependent variable—total spending. Using appropriate statistical procedures and selected measures of variables, it is possible to test whether or not the implications of the reduced-form equation have occurred in the past. If the implied relationships are not confirmed, then the relationship asserted by the reduced-form equation is said to have been refuted. However, not confirming the reduced form does not necessarily mean that the whole "model," and all of the

[8] For a detailed discussion of testing hypotheses in reference to monetary actions, see Albert E. Burger and Leonall C. Andersen, "The Development of Testable Hypotheses for Monetary Management," a paper presented at the annual meeting of the Southern Finance Association, November 8, 1968. It will appear in a forthcoming issue of the *Southern Journal of Business*, University of Georgia, Athens, Ga.

factors and causal relations contained in it, are denied. It may be only that one or more of the structural linkages of the model is incorrect, or that the empirical surrogates chosen as measures of monetary or fiscal influence are not appropriate.

Frequently one encounters statements or conjectures regarding factors which are asserted to influence economic activity in a specific way. These statements take the form of reduced-form equations, and are sometimes attributed to various theories of the determination of economic activity. As stated previously, this study does not attempt to test the causal linkages by which fiscal and monetary actions influence total spending, but is concerned only with the confirmation or refutation of rival conjectures regarding the strength and reliability of fiscal and monetary actions based on frequently used indicators of such actions.

Measuring the Empirical Relationships

As a step toward analyzing the three propositions put forth earlier, empirical relationships between the measures of fiscal and monetary actions and total spending are established. These relationships are developed by regressing quarter-to-quarter changes in GNP on quarter-to-quarter changes in the money stock (M) and in the various measures of fiscal actions: high-employment budget surplus (R-E), high-employment expenditures (E), and high-employment receipts (R). Similar equations were estimated where changes in the monetary base (B) were used in place of the money stock.

Changes in all variables were computed by two methods. Conventional first differences were calculated by subtracting the value for the preceding quarter from the value for the present quarter.[9] The other method used is an averaging procedure used by Kareken and Solow called central differences.[10] The structure of lags present

[9] Changes in GNP, R and E are quarterly changes in billions of dollars measured at annual rates, while changes in M and B are quarterly changes in billions of dollars. Changes in GNP, R and E are changes in flows, whereas changes in M and B are changes in a stock. Since all of the time series have strong trends, first differences tend to increase in size over time. Statistical considerations indicate that per cent first differences would be more appropriate. On the other hand, regular first differences provide estimates of multipliers which are more useful for the purposes of this study. Test regressions of relative changes were run and they did not alter the conclusions of this article.

[10] John Kareken and Robert M. Solow, "Lags in Monetary Policy" in *Stabilization Policies* of the research studies prepared for the Commission on Money and Credit (Englewood Cliffs, N.J.: Prentice-Hall, Inc., 1962), pp. 18–21.

in the regressions was estimated with use of the Almon lag technique.[11] The data are seasonally adjusted quarterly averages for the period from the first quarter of 1952 to the second quarter of 1968.[12]

As discussed previously, statements are frequently made from which certain relationships are expected to exist between measures of economic activity on the one hand and measures of monetary and fiscal actions on the other hand. Such relationships consist of a direct influence of an action on GNP and of an indirect influence which reflects interactions among the many markets for real and financial assets. These interactions work through the market mechanism determining the dependent variables listed in Exhibit 1. The postulated relationships are the total of these direct and indirect influences. Thus, the empirical relationship embodied in each regression coefficient is the *total* response (including both direct and indirect responses) of GNP to changes in each measure of a stabilization action, assuming all other forces remain constant.

The results presented here do not provide a basis for separating the direct and indirect influences of monetary and fiscal forces on total spending, but this division is irrelevant for the purposes of this article. The interested reader is referred to the Appendix for further elaboration of these points.

Using the total response concept, changes in GNP are expected to be positively related to changes in the money stock (M) or changes in the monetary base (B). With regard to the high-employment surplus (receipts minus expenditures), a larger surplus or a smaller deficit is expected to have a negative influence on GNP, and conversely. Changes in high-employment expenditures (E) are expected to have a positive influence and changes in receipts (R) are expected to have a negative influence when these variables are included separately.

Considering that the primary purpose of this study is to measure the influence of a few major forces on changes in GNP, rather than

[11] Shirley Almon, "The Distributed Lag Between Capital Appropriations and Expenditures," *Econometrica*, Vol. 33, No. 1, January 1965, pp. 178–196.

[12] As a test for structural shifts, the test period was divided into two equal parts and the regressions reported here were run for each sub-period and for the whole period. The Chow test for structural changes accepted the hypothesis that the sets of parameters estimated for each of the sub-periods were not different from each other or from those estimated for the whole period, at the five per cent level of significance. As a result, there is no evidence of a structural shift; consequently, the whole period was used.

to identify and measure the influences of all independent forces, the results obtain are quite good (Table I). The R^2 statistic, a measure of the per cent of the variance in changes in GNP explained by the regression equation, ranges from .53 to .73; these values are usually considered to be quite good when first differences are used rather than levels of the data. All of the estimated regression coefficients for changes in the money stock or the monetary base have the signs implied in the above discussion (equations 1.1 to 2.4 in Table I) and have a high statistical significance in most cases. The estimated coefficients for the high-employment measures of fiscal influence do not have the expected signs in all cases and generally are of low statistical significance. These regression results are discussed in greater detail below.

Money and the Monetary Base

The total response of GNP to changes in money or the monetary base distributed over four quarters is consistent with the postulated relationship (i.e. a positive relationship), and the coefficients are all statistically significant. The coefficients of each measure of monetary action may be summed to provide an indication of the over-all response of GNP to changes in monetary actions. These summed coefficients are also statistically significant and consistent with the postulated relationships. The results obtained for measures of monetary actions were not effected significantly when measures of fiscal actions other than those reported here were used in the regressions.

High-Employment Budget Surplus

As pointed out previously, the high-employment surplus or deficit is often used as a measure of the direction and strength of fiscal actions. Equation 1.1 summarizes the total response of GNP to changes in money and changes in the high-employment surplus. The coefficients of the high-employment surplus estimated for the contemporaneous and first lagged quarter have the expected sign, but the coefficients are of very low statistical significance and do not differ significantly from zero. The signs of the coefficients estimated for the second and third lagged quarters are opposite to the expected signs. The sum of the coefficients (total response distributed over four quarters) is estimated to have a positive sign (opposite the postulated sign) but is not statistically significant. These results provide no empirical support for the view that fiscal actions measured by the high-employment surplus have a significant influence on GNP. In principle, these results may have occurred either because

TABLE I Regression of Changes in GNP on Changes in Monetary and Fiscal Actions

First differences	Equation 1.1 ΔM	Equation 1.1 Δ(R-E)	Equation 1.2 ΔM	Equation 1.2 ΔE	Equation 1.2 ΔR	Equation 1.3 ΔM	Equation 1.3 ΔE	Equation 1.4 ΔB	Equation 1.4 ΔE	Equation 1.4 ΔR
t	1.57* (2.17)	-.15 (.65)	1.51* (2.03)	.36 (1.15)	.16 (.53)	1.54* (2.47)	.40 (1.48)	1.02 (.49)	.23 (.67)	.52 (1.68)
t-1	1.94* (3.60)	-.20 (1.08)	1.59* (2.85)	.53* (2.15)	-.01 (.03)	1.56* (3.43)	.54* (2.68)	5.46* (3.37)	.37 (1.36)	.02 (.07)
t-2	1.80* (3.37)	.10 (.55)	1.47* (2.69)	-.05 (.19)	-.03 (.10)	1.44* (3.18)	-.03 (.13)	6.48* (4.10)	-.21 (.84)	-.17 (.64)
t-3	1.28 (1.88)	.47* (1.95)	1.27 (1.82)	-.78* (2.82)	.11 (.32)	1.29* (2.00)	-.74* (2.85)	3.05 (1.54)	-.93* (3.10)	.14 (.39)
Sum	6.59* (7.73)	.22 (.45)	5.84* (6.57)	.07 (.13)	.23 (.32)	5.83* (7.25)	.17 (.54)	16.01* (5.67)	-.54 (.89)	.51 (.67)
Constant	1.99* (2.16)		2.10 (1.88)			2.28* (2.76)		1.55 (1.22)		
R²	.56		.58			.60		.53		
S.E.	4.24		4.11			4.01		4.35		
D-W	1.54		1.80			1.78		1.71		

Central differences	Equation 2.1 ΔM	Equation 2.1 Δ(R-E)	Equation 2.2 ΔM	Equation 2.2 ΔE	Equation 2.2 ΔR	Equation 2.3 ΔM	Equation 2.3 ΔE	Equation 2.4 ΔB	Equation 2.4 ΔE	Equation 2.4 ΔR
t	1.50 (1.84)	-.24 (.91)	1.58* (2.01)	.53 (1.52)	.32 (1.05)	1.54* (2.45)	.63* (2.21)	.61 (.28)	.28 (.73)	.87* (2.55)
t-1	2.11* (3.61)	-.23 (1.16)	1.57* (2.78)	.60* (2.44)	-.04 (.17)	1.63* (3.57)	.59* (2.61)	5.42* (3.16)	.50 (1.87)	-.07 (.27)
t-2	1.89*	.15	1.41*	-.15	-.11	1.43*	-.16	6.87*	-.27	-.33

	(3.18)	(.81)	(2.45)	(.60)	(.47)	(3.16)	(.71)	(3.92)	(1.04)	(1.31)
t-3	1.06	.52	1.26	-.96*	.18	1.13	-.86*	3.51	-1.26*	.35
	(1.36)	(1.90)	(1.72)	(3.15)	(.48)	(1.71)	(3.07)	(1.71)	(3.65)	(.87)
Sum	6.56*	.21	5.80*	.02	.34	5.74*	.19	16.41*	-.75	.82
	(8.16)	(.47)	(7.57)	(.04)	(.54)	(8.45)	(.77)	(6.95)	(1.37)	(1.16)
Constant	2.02*		2.00*			2.30*		1.24		
	(2.48)		(2.14)			(3.55)		(1.14)		
R²	.66		.72			.73		.67		
S.E.	3.35		3.03			2.97		3.26		
D-W	.88		1.14			1.13		1.05		

NOTE: Regression coefficients are the top figures, and their "t" values appear below each coefficient enclosed by parentheses. The regression coefficients marked by an asterisk (*) are statistically significant at the 5 per cent level. R² are adjusted for degrees of freedom. S.E. is the standard error of the estimate, and D-W is the Durbin-Watson statistic.

the high-employment surplus was not a good measure of fiscal influence, or because fiscal influence was not important during the sample period.[13]

Expenditures and Receipts

Simple textbook Keynesian models of income determination usually demonstrate, theoretically, that changes in tax rates exert a negative influence on economic activity, while changes in Government expenditures exert a positive influence. Equations 1.2 and 1.3 provide tests of these propositions. The signs of the coefficients estimated for tax receipts are the same as the hypothesized signs for only the first and second lagged quarters. However, since these coefficients (individually and the sums) are of low statistical significance, no importance can be attached to this variable. Inclusion of changes in receipts (ΔR) in equation 1.2 does not improve the overall results, in terms of R^2 and the standard error of estimate, compared with equation 1.3 from which receipts are excluded.

These results provide no support for theories which indicate that changes in tax receipts due to changes in tax rates exert an overall negative (or any) influence on economic activity. The results are consistent with theories which indicate that if the alternative to tax revenue is borrowing from the public in order to finance Government spending, then the influence of spending will not necessarily be greater if the funds are borrowed rather than obtained through taxation. They are also consistent with the theory that consumers will maintain consumption levels at the expense of saving when there is a temporary reduction in disposable income.

The signs of the coefficients estimated for high-employment expenditures in equations 1.2 and 1.3 indicate that an increase in Government expenditures is mildly stimulative in the quarter in which spending is increased and in the following quarter. However, in the subsequent two quarters this increase in expenditures causes off-

[13] It was suggested to the authors that a weighted high-employment budget surplus might be a better measure of fiscal influence than the usual unweighted series. For an elaboration of such a weighted series, see Edward M. Gramlich, "Measures of the Aggregate Demand Impact of the Federal Budget," in *Staff Papers of the President's Commission on Budget Concepts* (Washington, D.C.: U.S. Government Printing Office, October 1967). Gramlich provided weights from the FRB-MIT model of the economy for constructing a weighted series. It was further suggested that the level of the high-employment budget surplus was a more appropriate measure of fiscal actions. Coefficients of fiscal influence were estimated using both changes in the weighted series, and levels of the high-employment surplus. The results did not change any of the conclusions of this article.

setting negative influences. The overall effect of a change in expenditures distributed over four quarters, indicated by the sum, is relatively small and not statistically significant. These results are consistent with modern quantity theories which hold that Government spending, taxing and borrowing policies would have, through interest rate and wealth effects, different impacts on economic activity under varying circumstances.[14]

Three Propositions Tested

The empirical relationships developed relating changes in GNP to changes in the money stock and changes in high-employment expenditures and receipts are used to test the three propositions under consideration. The results of testing the propositions using changes in the money stock are discussed in detail in this section. Similar results are reported in the accompanying tables using changes in the monetary base instead of the money stock. Conclusions drawn using either measure of monetary actions are similar.

Proposition I

Proposition I states that fiscal actions exert a larger influence on economic activity than do monetary actions. A test of this proposition involves an examination of the size of the regression coefficients for high-employment expenditures relative to those for money and the monetary base.[15] Proposition I implies that the coefficients for ΔE would be larger, without regard to sign, than those for ΔM and ΔB.

The coefficients presented in Table I are not appropriate for this test because the variables have different time dimensions and are a mixture of stocks and flows. An appropriate measure is developed by changing these regression coefficients to "beta coefficients" which

---

[14] John Culbertson points out that in a financially constrained economy (i.e., no monetary expansion to finance Government expenditures), expenditures by the Government financed in debt markets in competition with private expenditures can very possibly "crowd out of the market an equal (or conceivably even greater) volume that would have financed private expenditures." He asserts that it is possible to have a short-lived effect of Government spending on total spending if the financial offsets lag behind its positive effects. The results obtained for ΔE in this article are consistent with his analysis. See John M. Culbertson, *Macroeconomic Theory and Stabilization Policy* (New York: McGraw-Hill, 1968), pp. 462–463.

[15] Since little response of GNP to ΔR was found, further discussions consider only ΔE.

TABLE II Measurements of the Relative Importance of Monetary and Fiscal Actions

FIRST DIFFERENCES (EQUATIONS 1.2 AND 1.4)

Quarter	Beta coefficients						Partial coefficients of determination					
	ΔM	ΔE	ΔR	ΔB	ΔE	ΔR	ΔM	ΔE	ΔR	ΔB	ΔE	ΔR
t	.24	.14	.05	.06	.09	.16	.07	.02	.01	*	.01	.05
t-1	.26	.20	*	.31	.14	.01	.14	.08	*	.18	.03	*
t-2	.24	-.02	-.01	.37	-.08	-.05	.12	*	*	.24	.01	.01
t-3	.20	-.30	.03	.17	-.36	.04	.06	.13	*	.04	.16	*
Sum	.94	.02	.07	.91	-.21	.16	.45	*	*	.38	.02	.01

CENTRAL DIFFERENCES (EQUATIONS 2.2 AND 2.4)

Quarter	Beta coefficients						Partial coefficients of determination					
	ΔM	ΔE	ΔR	ΔB	ΔE	ΔR	ΔM	ΔE	ΔR	ΔB	ΔE	ΔR
t	.26	.20	.09	.04	.11	.25	.07	.04	.02	*	.01	.11
t-1	.26	.23	-.01	.31	.19	-.02	.13	.10	*	.16	.06	*
t-2	.23	-.06	-.09	.40	-.10	-.09	.11	.01	*	.23	.02	.03
t-3	.20	-.36	.05	.20	-.47	.10	.05	.16	*	.05	.21	.01
Sum	.95	.01	.10	.95	-.27	.24	.53	*	.01	.49	.04	.03

* Less than .005.

eliminate these difficulties (Table II). These coefficients take into consideration the past variation of changes in each independent variable relative to the past variation of changes in GNP.[16] The size of beta coefficients may be, therefore, directly compared as a measure of the relative contribution of each variable to variations in GNP in the test period.

According to Table II, the beta coefficients for changes in money are greater than those for changes in high-employment expenditures for the quarter in which a change occurs and during the two following quarters. The coefficients for changes in the monetary base are greater for the two quarters immediately following a change in the base. In the lagged quarters in which the beta coefficients for ΔE are largest, a negative sign is associated with the regression coefficient, indicating a lagged contractionary effect of increased expenditures. As a measure of the total contribution over the four quarters, the sum of the beta coefficients for changes in money and the monetary base are much greater than those for changes in expenditures.

Proposition I may also be tested by the use of partial coefficients of determination. These statistics are measures of the percent of variation of the dependent variable remaining after the variation accounted for by all other variables in the regression has been subtracted from the total variation. Proposition I implies that larger coefficients should be observed for fiscal actions than for monetary actions. Table II presents the partial coefficients of determination for the variables under consideration. For the quarter of a change and the subsequent two quarters, these coefficients for ΔM are much greater than those for ΔE. With regard to ΔB, the coefficients are about equal to those of ΔE in the first quarter and are much greater in the two subsequent quarters. The partial coefficients of determination for the total contribution of each policy variable to changes in GNP over four quarters may be developed. Table II shows that the partial coefficients of determination for the over-all response of ΔGNP to ΔM and ΔB range from .38 to .53, while those for ΔE are virtually zero.

Other implications of the results presented in Table I may be used to test further the relative strength of the response of GNP to alternative government actions under conditions where "other things" are held constant. Three alternative actions are assumed taken by stabilization authorities: (1) the rate of government spending is increased by $1 billion and is financed by either borrowing from the public or increasing taxes; (2) the money stock is increased

[16] Arthur S. Goldberger, *Econometric Theory* (New York: Wiley, December 1966), pp. 197–200.

by $1 billion with no change in the budget position; and (3) the rate of government spending is increased by $1 billion for a year and is financed by increasing the money stock by an equal amount.

The impact on total spending of the first two actions may be measured by using the sums of the regression coefficients presented for equation 1.3. A billion dollar increase in the rate of government spending would, after four quarters, result in a permanent increase of $170 million in GNP. By comparison, an increase of the same magnitude in money would result in GNP being $5.8 billion permanently higher after four quarters.

The results of the last action are presented in Table III.[17] The annual rate of government spending is assumed to be increased by $1 billion in the first quarter and held at that rate for the following three quarters. This would require an increase in money of $250 million during each of the four quarters to finance the higher level of expenditures. Since we are interested only in the result of financing the original increase in expenditures by monetary expansion, expenditures must be reduced by $1 billion in the fifth quarter. If expenditures were held at the higher rate, money would have to continue to grow $250 million per quarter. According to Table III, GNP would rise to a permanent level $5.8 billion higher than at the beginning. This increase in GNP results entirely from monetary expansion.

According to these three tests, the regression results implied by Proposition I did not occur. Therefore, the proposition that the response of total demand to fiscal actions is greater than that of monetary actions is not confirmed by the evidence.

Proposition II

Proposition II holds that the response of economic activity to fiscal actions is more predictable than the response to monetary influence. This implies that the regression coefficients relative to their standard errors (this ratio is called the "t-value"), relating changes in E to changes in GNP, should be greater than the corresponding measures for changes in M and in B.. The greater the t-value, the more confidence there is in the estimated regression coefficient, and hence, the greater is the reliability of the estimated change in GNP resulting from a change in the variable. These t-values are presented in Table IV.

An examination of this table indicates greater t-values for the

[17] The authors wish to give special thanks to Milton Friedman for suggesting this illustration and Table III. However, the formulation presented here is the sole responsibility of the authors.

TABLE III Simulated Response of an Increase in Government Expenditures Financed by Monetary Expansion
(in millions of dollars)

Quarter	Increase in government expenditures			Required increase in money			Total response in GNP	
	Change in expenditures	Impact effect on GNP	Cumulative effect on GNP	Change in money stock	Impact effect on GNP	Cumulative effect on GNP	Impact effect on GNP	Cumulative effect on GNP
1	$1000	$400	$400	$250	$385	$385	$785	$785
2	0	540	940	250	775	1160	1315	2100
3	0	— 30	910	250	1135	2295	1105	3205
4	0	— 740	170	250	1458	3753	718	3923
5	— 1000	— 400	— 230	0	1072	4825	672	4595
6	0	— 540	— 770	0	682	5507	142	4737
7	0	30	— 740	0	323	5830	353	5090
8	0	740	0	0	0	5830	740	5830

TABLE IV   Measurement of Reliability of the Response of GNP to Monetary and Fiscal Actions
("t-values" of regression coefficients[1])

FIRST DIFFERENCES

Quarter	ΔM	ΔE	ΔR	ΔB	ΔE	ΔR
t	2.03	1.15	0.53	0.49	0.67	1.68
t-1	2.85	2.15	0.03	3.37	1.36	0.07
t-2	2.69	0.19	0.10	4.10	0.84	0.64
t-3	1.82	2.82	0.32	1.54	3.10	0.39
Sum	6.57	0.13	0.32	5.67	0.89	0.67

CENTRAL DIFFERENCES

Quarter	ΔM	ΔE	ΔR	ΔB	ΔE	ΔR
t	2.01	1.52	1.05	0.28	0.73	2.55
t-1	2.78	2.44	0.17	3.16	1.87	0.27
t-2	2.45	0.60	0.46	3.92	1.04	1.31
t-3	1.72	3.15	0.48	1.71	3.65	0.87
Sum	7.57	0.04	0.54	6.95	1.37	1.16

[1] t-values associated with equations 1.2, 1.4, 2.2 and 2.4 in Table I.

regression coefficients of the two monetary variables than for the fiscal variable, except for the third quarter after a change. Also, the t-values for the sum of the regresion coefficients for ΔM and ΔB are large, while those for ΔE are not statistically significant from zero. Since the regression results implied by Proposition II did not appear, the proposition is not confirmed.

Proposition III

Proposition III states that the influence of fiscal actions on economic activity occurs faster than that of monetary actions. It is tested by examining the characteristics of the lag structure in the regressions. Proposition III implies that beta coefficients for ΔE should be greater than those for ΔM in the quarter of a change and in those immediately following. It also implies that the main response of GNP to fiscal actions occurs within fewer quarters than its response to monetary actions.

The beta coefficients are plotted [on page 560].[18] A change in the money stock induces a large and almost equal response in each of the four quarters. The largest response of GNP to changes in the monetary base occurs in the first and second quarters after a change. The beta coefficients for changes in M are greater than those for changes in E for the quarter of a change and the following quarter, indicating comparatively smaller response of GNP to fiscal actions in these first two quarters. Moreover, the largest coefficient for ΔE occurs for the third quarter after a change.

The expected regression results implied by Proposition III were not found. Therefore, the proposition that the major impact of fiscal influence on economic activity occurs within a shorter time interval than monetary influence is not confirmed.

Summary

This section tested the propositions that the response of economic activity to fiscal actions relative to monetary actions is (I) larger, (II) more predictable, and (III) faster. The results of the tests were not consistent with any of these propositions. Consequently, either the commonly used measures of fiscal influence do not correctly

---

[18] The Almon lag structure was developed by using a fourth degree polynomial and constraining the coefficients for t-4 to zero. The regressions indicate that four quarters constitute an appropriate response period for both fiscal and monetary actions. Equations using up to seven lagged quarters were also estimated, but there was little response in GNP to fiscal and monetary actions beyond the three quarter lags reported.

MEASURES OF LAG RESPONSE

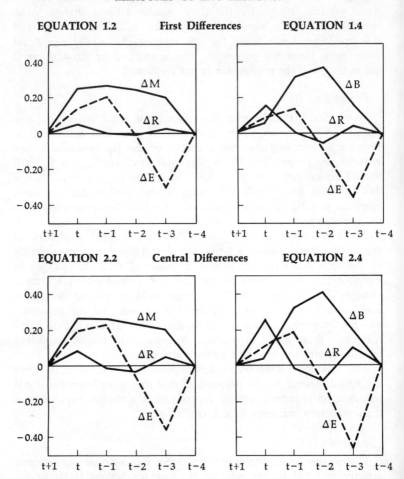

Beta coefficients are for changes in the money stock (ΔM), the monetary base (ΔB), high-employment expenditures (ΔE), and high-employment receipts (ΔR). These beta coefficients are calculated as the products of the regression coefficient for the respective variables times the ratio of the standard deviation of the variable to the standard deviation of GNP.

indicate the degree and direction of such influence, or there was no measurable net fiscal influence on total spending in the test period.

The test results are consistent with an alternative set of propositions. The response of economic activity to monetary actions compared with that of fiscal actions is (I′) larger, (II′) more predictable, and (III') faster. It should be remembered that these alternative propositions have not been proven true, but this is always the case in scientific testing of hypothesized relationships. Nevertheless, it is asserted here that these alternative propositions are appropriate for the conduct of stabilization policy until evidence is presented proving one or more of them false.

There is a major qualification to these statements. Since the propositions were tested using the period first quarter 1952 to second quarter 1968, it is implicitly assumed in making these statements that the general environment prevailing in the test period holds for the immediate future.

IMPLICATIONS FOR ECONOMIC STABILIZATION POLICY

Rejection of the three propositions under examination and acceptance of the alternatives offered carry important implications for the conduct of economic stabilization policy. All of these implications point to the advisability of greater reliance being placed on monetary actions than on fiscal actions. Such a reliance would represent a marked departure from most present procedures.

The finding that statements which assert that changes in tax rates have a significant influence on total spending are not supported by this empirical investigation suggests that past efforts in this regard have been overly optimistic. Furthermore, the finding that the response of total spending to changes in Government expenditures is small compared with the response of spending to monetary actions strongly suggests that it would be more appropriate to place greater reliance on the latter form of stabilization action.

Finding of a strong empirical relationship between economic activity and either of the measures of monetary actions points to the conclusion that monetary actions can and should play a more prominent role in economic stabilization than they have up to now. Furthermore, failure to recognize these relationships can lead to undesired changes in economic activity because of the relatively short lags and strong effects attributable to monetary actions.

Evidence was found which is consistent with the proposition that the influence of monetary actions on economic activity is more certain than that of fiscal actions. Since monetary influence was also found to be stronger and to operate more quickly than fiscal influence, it would appear to be inappropriate, for stabilization purposes, for monetary authorities to wait very long for a desired fiscal action to be adopted and implemented.

Evidence found in this study suggests that the money stock is an important indicator of the total thrust of stabilization actions, both monetary and fiscal. This point is argued on two grounds. First, changes in the money stock reflect mainly what may be called discretionary actions of the Federal Reserve System as it uses its major instruments of monetary management—open market transactions, discount rate changes, and reserve requirement changes. Second, the money stock reflects the joint actions of the Treasury and the Federal Reserve System in financing newly created Government debt. Such actions are based on decisions regarding the monetization of new debt by Federal Reserve actions, and Treasury decisions regarding changes in its balances at Reserve banks and commercial banks. According to this second point, changes in Government spending financed by monetary expansion are reflected in changes in the monetary base and in the money stock.

A number of economists maintain that the major influence of fiscal actions results only if expenditures are financed by monetary expansion. In practice, the Federal Reserve does not buy securities from the Government. Instead, its open market operations and other actions provide funds in the markets in which both the Government and private sectors borrow.

The relationships expressed in Table I may be used to project the expected course of GNP, given alternative assumptions about monetary and fiscal actions. Such projections necessarily assume that the environment in the period used for estimation and the average relationships of the recent past hold in the future. The projections are not able to take into consideration the influences of other inde-

TABLE V   Projected Change in GNP With Alternative Rates of Change in Money Stock[1]

| Quarter | Assumed rates of change in money stock[2] | | | |
	2%	4%	6%	8%
1968/III[3]	17.9	17.9	17.9	17.9
IV	14.6	16.0	17.5	19.0
1969/I	12.0	15.0	18.0	20.7
II	11.0	15.2	19.4	23.7
III	6.8	12.3	18.0	23.4
IV	8.0	13.7	19.4	25.2

[1] First differences of quarterly data. All variables are in billions of dollars. Projections are based on coefficients of equation 1.3 in Table I.

[2] Assumed alternative rates of change in the money stock from III/68 to IV/69.

[3] Preliminary estimate by the Department of Commerce.

pendent forces; therefore, they are not suitable for exact forecasting purposes. However, they do provide a useful measure of monetary and fiscal influences on economic activity.

An example of such projections using equation 1.3 is presented in Table V. Equation 1.3 related quarter-to-quarter changes in GNP to changes in the money stock and changes in high-employment expenditures, both distributed over four quarters.

Assumptions used in computing the projections of quarterly changes in GNP reported in Table V include: (a) high-employment expenditures were projected through the second quarter of 1969 under the assumption that Federal spending in fiscal 1969 will be about 5 per cent (or $10 million) greater than fiscal 1968; (b) Federal spending was assumed to continue increasing at a 5 to 6 per cent rate in the first two quarters of fiscal 1970; and (c) quarter-to-quarter changes in the money stock were projected from III/68 to IV/69 for four alternative constant annual growth rates for money: 2 per cent, 4 per cent, 6 per cent, and 8 per cent.

The highest growth rate of the money stock (8 per cent) indicates continued rapid rates of expansion in GNP during the next five quarters. The slowest growth rate of money (2 per cent) indicates some slowing of GNP growth in the fourth quarter of this year and further gradual slowing throughout most of next year.

The projections indicate that if the recent decelerated growth in the money stock (less than 4 per cent from July to October) is continued, and growth of Government spending is at about the rate indicated above, the economy would probably reach a non-inflationary growth rate of GNP in about the third quarter of 1969 and would then accelerate slightly. These projections, of course, make no assumptions regarding the Vietnam war, strikes, agricultural situations, civil disorders, or any of the many other noncontrollable exogeneous forces.

INTERNATIONAL
MONETARY
RELATIONS

PART VI

With few exceptions, the foregoing articles assume (implicitly or explicitly) the existence of a closed economy; a system without international trade or international money flows. Emphasis was on understanding the commercial banking system, the Federal Reserve System, and the nature and effectiveness of monetary policy. In addition, considerable attention was directed toward the relative effectiveness of and the optimum mix of monetary and fiscal policy for *domestic* economic stabilization.

The readings must now be expanded in scope to cover *international* banking and monetary relations. Given the present international monetary system, monetary and fiscal policies designed for domestic cyclical stabilization have significant international ramifications. The great need today for international equilibrium requires that these ramifications be studied and comprehended—especially if attaining internal stability calls for monetary and fiscal policies that deteriorate the balance of payments position. In addition, international monetary changes have implications for the appropriateness of domestic monetary and fiscal policy. For these reasons, some understanding of international monetary relations is essential.

The Employment Act of 1946 made it the Federal government's continuing responsibility to "promote maximum employment, production, and purchasing power." Since that time another policy objective has become crucially important: promoting and maintaining "equilibrium" in the U.S. balance of international payments. In fact, this has become so important that for some years during the 1958–1965 period, the U.S. government was reluctant to undertake adequate monetary and fiscal policies needed to reduce unemployment and stimulate domestic economic growth. It was feared that such measures would cause the U.S. payments position to deteriorate further. Indeed, the impact of the U.S. dollar problem on governments abroad has been so significant that it hindered reform of the international monetary system.

Selections in this part are divided into three segments. It was not intended that these selections should cover all aspects of international monetary relations. However, the papers clarify, extend, modify, and provide empirical data on relationships in money and banking textbooks, and together form an integrated body of knowledge.

Section A contains three readings on the nature, significance, and defects of the present international monetary system. The first two articles are from U.S. Treasury reports and are descriptive. The nature, functions, and significance of the international market for foreign exchange (that is, the foreign exchange market) are discussed in the first reading. The second identifies major characteristics of the present international monetary system. Not all these characteristics were envisioned at the Bretton Woods Conference in July 1944. Additionally, the second Treasury article underscores the importance for both individual nations and the international monetary system of an efficiently functioning balance of payments adjustment process.

Given this information about the international financial network encircling the Free World trading nations, it is now possible to analyze its alleged defects. And, indeed, this analysis is necessary. Smith, in a statement before the Subcommittee on International Exchange and Payments of the Congressional Joint Economic Committee maintains, as do most economists, that the major defects are associated with problems of adjustment, confidence, and liquidity. He then suggests some guidelines for reform. Note carefully that the three major problems are interrelated. While a solution to one problem may make solving one of the others more difficult, this need not be the case.

Section B embraces four selections dealing with different types of international monetary reform. The first three articles cover widely recognized reform measures, whereas the last explains the newly adopted Special Drawing Rights plan. Triffin, one of the first to recognize and propose a solution to the twin problems of international confidence and international liquidity, would eliminate these defects by creating an international clearing and reserve center (that is, an "international central bank") for national central banks. While not entirely the same, Triffin's reserve center has many similarities to Keynes' World War II International Clearing Union.

At another extreme, the reform proposed by Friedman involves adopting a system of freely fluctuating exchange rates in which there is no official intervention (to stabilize exchange rates). Such a system, he argues, not only would remove the defects but also would allow nations to freely use monetary and fiscal policy to achieve internal stabilization without having to consider the external impact of such measures. Wallich doubts the validity and feasibility of Friedman's proposal, arguing strongly in defense of fixed exchange rates. These two articles help put the controversy over fixed versus flexible exchange rates in proper perspective.

Neither Friedman's freely fluctuating exchange rate system (and its many variants) nor Triffin's International Central Bank proposal have received serious *official* support, although some academic support exists for both proposals, from members of the International Monetary Fund (IMF). However, some potentially significant progress has been made in the search for an international money. In September 1967 in Rio de Janeiro the members of the IMF unanimously adopted a resolution, the "Outline of a Facility Based on Special Drawing Rights in the Fund," calling for the creation of Special Drawing Rights. This then was translated into legal terms, the "Proposed Amendment to the Articles of Agreement to the International Monetary Fund," by the staff and Executive Directors of the IMF. In April 1968 it was endorsed at Stockholm by the Minister of the Group of Ten, and in the following month it was adopted by the Governors of the IMF. Upon being accepted by 60 percent of the members having 80 percent of the total voting power, the SDR plan enters into force. The nature, significance, and important features of this plan are explained by Davis in the last article of Section B.

Articles in Section C relate to some aspect of balance of payments equilibrium. More specifically, they deal with the U.S. dollar problem, the impact of inflation on the balance of payments, internal and external stabilization policy, and Eurodollars. Presented first is an excerpt from a U.S. Treasury report giving a historical review of the post-World War II dollar problem. This material gives special emphasis to the years since 1958 (in 1958 the deficit increased sharply and U.S. gold stock dropped more than $2 billion). It was not until after 1958 that the government became concerned about its payments imbalances; prior deficits from 1950 to 1956 (the Suez Canal crisis resulted in a small surplus in 1957) were relatively small and intentional, while those following 1958 were relatively large and unintentional. Immediately following that selection is President Johnson's Jan. 1, 1968, balance of payments message. This message presented the most comprehensive program ever inaugurated by the U.S. for eliminating or reducing future deficit balances. Both the scope of the program and the coerciveness of the capital controls under-scored the government's determination to solve the dollar problem. What may have been just as important, the government was equally determined at that time to convince other countries that the U.S. now meant business in solving its dollar problem. The over-all (liquidity) balance in the U.S. went from a deficit of $1.36 billion in 1966 to a deficit of $3.57 billion in 1967. In view of this sharp deterioration, foreign concern about the stability of the dollar was no small consideration.

The next two articles, by Dorrance and the Federal Reserve Bank of Chicago, discuss the implications of inflation and Eurodollars for domestic stabilization policy and the balance of payments. Dorrance's article evinces the effects of rapidly rising prices (in one country relative to the rest of the world) on a country's international trade in goods and services, international capital movements, and the country's exchange rate. Al-though unequal rates of inflation among countries is not the only factor that may impede a nation's international trade and investment or alter the equilibrium level of its exchange rate, it often is one of the most important considerations. Other important factors are income changes, structural changes in demand and supply, and relative changes in interest rates. In reference to the U.S., which is experiencing a payments problem combined with a significant rate of inflation, Dorrance's article implies that appropriate antiinflationary domestic monetary and fiscal policy should be instituted to help eliminate the dollar glut. The Chicago Federal Reserve Bank article brings in another factor that has affected the U.S. dollar problem. It discusses the meaning of Eurodollars and their impli-cations for domestic monetary policy and the U.S. payments balance. Since it appears now that the Eurodollar market is here to stay, its sig-nificance in the world economy must be understood.

The final article, by Mundell, deals with the problem of simultaneously achieving internal and external stability, assuming there are pegged ex-change rates and no changes in trade controls. Basically, Mundell asks this question: What type and combination of fiscal and monetary meas-ures are appropriate for achieving domestic stability at full employment with reasonable price level stability and international equilibrium? Internal and external equilibrium (goals) may call for compatible policies; for example, when a surplus balance of payments country experiences unemployment or when a deficit nation experiences inflationary conditions. However, internal stability may call for one set of monetary-fiscal policies, while external equilibrium may require an entirely different set of policies. This results when a surplus country experiences inflationary pressures or a deficit country has high unemployment. The latter situation can be very real, and was the condition that existed in the United States during 1958–1965.

All of the articles in this section deal with some aspect of international banking and monetary policy. Reflect on how they are interrelated. Search out the various threads that transform them from isolated papers into an integrated body of knowledge.

UNITED STATES
TREASURY DEPARTMENT

THE FOREIGN
EXCHANGE MARKET

40

Although its daily activity represents hundreds of millions of dollars in sales and purchases of the world's money, the Foreign Exchange Market is not housed in an impressive building on Wall
Street; you cannot buy a seat on this exchange; there are no ad-
vertisements soliciting public patronage of its facilities.

But this market, like any other, brings together the private buyers
and sellers of its commodity—in this instance, money itself—and
the rates at which the exchange of this commodity take place are
primarily the final products of the great ebbs and flows of supply
and demand caused by the free enterprise of the citizens of the free
world.[1]

In March 1961, the U.S. Treasury again became an active participant in the foreign exchange markets. Not since the 1930's had
our Government engaged in such operations—as foreign central
banks have done for many years to support their currencies generally and to guard against harmful effects of speculation. In February 1962, the Federal Reserve System joined the Treasury in this
activity. Together, they have worked effectively with the treasuries
and the central banks of the major free world nations to form a
strong, flexible, and alert defense to protect all the major currencies

Reprinted from United States Treasury Department (by Merlyn Nelson
Trued), "The Foreign Exchange Market," *United States Official Operations
in the Foreign Exchange and Gold Markets*, Washington, D.C.: Government Printing Office, 1965, pp. 1, 4–9.

[1] For an excellent and comprehensive discussion of the foreign exchange
market, see *The New York Foreign Exchange Market*, by Alan Holmes
and Francis Schott, published by the Federal Reserve Bank of New York.

from disorderly foreign exchange markets that might result from excessive speculative or other unsettling developments.

. . .

WHY THE U.S. GOVERNMENT PARTICIPATES

U.S. official operations in the foreign exchange markets are a logical outgrowth of the position of the dollar as the cornerstone of the international currency system; they are part of a pattern evolved over the last few years which has also brought about continuous consultation among the leading world monetary authorities. Official intervention in the exchange market—for that is what it is—arises from the desire of the free world nations to employ all appropriate means to assure the smooth functioning of payments arrangements that is essential to the continued growth of international trade and finance.

THE MARKET'S UNDERPINNINGS

There are certain ground rules under which the foreign exchange system of the world operates. Since these give the market its basic characteristics of fundamental importance, they should be known and understood before we look into the official operations by the United States Government in this market.

The key fact behind foreign exchange trading as conducted today is that all currencies used to any extent in international finance have a value officially defined in terms of the U.S. dollar or of gold, or of both.

Under the Articles of Agreement of the International Monetary Fund, to which virtually all the free world's nations have adhered, each country has committed itself to maintain the value of its currency in its market within a range of one percent on either side of an official parity.[2] The government of a country may, of course, acting in accordance with the rules set up in the Articles of Agreement, change the par value of its currency. Indeed, as will be discussed later, anticipation of such changes may on occasion be a predominant force in the market. Fortunately for major currencies, such changes have been limited in number since the wave of devaluations in 1949.

The United States, for its part, has met its obligation under the

---

[2] These limits are known in market parlance as the "ceiling" and the "floor."

Articles of Agreement by undertaking to sell gold at $35 per fine troy ounce, plus $\frac{1}{4}$ percent, on demand to all foreign central banks and monetary authorities, and to buy gold offered by such institutions at the same $35 price, less $\frac{1}{4}$ percent. This works out at $35.0875 and $34.9125.

The special role played by the U.S. dollar, along with the concept of fixed parities and margins for the world's currencies, has some important implications for official U.S. activities in foreign exchange. A foreign country meets its responsibility by buying and selling its currency against U.S. dollars; the foreign currency-dollar rate is thus the focal point. Exchange rates for that currency against other currencies (except the dollar) then become simply mathematical calculations. Thus, the French franc-Deutsche Mark rate would be calculated on the basis of the French franc-U.S. dollar and Deutsche Mark-U.S. dollar rates. If, for example, the Deutsche Mark rate moved from 3.97 DM to 4.00 per dollar while the French franc remained at 4.90 per dollar, the rate for the DM against the franc would be adjusted from 1.225 to 1.25 francs per DM. Rates for one foreign currency against another, so-called cross rates, thus are adjusted automatically through market arbitrage to reflect changes in the rates for each currency against the dollar. Indeed, most transactions in the market will go "through the dollar," the dollar thus serving as a vehicle currency in fashioning conversions of, say, Deutsche Marks into Italian lire. Accordingly, although no country with an important currency can neglect third currency effects of changes in dollar rates for its currency, its attention nevertheless can be largely concentrated on the dollar-local currency rate.

But for the United States, interest must range widely among all currencies traded significantly in the exchange market. While some rates are relatively more important than others, all must be viewed constantly since all are quoted in dollar terms. The pound sterling, for instance, widely used in international trade and finance, is the most actively traded currency apart from the dollar and accordingly is of primary importance. Generally speaking, however, official U.S. interest must be widely diffused and the administrative and analytical machinery somewhat broader than that of other nations.

A number of the major Western European countries have adhered also to the European Monetary Agreement under which each has committed itself to maintain the value of its currency in the spot market within three-fourths of one percent on either side of parity. Thus, for practical purposes, most of the world's major currencies are traded against the dollar within narrower limits than those permitted under the Articles of Agreement of the International Monetary Fund. But regardless of the particular margin involved, the principle remains the same in that each country has obligated itself to maintain the value of its currency within a certain range on either side of an established par value.

Thus, for example, the French franc has a fixed par value of 20.255 U.S. cents per French franc. If francs are in demand in the market and the price tends to rise, finally reaching a price of 20.4082 cents (i.e., ¾ percent above parity), the Bank of France is committed to supply French francs to the market in amounts sufficient to assure that the price will not increase further. In the process then, the Bank of France would be supplying francs to the market and taking in U.S. dollars, which dollars are, of course, added to its international reserves and thus remain available for selling at a later date should the French franc weaken. In the latter case, if the price were to drop to 20.1045 cents per franc, the Bank of France would undertake to purchase all French francs offered at that price, thus giving up U.S. dollar holdings which, of course, lowers its foreign exchange reserves.

All other major currencies follow a similar pattern. The pound sterling, for example, has a par value of $2.80 and the Bank of England is obligated to furnish all sterling demanded if the price increases to $2.82 per pound and to buy all sterling offered in the market if the price were to decline to as low as $2.78. It is most important to realize, however, that most monetary authorities, most of the time, enter the market well before the upper or lower limit of the permissible range has been reached. As discussed later, the central bank may enter the market at prices lying well within the range, for a variety of reasons.

So far, we have been discussing foreign exchange dealings in the spot market: that is to say, purchases and sales of a currency for immediate delivery. The term "immediate" may mean either one-day or two-day delivery depending on the particular currency involved. In either case, the essential nature of the transaction remains unchanged. But for several currencies there is also a foreign exchange market for so-called forward delivery. In this market purchases and sales of foreign exchange may be made at a price set today but for execution later: 30, 60, or 90 days—or even longer. The principal forward markets involve, of course, the major currencies which are used in international trade for purposes of invoicing and making payments. A United States exporter, for example, may accept payment in German marks under the terms of an agreed contract under which the marks will not be received until 90 days hence. During the 90-day period the U.S. exporter would be uncertain as to the exact amount of dollars he will receive in exchange for his marks. In order to ascertain the actual amount of dollars he will receive, he can offer the marks he will receive in the forward market and establish a certain rate, thus removing any risk he would otherwise run owing to possible changes in the market value of that currency.

As will be shown later, decision of an importer to sell his marks forward—or "cover" his transaction, as it is called—depends upon a variety of circumstances and has important implications for exchange dealings. For the moment, it is sufficient to note that forward markets do exist and that the rates prevailing in such markets are not subject to the margins within which spot dealings proceed. Forward quotations may thus lie well outside the range permitted for spot exchange; nevertheless, they remain subject to market forces, including the actual and permitted narrow range of spot rates, at least under normal conditions, and are, of course, responsive to official activity, if and when such activity is undertaken.

WHAT MAKES THE MARKET

In 1965, the United States exported to other countries some $26 billion worth of commodities and imported over $20 billion worth— a considerable proportion of all world exports of commodities, which may well have totaled over $160 billion. Such transactions, among others, are international in character and provide the grist for the workings of the foreign exchange markets.

All those who participate in a transaction in which any one of the participants receives or pays out a currency which he does not use domestically plays a role in the foreign exchange market. Thus, a Des Moines, Iowa, exporter of agricultural equipment making a sale to a German firm becomes a factor in the foreign exchange market: either he or the German customer will operate in a currency not his own.

The contract between these two parties may be invoiced in German marks or in U.S. dollars, or even in a third currency, perhaps in British pounds sterling. If the contract is concluded in terms of U.S. dollars, the U.S. exporter avoids any problems associated with the international nature of the transaction; the German importer, however, must face the problem of securing the dollars necessary to make payment.

Similarly, a U.S. investor wishing to purchase Canadian Treasury bills must secure Canadian dollars in order to make the purchase. Accordingly, both trade and financial transactions have an impact upon the foreign exchange markets.

The particular influence which any participant in the market exerts depends on a variety of considerations; such things, for example, as how much of what currency is involved, how that currency is sold or held or invested, and whether the participant seeks to "hedge" an operation in some manner so as to guard against losses from an adverse swing in the future value of the currency in which he is dealing.

If someone wishes to hedge, he may avail himself of the forward market mentioned earlier; that is he may sell or buy at a rate agreed upon for delivery at an agreed time in the future. Thus, the parties to the agreement know they will have to pay (or will receive) a particular currency some time hence. Although active forward markets are maintained for only a few currencies, they are those currencies which are most widely used in international transactions.

To take one example, let us suppose that the Des Moines exporter of agricultural equipment concludes a contract with a German importing firm, and that the contract calls for payment in dollars to the U.S. exporter three months from the date of the contract. The U.S. exporter knows the amount of his local currency, dollars, that he will be obtaining and hence, is not a direct participant in the market. However, the German partner to the contract has a payment obligation in dollars, and he must consider the various possible ways of making that dollar payment. He has a number of alternatives. He may take his local currency, Deutsche Marks, and purchase dollars in the "spot market," that is to say, for immediate delivery; he could then hold such dollars in an account in a U.S. bank and make payment on the due date. In the interim, he may invest those dollars in short-term money market obligations in the United States and thus earn an interest return. His German bank, through one of its correspondent banks in the United States, would be in a position to arrange such an investment.

On the other hand, the German importer may prefer to use his marks in his local operations for the three-month period. This actually might permit him to avoid borrowing marks for, say, working capital purposes. But he would then be exposed to an exchange risk, in case the dollar should become more expensive in terms of marks by the time the due date arrives, 90 days later. In the language of the foreign exchange market, he would in these circumstances probably want to "cover" his dollar obligation. He may choose to avoid the risk of uncertainty by buying the U.S. dollars in the forward market at the price prevailing today for dollars to be received in 90 days. To do so, he concludes a contract, normally with a commercial bank, that he will pay over to that bank a certain amount of German marks in three months, at which time the bank will put at his disposal the agreed-upon amount of dollars. The German importer then knows, in terms of his own currency, exactly how much he will be paying for the imported goods.

As a further alternative, illustrating the wide range of possibilities, the German importer may find it more convenient or cheaper to borrow sterling in London, sell the sterling for U.S. dollars immediately, invest those dollars in U.S. money market obligations and use the dollar proceeds as those obligations mature in 90 days to make payment; at the same time, he may contract to purchase sterling forward against marks. When his borrowing in London is due, he would pay marks for the sterling, and in turn employ the sterling to pay off the loan in London.

Obviously, the full range of possibilities of market operations is extensive, and the transactions may sometimes become quite complex. The particular method our German importer chooses depends upon a variety of factors, including relative interest rates in the different markets and the pattern of spot and forward exchange rates among the leading currencies, as well as the customary practices and habits of trading concerns and the facilities regularly available to them.

Essentially, however, the summation of the myriad of daily transactions involving payments or receipts of a foreign currency, makes up the principal volume of trading which flows through the foreign exchange market.

Normally, a participant in the foreign exchange market will, as noted previously, work through his commercial bank. That particular bank may itself have a foreign exchange department and operate actively in the market. If so, it will have accounts in banks abroad into which its purchases of foreign currencies can be deposited and out of which payments can be ordered when foreign exchange is sold. However, only a relatively few banks do in fact have these arrangements. It is unlikely, for example, that a smaller bank in the mid-West would have established direct relations with banks abroad. On the other hand, it is quite likely that it would have established a correspondent relationship with one of the large U.S. commercial banks—perhaps in New York, San Francisco, Chicago, or Boston—which does have such relationships abroad.

Thus, from the wide circle of individuals, businesses, and traders who participate in international commerce and finance, activity originating through a multitude of banks flows into a smaller group of banks which have direct connections and thus maintain deposit accounts with a number of banks in foreign countries. Accordingly, the forces in the market resulting from the offerings of currencies and demands for currencies, gradually become channeled into a limited number of banking institutions which form the heart of the foreign exchange market in each of the major countries of the world.

The motivation for banks to undertake foreign exchange activity is, of course, that of earning some return for the services performed. However, the earnings from this source are generally too small to cover the full range of expenses, day by day, and the banks rely upon other related activities to make their overall foreign operations profitable. The foreign exchange operations of those banks are here appraised in a very wide sense, as they attract other business within the bank's entire activity. The foreign exchange activities of the large banks are established as a means of servicing customer requirements in the broadest terms: that is, the conversion of currencies may well be only an incidental part of the total activity undertaken for a customer and hence, a minor part of the total services provided a customer and of the earnings received from all such services.

The need for a complex of inter-related operations to reach a level of activity large enough to make the maintenance of a foreign exchange department worthwhile helps to explain the limited number of banks that are active in the market. Through these institutions, which constitute the foreign exchange market in its most active sense, flow all the pressures upon the market that arise from transactions which may be undertaken by traders, financiers, speculators, investors, and tourists.

THE FLOW OF MARKET EFFECTS

Against this background it may be helpful to follow a hyopthetical flow of transactions through the market to show their potential effects upon our national economic and monetary policies. As seen earlier, transactions may arise from the activity of any international trader or financier whose order for a currency passes through his local bank to a large New York commercial bank which maintains accounts abroad and is a key participant in the foreign exchange markets.

When Supplies Increase

As continuing offerings of a particular currency—let us say sterling —are made to this and other commercial banks, the commercial bank makes payment to the seller in dollars, and receives its payment in sterling deposits (or balances) in its correspondent bank in

London. As the sterling deposits (that is, supplies of sterling) held by the commercial bank increase, the bank becomes increasingly reluctant to take additional amounts. Accordingly, the price which the bank will pay for that currency in terms of dollars will tend to decline. In the parlance of the market, the currency weakens. If the price should reach its lower limit, official action is automatically triggered: the Bank of England, as central bank of the country concerned is, at that point, committed by its agreement with the International Monetary Fund and the European Monetary Agreement to step into the market and buy all of its currency that is offered. Thus, the British Government would not permit the price of its currency to drop below $2.78 per pound sterling. In practice, of course, it may enter as a buyer of sterling well before that lower limit is reached.

Now, as the central bank buys supplies of its own currency, it pays out amounts of dollars which form, along with gold, its official exchange reserves. With payments of dollars thus being made, its foreign official reserves drop. As its available dollar balances decline, the central bank may find it necessary to replenish its dollar account. This it may do by selling out some of its short-term investments, normally U.S. Treasury bills, which it has made in the United States. Sales of such investments would have a potential impact on the money market. Accordingly, the Federal Reserve System, with its responsibility for monetary policy, would take these sales into account as it determines the type and amount of open market operations in which it will engage.

Should the pressure on a currency continue still further, the central bank may find it necessary to sell out some of its gold holdings, an action which is generally accomplished by sales of gold to the United States Treasury—the only government authority in the world which stands ready to buy or sell gold at a fixed price. The dollar proceeds of such gold sales then supplement existing dollar balances which the central bank may use to defend its currency in the market.

Payments of U.S. dollars by the foreign central bank may be made to the New York commercial bank out of the central bank's account at the Federal Reserve Bank of New York. This transfer of funds from the central bank's account at the "Fed" results, of course, in an increase in the reserves of U.S. commercial banks. Thus, such operations may affect commercial bank reserve positions, and, unless offset by other Federal Reserve operations, have an effect upon monetary conditions; in the example used, the lending capacity of U.S. banks would tend to be increased.

In practice, of course, intervention in the market by a central bank may be effected throughout the full range of the permissible fluctuations. Such intervention may serve to prevent too fast a drop or increase in a currency's value, rapid changes which might otherwise lead to unwarranted expectations in the foreign exchange market and hence, toward exaggerated movements of rates and shifts in foreign reserves of gold and dollars. Whether a central bank intervenes only at the margin or decides to make its influence felt at an earlier time, depends upon the particular circumstances and features of the market at a given moment.

When Demand Rises

Let us take an example using the reverse situation. Suppose that the foreign currency rather than being heavily offered, is in sharp demand. In this case, again using sterling for our illustration, traders and financiers would, on balance, be seeking to purchase sterling. The orders would again be channeled through the various commercial banks on to the center of the market—the large commercial banks with foreign departments. The sterling balances of those banks now tend to decline. As those balances decline, the price of the pound will tend to rise in terms of U.S. dollars. As the sterling balances of the commercial banks become minimal or threaten to become exhausted, the commercial bank will quote increasingly higher prices which may reach, or approach, the upper limit for sterling, $2.82. At that point the Bank of England, on behalf of the Exchange Equalization Account of the British Government, is committed to supply all sterling demanded against payment in dollars.

In the process of supplying the sterling, the Bank of England takes into its account an increasing accumulation of U.S. dollars and hence, its official foreign exchange reserves rise. As these balances increase, the central bank will normally invest some portion in interest-earning assets in the United States, thus earning a return on marketable instruments which can be promptly sold so cash reserves can again be readily available in case of need. Continued accumulation of dollars to the central bank's account may, at some point, result in a purchase of gold as it seeks to adjust its holdings of gold and foreign exchange in accordance with its customary, chosen preference. The purchase of gold will, of course, normally be made from the United States Treasury.

Thus again, in the process, the purchases of securities for the account of a foreign central bank has some potential effect upon the New York money market which, as in the reverse case, has implications for the Fed's overall operations in conducting monetary policy.

From the foregoing, one must infer that certain trends or indications, as they become visible, or even sensed, are signals that prompt official decisions to intervene or not to intervene in the foreign exchange markets by a particular nation's monetary authority. These developments in the market may relate to the actual level of the exchange rate in the spot market, the extent and rapidity of changes in that rate, the relationship of the forward exchange rate to the spot rate, the level and changes in official holdings of foreign exchange reserves, and shifts into and out of gold—all within the context of the market's tone at a particular moment. In the process of making such intervention effective, there are further implications, the most important of which involve the potential effects of the particular transaction on domestic U.S. commercial banking reserves and upon security prices in the money market.

It is the interrelationship of all these forces and developments in the market which have prompted over the years the majority of central banks to participate in foreign exchange activities, and to develop what are frequently very sophisticated techniques for achieving determined objectives.

UNITED STATES
TREASURY DEPARTMENT

THE INTERNATIONAL MONETARY
SYSTEM AND ADJUSTMENT
OF PAYMENTS IMBALANCES

41

A. THE INTERNATIONAL MONETARY SYSTEM—WHY AND HOW IT WORKS

An international monetary system provides means and methods of payments in order to facilitate international trade, capital and other transactions. In a world composed of various countries, each with its own currency, trade and capital movements across national borders have not only to be paid for as they are within any country, but have to be provided with a mechanism to convert one currency into another.

The American exporter to Italy usually wants to be paid in dollars—his currency. The Italian importer has lire. Some mechanism has to be provided to convert the lire into dollars to pay the American exporter. And if credit is involved, there needs to be a financing mechanism that crosses the frontier.

The requirements for handling international payments smoothly are:

• The various currencies should be convertible easily into each other.
• There needs to be confidence in the stability of the exchange rates of the major currencies against each other.
• The various countries need to have international reserves of unquestioned value so that if for a time their outpayments exceed their inpayments they can finance the difference by using these reserves.
• The system works more smoothly if owned reserves are supplemented by credit facilities to tide nations over periods of imbalance.

In a strict sense, the international monetary system is not a system at all. It is a series of arrangements, procedures, customs and

Reprinted from United States Treasury Department, "The International Monetary System and Adjustment of Payments Imbalances," *Maintaining the Strength of the United States Dollar in a Strong, Free World Economy*, Washington, D.C.: Government Printing Office, 1968, pp. 15–31.

institutions which have evolved over time and which are laced together by a network of formal and informal agreements. It has been partially codified as to objectives, principles and procedures by the Articles of Agreement of the International Monetary Fund (IMF). It has been aided by international cooperation on the part of the important central banks of the world—most notably through the so-called "swap network." It works partly through correspondent relationships of the major commercial banks of the world. Money and capital markets in the United States and Europe are important factors in making the system work. In recent years it has been strengthened by a series of consultative arrangements undertaken under the auspices of the Organization for Economic Cooperation and Development (OECD).

The system rests on five pillars:
* a dollar convertible into gold at $35 per ounce;
* other major currencies convertible into dollars at stated rates of exchange—under IMF rules they may vary plus or minus 1 percent from parity;
* adequate international reserves and credit facilities designed to support these relationships;
* a general presumption that a country will over time be in equilibrium in its international position—that surpluses will be offset by deficits on the average;
* in seeking to adjust from deficit to surplus, or *vice versa*, a country will take into account the consequences of its actions on the world community.

B. THE ROLE OF THE DOLLAR

In practice, all member countries of the IMF which have convertible currencies operate through their central banks or monetary authorities to keep their currencies in an established relationship to the dollar. For example, the exchange parity of the D-mark is 4 to the dollar, or $0.25. The IMF intervention limits are $0.2475 and $0.2525. In practice, the German Federal Bank intervenes within somewhat narrower limits. When the dollar is strong against the D-mark, the dollar price of the D-mark falls toward $0.2475. The Bundesbank supplies dollars from its reserves to buy up the excess D-marks. When the D-mark is strong against the dollar, its dollar price rises toward $0.2525. Then the Bundesbank supplies marks and buys dollars.

Each monetary authority acts essentially in the same way—intervening in its own markets to maintain the price of its currency *vis-à-vis* the dollar within the narrow band of plus or minus 1 percent from its parity.

The United States does not have to carry on operations like this. It fulfills its IMF parity obligations by freely buying and selling gold for dollars—only with monetary authorities and for legitimate monetary purposes, of course—at $35 per ounce.

The point is that virtually every country does its market interventions by buying or selling dollars. It does so because the dollar is the major transactions or vehicle currency and is widely used in the payment and receipt transactions of international trade and capital flows. It does so because the dollar is a reserve currency and most countries hold dollars in their international reserves.

The dollar is both a reserve currency and a vehicle currency because:
• it is strong, being backed by a strong economy;
• it can be invested profitably because there exists a big money and capital market in the U.S.;
• it is known and is acceptable as a store of value—that is, it holds its purchasing power better than most other currencies;
• it is in sufficient supply so that there are dollars that can be used or borrowed for transactions; and
• it is convertible by monetary authorities into gold so that they are willing to hold it.

The U.S. did not deliberately make the dollar a reserve currency or a transactions currency. The dollar evolved as such out of its basic strength.

But this strength can be called into question in two ways:
• If the supply of dollars in foreign hands becomes greater than the amount foreign central banks and private holders want to hold, either because of their basic needs or for other reasons.
• If declines in the U.S. gold reserve and consequent unfavorable effects on the relationship between U.S. gold and U.S. dollar liabilities raise questions as to the ability of the U.S. freely to convert outstanding dollars into gold at $35 per ounce.

It is to prevent such developments that the U.S. must achieve sustainable equilibrium in its payments position. Unless it does so, its liabilities to foreigners increase and its gold reserves decrease, and the monetary system becomes more vulnerable to a shrinkage in overall liquidity that can cause serious financial and business disruption through an international credit squeeze.

Foreign central banks and other official institutions hold some $16 billion of liquid dollar assets. Private foreigners hold another $16 billion.

The official holdings are reserves for the rest of the world and constitute nearly 30 percent of such reserves. But so long as they are not withdrawn in the form of gold, they have not reduced our reserves. Thus, our balances of payments deficit, unlike those of a nonreserve currency country, has been only partially reflected in a decline of gold reserves or in our reserve position in the IMF. A considerable part of our balance of payments deficit has been covered by an increase in our liabilities rather than by a reduction in our reserve assets.

While it is not necessary for a commercial bank to maintain liquid assets to cover all or even a major part of its liquid liabilities, the U.S. as a reserve center is a bank in a rather special sense, and needs to maintain a substantial reserve against its liabilities. It is important that our reserves be adequate to meet demands for conversion, and to maintain confidence in the bank on the part of the official and private dollar holders abroad.

Rising dollar liabilities which constitute reserves for other countries have permitted the world as a whole to build up its reserves more rapidly than would otherwise have been the case. A return of the United States to equilibrium would cut off this growth of reserves for these countries. It has become increasingly clear, therefore, that some other means of providing for the future growth in world reserves will be required. To this end, the members of the International Monetary Fund have now agreed on a plan for the deliberate creation of reserves through multilateral action. When this plan is in effect, the world would no longer be dependent upon gold and the deficits of the United States to provide for the expansion in world reserves which will be needed in the future.

Thus the role of the dollar as a reserve currency has been intertwined with the problem of our balance of payments and has also been related to the general problem of expanding world reserves. Through a multilateral system of reserve creation, we can relieve the dollar of its responsibility to provide for a growth in world reserves, and permit concentration on the balance of payments problem.

The following sections of this chapter set forth the elements of the international monetary system.

C. EXCHANGE RATES

One of the distinguishing features of the present international monetary system is the relative stability of exchange rates. Under the Articles of Agreement of the International Monetary Fund—

which since their adoption at Bretton Woods, New Hampshire, in 1944 have embodied the formal principles and procedures which underlie the present system—countries undertake to maintain exchange rates for transactions in their currencies within a margin of one percent of a declared par value. This par value may be changed, with the approval of the IMF, in the event of a "fundamental disequilibrium" in a country's balance of payments. For the most part, however, all the members of the IMF have shown a strong preference for stable exchange rates that are changed only infrequently.

In order to maintain their currencies within a margin of one percent of the declared par value, the monetary authorities of almost all countries other than the United States intervene when necessary in their exchange markets, buying or selling dollars against their own currency. There are a few exceptions to this method of official exchange-market intervention (notably in the sterling area), but for the most part the entire pattern of stable exchange rates is maintained by virtue of the fact that countries "peg" their exchange rates to the dollar.

Since most other countries peg their currencies to the dollar, the United States itself does not need to intervene in the exchange markets to maintain the value of the dollar in terms of other currencies. Although it may at times find it advantageous to do so in order to assure more orderly markets and more efficient and economical use of its reserves, the United States basically maintains its obligations regarding exchange stability in a very different manner: by freely buying and selling gold in transactions with monetary authorities (primarily central banks of other countries) at the price of $35 an ounce. No country other than the United States freely buys and sells gold. The whole exchange-rate system is therefore pegged to gold only through the commitment of the U.S. monetary authorities to buy and sell gold freely at the $35 price.

D. RESERVES

In order to weather periods of deficit in a system of stable exchange rates, monetary authorities must hold reserves of internationally-acceptable liquid assets. If a central bank had no reserves with which to purchase its own currency at times when its currency was in excess market supply, it would have no choice but to ask the IMF to approve a change in its par value.

Reserves are held primarily in the form of gold and dollar claims on the United States. Because dollars are held so widely in countries' reserves, the dollar is the main "reserve currency" of the international monetary system. Countries in the sterling and franc areas hold part of their reserves in sterling or French francs, and thus—to a much lesser extent—the pound and the franc also function as reserve currencies. Gold and reserve currencies are supplemented by reserve credit available from the International Monetary Fund (see below).

After an initial accrual of dollars resulting from market intervention, the country can either retain its reserve gain in the form of dollars or choose to convert the dollars into another reserve asset, usually gold. Conversely, a country necessarily experiences a reserve loss by the act of selling dollars in its exchange market, thereby reducing its dollar holdings. In order to stand ready to intervene in the market, central banks have to hold at least a working balance in dollars. This working balance can be replenished as necessary either by selling other reserve assets (such as dollar securities, time deposits, or gold) held by the monetary authorities or by drawing on the IMF or other credit facilities.

Many diverse factors enter into the decisions of central banks when they determine the proportions of their reserves to hold in gold, dollars, and other assets. Some central banks have traditionally held their reserves primarily in gold except for foreign-exchange working balances. Others have historically invested almost all their reserves in dollar or sterling assets. There are many different patterns of behavior in between these two extremes. Moreover, many countries have changed their reserve-composition policies over time.

One important motive for holding dollars is that they can be invested at interest. Gold does not earn any interest and actually costs something to store safely.

It has already been pointed out that the United States maintains its exchange stability obligations in a unique manner. It is equally true that the United States must of necessity have a unique policy with respect to its reserves. Whereas other countries use their reserves by buying or selling dollars in their exchange markets, the United States uses its reserves only to redeem excess dollars acquired by the monetary authorities of other countries.

This structural feature of the international monetary system has another important implication: when the United States does use its reserve assets to redeem outstanding dollar liabilities, this redemption—both in amount and timing—is determined by the reserve-asset preferences of foreign monetary authorities. The amount and timing of U.S. use of reserve assets is therefore not directly subject either to U.S. desires or to U.S. official policy actions. The

United States can influence the rate at which it gains or loses reserves only by influencing the attitudes and asset preferences of foreign monetary authorities. One of the major factors influencing foreign official attitudes, of course, is the prevailing appraisal of the strength or weakness of the U.S. balance of payments and reserve positions.

Just as the United States uses reserves in a unique manner, it must *hold* its reserves subject to considerations that are unique. Whereas other countries have a range of assets from which to choose that includes gold, dollars, other currencies, and reserve positions in the IMF, the United States has a much more restricted field of choice. It must hold assets which are acceptable to other countries when they call upon the United States to redeem our outstanding reserve-currency liabilities. While there is some scope for holding other countries' currencies in our reserves, it is clear that in the present system the United States must hold most of its reserves in gold.

Given the wide extent to which the dollar is used as the "intervention currency" and as a reserve currency, it is clear *that the stability of the entire international monetary system is intimately bound up with the behavior of U.S. reserves.* If a widespread feeling were to develop that U.S. reserve assets might be inadequate in comparison with the size of outstanding reserve-currency liabilities, or especially if U.S. reserve assets threatened to continue to decline simultaneously with a further large expansion of U.S. reserve-currency liabilities, dollar assets might be viewed with increasing distrust by individuals and governments all around the world. The U.S. Government fully appreciates the significance of the fact that the stability of the entire monetary system is interdependent with U.S. reserve and balance of payments policy. This fact and the desire to act responsibly in the face of it have been one of the primary considerations underlying U.S. balance of payments policy since the large payments deficits of 1958–60, accompanied by heavy gold losses, first underscored the existence of a problem.

E. OPERATIONS OF THE INTERNATIONAL MONETARY FUND

In addition to the gold and reserve currencies which countries hold in their reserves outright (sometimes referred to as "unconditional" liquidity since they are usable without any outside institution or government placing conditions on their availability), countries have access to a pool of currencies in the International Monetary Fund. The amount of resources a country may draw from the Fund is governed by its quota, which reflects its economic size and importance relative to other countries. When initially paying in its quota subscription, each country subscribes 25 percent in gold and 75 percent in terms of its own currency. In return for agreeing that the 75 percent balance of its own currency may be drawn upon in case of need to finance other countries' drawings from the currency pool, countries obtain the right to draw the currencies of others from the Fund themselves under certain stipulated conditions.

The right of a country to draw on its gold subscription ("gold tranche") is essentially beyond challenge; so also is its right to draw on any credit balance it acquired as a result of other countries having drawn its currency. These two amounts together are described as the country's "reserve position in the Fund"; it is also a form of unconditional liquidity. Most countries, including the United States, regard their reserve positions in the Fund as an asset fully liquid and usable in case of balance of payments need, and accordingly include the Fund reserve position in their published reserves.

Under circumstances which involve increasingly stringent analysis and discussion of a country's economic policies, members of the Fund may draw successive further amounts from the Fund up to 100 percent of their quotas. These further borrowings in a country's "credit tranches" are not comparable to reserves. They are conditional credit facilities (hence sometimes referred to as "conditional" liquidity). They carry specific repayment obligations and interest charges.

The role of the International Monetary Fund in supplying conditional liquidity to governments for the purpose of maintaining stability in exchange rates and the adjustment of payments imbalances has expanded greatly since the inauguration of the Bretton Woods system. The aggregate quotas of all members of the IMF are now some $21 billion. The appropriateness of quotas is reviewed every five years; the last round of general quota increases became effective in 1966. In addition to expanding the general level of quotas and selectively increasing the quotas of certain countries, the IMF was also strengthened in 1962 by an agreement among the ten main industrial countries (the "Group of Ten") known as the General Arrangements to Borrow (GAB). The GAB is an undertaking by these countries to lend the Fund specified amounts of their currencies (aggregating to the equivalent of about $6 billion) if the Fund decides that supplementary resources are needed to forestall or cope with an impairment of the international monetary system. The GAB arrangements have been activated several times in connection with large U.K. drawings from the Fund.

The U.S. quota in the IMF is $5.2 billion, out of total Fund quotas of about $21 billion. As of the end of 1967, the United States had approximately $400 million of its "gold tranche" and the full $5.2 billion of credit tranches available.

F. OTHER INSTITUTIONAL ARRANGEMENTS

In 1961, the new U.S. Administration began to foster the development of a new system of international short-term credits in the form of the "swap network" of the Federal Reserve System, and also introduced the so-called "Roosa bonds." Both of these provide a type of exchange protection to the lending country. That is, the lending country is repaid in a constant value in its own currency, and is thereby protected against an exchange adjustment by the borrowing country. The United States, at the center of the swap network, can borrow foreign currencies and sell them in the market in lieu of making gold sales, in the expectation that a subsequent reversal of part of the outflow will reduce the eventual drain on its reserves. In the meantime the swap partner holds dollars with a form of exchange protection. Similarly, the United States has, itself, been able to extend credit and acquire foreign currency with exchange protection when, for example, Italy or Canada or the United Kingdom had an outflow of funds. This network of short-term reciprocal borrowing of reserves, frequently called "a first line of monetary defense," now totals about $7.1 billion. It has helped to avoid gold losses resulting from short-term flows that were later reversed. When the United States has been drawn upon, other countries have been provided with dollars to hold their exchange rates stable.

Roosa bonds were designed to provide a longer-term instrument for the investment of dollars accumulated by foreign monetary authorities. Most of them have been denominated in the foreign country's currency as an added attraction to the purchasing country. A total of about $1.5 billion of these bonds was outstanding as of November 30, 1967.

Since its reopening in 1954, the free market for gold in London has re-emerged as the largest and most important center in the world for free-market gold transactions. During most of the period since that time the flow of gold to the London market, from new production and Russian sales, has exceeded the various demands on it. Accordingly, the residual supply of gold was absorbed by central bank purchases and by the U.S. Treasury at prices varying fairly closely around the U.S. fixed price of $35 per ounce. For short periods, sudden outbreaks of speculative demand for gold substantially exceeded the supply available to the market. Such a situation occurred in October 1960 when the market price rose to around $40 and aroused widespread anxieties concerning the international monetary system. The U.S. monetary authorities supported the Bank of England in intervening in the London market to stabilize the price within an acceptable range.

In the following year, after a similar but milder strain on the London market, the U.S. authorities suggested that, in view of the mutuality of interest among the monetary authorities of the major industrial countries in maintaining orderly conditions in the gold and exchange markets, an informal gold selling arrangement be arranged among the group of central banks that are members of the BIS or are associated with it. Under the arrangement, each member of the group (Belgium, France, Germany, Italy, the Netherlands, Switzerland, the United Kingdom and the United States) undertook to supply an agreed proportion of such net gold sales to stabilize the market as the Bank of England, as agent for the group, determined to be appropriate. The U.S. share was 50 percent. This informal arrangement has essentially been continued (without French participation since mid-year 1967 and with the U.S. share at 59 percent since then), both as to purchasing net gold acquisitions as well as supplying net market demand. Representatives of the central banks participating in the "pool" meet periodically at Basle to discuss all aspects of the gold and foreign exchange markets, providing a means thereby to coordinate exchange operating policies as well as to keep fully informed of developments in the London and other gold markets.

G. THE DOLLAR AS A TRANSACTIONS CURRENCY

In addition to its role as the international monetary system's major reserve currency, the dollar is also the primary international means of payment and a major medium for the international investment of short-term funds. This "transactions demand" for dollars has grown greatly over the whole postwar period. In recent years the growing importance of the Euro-dollar market has provided further illustrations of the central versatile role played by the dollar in private international financial transactions.[1]

Chart I, entitled "Liquid Liabilities to Foreigners," gives some indication of how rapidly U.S. liquid liabilities to nonofficial foreign-

---

[1] Euro-dollars are deposits in banks outside the United States, principally in European financial centers, that are denominated in U.S. dollars.

ers have grown in the recent past. Liquid liabilities to "other foreigners"—foreign commercial banks (including the foreign branches of U.S. banks) and other private foreigners—increased over the period 1957 to 1967 from approximately $6 billion to about $16 billion. These liquid dollar assets of foreigners held in the United States are invested in demand and time deposits and money market paper. The secular growth in foreign private dollar holdings can be expected to continue in the future *pari passu* with continued expansion in world trade and other international transactions.

The existence of very large outstanding dollar liabilities, not only to foreign official institutions ("reserve-currency" balances), but also to private foreign individuals and organizations ("transactions-currency" balances) underlines the importance of maintaining confidence in the dollar and, more generally, in the international monetary system itself. The following chapter of this paper, which deals with current problems facing the international monetary system, returns to this important point.

H. BALANCE OF PAYMENTS SURPLUS AND DEFICITS

When a country consistently loses reserves, it is in balance of payments "deficit." Conversely, if a country consistently gains reserves, it has a "surplus" in its balance of payments.

Strictly speaking, the matter is more complicated than that. "Surplus" and "deficit" are analytical concepts with a variety of possible definitions. For example, it may be appropriate in some circumstances to take into account changes in the foreign assets and/or liabilities of the country's commercial banking system—as well as changes in official reserves—in measuring a deficit.

The measurement of the U.S. balance of payments deficit is more complex than for other countries because of the unique position of the U.S. dollar, and was examined by a special review committee.[2] Following this report, the conclusion was reached that no single indicator of surplus or deficit was suitable for all purposes. The primary measure used in this paper is the balance on the "liquidity" basis, although for some purposes reference is made to the balance on the "official reserve transactions" basis.

Balance of payments surpluses and deficits sometimes are desired. This was the case in the early 1950's, for example, when

[2] See *The Balance of Payments Statistics of the United States A Review and Appraisal*, Report of the Review Committee for Balance of Payments Statistics to the Bureau of the Budget, E. M. Bernstein, Chairman (Washington, D.C.: U.S. Government Printing Office, April 1965).

Liquid Liabilities to Foreigners *(end of year 1956-63, end of month 1964; latest figures plotted: September)*

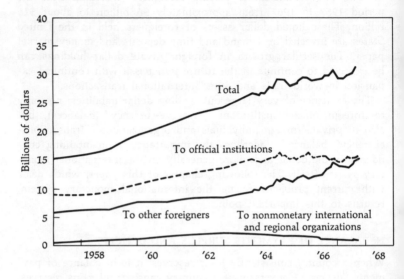

(on the definitions of surplus and deficit then in use) the European countries undergoing reconstruction had surpluses and the United States had deficits. These deficits and surpluses enabled the European countries to build up their reserves; the declines in the swollen U.S. gold reserves and the increases in our reserve-currency liabilities—representing as they did a redistribution and augmentation of the world's stock of reserve assets—were universally welcomed as such.

On the other hand, *large* and *persistent* payments imbalances, either surplus or deficit, are not sustainable and can give rise to instability in the international monetary system. There is an obvious limit to imbalances of the deficit type: countries can support their exchange rates with their reserves and credit facilities only so long as they have reserves or can arrange further credit. In the case of a reserve-currency country, there are limits to the willingness of private and official holders abroad to accumulate that currency. The limits on the ability of countries to run large and persistent surpluses are much less clear. What is clear, however, is that large and persistent surpluses impose strains on the international monetary system as great as those resulting from large and persistent deficits.

I. THE ADJUSTMENT PROCESS—BASIC OBJECTIVES

Each individual country has its own multiple economic and social objectives. These include full employment and a satisfactory rate of growth, reasonable price stability, an equitable distribution of income, and balanced regional and sectoral development. While seeking to attain these objectives, as already noted, countries must also avoid large and persistent imbalances in their external accounts. It is also widely agreed (in the words of the Convention setting up the Organization for Economic Co-operation and Development) that countries should "promote policies designed to contribute to the expansion of world trade on a multilateral, nondiscriminatory basis in accordance with international obligations."

The international monetary system set up at Bretton Woods and based on a pattern of stable exchange rates was then and is now believed by its participants to be the most appropriate system designed to foster these objectives. The system has evolved over time to meet changing needs and problems. It is once again going through a key evolutionary stage, as the work on proposed amendments to the IMF Articles of Agreement reaches completion, to establish a facility for deliberate reserve creation (see below) and to improve certain rules and practices of the Fund.

The simultaneous achievement of all the economic and social objectives described above, even for an individual country, is far from easy. Governments have only a limited number of policy tools at their disposal. They have not always been able or willing to use these tools in appropriate combinations. Governments in different countries attach different priorities to achievement of various internal and external aims. The nature of imbalances in payments, as well as the appropriate range and mix of instruments required to deal with them, can vary substantially from country to country in line with wide differences in economic and financial structure and in the nature of political institutions.

These difficulties have important implications for the speed and effectiveness with which the adjustment of payments imbalances can be attained. The adjustment process may work somewhat imperfectly, and in any case is apt to be gradual. In a few difficult cases, adjustment of payments imbalances may not take place at all, or will take place only with the costly sacrifice of some of the basic objectives that the system is intended to advance, unless a large measure of multilateral cooperation is brought to bear on the problem.

J. THE ADJUSTMENT PROCESS—NEED FOR MULTILATERAL COOPERATION

The need for multilateral cooperation in achieving and maintaining balance of payments equilibrium has become increasingly widely recognized in the last few years. An understanding of this need has been particularly advanced by an international working group formed under the auspices of the Organization for Economic Cooperation and Development (OECD). The Economic Policy Committee of the OECD established a Working Party in 1961 for the specific purpose of promoting better international payments equilibrium. This group, consisting of senior officials from Ministries of Finance and other key government agencies and Central Banks concerned with balance of payments questions, has met together at approximately six-to-eight week intervals ever since. In 1964, the Ministers and Governors of the ten countries participating in the General Arrangements to Borrow suggested that this OECD working party, known as Working Party 3, make a study of the balance of payments adjustment process with a view toward improving the process of continuing international consultation and cooperation.

The Working Party's report on this subject was issued in August 1966. In addition to endorsing the commonly agreed view that prolonged imbalance in either direction is in general undesirable, the Working Party also noted that

. . . the objectives of international consultation are broader and more general than the mere avoidance of imbalance. The purpose of consultation regarding adjustment policies is to ensure that the policies pursued by individual countries do not hinder others in the pursuit of the general aims of economic policy; more positively, the object is to ensure that as far as possible countries, while avoiding imbalance, collectively support each other in their policies.

The Working Party's report does not fail to point out that there are often inherent difficulties in managing an economy in a way which is consistent with domestic objectives, with the aims of its trading partners, with stable exchange rates, and with the general health of the world economy. But it also recognizes that there is clear room for improvement and that improvement is an urgent order of business. The report describes appropriate methods of dealing with these problems in different circumstances. It refers specifically to the need for clearer formulation of balance of payments aims; early identification and better diagnosis of payments problems; new and more selective instruments of economic policy; more timely action to correct inappropriate demand levels, competitive positions and capital flows; and a further strengthening of the processes of international consultation.

The U.S. Government has strongly supported the Working Party's report and its recommendations. At the recent meeting, November 30 to December 1, of the Ministers of the countries belonging to the OECD, for example, the United States representative, Under Secretary of State Eugene V. Rostow, said:

> We have no doubt that the Atlantic countries can resolve this problem, if they deal with it together, in ways which fortify the world monetary system and permit an early and assured return to growth patterns closer to our full employment objectives. All I am suggesting today is that we recognize that some aspects of the adjustment process require cooperative solutions and that we set about promptly to find them. Cooperation in handling the adjustment process, I suggest, is the next major step after Rio for us to take in improving our machinery for managing the monetary system.

K. THE ADJUSTMENT PROCESS—EQUILIBRIUM FOR THE SYSTEM AS A WHOLE

For any country to reduce its deficit or move into surplus, it is generally necessary for other countries to reduce surpluses or increase deficits. This is simply a statement of what must happen mechanically and statistically if payments imbalances are to be adjusted at all.

This inescapable interdependence of surpluses and deficits makes it very clear that countries must have compatible balance of payments aims if the whole system is not to be working at cross purposes. If all the countries in the system that are in surplus set their policies in such a way as to have continued surpluses, while deficit countries take active measures to eliminate their deficits, then either the deficit countries will still find themselves running deficits or else surplus countries will find that they have not been able to attain their targeted surpluses. All countries together cannot possibly achieve these inconsistent aims; someone is bound to be disappointed.

Virtually all countries take it as their balance of payments objective to be in surplus (and so to have growing reserves) over time. Few if any countries have indicated either a policy or a willingness to have their reserves fluctuate around a fixed level rather than around an upward trend.

It is understandable why countries tend to have this preference

for surpluses. The volume of trade and other international transactions has a strong upward trend. It is a reasonable presumption
that, because of this trend, the absolute size of imbalances will also
increase over time. These facts alone suggest that reserves should
likewise have an upward trend if they are to continue to be adequate
to support the fixed exchange rate against balance of payments
swings. Another factor leading countries not to attempt to reduce
their surpluses may be a propensity to discount an existing surplus
as partly or wholly "temporary;" it is natural and prudent to conduct affairs so as to prepare for "rainy weather" in the future, and
not to presume that current good fortune will continue. Even to
the extent that countries aim at a long-run objective of a zero surplus over time, which they tend not to do, they still probably react
more quickly to a deficit situation than when they are in surplus
(if only because countries in surplus are under much less urgent
and intense pressures to act to reduce the imbalance).

Given the set of prevailing attitudes which makes an upward
trend in reserves (balance of payments surplus) the targeted long-
run "norm" for each country taken individually, the obvious question suggests itself: when, if at all, can the international monetary
system as a whole be in equilibrium? Given that it is difficult enough
to bring about adjustment of payments imbalances even under ideal
conditions where deficit countries take actions to reduce deficits and
surplus countries willingly take cooperative actions to reduce their
surpluses, how can the system possibly function smoothly when
countries in surplus by and large do not want to see their surpluses
reduced?

Happily, there is a solution to this dilemma. It is not the case
that for every dollar of surplus in the system there must be an
exactly offsetting dollar of deficit. When the gross deficits and gross
surpluses (consistently defined) of all countries are offset against
each other, the sum of the surpluses can exceed the sum of the
deficits by the amount of new reserves being added to the system
which are not at the same time the liability of a particular country.
The key point of this relationship is that if new reserves of the
appropriate kind are flowing into the system, it *is* possible for some
countries to satisfy their preferences for reserve increases without
necessitating that other countries be in corresponding deficit.

Up to the present time, the only "new reserves" which have allowed this margin to exist have been increases in countries' monetary gold stocks. When newly-mined gold is sold to a monetary
authority, that government has a reserve gain without any other
country having experienced a deficit. When the dollar component

of world reserves increases, on the other hand, this increase in reserves does not allow the system as a whole to have a margin of surpluses exceeding deficits. When the rest of the world adds to its dollar reserves, these new assets are also an increase in U.S. reserve-currency liabilities, and there is therefore a U.S. deficit corresponding to the surplus of the rest of the world. However, gold is not the only reserve asset that is capable of permitting the system to have a situation in which the sum of surpluses exceeds the sum of deficits. Deliberately created new reserve assets, such as the proposed Special Drawing Rights (SDR) . . . will serve this function equally well.

Equilibrium for the system as a whole thus requires that new reserves—gold or new reserve assets such as SDR—be added to the system at such a rate that the sum of surpluses can exceed the sum of deficits by a reasonable margin. This condition for "equilibrium" of the system should be thought of as a necessary, but not sufficient, condition. Other considerations, such as the degree to which the system is promoting the achievement of its basic objectives, also need to be taken into account.

Only under these conditions is there a good chance of making countries' balance of payments aims mutually compatible; only then is there a plausible hope of attaining the objectives the system is intended to promote, including relative freedom from trade and payments restrictions while still getting the adjustment of payments imbalances to proceed smoothly.

What is a "reasonable" margin by which surpluses should exceed deficits? The answer to this question is not fully clear to the financial experts and economists who have studied this question. Broadly speaking, the rate at which new reserves should be added to the system should probably bear some relationship to the rate at which international transactions are expanding (though the two rates need not be the same and there is no necessity for a precise relationship). The margin should not be too small, and certainly should not be negative. Nor should the margin be an excessive one. At either of these two extremes, one would have to say that the system as a whole was in "disequilibrium."

It is important to be clear on the fact that the above condition for equilibrium of the system, if satisfied, in no way reduces the need for countries to avoid large and persistent imbalances in their external payments. It is still imperative for countries in large or prolonged deficit to reduce their imbalance. And it is just as important as ever for countries with large and persistent surpluses to reduce these surpluses to the point where they are moderate and broadly consonant with the rate at which reserves are growing in the system as a whole. The need for adjustment is not removed. The margin by which surpluses exceed deficits only means that, for each country individually and for the system as a whole, adjustment takes place around an upward trend in reserves rather than around a constant level.

WARREN L. SMITH

GUIDELINES FOR INTERNATIONAL MONETARY REFORM

42

I. THE PRESENT SYSTEM AND ITS DEFECTS

Any program for reform of the international monetary system must necessarily be based on a diagnosis of the ills of the present system. Accordingly, I shall begin by presenting my own view of the relevant features of the system and its weaknesses. As I see it, the basic principles of the system are as follows:

1. Each country is quite jealously insistent on its sovereign right to regulate internal demand for the purpose of maintaining suitable economic conditions at home in terms of employment and the behavior of its internal price level.

2. Free international movement of goods and of capital as a means of achieving efficient use of resources is a generally accepted goal, and substantial progress has been made in achieving it. In particular, since the advent of general currency convertibility in 1958, controls over the international flow of capital have been relaxed and investors have become increasingly inclined to shift funds

Reprinted from "Prepared Statement of Warren L. Smith," *Guidelines for International Monetary Reform*, Part I, Hearings Before the Sub-Committee on International Exchange and Payments of the Joint Economic Committee, 89th Cong., 1st Sess., July 27–29, 1965, pp. 60–70.

internationally in response to differential changes in expected rates of return.

3. Trade is conducted under a system of fixed exchange parities at any particular time, with actual exchange rates fluctuating only within very narrow limits around these parities. The maintenance of fixed parities is a highly prized objective; nevertheless, provision is made for parity adjustments under the rules of the IMF as a means of dealing with "fundamental" balance-of-payments disequilibria.

4. Countries hold limited supplies of monetary reserves in the form of gold, dollar balances, and (to a lesser extent) sterling balances. In addition, lines of credit are available at the IMF; portions of these credit lines are available virtually automatically and are practically the equivalent of "owned" reserves, while the remaining portions are available on conditions that become increasingly stringent as the amount borrowed increases. The reserves available and potentially obtainable set a limit—though a somewhat elastic one—on the cumulative size of a country's balance-of-payments deficit. Thus, each country operates subject to a "balance-of-payments constraint"—not in the sense that payments must always be in balance but in the sense that there is some limit on the size and duration of deficits that can be tolerated. It is important to note that there is no corresponding limit for surpluses.

A little more needs to be said concerning the goal of internal stability (item 1 in the above list). It is often said the countries seek the twin goals of "full employment" and "price stability." However, a more accurate way of describing the situation is as follows: There is in each country a "trade-off" between employment (or unemployment) and price stability; that is, over a considerable range the more unemployment is reduced by policies to expand the aggregate demand the higher is the price that must be paid in terms of inflation. This relation holds primarily because of the tendency for money-wage increases to outstrip increases in productivity even under conditions of substantial unemployment. The trade-off varies from country to country, depending on the organization, traditions, and aggressiveness of the labor movement, the price policies followed by industry, and so on, and from time to time depending upon the attendant circumstances. The trade-off may be influenced by policy measure—wage-price guideposts, income policies, etc.—but I am not aware of any cases in which efforts to change it have been notably successful. Not only does the trade-off between price stability and employment vary from country to country but so also do the relative weights attached to these two objectives in the hierarchy of values that govern the behavior of the authorities responsible for economic policy in the various countries. As a consequence, to the extent that each country is left free to decide what combination of price inflation and employment to select from the many choices open to it, price trends may vary from country to country.

Price stability is often given a high priority in the list of objectives of economic policy, not only for individual countries but for the world as a whole. It seems to me that the evidence is overwhelming, however, that price stability can really be attained on a continuing basis only at a cost in terms of unemployment and under-utilization of economic resources that is not only politically unacceptable but probably socially undesirable in most countries. This is true not only because the wage-price determination mechanism tends to set in motion a "creeping" rise in the price level before an acceptable level of unemployment has been reached, but also because prices are much more prone to rise in times and at places in which demand for goods and services is rising than to fall under conditions where such demand is declining. I believe that the achievement of an acceptable rate of utilization of economic resources requires that the world be willing to accept—and, indeed, under-write—a mild upward drift in the general level of prices, unless, of course, some as yet undiscovered means can be used to damp the tendency toward price and wage increases without reducing the overall level of demand.

There are three grave difficulties with the existing system as described above—admittedly in a slightly idealized way—which are relevant to the question of international monetary reform.

1. The first—and in many ways the most fundamental—difficulty is that the system contains no mechanism that can be depended upon to eliminate a balance-of-payments disequilibrium brought about by such disruptive forces as changes in tastes or technology. There are three possible ways of correcting a deficit or surplus by adjustment of the current account: through the use of trade or exchange controls, through an adjustment of exchange rates, and through internal price and income changes. Since all of these violate the principles of the system, they are ruled out. Consequently, when a country experiences a deficit, there is no assurance that the deficit will be eliminated before its limited supply of reserves is used up.

2. The system as it is now constituted is subject in extreme degree to destabilizing speculative tendencies which greatly complicate the problems of balance-of-payments adjustment. Although, as

indicated above, fixed exchange rates appear to be one of the generally accepted goals of economic policy, we do not now have a system of really fixed rates. Indeed, the present arrangements, under which exchange rates are fixed within very narrow limits at any particular time but are subject to readjustment from time to time to correct "fundamental" disequilibria in national balances of payments, seem ideally calculated to encourage speculation. Since opportunities for the investment of capital, viewed broadly, do not ordinarily vary widely as between major countries, even a mild suspicion that a country may devalue its currency can cause a speculative outflow of capital from that country. And, as more and more investors become familiar with the possibilities of transferring capital internationally, it seems probable that the potential size of speculative capital flows may become even larger. The result of this situation is that most countries will entertain the possibility of devaluation only in the most dire emergency, but the threat is nevertheless sufficient to induce speculation. And there is always the possibility that speculation will exhaust the country's reserves and force the devaluation that speculators are hoping for.

3. The third difficulty—and the one that I regard as least serious because easiest to correct—is that the present system contains no orderly arrangement for generating in a predictable way the increased quantities of international monetary reserves that are needed to meet the demands of a growing world economy. Increments to the world's monetary reserves are provided primarily by gold production (less the amount of gold that is absorbed in consumption and in hoards) and by additional dollars that are pumped into official reserves by U.S. deficits. Gold production is generally agreed to be capable of producing only a relatively small fraction of the additions to reserves that are needed, and the end to U.S. deficits, which may now be imminent, will shut off the flow of dollars.

The matter of speculative instability—the second of the three problems referred to above—merits some further amplification. The speculative threat to the stability of the system, which I believe is very serious, has two distinguishable aspects: (1) the threat imposed by the "overhang" of convertible claims against the monetary reserves of the reserve-currency countries—especially the United States—that are held by the monetary authorities of other countries; and (2) the danger of private speculative "runs" against currencies that are under pressure. The first of these dangers is present only in the case of reserve-currency countries. It has been an important factor in accentuating the difficulties of the United States, because as our continuing deficits have been settled partly in gold and partly through increases in the dollar holdings of foreign central banks, the ratio of our gold reserves to our outstanding dollar liabilities to foreign official agencies has declined, and fears that the dollar might have to be devalued have increased. This generates pressure for foreign central banks to convert outstanding dollars into gold and to insist on the settlement of current U.S. deficits in gold. This depletes U.S. gold reserves and weakens confidence in the dollar.

The second of the two dangers referred to above, that of private speculation against a currency that is under pressure, is, in my judgment, more fundamental and serious than the first and also more difficult to correct. In the first place, this threat is not confined to reserve-currency countries, although it may be more serious for such countries partly because it may be stimulated by reserve drains resulting from conversions of official holdings of reserve currencies. Under the present adjustable-peg exchange rate system, as long as there is some limit on the available supply of monetary reserves, any country whose currency comes under pressure as a result of a serious balance-of-payments deficit can easily get into a position where a devaluation of its currency (or the application of direct controls) is regarded as a serious possibility by private investors. This can quickly generate a speculative "run" which will reduce its reserves still further, thereby strengthening the fears of devaluation and leading to a self-generating increase in the rate of decline of its reserves. It is important to recognize that the entire stock of claims denominated in a particular currency is potentially available to participate in a private run on that currency. Since this includes claims held internally as well as externally, the possibilities are practically unlimited.

Of course, the system, which in its present form dates from the restoration of convertibility in 1958, has functioned after a fashion; indeed, in general, the world economy has prospered and international trade has expanded remarkably during this period. Actually, however, the system has survived only because its fundamental principles have been violated in various ways.

1. The underlying principle of free movement of goods and capital has been compromised through the imposition of trade restrictions for balance-of-payments reasons by Canada in 1962 and the United Kingdom in 1964. The United States has also persistently violated the principle by tying foreign aid, by discriminating in favor of American suppliers in its defense procurement policies, by the enactment of the so-called interest equalization tax, and, most recently, by the adoption of the voluntary program for limiting foreign loans by commercial banks initiated by President Johnson early in 1965.

2. Some minor use has been made of exchange rate adjustments in the Dutch and German revaluations of March 1961. Such adjustments, however, probably do more harm than good by weakening confidence in the overall stability of exchange rates and encouraging speculation.

3. In practice, domestic monetary and fiscal policies have not been entirely unaffected by the balance-of-payments situation. In part this is because, due to the less than perfect effectiveness of domestic monetary and fiscal tools, it has not always been feasible to offset completely the automatic corrective effects of deficits and surpluses on internal demand. Beyond that, deficit countries have found it necessary to adapt their domestic policies to the exigencies of the balance of payments—albeit reluctantly—when their international reserves have been seriously threatened. The leading example here is the United States, which has suffered from an unnecessarily high rate of unemployment and an irrecoverable loss of output amounting to perhaps $150 billion in the last 5 years, partly as a result of its balance-of-payments deficit. Actually, there is little evidence that policies to expand aggregate demand have been held back by fear that they would worsen the Nation's balance-of-payments position. But sufficiently expansionary fiscal policies have proved to be difficult to put into effect (as a consequence, in part of public antipathy to budget deficits and the growth of the public debt), while the need to avoid an accentuation of short-term capital outflows has acted as a constraint on monetary policy—the one flexible and acceptable instrument that might in the absence of a balance-of-payments constraint have been used to expand aggregate demand. No doubt similar considerations have to some extent operated in European countries to limit the use of restrictive monetary policies to check excessive inflation in the face of balance-of-payments surpluses. But it is quite clear that the present system has an inherent deflationary bias. The limited supply of reserves sets some upper bound on the size of a nation's cumulative deficit, whereas there is no equivalent upper bound to the size of a cumulative surplus and the associated expansion of monetary reserves.

Techniques of central bank cooperation through the use of currency "swaps" and intervention in foreign exchange markets to deal with minor speculative crises have been progressively developed and refined. To deal with more serious crises, massive supplies of foreign exchange have been mobilized to support threatened currencies and combat the activities of speculators. So far, these efforts have been successful in fending off disaster, but there is even now much concern about the position of sterling, and the financial world lives in fear of a forced devaluation of sterling or the dollar.

II. GUIDEPOSTS FOR REFORM OF THE SYSTEM

In my opinion, effective reform of the international monetary system requires a program which takes account of all of the problems referred to above. That is, a reform program should accomplish the following objectives:

1. Systematize the creation of monetary reserves and disconnect it from the vagaries of gold production and deficits of reserve-currency countries.

2. Eliminate or at least reduce the potentially dangerous speculative instability that is inherent in the present system. It is useful to separate this objective into two parts (although there is, of course, some connection between the two):

   (a) Tie down the "loose cargo" of officially held convertible claims which now constitute a threat to U.S. gold reserves.

   (b) Eliminate or reduce the propensity for private destabilizing speculation to develop in anticipation of devaluation of any currency that comes under pressure.

3. Take steps to strengthen the procedures that are available to maintain or restore balance-of-payments equilibrium.

It is not easy to devise a program that will achieve these results, but I shall discuss some of the possibilities.

A. Possible Contribution of an Overhaul of International Financial Arrangements

In much of the discussion, reform of the international monetary system has been viewed largely in terms of purely financial readjustments: reorganizing the IMF along one of several alternative lines, multilaterilizing the reserve-currency function now performed almost exclusively by the dollar and sterling, introducing some new form of international reserve asset to supplement gold and foreign exchange, and so on. While some financial reorganization must form a central part of any feasible program of reform, no proposal of this kind can by itself provide a full solution. Financial reforms along this line are capable of accomplishing only two of the objectives listed above: objective (1), the systematization of reserve creation, and objective (2a), the tying down of the overhang of official dollar claims. None of them would deal directly with either objective 2b), the curbing of private speculative propensities, or objective (3), the establishment of an effective balance-of-payments adjustment mechanism.

In deciding its stance with respect to proposals for international financial reform, I believe the United States should adhere to the following guideposts:

1. *The United States should oppose proposals which would move in the direction of imposing greater "discipline" on deficit countries to adopt generally restrictive domestic policies.*—The present system contains a deflationary bias in the sense that the pressure on deficit countries to undertake restrictive policies exceeds the pressure on surplus countries to adopt expansionary policies. If anything, this represents precisely the opposite kind of bias from that needed to achieve a healthy world economy. It would be most unfortunate if this bias were strengthened.

2. *The United States should oppose plans which limit participation in an arbitrary way to a small group of countries, such as the Group of Ten.*—Determination of the supply of monetary reserves is too important a question to be decided by a small group of countries with no opportunity for participation by the rest.

3. *The United States should weigh with great care the probable effect of any proposed plan on the reserve-currency status of the dollar.*—I do not believe we should automatically reject any proposal which would weaken the dollar's position. But we should give very serious thought to the question: Is the increase in the stability of the system that might result from the adoption of the plan worth the associated cost in terms of deterioration in the reserve currency position of the dollar? In arriving at an answer to such a question, it is necessary to distinguish between the role of the dollar as a private payments currency and its role as an official reserve currency. Many of the concrete benefits that the United States derives from the special position of the dollar in the world are derived from its use as a private payments currency rather than as a reserve currency. For example, the leading position of U.S. banks and other financial institutions in the financing of international trade is related to the position of the dollar as a private payments currency. Indeed, the predominant position of the dollar in private international trade and finance is almost certainly a valuable byproduct of the unparalleled efficiency and magnitude of our money and capital markets. I cannot see that any of the proposals for reforming the international financial system would be likely to weaken the position of the dollar as a private payments currency. None of the plans would interfere in any way with current practices relating to the conduct of private international transactions, and, in particular, none would involve the creation of a new monetary unit that would be used in the conduct of such transactions.

Leaving aside the issue of the use of dollars in financing private international transactions, the reserve-currency status of the dollar has both advantages and disadvantages for the United States. It almost certainly gives the United States a strategic advantage when it comes to financing a series of large deficits such as we have experienced in the last few years. Using the "official settlements" concept of the deficit which is advocated in the recent Bernstein report, the United States experienced an aggregate deficit of $12.6 billion in the period 1960–64, of which $3.5 billion was settled in gold, $1.9 billion was settled through debt prepayments by other governments, $1.2 billion reflected a change in the IMF position of the United States, and the remaining $5.9 billion represented an increase in U.S. liabilities to foreign official monetary institutions. It seems to me that if any of the proposed plans that would weaken the reserve-currency status of the dollar had been in operation during this period we would probably have had greater difficulty than we, in fact, experienced in financing this large deficit and would have found it necessary to settle a larger share of it through gold payments. On the other hand, the reserve-currency status of the dollar under the present system certainly does subject the United States to a serious element of speculative strain and risk. In deciding whether to accept a plan which would weaken or eliminate the reserve-currency status of the dollar, we would have to make a judgment as to whether the reduction in risk that would result would be worth the cost that might be imposed upon us in terms of reduced freedom of maneuver in seeking financing for some future series of balance-of-payments deficits. How we would come out in making such a judgment would presumably depend to a considerable extent on the details of the particular proposal that was put before us.

One of the dilemmas of international monetary reform is that most of the plans that would accomplish objective 2(a), the stabilization of outstanding official dollar claims, would be likely to prove objectionable on the basis of at least two—and possibly all three —of the guideposts listed above. This would be true of a CRU-type plan under which CRU's were issued on the basis of the participants' holdings of gold.[1] Such a plan would probably undermine the re-

[1] Several proposals have been made for reform of the international monetary system through the issuance of so-called composite reserve units (CRU's) which would constitute a new type of reserve asset. Under such plans, each country would deposit a specified amount of its currency with a managing agent (which might be a division of the IMF) and would receive in exchange an equal proportional claim, in the form of CRU's

serve-currency position of the dollar by giving participants an incentive to convert dollars into gold in order to qualify for a maximum quota of CRU's. It would also be limited to a select group of countries, and would, I suspect, be likely to represent a reversion toward the gold standard with a sharp increase in the deflationary pressures of deficit countries. The same objections might well apply to a posthuma-type plan, which would eliminate the special reserve currency status of the dollar by multilateralizing the reserve-currency function among the participating countries.

A CRU-type plan of the kind proposed by Dr. E. M. Bernstein would not be subject to these objections, because it would provide merely a way of increasing the supply of reserves without otherwise changing the present system substantially. On the other hand, the plan would do nothing to stabilize the outstanding stock of official dollar claims. While participation would initially be limited to a rather small group of countries, it might be feasible to admit other countries to participation as their currencies became convertible. The establishment of such a self-qualifying principle would get around the "exclusive club" aspect and eliminate the objection to the plan under the second guidepost mentioned above.

Actually, however, I cannot see what would be achieved by such a plan that could not be accomplished much more easily by simply extending automatic drawing rights under the IMF beyond the gold tranche. Such rights might, for example, be extended through the first credit tranche; i.e., up to the point where the Fund's holdings of a country's currency were equal to 125 percent of its quota. Not only would such an increase in automatic drawing rights provide a one-shot increase in effective reserves at the time it was adopted, but, in addition, such a change would mean that any future increases in quotas would add to effective reserves by an amount equal to 25 percent of the quota increase. If it was felt to be desirable to maintain the same volume of conditional drawing rights that are now available from the Fund, the upper limit on the Fund's holdings of a country's currency could be increased from the present 200 percent of its quota to 225 percent. If this were done, it would be necessary for the Fund to obtain access to addi-

---

(covered by a gold value guarantee and bearing a low rate of interest) against the pool of currencies established by similar deposits on the part of all participating countries. Further quantities of CRU's would be issued from time to time to provide for desired growth of world reserves. How such a plan would work would, in general, depend upon (a) the basis on which CRU's were issued; and (b) the way in which they were used after issuance.

tional resources from member countries to maintain the same balance between members' drawing rights and the Fund's foreign exchange resources that now exists.

In order to make such an increase in automatic drawing rights a successful means of increasing effective reserves, it would, of course, be necessary to obtain acceptance by participating countries of the principle that automatic drawing rights from the IMF are to be used regularly in the same way as "owned" reserves. It may be noted that an increase in automatic drawing rights through the first credit tranche of member countries' quotas would provide no additional immediately available reserves to those countries who had already borrowed beyond the first credit tranche so that the Fund's holdings of their currencies exceeded 125 percent of their quotas. Thus, the proposal would contain an automatic self-selecting mechanism which would limit the immediate benefits to countries that were not making extensive use of the Fund's resources. In order to make provision for continuous steady growth of world reserves, I can see no reason why provision could not be made for a general review of quotas more frequently than the 5-year intervals now provided for in the Articles of Agreement.

As a means of regulating the growth of reserves to meet the needs of a growing world economy, this simple proposal has much to recommend it. It would not, however, do anything to immobilize the existing overhang of official dollar claims. This problem might, however, be dealt with through the issuance by the United States of intermediate-term securities bearing a gold value guarantee. Such securities might be used to fund the existing overhang or a substantial part of it. The securities might contain a clause under which they would be redeemable at the Treasury if the holder country needed the proceeds to finance a balance-of-payments deficit. Interest could be paid at a rate sufficient to induce holders of a large portion of existing dollar balances to accept the securities. This rate would presumably be somewhat lower than the rate these holders would expect to earn on other investments during the life of the securities because of the protection against the risk of devaluation. Beyond the funding of the outstanding overhang of dollar balances, I can see no reason why the Treasury should not offer similar securities on a tap basis at interest rates adjusted to the current market as an investment for foreign official agencies which came into possession of dollars as a result of future U.S. deficits.

The unilateral issuance by the United States of a blanket gold guarantee that would be available to cover existing official dollar holdings—which is what this proposal amounts to—has never been regarded with favor by most U.S. officials. However, it is a very simple proposal which might serve to tie down the overhang of existing official dollar claims at a minimal cost to the U.S. Treasury. One objection that is sometimes raised against it is that if the United States should ever find it necessary to devalue the dollar, the compensation that would be required under the gold value guarantee would be excessively costly. In rebuttal of this argument, it should be recognized that dollar devaluation would be an incalculable shock to the entire international monetary system, and the institution of such a guarantee might substantially reduce the likelihood that it would ever be necessary. Moreover, even in the absence of a formal gold value guarantee, dollar devaluation without compensation to official holders would probably be regarded as a breach of faith on the part of the United States, particularly in relation to those countries, such as Canada and Japan, which have been holding a large proportion of their monetary reserves in the form of dollars rather than gold. Hence, if devaluation should become necessary, it might be judged appropriate to make some kind of restitution for losses to foreign official holders of dollar balances even in the absence of a preexisting formal guarantee. The other main argument against a unilateral blanket guarantee is that the offer of such a guarantee to official holders of dollars might be taken as a sign that the dollar was vulnerable and lead to a speculative run by private holders of dollar assets. This seems to me to be an exceedingly farfetched argument, although conceivably whether it had any foundation might depend upon the circumstances existing at the time the guarantee was offered. It might be best, for example, to unveil the guarantee plan at a time when the United States was experiencing no serious balance-of-payments difficulties. The gold value guarantee proposal seems to me to have sufficient merit to be worthy of serious consideration. Under the present system, the United States performs to a considerable extent the banking function for the international monetary system, and I can see no reason why in its banking role it should not provide the protection both to its own position and to the stability of the entire system that would be given by the issuance of obligations containing a gold value guarantee.

With respect to the appropriate level and rate of growth of world reserves, I would like to make two comments. First, in the present state of knowledge, I do not believe anyone can specify a rule that should govern reserve creation. The need for reserves in the future depends upon the magnitude, duration, and distribution of future balance-of-payments deficits, which depend in turn on the strength of the underlying forces producing such deficits and the speed of the adjustment mechanism in restoring equilibrium. These are matters that no one can predict. It is therefore necessary to adjust the supply of reserves to meet the requirements of the evolving situation on a more or less continuous basis. And under present arrangements, the speculative strains are so great that practically an unlimited supply of reserves must be available on a basis that speculators will regard as dependable in order to avoid the speculative ballooning of deficits and a runaway loss of such reserves as are available—note, for example, that despite the vast support already provided for sterling, a crisis still threatens.

Second, there is no close relationship between the quantity of international monetary reserves and the level of expenditures on goods and services. Almost none of the methods of creating additional reserves that have been proposed would involve the direct injection of reserves into the spending stream at the time they were created.[2] So far as I can see, the creation of reserves would generate inflationary pressure only if some of the recipient countries desired to follow a more expansionary internal policy but had been held back by a shortage of reserves which would not permit them to cover the balance-of-payments deficits that would result from the expansion. Creation of the additional reserves under circumstances in which no country's internal expansion was being held back by a lack of such reserves could be expected to have no immediate effect at all on aggregate demand in any country. Some discussions of the international monetary system seem to imply that if reserves are created at too rapid a pace, the world will immediately experience a soaring inflation. The quantity theory of money is of extremely dubious validity even as applied internally within a single country; it certainly has no direct application to international monetary reserves. Nor can I see any validity, at least as applied to the industrial countries, to the view that sometimes seems to be held that there always are a number of countries who are eagerly desirous of following a wildly inflationary internal policy and are only restrained from doing so by a lack of monetary reserves to cover the massive balance-of-payments deficits that would accompany such an inflation. On the contrary, as a general rule—to which there may, of course, be exceptions—I believe there is a strong

[2] Certain plans that create reserves by making development loans directly or indirectly to underdeveloped countries would constitute an exception: such countries would be likely to spend the proceeds of the loans on imports thus promptly injecting them into the world expenditure stream.

distaste for inflation based on its actual or presumed deleterious effects on the internal distribution of income and wealth and on the efficiency of the economy so that the opponents of inflation have quite sufficient influence on domestic policy in most countries and do not need the reinforcement that would be provided by a shortage of monetary reserves. Indeed, I believe the world is much more likely to suffer from a shortage than from an excess of reserves, and I therefore believe it is safer to err on the side of liberality in providing them.

B. Exchange-Rate Arrangements and the Problem of Private Speculation

As I have indicated, the instability of the present system is only partly due to the threat that hangs over reserve currency countries (especially the United States) as a result of the possibility of a drain on reserves resulting from a conversion of official claims. There is also a serious problem of private speculation—the curbing of which constitutes objective (2b) in the list given at the beginning of this section of the paper.

It seems to me that the adjustable peg exchange rate system that was established under the IMF has proved to be extremely unsatisfactory and has been a source of many of our recent international monetary difficulties. Exchange rates have to be either fixed or flexible; since we are unwilling to consider flexible exchange rates, the creation of a stable international monetary environment requires a vigorous effort to create a de facto system of fixed exchange rates. This can be accomplished only in the course of time if countries carefully avoid making any adjustments in exchange rates, thus gradually establishing confidence in existing parities. In order to accomplish this, it will be necessary to provide liberal supplies of monetary reserves and to take steps to shore up the adjustment mechanism.

Without advocating flexible exchange rates, which have (quite properly in my opinion) been ruled out of the discussion in these hearings, I wish to express my support for the establishment of a somewhat wider range of fluctuation of exchange rates around fixed parities than has recently been permitted. I would favor some widening of the margins of 1 percent either side of parity now permitted under the IMF rules. But even if such a change is not made, I believe that full advantage should at least be taken of the present 2-percent margin of fluctuation that is permitted. It has been common practice in the last few years for countries to stabilize exchange rates within much narrower margins than this.[3] If exchange rates were permitted to fluctuate at least within the full range of 2 percent now permitted, there would be somewhat greater risk in speculating against a currency than is presently the case. Indeed, if full confidence could gradually be established in the fixity of existing parities, even modest fluctuations around these parities within fixed limits might be expected to generate a stabilizing type of speculation such as took place in earlier times under the gold standard. For example, if exchange parities are fixed and the exchange rate rests at the lower limit of its permissible margin of fluctuation, the only possible direction in which it can move is upward. Under these conditions, an expectation of appreciation of the exchange rate might be expected to attract some speculative inflow of capital.

C. Improving the Techniques of Adjustment

Under a regime of fixed exchange rates, the traditional "rules of the game" for maintaining or restoring balance-of-payments equilibrium call for the adoption of a deflationary domestic policy by deficit countries and an expansionary policy by surplus countries. However, such a prescription seems plainly unacceptable today. Nearly all countries attach overriding importance to the achievement of domestic price-employment goals, and any substantial departure from these goals is usually politically unacceptable and in some cases plainly socially undesirable as well.

The problem is to find an arrangement which will leave individual countries reasonably free to regulate domestic demand so as to achieve their desired price-employment goals while at the same time providing some means of maintaining a reasonably satisfactory balance-of-payments position. I believe a significant improvement in this respect might be achieved by a more flexible and coordinated use of the instruments of monetary and fiscal policy.

The idea would be to develop a policy arrangement under which the Western industrial countries would agree to rely primarily on flexible fiscal policy, implemented chiefly through tax adjustments, to regulate internal demand to achieve domestic goals. Monetary policy would then be assigned the task of maintaining balance-of-payments equilibrium by establishing interest rates at levels which would induce a sufficient inflow or outflow of private capital to

[3] See R. Z. Aliber, "The Management of the Dollar in International Finance," Princeton Studies in International Finance No. 13 (Princeton, N.J.: Princeton University Press, 1964).

cover the deficit or surplus on current account (including Govern-ment military and foreign aid transactions) that would occur at target levels of income and employment.

Machinery would need to be set up to provide careful interna-tional coordination of the monetary policies of participating coun-tries. The objective would be to establish a matrix of interest rate differentials among countries which would be sufficient to achieve approximate overall equilibrium in the balance of payments of each country. Marginal adjustments would need to be made in interest rates from time to time to preserve equilibrium in the face of changes in underlying conditions. Strong efforts would be needed in order to avoid competitive increases in interest rates which would raise the general level or rates without contributing to the main-tenance of payments equilibrium. It would be highly desirable that steps be taken to increase the freedom of capital movements—es-pecially of long-term funds—in order to make capital flows adjust more sensitively to interest rate changes.

Under such a system, the mix of monetary and fiscal policies would be used to achieve internal and external equilibrium simul-taneously. The following table shows the direction in which taxes and interest rates should be adjusted in various situations.

Internal demand	Balance-of-payments position	Appropriate policy action
Below target	Deficit	Raise interest rates and lower taxes
Do	Surplus	Lower interest rates and/or lower taxes
Above target	Deficit	Raise interest rates and/or raise taxes
Do	Surplus	Lower interest rates and raise taxes

For example, if a country was experiencing excessive unemploy-ment (internal demand below target) and a balance-of-payments deficit at the same time, it would raise interest rates by central bank action to attract an inflow of capital. This rise in interest rates would by itself depress domestic demand still further below the op-timal level. Taxes should therefore be reduced to a sufficient degree not only to offset the restrictive effect of higher interest rates but beyond that to increase demand toward the desired level. By a sequence of marginal adjustments of this kind, it should be possible to approximate the desired employment level with a reasonably viable overall balance-of-payments position.

Of course, changes in Government expenditures could be employed rather than tax changes, but tax policy seems potentially a much more flexible instrument for making such fine adjustments. However, the administration of tax policy would have to be improved to permit more rapid adjustments than are now possible, not only in the United States but in many of the European countries. This might be accomplished here by giving the President some authority to initiate adjustments in personal income tax rates in accordance with the proposal advanced by the Commission on Money and Credit in its 1961 report or that recommended by the Council of Economic Advisers in its January 1962 annual report. Or, alternatively, some provision might be worked out for accelerated congressional action on tax proposals following an agreed pattern when such proposals were submitted by the President. No doubt the political difficulties of obtaining greater flexibility in fiscal policy would be substantial in some countries. But this problem will almost certainly have to be tackled anyway, because monetary policy is already sufficiently hamstrung by the balance-of-payments problem to make it an ineffective instrument of domestic policy in many countries. More use will have to be made of fiscal policy to achieve domestic goals even if no effort is made to achieve such far-reaching international coordination of policies as that described above.

One of the objections to this proposal might be that the use of the monetary-fiscal mix as a means of dealing with the balance of payments precludes its use to regulate capital formation for economic growth. Indeed, a country which experienced a chronic balance-of-payments deficit on current account might find that the high interest rates needed to attract capital to cover the deficit would deter investment and productivity improvement thereby weakening its competitive position still further. To overcome this difficulty and enable the country to regulate capital formation and thereby influence growth in the face of the adjustments in interest rates that would be needed to maintain balance-of-payments equilibrium, a second fiscal instrument could be employed. The best possibility for this purpose would probably be an investment tax credit, along the lines of the 7-percent credit introduced in the United States in the Revenue Act of 1962. The rate of tax credit could be adjusted periodically as seemed desirable—as, for example, to offset the restrictive effect on investment of a rise in domestic interest rates called for by balance-of-payments considerations. It is in principle possible to have—within limits at least—any desired level of investment in combination with any desired level of interest rates through appropriate use of fiscal incentives to shift the investment demand schedule.

It should be understood that this proposal for using flexible adjustments in the mix of monetary and fiscal policies is incapable of providing a full and permanent solution to the problem of balance-of-payments adjustment. If a country were to follow persistently an internal policy which caused its price level to rise too rapidly so that its competitive position deteriorated steadily, it would be forced to attract increasingly large inflows of capital to cover expanding current account deficits. This could scarcely continue indefinitely—for one thing, it would lead in the course of time to steadily increasing interest payments on the accumulating indebtedness, which would enlarge still further the current account deficit. What the proposal might hope to accomplish, however, would be to provide time to carry out the necessary underlying adjustments in an orderly way while preserving a reasonably viable balance-of-payments position in the meantime.

III. CONCLUDING COMMENTS

I have tried to outline the shortcomings of the present international monetary system and to suggest some ways of dealing with them. The most important point I have tried to make is that a coordinated attack on all the problems is necessary if success is to be achieved in improving the system. It may be noted that a coordinated program is likely to have some desirable cross effects that were not properly taken into account in my exposition. For example, a successful attack on the problem of speculative instability can be expected to reduce the size of balance-of-payments deficits and make the task to be performed by the adjustment mechanism less arduous than it would otherwise be. And, at the same time, an improvement of the adjustment mechanism should reduce speculative pressures and make them easier to cope with.

I want to emphasize that there is no program of international monetary reform—at least that can be discussed within the ground rules established by this subcommittee—that can "solve" the problems of balance-of-payments adjustment. If we were to succeed in putting into effect a program along the lines suggested by me—or I daresay by any of the other witnesses appearing at these hearings—we would still be faced with the same kinds of hard choices and tough decisions we have had to make during the last 4 or 5 years. The problems might be mitigated slightly but their fundamental nature would not be altered. It would be a mistake to expect miracles from international monetary reform. In fact, as I have tried to suggest, we should be extremely careful in this matter, because some of the reform proposals might make our problems more difficult rather than easier.

Having adhered sedulously to the ground rules of these hearings up to this point, I want to make a closing comment concerning flexible exchange rates. What we are really faced with is a situation in which there are more policy goals than there are policy instruments available to achieve them. As is widely recognized by economists, this is a situation that always creates a dilemma. If we were willing to give up the goal of fixed exchange rates, it might be possible to find a real solution to the problem.[4] While I can understand the fact that this possibility was ruled out of the discussion in these hearings, I hope it will not be dismissed completely.

[4] I have argued elsewhere that there are only two ways of achieving a fundamental solution: (1) to give up the goal of fixed exchange rates and adopt flexible rates, and (2) to give up the goal of national sovereignty over economic policy and adopt full economic integration as the individual States and regions have done in the United States. These solutions can be combined in a system of integrated regional blocks of countries with flexible exchange rates between blocs. See my paper, "Are There Enough Policy Tools?" *American Economic Review, Papers and Proceedings*, LX, May 1965, pp. 208–220.

PART VI-B // REFORMING THE INTERNATIONAL MONETARY SYSTEM

ROBERT TRIFFIN

THE LONG-RUN EVOLUTION OF OUR INTERNATIONAL MONETARY SYSTEM

43

A. A SINGLE RESERVE CENTER

The long-term consolidation of the international reserve system, and the adaptation of international reserve creation to the full, noninflationary growth potential of the world economy, would obviously be enormously facilitated by the adoption of a single clearing and reserve Center for national central banks. Each central bank would hold all of its monetary reserves—except for moderate, day-to-day working balances—in the form of international deposits with such a center.

Central banks would acquire, at the start, their initial reserve deposit with the Center by transferring to it their outstanding holdings of gold and other convertible reserve assets (see D below).

B. CASH SETTLEMENTS

The Center would then operate as a clearing agency for all subsequent international settlements not cleared by the private exchange market itself. Three types of operations would come under this heading:

1. Direct settlements among central banks would be effected by

Reprinted from Robert Triffin, "The Long-Run Evolution of Our International Monetary System," *The Evolution of the International Monetary System: Historical Reappraisal and Future Perspective*, Part III, Princeton Studies in International Finance No. 12, International Finance Section, Princeton University, 1964, pp. 30–42.

mere bookkeeping transfers, debiting the account of the payor, and crediting the account of the payee.

2. Stabilization interventions by central banks on the exchange markets involve either the purchase, or the sale, of foreign exchange by the bank concerned. The foreign currencies needed to reconstitute working balances depleted by such sales would be bought from the Center, through corresponding debits in the buying bank's reserve account. Conversely, foreign currencies—in excess of working balances—accumulated by a central bank in opposite stabilization interventions would be transferred to the Center and credited to the depositing bank's reserve account.

The reserve account of the central bank whose currency had been sold to the Center would be debited by the amount transferred. In the opposite case when a currency is bought from the Center, two alternative techniques could be considered. The simplest one would be for all central banks to authorize the Center to sell their currency directly against corresponding credits to their reserve account. The other would be for the Center to accumulate and maintain adequate working balances in the major currencies used in fact in such stabilization operations.

3. A third type of cash transaction would relate to the Center's purchases and sales of gold, and depend very much on the future policies jointly adopted among the world's monetary authorities regarding the suspension or continuation of the support extended by them up to now to the stabilization of gold-metal prices.

Under the radical reforms envisaged above, gold could well be dispensed with a medium of reserve accumulation, by the Center as well as by the national central banks. The essential requirement of a national currency is to be generally acceptable in payment within the country's borders. Such general acceptability can be elicited by other means than convertibility in gold metal, in one case as well as in the other, and we shall examine below how this could be done.

The continued guarantee of stable gold prices by the Center, or the world central banks, would then be tantamount to a decision to continue the traditional support given to gold-metal prices by the purchases of the monetary authorities. The main arguments in favor of such a policy would be.

1. to take advantage of the continued popular illusion that gold reserves alone can constitute an effective barrier against inflation and a proper backing for the liabilities of central banks—or of the proposed Center itself;

2. to avoid the bookkeeping losses that a demonetization of gold would almost certainly entail;

3. to avert a sudden disruption of the economies of the major gold-producing countries.

None of these arguments is very powerful, and the latter two problems could be solved, in a different manner, on their own merits. On the other hand, the continuation of gold support prices might well require very large purchases of gold, and unleash inflationary increases in world reserve assets and monetary liabilities, if the contemplated reform were to trigger large gold dishoarding by speculators. This would not be inconceivable, once people fully realized that such a reform had equipped central banks with ample means to dispense with gold altogether, and—at the very least—to rule out any probability of an increase in world gold prices in the foreseeable future.

If the decision were nevertheless adopted to support the world gold price at its present level, official interventions in the private gold market could be conducted either by the Center itself, or by the central banks. In the latter case, central banks would sell to the Center—against corresponding credits to their reserve account—any gold purchased in the course of such stabilization operations; and they would buy from the Center—against corresponding debits to their account—the gold they might need to sell.

Until the U.S.S.R. and the countries associated with it decided to join the Center, any of the techniques described above would strengthen the Western world against any possible abuse of the large gold stock—and gold production—of these countries for disruptive interventions, of an economic-warfare character, in the Western gold markets.

C. CREDIT OPERATIONS

The major central banks, at least, will probably wish to continue to increase their reserve levels—in future years as well as in the past—in order to facilitate the maintenance of international convertibility, at stable rates of exchange, of the rising amounts of their national currency issues needed to support expanding levels of production. The mechanism of reserve creation should adjust to this fact and promote a continuous adaptation of the world's reserve pool to the demand for reserves associated with feasible rates of noninflationary growth in world trade and production.

Under the reform suggested here, all—if gold price support is abandoned—or a large portion, at least, of the necessary reserve increases would have to be derived from the progressive expansion of the Center's loan-and-investment portfolio. The pace of overall increases should be determined jointly, in the light of—and in such a way as to combat or moderate—discernible inflationary or deflationary pressures of a worldwide character.

Prospective surplus countries, however, will probably want to incorporate in Treaty form some guarantees against inflationary abuses of the Center's lending potential, since indeed this potential would otherwise be unlimited.[1] Such a Treaty might specify, for instance, a presumptive ceiling of 3 to 5 percent in any twelve-month period, on the net expansion of the Center's global assets and liabilities. Such a ceiling would not necessarily be reached in any period of time—particularly at times of inflationary pressures—but it could not, in any case, be exceeded, except by qualified voting majorities of two-thirds, three-fourths, etc., of the total voting power.

Within these broad limitations, individual loan and investment operations would be designed to support mutually acceptable policies of member countries against temporary balance-of-payments pressures, thus providing a powerful stimulus for the long-run harmonization of members' policies, and the avoidance of unnecessary recourse to exchange restrictions, devaluation, or deflation by the deficit countries.

Desirable balance-of-payments disciplines upon countries following persistently inflationary policies would therefore be maintained, and indeed reinforced. No country could escape them through the automatic, but erratic and precarious, access to international borrowing enjoyed in the past by the reserve-currency countries—a type of borrowing the haphazard use and liquidation of which could unleash at any time highly disruptive forces upon these countries themselves, upon the rest of the world, and upon the stability of the international gold-exchange standard.

The nature of the Center's lending operations would have to be adapted to the character of the resources used by it. Since its overall portfolio would be called upon to expand continually—although at

[1] Excessive lending to deficit-prone countries would would merely increase *pari passu* the assets and liabilities of the Center. Subsequent drawings on their deposits by the borrowers could only reshuffle the Center's liabilities among its depositors, without producing any decline in overall liabilities. A worldwide Center would therefore be exempt from the discipline exercised upon a national central bank by national balance-of-payments deficits, in the same way as a national central bank can elude the discipline exercised upon commercial banks by losses of deposits from the more expansionary to the less expansionary banks of the system.

a variable rate—over the years to come, but rarely—if ever—to be substantially contracted, some of its loans and investments might be granted in theory for extended maturities. They might even take a form similar to that of the famed British "consols," without any repayment date whatsoever, but on which interest would be paid indefinitely by the borrowers. This would make it easier to channel the world's thirst for reserves into long-term development financing of the countries most in need of such assistance.

Yet, direct long-term loans to, or investments in, the underdeveloped countries by the Center may well be regarded as unadvisable as well as unnecessary in practice. They would, first of all, have to overcome powerful taboos in the financial community whose "orthodox" canons, inspired by commercial-banking criteria, would damn any long-term assets as inappropriate backing for the short-term liabilities of a monetary institution. Secondly, even though its total portfolio would not be subject to the threat of sudden and massive contraction, the Center should remain able to reshuffle its loans and investments among members, in order to counteract undesirable capital movements and other short-term disturbances in the international balance-of-payments pattern. Thirdly, long-term investments require a very different type of knowledge and expertise than those that should be relevant to stabilization interventions in the exchange market.

The bulk of the Center's assistance to long-term development financing should thus, in all probability, be channelled through—and cushioned by—intermediary institutions, specialized in such long-term lending. The Center might, for instance, distribute its investment portfolio between marketable obligations of international institutions, such as the International Bank for Reconstruction and Development, and other short-term or medium-term investments in the major financial centers—New York, London, Paris, Frankfurt, Amsterdam, etc.—enabling these to engage more boldly and actively in long-term lending, in the knowledge that temporary pressures on the country's reserves would be offset by a reshuffling of the Center's own investment portfolio.

Taken in conjunction with one another, the credit criteria suggested above would essentially tend to recreate some of the basic features of the adjustment mechanism of the nineteenth-century gold standard. Vast amounts of private long-term lending then cushioned, for long periods of time, the current-account deficits of developing countries and made more bearable and acceptable the discipline exercised upon monetary policy by residual balance-of-payments pressures. Fifty years of monetary and economic instability and the constant threat of governmental interference in private contracts have paralyzed, or perverted, much of these private capital flows in modern times. They can be revived, in part, and redirected by official policies designed to stabilize the international framework in which they take place. They have, in addition, been supplemented by official lending which can itself be further encouraged, and better distributed as between the U.S. and other countries, by the international underwriting of monetary stabilization policies.

Similarly, concerted international action is necessary today to harmonize relative rates of monetary and banking expansion in such a way as to preserve long-run balance in the international pattern of payments, without unnecessary recourse to trade or exchange restrictions or exchange-rate readjustments. Market pressures, arising from deposit losses and cash settlements by the more expansionist to the less expansionist banks, usually sufficed, in the nineteenth century, to ensure such harmonization among *individual* banks—and therefore, among national banking systems—*irrespective of the existence of national political borders.* This ceased to be true as:

1. Commercial banks' cash assets progressively shifted from internationally acceptable commodity moneys—gold and/or silver—to nationally issued credit money; *and*

2. Central banks' credit policies and monetary issues became more and more responsive to a variety of national objectives—such as price stabilization and satisfactory employment levels and growth rates—competing with, and often overriding, their initial concern with the maintenance of international reserve levels fully adequate to preserve full convertibility of their own liabilities into gold or foreign exchange, at stable rates.

International consultation among responsible national monetary authorities has thus become the only effective channel for the development of compatible and mutually supporting policies, and the minimization of unnecessary recourse to internationally disruptive, contagious, and mutually defeating policy measures. Unilateral action by the deficit countries alone to eliminate rapidly any emerging balance-of-payments disequilibria—whether lasting or temporary—often contributes to the unnecessary adoption and spread of deflation, devaluation and/or trade and exchange restrictions among member countries. Concerted action by surplus and deficit countries alike can certainly offer far more attractive, even though often slower-acting, means to correct such disequilibria over time, with a minimum of disruption of the national economies concerned. Conditional access to the Center's lending resources would (1) provide an added stimulus to such policy harmonization, and deterrent to unilateral action, (2) supplement the deficit country's ability to finance residual, temporary deficits through the depletion of its independent monetary reserves, and (3) discourage speculative capital movements which might otherwise create further, and possibly unbearable, drains on such reserves.[2]

D. CONSOLIDATION OF OUTSTANDING CURRENCY-RESERVE BALANCES

The transition from the old system to the new would, of course, involve a once-and-for-all type of credit operations determined by the Treaty itself, i.e. the transfer to the Center of the large currency-reserve balances now held by member countries.

The Center would, as a result, initiate its operations with large credit claims on the United States and the United Kingdom, inherited from many years of functioning of the gold-exchange standard. There would be no reason to liquidate systematically such investments, long incorporated into the international reserve system itself. Provisions for their amortization—through equivalent debits to the debtor's reserve account—should be limited in the following manner:

1. Voluntary amortization, at the request of the debtor;

2. Compensatory amortization up to the amounts of current reserve increases bringing their overall level above some agreed— "normal" (?)—ratio to the country's imports; and, possibly, if regarded as necessary,

3. An optional right for the Center to request additional amortization by no more than x percent—5 percent, for example—of the country's outstanding debt balance; such option, however, to be exercised only

   (a) when deemed necessary to meet other countries' legitimate requests for assistance without expanding the global loan and investment portfolio of the Center; and

   (b) when compatible with the preservation of an adequate reserve level and the pursuit of internationally acceptable policies by the debtor.

E. INTERNATIONAL GUARANTEES

All the claims and debts of the Center should obviously carry adequate guarantees against unilateral inconvertibility or exchange-

[2] Complementary—and partly alternative—measures aiming at a better adaptation of the world reserve pool itself to non-inflationary growth requirements of the world economy are amply discussed in other sections of this paper.

devaluation decisions, or default by the debtors. Some common unit of account, adapted from the EPU unit of account, could be used for that purpose in all Center transactions, and embody in effect an exchange guarantee in terms of whichever currency remains most stable in the future. Alternatively, this exchange guarantee could be expressed in terms of a weighted average of the major currencies used in world trade and payments.

Guarantees against default could be provided in two ways:

1. Through a commitment of all members to channel, as far as possible, through the defaulting country's account with the Center, all payments due to it until the default is made up;

2. Through a geographical distribution of the Center's gold assets, approximating, on a *pro rata* basis, the pattern of the Center's deposit liabilities to its members.

Such guarantees would indeed erect stronger safeguards against defaults than any ever devised in past international lending operations.

F. SURRENDERS OF NATIONAL SOVEREIGNTY?

Proposals such as these are lightly shrugged off in many circles as involving revolutionary surrenders of national sovereignty to a world-wide "super-bank," incapable in fact of discharging its responsibilities without the full backing of a supranational world government. The money created by a super-bank would be the most high powered ever generated by a man-made institution, yet it would have no supporting super-government to make good on its debts or claims. . . . Simply to establish the super-bank would require all countries of the world to give up their present reserves and accept instead the fiat issue of a super-authority existing without a super-state.[3] These emotional slogans bear little or no relation to the concrete content of the long term proposals developed above. They are even less relevant to the more modest suggestions for short or medium-term negotiations that will be outlined in the following section of this study, and which would merely streamline and rationalize the

[3] Robert V. Roosa, "Assuring the Free World's Liquidity," *Business Review Supplement*, Federal Reserve Bank of Philadelphia, September 1962, p. 8. More concrete objections are developed in the following paragraphs of the text, which quote the conflicts and disturbances which might arise from sudden shifts by individual countries from international deposits to national currency holdings or to gold metal. This might better be formulated, however, as a valid stricture on the present gold-exchange standard than as a criticism of proposals specifically designed to protect the international monetary system against such unnecessary sources of disturbance.

technical provisions endowing the International Monetary Fund with whatever level of lending capacity is deemed appropriate by its members, and is now derived from equivalent, but far more rigid, arbitrary and cumbersome capital subscriptions and other national commitments . . .

Reserve holders would retain, under the plan, far more control over the size and use of future accretions to world credit reserves than they have had—or now have—over the size and use of the IOU's dropped by the reserve-currency centers into the world's reserve pool. They would, it is true, renounce their present right to sudden and massive cashing of their credit reserves into gold metal, but they well know that such a right has already become largely theoretical and could not be exercised in fact on a large scale without bringing to an end the effective convertibility of the currencies involved, and without causing the collapse of the international gold-exchange standard itself.

Prospective borrowers, on the other hand, would in no way be forced to accept the advice—and the investments—offered them by the Center. They could refuse both, if they wish, particularly as the Center could not invest in their market without obtaining from the national authorities in charge the exchange guarantees described under E above.

Present reserve borrowers, moreover, would regain—through the transfer to the Center of their outstanding indebtedness to central banks—a degree of control over future monetary policies strongly handicapped today by the volatile character of this indebtedness.

Neither would the joint consultations and decisions relating to the Center's investments be revolutionary in character nor involve necessarily the setting up of supranational institutions or voting rules. The IMF and the EPU, for instance, have long functioned essentially along the lines suggested here without raising any objection to their supranational character.

Finally, the Center could hardly be described as a world central bank, since its reserve liabilities would circulate only among the national central banks themselves and these would retain full control over, and responsibility for, their currency issues, each within its own national territory. One consequence of this is that exchange readjustments could in no way be ruled out, and would indeed prove imperative at times for countries which failed to harmonize their monetary policies with those prevalent in the world community.

This raises a broad question which cannot be adequately explored within the confines of the present paper, i.e., the proper scope of institutional commitments to exchange-rate stability.

G. STABLE VERSUS FLUCTUATING RATES

This question is usually discussed in abstract terms as if the same solution were always advisable for all countries and at all times. I would prefer to answer it in terms very similar to those given to it in a recent paper of Ronald I. McKinnon.[4]

I have myself long expressed a preference for stable exchange rates, subject to readjustments only in the case of obvious failure to preserve adequate cost competitiveness for long-run equilibrium in the country's balance of payments at optimum levels of employment, economic growth, and trade and exchange liberalization. This preference was based on three main arguments.[5]

1. Stable exchange rates tend to spread and even out among the trading countries the inflationary and deflationary gaps arising from differential rates of national monetary and financial expansion. Balance-of-payments disequilibria and changes in monetary reserves provide, under this system, an alternative outlet to the development of domestic pressures—upward in the more expansionist countries, and downward in the less expansionist ones—upon prices and employment, and do indeed bear a far closer relationship to differential rates of monetary expansion than to differential changes in national price and cost levels.[6] The latter tend in fact to be kept roughly in line with one another through the impact of competition in internationally traded goods—and particularly by export competition in third markets—as long as domestic policies can be readjusted in time to avoid devaluation or trade and exchange restrictions, isolating national price levels from one another.

Freely floating rates—à la Friedman—would "bottle up" within each country's border the inflationary or deflationary pressures arising from every expansionist or contractionist error in domestic policies. Exchange-rate fluctuations would absorb the full brunt of the disequilibria formerly cushioned by reserve gains or losses, and help preserve competitiveness in each country's current-account

[4] "Optimum World Monetary Arrangement and the Dual Currency System," *Banca Nazionale del Lavoro Quarterly Review*, December 1963, pp. 366–396. See also a brief communication on "Optimum Currency Areas" in *The American Economic Review*, September 1963, pp. 717–725.

[5] See *Gold and the Dollar Crisis* (New Haven, Conn.: Yale University Press, 1960), pp. 82–86.

[6] See Robert Triffin and Herbert G. Grubel, "The Adjustment Mechanism to Differential Rates of Monetary Expansion Among the Countries of the European Economic Community," *Review of Economics and Statistics*, November 1962, pp. 486–491.

transactions; but they would also lift the barrier previously erected by stable exchange rates against divergent movements in national price and cost levels.

The upward flexibility of wage rates would, moreover, tend to sanction with permanent and irreversible wage increases any inflationary mistakes or mishaps in monetary and credit policies, and any consequent increases in foreign exchange rates, import costs, and consumers' prices; while deflationary errors would be unlikely to result in parallel, and offsetting, downward wage adjustments in a modern economy. Freely floating rates could hardly fail, therefore, to introduce a permanent bias toward currency depreciation—at least in terms of goods, if all countries adopted the system—and to elicit from Friedman's highly farsighted speculators one-way flights from the national currency into equities, real assets, gold, and/or foreign exchange, rather than alternating, and "stabilizing" capital inflows and outflows. Such de-stabilizing capital movements might, it is true, still be dubbed "equilibrating," but merely in the sense of accelerating the adjustment of exchange rates to price and cost disparities fostered by the system itself, and which might have been avoided under a system of stable exchange rates.

2. Secondly, "managed" floating rates—à la Meade—are too often advocated as though each country could determine by itself a desired rate in respect to all other countries. Exchange rates, however, express a relation between *several* currencies. Will the sterling-dollar rate, for instance, be abandoned by the United States to British management, or by the United Kingdom to U.S. management? And what will happen if the countries involved take a different view of the "desirable" rate between their currencies? (Meade himself is, of course, perfectly logical in his proposal, and recognizes that it involves the surrender of such management, by all countries, to an *International* Equalization Account).

3. Finally, I doubt whether floating rates can really provide, in the long run, a viable bridge between persistently divergent national monetary policies. They are far more likely to be a form of escapism, for which other and better methods could be substituted in the case of merely temporary lapses from responsible monetary management, and which would merely end in currency collapse in the case of protracted inflationary developments.

The spectacular growth and success of European monetary cooperation and policy harmonization since World War II seems to me to demonstrate the feasibility of an alternative path, far more deserving of support than the advocacy of exchange-rate-flexibility palliatives to monetary nationalism.

Yet, I would agree that these agreements are particularly applicable to the case of exchange relations between relatively small, highly open and competitive economies, capable of developing a satisfactory—and, in this case, highly desirable—degree of monetary cooperation and policy harmonization with one another. They are far less applicable to the exchange relations between larger countries, or groups of countries, which, because their external transactions are dwarfed by the size of their internal markets, are far better able to conduct effective monetary policies on their own, and are therefore far less interested and willing to subordinate their freedom of action to international consultation and effective policy harmonization.

Even in this case, however, the elimination of national currencies as an international reserve medium would remain a necessary prerequisite for the successful implementation and functioning of exchange-rate flexibility, particularly in the case of the present reserve-center countries.

H. WHETHER AND WHEN?

So-called realists will merely shrug their shoulders at the above proposals and dismiss them with the simple word: "Utopia!" They will prefer to "build directly upon the existing payments procedures to which governments and individuals are already well accustomed."[7] In the words of Erich Fromm, "it is, indeed, one of the irrationalities of human nature that we are prone to seek for easier, short-term solutions because we are afraid of the difficulties of the fundamental and real solutions. But in individual as in social life, it is the logic of facts that determines reality, not the logic of wishful thinking."[8]

This is why I have little doubt about the inevitability of a continued evolution of our international monetary institutions in a direction so clearly charted by the historical development of national monetary systems in every country of the world, and by similar trends already perceptible in the changing structure of the international reserve system itself over the last half century.

In every country, "commodity money" has been gradually displaced by "credit money." . . . Credit money remained at first unorganized, and its creation—or destruction—abandoned to the uncoordinated decisions and policies of multiple issue and deposit banks. The instability of such a system prompted the development of national central banks. These did not replace and eliminate pre-

[7] Robert V. Roosa, *op. cit.*, p. 12.
[8] Erich Fromm, *May Man Prevail?* (New York, 1961), pp. 207–208.

vious institutions, but assumed initially centralized clearing and reserve functions, out of which further instruments for policy co-ordination and orientation of bank credit and monetary expansion developed gradually over the years. As in the case of other human institutions, this evolution was rarely blueprinted in advance through conscious planning. It came, in most cases, as the unforeseen consequence of "short-term" expedients, adopted to meet pressing problems and crises, but which then developed a life of their own through the internal logic of institutional adaptation to man's changing environment.

Speaking of the development of the gold standard itself, Jacques Mertens noted that:

Most of those interventions do not flow from any clearly planned monetary policy and objectives. In general, the authorities intervene only in case of difficulties, during periods of monetary troubles. Time is then of the essence, and action is most often limited to partial and temporary measures. . . . What emerges are compromise solutions along the path of least resistance, whose merit in the eyes of the administrators is that they do not commit them in the future, but leave them a free hand to determine later final decisions whose timing is always postponed. It has certainly been one of the most tenacious illusions of the executive power to believe that by postponing decisions, by cumulating temporary expedients and half-measures, it retained its freedom of action. Have we not seen, on the contrary, that repeatedly and without wishing it, administrations have put their finger in the cog and have found themselves dragged on, against their will, toward unexpected results by measures which they considered as totally secondary or purely temporary?[9]

The displacement of "commodity money" by "credit money," in national monetary systems, finds an exact parallel in the incipient, but fast growing, displacement of "commodity reserves" by "credit reserves" in the international field. The proportion of credit reserves to total reserves has grown, for the countries of the Paris Club, from about 3 percent in 1885 and 7 percent in 1913 to 13 percent in 1949, 21 percent in 1957, and 28 percent in 1962. . . .

For the world at large, but excluding the two reserve-center countries of the gold-exchange standard, credit reserves totalled, in September 1963, $26.7 billion out of total reserves of $48.1 billion, i.e., more than 55 percent, as against less than 45 percent for gold itself.[10]

[9] Jacques E. Mertens, *La Naissance et le Développement de l'Étalon-Or* (Louvain and Paris, 1944), pp. 356–357.
[10] Calculated from pp. 15, 17 and 18 of the February 1964 issue of *International Financial Statistics*.

While the bulk of these credit reserves are still in the form of national currencies, a modest but growing portion is already held in the form of deposits with the IMF—under the name of "gold tranches,"—and national currency holdings themselves are becoming stabilized, little by little, by informal agreements, such as those long in effect in the sterling area and those more recently negotiated by the United States with the major dollar holders of Western Europe.

The main question facing us is not whether this evolution will continue over the sweep of history, but whether the international agreements necessary to that effect will be negotiated in time to avert further crises, such as that which swept away nearly overnight the "credit component" of the 1931 international reserves and brought about a protracted collapse of the international monetary system.

MILTON FRIEDMAN

FLEXIBLE EXCHANGE RATES

44

Discussions of U.S. policy with respect to international payments tend to be dominated by our immediate balance-of-payments difficulties. I should like today to approach the question from a different, and I hope more constructive, direction. Let us begin by asking ourselves not merely how we can get out of our present difficulties but

Reprinted from "Statement by Milton Friedman," *Contingency Planning for U.S. International Monetary Policy*, statements by private economists submitted to the Committe on International Exchange and Payments of the Joint Economic Committee, 89th Cong., 2d Sess., 1966, pp. 30–36. This statement, with minor differences, was originally made before the Joint Economic Committee during 1963. See "The International Monetary System: Functioning and Possible Reforms," *United States Balance of Payments*, Hearings Before the Joint Economic Committee, 88th Cong., 1st Sess., Part 3, Nov. 12–15, 1963, pp. 451–459.

instead how we can fashion our international payments system so that it will best serve our needs for the long pull; how we can solve not merely *this* balance-of-payments problem but *the* balance-of-payments problem.

A shocking and indeed, disgraceful feature of the present situation is the extent to which our frantic search for expedients to stave off balance-of-payments pressures has led us, on the one hand, to sacrifice major national objectives; and, on the other, to give enormous power to officials of foreign governments to affect what should be purely domestic matters. Foreign payments amount to only some 5 percent of our total national income. Yet they have become a major factor in nearly every national policy.

I believe that a system of floating exchange rates would solve the balance-of-payments problem for the United States far more effectively than our present arrangements. Such a system would use the flexibility and efficiency of the free market to harmonize our small foreign trade sector with both the rest of our massive economy and the rest of the world; it would reduce problems of foreign payments to their proper dimensions and remove them as a major consideration in governmental policy about domestic matters and as a major preoccupation in international political negotiations; it would foster our national objectives rather than be an obstacle to their attainment.

To indicate the basis for this conclusion, let us consider the national objective with which our payments system is most directly connected: the promotion of a healthy and balanced growth of world trade, carried on, so far as possible, by private individuals and private enterprises with minimum intervention by governments. This has been a major objective of our whole postwar international economic policy, most recently expressed in the Trade Expansion Act of 1962. Success would knit the free world more closely together, and, by fostering the international division of labor, raise standards of living throughout the world, including the United States.

Suppose that we succeed in negotiating far-reaching reciprocal reductions in tariffs and other trade barriers with the Common Market and other countries.[1] Such reductions will expand trade in general but clearly will have different effects on different industries. The demand for the products of some will expand, for others contract. This is a phenomenon we are familiar with from our internal development. The capacity of our free enterprise system to adapt

[1] To simplify exposition I shall hereafter refer only to tariffs, letting these stand for the whole range of barriers to trade, including even the so-called "voluntary" limitation of exports.

quickly and efficiently to such shifts, whether produced by changes in technology or tastes, has been a major source of our economic growth. The only additional element introduced by international trade is the fact that different currencies are involved, and this is where the payment mechanism comes in; its function is to keep this fact from being an additional source of disturbance.

An all-around lowering of tariffs would tend to increase both our expenditures and our receipts in foreign currencies. There is no way of knowing in advance which increase would tend to be the greater and hence no way of knowing whether the initial effect would be toward a surplus or deficit in our balance of payments. What is clear is that we cannot hope to succeed in the objective of expanding world trade unless we can readily adjust to either outcome.[2]

Suppose then that the initial effect is to increase our expendtures on imports more than our receipts from exports. How could we adjust to this outcome?

One method of adjustment is to draw on reserves or borrow from abroad to finance the excess increase in imports. The obvious objection to this method is that it is only a temporary device, and hence can be relied on only when the disturbance is temporary. But that is not the major objection. Even if we had very large reserves or could borrow large amounts from abroad, so that we could continue this expedient for many years, it is a most undesirable one. We can see why if we look at physical rather than financial magnitudes.

The physical counterpart to the financial deficit is a reduction of employment in industries competing with imports that is larger than the concurrent expansion of employment in export industries. So long as the financial deficit continues, the assumed tariff reductions

[2] Many people concerned with our payments deficits hope that, since we are operating further from full capacity than Europe, we could supply a substantial increase in exports, whereas they could not. Implicitly, this assumes that European countries are prepared to see their surplus turned into a deficit, thereby contributing to the reduction of the deficits we have recently been experiencing in our balance of payments. Perhaps this would be the initial effect of tariff changes. But if the achievement of such a result is to be sine qua non of tariff agreement, we cannot hope for any significant reduction in barriers. We could be confident that exports would expand more than imports only if the tariff changes were one sided, indeed, with our trading partners making much greater reductions in tariffs than we make. Our major means of inducing other countries to reduce tariffs is to offer corresponding reductions in our tariff. More generally, there is little hope for continued and sizable liberalization of trade if liberalization is to be viewed simply as a device for correcting balance-of-payments difficulties. That way lies only backing and filling.

create employment problems. But it is no part of the aim of tariff reductions to create unemployment at home or to promote employment abroad. The aim is a balanced expansion of trade, with exports rising along with imports and thereby providing employment opportunities to offset any reduction in employment resulting from increased imports.

Hence, simply drawing on reserves or borrowing abroad is a most unsatisfactory method of adjustment.

Another method of adjustment is to lower U.S. prices relative to foreign prices, since this would stimulate exports and discourage imports. If foreign countries are accommodating enough to engage in inflation, such a change in relative prices might require merely that the United States keep prices stable or even that it simply keep them from rising as fast as foreign prices. But there is no necessity for foreign countries to be so accommodating, and we could hardly count on their being so accommodating. The use of this technique therefore involves a willingness to produce a decline in U.S. prices by tight monetary policy or tight fiscal policy or both. Given time, this method of adjustment would work. But in the interim, it would exact a heavy toll. It would be difficult or impossible to force down prices appreciably without producing a recession and considerable unemployment. To eliminate in the long run the unemployment resulting from the tariff changes, we should in the short run be creating cyclical unemployment. The cure might for a time be far worse than the disease.

This second method is therefore also most unsatisfactory. Yet these two methods—drawing on reserves and forcing down prices— are the only two methods available under our present international payment arrangements, which involve fixed exchange rates between the U.S. dollar and other currencies. Little wonder that we have so far made such disappointing progress toward the reduction of trade barriers, that our practice has differed so much from our preaching.

There is one other way and only one other way to adjust and that is by allowing (or forcing) the price of the U.S. dollar to fall in terms of other currencies. To a foreigner, U.S. goods can become cheaper in either of two ways—either because their prices in the U.S. fall in terms of dollars or because the foreigner has to give up fewer units of his own currency to acquire a dollar, which is to say, the price of the dollar falls. For example, suppose a particular U.S. car sells for $2,800 when a dollar costs 7 shillings, tuppence in British money (i.e., roughly £1 = $2.80). The price of the car is then £1,000 in British money. It is all the same to an Englishman—or even a Scotsman—whether the price of the car falls to $2,500 while the price of a dollar remains 7 shillings, tuppence, or alternatively, the price of the car remains $2,800, while the price of a dollar falls to 6 shillings, 5 pence (i.e., roughly £1 = $3.11). In either case, the car costs the Englishman £900 rather than £1,000, which is what matters to him. Similarly, foreign goods can become more expensive to an American in either of two ways—either because the price in terms of foreign currency rises or because he has to give up more dollars to acquire a given amount of foreign currency.

Changes in exchange rates can therefore alter the relative price of U.S. and foreign goods in precisely the same way as can changes in internal prices in the United States and in foreign countries. And they can do so without requiring anything like the same internal adjustments. If the initial effect of the tariff reductions would be to create a deficit at the former exchange rate (or enlarge an existing deficit or reduce an existing surplus) and thereby increase unemployment, this effect can be entirely avoided by a change in exchange rates which will produce a balanced expansion in imports and exports without interfering with domestic employment, domestic prices, or domestic monetary and fiscal policy. The pig can be roasted without burning down the barn.

The situation is, of course, entirely symmetrical if the tariff changes should initially happen to expand our exports more than our imports. Under present circumstances, we would welcome such a result, and conceivably, if the matching deficit were experienced by countries currently running a surplus, they might permit it to occur without seeking to offset it. In that case, they and we would be using the first method of adjustment—changes in reserves or borrowing. But again, if we had started off from an even keel, this would be an undesirable method of adjustment. On our side, we should be sending out useful goods and receiving only foreign currencies in return. On the side of our partners, they would be using up reserves and tolerating the creation of unemployment.

The second method of adjusting to a surplus is to permit or force domestic prices to rise—which is of course what we did in part in the early postwar years when we were running large surpluses. Again, we should be forcing maladjustments on the whole economy to solve a problem arising from a small part of it—the 5 percent accounted for by foreign trade.

Again, these two methods are the only ones available under our present international payments arrangements, and neither is satisfactory.

The final method is to permit or force exchange rates to change—

in this case, a rise in the price of the dollar in terms of foreign currencies. This solution is again specifically adapted to the specific problem of the balance of payments.

Changes in exchange rates can be produced in either of two general ways. One way is by a change in an official exchange rate; an official devaluation or appreciation from one fixed level which the government is committed to support to another fixed level. This is the method used by Britain in its postwar devaluation and by Germany in 1961 when the mark was appreciated. This is also the main method contemplated by the IMF which permits member nations to change their exchange rates by 10 percent without consultation and by a larger amount after consultation and approval by the Fund. But this method has serious disadvantages. It makes a change in rates a matter of major moment, and hence there is a tendency to postpone any change as long as possible. Difficulties cumulate and a larger change is finally needed than would have been required if it could have been made promptly. By the time the change is made, everyone is aware that a change is pending and is certain about the direction of the change. The result is to encourage a flight from a currency, if it is going to be devalued, or to a currency, if it is going to be appreciated.

There is in any event little basis for determining precisely what the new rate should be. Speculative movements increase the difficulty of judging what the new rate should be, and introduce a systematic bias, making the change needed appear larger than it actually is. The result, particularly when devaluation occurs, is generally to lead officials to "play safe" by making an even larger change than the large change needed. The country is then left after the devaluation with a maladjustment precisely the opposite of that with which it started, and is thereby encouraged to follow policies it cannot sustain in the long run.

Even if all these difficulties could be avoided, this method of changing from one fixed rate to another has the disadvantage that it is necessarily discontinuous. Even if the new exchange rates are precisely correct when first established, they will not long remain correct.

A second and much better way in which changes in exchange rates can be produced is by permitting exchange rates to float, by allowing them to be determined from day to day in the market. This is the method which the United States used from 1862 to 1879, and again, in effect, from 1917 or so to about 1925, and again from 1933 to 1934. It is the method which Britain used from 1918 to 1925 and again from 1931 to 1939, and which Canada used for most of the interwar period and again from 1950 to May 1962. Under this method, exchange rates adjust themselves continuously, and market forces determine the magnitude of each change. There is no need for any official to decide by how much the rate should rise or fall. This is the method of the free market, the method that we adopt unquestioningly in a private enterprise economy for the bulk of goods and services. It is no less available for the price of one money in terms of another.

With a floating exchange rate, it is possible for governments to intervene and try to affect the rate by buying or selling, as the British Exchange Equalization Fund did rather successfully in the 1930's, or by combining buying and selling with public announcements of intentions, as Canada did so disastrously in early 1962. On the whole, it seems to me undesirable to have government intervene, because there is a strong tendency for government agencies to try to peg the rate rather than to stabilize it, because they have no special advantage over private speculators in stabilizing it, because they can make far bigger mistakes than private speculators risking their own money, and because there is a tendency for them to cover up their mistakes by changing the rules—as the Canadian case so strikingly illustrates—rather than by reversing course. But this is an issue on which there is much difference of opinion among economists who are agreed in favoring floating rates. Clearly, it is possible to have a successful floating rate along with governmental speculation.

The great objective of tearing down trade barriers, of promoting a worldwide expansion of trade, of giving citizens of all countries, and especially the underdeveloped countries, every opportunity to sell their products in open markets under equal terms and thereby every incentive to use their resources efficiently, of giving countries an alternative through free world trade to autarchy and central planning—this great objective can, I believe, be achieved best under a regime of floating rates. All countries, and not just the United States, can proceed to liberalize boldly and confidently only if they can have reasonable assurance that the resulting trade expansion will be balanced and will not interfere with major domestic objectives. Floating exchange rates, and so far as I can see, only floating exchange rates, provide this assurance. They do so because they are an automatic mechanism for protecting the domestic economy from the possibility that liberalization will produce a serious imbalance in international payments.

Despite their advantages, floating exchange rates have a bad press. Why is this so?

One reason is because a consequence of our present system that I have been citing as a serious disadvantage is often regarded as an advantage; namely, the extent to which the small foreign trade sector dominates national policy. Those who regard this as an advantage refer to it as the discipline of the gold standard. I would have much sympathy for this view if we had a real gold standard, so the discipline was imposed by impersonal forces which in turn reflected the realities of resources, tastes, and technology. But in fact we have today only a pseudo gold standard and the so-called discipline is imposed by governmental officials of other countries who are determining their own internal monetary policies and are either being forced to dance to our tune or calling the tune for us, depending primarily on accidental political developments. This is a discipline we can well do without.

A possibly more important reason why floating exchange rates have a bad press, I believe, is a mistaken interpretation of experience with floating rates, arising out of a statistical fallacy that can be seen easily in a standard example. Arizona is clearly the worst place in the United States for a person with tuberculosis to go because the death rate from tuberculosis is higher in Arizona than in any other State. The fallacy in this case is obvious. It is less obvious in connection with exchange rates. Countries that have gotten into severe financial difficulties, for whatever reason, have had ultimately to change their exchange rates or let them change. No amount of exchange control and other restrictions on trade have enabled them to peg an exchange rate that was far out of line with economic realities. In consequence, floating rates have frequently been associated with financial and economic instability. It is easy to conclude, as many have, that floating exchange rates produce such instability.

This misreading of experience is reinforced by the general prejudice against speculation, which has led to the frequent assertion, typically on the basis of no evidence whatsoever, that speculation in exchange can be expected to be destabilizing and thereby to increase the instability in rates. Few who make this assertion even recognize that it is equivalent to asserting that speculators generally lose money.

Floating exchange rates need not be unstable exchange rates— any more than the prices of automobiles or of government bonds, of coffee or of meals need gyrate wildly just because they are free to change from day to day. The Canadian exchange rate was free to change during more than a decade, yet it varied within narrow limits. The ultimate objective is a world in which exchange rates, while free to vary, are in fact highly stable because basic economic policies and conditions are stable. Instability of exchange rates is a symptom of instability in the underlying economic structure. Elimination of this symptom by administrative pegging of exchange rates cures none of the underlying difficulties and only makes adjustment to them more painful.

The confusion between stable exchange rates and pegged exchange rates helps to explain the frequent comment that floating rates would introduce an additional element of uncertainty into foreign trade and thereby discourage its expansion. They introduce no additional element of uncertainty. If a floating rate would, for example, decline, then a pegged rate would be subject to pressure that the authorities would have to meet by internal deflation or exchange control in some form. The uncertainty about the rate would simply be replaced by uncertainty about internal prices or about the availability of exchange; and the latter uncertainties, being subject to administrative rather than market control, are likely to be the more erratic and unpredictable. Moreover, the trader can far more readily and cheaply protect himself against the danger of changes in exchange rates, through hedging operations in a forward market, than he can against the danger of changes in internal prices or exchange availability. Floating rates are therefore far more favorable to private international trade than pegged rates.

Though I have discussed the problem of international payments in the context of trade liberalization, the discussion is directly applicable to the more general problem of adapting to any forces that make for balance-of-payments difficulties. Consider our present problem of a deficit in the balance of trade plus long-term capital movement. How can we adjust to it? By one of the three methods outlined: first, drawing on reserves or borrowing; second, keeping U.S. prices from rising as rapidly as foreign prices or forcing them down; third, permitting or forcing exchange rates to alter. And, this time, by one more method: by imposing additional trade barriers or their equivalent, whether in the form of higher tariffs, or smaller import quotas, or extracting from other countries tighter "voluntary" quotas on their exports, or "tieing" foreign aid, or buying higher priced domestic goods or services to meet military needs, or imposing taxes on foreign borrowing, or imposing direct controls on investments by U.S. citizens abroad, or any one of the host of other devices for interfering with the private business of private individuals that have become so familiar to us since Hjalmar Schacht perfected the modern techniques of exchange control in 1934 to strengthen the Nazis for war and to despoil a large class of his fellow citizens.

Fortunately or unfortunately, even Congress cannot repeal the laws of arithmetic. Books must balance. We must use one of these four methods. Because we have been unwilling to select the only one that is currently fully consistent with both economic and political needs—namely, floating exchange rates—we have been driven, as if by an invisible hand, to employ all the others, and even then may not escape the need for explicit changes in exchange rates.

We affirm in loud and clear voices that we will not and must not erect trade barriers—yet is there any doubt about how far we have gone down the fourth route? After the host of measures already taken, the Secretary of the Treasury has openly stated to the Senate Finance Committee that if the so-called interest equalization tax—itself a concealed exchange control and concealed devaluation—is not passed, we shall have to resort to direct controls over foreign investments.

We affirm that we cannot drain our reserves further, yet short-term liabilities mount and our gold stock continues to decline.

We affirm that we cannot let balance-of-payments problems interfere with domestic prosperity, yet for at least some 4 years now we have followed a less expansive monetary policy than would have been healthy for our economy.

Even all together, these measures may only serve to postpone but not prevent open devaluation—if the experience of other countries is any guide. Whether they do, depends not on us but on others. For our best hope of escaping our present difficulties is that foreign countries will inflate.

In the meantime, we adopt one expedient after another, borrowing here, making swap arrangements there, changing the form of loans to make the "figures" look good. Entirely aside from the ineffectiveness of most of these measures, they are politically degrading and demeaning. We are a great and wealthy nation. We should be directing our own course, setting an example to the world, living up to our destiny. Instead, we send our officials, hat in hand, to make the rounds of foreign governments and central banks; we put foreign central banks in a position to determine whether or not we can meet our obligations and thus enable them to exert great influence on our policies; we are driven to niggling negotiations with Hong Kong and with Japan and for all I know Monaco to get them to limit "voluntarily" their exports. Is this a posture suitable for the leader of the free world?

It is not the least of the virtues of floating exchange rates that we would again become masters in our own house. We could decide important issues on the proper ground. The military could concentrate on military effectiveness and not on saving foreign exchange; recipients of foreign aid could concentrate on how to get the most out of what we give them and not on how to spend it all in the United States; Congress could decide how much to spend on foreign aid on the basis of what we get for our money and what else we could use it for and not how it will affect the gold stock; the monetary authorities could concentrate on domestic prices and employment, not on how to induce foreigners to hold dollar balances in this country; the Treasury and the tax committees of Congress could devote their attention to the equity of the tax system and its effects on our efficiency, rather than on how to use tax gimmicks to discourage imports, subsidize exports, and discriminate against outflows of capital.

A system of floating exchange rates would render the problem of making outflows equal inflows into the market where it belongs and not leave it to the clumsy and heavy hand of government. It would leave government free to concentrate on its proper functions.

In conclusion, a word about gold. Our commitment to buy and sell gold for monetary use at a fixed price of $35 an ounce is in practice the mechanism whereby we maintain fixed rates of exchange between the dollar and other currencies—or, more precisely, whereby we leave all initiative for changes in such rates to other countries. This commitment should be terminated—as the corresponding commitment for silver already has been. The price of gold, like the price of silver, should be determined in the free market, with the U.S. Government committed neither to buying gold nor to selling gold at any fixed price. This is the appropriate counterpart of a policy of floating exchange rates. With respect to our existing stock of gold, we could simply keep it fixed, neither adding to it nor reducing it; alternatively, we could sell it off gradually at the market price or add to it gradually thereby reducing or increasing our governmental stockpiles of this particular metal. Personally, I favor selling it off (which would involve removing the present gold reserve requirement for Federal Reserve liabilities) and simultaneously removing all present limitations on the ownership of gold and the trading in gold by American citizens. There is no reason why gold, like other commodities, should not be freely traded on a free market.

HENRY C. WALLICH

EXCHANGE RATES: HOW FLEXIBLE SHOULD THEY BE?

45

Let me say at the outset that I conceive of my paper as a defense of fixed rates. The title indicates that I would like to see the pros and cons weighed because there are pros and cons, of course.

Flexible rates have achieved a high measure of acceptance in academic circles, but very little among public officials. This raises the question whether we have a parallel to the famous case of free trade: almost all economists favor it in principle, but no major country ever has adopted it. Does the logic of economics point equally irrefutable to flexible rates, while the logic of politics points in another direction?

The nature of the case, I believe, is fundamentally different. Most countries do practice free trade within their borders, although they reject it outside. But economists do not propose flexible rates for the States of the Union, among which men, money, and goods can move freely, and which are governed by uniform monetary, fiscal, and other policies. Flexible rates are to apply only to relations among countries that do not permit free factor movements across their borders and that follow, or may follow, substantially different monetary and fiscal policies. It is the imperfections of the world that seem to suggest that flexible rates, which would be harmful if applied to different parts of a single country, would do more good than harm internationally.

It is quite arguable that the Appalachian area would benefit if it could issue a dollar of its own, an Appalachian dollar which in that case would sell, probably, at 60 or 90 cents. Exports from that region would increase, and unemployment would diminish. A great many good things would happen, but we are also aware of what it would do to the economy of the United States—and, therefore, we do not propose that solution. The question is; Do we want to look upon the world as quite different from the United States, as hopelessly divided into self-contained units where cooperation and

Reprinted from Henry C. Wallich, "Exchange Rates: How Flexible Should They Be?" *The United States Balance of Payments*, Hearings Before the Joint Economic Committee, Congress of the United States, 88th Cong., 1st Sess., Part 3, "The International Monetary System: Functioning and Possible Reforms," Nov. 12–15, 1963, pp. 495–499.

efforts to coordinate policies are doomed to frustration? In that case, flexible rates may be the best way to avoid a very bad situation. But should we not try to establish within the world something that begins to approximate the conditions that prevail within a country, in the way of coordination of policies, freer flow of capital and of goods and so try to achieve the benefits of one large economic area within the world? That is what we should try for.

Now to resume: The proponents of flexible rates argue, in effect, that flexible rates can help a country get out of almost any of the typical difficulties that economies experience. This is perfectly true. If the United States has a balance-of-payments deficit, a flexible exchange rate allows the dollar to decline until receipts have risen and payments fallen enough to restore balance. If the United States has unemployment, flexible rates can protect it against the balance-of-payments consequences of a policy of expansion. We would then have less unemployment. If the United States has suffered inflation and fears that it will be undersold internationally, flexible rates can remove the danger.

All of these advantages are quite clear.

Other countries have analogous advantages. If Chile experiences a decline in copper prices, flexible rates can ease the inevitable adjustment. If Germany finds that other countries have inflated while German prices have remained more nearly stable, flexible rates could help to avoid importing inflation. If Canada has a large capital inflow, a flexible rate will remove the need for price and income increases that would otherwise be needed to facilitate the transfer of real resources.

There are other adjustments, however, that must be made in all of these cases. If a country allows its exchange rate to go down, some price adjustments still remain to be made. Furthermore, each time a country makes this kind of adjustment, allowing its exchange rate to decline, other countries suffer. If the U.S. dollar depreciates, we undersell the Europeans. It could be argued that if the U.S. price levels go down instead of the exchange rate, we also undersell the Europeans, and if because of a declining price level we have unemployment we would be buying still less from them. Nevertheless, there is a difference. A price adjustment tends to be slow and is likely to be no greater than it need be and tends to be selective for particular commodities. In contrast, an exchange rate movement is unpredictable. It can be large—we could easily have a drop of 10 or 20 percent in an exchange rate. It comes suddenly. And it compels other countries to be on their guard.

Why, given the attractions of flexible rates, should one advise policymakers to stay away from them? Since the dollar problem is the concrete situation in which flexible rates are being urged today, it is in terms of the dollar that they must be discussed. In broadest terms, the reason why flexible rates are inadvisable is that their successful functioning would require more self-discipline and mutual forbearance than countries today are likely to muster. Exchange rates are two sided—depreciation for the dollar means appreciation for the European currencies. To work successfully, a flexible dollar, for instance, must not depreciate to the point where the Europeans would feel compelled to take counteraction. I believe that the limits of tolerance, before counteraction begins today are narrow and that a flexible dollar would invite retaliation almost immediately.

In the abstract, the European countries perhaps ought to consider that if the United States allows the dollar to go down, it is doing so in the interests of all-round equilibrium. They ought perhaps to consider that with a stable dollar rate the same adjustment might have to take place through a decline in prices here and a rise in prices there. In practice, they are likely to be alive principally to the danger of being undersold by American producers if the dollar goes down, in their own and third markets. The changing competitive pressure would fall unevenly upon particular industries, and those who are hurt would demand protection.

The most likely counteraction might take one of two forms. The Europeans could impose countervailing duties, such as the United States also has employed at times. They could alternately also depreciate European currencies along with the dollar or, what would amount to almost the same thing, prevent the dollar from depreciating. This might involve the European countries in the purchase of large amounts of dollars. If they are to peg the dollar, they could minimize their commitment by imposing a simple form of exchange control that the Swiss practiced during the last war. The Swiss purchased dollars only from their exporters, also requiring their importers to buy these dollars thereby stabilizing the trade dollar, while allowing dollars from capital movements—finance dollars— to find their own level in the market.

The large volume of not very predictable short-term capital movements in the world today makes such reactions under flexible rates particularly likely.

•   •   •

A sudden outflow of funds from the United States, for instance (because of the fear of budget deficits or many other things that could happen), would tend to drive the dollar down. As a result, American exporters could undersell producers everywhere else in the world. It seems unlikely that foreign countries would allow a fortuitous short-term capital movement to have such far-reaching consequences. It would not even be economically appropriate to allow a transitory fluctuation in the capital account of the balance of payments to have a major influence on the current account. Such a fluctuation should not alter the pattern of trade, because the situation is likely to be reversed. Other countries therefore would probably take defensive action to make sure that no industry is destroyed and after several years may have to be rebuilt because of the ups and downs of short-term capital movements.

It can be argued that under flexible rates the effects of such a movement would be forestalled by stabilizing speculation on a future recovery of the dollar. This is possible. It is possible also, however, that speculation would seek a quick profit from the initial drop in the dollar, instead of a longer run one from its eventual recovery. Then short-run speculation would drive the dollar down farther at first. In any case there is not enough assurance that speculators will not make mistakes to permit basing the world's monetary system upon the stabilizing effects of speculation.

In the case of countries which import much of what they consume, such as England, a temporary decline in the local currency may even be self-validating. If the cost of living rises as the currency declines, wages will rise. Thereafter, the currency may never recover to its original level.

This points up one probable consequence of flexible exchange rates: A world wide acceleration of inflation. In some countries the indicated ratchet effect of wages will be at work. If exchange rates go down, wages will rise, and exchange rates cannot recover. In the United States the rise in the cost of imports would not be very important. But the removal of balance-of-payments restraints may well lead to policies that could lead to price increases. The American inflation of the 1950's was never defeated until the payments deficit became serious. Elsewhere, the removal of balance-of-payments disciplines might have the same effect. Rapid inflation in turn would probably compel governments to intervene drastically in foreign trade and finance.

• • •

The prospect that flexible rates would greatly increase uncertainty for foreign traders and investors has been cited many times. It should be noted that this uncertainty extends also to domestic investment decisions that might be affected by changing import competition or changing export prospects. It has been argued that uncertainties about future exchange rates can be removed by hedging in the future market. This, however, involves a cost even where cover is readily available. The history of futures markets does not suggest that it will be possible to get cover for long-term positions. To hedge domestic investment decisions that might be affected by flexible rates is in the nature of things impracticable.

The picture that emerges of the international economy under flexible rates is one of increasing disintegration. Independent national policies and unpredictable changes in each country's competitive position will compel governments to shield their producers and markets. The argument that such shielding would also automatically be accomplished by movements in the affected country's exchange rate underrates the impact of fluctuations upon particular industries, if not upon the entire economy. That international integration and flexible rates are incompatible seems to be the view also of the European Common Market countries, who have left no doubt that they want stable rates within the EEC. The same applies if we visualize the "Kennedy round" under the Trade Expansion Act. I think if we told the Europeans that, after lowering our tariffs, we were going to cast the dollar loose and let it fluctuate, we would get very little tariff reduction. They would want to keep up their guard.

If the disintegrating effects of flexible rates are to be overcome, a great deal of policy coordination, combined with self-discipline and mutual forbearance, would be required. The desired independence of national economic policy would in fact have to be foregone —interest rates, budgets, wage and prices policies would have to be harmonized. If the world were ready for such cooperation, it would be capable also of making a fixed exchange rate system work. In that case, flexible rates would accomplish nothing that could not more cheaply and simply be done with fixed rates. It seems to follow that flexible rates have no unique capacity for good, whereas they possess great capacity to do damage.

A modified version of the flexible rates proposal has been suggested. This version would allow the dollar and other currencies to fluctuate within a given range, say 5 percent up and down. This "widening of the gold points" is believed to reduce the danger of destabilizing speculation. It might perhaps enlist speculation on the side of stabilization, for if the dollar, say, had dropped to its lower limit, and if the public had confidence that that limit would not be broken, the only movement on which to speculate would be a rise. The spectacle of a currency falling below par may induce, according to the proponents, a strong political effort to bring it back. This proposal likewise strikes me as unworkable. For one thing,

I doubt that people would have a great deal of confidence in a limit of 5 percent below par, if par itself has been given up. Political support for holding this second line would probably be less than the support that can be mustered to hold the first. For another, the execution of the plan would still require the maintenance of international reserves, to protect the upper and lower limits. But with fluctuating rates, dollar and sterling would cease to be desirable media for monetary reserves. International liquidity would become seriously impaired. A third objection is that under today's conditions, the complex negotiations and legislation required, in the unlikely event that the plan could be negotiated at all, could not go forward without immediate speculation against the dollar before the plan goes into effect.

It remains only to point out that, even in the absence of a high degree of international cooperativeness, a system of fixed exchange rates can be made to work. It can be made to work mainly because it imposes a discipline upon all participants, and because within this discipline there is nevertheless some room for adjustment. The principal sources of flexibility are productivity gains and the degree to which they are absorbed by wage increases. Wages cannot be expected to decline. But their rise can be slowed in relation to the rate of productivity growth, in which case prices would become more competitive relative to other countries. With annual productivity gains of 2 to 3 percent in the United States and more abroad, it would not take many years to remove a temporary imbalance.

•   •   •

THOMAS E. DAVIS

THE NEW INTERNATIONAL
MONETARY PLAN
IN PERSPECTIVE

46

Recent developments in international finance, highlighted by the
devaluation of the British pound and speculative activity in the
London gold market, have created considerable public interest in
the future viability of the international monetary system. Policymakers, of course, have been vitally interested in this issue for a
number of years. In fact, more than four years ago, officials here
and abroad undertook a series of intensive studies designed to appraise the outlook for the functioning of the international monetary
system and to assess its probable future needs.[1] These studies generally agreed that the present system, based on fixed exchange rates
and the established price of gold, has proved its value as a foundation on which to build for the future. Moreover, it was agreed that
due to increasingly close cooperation between central banks and
the development of extensive official short-term credit facilities, the
present system has demonstrated a great capacity to adapt to changing circumstances and to meet successfully conditions of periodic
strain.

Despite the past success of the present system, officials and academicians alike also have agreed that the system is confronted by
certain actual or potential problems. Customarily, these problems
are grouped under three main headings: (1) insufficient effectiveness
in the balance of payments adjustment process, (2) the risk of potential instability resulting from a change of confidence in, and a subsequent shift between, existing international reserve assets, and
(3) the problem of assuring an adequate long-run supply of international reserve assets consistent with a desirable and noninflationary
economic growth rate in the world economy.

Reprinted from Thomas E. Davis, "The New International Monetary
Plan in Perspective," *Monthly Review* (February 1968), pp. 11–18, Federal Reserve Bank of Kansas City.

[1] See, for example, *Ministerial Statement of the Group of Ten and
Annex Prepared by Deputies*, August 1964; *Report of the Study Group on
the Creation of Reserve Assets*, Group of Ten, May 1965; *The Commu-
nique of Ministers and Governors and Report of Deputies*, July 1966; *The
Balance of Payments Adjustment Process*. A Report by Working Party
No. 3 of the Economic Policy Committee of the OECD, August 1966; and
the *Annual Reports* of the International Monetary Fund, 1964, 1965, and
1966.

In recognition of these three problems, continuous official efforts have been made during the past four years to explore and develop mutually acceptable methods to improve the international monetary system. As a result, considerable progress has been made in clarifying the issues and responsibilities involved in both the balance of payments adjustment problem and the "confidence" problem.[2]

The most notable accomplishment, however, has been directed toward the problem of assuring an adequate long-run supply of international reserves. This accomplishment occurred at the annual meeting of the International Monetary Fund (IMF) held in Rio de Janeiro, Brazil, in September 1967, when a resolution was unanimously adopted to proceed with a plan to establish, within the Fund, machinery for the creation of a new international reserve facility.[3] This facility, which is to take the form of special drawing rights (SDR's), is intended to meet the need, as and when it arises, for a supplement to existing international reserve assets. As specified in the approved resolution, the plan for the new facility is to be formally incorporated into a proposed amendment to the Fund's Articles of Agreement, which in turn is to be submitted for approval to the Fund's Board of Governors no later than March 31, 1968. Upon approval by the Fund's Board of Governors, the proposed amendment will be submitted to the 107 member countries of the IMF for their ratification—a process which will require an 80 percent majority of the voting power of IMF members and which is expected to be completed before the end of 1969. After ratification, the Fund will be able to activate the plan provided 85 percent of the weighted votes of the Fund members support the creation of special drawing rights.

In view of the widespread interest in the plan for creating special drawing rights, this article discusses the major factors underlying the need for supplementing existing international reserve assets, and reviews and comments on some of the principal features of the proposed plan.

THE NEED FOR A RESERVE SUPPLEMENT

Under the present international monetary system, international reserves consist of the aggregate stock of assets and facilities which

---

[2] *Ibid.*; see also "The Balance of Payments Adjustment Problem," *Monthly Review*, Federal Bank of Kansas City, November-December 1967.

[3] The formal resolution and complete description of the plan as contained in the "Outline of a Facility Based on Special Drawing Rights" appears in the *Federal Reserve Bulletin*, November 1967.

are unconditionally available to national monetary authorities to support the par value of their currencies in foreign exchange markets when their external payments are in deficit. Traditionally, reserves comprise countries' official holdings of gold and convertible foreign exchange, primarily dollars and sterling. In recent years, as countries have recognized that their reserve positions with the IMF serve the function of reserves, total international reserves have come to be considered as the sum of gold, foreign exchange, and IMF reserve positions held officially by all countries.[4]

It is widely recognized today that an adequate supply of international reserves is indispensable to the proper functioning of the international monetary system. Reserves provide the means by which a country can finance a temporary balance of payments deficit without resorting to undesirable measures designed to correct the deficit, such as deflationary domestic policies or restrictions on international trade and payments. Thus, an adequate supply of reserves not only affords a country more time in which it can implement desirable corrective policies when faced with an external deficit, but also serves as a basis for keeping trade and payments free from restrictions and for maintaining confidence in currencies in general.

Due to the importance of an adequate reserve supply, monetary authorities continually have been aware of the need to assure a satisfactory growth rate in the stock of international reserves. During the postwar period and throughout most of the 1950's, however, the growth in international reserves did not present a major problem. Reserves in the world outside the United States grew quite rapidly during the period without deliberate reserve action. Facilitating this growth were the moderate balance of payments deficits experienced by the United States, as well as the steady increase in the amount of gold produced and accumulated as part of official gold stocks. Often cited as evidence of the adequacy of reserves during this period is the dismantling of European trade restrictions and the introduction of widespread currency convertibility in 1958.

In recent years, monetary authorities have become increasingly concerned about the future adequacy of international reserves. In fact, a growing consensus has developed that the future supply of reserves emanating from existing sources is not likely to keep pace with the growing long-run need for reserves. This consensus is based partly on the expectation that, at the established price of gold,

---

[4] International reserves are customarily tabulated on a gross basis, i.e., without netting out liabilities. This is essential for the United States and the United Kingdom in view of their status as reserve currency countries.

the future growth in the stock of monetary gold will not be sufficient to meet legitimate reserve needs. It also is based on the expectation that future reserve growth is not likely to be met by increased U. S. dollar holdings to the same extent as in the past. Since the expected shortfall in future reserve growth provides the underlying rationale for the need to create a reserve supplement, further consideration is given below to the factors affecting both the need for and the supply of international reserves.

The expectation that the need for international reserves will increase over the long run generally is supported by two reasons. First, the long-run growth in world trade is likely to be accompanied by larger absolute swings in external payments imbalances, which in turn will require a larger stock of reserves with which to finance the imbalances. It should be emphasized, however, that no direct proportionality exists between the growth in world trade and payments and the need for reserves. This is because the need for reserves is related to the magnitude of payments imbalances, which while undoubtedly influenced by the growth of trade, can also be significantly affected by many other factors, such as the speed and efficiency of the balance of payments adjustment process and the equilibrating nature of international capital flows. Thus, while a qualitative assessment of future reserve needs can justifiably be based on the expected growth of world trade and payments, no satisfactory quantitative projection can be made on this basis alone. Second, as a matter of policy most countries today wish to see an increase in their international reserves over time, whereas no country is prepared to accept a long-run decline in its reserves. The United States, during most of the 1950's, was a notable exception to this latter statement. The striving of countries to accumulate reserves over the long run is attributed partly to their expectations of larger future payments imbalances, partly to their desire to assure their own financial and political independence, and partly to their desire to be able to meet future payments deficits without turning to unpleasant domestic corrective measures and restrictive international policies.

The expectation that the supply of international reserves will not be adequate to meet the secular increase in the need for reserves is related generally to the recent deceleration in the growth rate of reserves. As evidence of this deceleration, aggregate monetary reserves grew at an annual rate of only 2.0 per cent in 1966, which was considerably less than the average annual growth rate of 2.5 per cent between the end of 1950 and 1965, and markedly below the average growth rate of 3.5 per cent during the six-year period 1960–65. Moreover, during the first half of 1967, monetary reserves actually declined at an annual rate of 1.7 per cent. Thus, at the end of June 1967, monetary reserves totaled $71,020 million, or just slightly above the level reached at the end of 1965.

The factors contributing to the recent deceleration in the growth of international reserves generally are thought to be those which will continue to limit the future growth of reserves. These factors are best understood by reviewing the recent and prospective developments in each of the three components of monetary reserves, i.e., gold, foreign exchange, and reserve positions in the IMF.

Gold available for official reserves constitutes a residual remaining after new gold production in noncommunist countries and sales of gold by the Soviet Union have met the private absorption of gold for industrial, artistic, and professional uses and for hoarding and speculation. During the 15 years prior to 1966, official gold holdings of countries and international financial institutions rose at an average annual rate of $528 million, as private demand was less than the total amount of new gold supplied. In 1966, however, official holdings dropped $40 million, as private demand exceeded the amount of new gold supplied. In addition, throughout the first half of 1967, private demand continued to exceed the supply of new gold, so that official holdings dropped $210 million to a level of $42,975 million, or to just about the same level that prevailed at the end of 1964. Projections based on these developments—a steady and rapid increase in the private demand for gold combined with a slow rise in production—indicate that official gold holdings are unlikely to increase in the future at a desirable rate; unless, of course, supplemented by large Soviet gold sales. Indeed, if official holdings are sold to meet a rise in private demand in excess of new gold production, official holdings may tend to decline. For these reasons, it is generally thought that new additions to official gold holdings cannot be relied upon as a dependable source of future reserve growth.

Until recently, official holdings of foreign exchange have constituted one of the most rapidly growing components of international reserves. For example, between the end of 1950 and 1964 foreign exchange holdings grew at an average annual rate of $730 million, and during the five-year period 1960 through 1964, the annual increase averaged as much as $1,458 million. This growth in foreign exchange holdings was primarily in U. S. dollar liabilities, which was a consequence of the U. S. balance of payments deficits. While

International Reserve Assets *(in millions of U.S. dollars)*

	1950	1960	1964	1965	1966	Mid-1967
Gold held officially by countries	33,755	38,030	40,845	41,850	40,905	40,535
Total official gold holdings*	35,300	40,505	43,015	43,225	43,185	42,975
Foreign exchange	13,290	18,670	23,510	23,025	24,385	24,590
U. S. dollars	4,890	11,088	15,771	15,849	14,965	16,308
Other reserve currencies†	8,400	7,582	7,739	7,176	9,420	8,282
Reserve positions in IMF	1,671	3,570	4,155	5,376	6,330	5,897
IMF gold holdings	1,494	2,439	2,179	1,869	2,652	2,669
IMF net reserve creation‡	177	1,131	1,976	3,507	3,678	3,228
Total	48,715	60,270	68,505	70,250	71,620	71,020

* Includes gold held by countries and international organizations.
† Includes British pounds sterling plus a residual item including official monetary liabilities of countries other than the United States and United Kingdom.
‡ Equals Reserve Positions in IMF, minus IMF Gold Holdings.
SOURCE: International Financial Statistics.

U. S. deficits have continued since 1964, total U. S. dollar liabilities have risen only moderately above the level reached at the end of 1964, because the United States has financed its deficits mainly by drawing down its gold stock as well as its reserve position in the IMF. Total foreign exchange holdings also have risen only moderately since the end of 1964, increasing by $1,080 million to a level of $24,590 million at the end of June 1967. Moreover, most of this increase has reflected either temporary factors such as central bank currency swaps,[5] or special transactions like the transfer into British reserves in 1966 of assets formerly held as dollar securities by the British government. Thus, the recent slowdown in the growth of

[5] Formally, a currency swap is an exchange of currencies between two parties, reversible within a short period of time. As such, central bank currency swaps result in only a temporary increase in total reserve assets. For a discussion of U. S. swap transactions and facilities, see "Treasury and Federal Reserve Foreign Exchange Operations," *Federal Reserve Bulletin*, September 1967.

"ordinary" foreign exchange holdings, and the general realization that a further growth in U. S. dollar liabilities is likely to exert increasing pressure on U. S. gold reserves, are the primary reasons why it is considered unwise to depend on new additions to foreign exchange holdings as a major source of future reserve growth.

A reserve position in the IMF represents the amount that a member country may obtain, or draw, essentially automatically from the Fund, whenever the country is experiencing a balance of payments deficit.[6] In recent years, IMF reserve positions have been the most rapidly growing component of international reserves, rising from $4,155 million at the end of 1964 to $5,897 million in mid-1967. The major factors accounting for this increase were the large drawings on the Fund in 1965, particularly by the United Kingdom, and the net payment of gold to the Fund in 1966 in connection with the 25 percent increase in Fund quotas. In assessing the net contribution of this rise in Fund reserve positions to aggregate monetary reserves, it is necessary, of course, to omit the rise in Fund gold holdings. This is because a rise in Fund gold holdings involves an equivalent decrease in member countries' gold reserves. On this basis, net reserve creation by the Fund still has increased substantially in recent years, rising by $1,252 million from the end of 1964 to mid-1967. Nonetheless, since net reserve creation by the Fund reflects essentially medium-term credits extended to member countries by the Fund, the subsequent repayment of these credits will tend to cancel these temporary additions to international reserves; unless, of course, drawings increase at a rate not offset by repayments. Thus, under present arrangements, reserve positions in the IMF may not provide the basis for regular or permanent additions to the aggregate stock of international reserves.

In view of these factors, indicating that the supply of international reserves from traditional sources is unlikely to meet future needs, monetary authorities have found it advisable to establish a plan to provide for a permanent supplement to existing reserve assets. The major aspects of this plan are summarized in the following section.

[6] Specifically, a country's reserve position in the IMF consists of the country's gold tranche position at the Fund plus its outstanding lendings to the Fund. Normally, a country's gold tranche position is the amount by which the Fund's holdings of the country's currency is less than 100 per cent of the country's IMF quota. A country may draw beyond its gold tranche position, or in its credit tranches, up to the extent that the Fund holds not more than 200 per cent of its currency. However, drawings in the credit tranches are conditional in nature, requiring a degree of justification that increases with the amount of drawings outstanding.

THE PLAN FOR A RESERVE SUPPLEMENT

The plan to establish a supplementary reserve asset is basically quite simple in substance, but appropriately contains certain detailed provisions governing the activation, allocation, and use of the new asset. In essence, the plan would create a new international reserve asset in the form of special drawing rights (SDR's), which would be transferable among participating countries, and would be backed by a commitment of participating countries to accept them in exchange for convertible currencies. These SDR's would appear as book entries in a Special Drawing Account at the IMF and would be denominated in units of account equivalent to the gold value of one U. S. dollar. SDR's also would be guaranteed in terms of gold, and would carry a moderate rate of interest—as yet unspecified. It should be emphasized, however, that the value of the new reserve facility would rest fundamentally on the obligation of participants to accept it, in much the same way as the value of domestic fiduciary money derives from its status as legal tender.

Activation and Allocation of SDR's

The activation of the plan to create SDR's is to depend upon a widely recognized global need for reserve creation. Procedurally, the Managing Director of the IMF, after having satisfied himself that there is a need to supplement reserves, will undertake consultations to ascertain that there is broad support among the participants for the creation of SDR's in the amount he proposes. If the Executive Directors of the Fund agree with his proposal, it must then be approved by the Fund's Board of Governors by an 85 per cent majority of the voting power of the participating countries.

Since SDR's are intended to assure an adequate long-run growth rate in total reserves, the amount created usually will not vary from year to year in response to the payments positions or reserve needs of individual countries. Rather, the amount to be created normally will be for a specific period ahead—initially a five-year period—during which SDR's will be allocated at designated intervals. Underlying this principle is the belief that not only should SDR's be created on the basis of global reserve needs but that, given the present state of knowledge and institutional arrangements, it is neither feasible nor desirable to make short-term changes in the volume of world reserves to meet cyclical swings in international economic activity. In the case of unexpected major developments, however, there are provisions for changing the rate of issue within the specified period.

The allocation of SDR's will be made to all participating countries in proportion to their IMF quotas. For example, if a decision is made to create $1 billion of SDR's per year for five years, the United States, which currently has 24.6 per cent of total Fund quotas, would receive $246 million of the SDR's created each year—for a total of $1,230 million over the five-year period. Receiving an allocation of SDR's simply means that in each of the five years the Fund would credit the United States on the books of the Special Drawing Account with $246 million of SDR's.

The Use of SDR's

Since the plan calls for the establishment of a new and untried reserve asset, the most extensive provisions of the plan are directed toward the use of this asset. Generally, these provisions set forth rules on participating countries' eligibility to use and receive SDR's, their obligation to accept SDR's, and if necessary, their obligation to partially reconstitute the amount actually used. The major points in each of these provisions are summarized below.

Each participating country is entitled to use its SDR's to acquire an equivalent amount of convertible currencies only for balance of payments needs or in the light of developments in its total reserves. A country's exercise of this right is not subject to prior challenge, nor is it contingent on the adoption of appropriate policies designed to restore balance of payments equilibrium. In this latter sense, SDR's are unconditionally available—unlike the present credit facilities of the IMF, which are conditional in nature.[7] There is, however, a proviso attached to the unconditional use of SDR's. This proviso stipulates that no country should use SDR's merely to change the composition of its reserve assets. In the event that a country fails to observe this proviso, the Fund may direct transfers of SDR's to that country to offset such misuse.

Each participating country is obligated to accept SDR's, and to provide in exchange an equivalent amount of convertible currency up to an amount where its total holdings, including its allocations, are equal to three times its cumulative allocations. Put more simply, a country's acceptance obligation is always the difference between its actual holdings and three times its cumulative allocations. For example, if a country's initial allocations were $100 million and it

[7] See footnote 6.

used none of its SDR's, its acceptance obligation would be $200 million; and if it had transferred all of it initial allocations to other countries, its acceptance obligation would be $300 million. A country could, of course, accept and hold SDR's in excess of this amount.

The acceptance obligation, as indicated earlier, is the foundation of the plan since it provides the fundamental backing for the new asset. This obligation makes unncessary a pool of currencies like those used to back the present IMF credit facilities. Thus, great care was taken to make the obligations large enough to assure any participant that its holdings would be fully usable.[8]

Countries likely to receive a transfer of SDR's will normally be those with strong balance of payments or reserve positions. To assure this normal flow, the Fund, in its capacity as intermediary, will try to guide the transfer of SDR's to these countries in a manner designed to maintain over time an equal ratio in their holdings of SDR's to their total reserves. This rule is complemented by a special provision permitting a reserve currency country, such as the United States, that wants to buy balances of its own currency held by another country, to direct its transfer specifically to that country, provided the latter agrees. Regardless of how the transfers are arranged, whether directly between participants or indirectly through the Fund, they all are to be recorded in the Fund's Special Drawing Account by a debit to the account of the user and a credit to the account of the receiver.

Participating countries that use SDR's will incur an obligation to reconstitute, or restore, their position, depending on the amount and duration of use. The rules for reconstitution specify that over a five-year period a country's average net use is not to exceed 70 per cent of its average cumulative allocation. A country could, of course, exceed the 70 per cent use rate during the period, but would be obligated to restore its position at the end of the period. The primary

---

[8] As evidence of the adequacy of the acceptance obligation, it can be shown that the U. S. obligation is large enough to absorb a transfer of all of the EEC countries' holdings of SDR's, and the latter's total obligation is large enough to take a transfer of all U. S. holdings. For example, if $1 billion of SDR's were created annually, the United States would receive $1,230 million over a five-year period, and would have an acceptance limit of $3,690 million, which implies a potential additional acceptance obligation of $2,460 million. This would be more than enough to absorb the total allocation of the EEC countries, which—under the same assumptions and given their present share of IMF quotas of 18 per cent—would be $900 million. Conversely, the EEC acceptance obligation after five years would be $1,800 million, or more than enough to accommodate all of the U. S. allocation.

purpose of the reconstitution obligation is to prevent a country from financing persistent external deficits by the exclusive use of SDR's. However, to the extent that the balance of payments adjustment process works effectively, reconstitution will tend to work automatically through the usual process of a country moving from a deficit to a surplus position, and so becoming eligible to receive SDR's.

The reconstitution provision, to be sure, may impose a repayment obligation on part of a country's use of SDR's, but it does not significantly impair the quality of the asset. Indeed, that portion which is not required to be repaid, i.e., 70 per cent of the cumulative allocations, will constitute a stock of unconditionally available reserve assets and will be a permanent addition to the total supply of international reserves.

CONCLUSION

The plan to establish a new international reserve facility in the form of special drawing rights represents a major accomplishment in the continuing official effort to assure the future viability of the international monetary system. The plan provides a workable mechanism through which international reserves can be expanded on a permanent basis in accordance with the needs of the world economy, rather than being dependent—as in the past—on the uncertain by-product of such forces as the supply and private absorption of gold, the external payments position of reserve currency countries, and the decisions of participating countries concerning the composition of their reserves.

The plan, as indicated earlier, is designed specifically to meet the problem of the long-run adequacy of world reserves, and not the problem of external payments adjustment of individual countries nor the problem of confidence in the existing stock of reserves. It should be pointed out, however, that while a satisfactory solution to these latter problems is still recognized as being essential to the smooth functioning of the international monetary system, these problems may be ameliorated to some extent through the judicious and responsible activation of the plan. For example, adjustment policies adopted in an environment of an adequate growth rate in world reserves are likely to be more effective and also less harmful to world trade and payments than when reserves are not expected to increase at a sufficient rate. Moreover, through the collective determination of an adequate future supply of reserves, confidence is likely to be enhanced not only in the existing stock of reserves but also in the structural stability of the international monetary system in general.

The ultimate effectiveness of the plan will rest fundamentally, of course, on the degree to which countries support the plan and accept SDR's as equivalent to gold and dollars. In recognition of this principle, the provisions of the plan—particularly those dealing with the activation of the plan—are designed to assure the widest participation of all major countries or major groupings of countries, without whose support any decision to create reserves would be meaningless. Indeed, the most distinguishing feature of the plan is its implicit emphasis on the need for collective and cooperative international action through which the world community can control international reserves. It is primarily because of this feature that the agreement has been hailed in many quarters as the most significant achievement in international monetary affairs since the formation of the IMF at Bretton Woods in 1944.

UNITED STATES
TREASURY DEPARTMENT

U.S. BALANCE
OF PAYMENTS—
THE RECORD TO DATE

47

This chapter traces the evolution of the U.S. balance of payments
during the 1960's and the measures adopted to cope with the deficit.

In general, the United States has sought to improve its balance of
payments in ways that are conducive to (1) vigorous economic
growth at home and in the rest of the world, (2) reasonable price
stability at home and abroad, and (3) the preservation of an international framework for trading and investing that encourages the
best use of resources. The specific measures adopted have attempted
to avoid interfering with the maintenance of international security
and the flow of capital to developing nations while recognizing the
special role of the U.S. dollar in the international monetary system.

A. TRENDS SINCE WORLD WAR II

For more than a decade after the end of World War II, the economic
and financial policies of the United States and of other countries
were influenced by an overriding need to get the world economy
back on its feet. Tremendous progress was made—in physical reconstruction, in bringing the defeated countries, Germany, Italy, and
Japan, back into the currents of world trade, in gradually dismantling much of the pre-war and wartime paraphernalia of exchange controls and trade controls, in rebuilding monetary reserves,

Reprinted from United States Treasury Department, "U.S. Balance of
Payments—The Record to Date," *Maintaining the Strength of the United
States Dollar in a Strong, Free World Economy*, Washington, D.C.: Gov-
ernment Printing Office, 1948, pp. 53–62.

in reactivating the machinery of private credit. Severe inflation was halted. To help Europe and Japan get into the position of financing themselves internationally by trade instead of American aid, many currencies were devalued in 1949. Later, the French franc was again devalued in 1957 and 1958.

In this earlier period the United States had a balance of payments deficit, but it was not one that this nation or other nations were concerned about. The deficit may be said to have been almost deliberately created, to help rebuild the economies of the rest of the world and to rebuild the monetary reserves of the rest of world. The great problem for the whole world was the "dollar gap," and we were doing our best to close it.

In the mid-1950's, Europe and Japan were rapidly regaining their economic strength. Between the recessions of 1954 and 1958, the United States had a consumption and investment boom during which our price level for metals and machinery rose 20 percent (from the end of 1954 to the end of 1957). By the end of 1959 those prices—particularly important in determining our international competitive position—were nearly one-fourth higher than in 1954. With Europe and Japan steadily increasing their ability to produce goods for export, conditions were being created that would make it more difficult than before for the United States to achieve an *adequate* surplus in the current account of the balance of payments—that is, a current surplus sufficiently large to cover the flows of U.S. private and Government capital to the rest of the world.

Beginning in 1958, the United States has had a long series of large international payments deficits. These deficits, and our reserve losses, averaged much larger in 1958–60 than in the preceding ten years, and though reduced after 1960 they remained excessive. (See charts.)

Throughout the last ten years, except in 1958 and 1959, the United States has had large annual surpluses in net exports of goods and services (nonmilitary plus private remittances and pension payments). But these surpluses have been inadequate to cover the net outflow of capital and the government overseas costs of our security. Furthermore, in the last two years, this surplus has dropped somewhat at the same time that private capital outflows and the costs of maintaining security have risen.

The overall deficits have eaten into our net reserve position. During the past ten years our gold reserves fell from $23 billion to $12 billion, while our liquid liabilities to foreign central banks and governments increased from $9 billion to $16 billion. Nearly half of these gold losses occurred in the period 1958–60.

In addition, our other liquid liabilities increased by about $10 bil-

U.S. Balance of Payments on "Liquidity" Basis and Gold Sales

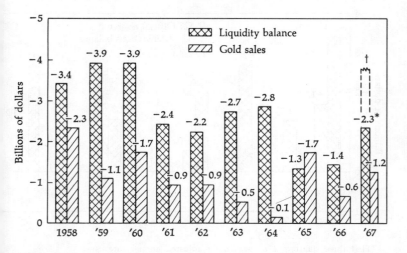

*First three quarters 1967 seasonally adjusted annual rate. †Preliminary full year estimate −$3.5 to −$4.0.

NOTE: Includes sales for domestic industrial and artistic purposes. Also includes acquisitions from IMF of $300 million of gold in 1960 and $150 million in 1961 and a payment of $259 million of gold for quota increases in 1965.

lion during the ten-year period in question. This growth of liquid liabilities to others than foreign central banks and governments served to hold down the amounts of the deficits that had to be financed by official reserve transactions, including gold sales.

After the end of the long steel strike in 1959 we had for five years an unprecedented degree of stability in U.S. industrial prices, while creeping inflation was going on in the rest of the world. (See Tables 1 and 2.) Along with that price stability we had an unprecedentedly long period of uninterrupted economic growth, and a great expansion of both our international receipts and our international expenditures.

In the period from 1960 to 1964, the U.S. balance of payments was characterized by a growing surplus on current transactions as the U.S. competitive position improved. In this period the trade surplus increased markedly, and receipts of income from foreign investments rose sharply. Also, the balance of payments cost of foreign aid was reduced through tying aid to U.S. goods and services, and net military outlays decreased as a result of economies and offset sales.

U.S. Balance of Payments on "Official Settlements" Basis and Gold Sales

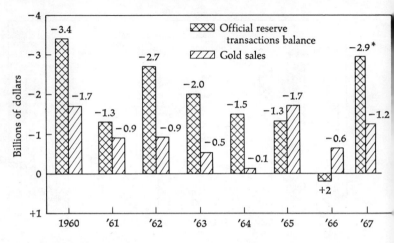

*First three quarters 1967 seasonally adjusted annual rate.

NOTE: The official settlements balance counts changes in dollar claims of foreign official monetary authorities—but not private holdings—in addition to reserve losses of the U.S. The liquidity balance counts changes in the liquid dollar holdings of all foreigners—private and public—as well as losses in reserves.

TABLE 1 Wholesale Prices for Manufactures—U.S. and Major Foreign Competitors (1960=100, national currency basis)

	1958–60 annual average	1961	1962	1963	1964	1965
European Economic Community						
France[1]	95.6	103.0	104.1	107.2	109.8	110.4
Germany[2]	99.2	102.3	104.6	105.8	106.6	109.2
Italy[2]	100.7	99.8	104.2	110.1	113.8	116.8
United Kingdom[3]	98.8	102.7	104.0	104.7	107.5	111.6
Canada[3]	99.4	101.0	102.8	105.0	105.9	107.9
Japan[2]	98.2	100.9	101.2	105.2	105.2	109.1
United States[3][4]	99.5	100.0	100.3	100.0	100.4	102.2

[1] Intermediate goods.

[2] Consumer goods.

[3] Manufactured goods.

[4] For purposes of international comparison, U.S. data represent an OECD re-weighting of official U.S. indices, and exclude manufactured foods.

SOURCE: Derived from data in "Main Economic Indicators," published by the Organization for Economic Cooperation and Development.

TABLE 2   Unit Labor Costs for Manufacturers—U.S. and Major
Foreign Competitors (1957=100, U.S. dollar basis[1])

	1958–60 annual average	1961	1962	1963	1964	1965
European Economic Community						
France	88	94	101	105	110	112
Germany	104	116	125	129	129	137
Italy	100	95	99	110	113	109
United Kingdom	104	111	114	113	114	120
Canada	100	94	88	87	86	87
Japan	101	100	109	113	111	118
United States	104	106	105	104	104	103

[1] Adjusted for changes in dollar parities of foreign currencies.
SOURCES: Derived from data published by the Bureau of Labor Statistics and the National Institute of Economic and Social Research.

The favorable trend in the balance on goods and services from 1960 to 1964 was offset, however, by a strong tendency for private capital outflow to increase—a tendency that was dampened first by the Interest Equalization Tax (mid-1963) and later, in 1965, by the voluntary programs to restrain direct investment in subsidiary companies abroad and loans abroad by U.S. financial institutions.

Though the overall balance of payments position was sharply improved in 1965 as the result of the voluntary restraint programs, the current account surplus began to worsen again. Especially from mid-1965 to the end of 1966, the underlying position worsened as a result of both the foreign exchange costs of the Vietnam War and the impact on the U.S. trade balance of the sudden upsurge in demand and rising prices. In 1967 there was a pause in the previously very rapid rise in imports, but as a result of the recessions in economic activity in some important foreign countries the rise in our exports also slowed.

B. U.S. BALANCE OF PAYMENTS PROGRAMS

In the period 1961–65, the Kennedy and Johnson Administrations launched a series of attacks on the balance of payments problem. These programs, described in Messages by President Kennedy in February 1961 and July 1963, and by President Johnson in February 1965, included in a broad spectrum of administrative and legislative measures designed:

* to increase American exports of goods and services;
* to increase inflows of portfolio capital and tourist receipts;
* to moderate private capital outflows;
* to reduce Federal Government foreign exchange outlays; and
* to strengthen international financial cooperation through such multilateral institutions as the International Monetary Fund and the Organization for Economic Cooperation and Development.

These Presidential recommendations for action shared a common philosophical underpinning, enunciated by President Kennedy in his February 1961 balance of payments message:

* The official price of gold will be maintained at $35 per ounce;
* National security and economic development programs will be carried forward:
* Maximum emphasis must be placed on expanding exports. This requires that costs and prices be kept low and that the Government help to enlarge foreign markets for American goods and services;
* A return to protectionism is not a solution; and
* The United States must take the lead in harmonizing economic policies among those industrialized nations whose behavior has a major influence on the course of world income and trade.

This statement of policy was in accord with the general objectives of the Eisenhower Administration, as set forth, for example, in the January 1961 Economic Report of the President.

During 1961–64, fiscal and monetary policy aimed at encouraging noninflationary economic expansion, and as already noted there was improvement in the current account of the balance of payments in this period. Selective fiscal and monetary measures also affected the capital account of the balance of payments. These actions included:

* reductions in corporate income taxes;
* liberalized depreciation allowances, to bring our rates more closely into line with those of our major foreign competitors;
* passage of the 7 percent investment credit;
* carefully designed monetary policies to keep domestic long-term interest rates low while moving shorter-term interest rates higher to minimize short-term capital outflows ("Operation Twist").

Over the four-year period 1961–64, an improvement of more than $3.7 billion took place in the following accounts:

* a higher commercial trade surplus ($1 billion);
* reduced overseas dollar spending for foreign aid ($400 million);
* economies in military spending abroad ($200 million);
* increased deliveries on military offset sales to foreign countries by the Department of Defense ($400 million);

• and an increase in profits and interest on past foreign investments ($1.7 billion).

The net *overall* improvement for 1964, however, fell far short *because of a sharp rise in overall private capital outflows,* including both short- and long-term bank credits and direct investment. The $3.9 billion deficit in 1960 was reduced to $2.8 billion in 1964.

The new balance of payments measures introduced by President Johnson in February 1965 served to check the rapid growth that had been developing in private capital outflows. His message called upon the business and banking community to do everything in their power to help to reduce overall private capital outflows. In addition, the President asked for legislation to remove tax barriers to foreign investment in the United States, an extension and broadening of the Interest Equalization Tax, further efforts to promote U.S. exports and foreign tourism in this country, and reductions in duty-free allowances for returning American tourists.

In response to the voluntary credit restraint programs, U.S. private capital outflows dropped substantially and the balance of payments deficit on the liquidity basis was cut from $2.8 billion in 1964 to $1.3 billion in 1965.

C. DEVELOPMENTS IN 1966 AND 1967

The year 1966 brought a halt to further progress toward equilibrium, owing primarily to:
• mounting direct costs of Vietnam, military expenditures related to Southeast Asia showing a further increase of $700 million over those of the preceding year;
• a $1.1 billion deterioration in our trade surplus which resulted from a flood of imports induced by unusually rapid and unbalanced increases in aggregate domestic demand and renewed inflationary pressures (associated in part with acceleration of defense outlays). U.S. export performance also was adversely affected by these factors, as well as by lagging economic growth in some major foreign markets.

On the other hand, U.S. capital outflow increased only a little in 1966, reflecting the continued effects of the Interest Equalization Tax, the Federal Reserve and Commerce Department voluntary restraint programs, as well as the tight credit conditions prevailing during much of the year. Meanwhile, there was a substantial increase in foreign capital inflow, as U.S. corporations sold securities abroad to finance direct investment abroad and as the Treasury Department launched a campaign to acquaint foreign central banks and others with certain long-term investments in the United States—notably certificates of deposit issued by commercial banks and certain federal agency bonds and participation certificates. Foreign purchases of these instruments were motivated by attractive interest returns as well as by the desire to reduce the large burden imposed upon the U.S. balance of payments by its growing overseas security and economic assistance efforts.

All in all, therefore, the liquidity deficit remained unchanged from 1965 to 1966. And the balance on the official settlements basis showed its first annual surplus, as the dollar holdings of foreign central banks fell substantially, reflecting the attraction of high interest rates for increased private dollar holdings in the Euro-dollar market and in the United States.

During the first three quarters of 1967 the balance of payments deficit was higher (at a seasonally adjusted annual rate) than in 1965–66.

The trade surplus increased only slightly from its depressed level of 1966. Imports leveled off with the slackening in aggregate demand in the U.S. economy in the first half of the year, but began to rise again toward the end of the year. Exports also leveled off, partly because economic activity in Western Europe was not expanding much during the spring and summer. Though activity was picking up in Germany in the autumn, conditions were still slack in a number of other countries.

There was a further increase in U.S. military expenditures in Vietnam in 1967 and a sizable increase in the outflow of U.S. private capital, particularly through purchases of foreign and international securities exempt from the IET, and through bank lending abroad. The larger capital outflow was in part a normal reflection of easier monetary conditions in the United States as compared with 1966. The improved liquidity of commercial banks helps to explain not only the increase in bank loans to foreign borrowers but also the repayment in the first half of the year of debt of head offices of banks to their branches abroad. The result of this reflow shows up in the very large deficit on the official settlements basis in the first half of the year.

In the final quarter of 1967 there was a large deficit—substantially larger than the quarterly average through September. This further deterioration was accounted for, mainly, by the following factors: liquidation by the U.K. Government of the $600 million balance in its portfolio of U.S. securities; speculative pressures in connection with the sterling devaluation; absence of substantial net foreign official acquisitions of long-term time deposits (as in 1966 and the

TABLE 3 U.S. Balance of Payments: 1958–1960, 1965, 1966, and January–September 1967 *(in billions of dollars)*

	Average 1958–1960	1965	1966	1967 Jan.–Sept. (annual rate)
Trade surplus	3.02	4.77	3.66	4.35
Surplus on total private and Government non-military current account[1]	4.26	8.00	6.94	7.11
Military and Government grant and capital transactions, net	−5.32	−5.26	−6.23	−6.60
Net military[2]	−2.89	−1.82	−2.75	−3.08
Of which: Increased expenditures related to Southeast Asia[3]	—	(−0.25)	(−0.95)	(n.a.)
Gross grant and capital outlays[4]	−3.19	−4.28	−4.68	−5.24
Repayments on Government credits and other Government capital receipts	0.76	0.85	1.20	1.72
(Net balance-of-payments cost of total Government-sector transactions)[5]	[6](−3.71)	(−2.59)	(−3.24)	−3.49
U.S. private capital, net	−3.06	−3.74	−4.21	−5.05
Other transactions, net	0.42	−0.33	2.14	2.25
Of which: Foreign capital	(0.41)	(0.08)	(2.45)	(3.17)
Of which U.K. Government portfolio	(—)	(−0.50)	(—)	(—)
Balance on liquidity basis	−3.71	−1.34	−1.36	−2.28
Balance on official settlements basis	n.a.	−1.30	0.23	−2.90

[1] Nonmilitary goods and services plus remittances and pensions. [2] Military expenditures less military cash receipts, as published by Commerce Department in balance-of-payment accounts. In 1958–60, less transfers under military sales contracts. [3] Increases over calendar year 1964 level. [4] Total foreign aid and credits, including outlays used on a "tied" basis to finance exports and other receipts of both private and Government sectors. [5] Excludes from net Government transactions that part of foreign aid and credits used on a "tied" basis to finance exports and other private-sector receipts. [6] 1960 only.

NOTE: Detail may not add to totals due to rounding.   SOURCE: Derived from Department of Commerce data.

first half of 1967); a deterioration in the trade surplus. (Complete data for the quarter are not yet available.)

Table 3 summarizes the U.S. balance of payments performance from 1958–60 through the first three quarters of 1967.

D. NEW ACTION PROGRAM

The British devaluation of sterling has reinforced the urgency of the need to improve the U.S. balance of payments. The British move created uncertainty and unrest in the international monetary system and doubts about the future stability of the dollar. These doubts arose in large part because of the persistence of large U.S. deficits and uncertainty as to whether the U.S. payments position would improve.

In these circumstances, it was urgent that the United States adopt strong measures to deal with the balance of payments problem. This it has done. Some of the new measures are clearly temporary. Others are of a long-run nature.

The U.S. program will inevitably create the need for adjustments elsewhere in the world. If the program is to lead to better and sustainable payments equilibrium, reduction of the U.S. deficit must be accompanied by reduction of surpluses in Western Europe.

The result will be a distinct slowdown in the rate of growth of world reserves, and as the United Kingdom repays its debts to the International Monetary Fund, possibly a decline in world reserves. This development will bring much closer the appropriate time for activation of the plan for creation of Special Drawing Rights.

PRESIDENT LYNDON B. JOHNSON

BALANCE OF PAYMENTS:
STATEMENT BY THE PRESIDENT
OUTLINING A PROGRAM OF ACTION—
JANUARY 1, 1968

48

WHERE WE STAND TODAY

I want to discuss with the American people a subject of vital concern to the economic health and well-being of this Nation and the free world.

It is our international balance of payments position.

The strength of our dollar depends on the strength of that position.

The soundness of the free world monetary system, which rests largely on the dollar, also depends on the strength of that position.

To the average citizen, the balance of payments, and the strength of the dollar and of the international monetary system, are meaningless phrases. They seem to have little relevance to our daily lives. Yet their consequences touch us all—consumer and captain of industry, worker, farmer, and financier.

More than ever before, the economy of each nation is today deeply intertwined with that of every other. A vast network of world trade and financial transactions ties us all together. The prosperity of every economy rests on that of every other.

More than ever before, this is one world—in economic affairs as in every other way.

Your job, the prosperity of your farm or business, depends directly or indirectly on what happens in Europe, Asia, Latin America, or Africa.

The health of the international economic system rests on a sound international money in the same way as the health of our domestic money. Today, our domestic money—the U.S. dollar—is also the money most used in international transactions. That money can be sound at home—as it surely is—yet can be in trouble abroad—as it now threatens to become.

In the final analysis its strength abroad depends on our earning abroad about as many dollars as we send abroad.

Reprinted from President Lyndon B. Johnson, "Balance of Payments: Statement by the President Outlining a Program of Action—January 1, 1968," *Weekly Compilation of Presidential Documents*, Vol. 4 (Jan. 8, 1968), pp. 20–26.

U.S. dollars flow from these shores for many reasons—to pay for imports and travel, to finance loans and investments, and to maintain our lines of defense around the world.

When that outflow is greater than our earnings and credits from foreign nations, a deficit results in our international accounts.

For 17 of the last 18 years we have had such deficits. For a time those deficits were needed to help the world recover from the ravages of World War II. They could be tolerated by the United States and welcomed by the rest of the world. They distributed more equitably the world's monetary gold reserves and supplemented them with dollars.

Once recovery was assured, however, large deficits were no longer needed and indeed began to threaten the strength of the dollar. Since 1961, your Government has worked to reduce that deficit.

By the middle of the decade, we could see signs of success. Our annual deficit had been reduced two-thirds—from $3.9 billion in 1960 to $1.3 billion in 1965.

In 1966, because of our increased responsibility to arm and supply our men in Southeast Asia, progress was interrupted, with the deficit remaining at the same level as 1965—about $1.3 billion.

In 1967, progress was reversed for a number of reasons:

- Our costs for Vietnam increased further.
- Private loans and investments abroad increased.
- Our trade surplus, although larger than 1966, did not rise as much as we had expected.
- Americans spent more on travel abroad.

Added to these factors was the uncertainty and unrest surrounding the devaluation of the British pound. This event strained the international monetary system. It sharply increased our balance of payments deficit and our gold sales in the last quarter of 1967.

THE PROBLEM

Preliminary reports indicated that these conditions may result in a 1967 balance of payments deficit in the area of $3.5 to $4 billion —the highest since 1960. Although some factors affecting our deficit will be more favorable in 1968, my advisers and I are convinced that we must act to bring about a decisive improvement.

We cannot tolerate a deficit that could threaten the stability of the international monetary system—of which the U.S. dollar is the bulwark.

We cannot tolerate a deficit that could endanger the strength of the entire free world economy, and thereby threaten our unprecedented prosperity at home.

A TIME FOR ACTION

The time has now come for decisive action designed to bring our balance of payments to—or close to—equilibrium in the year ahead.

The need for action is a national and international responsibility of the highest priority.

I am proposing a program which will meet this critical need, and at the same time satisfy four essential conditions:

- Sustain the growth, strength, and prosperity of our own economy.
- Allow us to continue to meet our international responsibilities in defense of freedom, in promoting world trade, and in encouraging economic growth in the developing countries.
- Engage the cooperation of other free nations, whose stake in a sound international monetary system is no less compelling than our own.
- Recognize the special obligation of those nations with balance of payments surpluses to bring their payments into equilibrium.

THE FIRST ORDER OF BUSINESS

The first line of defense of the dollar is the strength of the American economy.

No business before the returning Congress will be more urgent than this: to enact the anti-inflation tax which I have sought for almost a year. Coupled with our expenditure controls and appropriate monetary policy, this will help to stem the inflationary pressures which now threaten our economic prosperity and our trade surplus.

No challenge before business and labor is more urgent than this: to exercise the utmost responsibility in their wage-price decisions, which affect so directly our competitive position at home and in world markets.

I have directed the Secretaries of Commerce and Labor, and the Chairman of the Council of Economic Advisers to work with leaders of business and labor to make more effective our voluntary program of wage-price restraint.

I have also instructed the Secretaries of Commerce and Labor to work with unions and companies to prevent our exports from being reduced or our imports increased by crippling work stoppages in the year ahead.

A sure way to instill confidence in our dollar—both here and abroad—is through these actions.

THE NEW PROGRAM

But we must go beyond this, and take additional action to deal with the balance of payments deficit.

Some of the elements in the program I propose will have a temporary but immediate effect. Others will be of longer range.

All are necessary to assure confidence in the American dollar.

TEMPORARY MEASURES

1. Direct Investment

Over the past 3 years, American business has cooperated with the Government in a voluntary program to moderate the flow of U.S. dollars into foreign investments. Business leaders who have participated so whole-heartedly deserve the appreciation of their country.

But the savings now required in foreign investment outlays are clearly beyond the reach of any voluntary program. This is the unanimous view of all my economic and financial advisers and the Chairman of the Federal Reserve Board.

To reduce our balance of payments deficit by at least $1 billion in 1968 from the estimated 1967 level, I am invoking my authority under the banking laws to establish a mandatory program that will restrain direct investment abroad.

This program will be effective immediately. It will insure success and guarantee fairness among American business firms with overseas investments.

The program will be administered by the Department of Commerce, and will operate as follows:

- As in the voluntary program, overall and individual company targets will be set. Authorizations to exceed these targets will be issued only in exceptional circumstances.
- New direct investment outflows to countries in continental Western Europe and other developed nations not heavily dependent on our capital will be stopped in 1968. Problems arising from work already in process or commitments under binding contracts will receive special consideration.

- New net investments in other developed countries will be limited to 65 percent of the 1965–66 average.
- New net investments in the developing countries will be limited to 110 percent of the 1965–66 average.

This program also requires businesses to continue to bring back foreign earnings to the United States in line with their own 1964–66 practices.

In addition, I have directed the Secretary of the Treasury to explore with the Chairmen of the House Ways and Means Committee and Senate Finance Committee legislative proposals to induce or encourage the repatriation of accumulated earnings by U.S.-owned foreign businesses.

2. Lending by Financial Institutions

To reduce the balance of payments deficit by at least another $500 million, I have requested and authorized the Federal Reserve Board to tighten its program restraining foreign lending by banks and other financial institutions.

Chairman Martin has assured me that this reduction can be achieved:

- Without harming the financing of our exports;
- Primarily out of credits to developed countries without jeopardizing the availability of funds to the rest of the world.

Chairman Martin believes that this objective can be met through continued cooperation by the financial community. At the request of the Chairman, however, I have given the Federal Reserve Board standby authority to invoke mandatory controls, should such controls become desirable or necessary.

3. Travel Abroad

Our travel deficit this year will exceed $2 billion. To reduce this deficit by $500 million:

- *I am asking American people to defer for the next 2 years all nonessential travel outside the Western Hemisphere.*
- *I am asking the Secretary of the Treasury to explore with the appropriate congressional committees legislation to help achieve this objective.*

4. Government Expenditures Overseas

We cannot forego our essential commitments abroad, on which America's security and survival depend.

Nevertheless, we must take every step to reduce their impact on our balance of payments without endangering our security.

Recently, we have reached important agreements with some of our NATO partners to lessen the balance of payments cost of deploying American forces on the Continent—troops necessarily stationed there for the common defense of all.

Over the past 3 years, a stringent program has saved billions of dollars in foreign exchange.

I am convinced that much more can be done. *I believe we should set as our target avoiding a drain of another $500 million on our balance of payments.*

To this end, I am taking three steps.

First, I have directed the Secretary of State to initiate prompt negotiations with our NATO allies to minimize the foreign exchange costs of keeping our troops in Europe. Our allies can help in a number of ways, including:

- The purchase in the United States of more of their defense needs.
- Investments in long-term United States securities.

I have also directed the Secretaries of State, Treasury, and Defense to find similar ways of dealing with this problem in other parts of the world.

Second, I have instructed the Director of the Budget to find ways of reducing the number of American civilians working overseas.

Third, I have instructed the Secretary of Defense to find ways to reduce further the foreign exchange impact of personal spending by U.S. forces and their dependents in Europe.

LONG-TERM MEASURES

5. Export Increases

American exports provide an important source of earnings for our businessmen and jobs for our workers.

They are the cornerstone of our balance of payments position.

Last year we sold abroad $30 billion worth of American goods.

What we now need is a long-range systematic program to stimulate the flow of the products of our factories and farms into overseas markets.

We must begin now.

Some of the steps require legislation:

I shall ask the Congress to support an intensified 5 year, $200 million Commerce Department program to promote the sale of American goods overseas.

I shall also ask the Congress to earmark $500 million of the Export-Import Bank authorization to:
  • *Provide better export insurance.*
  • *Expand guarantees for export financing.*
  • *Broaden the scope of government financing of our exports.*
Other measures require no legislation.

I have today directed the Secretary of Commerce to begin a Joint Export Association Program. Through these associations, we will provide direct financial support to American corporations joining together to sell abroad.

And finally, the Export-Import Bank—through a more liberal rediscount system—will encourage banks across the Nation to help firms increase their exports.

6. Nontariff Barriers

In the Kennedy Round, we climaxed three decades of intensive effort to achieve the greatest reduction in tariff barriers in all the history of trade negotiations. Trade liberalization remains the basic policy of the United States.

We must now look beyond the great success of the Kennedy Round to the problems of nontariff barriers that pose a continued threat to the growth of world trade and to our competitive position.

American commerce is at a disadvantage because of the tax systems of some of our trading partners. Some nations give across-the-board tax rebates on exports which leave their ports and impose special border tax charges on our goods entering their country.

International rules govern these special taxes under the General Agreement on Tariffs and Trade. These rules must be adjusted to expand international trade further.

In keeping with the principles of cooperation and consultation on common problems, I have initiated discussions at a high level with our friends abroad on these critical matters—particularly those nations with balance of payments surpluses.

These discussions will examine proposals for prompt cooperative action among all parties to minimize the disadvantages to our trade which arise from differences among national tax systems.

We are also preparing legislative measures in this area whose scope and nature will depend upon the outcome of these consultations.

Through these means we are determined to achieve a substantial improvement in our trade surplus over the coming years. In the year immediately ahead, we expect to realize an improvement of $500 million.

7. Foreign Investment and Travel in the United States

We can encourage the flow of foreign funds to our shores in two other ways:

- *First, by an intensified program to attract greater foreign investment in U.S. corporate securities, carrying out the principles of the Foreign Investors Tax Act of 1966.*
- *Second, by a program to attract more visitors to this land. A special task force, headed by Robert McKinney of Santa Fe, N. Mex., is already at work on measures to accomplish this. I have directed the task force to report within 45 days on the immediate measures that can be taken, and to make its long-term recommendations within 90 days.*

MEETING THE WORLD'S RESERVE NEEDS

Our movement toward balance will curb the flow of dollars into international reserves It will therefore be vital to speed up plans for the creation of new reserves—the special drawing rights—in the International Monetary Fund. These new reserves will be a welcome companion to gold and dollars, and will strengthen the gold exchange standard. The dollar will remain convertible into gold at $35 an ounce, and our full gold stock will back that commitment.

A TIME FOR RESPONSIBILITY

The program I have outlined is a program of action.

It is a program which will preserve confidence in the dollar, both at home and abroad.

The U.S. dollar has wrought the greatest economic miracles of modern times.

It stimulated the resurgence of a war-ruined Europe.

It has helped to bring new strength and life to the developing world.

It has underwritten unprecedented prosperity for the American people, who are now in the 83d month of sustained economic growth.

A strong dollar protects and preserves the prosperity of businessman and banker, worker and farmer—here and overseas.

The action program I have outlined in this message will keep the dollar strong. It will fulfill our responsibilities to the American people and to the free world.

I appeal to all of our citizens to join me in this very necessary and laudable effort to preserve our country's financial strength.

Note: The statement was released at San Antonio, Texas.

WILLIAM MC CHESNEY MARTIN

THE PRICE OF GOLD IS NOT THE PROBLEM

49

The international monetary system has been the subject of much uncertainty in recent months. The devaluation of sterling in November provided a shock which, against the background of a persistent deficit in the U.S. balance of payments, precipitated fundamental questioning as to the evolution of the international monetary system, the role of the dollar, and the price of gold. A number of observers in the United States and abroad have come to the conclusion that an increase in the official price of gold would be desirable; others have decided that, even if it is undesirable, a rise in the gold price is inevitable.

I am firmly of the belief that a higher gold price is neither necessary nor desirable. In reviewing with you the problems of the international monetary system, I want to make it unmistakably clear that the future evolution of the system can and should be based on the present price of gold.

There is no doubt that the problems facing the international monetary system are serious. I have no wish to underestimate their gravity. Consideration of the various solutions that have been proposed must be based on a clear understanding of the nature of the prob-

Reprinted from William McChesney Martin, "The Price of Gold Is Not the Problem," *Federal Reserve Bulletin*, Vol. 54 (February 1968), pp. 115–121.

lems that we face. This is a time for cool-headed appraisal in the light of history and not for unmindful acceptance of panaceas that risk overturning a system that has provided the monetary framework for an unprecedented expansion of world income and trade in the period since Bretton Woods.

The case I shall put to you in what follows can be summarized in two straight-forward propositions.

First, it is imperative to adjust the balance of payments of the United States away from large and persistent deficit and of continental Europe away from large and persistent surplus. A higher gold price would do nothing to bring about those adjustments.

Second, the nations of the world need a means of increasing their reserves in a way that is not dependent on continuing deficits in the U.S. balance of payments. I am confident that the Rio Agreement on Special Drawing Rights (SDR's) can fulfill this function at the present price of gold.

THE DOLLAR AND THE U.S. BALANCE OF PAYMENTS

The root of the present imbalance in international payments can be traced back to the early years after World War II. At that time the United States initiated a program of international assistance designed to promote the economic recovery of war-damaged countries. In the process, the United States deliberately created a deficit in its balance of payments, while countries in Europe and elsewhere deliberately sought to achieve surpluses. An important by-product of the recovery program was that it increased the depleted reserves of the war-torn countries—by putting them in a position to accumulate dollar balances and by redistributing U.S. gold reserves —which at the end of 1948 comprised more than 70 per cent of world gold holdings.

Policies designed to encourage a U.S. payments deficit took many forms. We provided funds through the Marshall Plan in amounts larger than was necessary for countries in Europe to purchase badly needed American goods, thus making it possible for aid recipients to accumulate dollar reserves. We deliberately kept the aid untied by encouraging the spending of U.S. grants and loans in countries other than the United States. Much of the aid was in the form of grants rather than loans, so as to avoid burdening the future payments positions of the recipients. We provided special inducements for direct investment by American corporations abroad. We even encouraged European countries to liberalize their imports from each other while they continued to restrict their imports from the United

States, and later we supported the formation of the Common Market.

In these and other ways the United States adjusted its policies—and its citizens responded in their actions as importers, lenders, investors, and travelers—to the maintenance of a deficit in its balance of payments. In other words, the United States accustomed itself to an outflow of government and private capital in excess of its surplus on goods and services—with the result, as intended, that U.S. dollar liabilities increased and U.S. gold reserves fell. The countries of continental Europe made a corresponding adjustment to a surplus position—that is, to an inflow of capital from abroad combined with a pattern of transactions on current account that resulted in steady and sizable increases in their gold and dollar reserves. It was during this period that the dollar became the world's major reserve currency.

It is significant that in those early years we did not describe these payments positions as "deficits" and "surpluses." Many a newspaper article and book were written at that time about the persistent U.S. "surplus" and the intractable dollar shortage. The build-up of U.S. dollar balances abroad, together with the sale of U.S. gold to other countries, was universally regarded as desirable. And so it was.

But, like the man who came to dinner, the U.S. deficit, though invited, stayed too long. And so did the European surpluses. Both became chronic.

A continuing U.S. deficit of substantial size is neither desirable nor tolerable. Such a deficit saps the international liquidity position of the nation, by continually building up liquid liabilities abroad or continually reducing U.S. reserves, or both. A steady worsening of our liquidity position—even while our net worth is improving—cannot be sustained indefinitely. As a reserve currency, the dollar is widely held around the world. It is natural that holders of dollars look to our gold and other reserves, expecting us to maintain a reasonable relationship between our liquid reserves and our short-term liabilities, just as depositors look to the funds held in reserve by their banks.

The United States as a bank to the rest of the world was in the early postwar years a bank with *too* strong a liquidity position. By means of the Marshall Plan and the other policies I have mentioned, the bank embarked on a deliberate program that transformed its liquid assets into less liquid form, while its liquid liabilities expanded. In the process, the bank basically improved its position, while contributing significantly to world economic growth, for it acquired sound and high-yielding long-term assets around the world as a counterpart to its increasing liabilities. But its liquidity deteriorated, since its most liquid asset—its gold reserves—declined while its liabilities expanded.

This drawing-down in the bank's liquidity position—once welcome—has now gone on for too long. The time has come to arrest it, and to do so decisively. As this happens, the bank's depositors —the rest of the world—must adjust to a slowdown in the lending and deposit-creating activities of the bank by providing other sources of capital and by establishing another means of increasing international reserves.

In other words, the world payments pattern is going through a period of transition—away from the pattern I have described—and the transition is understandably a painful one, since it requires a modification of so many policies and habits established earlier. The United States must cut the suit of its payments abroad to fit the cloth of its receipts from abroad. And the countries of continental Europe must do the reverse—they must find ways to export capital in an amount equal to the excess of their exports over their imports of goods and services—or else they must reduce their export surpluses. And the adjustment by both sides should be carried out in a way that is compatible with the healthy and inflation-free growth of the world economy.

The U.S. balance of payments program, announced on January 1 by President Johnson, should produce substantial results. That program is more severe than would have been needed had timely action on the domestic stabilization front been taken a year or more ago. Furthermore, the new program necessarily represents a step backward—temporarily—from our aspirations for freer world investment and trade. While the various features of the program are serving a necessary stop-gap purpose, it is essential that the United States strengthen its underlying payments position. This means, at the very least, that it is vital for the United States to pursue effective stabilization policies that promote price stability and a competitive cost structure.

The results of the balance of payments program will be sustainable only if the reduction of the U.S. deficit has as its counterpart a reduction of European surpluses. This is so because there are not many countries outside of continental Europe that earn large surpluses or that have strong enough reserves to be able to adjust to a substantial improvement of the U.S. payments balance.

I am pleased to say that the reactions of European officials to the announcement of the U.S. program seem by and large to be highly constructive. They have made it clear that they understand the economic necessity I have just mentioned and that they intend to adopt policies designed to facilitate rather than interfere with the adjustment of the payments imbalance.

European officials recognize the need to prevent a reduction in total demand in their economies as U.S. foreign investment and other forms of spending in Europe decrease. They recognize the need to offset through their monetary policies tendencies for the reduction in the flow of dollars to Europe to tighten monetary conditions there and, more broadly, they recognize the need to encourage capital outflows from their markets. And they acknowledge that the pursuit of such policies may result in reductions in their own reserves.

Thus, we have before us the possibility, *if stated intentions on both sides of the Atlantic are implemented with proper actions,* of a highly successful effort of international cooperation—aimed at rectifying the imbalance in international payments and completing the transition away from the payments pattern that was established, in response to need, in the earlier postwar period.

In the light of this way of looking at the balance of payments adjustment problem, I can now put to you the following question: Is there any reason to think that a higher gold price would help to bring about the needed adjustment?

It can be taken for granted that a unilateral devaluation by the United States is impossible; a change in the price of gold in terms of dollars would undoubtedly be accompanied by an equal change in terms of virtually all other currencies.

Would the U.S. balance of payments improve as the result of such an increase in the price of gold? Only to the extent that the enlarged foreign exchange earnings of gold producing countries led them to increase their purchases from the United States. But this would be a very small benefit compared with the magnitude of the U.S. payments deficit and would be far outweighed by the many disadvantages that would accompany an increase in the gold price. Would American corporations have less incentive to invest abroad? Would Americans travel less? Would developing nations need less aid? Would our imports decrease? Would our military spending in Europe and Asia seem less pressing—if the price of gold were higher? The answer in each case is clearly no.

Would European surpluses decline as the result of a higher gold price? Not at all. In fact, insofar as gold producing nations increased their purchases from Europe, these surpluses would be aggravated.

It seems perfectly clear that a revaluation of gold would make little or no contribution to an adjustment of the imbalance in international payments.

There are those who will accept the point I have just made but will say that an increase in the gold price will buy time for the United States. Buy time for what? They can only mean that it would delay the need for forceful measures to improve the balance of payments—that it would permit the United States to avoid distasteful curbs on capital outflows or other payments abroad and continue to incur deficits, thus putting off the painful adjustment to a healthier balance of payments. It seems clear to me that a measure known to be intended to buy time, if it is not accompanied by action to improve the underlying problem, will in fact buy relatively little time—for markets will anticipate the lapse of the period of bought time and act accordingly. Thus, a rise in the gold price is not an alternative to measures to strengthen the balance of payments. Such measures are required in any event and cannot be avoided by an increase in the price of gold.

The United States can and must pursue domestic fiscal and monetary policies that keep its economy and its price level under control. This is the paramount economic issue of 1968. And it must for the time being persevere with supplementary balance of payments measures to help restore its external payments to equilibrium as quickly as possible. Tinkering with the international price of gold is in no sense a substitute for actions that face up to these hard facts of life.

THE DOLLAR AND INTERNATIONAL LIQUIDITY

I turn now from the balance of payments problem itself to the relation between the U.S. balance of payments and international liquidity and the relevance of this to the price of gold.

It became clear soon after the war that as economic recovery and economic growth proceeded, countries wished to see their gold and foreign exchange reserves increase.

The balance of payments pattern that was established in the postwar period provided a built-in mechanism for expanding not only the reserves of the war-torn countries but also for expanding world reserves. Insofar as other countries added dollars to their reserves instead of using dollar accruals to buy gold from the United States, the U.S. deficit enlarged the reserves of other countries without reducing U.S. reserves. And even when other countries began to use a part of their dollar receipts to purchase gold from the United States, their reserves rose faster than our reserves fell—and world reserves expanded accordingly. But this process had the inevitable effect of reducing the international liquidity position of the United States.

The balance of payments adjustment that must now be accomplished will cut off this major source of reserve growth. Yet the desire of countries around the world to increase their reserves has not diminished and will not diminish. Thus another source of reserve growth will be needed.

It is understandable that nations wish to see their reserves increase over time. Individuals and businesses expect their liquid assets to grow as their incomes grow. Liquid assets are there to be used in times of temporary shortfalls of receipts below payments. But no individual or business and no nation can afford to see its liquid reserves diminish persistently. Taking all nations together we have observed, and will no doubt continue to observe, a tendency to add to reserves over time. What is needed is a steady and dependable supply of new reserves to satisfy this basic desire of nations to increase their reserves—a supply that is neither excessive nor deficient but consistent with the noninflationary growth of the world economy. A once-for-all or once-in-a-generation increase in the value of gold reserves resulting from an increase in the gold price is no substitute for a gradual and steady accretion of new reserves. It is precisely this need that the Special Drawing Rights are designed to fulfill.

It has been clear for many years that new gold production alone cannot provide the necessary increase in world reserves. It is equally clear that dollars cannot and should not any longer satisfy a major part of the desired growth in the reserves of other countries. This was the basis for the unanimous decision of the members of the International Monetary Fund at Rio last September to proceed with the plan for Special Drawing Rights.

It has been said, and correctly, that the Rio agreement is a landmark in international monetary history. It is a landmark because it introduces a new concept—the deliberate creation of international reserves as a supplement to existing reserves of gold and foreign exchange. The Federal Reserve System is based on the proposition that "money will not manage itself." The SDR Agreement can be said to be based on the view that international money will not manage itself either. The willingness of monetary authorities to cooperate, through the International Monetary Fund, in the creation of Special Drawing Rights has unmistakable implications: it means that the world will be assured of a growing supply of reserves *at the present price of gold.*

Events of recent months—the shock to the international monetary system following the devaluation of sterling and the strong reinforcement of the U.S. balance of payments program—lend greater timeliness to the implementation of the Rio Agreement. Once the SDR Amendment is completed by the Executive Board of the International Monetary Fund and approved by its Board of Governors, I would hope that governments would proceed promptly to seek ratification from their legislatures.

THE ROLE OF GOLD

I have said that neither of the two major problems facing the international monetary system calls for an increase in the price of gold. Such a step is neither necessary nor desirable as a solution to the problem of international payments imbalance or to the problem of assuring adequate growth in international reserves. It would be highly disruptive and highly inequitable. A small increase in the gold price would inevitably engender expectations of additional increases in the not-distant future, thus leading both private and official holders of dollars to convert them into gold and negating the increase in international liquidity that the gold price rise was designed to achieve. An increase in the price of gold of sufficient magnitude to avoid arousing expectations of another such move soon would have to be very large. It would undoubtedly be inflationary, for it would expand, by a corresponding amount, both the reserves of gold-holding countries and the purchasing power of private gold holders. Neither a large nor a small rise in the price of gold would increase international reserves in an orderly and equitable manner. Countries with small gold reserves would share very little in the increase in reserves. Other means of increasing reserves of countries—particularly those holding little gold—would be required in any event.

The recommendation of a higher gold price based on the fact that the general price level has risen greatly since the early 1930's while the price of gold has been unchanged mistakenly views gold more as a commodity than as a measure of monetary value and a monetary reserve asset. To raise the price of gold because the general price level has risen would be like increasing the length of the yardstick because the average height of human beings has increased.

In addition to these general economic considerations, which argue strongly against raising the gold price, there are considerations of special concern to the United States. A rise in the gold price would break faith with the many nations around the world that have held dollars on the basis of confidence that the United States would stick to its commitment regarding the price of gold.

Those who recommend an increase in the price of gold or are willing to tolerate it seem to me to have decided that monetary management is impossible on an international scale and that we must yield to blind and immutable forces that somehow govern economic destiny. Given the magnificent record of international monetary and economic cooperation we have witnessed in the past 20 years, I refuse to accept the cynical and desperate view that man must turn back to greater dependence on gold.

Let me be unmistakably clear: in my judgment an increase in the gold price would be wholly detrimental to the best interests of both the United States and the international monetary system.

I have been quoted as saying that gold is a barbarous metal. But it is not *gold* that is barbarous; that wasn't my point. Quite the contrary: gold is a beautiful and noble metal. What *is* barbarous, when it occurs, is man's enslavement to gold for monetary purposes.

It is important to sort out clearly just what the role of gold is for the United States and for the world economy. The reserves of the United States are mainly in the form of gold, and the international monetary system has as one of its foundations the convertibility of the dollar into gold at $35 per ounce. There are some who believe that the U.S. balance of payments problem could somehow be solved if we cut the link between the dollar and gold. I believe this view is mistaken. In the circumstances ruling in recent years, the United States would have had a balance of payments problem, whatever form our reserves happened to take—for the deficit in our payments inevitably led to a reduction of our reserves. We cannot attribute the payments imbalance to the link between the dollar and gold. We can't solve the payments problem by either cutting the link with gold or by reinforcing dependence on gold by raising its price.

Monetary history, both within and among countries, reveals a steady progression away from exclusive dependence on gold as a monetary instrument. In very few countries now is gold any longer used domestically for monetary purposes—either as a medium of exchange or as a regulator of monetary policy. Supplements to and substitutes for gold have been developed and have taken over gold's role as a monetary asset.

The same development has occurred internationally, and today gold comprises only a little more than half of world monetary reserves, with foreign exchange (mainly dollars and sterling) and reserve positions in the IMF making up the other half. The creation and use of SDR's will permit a continuation of this process by which dependence on gold gradually diminishes over time.

Thus gold, which was the major international reserve asset in the past, will continue to be held and used by monetary authorities. But its importance will gradually decline over time as SDR's supply the major part of reserve growth. This evolution, which recognizes the monetary importance of gold but avoids excessive dependence on it, seems to me to be the only rational course for the international monetary system to take.

CONCLUDING OBSERVATIONS

I do not wish to leave you with a false sense of reassurance. The international economy has been passing through critical times and there are serious problems ahead—in the payments relations between the United States and Europe, and in the payments positions of countries in the rest of the world as the U.S. deficit and continental European surpluses are reduced. Meanwhile, other economic problems need continuing attention, including an adequate flow of capital from the advanced to the developing nations and an effective use of such capital. We must never forget that monetary matters and institutions are not an end in themselves but a means to the end of satisfactory economic growth and stability.

While avoiding false optimism, I *do* want to leave you with a sense of confidence regarding international monetary problems. A rational and orderly way is discernible through the twin challenges of balance of payments adjustment and adequate growth of international liquidity—a way that takes the Bretton Woods system and the gold exchange standard as a foundation and supplements them as needed with continued international cooperation, on which so much past progress has been based. I have no doubt that our present international monetary system, supplemented and modified gradually over time, can continue to provide a framework for sustained expansion of world trade and payments and, in turn, for uninterrupted advance in living standards throughout the world.

GRAEME S. DORRANCE

RAPID INFLATION
AND INTERNATIONAL
PAYMENTS

50

While the Fund is vitally interested in encouraging the economic
development of all its members, its interests are naturally concentrated in its special sphere of responsibility, as outlined in the first
of its Articles of Agreement:

To facilitate the expansion and balanced growth of international trade,
and to contribute thereby to the promotion and maintenance of high
levels of employment and real income and to the development of the productive resources of all members as primary objectives of economic
policy.

Hence, the Fund is directly concerned with everything that influences the expansion and balanced growth of international trade, in
the broadest sense, and particularly in the relation between the
growth of a country's trade and its economic progress. Among the
negative influences, rapid inflation is disastrously prominent.

Serious inflation does not limit its ravages to those on the home
economy. It also leads to a worsening of the country's international
position. This can be seen directly in a country's international trading position, its international capital transactions, and its exchange
rate. More broadly, the worsening of a country's position in these
specific fields can seriously damage its general development.

RAPID INFLATION AND TRADE

The effect of inflation on international trade may be described quite
simply. When prices and costs in any country rise rapidly, goods
produced in the country soon become more expensive than similar
goods produced abroad. Unless the exchange rate changes (the exchange rate problem will be discussed later) this encourages imports and discourages exports.

Reprinted from Graeme S. Dorrance, "Rapid Inflation and International
Payments," *The Fund and Bank Review: Finance and Development*, International Bank for Reconstruction and Development, Vol. II (June 1965),
pp. 65–70.

As prices in a country rise more rapidly than in the rest of the world, not only does the rest of the world buy less of its exports, but people in that country tend to turn from buying these increasingly expensive products of their own industries to the relatively cheaper foreign goods. Far from fostering purchases from home producers, which would encourage home output and the substitution of home produced goods for imports, inflation has the opposite effects: imports are encouraged while the growth of domestic industry is discouraged. The effects are not only quantitative but qualitative. Scarce foreign exchange tends to be dissipated on excessively large imports of consumption goods which might well be foregone in order to encourage the development of new industries. On the other hand, the growth of vibrant export industries tends to be stunted, and production of goods which would be acceptable as import substitutes is discouraged.

While the expansion of imports and contraction of exports have a generally depressing effect on a country's growth, the impact of inflationary pressures on specific imports and exports may prove to be of more direct harm. The effects of strong inflation on a country's traditional exports may in many instances be delayed. Producers in well-established activities yielding primary goods greatly in excess of a country's possible needs (e.g., coffee in Brazil, copper in Chile, rubber in Indonesia, and fish in Iceland) cannot turn to other production quickly, nor can they take advantage of inflationary demand at home. Consequently, the harmful effects of inflationary pressures on the output of traditional exports may be exerted over the long term rather than immediately. This long-term effect of inflation should not be underestimated. While their more stable competitors have advanced, Argentina, Bolivia, Brazil, Chile, and Haiti, with long histories of inflation, have not been able to maintain the volume of their exports at even pre-1913 levels.[1]

Yet striking as such long-term effects may be, the immediate effects of inflation on exports may be even more harmful in a country that seeks to encourage initiative, experimentation, and enthusiasm for new methods of production. Development of new products is often made easier if there is a prospect that some export sales may be achieved eventually, bringing with them the benefits of fairly large-scale production. If inflation makes the international competitive position of these producers more difficult, they may be discouraged from undertaking new activities, and diversification of the economy will be hampered. Thus, a comparison of two groups

[1] The evidence on this point is contained in J. Herbert Furth, "On United Nations Economics," *World Politics*, January 1960, pp. 264–271.

of countries, one with relative price stability from 1953 to 1959, and the other with rapid inflation in the same period, showed a marked expansion of traditional exports in the former and relative stagnation in the latter. Perhaps more significantly as an indicator of progress, new or relatively minor exports from the stable countries rose in this period by almost one half, while for the inflating countries these exports remained unchanged on balance.[2]

The effect of strong inflation on the structure of imports can also retard progress. Declining exports and rising import demands will by themselves lead to balance of payments difficulties. As discussed later, international capital transactions are likely to aggravate these difficulties. In order to cope with these problems, the authorities in an inflating country are frequently forced to restrict imports. These restrictions form an element in general economic policies which are usually directed, in part, toward protecting the living standards of those most hurt by inflation. Social policies that are in themselves desirable—and that may even be indispensable—tend to encourage the import of goods considered to be essential or of high social value. It is upon such goods that the least restriction is imposed and the lowest rates of tax are levied. Because countries are best able to produce certain specific goods that are nutritious or otherwise desirable, these goods come to be regarded as necessities of life in their countries of production (e.g., beans or maize in much of Latin America, or rice in Asia), while they are considered luxuries or semiluxuries in other countries where they are expensive or impossible to produce. The most severe restrictions or highest taxes are placed on imports of nonessentials or products which have not been important imports in the past. This policy, which may be required for social tranquillity, results in exposing the domestic producers of essentials to the full rigor of foreign competition, while protecting the domestic producers of nonessentials and making the import of new products difficult. This can well result in discouragement of domestic production of goods that are either desirable or which the country is best able to produce, and an encouragement of production of goods that are not particularly desirable or which the country is not well-suited to produce. Many a multiple exchange rate system (a device which includes exchange taxes and subsidies on imports or exports and is frequently adopted to minimize the effect of inflation on the balance of payments) might well be interpreted as an ingenious plan to discourage dairy farm-

[2] The data for this comparison are contained in G. Lovasy, "Inflation and Exports in Primary Producing Countries," IMF *Staff Papers*, IX, March 1962, pp. 37–69.

ing and the improvement of children's welfare, while encouraging the production of alcoholic beverages.

Discouraging the import of new products, particularly if administrative controls are the means of discouragement, may well impede development. The import of materials or new types of equipment may be essential for the growth of new industries and the diversification of the economy. On occasion, strict import quotas based on historic trade patterns have prevented the import of necessary spare parts and forced the closing, at least temporarily, of vital new industries.

RAPID INFLATION AND CAPITAL MOVEMENTS

Strong inflation does not limit its havoc to transactions in goods and services: it also distorts the international movements of capital. First it discourages the flow of capital, and hence of resources, to developing countries. Perhaps even more tragically, it fosters flight of capital from the latter countries.

One of the differences between stable and inflationary economies is that investors can make reasonable estimates of future money costs and money receipts in the stable countries, while this is impossible once inflation is well under way. Further, this uncertainty bears most heavily on foreign investors. All the chances in the lottery are stacked against them. International investment is in any event likely to be more hazardous than domestic investment. With inflation, the hazards involved in movements of international capital are increased by the unpredictability of exchange rates. Not only are the net returns on investment in the developing country's currency unknown, but the returns in terms of the investor's currency are even more speculative. So it is not surprising that foreign investors tend to shy away from countries with extreme inflation, and that such countries tend to cut themselves off from access to resources from abroad.

While a strong inflation by itself is thus likely to frighten capital away from a developing country, the policies frequently adopted by governments to ease the burdens of rising prices may have an effect that is even greater in discouraging national progress. As suggested above, strong inflation usually leads to the adoption of payments restrictions. Among the first candidates for restriction are payments on foreign capital. Even if assurances are given that foreign investors will be favorably treated, experience has taught these investors to be wary of restrictive systems, which usually contain considerable scope for administrative arbitrariness. Thus the almost inevitable exchange restrictions brought by strong inflation do more than discourage capital from fostering development. They so frighten capital away, and even encourage repatriation, that measures designed to conserve foreign exchange may in fact dry up a country's resources and actually dissipate its reserves.

It is hard to rank the effects of inflation on a country's balance of payments on any scale of severity. However, the effect of a strong inflation on capital flight must stand high on any such list. This capital flight has not only economic but also severe social effects. The inevitability of exchange rate depreciation in the uncertain world of a rapidly inflating country means that there is one sure prospect: if people can get their money out of the country, they will be able to benefit in the future. Thus, to quote an extreme example, if a Brazilian receiving at all times only the current minimum wage had started at the beginning of 1959 to save 1 per cent of his wages, and if he had been able to lend these savings at an interest rate of 1 per cent a month, he would have accumulated approximately 15,000 cruzeiros by the end of 1964; if he had instead used these savings to buy a dollar bill each time he had accumulated enough cruzeiros to do so, he would have had a bundle of dollar bills worth approximately 45,000 cruzeiros at the end of 1964. It is little wonder that the incentive to capital flight becomes all-pervasive in an unstable economy, and that savings which might be used to develop the country fly abroad.

It may be maintained that the harmful effects of inflation on capital inflows may be mitigated, and the flight of capital prevented, by exchange controls. Such arguments ignore the experience of virtually all exchange controllers that such controls cannot be effective when pressures on them are great, and often they may even have a tendency to induce capital flight.

RAPID INFLATION AND THE EXCHANGE RATE

Exchange rate movements are often front page news in a country where inflation is rampant. It may be taken that once inflation is under way the exchange rate must break. Rising prices leading to an increased demand for imports and an unwillingness to export cannot persist without complete collapse of the economy, unless the exchange rate moves to offset the rise in domestic prices. In fact, the rush to import, the collapse of exports, the slowdown in capital inflows, and the flight from the home currency all produce such pressures on the exchange rate that eventually it is likely to deteriorate even faster than prices are rising. This rapid worsening of the rate makes import prices rise more rapidly still and magnifies, in terms of national currency, the profits to be made from capital flight, thereby aggravating the pressure on the exchange.

If exchange depreciation were allowed to progress fast enough it might serve to reduce imports adequately, encourage export production, and eventually encourage the belief that future capital flight would not be profitable. On occasion, a freely moving exchange rate may indeed redress the harmful effects of inflation on the balance of payments. However, if this happens, the prices of imports will rise more rapidly than other prices, a situation which could be unfavorable to those imports that are frequently essential to maintain the standard of living or the continued operation of domestic industry. Further, the foreign exchange value of a country's currency is often taken as a symbol of its real worth, despite the overvaluation that has developed owing to rapid inflation. Governments therefore try to hold the rate in an attempt to soften the sufferings caused by inflation and to help retain that confidence in the currency which is essential if monetary stability is sought, even as a distant ambition. Recent history is replete with examples of such attempts to stem the tide of exchange depreciation. Before these attempts fail, as in a rapid inflation they are bound to, the worst effects of the eventual depreciation are observed. With strong beliefs developing that the exchange rate cannot be held indefinitely, importers rush to buy goods before prices rise, and exporters hold up their sales in the hope of better days; with depreciation confidently expected, capital is sent out of the country in the belief that it can be brought back soon at a large profit. Attempts to peg the rate lead to the worst of both worlds. The harmful effects of a depreciation are not even delayed, while the handicaps of a fixed rate out of line with reality are experienced. In brief, a strong inflation necessarily involves a depreciation of the exchange rate, with the adverse effects of such a movement on the economy. Yet, even though a worsening of the rate may impose burdens on a country, to attempt to hold the rate when inflation is rampant may have even more serious consequences.

FEDERAL RESERVE BANK
OF CHICAGO

EURODOLLARS—AN
IMPORTANT SOURCE OF FUNDS
FOR AMERICAN BANKS

51

Interest rates—under pressure from inflation, strong credit demands, and restrictive monetary policy—have moved to near-record highs. The public's demand for certificates of deposit at banks has declined as yields on competing money-market instruments moved above the maximum rates banks are allowed to pay for time deposits. And reserve and liquidity positions of banks have been squeezed as CDs ran off.

In these circumstances, banks have reduced their holdings of government securities and increased their borrowing from Federal Reserve banks while adjusting their loan and investment policies. At the same time, some banks, particularly those with foreign branches, have turned to a source of funds virtually unknown only a few years ago—the Eurodollar market.

Liabilities of American banks to their foreign branches (mostly "borrowings" of Eurodollars) stood about $10 billion in late May, after having risen about $3 billion since the end of 1968 and more than $8 billion since mid-1966. Eurodollars have apparently found a permanent place in the American financial structure.

WHAT ARE EURODOLLARS?

Eurodollars are dollar-denominated deposits at commercial banks outside the United States. Most, but not all, are in Europe. Such deposits can be initiated by:

• Foreign holders of dollar-deposits at American banks transferring their deposits to foreign banks.
• Foreigners receiving payments by checks drawn on accounts at American banks, depositing the dollars in banks in their countries.

Reprinted from "Eurodollars—An Important Source of Funds for American Banks," *Business Conditions* (June 1969), pp. 9–20, Federal Reserve Bank of Chicago.

• Americans transferring their dollar deposits in American banks to foreign banks.

• Holders of convertible currencies (such as German marks) exchanging them for dollars and depositing them in a foreign bank.

The bank receiving the deposit establishes a dollar-denominated liability to its depositor. This is Eurodollars.

But the process by which Eurodollars come into existence does not usually stop there. The original dollar deposit can be loaned and redeposited and, in the process, new dollar-denominated liabilities, and assets, created. Thus, the total of Eurodollars outstanding—currently estimated at well over $20 billion dollars—can be viewed as a superstructure of dollar-denominated deposits in foreign banks underpinned by dollar deposits in American banks.[1]

ORIGIN OF EURODOLLARS

Eurodollars are only one of several foreign-currency denominated deposits loaned and borrowed by banks and corporations throughout the world. Deposits denominated in British pounds (Eurosterling), German marks (Euromarks), Swiss francs (Eurofrancs) are held and traded by banks outside the countries to which these currencies are domiciled.

This practice, which dates back to the early history of banking, stems from its convenience and profitability to banks and businesses engaged in international transactions. Deposits denominated in pound sterling were common in the 1920s, when the pound was a major trading currency.

The growth of dollar-denominated deposits since the dollar emerged after World War II as the major exchange medium in international transactions was hampered at first by exchange restrictions imposed abroad. A limited market in dollar-denominated deposits, nevertheless, developed in the early 1950s as a result of practices followed by some communist countries. Anxious to hold dollars but concerned that their deposits might be blocked or confiscated in return for the expropriation of American property if held in their name in American banks, these countries placed their dollars with banks in Western Europe. These banks then lent the dollars to

---

[1] Unlike the U. S. dollars held by foreigners, Eurodollars are not direct claims on the resources of the United States. They are only claims on foreign banks, and it remains for these banks to provide the dollars from their reserves when the claims are exercised. The "creation" of Eurodollars by foreign banks does not lead to an expansion of U. S. liabilities to foreigners.

Europeans, while maintaining dollar-denominated liabilities on their books in favor of the East-Europeans.[2]

The move by many countries to virtually free convertibility of currencies in 1958 gave banks and residents of those countries an opportunity to hold dollar deposits and to invest dollars at yields higher than those offered by American banks. Removal of exchange restrictions also allowed banks and residents of other countries to swap their currencies for dollars and invest the proceeds in the Eurodollar market.

Certain institutional features in the domestic economies of the United States and many European countries encouraged development of the market in Eurodollars. One of the most important was the Federal Reserve regulation governing the payment of interest on deposits by American banks. Regulation Q prohibits payment of interest on demand deposits held in American banks deposits with maturities of less than 30 days and prescribes the maximum rates banks can pay on time deposits. With the prescribed rates considerably lower at times than the rates foreign banks paid on dollar deposits, this regulation provided a powerful incentive for holding dollar deposits abroad.

Another factor was the dissimilarity in economic growth in the late 1950s between the United States and major European countries. In the United States, the economy was sluggish and interest rates low, while in Europe, largely as a result of postwar reconstruction and creation of the Common Market, there was a boom accompanied by high interest rates. These encouraged retention of funds in Europe.

Still another factor was the shortage of money-market instruments suitable for short-term investment in Europe. Given the preference of European investors for liquid assets and the relative underdevelopment of the money markets there, the Eurodollar deposit provided users and suppliers a convenient means of profitably employing short-term funds.

---

[2] The following possibly apocryphal but nevertheless plausible story suggests how communists may have been instrumental in giving a name to dollar-denominated deposits. One of the major suppliers of dollar deposits to European banks in the early 1950s was a "branch" of the Russian state bank in Paris, the Banque Commerciale pour l'Europe du Nord, S.A., whose international cable code is "Eurobank." Since most transactions in foreign-exchange markets are transacted by cable, transfers of dollars to or from that bank bore its cable-code designation. Foreign-exchange traders and banks engaged in dollars transactions soon began to refer to dollar deposits obtained from that bank as "Eurodollars." The name apparently stuck even after other suppliers entered the market.

Interest Rates on All Maturities of Eurodollar Deposits Have Reached New Highs in 1969

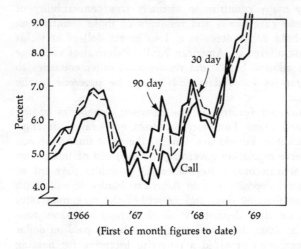

(First of month figures to date)

As the international movement of trade and capital increased, there was increasing need for convenient short-term financing in a generally acceptable currency. Unlike British banks after World War I, American banks were slow to capitalize on the special position of the dollar after World War II. In the late 1950s and early 1960s, many American banks with strong domestic ties were just beginning to recognize the growing need for international banking services. Their failure to provide such financing earlier left a vacuum in international financial markets that was quickly filled by European banks using Eurodollar deposits. By 1959, Dutch, Swiss, Scandinavian, and German banks had become substantial lenders of Eurodollars. As the demand for Eurodollars increased—and with it the interest rates offered on such deposits—these banks sometimes found suppliers even among central banks of Europe and Asia. The Eurodollar market was rapidly developing into a truly international market.

FUNCTIONING OF THE MARKET

Transactions in the Eurodollar market consist primarily of the acceptance and placement (borrowing and lending) of dollar deposits. Maturities of deposits and loans range from "call" to one year and more, with most falling between one and six months.

Several factors influence supply and demand in the market. In addition to interest rates on various maturities, users and suppliers of Eurodollars must also consider the cost of converting dollars into other currency (or vice versa) and the cost of insurance against exchange rates changing while the Eurodollar deposit or loan is outstanding—the cost of "forward cover."

A variety of participants are attracted to the market by the flexibility with which it can meet individual needs. Corporations, banks, and sometimes individuals have developed the practice of placing funds in the Eurodollar market temporarily when yields are attractive. But the supply is not limited to commercial sources. Official monetary institutions also place funds in the market for various reasons and through various means. The Swiss National Bank and the Bank for International Settlement in Basle, for example, placed more than $800 million in the market late last year to ease seasonal pressures and the impact of speculative flows of funds that were threatening to disrupt trade by causing sharp fluctuations in interest rates.

Foreign central banks have also on occasion used the Eurodollar market to control the liquidity position of the banking system in their countries. For example, as a result of rumors last November and again this spring that the German mark would be revalued, large amounts of funds flowed into Germany, causing both a rapid and undesired increase in the liquidity of the German banking system and a severe strain on the availability of funds in the Eurodollar market. The German Federal Bank, wanting funds to be cycled back into an international market, offered to provide forward cover for funds placed in the Eurodollar market at a cost considerably below the forward rate in the commercial market. Taking advantage of this offer, German commercial banks channeled a large amount of funds in the Eurodollar market and, in the process, reduced their excessive liquidity.

USES OF EURODOLLARS

The most common use of Eurodollars has probably been in financing international trade, at least until recently. More than a third of the current $230 billion annual volume of world trade is financed by dollars, only part of which is supplied by American banks. The ability of American banks to meet world needs for short-term dollar credit in financing trade between foreign countries has been especially limited since initiation of the Voluntary Foreign Credit Restraint Program in 1965. The Eurodollar market provides a convenient alternative.

Dollar Deposits in European Banks Originate in All Corners of the Globe . . .

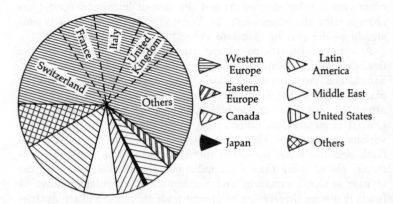

SOURCE: *Thirty-Eighth Annual Report of the Bank for International Settlements,* June 1968. Data cover dollar liabilities of banks in eight European countries to nonresidents at the end of 1967.

Converted into domestic currencies, Eurodollars have also been used in some countries, Japan, for example, in financing domestic credit needs. In other countries, such as Britain, they have been used in financing local governments. American companies expanding their operations abroad have relied heavily on the Eurodollar market for working capital. Foreign commercial banks have frequently borrowed in the Eurodollar market to supplement their liquidity needs and raise funds for domestic needs.

AMERICAN BANKS IN THE MARKET

Through branches abroad, American Banks have been heavily involved in the Eurodollar market from the beginning and they have shared in its growth. Between 1960 and 1968, total deposits at the branches of American banks in the United Kingdom—the center of the Eurodollar market—increased from $1.1 billion to $11.7 billion. At the end of 1968, almost 90 percent of the deposits of these branches were denominated in currencies other than sterling—presumably dollars.

Foreign branches of American banks have followed much the same pattern in their Eurodollar activities as other foreign banks. They have used Eurodollar deposits to make loans to corporate customers and to participate in the interbank Eurodollar market.

... and They Are Used Throughout the World.

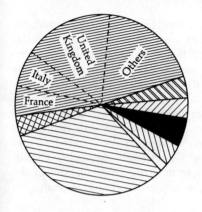

SOURCE: *Thirty-Eighth Annual Report of the Bank for International Settlements,* June 1968. Data cover dollar claims of banks in eight European countries on nonresidents at the end of 1967.

They have also "swapped" Eurodollars into other currencies so they could make foreign-denominated loans. But in addition to these usual practices of foreign banks, they have also placed Eurodollar deposits at the disposal of their home offices in the United States.

Until late 1964, liabilities of American banks to their overseas branches were never more than $1 billion. The balances rose slightly in 1965, but until mid-1966 they remained well below $2 billion.

In late 1966, the picture changed. American banks came under a severe squeeze from strong credit demands and restrictive monetary policy. As interest rates rose in the money market, banks had a large runoff of CDs. To cushion the impact, banks turned to their branches for Eurodollars. Liabilities of American banks to their foreign branches rose sharply, reaching $4.3 billion by December 1966.

As monetary pressures eased in early 1967, American banks reduced their use of Eurodollars, but the level of borrowing remained high by pre-1966 standards. In the second half of 1967, it began rising again until, in November, the volume of borrowing passed the peak reached in 1966.

With the continued buildup in monetary pressures in 1968, liabilities of American banks to their foreign branches surged ahead. After a short decline from the large amounts outstanding in late 1968—due partly to unsettled conditions in foreign-exchange markets and partly to seasonal patterns—the rate of increase rose in the wake of tightening credit conditions in early 1969. Toward the end of April, the total outstanding had reached more than $10 billion.

It is possible to view 1966 as a turning point in the Eurodollar activities of American banks. Their experience with the Eurodollar market during the credit crunch of that year demonstrated the market's flexibility in meeting their needs. Banks discovered that the capacity of the market to generate large amounts of funds in response to movements of interest rates was conducive to active competition for call deposits and time deposits with maturities of less than 30 days. At the same time, the absence of rate ceilings on time deposits abroad allowed them to compete for longer-term deposits in the Eurodollar market at a time when Regulation Q prohibited such competition in American markets. These features of the Eurodollar market gave the banks greater flexibility in managing their liabilities.

The competitive advantage of the Eurodollar market as a source of funds for American banks has also been strengthened by certain technical factors that tend to reduce the effective cost of Eurodollar funds. The Eurodollar balances American banks obtain through their foreign branches are carried on the books as liabilities to the branches. Because of a Federal Reserve Board ruling that a bank and its branches form a single legal entity, balances due a branch are not treated as deposits in assessing reserve requirements and Federal Deposit Insurance Corporation insurance fees. The result is a lower effective cost of Eurodollar time deposits obtained through an overseas branch than similar deposits obtained in the American market at the same interest rate. A bank has full use of the funds it receives from the Eurodollar market, while it must pay the insurance fee on funds obtained in the domestic market and set part of the funds aside as reserves.

The effective cost of Eurodollars is further reduced by factors arising from rules governing the transfer of funds between branches and their home offices. The rules allow a bank to reduce its total deposit liabilities subject to reserve requirements for one day by the amount of funds being transferred between it and the branches.[3] This enables the bank to invest, for one day, the funds that it would otherwise be required to hold as idle reserves.

All these considerations no doubt played a part in increasing the reliance of American banks on the Eurodollar market both in day-to-day management of their reserves and as a source of loanable funds.

---

[3] The Board of Governors of the Federal Reserve System recently proposed an amendment to its rules governing member bank reserves that would prevent such reduction.

Use of Eurodallars by U.S. banks has been on the rise since 1966

The Effective Cost of Short-term Eurodallars Stays Below the Cost of Fed Funds

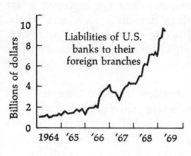

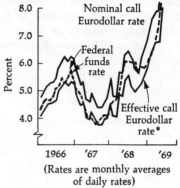

(Rates are monthly averages of daily rates)

SOURCE: *Federal Reserve Bulletin.* For weekly data see May 1968, page A104 (1964-68 data) and May 1969, page A83 (1969 to date).

* The effective rate was computed by adjusting the nominal rate for saving in reserves.

Banks have sometimes been led to tap the market because of the favorable constellation of interest rates that made borrowing in the Eurodollar market cheaper. The persistent favorable differential between the one-day Eurodollar rate (adjusted for "cost-savings" to banks using funds of such maturity) and the rate on Federal Funds was probably one reason for the continued large borrowing of Eurodollars. At other times, it has been the effect of Regulation Q that, by keeping banks from obtaining funds in this country, caused them to turn to the Eurodollar market. Sharp increases in the liabilities of American banks to their branches in late 1966 and again in late 1968 have undoubtedly been the result of these developments.

IMPLICATIONS FOR CREDIT POLICY...

The increased activity of American banks in the Eurodollar market has added a new dimension to the Federal Reserve's responsibilities for monetary management. The problem has been, on the one hand, the possible impact of Eurodollar borrowing on bank reserves and, therefore, on the ability of the banking system to extend credit and, on the other, the possible redistribution of reserves in favor of banks borrowing in the Eurodollar market.

For an individual bank, a Eurodollar deposit obtained by its branch and transferred to the home office represents a net addition to its ability to extend loans and acquire other earning assets. But the deposit obtained by the branch and carried on its books as a dollar-denominated liability to foreigners does not represent a net addition to resources of the American banking system as a whole. Such a deposit has already existed in the American banking system —held in most instances by a foreigner in another American bank. Thus, one bank's gain is another's loss. Total reserves of the entire banking system remain unaffected.[4]

But because of the technical distinction between "deposits" and "due to branch" accounts, the effect of Eurodollar borrowing is a transformation of deposit liabilities subject to reserve requirements into reserve-free liabilities. For the banking system as a whole, required reserves are reduced (or excess reserves expanded) by the amount formerly needed to back the original deposit. Given the current reserve requirements for various classes of deposits, such a reduction in required reserves can range from 3 percent of the amount of Eurodollars transferred (if the original deposit was a time deposit at a bank with total deposits of less than $5 million) up to 17.5 percent (if the deposit was a demand deposit in a reserve city bank with total deposits of more than $5 million).

This potentially expansionary effect of Eurodollar borrowing by American banks can be readily offset, however, by the Federal Reserve through its open-market operations. The monetary authority's control over the aggregate reserve base is in no way diminished by banks borrowing in the Eurodollar market.

In some respects, however, the redistribution of reserves in favor of banks with ready access to the Eurodollar market remains a relevant issue. Some observers have argued that the ability of some banks to compete for time deposits that are exempt from reserve requirements—especially at times when regulation limits the power of other banks to compete—can lead to a disproportionate share of the "burden" of restrictive monetary policy being borne by banks without access to the Eurodollar market. Banks without foreign branches may be forced to sell more securities (usually at capital losses) or to reduce their lending more than banks with such access.

---

[4] Since a branch bidding for dollars abroad does not know what American bank they are deposited in until the transaction is completed, banks often purchase their own deposits. If they did not purchase them, however, the deposits would probably be purchased by another bank and, therefore, lost to the bank holding them.

Analysis of the available evidence shows, however, at least for the most recent experience, that this concern may have been exaggerated. During the current period of monetary restraint, total assets of the American banks that borrow most of the Eurodollars have declined relative to the total assets of other large banks. Their total deposits have also declined, relative to those of other large banks, reflecting mostly the fairly large runoffs of large CDs. Borrowing by these banks from domestic sources has declined as a proportion of all such borrowing by large American banks, indicating that borrowing of Eurodollars has merely substituted for domestic sources of funds.

But more subtle aspects of the situation nevertheless emerge. Banks borrowing in the Eurodollar market increased their share in the total business loans outstanding. As domestic monetary policy became restrictive, the ready access of some large banks to Eurodollars may have allowed them to avoid curtailment of business lending to some extent.

... AND BALANCE OF PAYMENTS

While it is not clear that the Eurodollar activities of American banks present no conflict with the domestic objectives of U. S. monetary policy, there is no doubt that recent increases in Eurodollar borrowing by American banks have contributed significantly to the achievement of an important international objective—improvement of the country's balance of payments. The huge surpluses recorded on the official reserve transaction basis in 1968 and again in the first quarter of this year can be attributed largely to the activities of American banks in the Eurodollar market during those periods.

Active bidding for Eurodollar funds by American banks contributed to rising interest rates in the Eurodollar market. This—and at times speculation flights out of particular currencies—attracted increasing numbers of foreign investors who converted their currencies into dollars and made them available to American banks.

As the volume of conversion increased, more pressure was put on exchange rates and foreign central banks were brought into the foreign-exchange markets. The central banks, obligated under international agreements to maintain exchange rates of their currencies within a small range relative to the dollar, provided the market with dollars out of their reserves to keep the dollar-exchange rates of their currencies from dropping below agreed limits. Thus, in many instances, the dollars acquired by American banks came directly from the reserves of the foreign central banks.

Since the reduction in dollar holdings of foreign central banks counts as items improving this country's balance-of-payments on the official transactions basis, borrowings by American banks contributed to the achievement of a surplus.[5]

EURODOLLARS IN PERSPECTIVE

The emergence and growth of the Eurodollar market has provided a fascinating demonstration of the capacity of competition and free markets to develop new institutions in response to economic needs.

The market has not yet been tested under all conditions, however. Its fluidity and responsiveness to changing conditions, which contributed so significantly to its growth, could create severe strains for some participants in the future. But one thing seems certain: the market has established itself as a significant and continuing force tending to link national and international money markets—and therefore national economies—more closely.

EURODOLLARS AND EXCHANGE RATES

The cost of borrowing Eurodollars is influenced, in addition to interest rates, by a whole constellation of exchange rates. Here is an example using hypothetical figures to illustrate the point.

A German importer wants to borrow funds to buy goods from a British exporter. He needs the equivalent of 1 million pounds for

[5] Without precise data, the effect of recent Eurodollar borrowing by American banks on the liquidity balance—which is computed as the total change in liquid liabilities to foreigners, both official and private—is harder to establish. Nominally, Eurodollar borrowing by American banks results in a shift in the ownership claims on the United States from foreign holders to the branches of American banks abroad. But because foreign branches of American banks are foreign entities, the transfer of funds does not change the amount of foreign claims on the United States. Whether a shift in claims between foreign holders and foreign branches of American banks changes the liquidity balance depends on the maturity of the original claim.

If the claim was long term (with a maturity of more than one year) before it was transformed into a short-term Eurodollar deposit, the transfer would increase the liquidity deficit. American banking's short-term liabilities to foreigners would be increased and its long-term liabilities reduced. And since only the changes in liquid liabilities are counted in computing the balance of payments on this basis, the deficit would be increased.

If, however, the original claim was short term, the transfer into Eurodollars and repatriation by branches of American banks would not change the liquidity deficit.

three months. To raise this amount, he can borrow German marks at his own bank at, say, 10 percent a year and convert the marks into pounds at 9.6 marks per pound. After three months, he would repay the bank 9,840,000 marks (principal plus interest).

Alternatively, he can borrow Eurodollars, again say, at 10 percent, and convert them into sterling at $2.39 per pound (the current rate). If at the maturity of the loan, he can obtain dollars for marks at 4 marks per dollar, his total cost will be 9,799,000 marks (9,560,000 marks to purchase $2,390,000 for repayments of principal plus 239,000 marks to purchase $59,750 for payment of three months' interest). This is 41,000 marks cheaper than if he had borrowed marks for exchange into pounds.

The advantage exists, however, only as long as the borrower can be sure that when the loan matures he can purchase dollars with marks at 4 marks per dollar. The advantage of borrowing in the Eurodollar market would be wiped out if the mark depreciated to say, 4.03 marks per dollar, the lower limit allowed under international agreements. At that rate, the borrower would have to pay out, 9,872,492 marks in repayment of the dollar loan—more than if he had borrowed marks.

To ensure against such a drop in the exchange rate, he can "hedge" his loan in the "forward" foreign exchange market.

In that market, foreign-exchange dealers contract to buy or sell foreign currencies for future delivery at specified rates of exchange. The rates at which they offer such contracts are posted as forward rates.

Forward rates of various currencies can be higher or lower than the spot rates, depending usually on relative interest rates in the different countries but also on the market's estimates of future movements in rates.

The German importer could protect himself against the possibility of an unfavorable change in the mark-dollar exchange rate by buying "90-day forward dollars"—a contract specifying delivery to him of dollars for German marks three months later. Dollars for delivery in 90 days were recently selling in the German exchange market at a discount of about 7 percent a year—this is about 3.930 marks per dollar. At that rate, the importer would have to pay 9,627,517 marks for the $2,449,750 he needed to repay his Eurodollar loan. That would be 212,483 marks less than if he had borrowed marks instead of Eurodollars. Clearly, it would be to his advantage to finance his imports in the Eurodollar market.

ROBERT A. MUNDELL

THE APPROPRIATE USE OF
MONETARY AND FISCAL POLICY
FOR INTERNAL AND
EXTERNAL STABILITY

52

This paper deals with the problem of achieving internal stability
and balance of payments equilibrium in a country which considers
it inadvisable to alter the exchange rate or to impose trade controls.
It is assumed that monetary and fiscal policy can be used as independent instruments to attain the two objectives if capital flows are
responsive to interest rate differentials, but it is concluded that it is
a matter of extreme importance how the policies are paired with the
objectives. Specifically, it is argued that monetary policy ought to
be aimed at external objectives and fiscal policy at internal objectives, and that failure to follow this prescription can make the disequilibrium situation worse than before the policy changes were
introduced.

The practical implication of the theory, when stabilization measures are limited to monetary policy and fiscal policy, is that a surplus
country experiencing inflationary pressure should ease monetary
conditions and raise taxes (or reduce government spending), and that
a deficit country suffering from unemployment should tighten interest rates and lower taxes (or increase government spending).[1]

THE CONDITIONS OF EQUILIBRIUM

Internal balance requires that aggregate demand for domestic output
be equal to aggregate supply of domestic output at full employment.
If this condition is not fulfilled, there will be inflationary pressure
or recessionary potential according to whether aggregate demand exceeds or falls short of, respectively, full employment output. It will
be assumed here that, during transitory periods of disequilibrium,
inventories are running down, or accumulating, in excess of desired

Reprinted from Robert A. Mundell, "The Appropriate Use of Monetary
and Fiscal Policy for Internal and External Stability," *Staff Papers*, International Monetary Fund, Vol. IX (March 1962), pp. 70–77.
[1] This possibility has been suggested, and to a limited extent implemented, elsewhere. See, for example, De Nederlandsch Bank N.V., *Report
for the Year 1960* (Amsterdam, 1961).

changes, according to whether the disequilibrium reflects a state of inflationary or recessionary potential.

External balance implies that the balance of trade equals (net) capital exports at the fixed exchange parity. If the balance of trade exceeds capital exports, there will be a balance of payments surplus and a tendency for the exchange rate to appreciate, which the central bank restrains by accumulating stocks of foreign exchange. And likewise, if the balance of trade falls short of capital exports, there will be a balance of payments deficit and a tendency for the exchange rate to depreciate, which the central bank prevents by dispensing with stocks of foreign exchange.

In what follows it is assumed that all foreign policies and export demand are given, that the balance of trade worsens as the level of domestic expenditure increases, and that capital flows are responsive to interest rate differentials. Then domestic expenditure can be assumed to depend only on fiscal policy (the budget surplus) and monetary policy (the interest rate) at the full employment level of output. The complete system can thus be given a geometric interpretation in the two policy variables, the interest rate and the budget surplus[2] (Diagram 1).

In the diagram, the FF line, which will be referred to as the "foreign-balance schedule," traces the locus of pairs of interest rates and budget surpluses (at the level of income compatible with full employment) along which the balance of payments is in equilibrium. This schedule has a negative slope because an increase in the interest rate, by reducing capital exports and lowering domestic expenditure and hence imports, improves the balance of payments; while a decrease in the budget surplus, by raising domestic expenditure and

[2] The assumptions could be made less restrictive without detracting from the generality of the conclusions. Thus, an assumption that capital imports directly affect domestic expenditure, as in theoretical transfer analysis, would tend to reinforce the conclusions. Even the (plausible) assumption that, in addition to capital flows, capital indebtedness is responsive to the rate of interest (to take account of the "stock" nature of much of international floating capital) would not change the conclusions, although it may affect the quantitative extent of the policy changes required.

Notice, however, that I have implicitly assumed away strong "Pigou" effects, speculation on international markets that is related to the size of the (positive or negative) budget surplus, forward rate movements that more than offset interest-rate-differential changes (an unlikely occurrence), and concern about the precise composition of the balance of payments; the last assumption may mean that the method of achieving equilibrium suggested below is desirable only in the short run.

DIAGRAM I

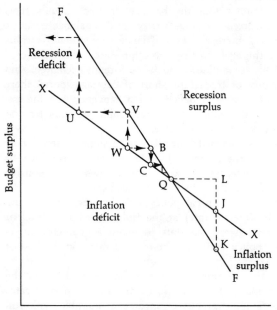

hence imports, worsens the balance of payments. Thus, from any point on the schedule an increase in the rate of interest would cause an external surplus, which would have to be compensated by a reduction in the budget surplus in order to restore equilibrium. Points above and to the right of the foreign-balance schedule refer to balance of payments surpluses, while points below and to the left of the schedule represent balance of payments deficits.

A similar construction can be applied to the conditions representing internal balance. The *XX* line, or "internal-balance schedule," is the locus of pairs of interest rates and budget surpluses which permits continuing full employment equilibrium in the market for goods and services. Along this schedule, full employment output is equal to aggregate demand for output, or, what amounts to the same condition, home demand for domestic goods is equal to full employment output less exports. There is, therefore, only one level of home demand for domestic goods consistent with full employment and the given level of exports, and this implies that expenditure must be constant along *XX*. The internal-balance line must therefore have a negative slope, since increases in the interest rate are associated with decreases in the budget surplus, in order to maintain domestic expenditure constant.

Both the internal-balance and the foreign-balance schedules thus have negative slopes. But it is necessary also to compare the steepness of the slopes. Which of the schedules is steeper?

It can be demonstrated that FF must be steeper than XX if capital is even slightly mobile, and by an amount which depends both on the responsiveness of international capital flows to the rate of interest and on the marginal propensity to import. The absolute slope of the internal-balance schedule XX is the ratio between the responsiveness of domestic expenditure to the rate of interest and the responsiveness of domestic expenditure to the budget surplus. Now, if it is assumed for a moment that capital exports are constant, the balance of payments depends only on expenditure, since exports are assumed constant and imports depend only on expenditure. In other words, if capital exports are constant, the slope of FF also is the ratio between the responsiveness of domestic expenditure to the rate of interest and the responsiveness of such expenditure to the budget surplus. Therefore, apart from the effects of changes in capital exports, the two slopes are the same. It is then possible to see that the responsiveness of capital exports to the rate of interest makes the slope of FF greater in absolute value than the slope of XX.[3]

Consider, for example, what happens to an initial situation of over-all equilibrium at Q as this equilibrium is disturbed by an increase in the rate of interest equal to QL. Because of the higher rate of interest, there would be deflationary pressure and a balance of payments surplus at the point L. If the budget surplus is now lowered, the deflationary pressure can be eliminated at a point like J on the internal-balance schedule. But at J, expenditure is the same as it was at Q, and this means that imports, and hence the balance of *trade*, must be the same as at Q. The balance of *payments* is therefore in surplus at J because of capital imports attracted by the higher rate of interest; this makes necessary a further reduction in the budget surplus in order to bring the balance of payments again

[3] Both the absolute and relative values of the slopes depend on the particular fiscal policy in question. The discussion in the text applies to income tax reductions because that instrument tends to be neutral as between home and foreign spending. The conclusions would be strengthened or weakened, respectively, as the particular fiscal policy was biased toward or against home goods; the more the change in the budget surplus results from a change in spending on home goods, the greater is the difference between the slopes of XX and FF.

into equilibrium. It follows, then, that the point K on the foreign-balance schedule is below the point J on the internal-balance schedule, and that FF is steeper than XX. It can then also be concluded that the absolute difference in slopes is greater, the more mobile is capital (because this causes a larger external surplus at J) and the lower is the marginal propensity to import (because this necessitates a larger budget deficit to correct any given external surplus).[4]

In Diagram I, the two schedules separate four quadrants, distinguished from one another by the conditions of internal imbalance and external disequilibrium. Only at the point where the schedules intersect are the policy variables in equilibrium.

TWO SYSTEMS OF POLICY RESPONSE

Consider now two possible policy systems determining the behavior of fiscal policy and monetary policy when internal and external balance have not been simultaneously achieved. The government can adjust monetary policy to the requirements of internal stability, and fiscal policy to the needs of external balance, or it can use fiscal policy for purposes of internal stability and monetary policy for purposes of external balance.

It will be demonstrated first that the policy system in which the interest rate is used for internal stability, and fiscal policy is used for external equilibrium, is an unstable system. Consider, for example, a situation of full employment combined with a balance of payments deficit, represented by the point W. To correct the deficit by fiscal policy, the budget surplus must be raised from that indicated by W to that given by V. At V there will be equilibrium in the balance of payments, but the increased budget surplus will have caused recessionary pressure. If now the threatening unemployment is to be

---

[4] The assumption that imports depend only on expenditure, while the latter depends partly on the rate of interest, means that imports are affected by the rate of interest, although the *share* of imports in expenditure is not. This assumption could be relaxed without fundamentally altering the results, although an exception—remote in practice but possible in theory—does arise, if import goods are highly responsive to the rate of interest while home goods are not, capital flows are only slightly responsive to the rate of interest, and the marginal propensity to buy imports is high relative to the marginal propensity to buy home goods. Under these conditions, it is possible that XX may be steeper than FF. More formally, then, it is necessary to limit the present conclusions to countries in which the ratio of the effect of budget policy on the balance of payments to its effect on domestic excess demand is less than the ratio of the effect of the interest rate on the balance of payments to its effect on excess demand.

prevented by monetary policy, the rate of interest must be lowered from that indicated by V to that described by U. But at U there is again a balance of payments deficit, which in turn necessitates a further increase in the budget surplus. The process continues with the interest rate and the budget surplus moving ever further from equilibrium.[5]

To show formally that the system is unstable, it is sufficient to note that the payments deficit at U, after the first round of policy changes, exceeds the deficit at W. This is evident since it is known that the balance of *trade* at U and W is the same but, because of the lower rate of interest, the balance of *payments* at U is worse. It follows that this type of policy reaction is unstable.

On the other hand, the opposite type of policy response is stable. Suppose that the authorities adjust the interest rate to correspond to the needs of external equilibrium and adjust fiscal policy to maintain internal stability. Then from the same disequilibrium point W, the rate of interest would be raised to B, thereby correcting the external deficit. But the tendency toward unemployment generated by the restrictive credit policy must now be corrected by a reduction in the budget surplus or increase in the budget deficit. At C there is again internal balance of payments deficit, as at W. But it is now possible to see that the deficit at C is *less* than the deficit at W. This follows, as before, because the balance of *trade* at C is identical with that at W but, since the rate of interest is higher at C, the balance of *payments* deficit must be less. The system is therefore stable.

The diagrammatic argument can be absorbed at once when it is realized that at W—or anywhere in the quadrant representing a deficit and recession—the interest rate is lower, and the budget surplus is higher, than is appropriate to the over-all equilibrium at Q. The use of fiscal policy for external balance, and monetary policy for internal balance, drives the interest rate and budget surplus further away from equilibrium, while the alternative system moves the instruments closer to equilibrium.

The same argument applies to an initial disequilibrium in the opposite quadrant, representing inflationary pressure and external surplus. To restore equilibrium, the interest rate must be reduced,

[5] It need hardly be mentioned that the demonstration of instability in this instance (or of stability in the subsequent analysis) is not dependent upon the particular assumption that the government corrects imbalance first in one sector and then in the other, an assumption which is made only for expositional convenience. The conclusions follow, for example, even if the authorities simultaneously adjust fiscal and monetary policies.

and fiscal policy must be made more restrictive. Only if monetary policy is used for the external purpose, and fiscal policy for the internal purpose, will correction of the disequilibrium automatically ensue.[6]

In the other two quadrants, monetary and fiscal policies will be moving in the same direction under either system of policy response, because both tighter monetary policy and an increased budget surplus correct inflationary pressure and external deficit, and both easier monetary policy and a reduced budget surplus tend to alleviate recession and external surplus. The distinction between the two policy systems appears less important in these phases of the international trade cycle; it nevertheless remains, since inaccurate information about the exact location of the point Q could propel the situation into one of the quadrants involving either recession and deficit or inflation and surplus.[7]

CONCLUSIONS

It has been demonstrated that, in countries where employment and balance of payments policies are restricted to monetary and fiscal instruments, monetary policy should be reserved for attaining the desired level of the balance of payments, and fiscal policy for preserving internal stability under the conditions assumed here. The opposite system would lead to a progressively worsening unemployment and balance of payments situation.

The explanation can be related to what I have elsewhere called the Principle of Effective Market Classification: policies should be paired with the objectives on which they have the most influence.[8]

[6] Even if the authorities do not wish to pair instruments and targets, they can use the information provided by the analysis to determine the relation between *actual* policies and *equilibrium* policies. Thus, situations of deficit and recession imply that the budget surplus is too high and the interest rate is too low, while situations of surplus and inflation imply the opposite. In this manner, appropriate policies can be determined by observable situations of target disequilibria.

[7] The system can be generalized for a two-country world by assuming that the other country adjusts fiscal policy to maintain internal stability. The only difference in the conclusion is that the conditions of dynamic stability of the adjustment process are slightly more restrictive, requiring that the marginal propensities to import be, *on the average*, no greater than one half; this is the usual asumption necessary to rule out any "reverse transfer" that is due to policies affecting expenditure.

[8] "The Monetary Dynamics of International Adjustment Under Fixed and Flexible Exchange Rates," *Quarterly Journal of Economics*, LXXIV (1960), pp. 249–250.

If this principle is not followed, there will develop a tendency either for a cyclical approach to equilibrium or for instability.

The use of fiscal policy for external purposes and monetary policy for internal stability violates the principle of effective market classification, because the ratio of the effect of the rate of interest on internal stability to its effect on the balance of payments is less than the ratio of the effect of fiscal policy on internal stability to its effect on the balance of payments. And for precisely this reason the opposite set of policy responses is consistent with the principle.

On a still more general level, we have the principle that Tinbergen has made famous: that to attain a given number of independent targets there must be at least an equal number of instruments.[9] Tinbergen's Principle is concerned with the *existence* and location of a solution to the system. It does not assert that any given set of policy responses will in fact lead to that solution. To assert this, it is necessary to investigate the stability properties of a dynamic system. In this respect, the Principle of Effective Market Classification is a necessary companion to Tinbergen's Principle.

[9] J. Tinbergen, *On the Theory of Economic Policy* (Amsterdam, 1952).

INDEX

Africa, prehistoric, exchange in, 15
Asia Minor, ancient, exchange in, 18, 20–22, 26–29
Asia, prehistoric, exchange in, 15
Asset management services, 82–83

Babylon, exchange in, 20, 27
Balance of payments, 581–598
  capital movements, 660, 663, 665–666, 672–674, 676, 691
  disequilibrium, adjustment of, 593–598, 600, 612–615, 677–686
  Eurodollars, 703–704
  fiscal and monetary policies, 520–524, 603, 612–615, 639–640, 706–713
  foreign aid, 659–660, 661, 678–679
  gold price, 677–686
  inflation, 437, 521–522, 690–691
  interest rates, 520–524, 664–665
  military expenditures, 661, 663, 664, 670, 673–674
  money supply, 393–394, 407, 419–420
  Operation Twist, 521–522, 664
  price levels and, 599–600; restraints proposed, 671–672
  reserves, 583–584, 585–587, 650, 677–686
  speculation, 600–602
  surplus and deficits, 591–592, 599
  travel, international, 665, 673, 676
  unemployment, 433–434, 598, 599–600, 603, 613
  United States, 639–686; Eisenhower policy, 664; foreign aid, 659–660, 661, 678–679; foreign capital inflow, 665–666, 676; gold reserves, 660–661, 677–686; Johnson policy, 663–665, 669–677; Kennedy policy, 663–665; military expenditures and, 661, 663, 664, 670, 673–674; private capital outflow, 660, 663, 665, 666, 672–674

wage-price restraints proposed, 671–672
  See also Foreign exchange
Banks and banking, intermediary function of, 33–34
  policy lags, 525–535
  See also forms, subjects
Barter, 6–7, 14–30 passim
Borrowing and lending, 8–9
  See also Debt
Branch banking, 103–106, 107–110
  competition, 109–110, 113–119
  credit cards, 174–175
  international, and Eurodollars, 698–703
Bronze Age, exchange in, 20–30
Budgets, national, 184, 494–497
  policy effect measure, 543–544, 549–563
Buybacks, 161–162

Canada, central banking, 183, 227
Capital, corporate sources of, 52–57
  distribution, price changes and, 384–387
  flow, balance of payments and, 660, 663, 665–666, 672–674, 676, 691; inflation and, 690–691; money supply, 393
  formation, debt and, 32–34
  liquidity and, 146–150
  See also Foreign exchange
Central banking, 181–188
  credit control, 181, 185–187, 191–200
  functions of, 181–183, 185, 389–390
  government relationships, 183–188
  international banking, 181, 185, 570–573, 578–580, 582; Eurodollars, 697–698, 703–704; international banking reforms proposed, 617–630
  monetary policy and, 185–188, 372–390
  See also Federal Reserve

Central Europe, ancient, exchange in, 23

China, ancient, exchange in, 15, 20, 21, 27
central banking, 183

Clayton Act, 100

Clearing services, 80–82

Commercial banks and banking, asset management services, 82–83
branches, 103–106, 107–110; competition and, 109–110, 113–119; credit cards, 174–175; international, and Eurodollars, 698–703
central banks, relationships with, 181, 185–187
clearings, 80–82
competition, 94, 99–111, 175; non-monetary intermediaries, 323–339; structure and, 111–120
correspondent banking, 79–91, 141, 157, 174–175; foreign exchange, 575–577, 582
costs, 125
credit, central bank policy control of, 186–187; creation, 96, 342–343, 345–346; policy lags, 527–528, 530
credit cards, 168–177
diversification, 97–99
earnings, 93, 121, 165; correspondent banking, 84–90; credit cards, 172–173, 174
equity transfers, 83–84
failures, 71–79, 100–103
Federal-funds market, 122–123, 138–141, 154–167
insurance, deposit, 75–77
interbank balances, 84–90
intermediary function of, 33–34
international banking, 575–580, 582; Eurodollars, 150–152, 153, 693–705; loan restrictions, 673
liquidity, 78–79, 120–153, 697–698
management practices, 73–75, 79; competition and, 117–118
mergers, 102, 103, 107, 114
monetary policy and, 95–96; lags, 525–535
"money" creation by, 308–318
money supply and, 93, 94, 109, 308–318
nonfinancial enterprises, 97–99

number of, 77–79, 103–107
ownership, changes in, 71–73, 76–77; holding company, 98, 99
policy focus on, 66–67
rates, see Interest rates; Rates
regulation of, 67, 76–77, 93–99, 100–101, 154–155
reserves, see Liquidity; Reserves
securities, government, dealers market in, 242, 247; holdings, 263–264, 266
services, 80–91, 101–102, 103, 116; credit cards, 168–177, diversification, 97; foreign exchange, 575–577
speculation, 71–73
stocks, marketing of, 83, 84, 146–149
structure, 91–99, 111–120
suspensions, 77–79
time deposits, 64–65, 133–138, 140

Committee for Economic Development, 297–298

Competition, banking, 94–95, 99–120
credit card systems, 175; non-monetary intermediaries, 323–339
prices and, 458–460, 469–470

Consols, 296–297

Consumer Price Index, 440–446

Consumer debt, 39–50
See also Debt

Contracts, monetary instability and, 11–12

Copper as exchange medium, 20–21, 22, 30

Corporate debt, 39, 51–57
See also Debt

Correspondent banking, 79–91
borrowing of reserves, 141
credit cards, 174–175
Federal-funds market, 141, 154–167
foreign exchange, 575–577, 582
interbank balances, 84–90
reserve borrowing, 141

Costs, business fluctuations and, 465–474
See also Prices and price levels

Credit, availability doctrine, 339–345, 346–353
creation, 96, 345–346, 351–352
discount rate, 185–186, 193, 195, 199

Credit (*Continued*)
  international, 581–582, 599; composite reserve units (CRU's), 606–607; Eurodollars, 150–152, 153, 693–705; International Monetary Fund, 587–589, 607–608; level of, 609–611; Roosa bonds, 589; special drawing rights, 597, 648, 654–658, 678, 684
  "lock-in" effect, 343–345
  monetary policy effect on, 493–494
  money and, 5–13 *passim*
  open-market operations, 191, 192, 195–198, 201
  policy lags, 527–528, 530
  productive, system of, 129
  regulation by central banks, 181, 185–187, 194–195
  reserve requirements, 181, 185–187, 194–195
  trade, 54–55
Credit cards, bank, branch banking, 174–175
  cardholder characteristics, 172
  correspondent banking, 174–175
  distribution policies, 170–171
  income from, 173, 174
  interchangeability, 175–176
  loan portfolio ratio, 173–174
  management plans, 171–172
  pricing, 172–173
Crete, ancient, exchange in, 17, 21–22, 27
Currency, 102
  convertibility, 571, 581, 582, 598, 599, 649, 695; depreciation and devaluation, 668, 677, 692; Eurodollars and, 695; speculation, 601–602, 610

Debt, 31–57
  accounts receivable and, 52–53, 54–55
  asset size and, 55–57
  consols, 296–297
  consumer, 39–50
  corporate, 39, 51–57; Corporate Gross Product and, 51–52
  creation of, 32–34
  floating or short-term, 293–295
  funding, 293–295
  Gross National Product and, 35–36, 37–39

  household, 39–40
  income, liquidity and, 37–39, 44–50, 51–52
  instalment credit and, 40–49
  intermediation and, 33–34
  management, 280–307, 404, 407; countercyclical, 296–300; neutrality doctrine, 304–306; portfolio view of, 544; procyclical, 300–304
  money as symbol of right to goods, 8–9
  mortgages, residential, 39–40, 47
  open-market operations and, 202
  private, 36–57
  public, 34–37
  total, 34–37
Demand deposits, 62–64, 66–67
  Eurodollar market, 151
  liabilities management theory, 133–134, 152
  money supply, 93, 100
  rates, 103, 134
Deposits, insurance of, 75–76, 79
      See also Demand deposits; Eurodollars; Time deposits

Eastern Europe, ancient, exchange in, 23
Economy, central banking and, 183–187, 190
  debt and, 31–57
  goals, national policy, 430–439
  inflation, international trade and, 687–690
  market variables, 537–539
  measures of, 539–545
  stabilization, debt management, 295–307; fiscal and monetary actions and, 536–563, 706–713; internal and external, and fiscal and monetary policy, 706–713; money supply, 354–402; policy coordination, 497–501, 515–524
  trade, international, and economic development, 688–690
      See also specific aspects
Egypt, ancient, exchange in, 20–21, 26
Eisenhower, balance of payments policy, 664
Employment, *see* Unemployment
Employment Act, 430–439

Eurodollars, 693–705
 balance of payments, 703–704
 central banking, 697–698, 703–704
 commercial banking, 150–152, 153,
  693–705; reserves, 151, 700, 701–
  703
 exchange rates, 704–705
 interest rates, 695–696, 700, 701,
  703
 investment, short-term, and, 695–
  696
Exchange mediums, money, 4
 precoinage, 13–30
Export-Import Bank, and export increase, 675

Federal Advisory Council, 191, 194
Federal Deposit Insurance Act, 75–77
Federal-funds market, 154–167
 buying and selling on, 158–162
 effect of, 164–165
 growth patterns, 165–167
 liquidity and, 122–123, 138–141,
  152–153, 154–155
 rates, 139, 140, 162–164
 repurchase agreements and buybacks, 161–162
 secured loans, 161
 structure of, 156–158
 volume, 157–158, 165–167
Federal Open Market Committee,
  191, 192, 195–198, 201–203, 249,
  250, 253, 408, 411–416
  See also Open-market operations
Federal Reserve Banks, 191–200
 branches, 193
  See also Federal Reserve System
Federal Reserve Board, 191–194, 195,
  199
  See also Federal Reserve System
Federal Reserve System, 189–200
 borrowing from, 141–144, 153,
  203–216, 224–230, 254–267
 clearing services, 81–82
 commercial banking, regulation
  of, 67, 103, 146, 155–156
 credit, availability doctrine, 339–
  353; control of, 200–239; disposable income and, influence
  on, 493–494

debt management, 404, 407
discount policy and rates, 141–142,
 144, 199, 203–230, 254–267; announcement effect, 216–223;
 basic borrowing privilege, 269–
 271; changes in rate, 225–230,
 258–261, 269; collateral, 266,
 268; cost factor, 204–216; credit-
 deficit areas, 274–275; free reserves, 211–216; interest and,
 227–229; nonmember banks,
 266–267, 274; open-market operations, 207–211, 275; penalty
 rates, 204–205, 260–262; preferential rates, 283–284, 287; reform, 224–230, 266–275; seasonal
 credit, 269, 271–274; short-term
 rates, 285–286, 287–288; Treasury
 bill rates, 216, 225–227; Treasury opposition to, 282–284, 285–
 291
economic response to monetary actions of, 540–563
Eurodollar market, 701–702
Federal-funds market, 154–156
foreign exchange, 570–571, 578–
 579; international credits, 589;
 loan restrictions, 673
guidelines for, 402–408
liabilities management theory and,
 136–138
liquidity maintenance, 78, 123,
 225, 254–275
monetary base control, 540–543
money supply, 367, 392–393, 403,
 409–425
open-market operations, 191, 192,
 195–198, 201–203, 255–257, 407,
 408, 411–416, 702; dealer market, 241, 247, 249–254; discount
 policy and, 207–211, 275; foreign
 exchange, 578–579; reserve requirements and, 232–233; Treasury attitude, 284–285
power structure, 190–200
regionalism, 198–200
reserve requirements, 126–127, 230–
 238, 266–267
short-term note regulation, 146
Treasury controversies, 280–292
war financing, 281–282, 285–287
withdrawals from, 267, 268
  See also Monetary policy

Federal Trade Commission Act, 100
Financial intermediaries, 58–79
    claims, demand deposits, 62–64; growth of, 60–62; time deposits, 64–66
    debt and, 33–34
    foreign loans, restrictions on, 673
    primary issue ratios, 321–324, 330–332
    "money" creation, 308–318
    saving-investment process, 319–338
Fiscal policies, balance of payments, 603, 612–615, 639–640, 663–668, 706–713
    budgets, 184, 494–497
    discretionary action, 496–497, 499, 500, 508–509, 532
    economic response to fiscal and monetary actions, 536–563; measures of, 543–545
    government expenditures, composition, 492; financing and influence of, 544–545, 562; overseas, and balance of payments, 664, 673–674; policy lags, 527, 529–530; stabilizing influence of, 495–496
    inflexibility of, 494–497
    Keynesian, 356–357, 364–365, 376, 507–508, 539, 542, 543–544
    lags, 495, 525–535, 559–561; action lag, 526, 528–529, 531–532, 533; duration, 528–530; inside lags, 526, 528–529, 532–533; measurement of, 532–535; outside lags, 526–528, 529–530, 531, 533–535; public policy and, 530–532; recognition lag, 525–526, 530, 531–532, 533
    mechanics of, 488–492
    monetary policy coordination, 497–501, 515–524
    stabilizers, automatic, 495–496, 499
    taxes, structure of, 491–492, 500, 509–511, 513–515, 518–520
Foreign aid, 659–660, 661, 678–679
Foreign exchange, balance of payments, see Balance of payments
    central banks, 181, 185, 570–573, 578–580, 582; reform plan for, 617–630

commercial banking, 575–580, 582
credit and reserves, 578, 579, 581–584, 585–587, 599; balance of payments and, 583–584, 585–587, 650, 677–686; composite reserve units (CRU's), 606–607; dollar reserves, 582–587, 596–597, 601–602, 605–609; gold reserves, 585–587, 596, 601–602, 651–653, 677–686; increments to, 596–597, 601, 610, 649–653; International Monetary Fund, 587–589, 607–608, 648–658; level of, 609–611; reforms proposed, 605–611, 617–630; Roosa bonds, 589; special drawing rights, 597, 648, 654–658, 678, 683, 684; swap network, 589; U.S., 678–679
currency, convertibility, 571, 581, 582, 598, 599, 649, 695; depreciation, 668, 672, 692; market, 571–574; speculation, 601–602, 610
dollar role in, 571; reserves, 582–587, 596–597, 601–602, 605–609; transactions, 573–576, 590–591, 605
domestic policies and, 594–595, 598–600, 603, 605, 612–615, 639–640, 663, 668
earnings, repatriation to U.S., 673
economic development and, 688–690
Eurodollars, see Eurodollars
foreign investment and travel in U.S., 665, 676
forward market, 573–574, 575–576, 705
gold, currency value, 571; demonetization, 618–619, 685–686; market, free, 589–590, 646; price, 572, 583, 585, 590, 618–619, 640, 677–686; purchases, 572, 579; reserves, 585–587, 596, 601–602, 651–653, 678–679; tranche, 588–589; value guarantee of dollar holdings, 608–609
government participation in, 570–573, 578–580
inflation and, 419–420, 687–692
instability of, 12–13
investment and, 574, 598–599, 601;

Foreign exchange (*Continued*)
 restrictions proposed on U.S., 672–673
 liquidity, 587–598
 market, 570–580
 purchasing power parity, 387
 rates, *see* Rates
 restrictions, 602, 649, 672–673, 690–691, 698
 reserves, *see* Reserves
 speculation, 589–590, 600–602, 603, 610, 611–612
 spot market, 572–573, 575, 705
 tariffs, 631–633
 trade, 573–575, 638–639; and post-war reconstruction, 659–660, 678–679
 travel, international, 665, 673, 676
France, central banking, 184, 573
Full Employment Act, 255

Gold, exchange medium, 20, 23–30
 foreign exchange, currency value, 571; demonetization, 618–619, 685–686; market, free, 589–590, 640; price, 572, 583, 585, 590, 618–619, 640, 677–686; purchases, 572, 579, 585; reserves, 585–587, 596, 601–602, 650, 651–653, 678–679; tranche, 588–589; value guarantee of dollar holdings, 608–609
Government, budgets, 184, 494–497, 543–544, 549–563
  See also Fiscal policies, government expenditures
 central banks and, 181–188
 debt, 36–37; management, 280–307, 404, 407, 544
 policy, *see* Fiscal policy; Monetary policy; under specific subjects
 securities, bank holdings, 263–264, 266; dealer market, 241–254; open-market operations, 191, 192, 195–198, 201–203, 247, 249–254, 407, 408, 411–416, 702
Great Britain, central banking, 182–183, 184, 573
 devaluation, 668, 677
 Eurodollar market, 698
Greece, ancient, exchange in, 17–19, 22, 27–30

Gross National Product, debt and, 35–36
 deflator, 432, 440–442, 449–450
 primary issue ratio, 320–322
 private, 37–39
 public, 35–36

Implicit Price Index, 440–443, 449–450
Income, cash balances, 368–370
 debt and, 37–39, 44–50, 51–52
 disposable, Federal Reserve influence on, 493–494; tax effect on, 495; Treasury operations and, 489–491
 distribution, inflation and, 452–455
 money supply, lag, 530; velocity and national income, 366–367
India, ancient, exchange in, 17, 21, 27
Industrialization, international trade and, 688–690
Inflation, 451–461
 balance of payments and, 437, 521–522
 capital movements and, 690–691
 central bank control of, 183
 debt management, 281, 294, 295–298
 demand-pull, 456–457
 exchange rates and, 419–420, 691–692
 income distribution, 452–455
 international monetary reserves and, 610–611
 market power (cost-push), 459–460, 463, 473
 measures of, 439–451
 money supply and, 363–366, 406–407, 408
 price, 439–451
 structural (demand shift), 460–461, 463–465, 473
 trade, international, 687–690
 unemployment and, 430–487; inverse relationship of, 503–506
 wage/productivity relationship, 391–392
 wealth distribution, 455–457
Instalment credit, 40–49
 credit cards, bank, 168–177
Interest rates, balance of payments and, 520–524, 613–614, 664–665

Interest rates (*Continued*)
  ceilings on, and deposit shifts, 265–266
  debt management, 291, 297, 303, 305–306
  demand deposits, 134
  direct finance ratios and, 332–335
  Eurodollars, 695–696, 700, 703
  income and inflation, 453–454
  international, 523
  liquidity, 123–128, 133–153; trap, 378–379
  monetary policy, 257, 394, 523
  money supply and, 393, 394–395, 422–423
  nonmonetary intermediation and, 326–328
  pegged, 391
  policy, 257, 394–395; lags, 527–528, 530, 534
  portfolio theory, 540, 542
  reserve requirements and, 234–235
  unstable, 394–395, 422–423
  velocity and, 336–339
  See also Rates
International Monetary Fund, 571–572, 582–598 *passim*, 607–608, 648–658, 678, 683–684
  special drawing rights, 597, 648, 654–658, 678, 684
International monetary system, 581–582
  cooperation, multilateral, 523, 603, 617–630, 664
  foreign exchange market, 570–580
  payments imbalances, 581–598; *see also* Balance of payments
  reform of, 598–658; guidelines for, 604; reserves and credit, 605–609, 617–630
  sovereignty, 624–625
  See also Foreign exchange; under specific subjects
Investment, credit suspension, 513–515
  debt and, 32–34
  Eurodollars and short-term, 695–696
  foreign exchange, 574, 598–599, 601; foreign investment and travel in U.S., 665, 676; gold price and, 681; restrictions on, 663, 665, 672–673

  portfolio theory of, 540, 542
  saving process, 319–338
  stabilization, 512–515
  stimulation, 518–520, 523–524
  tax incentives, 518, 523–524; balance of payments and, 524–525, 614
Iron, as exchange medium, 20, 29–30
Italy, ancient, exchange in, 17–18, 22–23, 29

Johnson, balance of payments policy, 663–664, 669–677

Kennedy, balance of payments policy, 663–664
Kennedy Round, 675
Keynesianism, 355–358, 364–365, 376, 507–508, 539, 542, 543–544

Liquidity, anticipated income theory, 132–133
  capital funds, 146–150, 153
  cash asset ratios, 121–127
  commercial banking, 78–79, 120–153
  commercial loan theory, 128–130
  cyclical, 126–153
  debt and, 37–39, 44–50
  emergencies and reserve requirements, 238
  Eurodollars, 150–152, 153, 697–698
  Federal-funds market and, 122–123, 138–141, 152–153, 154–155
  inflation and, 295–298
  international, 587–598
    See also Balance of payments
  liabilities management theory, 133–153
  procyclical debt management and, 301–303
  Reserve borrowing and, 141–144, 153, 203–216, 254–275; collateral, 266, 268
  shiftability theory, 130–132
  short-term notes, 144–146, 153
  See also Reserves

Marshall Plan, 678, 679
Metals, as exchange mediums, 19–30
  See also Gold

Military, expenditures of, and balance of payments, 661, 663, 664, 670, 673–674
Monetarist economics, 358–362
Monetary policy, announcement effects, 216–223, 235–236
  balance of payments, 394, 520–524, 612–615, 639–640, 663–668, 706–713
  budgets, 184, 494–497, 543–544, 549–563
  commercial banking and, 95–96, 525–535
  credit availability, 339–353
  debt management, 280–307
  economic response to, 536–563; measures of, 540–543
  fiscal policy coordination, 497–501, 515–524
  goals, 404–405
  interest rates, 257, 394, 523
  lags, 403–404, 495, 525–535, 559–561; action lag, 526, 528–529, 531–532, 533; duration, 528–530; inside lag, 526, 532–533; measurement, 532–535; outside lag, 526–528, 530, 533–535; recognition lag, 525–526, 530–531, 533; reserve changes, 236–237
  mechanics of, 492–493
  money role in, 411–412
  money supply, 257, 354–363, 374–382, 390–402
  rules versus authority, 354–424; central banking, 372–390; guidelines, 402–408; money supply, 354–363, 374–382, 390–402
  securities, government, dealer market in, 241, 249–254
  timing and effect of, 213–223, 387–389, 399–400, 403–404
    See also Central banking; Federal Reserve System
Money, 3–13
  advantages of, 5–7
  creation of, by financial intermediaries, 308–318
  definition, 4–5, 67, 361, 395, 410, 412
  disadvantages of, 8–13
  value, instability of, 9–13
  words for, derivation of, 18
    See also Money supply

Money supply, 354–371, 409–425
  balance of payments, 393–394, 407, 419–420
  commercial banks and, 93–94, 100, 308–318
  exchange rates, 393
  growth rate, 390–425
  inflation and, 365–366, 406–407, 408
  interest rates and, 394–395, 418–420, 422–423
  monetary base and, 413–425, 540–543
  nonmonetary substitutes for and level of, 323–324
  policy lags, 527–528, 530, 534–535
  policy response, 257, 549, 555–563
  quantity theory of, 364–371, 374–387, 397, 540–543; international monetary system and, 610–611
  stock, nominal and real, 368–369, 417–420
  time deposits and, 395
  velocity, 360–361, 366–367, 396–399; interest rates, 336–339
    See also Money
Mortgage debt, residential, 39–40, 47
Mutual savings banks, rates and capital, 138
  time deposits, 65–66

New Zealand, central banking, 184–185
Northern Europe, ancient, exchange in, 23
Neolithic Age, exchange in, 15–16, 20

Open-market operations, 191, 192, 195–198, 201–203, 255–257, 407, 408, 411–416, 702
  dealer market, 241, 247, 249–254
  discount policy, 207–211, 275
  foreign exchange, 578
  reserve requirements, 232–233
  Treasury attitude, 284–285
Ox unit of value, 17–19

Persia, ancient, exchange in, 17
Phoenicia, exchange medium in, 27
Prehistory, exchange in, 15–17, 20
Prices and price levels, 457–458
  balance of payments, 599–600
  central banking and, 183, 187–188

Prices and price levels (*Continued*)
  competitive, 458–460, 469–470
  distribution effects, 384–387
  economic growth, 432–434
  exchange rates, 633–634
  expansion periods, 465–470
  indexes, 440–450
  inflation, 439–451, 457–461
  monetary policy, 382–384
  money supply, 354–363, 365–371, 382–384
  recession periods, 470–472
  unemployment, 433, 474–475, 486–487; long-run equilibrium theory, 481–486; trade-off (Phillips) curve, 432, 475–481
Private debt, 36–57
  See also Debt
Production, money and capitalistic, 6–9
Profits, inflation and, 453
Public debt, 34–37
  See also Debt
Purchasing power, 431–432
  debt and, 32–34; consumer credit, 40–50
  money and, 5–6
  parity, 387

Quantity Theory of Money, 364–371, 374–387, 397, 540–543
  international monetary system and, 610–611

Radcliffe Report, 374–376
Rates, capital notes, 149
  central bank, 185–186, 193, 195, 199; *see also* Federal Reserve System, discount policy and rates
  Eurodollar market, 152
  federal funds, 139, 140, 144, 162–164
  foreign exchange, 393, 407, 419–420, 433–435, 437, 572–574; dollar depreciation and, 633–634, 639, 642–644; dollar "peg," 582–583, 585; Eurodollars and, 704–705; fixed versus fluctuating, 626–628, 641–645; floating, 393, 626–628, 631, 635–640; fluctuation, desirability of, 611–612, 645–646; forward market, 574, 705; infla-

tion and, 419–420, 691–692; parity, 571–573, 582–583, 584–585, 599; prices and, 633–634; spot market, 572–573, 705
  short-term, 146, 153, 285–286, 287–288, 522
  time deposits, 136–137, 152
  Treasury bills, 216, 225–227, 285
  See also Interest rates
Regulation bank, 76–77, 93–99, 100–101
  credit, 181, 182–183
  rates, *see* Rates
  See also specific subjects
Repurchase agreements, 161–162, 197–198, 246–247, 250–251
Reserves, Federal-funds market, 140, 154–167, 263
  cash, 126–127
  central bank, 181, 185–187, 194–195
  credit and deposit expansion, 315–318
  Eurodollars and, 151, 700, 701–703
  excess, 126, 211–216, 286–287
  Federal Reserve requirements, 126–127, 230–238, 266–267; announcement effect, 235–236; emergencies, liquidity in, 238; open-market operations and, 232–233; policy lag, 236–237
  foreign exchange, 578, 579, 581–584, 585–587, 599, 629, 649–658; gold, 585–587, 596, 601–602, 650, 651–653, 677–686; increments to, 596–597, 601, 610, 649–653, 682–684; International Monetary Fund, 587–589, 607–608, 648–658, 683–684; reform, 605–609, 617–625; special drawing rights, 597, 648, 654–658, 678, 683–684; swap network, 589
  free, 211–216, 317
  Reserve balances, *see* Federal-funds market
  short-term notes and, 145, 146
  time deposits, 134–138, 148, 263
  See also Liquidity
Retailing, bank credit cards and, 176–177

Savings, debt and, 32–34
  investment process, 319–337

Savings and loan associations, 65–66, 95, 137–138
Securities, *see* Government securities; Stocks and securities, bank
Shells, as exchange medium, 15–16
Sherman Act, 100
Short-term financing, 143–146, 153
   rates, 285–286, 287–288
Silver, as exchange medium, 20, 26–30
Special drawing rights (SDR's), 597, 648, 654–658, 678, 684
Speculation, commercial banking, 71–73
   foreign exchange, 589–590, 600–602, 603, 610, 611–612
Sterling, devaluation, 668, 677
Stocks and securities, bank, 83, 84, 146–149, 153
Syria, ancient, exchange in, 20, 26

Tariffs, reduction of, 631–633, 675
Taxes, balance of payments, 613–614
   corporate funds and indebtedness, 52
   investment stimulation, 518, 523–524; credit suspension, 513–515
   policy lag, 527, 529–530, 533
   spending versus, 492
   stabilizers, automatic, 495–496
   structure effects, 491–492, 500, 509–511, 513–515, 518–520
Time certificates of deposit (CD's), 134–138, 263
Time deposits, 64–66
   Eurodollar market, 151, 700
   interest ceilings, 265–266
   liabilities management, 133–138, 140
   money supply, 393, 394–395
Trade, international, 573–575, 638–639
   economic growth and, 687–690; Eurodollars, 696, 698, 704–705; inflation and, 687–690; postwar reconstruction, 659–660, 678–679; restrictions, 602, 649; tariffs, 631–633, 675
   exports, U.S., and balance of trade betterment, 674–675
      See also Foreign exchange
Travel, abroad, 673
   foreign in U.S., 665, 676

Treasury, bills, 144, 242, 248, 251–253; rate, 225–227, 285–286
   debt management, 282–283, 291, 293–301
   economic response to actions of, 488–492, 540–563
   Federal Reserve, Accord, 154, 203, 211, 233, 254, 290
   Federal Reserve controversies, 280–292
   foreign exchange, 570–571, 579
   war financing, 281–282, 285–287

Unemployment, balance of payments, 433–434, 598, 599–600, 603, 613
   economic growth, 432–433
   "full employment," 436
   inflation, 430–487; demand-pull, 458–459; inverse relationship of, 503–506; market power, 459–460
   prices, 474–475, 486–487; long-run equilibrium, 481–486; trade-off (Phillips) curve, 432, 475–481
   tariff reductions, 631–633, 675
   technology, 432, 433
   wages and productivity, 391–392

Value, money as standard of, 4–5
   precoinage units of, 13–30; metallic mediums, 19–30; ox unit of, 17–19; shells, 15–16
Velocity, 360–361, 366–367, 396–399
   interest rates, 336–339

Wages, balance of payments and restraints on, 671–672
   inflation and income distribution, 453
   money and, 5–13 *passim*
   productivity relationships, 391–392, 468, 476–477, 646
   structural (demand shift) inflation, 460–461, 468–469
   unemployment and, 475–487
Wealth, concepts of, 59–60
   distribution, 9–11, 455–457
   inflation and, 455–457
   monetary instability and, 9–13
Weighing, introduction of, 22
Wholesale Price Index, 440–443, 446–449